THE *NEW* ILLUSTRATED ENCYCLOPEDIA OF

COUNTRY MUSIC

THE *NEW* ILLUSTRATED ENCYCLOPEDIA OF

COUNTRY MUSIC

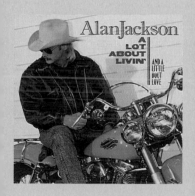

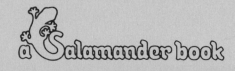

a Salamander book

Published by Salamander Books Limited
LONDON

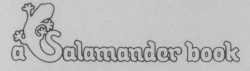

a Salamander book

Published by Salamander Books Ltd
129–137 York Way
London N7 9LG
United Kingdom

This revised edition published 1994

© Salamander Books Ltd 1977, 1986, 1994

ISBN 0 86101 763 3

Credits

Editor: Lisa Dyer
Designer: Paul Johnson
Research Assistant: Sandra Paine
Filmset by Flair plan Phototypesetting Ltd
Colour Reproduction by Scantrans Pte Ltd, Singapore
Printed in Spain by Cronion F.A.

Picture Credits

Many of the photographs in this book were provided by the record companies mentioned in the Acknowledgments, and we are very grateful for their help. Additionally we would like to again thank Douglas B. Green and Grease Brothers for pictures supplied for the original edition and re-used here, and also the following individuals and companies: Barry Hollis; Ron Keith; Photo Guild, Nashville; Mark Tucker and Ian Tilbury. Very grateful thanks also go to London Features International for supplying many of the new transparencies in this edition.

Acknowledgments

The author acknowledges the debt he owes to the following: Malone and McCulloch's *Stars Of Country Music;* Melvin Shestack's *Country Music Encyclopedia;* Stambler and Landon's *Encyclopedia Of Folk, Country And Western Music;* Kenn Kingsbury's *Who's Who In Country And Western Music;* Jerry Osborne's *55 Years Of Recorded Country/Western Music;* Bill C. Malone's *Country Music U.S.A.;* Rick Marshall's *Encyclopedia Of Country And Western Music;* John Morthland's *The Best Of Country Music;* Leslie Halliwell's *Filmgoer's Companion; Country Music People; Country Rhythms; Country Music Round-Up; Billboard; Music City News; Country Song Roundup;* CMA's *Close-Up; NME; Melody Maker* and Joel Whitburn's essential series of chart books.

I would also like to thank all the record companies who supplied many of the record and CD sleeves and illustrations used in this book. Special thanks are also due to: Byworth-Wootton (Europe's country publicists par excellence); Cathy Gurley and Evelyn Shriver and their respective Nashville office staff; B. Craig Campbell of Aristo Media, Nashville; Yumi Kimura of Warner, Nashville; Sarah Wells of Nashville Connection; Constance Woolsey; George Strait; Dave Hastings of Record Corner; John Slyfield of Upfront Video; and, of course, Roy Thompson, Fred Dellar, Dave Redshaw and Douglas B. Green, without whose special work this volume would not exist.

Author and Consultant

ALAN CACKETT is a freelance journalist best known for his contributions to *Country Music People*. In the late '60s he edited and published Britain's first monthly country music magazine – *Country Record Exchange* and *Country Music Monthly*. He has contributed a regular country music column for the *Kent Evening Post/Kent Today* and has also written for *Record Mirror* and *Sounds*, as well as providing pop music and country music columns for the Kent Messenger Group of publications. For the past seven years Alan has been promoting country music shows and festivals, featuring both UK and US talent, through his company Good 'N' Country. He contributed to the last edition of this encyclopedia and continues to be one of Britain's most informed music journalists, with strong connections to the US country scene.

Special Consultant

ALEC FOEGE is a contributing editor at *SPIN* Magazine, for which he has covered music. A former senior editor at *SPIN*, he has also written for many other publications, including *Rolling Stone*, *Variety*, *Vogue* and *New York Woman*. He lives in New York, where he recently wrote his first book.

Contributors

FRED DELLAR is one of the busiest journalists on the British music scene. He began his career providing rock and country articles for *Audio Record Review* (now *Hi-Fi News*) in 1968 and has since contributed to a huge number of publications, though he is probably best known for his Fred Fact column in *New Musical Express*.

DOUGLAS B. GREEN is one of America's leading country music historians. Once head of the Oral History Project at the Country Music Foundation in Nashville, he has written several well-received books and has contributed to some two score music publications, including liner notes for several country albums. He heads a band of his own, Riders In The Sky, and is a member of the Grand Ole Opry.

ROY THOMPSON is a country music fanatic who met Fred Dellar while working for a publishing company. Roy, who owns one of the largest collections of country records in England, has worked with Fred on a number of musical projects.

Foreword

Country music is the music of the past and the present. It has a lot to say to people of all ages and from all walks of life. At one time, country's core fans were much older than today's audiences, which more closely resembles a crowd of young rock and roll fans. They, of course, represent the future of country music. Yet, today's country music is really not all that different from the country music of yesteryear. You can still hear the influences of the singing cowboys from western movies – the lonesome yodel of Jimmie Rodgers, the heartache of Hank Williams and the western swing of Bob Wills. All of them are there in our country music of today.

Country music is all about communication, that ability to move the listener, whether it be to tears with the sad songs of real life or to whoop it up with the kickin' beat of a Texas dance hall. And that's the way it's always been with country music. Our music breaks down all kinds of barriers as it crosses international boundaries, bringing the people of the world together in an appreciation of the music.

In the pages of this reference work, you will come across singers, musicians and performers from all around the world who have helped to make country music truly international. It's a music that has absorbed the sounds and traditions of such far flung countries as Ireland, Scotland, Czechoslovakia, Germany, Mexico, England, Australia and many others.

For more than 200 years America has been home to immigrants from all corners of the world who come in search of the American Dream. Nowhere is this dream more apparent than within country music. For years, aspiring writers, singers and musicians have flocked to Nashville in the hope of gaining fame and fortune. I'm living proof that it can happen, that those dreams really can come true. This book has stories of others who not only sought that pot of gold, but eventually found it. They have all enriched our musical heritage with their own styles, which over the years has evolved into the whole of country music.

I believe that this book brings that rich heritage into perspective, historically and musically, and is essential reading for anyone with an appreciation of country music.

George Strait

Introduction

It has been 18 years since the first edition of this encyclopedia was published, and since that time the fortunes of country music have undergone many changes. At the time of writing this the music is enjoying a boom in America with country music record sales at an all-time high, and several of the major stars registering high placings on the American pop charts.

I guess the biggest phenomenon of the early '90s has to be Garth Brooks, who has amassed record sales exceeding 30 million albums, and set new attendance records virtually everywhere he has appeared. Garth's success in both the American pop and country charts has opened the door for others, and so we have witnessed many other country names, including Reba McEntire, Wynonna, Travis Tritt, Billy Ray Cyrus, George Strait, Brooks & Dunn, etc, storming the American pop charts.

All of these relatively new stars owe a great debt to the pioneers of country music. Reba will be the first to pay tribute to such stars of the past as Patsy Cline, Loretta Lynn and Ray Price. Garth openly admits it was George Strait who opened his ears to country music, and that George Jones is the king.

Going back further, both George Jones and George Strait owe their start to such legends as Roy Acuff and Merle Haggard respectively. So the country music story is on-going, and within the pages of this book I have attempted to document the history of country music; from its early beginnings of the very first commercial country music recordings of the '20s through the early days of the Nashville Sound of the '50s to the revitalized New Traditional Sound of the '80s and then on to the future stars of the '90s.

It is a rich heritage of sounds and styles; bluegrass to comedy, smooth pop-country balladry to hard-core honky-tonk, Texas swing to Louisiana Cajun, West Coast country to cowboy ballads. These and many other facets of country music are covered within the pages of this book.

Major artists are listed in alphabetical order, classified under their surnames, while groups are listed under their full title – The Kentucky HeadHunters, for instance, being logged under 'K'. The past few years has seen the emergence of many new names into country music, so it has been necessary to enlarge the all-embracing appendix, which lists performers who, though making important contributions to the history of country music, were deemed not of the stature to be included in the main body of the book. Also included in the appendix is information on such items as the Country Music Association, important centres such as Austin, musical styles and other relevant information to the history of country music.

The emphasis of this book is placed heavily on the musicians, writers and singers who have made country music a worldwide phenomenon of cultural and commercial standing. Major hit singles and albums are noted, plus details of awards, whether it be for sales or from the various governing bodies such as the CMA or the Academy of Country Music.

Some choose to claim a huge array of hit singles in their press releases; a 'nationwide No.1' in one singer's handout probably relates to a record that merely went Top 20! To keep accuracy and consistency to the fore, unless otherwise stated, the chart references all relate to *Billboard* magazine's country music charts, which I feel is the most authentic and accurate of its type. I have also used the *Billboard* pop and rock charts for any references to country music artists and records that have 'crossed over'.

Since the last edition of the encyclopedia in 1986 much has changed. Many of the singers and musicians whose lives were documented have sadly gone, while others have taken their places. This has resulted in a completely revised and newly written book. I thank Sandie Paine for her exhaustive research work, and I am also indebted to the invaluable input of Fred Dellar, Roy Thompson, Douglas B. Green and David Redshaw to the original edition, which has formed the basis for much of this new edition.

I am extremely proud of the results. We have not achieved perfection, because I do not think any such thing is possible on such an all-embracing project. For instance, it is difficult to even pin down definite dates of birth because some people will not reveal such details, while others just downright lie about their time of arrival. This is very much the case with many of the new young stars currently emerging on the scene. Image is all important to their career standing, and sometimes it is felt that truth about age might damage that image.

Despite providing the most comprehensive country music encyclopedia it is possible to devise, perfection is not claimed. In fact I look to you to supply any details that you feel should be revised, and information about any artist you feel may have been neglected.

Alan Cackett

Roy Acuff

Son of a Baptist minister, Roy Claxton Acuff was born September 15, 1903, in a three-room shack in Maynardsville, Tennessee. As a child, Roy learnt jew's-harp and harmonica. However, it seemed that he was destined to become an athlete. Following a move to Fountain City, near Knoxville, Acuff (at that time nicknamed 'Rabbit' because he weighed only 130 pounds) gained 13 letters at high school, eventually playing minor league ball and being considered for the New York Yankees. Severe sunstroke put an end to this career, confining Acuff to bed for much of 1929 and 1930.

Following this illness, Acuff, whose jobs had included that of callboy on the L&N Railroad, hung around the house, learning fiddle and listening to records by old-time players – also becoming adept with a yoyo.

In spring 1932, he joined a travelling medicine show, led by a Dr Haver, playing small towns in Virginia and Tennessee. By 1933 he formed a group, the Tennessee Crackerjacks, in which Clell Summey played dobro, thus providing the distinctive sound that came to be associated with Acuff (Pete 'Bashful Brother Oswald' Kirby providing the dobro chords in later Acuff aggregations). Soon he obtained a programme on Knoxville radio station WROL, moving on to the rival KNOX for the Mid-day Merry-Go-Round show. On being refused a raise (each musician received fifty cents per show) the band returned to WROL once more, adopting the name of the Crazy Tennesseans.

Acuff married Mildred Douglas in 1936, that same year recording two sessions for ARC (a company controlling a host of labels, later merged with Columbia). Tracks from these sessions included **Great Speckled Bird** and **Wabash Cannonball**, two classic items, the latter having a vocal by Dynamite Hatcher.

Making his first appearance on the Grand Ole Opry in 1938, Acuff soon became a regular on the show, changing the name of the band once more to the Smoky Mountain Boys. He won many friends with his sincere, mountain-boy vocal style and his dobro-flavoured band sound, and eventually became as popular as Uncle Dave Macon, who was the Opry main attraction at the time.

In 1942, together with songwriter Fred Rose, Acuff organized Acuff-Rose, a music publishing company destined to become one of the most important in country music. During that same period, Acuff's recordings became so popular that he headed Frank Sinatra in some major music polls and reportedly caused Japanese troops to yell 'To hell with Roosevelt, to

Time, Roy Acuff, a 1971 offering. Courtesy Hickory Records.

hell with Babe Ruth, to hell with Roy Acuff' as they banzai-charged at Okinawa. The war years also saw some of his biggest hits, including **Wreck On The Highway** (1942), **Fireball Mail** (1942), **Night Train to Memphis** (1943), **Pins And Needles** and **Low And Lonely** (1944).

Nominated to run as governor of Tennessee in 1944 and 1946, Acuff failed to get past the primaries. But in 1948 he won the Republican primary, although failed to win the ensuing election. Nevertheless he gained tremendous support, earning a larger slice of the vote than any previous Republican candidate had ever earned in that particular political confrontation. Also in 1948, Acuff opened his Dunbar Cave resort, a popular folk music park, which he owned for several years.

Four years later, after being requested to change his style by Columbia, Acuff left the label, switching in turn to MGM, Decca and Capitol. And though his live performances still continued to go well and his publishing empire seemed ever-expanding, Acuff's record sales failed to maintain their previous high – **So Many Times** (1959), **Come And Knock** (1959) and **Freight Train Blues** (1965), all on his own Hickory label, being the only releases to create any real interest during the '50s and '60s.

However, his tremendous contribution to country music was recognized in November 1962, when Acuff became the first living musician to be honoured as a member of the Country Music Hall Of

Above: The King of Country Music, Roy Acuff, died in 1992, after a career spanning over half a century. He was the first living member of the Country Music Hall Of Fame.

Fame. Known as the 'King of Country Music', Roy Acuff has sold more than 30 million records throughout the years – his most successful disc being his Columbia version of **Wabash Cannonball**, which went gold in 1942. His film appearances include 'Grand Ole Opry' (1940), 'Hi Neighbor' (1942), 'My Darling Clementine' (1943), 'Sing, Neighbor, Sing' (1944), 'Cowboy Canteen' (1944) and 'Night Train To Memphis' (1946).

Severely injured in a road accident during 1965, Acuff was back and touring within a few months, at one stage making several visits to the Vietnam War front. On May 24, 1973, he entertained returned POWs at the White House and, on March 16, 1974, was chosen to provide the President with yoyo lessons at the opening of the new Nashville Opryhouse, an incident which Acuff considered to be one of the high points in his career.

He guested on the Nitty Gritty Dirt Band's triple album set **Will The Circle Be Unbroken?** in 1972, lending credence to contemporary and country-rock music. He continued to appear regularly on the Grand Ole Opry throughout the '70s and '80s, but cut down on his previously extensive touring schedule, until by the early '90s his only appearances were

infrequent guest spots at Opryland. He died on November 23, 1992, following a short illness, and was buried just four hours later. He had requested a swift service and burial because he did not want his funeral turned into a circus.

Recommended:
Roy Acuff And His Smoky Mountain Boys (Capitol/–)
How Beautiful Heaven Must Be (Pickwick/–)
King Of Country (Hickory/–)
Smoky Mountain Memories (Hickory/DJM)
That's Country (Hickory/–)
Columbia Historic Edition (Columbia/–)
Steamboat Whistle Blues (Rounder/–)
The Great Roy Acuff (–/Stetson)
Two Different Worlds (–/Sundown)

Country Music Hall Of Fame, Roy Acuff. Courtesy Hickory Records.

Alabama

Jeff Cook (born August 27, 1949, Fort Wayne, Alabama), lead guitar, keyboards, fiddle; Teddy Gentry (born January 22, 1952, Alabama), bass; Randy Owen (born December 13, 1949), guitar; Mark Herndon, drums.

This American country-rock group has been one of the most successful country acts of recent years, with the majority of their singles hitting No.1 on the country charts, and all albums having reached gold or platinum status. Initially formed in 1969 at Fort Wayne, Alabama, as Wildcountry, the group was a semi-professional outfit with the nucleus of cousins Jeff Cook and Randy Owen, plus Teddy Gentry. They turned fully professional in 1973 when they landed a club residency in Myrtle Beach, South Carolina.

Southern Star, Alabama. Courtesy RCA Records.

By this time they had started writing songs and Teddy Gentry's **I May Never Be Your Love, But I'll Always Be Your Friend**, was recorded by Bobby G. Rice and made the country charts in 1975. The band had recorded for small labels as Wildcountry in the mid-'70s and made the name change to Alabama when they signed to GRT Records at the beginning of 1977, making their first mark on the country charts with **I Want To Be With You**.

At this time Alabama were undertaking tours all across the southern states, but without a major record deal or hit singles they were struggling. In 1976 original drummer John Vartanian decided to quit, and the group spent several months as a three-piece until they found Mark Herndon, the fourth member of Alabama. Larry McBride, a Dallas businessman, took an interest in the group and signed them to a management deal. He set up MDJ Records and the group's first record, **I Wanna Come Over**, made the country charts in the autumn of 1979. Under the production of Harold Shedd they came up with another hit, **My Home's In Alabama**.

The group signed with RCA Records at the beginning of 1980 and hit the top of the country charts with **Tennessee River**, following up with **Why Lady Why, Feels So Right** (also Pop Top 20), **Mountain Music, Love In The First Degree** (also Pop Top 20), **The Closer You Get, 40 Hour Week, Take Me Down** (also Pop Top 20), **Can't Keep A Good Man Down, Song Of The South** and **Jukebox In My Mind**. All albums have gone gold and many have gone multi-platinum.

Alabama have been named CMA Group Of The Year consistently since 1981, and also won Entertainer Of The Year in 1982, 1983 and 1984. In 1986 they joined pop-soul singer Lionel Ritchie in the studio and sang harmonies on **Deep River Woman**, a major pop-country hit. Alabama's commercial success changed the thinking in Nashville away from the solo performer. They have created the group sound rather than a singer accompanied by a group of musicians and set things in motion for other outfits such as Atlanta, Exile and Bandana, and, later, Restless Heart, Confederate Railroad, Desert Rose Band and Kentucky Headhunters.

Though they could have turned their back on country music, Alabama are keen to retain their country connection. This is reflected in their song content,

Below: Alabama created the group sound in country music during the '70s, leading the way for such '90s bands as Confederate Railroad and the Desert Rose Band.

instrumental arrangements and overall musical presentation.

Recommended:
The Closer You Get (RCA/–)
Feels So Right (RCA/–)
Mountain Music (RCA/–)
Southern Star (RCA/–)
Pass It On Down (RCA/–)
American Pride (RCA/–)

Deborah Allen

One of Nashville's leading songwriters, Deborah Allen was born Deborah Lynn Thurmond on September 30, 1953 in Memphis, Tennessee, and always dreamt of being a country singer. The black-haired beauty first made the move to Nashville in 1972, worked as a waitress, then landed a job at Opryland, where she sang and danced in the chorus line. Two years later she was in Los Angeles, working on Jim Stafford's TV Variety Show.

She made a move back to Nashville in 1977 and signed a writer's contract with MCA Music, providing hit songs for such stars as: Janie Fricke, who scored her first No.1 country hit with Deborah's **Don't Worry 'Bout Me Baby**; John Conlee with **I'm Only In It For The Love**; Tanya Tucker with **Can I See You Tonight**; and Patty Loveless with **Hurt Me Bad (In a Real Good Way)**.

Deborah first made an impression on the record-buying public during 1979 when her vocals were added to already-recorded tracks by the late Jim Reeves, resulting in a trio of Top 10 singles. This led to a recording contract with Capitol for whom she recorded the album, **Trouble In Mind**, a highly acclaimed mix of country, folk and gospel, and scored Top 20 hits with **Nobody's Fool** and **You (Make Me Wonder Why)**.

In 1983 she joined RCA and immediately came up with the crossover hit, **Baby I Lied**, which she co-wrote with Rafe Van Hoy, whom she married in 1982. Van Hoy was also Deborah's producer and her first RCA album, **Cheat The Night**, contained the further Top 10 hits **I've Been Wrong Before** and **I Hurt For You**. Her next album, **Let Me Be The First**, was the first all-digitally produced Nashville album in history. It received overwhelming critical acclaim, and Allen was touted as a major star of the future. Instead RCA went through traumatic executive changes, and when her contract was up for renewal in 1988, Deborah declined and found herself in an artistic wilderness.

She continued with her writing and singing on demo sessions, then late in 1992 she landed a new record deal with Giant, and produced **Delta Dreamland**, a superb album of self-composed songs with a distinctive nod to her rich Memphis musical heritage blending in country, R&B, pop and gospel influences.

Recommended:
Trouble In Mind (Capitol/–)
Cheat The Night (RCA/–)
Delta Dreamland (Giant/–)

Rex Allen

Known as the 'Arizona Cowboy', Allen was born Willcox, Arizona, December 31, 1924. A rodeo rider in his teens, he learnt to play guitar and fiddle at an early age. He took

an electronics course at University College of Los Angeles but opted instead for a singing career, finding his first job with radio station WTTM, Trenton, New Jersey, during the mid '40s. Like Gene Autry before him, he was a popular singer on the NBD before entering films. In 1951 he was awarded his own Hollywood radio show by CBS, subsequently getting high ratings.

He has since recorded for Decca, Mercury, Buena Vista and others, and has made films for Fox, Republic and Universal, having the distinction of being the last of the singing cowboys on screen. He had a Top 20 hit with **Don't Go Near The Indians** in September 1962, having previously won a gold disc for his version of **Crying In The Chapel** in 1953.

He is perhaps best known nowadays for his singing and narration chores in various Disney productions.

Recommended:
Golden Songs Of The West (Vocalion/–)
Under Western Skies (–/Stetson)
Boney-Kneed, Hairy-Legged Cowboy Songs (–/Bear Family)
Mister Cowboy (–/Stetson)
Voice Of The West (–/Bear Family)

Rex Allen Jr

The son of singing cowboy Rex Allen was born on August 23, 1947 in Chicago and made quite an impression on the country scene with such hit singles as **Two Less Lonely People, Lonely Street** and **Me And My Broken Heart**. He started while still a youngster, playing rodeos and state fairs with his father.

A move to Nashville in the early '70s set him up for a promising career in country music, signing with Shelby Singleton's SSS International label. A change to Warner Brothers Records in 1973 started a long run of hit singles and distinctive albums, such as **Oklahoma Rose** and **The Singing Cowboys**, featuring guest appearances by his father and Roy Rogers. He moved to the smaller Moonshine Records in 1984 and produced the excellent album **On The Move** which, like many of his previous recordings, he co-produced. By the early '90s he had become a regular on the Statler Brothers Show on American cable television.

Recommended:
Ridin' High (Warner Bros/–)
Brand New (Warner Bros/Warner Bros)
Oklahoma Rose (Warner Bros/–)
Cats In The Cradle (Warner Bros/–)
On The Move (Moonshine/–)

Rosalie Allen

Known as 'The Prairie Star' in her heyday, Rosalie Allen was a great cowgirl yodeller in an era full of them. Actually, she was born Julie Marlene Bedra, the daughter of a Polish-born chiropractor, in Old Forge, Pennsylvania, on June 6, 1924.

Entranced by the cowboy image and music, she gained a radio spot with long-time New York City favourite Denver Darling in the late '30s, and through the '40s and '50s she was a fixture of the northeast states. She signed with RCA, her biggest solo efforts being yodelling spectaculars **I Want To Be A Cowboy's Sweetheart** and **He Taught Me How To Yodel**. She was frequently paired with

Elton Britt, another legendary yodeller, for a number of records.

She turned to a career as a disc jockey over WOV in the '50s, preferring not to travel, and gradually left her performing and recording career behind.

For several years she owned a record shop in New Jersey, specializing in country music. She currently lives in rural Alabama.

Allman Brothers Band

Although they are not a country outfit, this southern-rock band, formed by brothers Duane and Gregg Allman in 1969, has been influential with many country acts, especially the bands that came to the forefront in Nashville in the '80s and '90s. Originally an R&B based rock band, they started leaning more towards a melodic country-rock style following Duane's fatal motorcycle crash on October 29, 1971, which was typified in such numbers as the instrumental hit, **Jessica**, and **Ramblin' Man**. The latter became a small country hit for Gary Stewart in 1973. The band split in 1977, but have reunited on several occasions since, making it back into the rock charts with the **Seven Turns** album in 1990. The Allmans were the most important and influential of all the southern boogie outfits.

Bill Anderson

Nicknamed 'Whispering Bill' because of his lack of any real voice, Anderson was born Columbia, South Carolina, November 1, 1937. Training initially to be a journalist, he obtained a BA degree at the University of Georgia, singing and acting as a disc jockey in his spare time. Along the way, he worked as a sports writer for the weekly 'DeKalb New Era' and as correspondent for the 'Atlanta Journal', opting for a full-time musical career in 1958 after Ray Price heard him singing his self-penned **City Lights** on a car radio and promptly covered it, thus earning a gold disc.

Many other Anderson songs were then recorded by Hank Locklin, Jim Reeves, Porter Wagoner, Faron Young, Jean Shepard, and others, while his own discs (for Decca) also sold well. However, his real breakthrough as a recording artist came in 1962, with a cross-over hit **Mama Sang A Song**, this being followed by **Still** and **8 × 10**, both covered in Britain by singing comedian Ken Dodd. Since that time, Anderson has waxed a stream of hits including **I Get The Fever** (1966), **For Loving You** with Jan Howard (1967),

The Bill Anderson Story. Courtesy MCA Records.

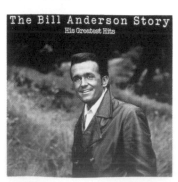

Wild Weekend (1968), **Happy State Of Life** (1968), **My Life** (1969), **But You Know I Love You** (1969), **Quits** (1971), **The Corner Of My Life** (1973), and many others.

Live From London, Bill Anderson. Courtesy MCA Records.

Anderson discovered Mary Lou Turner, who became another successful duet partner in the '70s (**Sometimes** and **I Can't Sleep With You**). When his records failed to make an impression, he turned to disco songs and came up with disco-country numbers such as **I Can't Wait Any Longer** and **Three Times A Lady**.

In recent years he has become a TV personality, starting with his own syndicated Bill Anderson Show in the '60s and leading up to game shows like Mister and Mrs. Bill is now an elder statesman of the Grand Ole Opry, where he regularly reprises his many hits for country fans, old and new.

Recommended:
The Bill Anderson Story (MCA/MCA)
Don't She Look Good? (MCA/–)
Always Remember (MCA/–)
Whispering Bill (MCA/–)
Live From London (–/MCA)
Ladies Choice (MCA/Bulldog)
Bright Lights And Country Music
    (Decca/Stetson)
Golden Greats (–/MCA)
Country Music Heaven (Curb/–)

John Anderson

This honky-tonk country singer with a rich bluesy vocal style was born December 12, 1955 in Apopka, Florida. He played in a rock'n'roll band called Living End while still in high school in Florida. One week after graduation he moved to Nashville and for two years he was singing in lounge bars with his older sister Donna. Anderson signed a recording contract with the small Ace Of Hearts label, releasing his first single **Swoop Down Sweet Jesus** in 1974 and landed a writer's contract with Al Gallico Publishing. For the next three years he tried his hand at various jobs during the day while working the Nashville clubs and bars. A move to Warner Bros Records in 1977 started a consistent run of chart successes with hard country songs like **The Girl At The End Of The Bar**, **Your Lying Blue Eyes** and the reflective **1959** in 1980.

Hailed as the new George Jones and Lefty Frizzell, John scored No.1 hits with **Wild And Blue**, **Swingin'**, a hardcore country blues number which crossed into the American pop charts in 1983, and **Black Sheep**. A further Top 3 hit with **She Sure Got Away With My Heart** in 1984 saw John's records start to miss the

higher reaches, though he did make a return to the Top 10 with **Honky Tonk Crowd** in 1986. The following year he joined MCA Records and made a couple of good albums, but his only notable success came with **Somewhere Between Ragged And Right**, which featured Waylon Jennings on harmony vocals in 1988. Next he signed with Universal, and, although he was working with Bernie Taupin and Paul Kennerley and touring regularly, he failed to make an impact on the charts.

Below: John Anderson made an impact in 1992 with Seminole Wind.

Above: Lynn Anderson has spent a lot of time collecting funds for charity.

In 1991 he signed with BNA Records, and he was back at the top of the charts with **Straight Tequila Night**. Taken from his **Seminole Wind** album, this went platinum in 1992 and Anderson was back as one of the finest country vocalists and writers on the contemporary scene. He worked with Mark Knopfler, who provided him with the song **When It Comes To You**; other guests on the album included Carl Jackson, Buddy Emmons and Dann Huff. Another track from the album, **Let Go Of The Stone** also hit No.1 in the charts.

Recommended:

Wild And Blue (Warner Bros/Warner Bros)
I Just Came Home To Count The
   Memories (Warner Bros/–)
Best Of (Warner Bros/Warner Bros)
Eye Of A Hurricane (Warner Bros/–)
Tokyo, Oklahoma (Warner Bros/–)
Seminole Wind (BNA/–)
Solid Ground (BNA/–)
Blue Skies Again (MCA/–)

Lynn Anderson

Singer Lynn Rene Anderson, daughter of
Casey and Liz Anderson, country
performers of the '50s and '60s, was born
in Grand Forks, North Dakota, September
26, 1947. Later, the family moved to
Sacramento, where Lynn became an
equestrian success.

During 1966 she joined Chart Records,
recording around 100 songs for the label
and producing 17 hits during the late '60s,
the biggest of these being a cover version
of Ben Peters' **That's A No No** (1969).
After marrying producer-songwriter Glen
Sutton, Lynn signed for Columbia Records,
her first single for the label being **Stay
There Till I Get There**, a hit written by
her husband. In the same year (1970),
Lynn's recording of **Rose Garden** became
a monster hit winning her a Grammy and
the CMA Female Vocalist Of The Year
awards.

Other hits include **You're My Man**,
Keep Me In Mind, **Top Of The World**,
I've Never Loved Anyone More and
Isn't It Always Love. She and Sutton
were divorced in the mid-'70s and for
several years Lynn concentrated on her
horse-riding skills. In 1983 she signed to
Permain Records and made a return to the
Top 10 with **You're Welcome Tonight**, a
duet with Gary Morris. This was followed
by a short stay with Mercury, for whom

**Below: Lynn Anderson comes from a
country music family.**

she recorded a few minor hits, including a
revival of the Drifters' **Under The
Boardwalk** in 1988.

Recommended:

Rose Garden (Columbia/CBS)
What A Man My Man Is (Columbia/CBS)
I've Never Loved Anyone More
  (Columbia/CBS)
Outlaw Is Just A State Of Mind
  (Columbia/CBS)
All The King's Horses (Columbia/–)
Rose Garden/How Can I Unlove You?
  (Columbia/–)
Country Girl (–/Embassy)
Lynn Anderson Is Back (Permain/–)
Country Store (–/Starblend)

Eddy Arnold

A country crooner with a smooth, very
commercial voice, Arnold has probably sold
more records than any other C&W artist.
Born on a farm near Henderson,
Tennessee, on May 15, 1918, Richard
Edward Arnold first became interested in
music while at elementary school, his
father – an old-timer fiddler – teaching him
guitar at the age of ten.

Arnold left high school during the early
'30s to help his family run their farm.
During this period he played at local barn
dances, sometimes travelling to such dates
on the back of a mule. He made his radio
debut in Jackson, Tennessee during 1936,
six years later gaining a regular spot on
Jackson station WTJS. His big break came
as singer/guitarist with Pee Wee King's
Golden West Cowboys providing exposure
on Grand Ole Opry.

As a solo act he signed for RCA in 1944,
sparking off an amazing tally of hit records
with **It's A Sin** and **I'll Hold You In My
Heart** in 1947, the latter becoming a
million-seller. This achievement was
matched by later Arnold recordings:
**Bouquet Of Roses, Anytime, Just A
Little Lovin' Will Go A Long Long Way**
(1948); **I Wanna Play House With You**

(1951) and **Cattle Call** (1955), while many
others sold nearly as many.

Arnold's records sold to people who
normally bought straight pop, so his TV
appearances were not confined to just
Grand Ole Opry and country shows; he
guested on programmes hosted by Perry
Como, Milton Berle, Arthur Godfrey, Dinah
Shore, Bob Hope, Spike Jones and other
showbiz personalities. Arnold also had his

**Eddy. Courtesy RCA Records. A fine
Owens Bradley-produced album.**

own syndicated TV series, Eddy Arnold
Time, plus other shows on NBC and ABC
networks.

Though his record sales dropped slightly
by the end of the '50s. **What's He Doing
In My World? Make The World Go
Away, I Want To Go With Me,
Somebody Like Me, Lonely Again,
Turn The World Around** and **Then You**

**The Best Of Eddy Arnold. Courtesy
RCA Records.**

**Above: 20 Of The Best, Eddy Arnold.
Courtesy RCA Records. The album
contains some of his finest –
including Cattle Call, Make The
World Go Away and Bouquet Of
Roses.**

Can Tell Me Goodbye, all topped the
country charts during the '60s. Arnold,
nicknamed 'The Tennessee Plowboy', had
sold well in excess of 60 million discs.

In 1966, Arnold was elected to the
Country Music Hall Of Fame.

Recommended:

Cattle Call (RCA/Bear Family)
So Many Ways/If The World Stopped
  Turnin' (MGM/–)
Country Gold (RCA/–)
Pure Gold (RCA/–)
Eddy (RCA/RCA)
A Legend And His Lady (RCA/–)
Famous Country Music Makers (–/RCA)
Hand Holding Songs (RCA/–)
Last Of The Love Song Singers (RCA/–)

Ernie Ashworth

Born in Huntsville, Alabama on December
15, 1928, Ernie Ashworth played guitar and
sang on local radio stations in his teens,
later moving to Nashville and working for
station WSIX. Carl Smith and Little Jimmy
Dickens were among those to record
Ashworth's songs, prompting MGM to sign
him to a recording contract in 1955, a
number of the discs being cut for the label
under the name of Billy Worth. Wesley
Rose, who had initiated the MGM contract,
won Ashworth another deal, this time with
Decca, his first release **Each Moment
(Spent With You)** becoming a major hit in
May 1960. After further successes with
You Can't Pick A Rose In December
and **Forever Gone** came a move to
Hickory Records, the hits continuing via
Everybody But Me (1962), his first
Hickory single, and **Talk Back Trembling
Lips**, a No.1 in the 1963 country charts.

A consistent hit-maker throughout the
'60s, Ashworth's **A Week In The
Country, I Love To Dance With Annie**
and **The DJ Cried**, all figured in the
country charts.

Asleep At The Wheel

Wheel, a western swing unit, began life on vocalist-guitarist Ray Benson's rent-free 1,500-acre farm, near Paw Paw, West Virginia, where he, Leroy Preston (vocals, guitar) and Reuben Gosfield often called 'Lucky Oceans' (pedal steel guitar) formed a small country band. With various changes, the band gained further shape when female vocalist Chris O'Connell, just out of high school, became the fourth permanent member. Following a move to San Francisco, pianist Floyd Domino joined, bringing jazz influence to the band.

Above: Asleep At The Wheel's fiddle sound recreated '40s western swing.

The first UA album by the Wheel was near country in character but subsequent albums for Epic, Capitol, MCA have seen the band employing more diverse material, linking country, R&B and jazz in best western swing tradition, often employing contributions by guesting ex-Texas Playboy Johnny Gimble. They won a Grammy for their version of Count Basie's **One O'Clock Jump** in 1978, and in 1980 appeared on the soundtrack of 'Roadie'.

They do what they do and it's often full of surprises. In fact the only thing about the band that can be guaranteed is that the Wheel will feature a changed personnel next time you hear them – at the last count some 60 musicians claim to have worked with the band at one point or another!

Recommended:
Ten (Epic/Epic)
Alive And Kicking (Arista/Arista)
Western Standard Time (Epic/Epic)
Comin' Right At Ya (UA/–)
Texas Gold (Capitol/Capitol)
Wheelin' And Dealin' (Capitol/Capitol)
Collision Course (Capitol/Capitol)
Pasture Prime (MCA Dot/Demon)

Bob Atcher

Robert Owen Atcher, born in Hardin County, Kentucky on May 11, 1914, grew up in North Dakota in a family of folk singers and championship fiddlers, and the duality of these locations gave him a broad knowledge of both traditional folk songs and cowboy songs, although he proved to be a very commercial country singer during his long association with Columbia Records (1937–58).

Bob's clear tenor voice was a fixture and a cornerstone of the once-thriving country music scene in Chicago; he appeared there on WJJD and WBBM and on a host of network programmes from 1931–34 and 1937–48, then joined the National Barn Dance as its top star from 1948 right through to its demise in 1970.

He recorded for Kapp and Capitol as well as Columbia Records (his biggest hit for them was a comedy version of **Thinking Tonight Of My Blue Eyes**), wrote songs, pioneered television in Chicago, and appeared as a singing cowboy in several Columbia pictures.

Although he continued to perform, Atcher's interest gradually turned to the civic, and he spent nearly two decades as mayor of the Chicago suburb of Schaumburg.

Collision Course, Asleep At The Wheel. Courtesy Capitol Records.

His past albums have included **Early American Folk Songs, Songs Of The Saddle, Dean Of The Cowboy Singers** (all Columbia); **Bob Atcher's Best** (Harmony) and **Saturday Night At The Old Barn Dance** (Kapp).

Chet Atkins

Chester Burton Atkins was born June 20, 1924, on a 50-acre farm near Luttrell, Tennessee. His elder half-brother, Jim, was a proficient guitarist who later went on to play with Les Paul. At 18, Chet became fiddler on station WNOX in Knoxville, Tennessee, then toured with Archie Campbell and Bill Carlisle, playing

20 Of The Best, Chet Atkins. Courtesy RCA Records.

fiddle and guitar. After marrying Leona Johnson in 1945, Atkins joined Red Foley in 1946, then moved to Nashville in 1950 with the Carter Sisters and Mother Maybelle, signing a record contract with RCA and initially cutting more vocals than instrumentals – the latter got the airplay.

He became top session guitarist for RCA's Nashville sessions at the end of the '40s, moving up to the post of A&R assistant under Steve Sholes in 1952. After

assisting Sholes on Presley's **Heartbreak Hotel** sessions in 1955, Atkins was placed in charge of the new RCA studio, becoming Nashville A&R manager in 1960 and vice-president of RCA Records just eight years later, holding the post until 1982, when he left the label.

A guitarist able to tackle many styles, Atkins has appeared at the Newport Jazz Festival and was featured soloist with the Atlanta Symphony Orchestra. He has produced hit records for Hank Snow, Waylon Jennings, Perry Como, Al Hirt and many, many others, and also had his own major hits with **Poor People Of Paris** (1956), **Boo Boo Stick Beat** (1959), **One Mint Julep** (1960), **Teensville** (1960) and **Yakety Axe** (1965), among others. Along with Floyd Cramer, Hank Garland and others, he is credited with creating the highly commercial Nashville Sound that brought pop acts scurrying to record in the

Above: Chet Atkins teamed with Mark Knopfler on his Neck And Neck album.

area. For 14 consecutive years he won Best Instrumentalist award in the 'Cashbox' poll.

He signed with Columbia Records in 1983 and at that time added the initials C.G.P. (Country Guitar Picker) after his name. Though he had now returned to his first love of guitar picking, his recordings tended to lean towards Jazz/New Age. He made a big impact with his album **Stay Tuned**, which featured guest guitarists Larry Carlton, George Benson, Mark Knopfler and Earl Klugh. Further albums for Columbia, such as **Street Dreams**, **Sails** and **Chet Atkins C.G.P.**, all maintained a modern jazz sound. He achieved notable commercial success in 1991 with **Neck And Neck**, which found him teaming up once again with Mark Knopfler, who produced the album and also sang.

With more than 100 albums to his credit covering all styles of music and having guided the careers of Jerry Reed, Jim Reeves, Hank Locklin, etc, he is one of Nashville's leading country figures. He was elected to the Country Music Hall Of Fame in 1973 as the youngest inductee.

Recommended:
Country Pickin' (Camden/–)
Finger Pickin' Good (Camden/–)
For The Good Times (RCA/–)
Me And Jerry Reed (RCA/–)
Superpickers (RCA/RCA)
Chester And Lester (RCA/RCA)
Me And Chet Atkins with Jerry Reed (RCA/RCA)
Famous Country Music Makers (–/RCA)
Atkins-Travis Traveling Show (RCA/RCA)
Stay Tuned (Columbia/CBS)
C.G.P. (Columbia/Columbia)
Sneaking Around with Jerry Reed (Columbia/–)
Neck And Neck with Mark Knopfler (Columbia/Columbia)

Gene Autry

Orvon Gene Autry, the most successful of all singing cowboys to break into movies, was born in Tioga, Texas, September 29, 1907. Taught to play guitar by mother Elnora Ozment Autry, Gene joined the Fields Brothers Marvelous Medicine Show while still at high school, but after graduation in 1925 became a railroad telegrapher with the Frisco Railway at Sapulpar, Oklahoma. Encouraged by Will Rogers following a chance meeting, Autry took a job on radio KVOO, Tulsa, in 1930, billing himself as 'Oklahoma's Singing Cowboy', and singing much in the style of Jimmie Rodgers.

In 1929 he had visited New York and began recording with such labels as Victor, Okeh, Columbia, Grey Gull and Gennett (often under a pseudonym), sometimes working with Jimmy Long, a singer-songwriter-guitarist, once Autry's boss on the Frisco line. On many he was assisted by Frank and Johnny Marvin. Shortly after, Autry began broadcasting regularly on the WLS Barn Dance programme for Chicago,

Below: Singing cowboy Gene Autry appears here in a still from the movie 'The Last Roundup'.

his popularity gaining further momentum with the 1931 release of **Silver Haired Daddy Of Mine** (penned by Autry and Long), a recording that eventually sold over five million copies.

Next came a move to Hollywood where, following a performance in a Ken Maynard western 'In Old Santa Fe', he was asked to star in a serial 'The Phantom Empire'. Thereafter, Autry appeared in innumerable B movies, usually with the horse, Champion. His list of hit records during the '30s and '40s – he was easily the most popular singer of the time – is awesome, including **Yellow Rose Of Texas** (1933), **The Last Roundup** (1934), **Tumbling Tumbleweeds** (1935), **Mexicali Rose** (1936), **Back In The Saddle Again** (1939), **South Of The Border** (1940), **You Are My Sunshine** (1941), **It Makes No Difference Now** (1941), **Be Honest With Me** (1941), **Tweedle-O-Twill** (1942) and **At Mail Call Today** (1945).

Autry enlisted in the Army Air Corps in July 1942 and became a pilot flying in the Far East and North Africa with Air Transport Command. Discharged on June 17, 1945, he formed a film company, continuing to star in such movies as 'Sioux City Sue' (1947), 'Guns And Saddles' (1949) and 'Last Of The Pony Riders' (1953). He also appeared in the long-running 'Melody Ranch' radio programme from 1939 until 1956.

His other activities included opening a chain of radio and TV stations and running a record company, a hotel chain and a music publishing firm, plus a major league baseball club, the California Angels. Since **Silver Haired Daddy**, Autry has had three other million-selling discs in **Here Comes Santa Claus** (1947), **Peter Cottontail** (1949) and the other nine million-seller **Rudolph The Red Nosed Reindeer** (1948).

Writer of scores of hit songs, Gene Autry has also starred at a series of annual rodeos held in Madison Square Garden and even had an Oklahoma town named after him. In 1969 he was elected to the Country Music Hall Of Fame.

Recommended:
Country Music Hall Of Fame (Columbia/–)
All American Cowboy (Republic/–)
Cowboy Hall Of Fame (Republic/–)
Favorites (Republic/Ember)
South Of The Border (Republic/Ember)
Live From Madison Square Garden (Republic/Ember)

Hoyt Axton

Born on March 25, 1938 in Comanche, Oklahoma, the son of teachers John Thomas Axton and his wife Mae – a lady who worked for Grand Ole Opry and wrote many fine songs including **Heartbreak Hotel**, Axton began playing guitar and singing in West Coast clubs during 1958.

After a brief spell in the Navy, he cut his first record **Follow The Drinking Gourd** in Nashville, along with sessionmen Jimmy Riddle (harmonica) and Grady Martin (guitar). Axton's **Greenback Dollar** became a hit when recorded by the Kingston Trio in 1963, while **The Pusher**, another Axton song, was heard by John Kay in 1964 and subsequently became an enormous success for Kay's rock group, Steppenwolf. Other Axton compositions, **Joy To The World** and **Never Been To Spain**, proved winners for Three Dog Night and **No No Song** scored for Ringo Starr in 1976.

While Axton was once thought of primarily as a folk singer, he is now considered as one of the finest writers in country music, his songs being recorded by Waylon Jennings, Tanya Tucker, John Denver, Glenn Yarborough, Lynn Anderson, Glen Campbell, Commander Cody and many others. He featured in the country charts during the late '70s with **Flash Of Fire**, **A Rusty Old Halo** and **Della And The Dealer**, the latter making an impression in Britain. Axton has also made his mark in films, appearing in 'The Black Stallion', 'Gremlins', and many more. He

Above: Hoyt Axton is probably best known as the songwriter of Joy To The World.

also has his own record company, Jeremiah, named after the bullfrog in the song **Joy To The World**.

Recommended:
Life Machine (A&M/A&M)
Southbound (A&M/A&M)
A Rusty Old Halo (Jeremiah/Youngblood)
Spin Of The Wheel (DPI/–)
Road Songs (A&M/A&M)

Free Sailin', Hoyt Axton. Courtesy MCA Records.

The Bailes Brothers

Homer Bailes, fiddle, vocals; Johnny Bailes, guitar, vocals; Kyle Bailes, string bass, vocals; Walter Bailes, guitar, vocals.

Despite the number of Bailes Brothers members, the act of that name rarely consisted of all four brothers. The heart of the act, however, comprised Johnny and Walter, whose song writing and singing made them one of the most popular groups of the 1940s.

Johnny was actually the first to work professionally, teaming up with Red Sovine in 1937. By the time he had gone to Beckley, West Virginia (1939), he had not only acquired the services of Skeets Williamson but also those of his sister Laverne, who became known as Molly O'Day. Yet another band member was Little Jimmy Dickens. During the same period, Kyle and Walter were billing themselves as the Bailes Brothers; before long it was Walter and Johnny.

In 1942, Roy Acuff heard them and arranged for an audition – which was successful – for the Grand Ole Opry, a tenure which lasted through to 1948 when they joined the Louisiana Hayride. It was during the Opry years that they recorded many of the songs that made them famous: **Dust On The Bible**, **I Want To Be Loved**, **Remember Me**, **As Long As I Live** and others, mainly for the Columbia Records label.

The act eventually broke up in 1949, Homer and Walter entering the ministry,

although both Johnny and Walter, and Homer and Kyle, worked as gospel duets intermittently in the '50s. By the late '70s, Kyle was in the air-conditioning business and Johnny was managing one of Webb Pierce's radio stations, leaving Walter, though actively involved in church work, as the other brother still performing on a semi-regular basis, doing gospel numbers (largely self-written) like his classic **Whiskey Is The Devil In Liquid Form**.

Recommended:
The Bailes Brothers: Johnny And Homer (Old Homestead/–)
I've Got My One Way Ticket (Old Homestead/–)

Razzy Bailey

A rough-voiced singer with a penchant for country blues, Rasie (later Razzy) Bailey was born on February 14, 1939 on a Five Points Alabama farm which had no running water or electricity. A back porch picker, he learned guitar and joined a string band sponsored by the Future Farmers Of America. He then became, in turn, a truck driver, an insurance salesman, a furniture company representative and a meat cutter for a butcher, trying to keep both a band and a family together, the former wanting to quit and his wife first seeking a divorce and then psychiatric help. In 1972, he recorded just one release for MGM and in 1975 he cut **Peanut Butter** for Capricorn, but nothing really jelled, though his marriage miraculously held together.

But in 1976, amid a contract hassle, he was told by a psychic that not only his contractual problems would be cleared up but another artist would record a Bailey song and that it would change his whole way of life. Soon after, Dickey Lee recorded Razzy's **9,999,999 Tears** and had a Top 5 hit. Another of the psychic's predictions came true when RCA signed Bailey in 1978 and his first single, **What Time Do You Have To Be Back In Heaven** went Top 20, followed by **Tonight She's Gonna Love Me (Like There Was No Tomorrow)** (1978), **If Love Had A Face**, **I Ain't Got No Business Doin' Business Today**, **I Can't Get Enough Of That** (all 1979) and **Too Old To Play Cowboys** (1980), his first chart-toppers coming with **Loving Up A Storm** and **I Keep Coming Back**, in 1980.

By 1981 he was 'Billboard' magazine's Country Singles Artist Of The Year, and played many major venues.

Many artists wait until their record sales plummet before they jump labels but Razzy switched from RCA to MCA while still a happy hit-maker in 1984. And at last his feel for things raunchy and bluesy seemed to be paying off. His last Top 20 hit for RCA was a version of Wilson Pickett's **In The Midnight Hour**, while his first album with his new label, **Cut From A Different Stone**, saw Bailey linking with soul guitar ace Steve Cropper to write several songs, also reprising Eddie Floyd's R&B classic **Knock On Wood**.

He continued his association with country-blues with the excellent **Blues Juice** album for King Snake Records in

Makin' Friends, Razzy Bailey. Courtesy RCA Records.

1989, which featured a whole host of country and blues pickers lending their support to his raspy vocal work.

Recommended:
Makin' Friends (RCA/RCA)
Razzy Bailey's Greatest Hits (RCA/–)
The Midnight Hour (RCA/–)
Cut From A Different Stone (MCA/–)
Blues Juice (King Snake/–)

Baillie And The Boys

This East Coast trio hit the big-time in Nashville in the late '80s after a twenty year wait in the wings. Michael Bonagura and Alan LeBoeuf teamed up in New Jersey in 1968 to form a band called London Fog, playing a mixture of originals and Top 40 covers. They met Kathie Baillie, a talented session singer, in 1973, and the trio provided back-up vocals for such diverse pop acts as Gladys Knight, Talking Heads and the Ramones. The trio split in 1977 when LeBoeuf landed a starring role in the Broadway show 'Beatlemania'. In the meantime, Kathie and Michael married, and, in 1981, with Alan back with

Above: People used to ask Razzy if he was a pop singer or an R&B artist. But he is really into the country blues.

them, the re-formed trio moved to Nashville, where they landed a job as back-up vocalists for Ed Bruce.

Their talents as writers, singers and musicians led to steady work in the studios and in 1984 they were signed as writers to Picalic Music. Two years later they landed a record deal with RCA, and the blend of three-part harmony, strong musicianship and impressive writing skills created such

The Lights Of Home, Baillie And The Boys. Courtesy RCA Records.

country Top 10 entries as **Oh Heart** (1987), **Wilder Days**, **Longshot** (1988), **She Deserves You**, **(I Wish I Had A) Heart Of Stone**, **Can't Turn The Tide** (1989) and **Fool Such As I** (1990).

LeBoeuf left again in 1989 and Kathy and Michael continued as a duo, utilizing back-up musicians for live shows. They put out a cover version of Fairground Attraction's **Perfect**, which became a minor country hit in 1990, and made it back into the Top 20 with **Treat Me Like A Stranger** (1991), but have done nothing chart-wise, since 1991.

Recommended:
Turn The Tide (RCA/–)
The Lights Of Home (RCA/–)

Moe Bandy

A provider of undiluted honky-tonk, Bandy was born in Meridan, Mississippi, February 12, 1944, one of six children born to a piano-playing mother and a guitar-picking father. The family settled near San Antonio, Texas, when Moe was six, his father there organizing a band called the Mission City Playboys. A guitar player from an early age, Bandy initially preferred

bronco-busting and opted for a rodeo career until a surfeit of broken bones convinced him to return to a less hazardous occupation. At the age of 19, he formed a group, Moe Bandy and the Mavericks, eventually gaining his first record contract with Satin, a local label. Then came stints with Shannon (during which Bandy first met producer Ray Baker) and GRC, the latter releasing **I Just Started Hating Cheatin' Songs Today** (1974), Bandy's first hit. The label released three more Top 20 hits – **It Was Always So Easy** (1974), **Don't Anybody Make Love At Home Anymore?** and **Bandy The Rodeo Clown** (1975), after which GRC folded and Moe moved on to Columbia and renewed success with **Hank Williams You Wrote My Life** (1975).

With Baker masterminding his career (acting as producer and also as song-finder, sometimes finding well over a thousand songs which were whittled down to a final 20), Bandy became a hit-making machine, logging two Top 20 songs in 1976, three in 1977, and three in 1978, peaking in 1979 when he provided five records including two chart-toppers, **Just Good Ol' Boys** (with Joe Stampley) and **I Cheated Me Right Out Of You**.

Still singing songs about seeing life through a bottle or of love gone sour, Moe has refused to cross over in search of pop success and throughout the '80s he continued to hit the charts with such honky-tonkers as **She's Not Really Cheatin' (She's Just Gettin' Even)**, **It Took A Lot Of Drinkin' (To Get That Woman Over Me)**, **Till I'm Too Old To Die Young**, **You Haven't Heard The Last Of Me** and **Daddy's Honky Tonk**. The latter was another duet with Joe Stampley, Bandy's partner on the 1984 Top 10 **Where's The Dress?**, a hilarious send-up of the pop transvestite scene.

A frequent award winner, Moe Bandy was also linked with Stampley at the 1980 CMA Awards ceremony; on this occasion the twosome won the Vocal Duo Of The Year category. **Americana**, a Top 10 success for Bandy in 1988, painted a patriotic look at how small town America has hardly changed over the years. Sadly, things have changed for Moe Bandy. He is no longer on a major label, but has established a nice niche in Branson, Missouri, where he has his own theatre, packing the country fans in with a healthy diet of good ole honky-tonk music.

Recommended:
Bandy The Rodeo Clown (GRC/–)
Hank Williams You Wrote My Life (Columbia/–)
Soft Lights And Hard Country Music (Columbia/CBS)
It's A Cheatin' Situation (Columbia/CBS)
Just Good Ol' Boys – with Joe Stampley (Columbia/CBS)
Many Mansions (MCA/MCA)
You Haven't Heard The Last Of Me (MCA/–)
No Regrets (Curb/–)
Live In Branson (Laserlight/–)

R. C. Bannon

From Dallas, Texas, Bannon initially moved into Nashville as a DJ, holding down a five year residency at the city's Smuggler's Inn. Prior to this, he had spent many years on the road, performing at clubs throughout the Southwest, at one point acting as warm-up act for Marty Robbins.

In Nashville he was introduced to songwriter Harlan Sanders who nudged Warner Brothers Music into signing

Bannon as a writer. By 1977 he had gained a recording contract with Columbia, logging a trio of minor hits that year and a couple in 1978. But the big breakthrough came in 1979 when he married Louise Mandrell, the two of them also getting together on record for Epic and recording a number of chart duets, one of which, **Reunited**, went Top 20. However, his own solo career refused to move up a gear and 1980 brought only three further mid-chart singles, leaving Bannon searching for the right song to really establish himself as a headline act. He has, however, worked on arrangements for television and wrote **One Of A Kind Pair Of Fools**, a No.1 hit for Barbara Mandrell in 1983.

Recommended:
R. C. Bannon Arrives (Columbia/–)
Inseparable – with Louise Mandrell (Epic/–)

Bobby Bare

The provider of such million-selling singles as **Detroit City** and **500 Miles Away From Home** and one of country's ranconteurs supreme, Bare was born in Ironton, Ohio, April 7, 1935. Motherless at the age of five, his sister being sent for adoption because of the father's inability to feed the whole family, Bare became a farm worker at 15, later obtaining a job in a clothing factory. He built his own guitar and learned to play, eventually winning a job with a country band in the Springfield-Portsmouth area, for which he received no pay. He recorded his own song **All American Boy** in 1958, then joined the army, the tapes of his song being offered to various record companies and taken up by Fraternity, who released the disc as by 'Bill Parsons'. But although the single became the second biggest selling record in the USA in December, Bare hardly benefited financially, having sold the song rights for $50.

Upon service discharge, Bare began performing and writing once more, contributing three songs for the Jimmy

Below: Bobby Bare is still commanding a loyal following in Europe, though less of one at home.

Clanton-Chubby Checker movie 'Teenage Millionaire', a year later having his own hit record with an RCA release, **Shame On Me**. Richard Anthony then recorded a French version of **500 Miles Away From Home** (a folk song adapted and arranged by Bare, Hedy West and Charles Williams) and obtained a gold disc; Bare also achieved hit status with the same song. A year later, Bare appeared in an acting role in the cavalry western 'A Distant Trumpet' and also provided RCA with further hits via his versions of Hank Snow's **Miller's Cave** and Ian and Sylvia's **Four Strong Winds**.

After numerous other hit singles including **The Streets Of Baltimore** (1966) and **(Margie's At) The Lincoln Park Inn** (1966), Bare left RCA to join Mercury in 1970 supplying his new label with such Top 10 country hits as **How I Got To Memphis** (1970), **Come Sundown** (1970) and actually charting with every release. But he rejoined RCA (1972) and began working on a series of fine albums, commencing with one of his most successful, **Lullabies, Legends and Lies** (1973), an album penned almost entirely by Shel Silverstein and one that spawned such Top 10 hits as **Daddy What If** (1973) and **Marie Laveau**, a 1974 No.1. After an album with his whole family, **Singing In The Kitchen** (1974), he moved on to produce **Hard Time Hungries** (1975), another critically acclaimed LP. Other hit singles followed but, unhappy with RCA, Bare signed for Columbia in 1978, first cutting **Bare** (1979), a well-received, self-produced album. He then moved on to make **Sleeper Wherever I Fall**, reputed to have cost nearly $100,000, making it one of the most expensive albums ever to have been made in Nashville at that time.

Managed by rock mogul Bill Graham at this period, it seemed that Bare would once more cross over into the pop market. But, despite a number of other exemplary albums and a potentially chart-busting single in **Numbers** (1980), a Shel Silverstein-written parody of the movie '10', Bare's recording career gradually lost impetus and, despite the kudos gained by hosting the highly acclaimed Bobby Bare And Friends TV show on the Nashville Network. By the mid-'80s, Bare – still without any well-deserved CMA award –

Drunk & Crazy, Bobby Bare. Courtesy CBS Records.

eventually signed to EMI America in 1985, but failed to score any major chart successes, and is now content to make regular tours of Europe.

Recommended:
Famous Country Music Makers (RCA/RCA)
Lullabies, Legends And Lies (RCA/RCA)
Hard Time Hungries (RCA/RCA)
Bare (Columbia/CBS)
Sleeper Wherever I Fall (Columbia/CBS)
Drinkin' From The Bottle, Singin' From The Heart (Columbia/CBS)
The Mercury Years (–/Bear Family)
Ain't Got Nothin' To Lose (Columbia/CBS)

Dr Humphrey Bate (And The Possum Hunters)

Oscar Albright, bass; Alcyone Bate, vocals, ukelele, piano; Buster Bate, guitar, tipple, harmonica, jew's-harp; Dr Humphrey Bate, harmonica; Burt Hutcherson, guitar; Walter Leggett, banjo; Oscar Stone, fiddle; Staley Walton, guitar.

The harmonica-playing leader of the most popular string band on the Grand Ole Opry, Dr Bate – a graduate of the Vanderbilt Medical School who earned his living as a physician – was born in Summer County, Tennessee, in 1875. He had fronted a great many popular local string bands before he began to play on Nashville radio in 1925, joining the forerunner of the Opry late in that year. Not long after, they recorded a number of tunes and songs for Brunswick Records. After Dr Bate's death in 1936, Oscar Stone headed the band until 1949, when Staley Walton and Alcyone Bate took over the leadership of the Possum Hunters, whose remaining members were absorbed when four old-time Opry bands were amalgamated into two during the '60s. Bate's daughter, Alcyone Beasley, joined her father's band at the age of 13 as a vocalist, eventually becoming pianist with the Crook Brothers and logging well over half a century as an Opry member.

reputation with their version of **Let Your Love Flow**, a song written by Neil Diamond's roadie Larry Williams, thus providing the brothers with a US pop No.1 in 1976. Fashioning a rock-styled, yet often acoustic-based, kind of country music, the Bellamy Brothers achieved their second major success with **If I Said You Had A Beautiful Body Would You Hold It Against Me** (1979), a song which was voted Single Of The Year by the CMA of Great Britain.

Since that time there have been no further pop hits for the Bellamys, but plenty of success on the country circuit with such No.1s as **Sugar Daddy** (1980), **Dancin' Cowboys** (1980), **Do You Love As Good As You Look** (1981), **For All The Wrong Reasons** (1982), **I Need More Of You** (1985) and **Too Much Is Not Enough** (1986), the latter in partnership with the Forester Sisters.

In 1987, now signed to MCA/Curb, the brothers started a series of nostalgic songs, such as **Kids Of The Baby Boom** and **Rebels Without A Clue**, which kept them high in the country charts. Another label change in 1991 saw them on Atlantic, but struggling. They continue as a popular touring act, and such songs as **Let Your Love Flow** and **If I Said You Had A Beautiful Body** have become standards.

Recommended:
Rebels Without A Clue (MCA-Curb/–)
Crazy From The Heart (MCA-Curb/–)
Country Rap (MCA-Curb/–)
Reality Check (MCA-Curb/–)

The Bellamy Brothers Best. Courtesy MCA/Curb Records.

Beausoleil

Tommy Alesi, drums; Jimmy Breaux, accordion; Tommy Comeaux, bass, mandolin; David Doucet, guitar, vocals; Michael Doucet, guitar, vocals; Billy Ware, percussion.

One of the most popular American Cajun bands, Beausoleil have probably found as much fame as it is possible to find by staying true to the tradition of their music. Formed by Michael Doucet, a superb fiddle player, excellent singer and knowledgeable scholar on Cajun music, Beausoleil have successfully combined the essence of traditional Cajun music with a contemporary edge.

Doucet came from a musical family in Lafayette, Louisiana, but it was a mish-mash of jazz, classical, French and big band that his relatives played. Though he grew up with Cajun music, it was not until he went to college at the Louisiana State University in the late '60s and studied American folklore, that he started taking Cajun music seriously. By the mid-'70s he was playing traditional music with Marc and Ann Savoy as the Savoy-Doucet Cajun

Bayou Cadillac, Beausoleil. Courtesy Rounder Records.

Band. He later formed Beausoleil and has been successful in promoting Cajun music to an increasingly enthusiastic and ever-widening audience. Their music was featured in the 1987 movie 'The Big Easy', while Doucet has found time to be involved in other projects, including producing radio and TV programmes. The nucleus of the band backed up Mary-Chapin Carpenter on her 1991 hit recording **Down At The Twist And Shout**. They also appeared on that year's CMA Awards Show, backing up Carpenter. Beausoleil have recorded for various labels since the early '80s.

Recommended:
Dance De La Vie (Rhino/–)
Hot Chili Mama (Arhoolie/–)
Bayou Deluxe (Rhino/–)
Bayou Boogie (Rounder/–)
Bayou Cadillac (Rounder/–)

Carl Belew

Singer-songwriter and guitarist Carl Robert Belew was born in Salina, Oklahoma, April 21, 1931. For many years he played minor venues and country fairs, eventually gaining a spot on Shreveport KWKH's Louisiana Hayride and obtaining a recording contract with Decca. His first major hit for the label was **Am I That Easy To Forget?**, a self-penned song that became a Top 10 country hit in 1959, the success of this disc being matched by **Hello Out There**, an RCA release waxed by Belew in 1962. Other hits followed throughout the mid-'60s, namely **In The Middle Of A Memory**, **Crystal Chandelier**, **Boston Jail**, **Walking Shadow**, **Talking Memory**, **Girl Crazy** and **Mary's Little Lamb**.

After 1968 Belew's name was absent from the charts for a long period, returning in 1971 when **All I Need Is You**, a duet recorded with Betty Jean Robinson,

Above: The first string band to play the Opry – Dr Bate And The Possum Hunters.

became a mini-hit. A further success with **Welcome Back To My World**, an MCA release in 1974, augered well for furthering his career, but chart success was not to be his. He continued to tour regularly until cancer claimed his life in November 1990.

Recommended:
Carl Belew (Vocalion/–)
12 Shades (Victor/–)
Songs (Vocalion/–)

Bellamy Brothers

David, who plays guitar and keyboards, was born September 16, 1950, and Howard, who plays guitar, was born February 2, 1946 in Darby, Florida. The sons of a farmer who played dobro and fiddle in a bluegrass band, they were raised in a musical environment and made their first professional appearance in 1958. David joined soul band the Accidents in 1965 and played organ behind Percy Sledge, Little Anthony and the Imperials,.

During 1968 the brothers formed a pop band, Jericho, playing the club circuit in Georgia, Mississippi and South Carolina, but disbanded in 1971 and returned to the family farm. There the duo began songwriting, also providing jingles for the local radio and TV stations.

After one of David's songs, **Spiders And Snakes**, proved to be a two-million-seller for Jim Stafford in 1973, they headed for California, and embarked on a recording career, making an initial impact with **Nothin' Heavy**, a regional hit (1975). They moved on to gain an international

Matraca Berg

A dynamic singer-writer, Matraca Berg looked set to take country music by storm in 1990, but has so far failed to fulfil the commercial success her talent promises. She was born in 1954 into a musical family. Her mother, Icie Callaway Kirby, was a member of the Callaway Sisters, a quartet that performed on country shows throughout the '50s and '60s. The family moved to Nashville in the early '60s and Icie soon became an in-demand session singer and songwriter. Matraca was constantly around the music business and naturally followed in her mother's footsteps. Her first breakthrough came as a writer, penning **Fakin' Love**, a country No.1 for T. G. Sheppard and Karen Brooks in 1982 and **The Last One To Know**, this time a No. 1 for Reba McEntire in 1987, which was also nominated for a Grammy. This led to a record deal with RCA, and her acclaimed **Lying To The Moon** album, which spawned such country hits as **Baby, Walk On** and **The Things You Left Undone** (both 1990), and **I Got It Bad** and

I **Must Have Been Crazy** (both 1991). Matraca made a big impact in Europe with I **Got It Bad**, which became a hit in Holland and gained extensive radio plays throughout Britain. Although she has continued to write and sing on sessions, Matraca Berg has not yet built upon the solid base of her excellent first album.

Recommended:
Lying To The Moon (RCA/–)

Clint Black

Black is one of the most visible country stars on the American tour circuit, which has led to him gaining multi-platinum awards for all three of his albums and an impressive run of chart-topping singles.

Though born in Long Beach, New Jersey on February 4, 1962, Black and his family are all Texans. The family home was in Houston, and Clint grew up to the strains of classic George Jones and Merle Haggard. He was playing harmonica and guitar by the age of 15. An older brother had a band and Clint sang harmony and played bass with them. A chance meeting with local musician Hayden Nicholas in 1980 led to a promising songwriting partnership. The pair formed a band and for the next seven years played the bars and honky-tonks right across Texas.

Demos of their songs reached Bill Ham, the manager of ZZ Top, who immediately struck up a management agreement with Black and negotiated a record contract with RCA Nashville at the end of 1987. Armed with a supply of original songs, Black produced a classic album of stirring honky-tonk ballads that endeared him to the working man. His first single, **Better Man**, climbed to the top of the charts in early 1989, followed by the album's excellent title song, **Killin' Time**. Two more singles from the album, **Nobody's**

Home and **Walkin' Away** also topped the charts, while a fifth single, **Nothing's New**, reached No.3. No performer in any style of music had achieved that level of success with their debut album. **Killin' Time** not only topped the country album charts, but also crossed over into the pop listings, and within a year of release had reached platinum status.

Black's dance style of honky-tonk had evolved from his Texas upbringing and years of playing the clubs. His quivering, traditional-sounding vocals and common-man songs gained him a huge following and his second album, **Put Yourself In My Shoes**, went platinum just two months after release in November 1990. The title song went to No.5, then he was back at No.1 with **Loving Blind** and **Where Are You Now** both 1991 hits. That same year he married soap-star Lisa Hartman.

A management disagreement between Black and Bill Ham kept Clint out of the studios for almost two years, though he did record a duet with legendary cowboy-star Roy Rogers – **Hold On Partner**, a minor country hit at the end of 1991. Meanwhile Clint maintained a busy touring schedule, dispensed with Ham's services, and returned to the studio to co-produce his third album, **The Hard Way**. This was released in the summer of 1992, but saw him in dispute with RCA, because the album was completed behind schedule. The wait was well worthwhile. This was Black's finest album, containing such hit singles as **We Tell Ourselves**, **Burn One Down** (1992) and **When My Ship Comes In** (1993).

In 1992 Black put together the most ambitious concert tour ever undertaken by a mainstream country performer. He played 150 dates before 1.5 million people from July 1992 through to March 1993. He added four additional band members to his five-piece backing outfit, and had a quarter-of-a-million dollars stage set specially built with dual video screens.

Above: The Bellamy Brothers have become country chart regulars.

Recommended:
Killing' Time (RCA/RCA)
Put Yourself In My Shoes (RCA/RCA)
The Hard Way (RCA/RCA)

The Blue Sky Boys

Bill Bolick, vocals, mandolin; Earl Bolick, vocals, guitar.

Both born in Hickory, North Carolina: Bill on October 28, 1917, Earl on December 16, 1919, they were sons of Garland Bolick, who grew tobacco and worked in a textile mill. The Bolicks began playing traditional material, working in and around the Hickory area. In 1935, Bill sang for the East Hickory String Band – a name later changed to the Crazy Hickory Nuts, after J. W. Fincher of the Crazy Water Crystal Company who had offered them a job in Nashville – and the same year, the brothers began singing duets on the local radio station. In 1936, they recorded for Victor, whose A&R man believed them to be copies of the Monroe Brothers.

Their first release – on Bluebird – was **The Sunny Side Of Life**, written by Bill. During the late '30s and early '40s, the Bolicks' mixture of old-time and religious music became very popular but, following World War II, country fans began seeking something more commercial.

In 1951, the Blue Sky Boys broke up. Persuaded by Starday Records to come out of retirement in 1963 and cut an album titled **Together Again**, they also decided to play the odd date or two at folk festivals and colleges. They also recorded an album for Capitol in 1965 and another for Rounder as late as 1976.

But these albums and the occasional live dates were but gestures. After 1951 the Boys – soured by their experiences in the music business – never returned to full-time music careers.

Recommended:
The Blue Sky Boys (Rounder/–)
The Sunny Side Of Life (Rounder/–)
Presenting The Blue Sky Boys (JEMF/–)

Dock Boggs

Possessor of a unique banjo style, Moran Lee 'Dock' Boggs was born Norton, Virginia, February 7, 1898. A miner for 41 years, Boggs played five string banjo merely as a hobby.

Acquiring his unusual playing style (using two fingers and a thumb instead of the normal one finger and thumb claw hammer method) from a black musician he met in Norton, Boggs gradually developed his technique and recorded a number of sides for Brunswick in 1927. But upon his retirement from mining, Boggs turned more of his attention to music and found himself to be an in-demand performer at various folk festivals where his playing, his eerie, haunting songs like **Oh Death** and his nasal vocal delivery, attracted much attention, encouraging Mike Seeger to record Boggs for the Folkways label. He died in 1971.

Recommended:
Dock Boggs Volumes 1 & 2 (Folkways/–)
Dock Boggs Volumes 3 & 4 (Folkways/–)

The Blue Sky Boys (Bill and Earl Bolick). Courtesy RCA Records.

Suzy Bogguss

A real country girl, Suzy Bogguss was born on December 30, 1956 in Aledo, Illinois; growing up in a farming family near a small town in rural America. The youngest in a family of four, she recalls listening to a diverse mix of music from country to big band and '60s pop. She sang in the Aledo Presbyterian Church choir, then later branched out to accompanying herself on guitar and playing coffee houses at Peoria, Illinois. At college she graduated as a metalsmith, gaining an art degree and planning to open a studio for jewellery design. But the pull of music became too strong, so she took to booking dates into clubs and coffee houses. Driving a camper truck and accompanied by her pet dog and cat, she worked all across the Midwest.

A determined lady, Suzy recorded her own cassette in Nashville in 1985 and sold it at her show dates. The following year she was signed as the headlining female performer at Dollywood for the summer

Legendary Singer And Banjo Player, Dock Boggs. Courtesy Folkways.

season. A contract with Capitol Records followed, and she made her first impact on the charts with **I Don't Want To Set The World On Fire** (1987). Further minor hits followed and Suzy finally cracked the Top 20 with **Cross My Broken Heart** (1989). Her first album, **Somewhere Between**, proved influential with British female performers, with several of the songs gaining cover versions.

Although she was touring regularly, Suzy was struggling to make a big impact with her records, but she did return to the Top 20 with a duet, **Hopelessly Yours** (1991), with Lee Greenwood, and a solo revival of **Someday Soon** (1991). Since then she has hardly looked back. Her third album, **Aces**, was the big breakthrough she needed with such Top 10 singles as **Outbound Plane**, **Letting Go** and the title song. The album went gold in the summer of 1992 and that September Suzy Bogguss was presented with the Country Music Association Horizon award. She was back in the Top 10 in the spring of 1993 with **Drive South**, a song taken from her second gold album, **Voices In The Wind**.

Recommended:
Somewhere Between (Capitol/–)
Moment Of Truth (Capitol/Capitol)
Aces (Capitol/Liberty)
Voices In The Wind (Liberty/Liberty)

Johnny Bond

Singing cowboy film star, Johnny Bond, was born Cyrus Whitfield Bond, at Enville, Oklahoma, on June 1, 1915.

After his family moved to a Marietta, Oklahoma farm in the '20s, he bought a 98 cent ukelele through a Montgomery Ward catalogue and began playing it, moving on to guitar and becoming proficient on that instrument by the time he'd entered high school. In 1934, Bond made his debut on an Oklahoma City radio station. Three years later, he joined the Jimmy Wakely Trio (known as the Bell Boys) – a group heard by Gene Autry – and signed for Autry's Melody Ranch show in 1940.

That same year, Bond began recording for Columbia Records, with whom he recorded **Cimarron**, **Divorce Me, C.O.D.**,

Tennessee Saturday Night, **Cherokee Waltz**, **A Petal From A Faded Rose** and many others. His strong association with Autry also led to minor parts and sidekick roles in scores of films, while during the '50s and '60s he guested on TV shows hosted by Autry, Spade Cooley and Jimmy Wakely, becoming co-host of Compton's Town Hall Party Show and partner with Tex Ritter in music publishing.

A fine songwriter, Bond is responsible for such standards as **Cimarron, I Wonder Where You Are Tonight, Gone And Left Me Blues, Your Old Love Letters, Tomorrow Never Comes** plus around 500 other compositions. His contract with Autry's Republic Records provided that label with **Hot Rod Lincoln**, a Top 30 pop hit in 1960; a 1965 recording of **Ten Little Bottles** giving another company, Starday, a top-selling single. In the late '60s he signed for Capitol, cutting an album with Merle Travis, and then, after seeing one of his Starday tracks **Here Come The Elephants** become a mild hit (1971), moved on to Lamb And Lion who released one album, **How I Love Them Old Songs** (1975).

Bond toured the UK in 1976, the same year that his book 'The Tex Ritter Story' was published by Chappell. A writer of some talent he also wrote a book on Gene Autry plus 'Reflections', an autobiography.

His death occurred in Burbank, California, on June 12, 1978, after an illness which lasted for almost a year.

Recommended:
The Best Of Johnny Bond (Starday-Gusto/–)

Debby Boone

Daughter of singer Pat Boone and granddaughter of Red Foley, Debby was born Hackensack, New Jersey, September 22, 1956.

An onstage performer at an early age, Debby, her sisters and her mother (singer-actress Shirley Jones) provided the backing for Pat's act as the Boone Girls. Debby and her sisters later formed a gospel quartet, the Boones, before she opted to go solo, gaining a massive hit with **You Light Up My Life** (1977), claimed to be the biggest-selling single in over 20 years, the record providing her with a Grammy as Best New Artist. It also gave Debby her first major country hit and won her the Top New Vocalist category at the Academy Of Country Music presentations in 1978. That same year Debby achieved another country chart hit **God Knows**, following this with such climbers as **My Heart Has A Mind Of Its Own** and **Breakin' In A Brand New Broken Heart** in 1979, the year that she was nominated in the Top Female Vocalist category at the CMA Awards. By 1980 she had her first country No. 1 in **Are You On The Road To Lovin' Me Again**.

An autobiography 'Debby Boone – So Far' was published in 1981.

Recommended:
Debby Boone (Warner Bros/–)
Love Has No Reason (Warner Bros/–)

Larry Boone

One of the very best honky-tonk singers and country songwriters to emerge in the '80s, Larry Boone, from Cooper City, Florida, has probably enjoyed more success

The Best Of Debby Boone. Courtesy Warner Bros Records.

as a writer than recording star, although he has consistently hit the country charts and produced several acclaimed albums.

Before taking the route to Nashville and a career in country, Boone dabbled with the idea of becoming an athlete. For a time he was a sports writer, and with his academic credentials he became a substitute teacher. He eventually reached Nashville in 1980, but it was to be several years before he was to make his mark. Initially he played at the Wax Museum, a Nashville tourist attraction. His warm, mellow country voice came to the attention of Gene Ferguson, who signed him to a management contract. He started to make an impact as a writer, then he landed a record deal with Mercury in 1986 and proceeded to chalk up several minor hits such as **Stranger Things Have Happened** (1986), **Roses In December** (1987) and making the Top 10 with **Don't Give Candy To A Stranger** (1988). By this time he was an accomplished stage performer and was regularly providing fellow country stars Lacy J. Dalton, Ed Bruce, John Conlee and Don Williams with hit songs.

Boone continued to make the Top 20 with **I Just Called To Say Goodbye Again** (1988) and **Wine Me Up** (1989), and looked set for success when he joined Columbia Records in 1990. He co-wrote the majority of the songs on **One Way To Go**, his first album for the new label, but instead of hitting the big-time, his career faltered. He only managed a couple of minor hits with **I Need A Miracle** and **To Be With You** (both 1991). Boone was still with Columbia in 1993, and went back in the charts with **Get In Line**.

Recommended:
Swinging Doors, Sawdust Floors
(Mercury/Mercury)
Down That River Road (Mercury/–)
One Way To Go (Columbia/–)

Don Bowman

Top country comedian of the '60s, Bowman was born in Lubbock, Texas, August 26, 1937. While a child he sang in church, later learning to play guitar – though part of his stock in trade is that he professes to play it badly! During Bowman's school years he became a DJ though he was forced to sell hub caps and pick cotton.

Becoming more established as a DJ, at one time working with Waylon Jennings, he began working more of his own routines into shows, eventually opting to become a full-time fun maker, appearing at clubs in the South and Southwest. In the mid-'60s, Chet Atkins signed Bowman to RCA, the result being **Chet Atkins Made Me A Star**. In 1966 came smaller successes with **Giddy Up Do-Nut** and **Surely Not**, which helped Bowman win the 'Billboard' award as favourite C&W Comedian Of The Year.

His others hits have included **Folsom Prison Blues No.2** (1968) and **Poor Old Ugly Gladys Jones** (1970).

Recommended:
Support Your Local Prison (RCA/–)
All New (Mega/–)

Boxcar Willie

A singer whose train whistle impressions helped him become a UK favourite before he had established any real reputation in his homeland, Boxcar was born Lecil Martin, Sterret, Texas, September 1, 1931. The son of a railroad worker, he worked in many jobs while pursuing a part-time profession as an entertainer for 37 years. Determined to become a top-line country artist, he assumed a hobo-like persona during the mid-'70s and moved to Nashville, giving himself three years in which to make the grade. Seen by Scottish agent Drew Taylor at Nashville's Possum Hollow Club in 1977, he was signed to play his first British tour the following year, playing to small clubs. Gradually, after further tours, he built something of a reputation and gained a spot on the 1979 Wembley Festival bill where he proved a sensation. Also in 1979 he made his first appearance on the Grand Ole Opry winning a standing ovation.

Boxcar Willie, a 1979 release by the sage of the train who has a strong following in the US and Europe. Courtesy Big R Records.

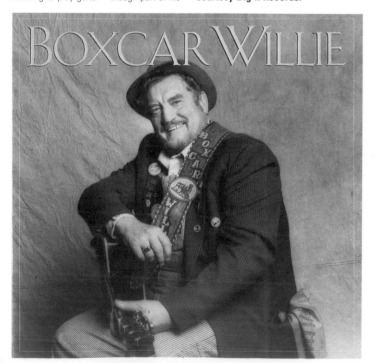

He returned to Wembley for a further triumph in 1980, reaching the Top 5 in the UK album charts that year with a TV-advertised album, **King Of The Road**. In the US he logged his first single in the country charts, his **Train Medley** nudging into the Top 100.

A fine entertainer who deals mainly in material of a traditional nature, Boxcar has remained a major crowd-puller in Europe, but has failed to make much of an impact in the USA. He now owns a theatre in Branson, Missouri, where his larger-than-life personality delights the inquisitive country fans.

Recommended:
King Of The Road (–/Prism)
Daddy Was A Railway Man (–/Big R)
Live In Concert (–/Pickwick)

Bill Boyd

Singer, guitarist, bandleader and film actor, William Boyd was born in Fannin County, Texas, on September 29, 1910.

A true cowboy raised on a ranch, Boyd, together with his brother Jim (born on September 28, 1914), formed Alexander's Daybreakers in the late '20s, this group eventually becoming the Cowboy Ramblers, a Greenville, Texas, band. They began recording for Bluebird in 1934, initially cutting versions of traditional numbers plus cowboy songs like **Strawberry Roan** – of these, **Under The Double Eagle** (1935), a fiddle and guitar version of the popular march, proved most successful. Boyd, whose band grew from a four-man string band in 1934 to a ten-man western swing outfit in 1938, recorded over 300 sides for RCA, including such best-sellers as **New Spanish Two Step** and **Spanish Fandango** (1939) plus **Lone Star Rag** (1949), and had his own radio show on station WRR, Dallas for many years. His last recording session was February 7, 1950 and he retired soon after. He died on December 7, 1977.

After his brother's death, Jim Boyd, who had worked with the Light Crust Doughboys in 1938–39 and the Men Of The West in 1949–51, continued the family tradition, performing with the Light Crust Doughboys before modern-day audiences in the Dallas-Forth Worth area.

Recommended:
Bill Boyd's Cowboy Ramblers (Bluebird/–)
Bill Boyd And His Cowboy Ramblers
1934–47 (Texas Rose/–)

Owen Bradley

A Nashville producer, musician and executive, Owen Bradley had as much, if not more, to do with the creation of the Nashville Sound and the growth of the studios than any other individual.

Born on October 10, 1915, in Westmoreland, Tennessee, Bradley was a band-leading pianist who had one of the most popular dance bands in the Nashville area for some time and served as director of WSM radio from 1940–58, leading their staff orchestra from 1947. That same year, Decca's Paul Cohen asked Bradley to do some producing for him in Nashville. Bradley accepted and by 1952 he and his younger brother Harold (later a leading Nashville session musician) had built their first studio.

By 1956 they had built their legendary Quonset hut on 16th Avenue South, which was the beginning of large scale Nashville studio activity and of the area which has come to be known as Music Row. In the Studio, which became known as Bradley's Barn, Bradley became instrumental in pioneering the so-called Nashville Sound during the '50s, smoothing out country music and providing it with a more pop, uptown treatment, often featuring lush strings and background voices.

Bradley, whose own recording career had started with the Bullet label, made many successful records of his own during the '50s. But as MCA's chief staff producer he achieved more fame, producing just about every one of their major artists.

He was quite open about dispensing with steel guitars, fiddles etc, and pursuing a sophisticated recording sound which many felt was castrating country as an individual form. But Bradley, with the Nashville Sound, formulated a safe, broadly appealing sound and can justifiably be said to have brought country music in from the cold when it needed help most. Had the music not gone through this stage of its development, it might well not enjoy its current acceptability.

In 1958 he moved up the corporate ladder to become country A&R director, a position he held for over a decade until his promotion to vice-president of MCA's Nashville operation. In 1974 he was elected to the Country Music Hall Of Fame and, after retirement from MCA, continued to produce independently until he retired in 1982. Canadian new-wave country singer k. d. lang coaxed Bradley out of retirement in 1988 to produce her **Shadowlands** album, which was as much a tribute to Bradley, the producer, as it was to lang's distinctive vocal work. The project turned out to be one of the biggest successes of Bradley's long career and helped rekindle interest in the recordings of Patsy Cline, which he had produced more than 25 years earlier.

Recommended:
Big Guitar (–/Charly)

Elton Britt

Born in Marshall, Arkansas, June 27, 1917, Elton Britt's real name was James Britt Baker. He was the son of a champion fiddle player. While still at school he learnt guitar on a model purchased from Sears Roebuck for $5.

When only 14, he was discovered by talent scouts who signed him to a year's contract with station KMPC, Los Angeles, where he appeared with the Beverly Hillbillies. In 1937 he signed for RCA Records, staying with the label for over 20 years, during which time he recorded 672 singles and over 50 albums. Following this, he moved on to record for Decca, Ampar and ABC-Paramount.

Britt, who was considered to be one of the world's greatest yodellers, obtained the first gold disc awarded to any country star when, in 1944, his version of **There's A Star Spangled Banner Waving Somewhere**, originally released in May 1942 as a B-side, reached the million sales mark. His other successful singles include **Chime Bells** (1948), **Jimmie Rodgers Blues** (1968) and **Quicksilver** (1949), the latter being one of the many duets he recorded with Rosalie Allen.

Britt, who died June 23, 1972, appeared in several films and made many TV appearances during the '50s and '60s, although he was a semi-retired gentleman farmer from around 1954 to 1968.

Recommended:
16 Great Country Performances (ABC/–)
Elton Britt Yodel Songs (RCA/Stetson)

Brooks & Dunn

This pair of rowdy, good-natured country rockers teamed up in 1991 and delivered **Brand New Man**, the most successful debut album ever released by a country duo or group. The album not only went multi-platinum, but also produced four No.1 singles and a fifth that hit Top 5. In 1993, the album won ACM award for Album Of The Year, and single **Boot Scootin' Boogie** won Single Of The Year.

Kix Brooks was born Leon Eric Brooks, May 12, 1956, Shreveport, Louisiana, just down the street from Johnny Horton. His first paying gig was performing with Horton's daughter, and later he became a veteran of the road, settling for a time in both Fairbanks, Alaska and New Orleans. He moved to Nashville in the early '80s and started penning hits for John Conlee (**I'm Only In It For The Love**), Nitty Gritty Dirt Band (**Modern Day Romance**) and Highway 101 (**Who's Lonely Now**). He recorded as a solo for Avion Records (1983), then later joined Capitol Records, releasing an excellent rock-styled album in 1989 and scoring a minor hit with the self-penned **Sacred Ground**.

Ronnie Dunn, like Brooks, spent years working the road. He was born June 1, 1954, in Coleman, Texas, and attended Abilene Christian College, but was thrown out for performing in honky-tonks. He moved to Tulsa where he formed the house band at Duke's night club (his bass player

Hard Workin' Man, Brooks & Dunn. Courtesy Arista Records.

was Garth Brooks' sister Betsy Smittle). In Oklahoma he recorded for Churchill Records, making his chart debut with **It's Written All Over Your Face** (1983). After winning the 1989 Marlboro National Talent Contest he relocated to Nashville.

Both Brooks and Dunn were trying to land solo deals in 1990 when they were introduced to each other by Arista Records' Tim DuBois, who suggested they write together. The ploy paid off, and DuBois signed them as a duo to Arista, and their first single, **Brand New Man** (1991), soared to the top of the charts and paved the way for the album of the same name, which crossed over to the pop charts. Further No.1s came with **Next Broken Heart** (1991), **Neon Moon** and **Boot Scootin' Boogie** (both 1992), the latter gaining a special dance mix, which took Brooks & Dunn's music to a whole new audience outside mainstream country.

The pair make a formidable combination in concert; Dunn is the less flamboyant of the two, but his vocal intensity somehow matches Brooks' manic leaps, duckwalks and near-violent guitar work and his more rock-edged voice. They picked up the Country Music Association Vocal Duo Of The Year Award in 1992. Their second album, **Hard Workin' Man** (1993), also gained platinum status and presented the duo with another No.1 in the title song.

Recommended:
Brand New Man (Arista/–)
Hard Workin' Man (Arista/–)
Kix Brooks (Capitol/–)

Garth Brooks

The Country Music Superstar of the '90s, Brooks was born on February 7, 1962, in Tulsa, but raised in Yukon, Oklahoma, where country music played a role in the Brooks' household, but not a dominant one. His mother, Colleen Carroll Brooks, had been a country performer in the mid-'50s, recording for Capitol Records and she was a regular on Red Foley's Ozark Jubilee TV show. By the time Garth was born she had retired from a professional career and the Brooks' house reverberated with as much rock and pop music as country.

A keen sportsman, Garth attended Oklahoma State University, Stillwater, on a track scholarship (javelin) with no set plans for a music career, although he had sung occasionally at Yukon High School. It was not until 1984 when he realized that a sports career was not for him, so he went into advertising and started to take music seriously. He had been performing around Stillwater for some months, and in the summer of 1985 he left for Nashville and a career in country music, only to return home four days later, dejected by rejection.

He joined a local band, Santa Fe, as lead singer, and for the next year played the Southwest circuit performing a mix of nostalgic pop hits and modern country. Garth had become a big fan of singer-writers James Taylor and Dan Folgelberg, rock bands Boston and Kansas, and the modern country of George Strait.

In early 1987 Garth, his new wife Sandy (whom he married in May 1986) and Santa Fe moved to Nashville. It was Garth who made the impact, singing jingles and on demos for publishers, and holding down a day-time job in a boot store at the same time. He signed a writer's contract in November 1987 and by the end of the next

Above: Brooks & Dunn keep up their boot scootin' stage antics at the 1993 Nashville Fan Fair.

year had joined Capitol Records, working in the studio with Allen Reynolds. His first single, **Much Too Young (To Feel This Damn Old)**, slowly climbed into the Top 10 in the summer of 1989, and his first album, **Garth Brooks**, gave no indication of what was to come. It was a straight country set with plenty of fiddle and steel guitar and good songs, gaining favourable reviews in all the country music press. His second single, **If Tomorrow Comes**, hit the top of the charts, but it was his fourth release, **The Dance**, accompanied by an evocative video, which opened the floodgates. **The Dance** soared to the top of the charts and pushed the album into the pop charts, and from there was no stopping Garth Brooks.

During the next few years he was everywhere. He had further country No.1s with **Friends In Low Places** and **Unanswered Prayers** (1990), **Two Of A Kind, Workin' On A Full House, The Thunder Rolls** and **Shameless** (1992). With his third album, **Ropin' The Wind**, he set a new precedent, when on day of release in September 1991, advance orders stood at 4 million and the record entered the pop charts at No.1. This had never happened to a singer wearing a cowboy hat who phrased his words with an unmistakable southern drawl. At the same time, his two previous albums, **Garth Brooks** and **No Fences**, which had both gained platinum status, were in the pop Top 10, and for some weeks Brooks held both the No.1 and No.2 position in the pop charts. This kind of success helped lead to a new awareness of country music in America and opened the doors for many other country stars to taste pop chart success.

Ropin' The Wind, Garth Brooks. Courtesy Capitol Records.

As successful as his recordings have been, it is as an onstage performer that Brooks has taken country music to a new high and reached out to a younger audience. He is very visual, and rides a continual wave of energy in true rock rather than country, as he runs around the stage, involves his fellow musicians in his crazy antics and really communicates with his fans. In 1991 and 1992 he outsold every pop and rock act at the major American stadiums, setting new records for selling thousands of show tickets in mere minutes.

The Brooks phenomenon continued with his fourth album, **The Chase**, which also had high advance orders prior to release in September 1992, gaining instant platinum status, entering the pop charts at No.1 and providing such country chart-toppers as **We Shall Be Free, Somewhere Other Than The Night** and **Learning To Live Again**. Simultaneously, he released **Beyond The Season**, a Christmas album which hit No.2 on the pop and country charts and gained yet another multi-platinum award.

He has won more than 50 major industry awards, three times winning CMA's Entertainer Of The Year. His album sales (for six releases) have topped 35 million in a career of less than five years, which makes him possibly the most successful country music entertainer of all time. But the man maintains his close affinity to country music. His Stillwater Band utilizes fiddle and steel guitar, his songs cover a wide range from cowboy ballads through raucous honky-tonkers to country swing and rock. His family are closely involved with his career, with his sister, Betsy Smittle, playing bass in the band, and his brother, Kelly, acting as road manager.

Although Garth talked about retiring from touring to spend more time with his family in 1992, all the indications are that he will be around for a good many years to come. He is a natural writer, a versatile singer and an exciting performer, who has made country music the music of the early 1990s, showing that it can be acceptable right across the USA and as an equal to rock, pop, soul, jazz or any other musical style.

Recommended:
Garth Brooks (Capitol/Capitol)
No Fences (Capitol/Capitol)
Ropin' The Wind (Capitol/Capitol)
The Chase (Capitol/Capitol)
Beyond The Season (Capitol/Capitol)

The Browns

The Browns – Ella Maxine Brown, born in Sampti, Louisiana, April 27, 1932; her brother Jim Edward, born in Sparkman, Arkansas, March 1, 1934; and younger sister Bonnie, born in Sparkman, Arkansas, July 31, 1937 – began as a duo in the early '50s when Jim and Maxine won a talent contest on Little Rock's KLRA radio station. In 1955, following an extensive concert tour, Bonnie came in to form a trio, the threesome becoming a headline act on the Ozark Jubilee show. Initially signed to Abbott Records, the Browns moved to RCA after being brought to the label's attention by Jim Reeves. They scored an initial hit with a version of the Louvin Brothers' **I Take A Chance** in 1956 and after Jim Ed had completed his army service, they recorded **The Three Bells**, an adaptation of Edith Piaf's Euro-hit **Les Trois Cloches**, which proved to be a 1959 million-seller.

he teamed with Helen Cornelius and grabbed a country No.1 with **I Don't Want To Marry You**, followed this with another duet, **Saying Hello, Saying I Love You, Saying Goodbye**, which only just missed the top spot. Since that time Brown and Cornelius have also had many major records, such as **If The World Ran Out Of Love Tonight** (1978), **Lying In Love With You** (1979), and **Morning Comes Too Early** (1980), the twosome's final chart record for RCA being **Don't Bother To Knock** (1981). An award winner way back in 1967, when the Browns won the Cash Box poll as the best country vocal group,

Angel's Sunday, Jim Ed Brown. Courtesy RCA Records.

Jim Ed also shared the CMA vocal duo award with Helen Cornelius ten years later. These days you'll find Jim Ed regularly hosting the Grand Ole Opry in Nashville, where he is rightly regarded as one of the great country stars of yesteryear.

Recommended:
Morning (RCA/RCA)
Barrooms And Pop A Tops (RCA/–)
I Don't Want To Have To Marry You – with Helen Cornelius (RCA/RCA)
I'll Never Be Free – with Helen Cornelius (RCA/–)

Marty Brown

Marty Brown, the kid from the small town, burst on the country scene in 1992 with the catchy single, **Every Now And Then**, which, with the help of an excellent video, rapidly climbed the charts. Born and raised in Maceo, Kentucky, Brown served his dues working clubs and honky-tonks. With a yodel and a hint of sadness in his voice, Brown evokes comparisons to the legendary Hank Williams Sr.

After years of knocking on doors in Nashville, he finally landed a contract with MCA Records in 1991, and his first album, **High And Dry**, introduced a sound that was so country it made the New Traditionalists sound slick and ultra-modern. In support of the album, Marty and his band, The Maceo Misfit, undertook a 12-state High And Dry Cadillac Tour, when he visited 45 Wal-Mart stores in the south-west in 42 days in his '69 red Cadillac DeVille Convertible. His second album, **Wild Kentucky Skies**, further showcased his solid writing and undiluted country styling.

Recommended:
High And Dry (MCA/–)
Wild Kentucky Skies (MCA/–)

I Don't Want To Have To Marry You, Jim Ed Brown. Courtesy RCA Records.

Hits such as **Scarlet Ribbons** (1959), **The Old Lamplighter**, **Teen-Ex**, **Send Me The Pillow You Dream On**, **Blue Christmas** (all 1960) and **Ground Hog** (1961) followed, plus a number of well-received overseas tours.

In 1963, the Browns became Opry members, but Bonnie and Maxine, both married, wanted to spend more time with their families. As a result, the group disbanded in 1967, despite having chart success that same year with **I Hear It Now** and **Big Daddy**. Maxine later returned to record as a solo artist for Chart, scoring with **Sugar Cane Country** (1968), while Jim Ed began a solo career on RCA.

Recommended:
20 Of The Best Of The Browns (–/RCA)
Looking Back To See (–/Bear Family)
Rockin' Rollin' Browns (–/Bear Family)

Above: The Browns' biggest record was a cover of an Edith Piaf song.

Jim Ed Brown

In 1965, Bonnie and Maxine of the Browns persuaded Chet Atkins to record Jim Ed as a solo artist, his first single, **I Heard From A Memory Last Night**, being a chart entry. Following this, Jim Ed began to record more frequently as a soloist, enjoying hits with **I'm Just A Country Boy**, **A Taste Of Heaven** (1966), **Pop A Top**, **Bottle, Bottle** (1967) and others. When the Browns disbanded in 1967, Jim Ed was easily able to reshape his stage act and continue as a star attraction.

Throughout the '70s and early '80s, Jim Ed's Midas touch continued to function. In 1970 he charted with **Morning**, a song successfully covered by singer Val Doonican in Britain, while Top 10 entries also came with **Southern Loving**, **Sometime Sunshine** (1973), and **It's That Time Of Night** (1974). During 1976

Milton Brown

One of the founders of western swing, Brown was born in Stephenville, Texas, September 8, 1903. In 1918 his family moved to Fort Worth. Following a meeting with Bob Wills in 1931, he began singing professionally as part of Wills' Fiddle Band. Then followed a number of sponsored radio shows, the band name-changing to the Aladdin Laddies when promoting Aladdin Mantle Lamps, and the Light Crust Doughboys as pluggers of Light Crust Flour.

Following some personnel changes, the band cut some sides for Victor in the guise of the Fort Worth Doughboys. But soon after, Brown formed his own unit, the Musical Brownies, to play on radio KTAT, Fort Worth, the lineup eventually stabilizing at Milton Brown (vocals), Durwood Brown (guitar and vocals), Jesse Ashlock and Cecil Brower (fiddles), Wanna Coffman (bass) and Fred 'Papa' Calhoun (piano). This line-up – minus Ashlock – recorded a number of sides for Bluebird in April 1934, the fiddler returning for the band's second Bluebird session in August of that year.

With the addition of jazz-playing guitarist Bob Dunn – the first in country to electrify his instrument – a complete western swing sound was achieved. At the same time, Brown concluded a contract with the new Decca and with this label the Brownies began cutting a miscellany of titles ranging from jazz items like **St Louis Blues**, **Memphis Blues** and **Mama Don't Allow** through to such western songs as **Carry Me Back To The Lone Prairie** and **The Wheel Of The Wagon Is Broken**. But, just when the band began moving into top gear, Brown died following a car accident. Though rushed to hospital, Brown died on April 13, 1935. A passenger, vocalist Katherine Prehoditch, was instantly killed.

For a while the Brownies continued to fulfil contractual obligations but the band finally folded in early 1938. Brown is considered, along with Wills, as the co-founder of western swing.

Recommended:
Taking Off (String/–)
Dance-O-Rama (Rambler/–)
Easy Ridin' Papa (–/Charly)

T. Graham Brown

T. Graham Brown turned out to be the real revelation of the New Country Movement that started gaining momentum in Nashville in the late '80s. A throwback to '50s rockabilly and '60s R&B, he brought a

I Write It Down, Ed Bruce. Courtesy MCA Records.

Above: Ed Bruce was once a Memphis rockabilly who sold used cars.

black, soulful edge to country, resulting in a string of Top 10 country hits including **Hell And High Water** (1986), **Don't Go To Strangers** (1987) and **Darlene** (1988).

Anthony Graham Brown was born October 30, 1954, in Atlanta, Georgia. Following graduation, he moved to Athens to attend the University of Georgia. Brown and college buddy Dirk Howell, played rock, pop and beach music as Dirk And Tony at the Athens Holiday Inn, but when Dirk opted for the straight life, Brown decided to form a band.

Modelling himself on David Allan Coe, he fronted a band called Reo Diamond. With the advent of Urban Cowboy at the end of the '70s, Brown's raunchy country was no longer in vogue, so he formed T.

Graham Brown's Rack Of Spam, and played soul and R&B music. By this time he was married, and with his wife Sheila's support he moved to Nashville in 1982, hoping to make a career in country music.

He signed a writer's contract with CBS Songs and was taken under the wings of veteran tunesmith Harlan Howard. He gained work singing on demos and also did jingles for Kraft, McDonald's and Coca Cola, among others. In 1984 he was signed to a recording contract by Terry Choate at Capitol and made the country charts with **Drowning In Memories** the following year. His first Top 10 record was **I Tell It Like It Used To Be** (1985), and for the next few years he was hardly absent from the charts. His mix of blues, rock, R&B, soul and country blended with his big, gravelly voice, and gave Brown one of the most distinctive sounds in country. He has

continued to make jingles, a lucrative sideline to his hits, which have included **Brilliant Conversationalist** (1987), **The Last Resort** (1988), **Come As You Were** (1989) and **Don't Go Out** (1990), the latter a duet with Tanya Tucker.

Recommended:
Brilliant Conversationalist (Capitol/Capitol)
Bumper To Bumper (Capitol/Capitol)
I Tell It Like It Used To Be (Capitol/Capitol)
You Can't Take It With You (Capitol/–)

Ed Bruce

Recording for Phillips under the name Edwin Bruce (he was born William Edwin Bruce Jr on December 29, 1940 in Keiser, Arkansas), this singer had a brief career as a '50s rocker. By the mid-'60s he'd moved to Nashville, there recording over a dozen singles for RCA with the aid of producer Bob Ferguson, having mild chart reaction with **Walker's Woods** (1967), **Last Train To Clarksville** (1967), and **Painted Girls And Wine** (1968), his rich voice also being heard on an album, **If I Could Just Go Home**.

In 1968, Bruce joined Monument Records cutting a fine album, **Shades Of Ed Bruce**, also having minor singles success with **Song For Jenny** and **Everybody Wants To Go Home** (1969). However, despite his strong commercial appeal, it wasn't until the '70s and an association with UA Records that Bruce finally established himself as a record seller of any consequence, his **Mamas Don't Let Your Babies Grow Up To Be Cowboys** moving high into the charts during early 1976. The song, written by Bruce and his wife Patsy, was later covered by Waylon Jennings and Willie Nelson whose joint version climbed to No.1 in 1978, gaining Bruce a nomination both for a Grammy and for the CMA's Song Of The Year.

In the wake of his last single for UA, a version of Alex Harvey's **Sleep All Mornin'**, Bruce signed for Epic (1977), only mustering mid-chart singles from 1977 to 1979.

Throughout 1979 Bruce spent his time writing and recording, fashioning new material for his new label, MCA, for whom he signed in 1980. That year he logged three major singles, **Diane**, **The Last Cowboy Song** and **Girls, Women And Ladies** plus **Ed Bruce**, which re-established him as a major country music name. Well-known on TV ads where he had dressed in Daniel Boone manner to advertise Tennessee – gaining Bruce the title of The Tennessean – his acting career flourished initially when he was signed to appear in The Chisholms mini-series.

Since that time there have been such other excellent albums as **One To One** (1981) and **I Write It Down** (1982), along with hit singles that include **Everything's A Waltz**, **You're The Best Break This Heart Ever Had** (1981), **Love's Found You And Me**, **Ever Never Lovin' You** (1982), **My First Taste Of Texas** and **After All** (1984). Over the years Ed Bruce has written hits for such artists as Kitty Wells, Tanya Tucker, Crystal Gayle, Tommy Roe, Kenny Price and Charlie Louvin. 1984 found Ed back on RCA gaining Top 5 hits with **You Turn Me On (Like A Radio)** and **Nights**. Now divorced from wife Patsy, Ed's career in recent years has gone into rapid decline and he no longer has a major record label deal.

Recommended:
Shades Of Ed Bruce
   (Monument/Monument)
Ed Bruce (UA/–)
The Tennessean (Epic/–)
I Write It Down (MCA/MCA)
The Best Of Ed Bruce (–/MCA)
Night Things (RCA/RCA)
Rock Boppin' Baby (–/Bear Family)

Cliff Bruner

The leader of an early swing/honky-tonk band, Cliff Bruner was born April 25, 1915, in Houston, Texas, and got his start as a fiddler in Milton Brown's Musical Brownies, cutting 48 sides with Brown before the bandleader's death in 1935.

At that point Bruner formed his own band, the Texas Wanderers and began a long recording association with Decca in 1937. His biggest hit on the label was the first version released of Floyd Tillman's **It Makes No Difference Now** (1938), although one of the band's most historic milestones was cutting the first truck driving song on record: Ted Daffan's **Truck Driver's Blues** (1939).

Bruner – who also recorded for the Ayo label in the '40s – became increasingly inactive as the years passed and by the early '50s had become an insurance salesman and executive, performing only occasionally. By the late '70s he was living in the Houston suburb, League City.

Boudleaux And Felice Bryant

Boudleaux Bryant, born in Shellman, Georgia on February 13, 1920, originally aimed at a career in classical music, studying to become a concert violinist and, in 1938, playing a season with the Atlanta Philharmonic. Then came a switch to more popular music forms, Bryant joining a jazz group for a period. It was during this time he met his wife-to-be Felice Scudato (born Milwaukee, Wisconsin, August 7, 1925), then an elevator attendant at Milwaukee's Shrader Hotel. After marriage, the duo began writing songs together, in 1949 sending one composition, **Country Boy**, to Fred Rose who published the song, thus providing Little Jimmy Dickens with a Top 10 hit.

In 1950 the Bryants moved to Nashville and began writing hit after hit, supplying Carl Smith with a constant supply of chart-busters, one of these songs, **Hey Joe** (1953), becoming a million-seller when covered by Frankie Laine. During 1955, Eddy Arnold charted with the Bryants' **I've Been Thinkin'** and **The Richest Man**, but it was the duo's association with the Everly Brothers that brought the songwriting team their biggest string of successes with **Bye Bye Love**, **Wake Up Little Susie**, **Problems**, **Bird Dog**, **All I Have To Do Is Dream**, **Poor Jenny** and **Take A Message To Mary**, all ending up on million-selling discs.

Other Bryant hits have included: **Raining In My Heart** (Buddy Holly, 1959); **Let's Think About Living** (Bob Luman, 1960); **Mexico** (Bob Moore, 1960); **Baltimore** (Sonny James, 1964); **Come Live With Me** (Roy Clark, 1973); and the oft-recorded **Rocky Top**, which Felice and Boudleaux wrote in just ten minutes. In 1974 'Billboard' was able to publish a list of well over 400 artists who had recorded songs by the Bryants, and in 1986 the duo were honoured by being elected to the Songwriters' Hall Of Fame. The following year Boudleaux died on June 30, following a short illness. Deservedly this talented husband and wife team was inducted into the Country Music Hall Of Fame in 1991, when Felice was able to make a tearful speech of acceptance.

Jimmy Buffett

Singer-songwriter Jimmy Buffett brought a good-time feel to country music in the mid-'70s with his songs about boats, beaches, bars and beautiful women. Born December 25, Pascagoula, Mississippi, Buffett was

Above: Jimmy Buffett is also a Florida resident and popular novelist.

raised in Mobile, Alabama. He gained a BS degree in history and journalism from the University of Southern Mississippi and started his singing career in the bars of New Orleans. In 1969 he moved to Nashville, landed a job as the Nashville correspondent for 'Billboard' magazine, and started building a reputation for his lyrical songs and solo performances.

He signed a recording contract with Barnaby Records and, working in the studio with Buzz Cason, made the **Down To Earth** album (1970), which flopped. A second album, **High Cumberland Jubilee**, was never released, and a disillusioned Buffett moved to Florida. In the meantime, Tompall & The Glaser Brothers recorded some of his songs, and, in 1972, he received an offer from ABC Dunhill Records to return to Nashville.

A White Sport Coat And A Pink Crustacean received rave reviews and presented Buffett with his first minor country hit in **The Great Filling Station Holdup** (1973). He made a bigger impact the following year with **Come Monday**, which made the pop charts. During the next few years he emerged as one of the biggest concert attractions and album-sellers on the American music scene. He made the country Top 20 with **Margaritaville** (1977) and also crossed over into the pop Top 10. Soon albums like **Changes In Latitudes, Changes In Attitudes** (1977), **Son Of A Son Of A Sailor** (1978), **You Had To Be There** (1978) and **Coconut Telegraph** (1980), all gained platinum awards.

Many of his songs reflect his lifestyle in the Florida Keys where he spends much of his time on his boat or in his Margaritaville store. He has maintained a large and loyal following over the years with a glossy fan magazine. He is also now a popular novelist. His albums have continued to sell in vast quantities and he was one of the first artists to have all his back catalogue (16 albums) made available on CD. He was back in the country Top 20 with **If The Phone Doesn't Ring, It's Me** (1985), and though he has had songs recorded by Lefty Frizzell, Merle Haggard, Crystal Gayle and Waylon Jennings, Buffett has remained outside the country music mainstream.

Recommended:
Boats, Beaches, Bars & Ballads (MCA/–)
Floridays (MCA/–)
Son Of A Son Of A Sailor/Coconut
   Telegraph (MCA/–)
Feedin' Frenzy (MCA/–)

The Burch Sisters

Cathy, Charlene and Cindy Burch came to prominence in Nashville in the late '80s when they landed a recording contract with Mercury Records. This followed several years of building up a healthy reputation around their home town of Screven, Georgia.

The three sisters were born in Jacksonville, Florida, and moved to Georgia in their teens. Coming from a musical family, the girls perfected their pure-country harmonies on a mixture of country standards and gospel songs. In 1986 they won a State talent contest and started to take their music more seriously. Financing a recording session in Atlanta, they hawked the finished tape around the Nashville studios and were lucky enough to be signed to Mercury in 1987. The Burch Sisters scored a handful of chart singles during the next three years, including

Everytime You Go Outside I Hope It Pours (1988) and **Old Flame, New Fire** (1989). The girls have always remained in the shadow of more famous girl vocal groups, and by 1992 the act had split and Cathy Burch signed a solo recording contract with Giant Records in March 1993.

Recommended:
New Five (Mercury/–)

Billy Burnette

William Burnette III was born May 8, 1953, in Memphis, Tennessee. His father was rockabilly guitarman Dorsey Burnette, and his uncle was rockabilly legend Johnny Burnette, and they comprised two-thirds of the Johnny Burnette Rock'n'Roll Trio, a red-hot rockin' '50s bop act that hiccupped its way to fame and fortune. Billy grew up surrounded by music, and when he was only seven he had Ricky Nelson's band back him up on his very first single, **Hey Daddy** on Dot Records. At this time the Burnette brothers were based in Los Angeles, making their mark as writers with hits for Nelson (**Believe What You Say, Waitin' In School**), and scoring their own solo pop hits.

Young Billy learned to play guitar at an early age and performed worldwide as part of Brenda Lee's shows. In the early '70s he led the band behind his father, later moving back to Memphis where he worked in the studios with Chips Moman. A contract with Polydor Records followed in 1979 and he made his debut on the country charts with **What's A Little Love Between Friends** (1979). He then moved to Nashville where he began writing hit

Below: After starting with the family rockabilly band, then two years with Roger Miller and a six-year-stint with Fleetwood Mac, Billy Burnette went solo with a back-up band.

songs for such diverse acts as Charlie Rich, Eddy Raven, Ray Charles, Everly Brothers and Charley Pride. He also spent two years as a singer and guitarist with Roger Miller.

In 1985 Billy signed with Curb Records and was nominated by the Academy of Country Music as the Top New Male Vocalist the following year and seemed poised for major success, but was sidetracked when Fleetwood Mac asked him to join the band when Lindsey Buckingham left in 1987. He spent six years with Mac, touring around the world and recording two multi-platinum albums with them. He brought a country influence to the group and his song, **When The Sun Goes Down**, received a smattering of country airplay. Billy left Fleetwood Mac in 1992 and headed back to Nashville to resume his solo career. He signed with Capricorn Records, and with a batch of songs he had co-written with Paul Kennerley, Dennis Morgan, Ronnie Rogers, Deborah Allen and Rafe VanHoy, he produced the **Coming Home** album (1993) which aptly displayed his energetic brand of country music with an edge.

Recommended:
Coming Home (Capricorn/–)

Johnny Bush

Born in Houston, Texas, on February 17, 1935, Bush – voted Most Promising Male Vocalist Of The Year by Record World in 1968, an accolade duplicated by Music City News 12 months later – moved to San Antonio, Texas in 1962, obtaining his first musical job at the Texas Star Inn, where he played rhythm guitar and sang.

At a later stage, he opted to become a drummer, eventually joining a band organized by his friend Willie Nelson during the early '60s. After a year's stay with this outfit, he then became a member of Ray Price's Cherokee Cowboys, with whom he played for three years before

returning to Nelson's side once more. With Nelson he became front man for the band, the Record Men, also branching out as a solo artist on Stop Records, his first release for the label, a Nelson original titled **You Ought To Hear Me Cry**, being a mild hit in 1967. His next release, **What A Way To Live**, yet another Nelson song, climbed even further up the charts.

Primarily a honky-tonk singer in the Ray Price tradition, Bush switched from Stop – with whom he had major hits with **Undo The Right** (1968) and **You Gave Me A Mountain** (1969) – to RCA in 1972, enjoying his greatest-ever disc success with Willie Nelson's **Whiskey River**.

Throughout 1973 the hits kept on coming but began to peter out during the following year, Bush's name then being absent from the chart until 1977 when he had low-level success with **You'll Never Leave Me Completely**, a Gusto-Starday release.

Recommended:
You Gave Me A Mountain (Stop/Stop)
Undo The Right (Gusto/–)
Whiskey River (RCA/RCA)

Carl And Pearl Butler

A highly popular duo during the '60s, honky-tonk vocalist Carl Roberts Butler (born Knoxville, Tennessee, June 2, 1927) and his wife Pearl (born Pearl Dee Jones, Nashville, Tennessee, September 20, 1930) first performed as a team in 1962. Prior to this, Carl had been a highly successful recording artist with Capitol and Columbia, having hits for Columbia with **Honky Tonkitis** (1961) and **Don't Let Me Cross Over** (1962), the latter being released as a Carl Butler solo item but featuring Pearl on harmony vocals.

When **Don't Let Me Cross Over** became a country No.1, the Butlers

realized they had hit on a winning formula and began recording as a duo, logging a fair number of chart entries during the '60s, including: **Loving Arms** (1963), **Too Late To Try Again** (1964), **I'm Hanging Up The Phone** (1964) and **Just Thought I'd Let You Know** (1965).

Granted Opry status in 1962, the Butlers were influential, with Gram Parsons borrowing their country-gospel style when he recorded their **We'll Sweep Out The Ashes In The Morning**. Carl was also a gifted songwriter, penning **If Teardrops Were Pennies**, a hit for Carl Smith (1951). Later Ricky Skaggs had a No.1 hit with a revival of **Crying My Heart Out Over You** (1982). Members of the Salvation Army, the Butlers were involved in various rehabilitation programmes leading to a Meritorious Service Award in 1970. The couple continued performing and recording well into the '80s. Pearl died of thyroid complications on March 3, 1988, and Carl suffered a fatal heart attack on September 4, 1992.

Recommended:
Greatest Hits (Columbia/–)

Jerry Byrd

Born in Lima, Ohio, March 9, 1920, Jerry Byrd went on to become one of the genuine giants of the electric steel guitar. Unequalled for purity of tone and taste, he was in demand for record sessions for years, although he was never comfortable with the increasingly popular pedal steel style, preferring Hawaiian stylings. Finally, growing weary of Nashville and the music business, he chucked it all and caught a plane to Honolulu where he became revered as practically a national monument for his advancement of the Hawaiian guitar.

Recommended:
Master Of Touch And Tone (Midland/–)

Above: Sweetheart Of The Rodeo, the Byrds. Courtesy CBS Records. One of the first and finest of all country rock albums. The design was taken from a catalogue of western clothes.

The Byrds

Initially an LA folk-rock group formed in 1964, the Byrds recorded a country-influenced album **The Notorious Byrd Brothers** in 1968, using such guest musicians as Lloyd Green, John Hartford, Earl Ball and Byrd-to-be, Clarence White. That same year, the group, heavily influenced by newcomer Gram Parsons, produced **Sweetheart Of The Rodeo**, arguably the first real country-rock album, containing songs penned by the Louvin Brothers, Woody Guthrie, Merle Haggard and others. Thereafter, most Byrds albums featured some country-style tracks, despite the fact that Gram Parsons quit the group later in 1968.

The group, which folded in 1972, featured several musicians who have made some contribution to the expansion of country music. Gram Parsons and Chris Hillman formed the Flying Burrito Brothers in 1969. Parsons was also a major influence on '70s country-rock and he discovered Emmylou Harris. Hillman has played in several country-styled outfits, the most recent being the highly successful Desert Rose Band.

Recommended:
Sweetheart Of The Rodeo (Columbia/Edsel)

The Callahan Brothers

Homer C. ('Bill') Callahan, guitar, mandolin, bass and vocals; Walter T. ('Joe') Callahan, guitar and vocals.

Natives of Laurel, North Carolina (Walter born on January 27, 1910 and Homer born on March 27, 1912), the Callahan Brothers became a popular duet team of the south-eastern style in the 1930s, and by 1933 were already busy on radio and were recording for the ARC labels. They spent some time at WHAS in Louisville and WWVA in Wheeling before serving other stretches at WLW (1937–39) and KVOO in Tulsa, before settling down in the North Texas area, basing their operations from either Dallas or Wichita Falls for over a period of ten years.

It was here, for reasons best known to themselves, that they changed their names from Walter and Homer to Bill and Joe, and changed their music as well, performing more and more western and swing material, the highlight probably being their double-yodel version of **St Louis Blues**. Except for a single session with Decca (1941) and one Bill Callahan session with Cowboy Records, their 91 recorded sides were with ARC or Columbia, over a period stretching from 1934 to 1951. They became increasingly inactive in the '50s and '60s. Bill Callahan died on September 10, 1971.

Recommended:
The Callahan Brothers (Old Homestead/–)

Archie Campbell

Honoured as Comedian Of The Year in 1969 by the CMA, Campbell has been writer and star of the Hee Haw TV show.

Born in Bulls Gap, Tennessee, on November 17, 1914, his career really rocketed through stints on WNOX, Knoxville in 1949, an eventual TV show on WATE, Knoxville (1952–58), coming his way. He joined the Prince Albert portion of the Grand Ole Opry in 1958, also signing a recording contract with RCA, for whom he cut a number of comedy routines including **Beeping Sleauty** and **Rindercella**.

On the serious side, he scored with the narration **The Men In My Little Girl's Life** (1965), as well as duets with Lorene Mann, the most popular being **At The Dark End Of The Street** (1968). Away from showbusiness, Campbell was a talented sculptor, poet and painter and also a keen golfer. He died of a heart attack in Knoxville on August 29, 1987.

Recommended:
Live At Tupelo (Elektra/–)
Bedtime Stories For Adults (RCA/–)

Glen Campbell

The seventh son of a seventh son, singer-songwriter-guitarist-banjoist Glen Campbell was born in Delight, Arkansas, on April 22, 1936. A reasonable guitarist at the age of six, he joined Dick Bills' (his uncle) western band while a teenager, later forming his own outfit in New

Below: Archie Campbell – a multi-talented comedian and country singer.

Glen Campbell, a 1962 album. Courtesy Capitol Records.

Mexico, where he met Billie Nunley and married her.

Armed with his 12-string, in 1960 he opted to become one of Hollywood's busiest session musicians but found time to cut sides as a solo performer, one, **Turn Around, Look At Me**, becoming a 1961 pop hit on the local Crest label. Signed immediately to Capitol, Campbell graced the 1962 charts with Al Dexter's **Too Late To Worry, Too Blue To Cry** and Merle Travis' **Kentucky Means Paradise**, and in the mid-'60s supplied a couple of other minor hits while continuing his work as a sideman with the Beach Boys, Jan and Dean, Association, Rick Nelson, Elvis Presley and many others.

Then in 1967 he recorded John Hartford's **Gentle On My Mind**, following this monster hit with an even bigger one in **By The Time I Get To Phoenix**, a song written by Jimmy Webb. From then on came a succession of high selling albums and singles in the '70s. The most successful of the latter were **Wichita Lineman, Galveston, Where's The Playground, Susie?, Try A Little Kindness, Honey Come Back, It's Only Make Believe, All I Have To Do Is Dream** — with Bobbie Gentry, **Dream**

Above: Glen Campbell and a friend of Colonel Sanders on the Louisiana Hayride in a scene from 'Norwood'.

Baby, Country Boy, Rhinestone Cowboy and Southern Nights.

Campbell made the headlines over his on-off affair with singer Tanya Tucker while they toured and recorded together, and, in a barrage of publicity, they finally split up in 1981. He left Capitol Records that same year, and has since recorded with Atlantic, MCA, Universal and a return to Capitol. Although he has never regained the commercial success he enjoyed in the late '60s and early '70s, Campbell has been a regular in the country Top 10 with such songs as **Faithless Love** (1984), **Still Within The Sound Of My Voice** (1987), **The Hand That Rocks The Cradle** (a duet with Steve Wariner in 1987) and **She's Gone, Gone, Gone** (1989).

Possessor of 12 gold records, featured artist on countless TV shows, including his own Glen Campbell Show, co-star with John Wayne in the film 'True Grit' (1969) and star of 'Norwood' (1969), Campbell is also a golf fanatic, hosting the Glen Campbell Los Angeles Open.

Recommended:
Glen Travis Campbell (Capitol/Capitol)
I Remember Hank Williams (Capitol/ Capitol)
Rhinestone Cowboy (Capitol/Capitol)
Ernie Sings And Glen Picks (Capitol/ Capitol)
Old Home Town (Atlantic-America/ Atlantic-America)
It's Just A Matter Of Time (Atlantic-America/Atlantic-America)
Unconditional Love (Capitol/Capitol)

Left: Glen duetted with Steve Wariner on The Hand That Rocks The Cradle.

Still Within The Sound Of My Voice (MCA/MCA)
Walkin' In The Sun (Capitol/Capitol)
Somebody Like That (Liberty/Liberty)

Henson Cargill

From a family of political and legal background, Henson Cargill was born February 5, 1941 in Oklahoma City. He was brought up on a ranch. He studied at Colorado State, worked for a time as a deputy sheriff in Oklahoma City, then headed for Nashville.

When he first arrived in Nashville he started out performing with the Kimberleys, then, with the aid of guitar-playing producer Fred Carter Jr, he made his recording debut with **Skip A Rope**, which earned him a contract with Monument Records and a 1967 million-seller. He followed with such major hits as **Row, Row, Row** (1968), **None Of My Business** (1969) and **The Most Uncomplicated Goodbye** (1970). Then Cargill went through such labels as Mega, Atlantic and Copper Mountain without exactly setting the charts on fire. In the mid-'70s he moved to Stillwater, Oklahoma where he operated a large cattle ranch. After a ten-year lay-off, Henson returned to the studios in 1990 to produce the **All-American Cowboy** album for Amethyst.

Recommended:
Coming On Strong (Monument/ Monument)
Henson Cargill Country (Atlantic/–)
All-American Cowboy (Amethyst/–)

Bill And Cliff Carlisle

Cliff Carlisle, born in Taylorsville, Kentucky, on May 6, 1904, was among the first top-line dobro players. As a boy he toured as a vaudeville act, first recording for Gennett in 1930 with guitarist Wilbert Ball. An excellent yodeller, Cliff – who backed Jimmie Rodgers on some of his recordings – eventually formed a duo, the Carlisle Brothers, with his younger brother, Bill (born in Wakefield, Kentucky, December 19, 1908), playing dates in the Louisville-Cincinnati area. The brothers, who spiced their vocal and instrumental act with a fair degree of comedy, obtained regular radio exposure on station WLAP, Lexington, Kentucky during 1931, and six years later had their own show, The Carlisle Family Barn Dance, on radio station WLAP, Louisville.

In 1947 Cliff retired and for many years lived in Lexington, Kentucky. He died, following a heart attack on April 2, 1983. Bill went on to form a new group, the Carlisles. In 1954, following hits with **Rainbow At Midnight**, **No Help Wanted** and **Too Old To Cut The Mustard**, the Carlisles joined the Grand Ole Opry, remaining cast members to this day, scoring a further hit with **What Kinda Deal Is This?** (1966).

During his career, Bill Carlisle has won over 60 various country awards, his past albums include **Fresh From The Country** (King) and **The Best Of Bill Carlisle** (Hickory).

Recommended:
The Carlisles – Busy Body Boogie (–/Bear Family)

Paulette Carlson

Paulette Tenae Carlson from Northfield, Minnesota, made a big impression in the late '80s as lead singer with Highway 101, a country-rock outfit that scored No.1 hits **Somewhere Tonight** (1987) and **(Do You Love Me) Just Say Yes** (1988).

This talented singer, writer and guitarist moved to Nashville in 1981 and signed a writer's contract with the Oak Ridge Boys' publishing company. The following year she demoed some songs for an RCA singles deal and enjoyed a handful of minor hits including **You Gotta Get To My Heart (Before You Lay A Hand On Me)** (1983) and **I'd Say Yes** (1984). At this time she also had songs recorded by Tammy Wynette and Gail Davies and also sang back-up for the latter.

In 1986 she was brought in as lead singer for Highway 101, her crisp, rocky and clear vocals sitting perfectly in the blend of traditional country and rock'n'roll backbeat. Paulette used the group as a stepping stone for a solo career, and, at the end of the 1990, branched out with a solo deal with Capitol/Liberty Records that resulted in a Top 20 entry with **I'll Start With You** (1991). Her first album, **Love Goes On**, turned out to be a patchy affair. Paulette took almost a year off to have daughter Cali, so her fortunes as a solo star have yet to be realized, though she was back in the studios in the spring of 1993 working on her second solo album.

Recommended:
Love Goes On (Capitol/–)

Below: Paulette Carlson no longer travels Highway 101 as she steps out on her own.

Mary-Chapin Carpenter

Mary-Chapin Carpenter, third of four daughters, was born on February 21, 1958, in Princeton, New Jersey. Her father was an executive for 'Life' magazine and for some years the family lived in Japan. In 1974 they moved to Washington DC, by which time Mary-Chapin had learned guitar. She thrived on the local music

Come On Come On, Mary-Chapin Carpenter. Courtesy Columbia.

scene and, after gaining a degree from Brown University, she regularly appeared at the Birchmere, an acoustic-based nightclub. She met guitar player John Jennings in 1982, and he has since played a major role in her career development. Four years later she collected five awards at Washington DC's Wammie Awards and then started work on a demo tape. The original plan was to produce a gig tape, but the tape reached Columbia Records and in 1987 that demo became the basis of her debut album, **Hometown Girl**.

A throwback to singer-songwriters of the '70s, Mary-Chapin's music was literate, personal and beautifully melodic. That first album, co-produced by Jennings, was dismissed by country as being too 'folksy'. Gradually she has opened her music to more commercial possibilities, stretching country music's parameters along the way. A second album, **State Of The Heart** (1989), made both the pop and country charts and produced such Top 20 country hits as **How Do** and **Never Had It So Good** (1989), as well as **Quittin' Time** and **Something Of A Dreamer** (1990).

By this time she was working with a band, and, although she had initially written for herself to perform as a solo act, she was now creating songs that could utilize fuller instrumentation. This was evident in her breakthrough album, **Shooting Straight In The Dark** (1990), which gained gold status. The album included a revival of an old Gene Vincent hit, **Right Now** (1991), which was another Top 20 country hit, and **Down At The Twist And Shout**, a rousing Cajun number featuring three members of Beausoleil. This song hit No.2 on the country charts, won a Grammy in 1992, and led to Mary-Chapin Carpenter being named CMA's 1992 Female Vocalist Of The Year.

Carpenter is rightly hailed as a musical phenomenon, always crossing borders and breaking new ground with her blending of blues, folk, pop, rock, modern country and much more. There have been further major country hits with **Going Out Tonight** (top 20 in 1991), the raunchy **I Feel Lucky** (1992), a duet with Joe Diffie on **Not Too**

Much To Ask (1992) and Top 5 again with Lucinda Williams' **Passionate Kisses** (1993). The **Come On, Come On** album was named one of the Top 50 albums by Britain's Q Magazine. The album soared high into the country and pop charts and gained Carpenter her first platinum.

The CMA nominated the album Album Of The Year in 1993, and Mary-Chapin was named for Female Vocalist again.

Recommended:
State Of The Heart (Columbia/CBS)
Hometown Girl (Columbia/–)
Shooting Straight In The Dark (Columbia/Columbia)
Come On, Come On (Columbia/Columbia)

Fiddling John Carson

An old-timer fiddler, he became (on June 14, 1923, in Atlanta, Georgia) the first country musician to be recorded by field recordist Ralph Peer. The tracks cut, **Little Old Log Cabin In The Lane** and **That Old Hen Cackled And The Rooster's Goin' To Crow**, were initially released on 500 unlabelled discs, all immediately sold at a local old-time fiddlers' convention. Following a re-release on Okeh, Carson was awarded a contract with the label.

Born on March 23, 1868, in Fannin County, Georgia, Carson was the fiddler champion of Georgia seven times, and he made his radio debut on September 9, 1922. Often working with a string band, the Virginia Reelers (which included his daughter Rosa Lee Carson, also known as Moonshine Kate), he cut around 150 discs for Okeh between 1923 and 1931. Following the Depression, Carson moved to RCA, mainly re-cutting earlier successes.

In later life an elevator operator, Carson died December 11, 1949.

Recommended:
That Old Hen Cackled (Rounder/–)

Martha Carson

A country gospel singer whose repertoire appealed not only to Opry fans but also the audiences at such ritzy venues as New York's Waldorf Astoria, Martha Carson was one of the most popular vocalists in her genre during the 50s.

Born Irene Ambergay, in Neon, Kentucky, on March 19, 1921, her first broadcasts were relayed over station WHIS, Bluefield, West Virginia in 1939. During the '40s she toured as one half of Martha and James Carson, the other half of the duo being her husband, the singing and mandolin-playing son of Fiddlin' Doc Roberts. They were longtime fixtures of the WSB Barn Dance in Atlanta becoming known as the Barn Dance Sweethearts. Together they recorded many magnificent sides, including **The Sweetest Gift, Man Of Galilee** and **Budded On Earth**.

Divorced in 1951, Martha began gracing the Opry with her fervent style during the following year. Martha is the writer of well over 100 songs, including **I'm Gonna Walk And Talk With My Lord, I Can't Stand Up Alone** and **Satisfied**.

Recommended:
Explodes (–/Bear Family)
Satisfied (–/Stetson)

1961. Maybelle Carter, plus Helen and Anita, also joined Johnny Cash, and became regulars on his TV show in 1966. After Mother Maybelle passed away on October 23, 1978, the Carter Family carried on with Anita's daughter Lori, Helen's son David and June's daughter Carlene, along with their mother, all appearing as part of the Carter Family Road Show.

Recommended:
Famous Country Music Makers (–/RCA)
Carter Sisters – Maybelle, Anita, June & Helen (–/Bear Family)
Musical Shapes – Carlene Carter (–/F-Beat)
Favorite Family Songs (Liberty/–)
Traveling Minstrel Band (Columbia/–)
Clinch Mountain Treasure (County/–)

Maybelle Carter

During the '60s Maybelle became a mother figure to the New Generation folkies (it was at a time when singers like Joan Baez had begun to discover and re-record Carter Family songs) and appeared on many folk bills throughout the country, winning much acclaim at the Newport Folk Festival of 1963. At a later Newport Festival, in 1967, she reunited with Sara Carter to record the live album **An Historic Reunion**, their first recording together for 25 years. In 1971, she also appeared on Nitty Gritty Dirt Band's **Will The Circle Be Unbroken** album. She died on October 23, 1978 in Nashville.

Recommended:
Mother Maybelle Carter (Columbia/–)
Sara And Maybelle Carter (Columbia/–)

Lionel Cartwright

Cartwright, a hillbilly from West Virginia, has progressed steadily with his own songs, going against the trend of the twangy, cowboy-hatted country of the early '90s and hitting paydirt with his chart-topping **Leap Of Faith** (1991).

He had piano lessons as a child and later picked up chords on his elder brother's guitar. In his early teens he landed a spot on a radio show in Milton, West Virginia and later featured as singer/musician on Columbus, Ohio's WMNI Country Cavalcade. The next step was the WWVA Jamboree in Wheeling, West Virginia.

Lionel moved to Nashville in the early '80s and soon landed a position as musical director for the Nashville Network and worked on the TNN sit-com 1–40 Paradise as musical director and had a small acting role in the series. A recording contract with MCA in 1988 led to a chart debut with **You're Gonna Make Her Mine** (1988), and the following year he made the Top 5 with **Give Me His Last Chance**. Further Top 10 hits came with **I Watched It All (On My Radio)** and **My Heart Is Set On You** (both 1990), as well as the chart-topping **Leap Of Faith** and **Family Tree** (both 1991). His albums have been high quality, with his self-penned songs about real-life situations.

Carlene Carter

Keeping the famous Carter Family name alive, Carlene Carter, the daughter of June Carter and her husband Carl Smith, was born in Nashville, Tennessee, September 26, 1955. Married at 15, she toured as part of the Carter Family while still at school, but later rebelled, working as a model, then moving to London where she signed with Warner Brothers Records and made her first album, **Carlene Carter** (1977) with rock singer Nick Lowe, who became her third husband in 1979; the couple later separated. She made her first appearance on the country charts with **Do It In A Heartbeat** that same year, and also recorded with rocker Dave Edmunds, Graham Parker's the Rumour and members of the Squeeze, as she directed her music towards a young rock audience.

In 1984 she was in the London production of the show 'Pump Boys And Dinettes' and made a short film, 'Too Drunk (To Remember)'. A return to Nashville found her recording with country-rock band Southern Pacific (1989) and finally making a big impact in country the following year when she signed with Reprise Records and scored two Top 5 hits with **I Fell In Love** and **Come On Back**. Both were taken from her acclaimed **I Fell In Love** album, comprised mainly of self-composed songs backed up by some of music's finest pickers and singers.

Recommended:
I Fell In Love (Reprise/–)
Musical Shapes/Blue Nun (–/Demon)

The Carter Family

One of the most influential groups in country music, the original line-up was headed by Alvin Pleasant (A.P.) Delaney Carter, born in Maces Spring, Virginia, on April 15, 1891. One of nine children, A.P. initially sang in a church quartet alongside two uncles and an elder sister. Later he met Sara Dougherty (born in Wise County, Virginia, on July 21, 1898), a singer, guitarist, autoharp and banjo player, and they married on June 18, 1915. The third member of the group, Maybelle Addington (born in Nickelsville, Virginia, on May 10, 1909), joined after marrying A.P.'s brother, Ezra Carter, in 1926. She too played guitar, autoharp and banjo.

The Carter Family were first recorded by Ralph Peer for Victor on August 1, 1927 (at the same session that Jimmie Rodgers cut his first sides) completing six titles, including **Single Girl, Married Girl**, at a makeshift studio in Bristol, Tennessee. After some success the family began a whole series of sessions for Victor, often recording A.P.'s own songs, though **Wildwood Flower**, a traditional item cut on May 9, 1928, proved to be the group's biggest seller, registering over a million sales for 78 rpm discs alone. Another important recording date occurred during June 1931, when Peer cut sides featuring the collective talents of the Carters and Jimmie Rodgers.

After recording around 20 songs at one Victor session on December 11, 1934, the family moved on to ARC, waxing some 40 titles for that label during May 5–10, 1935. Sara and A.P. obtained a divorce during the following year but continued working together in the group, next recording for Decca before moving to Texas to appear on various radio stations. During this three-year period, other members of the Carter Family joined the group – Anita, June and Helen (Maybelle and Ezra's three daughters) and Janette and Joe (Sara and A.P.'s children). Sara then remarried, to Coy Bayes, and though the Family cut further sides for Columbia and Victor (the last session by the original Carter Family taking place on October 14, 1941) they disbanded in 1943, having waxed over 250 of their songs including **Wabash Cannonball**, **Lonesome Valley** and **I'm Thinking Tonight Of My Blue Eyes**.

Maybelle then formed a group with her three daughters and began a five-year stint on station WRVA, Richmond, Virginia, after which came a switch to Nashville, where the quartet became regulars on Grand Ole Opry. A.P. began his career again too, working on some sides for the Acme label during 1952–6. But this version of the Carter Family – employing Sara, Joe and Janette – made little impact. A.P. died on November 7, 1960, ten years before the Carter Family's election to the Country Music Hall Of Fame. Sara Carter died on January 8, 1979, in Lodi, California following a long illness.

Following A.P.'s death, Maybelle and her daughters began working as the Carter Family (previously they'd appeared as the Carter Sisters And Mother Maybelle). June Carter eventually went solo and became part of the Johnny Cash Road Show in

A multi-talented instrumentalist, brilliant songwriter and heart-tugging singer, with rugged, boyish good looks, Lionel Cartwright has built up a sizeable following among younger female country music fans.

Recommended:
Lionel Cartwright (MCA/MCA)
I Watched It On The Radio (MCA/–)
Chasin' The Sun (MCA/–)

Johnny Cash

Winner of six CMA awards in 1969 (Best Male Vocalist, Entertainer Of The Year, Best Single, Best Album, Outstanding Service and even one award with June Carter for Best Vocal Group), John R. Cash was born in Kingsland, Arkansas, February 26, 1932, son of a poverty-stricken cotton farmer, Ray Cash and his wife Carrie. In 1935 the Cash family moved to the government resettlement Dyess Colony, surviving the Mississippi river flood of 1937, an event documented in a 1959 Cash song, **Five Feet High And Rising**. One son, Roy, put together a country band, the Delta Rhythm Ramblers, which broadcast on KCLN, Blytheville. However, tragedy struck the Cash family in 1944 when son Jack died after an accident with a circular saw, which had a lasting effect on the young John.

After high school graduation in 1950, J.R. took various menial jobs, but by July of that year he had enlisted in the air force for a four-year term. It was while serving in Germany that Cash learned guitar and wrote his first songs. Upon discharge in July 1954, he married Vivian Liberto and headed for Memphis where he became an electric appliance salesman.

In Memphis he met guitarist Luther Perkins and bassist Marshall Grant and began performing with them – for no pay – on station KWEM. Eventually they gained an audition with Sam Phillips at Sun

Right: Johnny Cash has cut albums in San Quentin and Folsom prisons and shot a documentary film in the Holy Land. But his album with Bob Dylan still remains unissued.

Heroes, Johnny Cash and Waylon Jennings. Courtesy CBS Records.

Records and their first single, **Hey Porter/Cry, Cry, Cry** – listed as by Johnny Cash and The Tennessee Two – became a hit, selling more than 100,000 copies. The follow-up, **Folsom Prison Blues**, another Cash original, was also a success and led to Cash joining KWKH's Louisiana Hayride

in December 1955. He also began touring extensively, and after **I Walk The Line**, a cross-over hit that sold a million, and **There You Go**, another 1956 winner, he joined the Grand Ole Opry.

He played a maniacal killer in a 'B' movie entitled 'Five Minutes To Live' (1958), then came tours in Canada and Australia and a lucrative new record deal with Columbia. Drummer W. S. Holland joined the Tennessee Two in 1960 (at which point they became the Tennessee Three), Cash and his enlarged band being much in demand and playing nearly 300 gigs a year; he was pill-popping to provide enough energy.

Cash first began working with June Carter in December 1961. The following year saw a heavier work schedule that included a 30-hour tour of Korea and a disastrous Carnegie Hall date. At the Newport Folk Festival of 1964 he sang with Bob Dylan and started widening his audience outside of the usual mainstream country. But the pill-popping worsened and, in October 1965, Cash was arrested by the narcotics squad in El Paso and received a 30-day suspended sentence and $1,000 fine. The following year he was jailed once more – for embarking on a 2am flower-picking spree! Also in 1966, Carl Perkins became a regular part of the Johnny Cash touring show.

Though in poor health and with his weight down to 140 pounds, his recorded work maintained a high standard, but his personal life continued heading ever downwards, with Vivian Cash suing him for divorce in mid-1966. The pill addiction continued, but with help from June Carter

he undertook treatment, gradually fighting back until by the close of the '60s he was restored to complete health once more.

Since signing to Columbia in 1958, Cash had cut a tremendous quota of hit singles – the biggest of these being **All Over Again** (1958), **Don't Take Your Guns To Town** (1959), **I Got Stripes** (1959), **Ring Of Fire** (1963), **Understand Your Man** (1964), **It Ain't Me Babe** (1964), **Orange Blossom Special** (1965), **The One On Your Right Is On Your Left** (1966), **Folsom Prison Blues** (1968), **Daddy Sang Bass** (1968) and **A Boy Named Sue** (1969). More importantly, he had also cut some of the most striking albums to emerge from country music – including **Ride This Train** (1960), a kind of musical hobo-ride through America; **Blood, Sweat And Tears** (1964), a tribute to the working man; **Bitter Tears** (1964), regarding the mistreatment of the American Indian; **Ballads Of The True West** (1965), a double-album glance at western folklore; and **At Folsom Prison** (1968), an award-winning affair recorded in front of perhaps

Look At Them Beans, Johnny Cash. Courtesy CBS Records.

the world's toughest, but most appreciative audience.

His partnership with June Carter, whom he married in March, 1968 (Merle Kilgore was best man), proved successful both on and off stage, the duo gaining a Grammy for **Jackson**, judged the Best Country Performance by a group during 1967. And as the '60s rolled away, the CMA showered a whole flood of awards on the craggy-faced man in black, while the film critics applauded his portrayal of an ageing gun-fighter in 'The Gunfight', a 1970 release in which he pitted his acting ability against Kirk Douglas. During the '70s, Johnny Cash turned increasingly towards religion, visiting Israel to make a film about life in Holy Land, and appearing on shows headed by evangelist Billy Graham.

Though he continued to make superb albums, his run of hit singles slowed down to a mere trickle. Since **One Piece At A Time** in 1976, he has only hit the Top 5 in

Bitter Tears, Johnny Cash. Courtesy CBS Records.

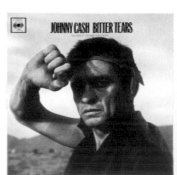

the country charts with **There Ain't No Good Chain Gang** (a duet with Waylon Jennings, 1978), **(Ghost) Riders In The Sky** (1979) and **Highwayman** (with Waylon Jennings, Willie Nelson and Kris Kristofferson, 1985). He was elected to the Country Music Hall Of Fame in 1980, but in 1983 Cash nearly died before undergoing abdominal treatment at Nashville's Baptist Hospital. "It was abuse", he claimed, admitting that he had once more begun dabbling with pills, "Many, many long years of abuse."

But he has since pulled back, resuming his touring career, signing with Mercury Records in 1987 and tackling songs of various dimensions. But thanks to his obvious sincerity and his crumbling rock of a voice (often placed out front over the most meagre of rhythm patterns) everything he sings about, no matter how sentimental, always comes out sounding completely believable.

Recommended:

At Folsom Prison (Columbia/CBS)
At San Quentin (Columbia/CBS)
Blood, Sweat And Tears (Columbia/–)
Man In Black (Columbia/CBS)
Ride This Train (Columbia/Bear Family)
Ballads Of The True West
   (Columbia/Embassy)
America (Columbia/CBS)
Silver (Columbia/CBS)
Rockabilly Blues (Columbia/CBS)
The Adventures Of Johnny Cash
   (Columbia/CBS)
Water From The Wells Of Home
   (Mercury/Mercury)
Bitter Tears (Columbia/Bear Family)
Heroes – with Waylon Jennings
   (Columbia/CBS)
Johnny 99 (Columbia/CBS)

Rosanne Cash

The eldest daughter of Johnny Cash and his first wife, Vivian Liberto, Rosanne was born on May 24, 1955, in Memphis, Tennessee at a time when her father's career was just starting to take off. Her parents were divorced when she was eleven, and Rosanne and her three sisters lived with their mother in California. Inevitably, she moved to Nashville following graduation, working with the Johnny Cash Roadshow, singing back-up vocals to her famous father. In 1975 she left to pursue her interest in acting, moving to London with the intention of enrolling in drama school. Instead she landed a job at CBS Records, the same label her father recorded for.

A year later she returned to America and studied drama at Nashville's Vanderbilt University, then moved back to California to study method acting at the Lee Strasberg's Theatre Institute. A vacation in Germany during the Christmas break led to a change in career direction. She was offered a recording contract by Ariola Records and after completing her studies, returned to Munich in the summer of 1978 to record her first album. The album completed, she moved back to Nashville to make music her career.

Teaming up with Rodney Crowell, whom she married in 1979, she signed with Columbia Records. With Crowell handling production, she recorded the acclaimed **Right Or Wrong** album. Though not a huge success, there were three country hits, including a duet with Bobby Bare, **No Memories Hangin' 'Round** (Top 20 in

Seven Year Ache, Rosanne Cash. Courtesy CBS Records.

1979). The next album, **Seven Year Ache**, continued with progressive country meshed with a definite rock attitude. Surprisingly, it provided Rosanne with her first country No.1s in the self-penned title song, **My Baby Thinks He's A Train** and **Blue Moon With A Heartache** (both 1981). The album gained gold status.

Uncompromising in her attitude to music and her life, Rosanne has refused to take the accepted 'star route' in promoting her career. **Somewhere In The Stars**, released towards the end of 1982, failed to

Below: Rosanne cut her newest album, The Wheel, in 1993, without Rodney Crowell.

match the commercial success of its predecessor, mainly because Rosanne decided it was more important to organize her life around her family. She spent the next two years raising her two daughters, Caitlin and Chelsea. The album still produced two Top 10 hits with **Ain't No Money** and **I Wonder** (both 1982).

This period of inactivity gave her the time to write material for **Rhythm And Romance** (1985), which not only went gold, but included such No.1 hits as **I**

Don't Know Why You Don't Want Me and **Never Be You**. Rosanne won a Grammy for Best Female Vocalist Performance in 1986, and the next album, **King's Record Shop**, followed much quicker. Titled after a record store in Louisville, Kentucky, this album had No.1s with **The Way We Make A Broken Heart** (1987), a revival of her father's **Tennessee Flat Top Box**, **If You Change Your Mind** and **Runaway Train** (all 1988). Sandwiched between these was yet another No.1, **It's Such A Small World**, a duet with Rodney Crowell that was included on his **Diamonds & Dirt** album in 1988.

Maintaining an integrity rare in country music, Rosanne has been a pioneer for

Six White Horses, Tommy Cash. Courtesy Epic Records.

female rights. This came through strongly on **Rosie Strikes Back**, a song which encourages a woman who suffers physical abuse to stand up for herself. A remarkable decade was captured in the compilation **Hits 1979–1989**, which featured ten of her past hits, plus yet another No.1, a revival of the Beatles' **I Don't Want To Spoil The Party** (1989).

The following year rumours were rife that her marriage to Crowell was in trouble, and were heightened by the doomy, introspective songs of **Interiors** (1990). There were no major hit singles, though an excellent video of the album was also released and, artistically, it was a superb set of meaningful songs. The pair did separate and filed for divorce in November 1991, but they made it clear they remained close friends. It was the start of a new beginning when Rosanne entered the studio without Crowell to record **The Wheel** (1993). There was an optimistic air to many of the songs, which were all self-written, and a commercial edge which should keep Rosanne at the forefront of modern-day country music.

Recommended:

Right Or Wrong (CBS/–)
Seven Year Ache (CBS/–)
Somewhere In The Stars (CBS/CBS)
Rhythm And Romance (CBS/CBS)

Tommy Cash

Younger brother of superstar Johnny Cash, Tommy was born in Mississippi County, Arkansas, on April 5, 1940.

He learnt the guitar at 16 after watching his brother play chords and listening to other guitarists. His first public appearance was as a performer at Treadwell High School in 1957; he then joined the army at 18, becoming a disc jockey for AFN, Frankfurt, Germany and having his own show, Stickbuddy Jamboree. He met his wife Barbara during this period.

Tommy Cash

Cash began appearing with a band at various service clubs and eventually launched his professional career by performing alongside Hank Williams Jr at Montreal in January, 1965. He recorded for Musicor and United Artists, but it was not until he signed to Epic in 1969 that he made a commercial breakthrough with **Six White Horses**, a hit in 1969, and **Rise And Shine** and **One Song Away**, hits in 1970. During the '70s, Cash continued to tour with his band, the Tom Cats.

A regular visitor to Britain and Europe, Cash recorded a **25th Anniversary Album** with guest appearances from George Jones, Tom T. Hall, Connie Smith and brother Johnny Cash, in 1990.

Recommended:
Six Horses/Lovin' Takes Leavin' (Epic/–)
Only A Stone (Elektra/–)
25th Anniversary Album (Playback/Cottage)

Ray Charles

Although best known as an R&B performer, Ray Charles has made a telling contribution to the cause of country music. Born Ray Charles Robinson, in Albany, Georgia, on September 30, 1930, he could play piano before he was five. At six he contracted glaucoma, which eventually left him blind. Later he learned composition and became proficient on several instruments, leaving school to work with dance bands around Florida.

He went on to work with a Nat Cole R&B-styled group, then switched style and utilized a more fervent, gospel-styled approach, signing with Atlantic Records in 1953 and piling up an imposing array of pop, rock and R&B hits. Though he covered country songs, it was not until 1962, when he made the remarkable **Modern Sounds In Country Music** for ABC Records, that he really edged into country. The album sold a million copies and spawned some massive pop hit singles. Charles' success paved the way for many other black artists to cut Nashville-oriented albums. These include Esther Phillips, Dobie Gray, Joe Tex, Bobby Womack and Millie Jackson.

After fashioning a sequel to **Modern Sounds**, he moved on yet again, touching all bases, but settling for none, seemingly losing direction. However, in 1982, he returned to country music once more, recording in Nashville and releasing the excellent **Wish You Were Here Tonight** album for Columbia. This time the Nashville connection lasted for three years and included the subsequent album,

Below: Ray Charles adds a soulful edge to traditional country music.

Friendship (1984), a collection of duets that found Ray swopping vocal licks with Johnny Cash, Mickey Gilley, Ricky Skaggs, Hank Williams Jr and others. The partnerships with George Jones (**We Didn't See A Thing**), B. J. Thomas (**Rock And Roll Shoes**) and Willie Nelson (**Seven Spanish Angels**) all furnished hit singles. Ray Charles was inducted into the Rock'n'Roll Hall Of Fame in 1986, and still continues to record and perform all styles of music in his own inimitable fashion.

Recommended:
Modern Sounds In Country & Western Music (ABC/HMV)
Wish You Were Here Tonight (Columbia/CBS)
Do I Ever Cross Your Mind (Columbia/CBS)
Friendship (Columbia/CBS)

Mark Chesnutt

Born September 6, 1963, in Beaumont, Texas, Mark Chesnutt has established himself as one of the most solid new honky-tonk traditionalists with a series of Top 10 hits. His first two albums achieved gold status. Known as 'The Human Jukebox', Mark is said to have the words to as many as 1,000 country songs all ready to sing when required. This has come from years of hanging around honky-tonks and listening to nothing but classic country albums.

His father, Bob Chesnutt, was a regional Texas star who had several singles on an independent Nashville label in the late '60s and early '70s. When Mark was 16 he started going to clubs, initially to watch his father perform, but then started to sing himself. He quit school in the 11th grade to develop a career in country music and made his recording debut for the AXBAR label in San Antonio. The next few years saw Mark and his band working the night-clubs around Beaumont. With his father's guidance he made some demo tapes which were sent to Nashville. Another independent deal was struck up with Cherry Records in Houston. One of his singles, **Too Cold At Home**, came to the attention of MCA Records, who signed Mark and re-released the song, pushing it up to No.3 (1990) in the country charts.

The first album, titled after that hit, was endorsed by George Jones in the sleeve notes, and contained Mark's No.1, **Brother Jukebox** (1990) and two more Top 5 hits with **Blame It On Texas** and **Your Love Is A Miracle** (both 1991). The album made a big impact on both the pop and country charts and became the biggest selling debut LP in MCA Nashville's long history. To capitalize on that success, Mark and his band undertook more than 300 show dates in 1991 and he still found time to record a second album, **Longnecks And Short Stories**. He enjoyed another No.1 with **I'll Think Of Something** (1992), and maintained his Top 10 consistency with the wild **Bubba Shot The Jukebox** (1992) and **Ol' Country** (1993). Chesnutt's only setback was the sudden death of his father in 1991 from a massive heart attack.

Recommended:
Longnecks And Short Stories (MCA/–)
Too Cold At Home (MCA/–)
Almost Goodbye (MCA/–)

Right: The well-respected songwriter Guy Clark provides hit songs for many country stars.

Above: Texas honky-tonker Mark Chesnutt plays one of his many hits.

Guy Clark

One of country music's finest songwriters, Clark, who was born on November 6, 1941, in Rockport, Texas, spent most of his early life in the town of Monahans, living with his grandmother in a run-down hotel, which provided the inspiration for many of his later songs.

During the '60s he moved to Houston, there working as an art director on a local TV station, and meeting Jerry Jeff Walker and Townes Van Zandt. He briefly performed in a folk trio with K. T. Oslin, playing the coffee house circuits of Houston, Dallas and Austin. Clark moved to Los Angeles, where he utilized his talent for constructing classical guitars and dobros and landed a writer's contract with Sunbury Music.

He headed back home via Oklahoma City, where he met and married Susanna, a gifted artist and songwriter in her own right. Finally the creative trail brought Clark to Nashville, where he recorded his first album, but scrapped it due to personal dissatisfaction. By this time his songs, such as **Desperados Waiting For A Train**, **L.A. Freeway** and **Texas 1947**, were being recorded by Jerry Jeff Walker, Johnny Cash and others. A return to the studio in late 1974 resulted in the **Old No.1** album, which critics acclaimed as the finest album for many years.

Clark's second RCA album, **Texas Cookin'**, was equally impressive, but failed to provide any hit singles, even though there were guest appearances by Waylon Jennings, Emmylou Harris, Rodney Crowell and Hoyt Axton. Clark writes almost poetically about losers and low-life ladies. He joined Warner Bros Records in 1978 and during the next five years recorded three more superb albums. He made brief appearances on the charts with singles **The Partner Nobody Chose** (1981) and **Homegrown Tomatoes** (1983).

A father figure to the new breed of singer-songwriters, Clark has never enjoyed the commercial success his talent would suggest, but has become an in-demand performer and well-respected songwriter. He has provided hit songs for Emmylou Harris, Steve Wariner, Gary Stewart, Ricky Skaggs and others. In 1988 he was back in the studios again, recording **Old Friends**, an album for Sugar Hill, which was picked up for European release on U2's Mother Records. This led to several European trips, where his intimate solo shows gained him a cult following among young music fans. He's now based mainly in Nashville, where his wife Susanna is busy as a visual artist, and he spends time co-writing with modern country writers, such as Richard Leigh, Roger Murrah, Jim McBride, Verlon Thompson and Lee Roy Parnell. Another brilliant album, **Boats To Build**, surfaced on Asylum in 1992, but lack of promotion

from the record company meant that not too many know of its existence.

Recommended:
Old No. 1 (RCA/Edsel)
Texas Cookin' (RCA/Edsel)
The South Coast Of Texas (Warner Bros/–)
Better Days (Warner Bros/–)
Boats To Build (Elektra/–)

Roy Clark

Multi-talented star of the Hee Haw TV series, Roy Linwood Clark was born in Meherrin, Virginia, on April 15, 1933. Son of a guitar-playing tobacco farmer, Clark soon picked up the rudiments of guitar techniques but at an early age became even more proficient on banjo. Following a move to Washington DC, Roy played as part of the Clark family group, performing at local square dances and eventually winning a solo spot on the Jimmy Dean TV Show – but getting fired due to perpetual lateness. A subsequent job found him getting fired by Marvin Rainwater – this time for earning more applause than the star himself. Better luck followed when, as a cast member of a George Hamilton IV TV series, he gained wide recognition.

Recording initially for Four Star as Roy Clark And The Wranglers, he later moved on to Debbie, Coral and Capitol, enjoying his first sizeable hit with a Capitol single, **Tips Of My Fingers**, in 1963. Following a contract with Dot, the hits really began to proliferate, via titles like **Yesterday When I Was Young** (1969), **I Never Picked Cotton**, **Thank God And Greyhound** (both 1970), **A Simple Thing Called Love** (1971), **Come Live With Me** (1973), **Honeymoon Feeling** (1974) and **If I Had To Do It All Over Again** (1976).

A jovial international ambassador for country music, Clark was presented with the CMA Entertainer Of The Year award in 1973. Since the early '80s he has recorded for Churchill Records (a label formed by his manager Jim Halsey), Silver D and Hallmark, providing each with minor hits. He joined the Grand Ole Opry in 1987.

Recommended:
My Music And Me (Dot/–)
Roy Clark Sings Gospel (Word/Word)
A Pair Of Fives – with Buck Trent (Dot/ABC)
Back To The Country (MCA/MCA)
Live From Austin City Limits (Churchill/–)
The Entertainer (Dot/Ember)
I'll Paint You A Song (–/Ember)
20 Golden Pieces (–/Bulldog)
Makin' Music (MCA/MCA)

Jack Clement

Few people have mastered more phases of the music business than Jack 'Cowboy' Clement, who was born on April 5, 1931, in Memphis, Tennessee. As a youth he mastered a variety of instruments and played all kinds of music from big band to bluegrass as he worked his way into the production end of the business, where he fell in with Sam Phillips at Sun Records as a session musician, engineer and producer. During that era, Clement also wrote a great many songs including **Guess Things Happen That Way** and **Ballad Of A Teenage Queen** for Johnny Cash.

Since the mid-'60s he has concentrated his energies in Nashville, where he built an extremely successful publishing firm – Jack Music – ran Jack Clement Studio, assisted in the careers of Charley Pride, Tompall and the Glasers and continued to write as well. He even found time to produce a horror film, 'Dear Dead Delilah'. In 1971 he formed JMI Records, working with Allen Reynolds, Bob McDill and Don Williams, but the company folded in 1974.

Clement made a comeback in the late '70s as a producer with Johnny Cash and Waylon Jennings and started recording for the first time in almost 20 years for Elektra. Amongst his most notable songs are **Miller's Cave, I Know One, A Girl I Used to Know** and **The One On The Right Is On The Left**.

Recommended:
All I Want To Do In Life (Elektra/Elektra)

Vassar Clements

A much respected fiddle player who worked for some time as a sessioneer in Nashville before finding a degree of solo fame. Born on April 25, 1928, at Kinard, South Carolina, Vassar has been in the bands of Bill Monroe, Jim and Jesse, Faron Young and the contemporary-slanted Earl Scruggs Revue.

He appeared on the Nitty Gritty Dirt Band's **Will The Circle Be Unbroken** and his consequent familiarity to the general public after years of being a name among recording sessions credits has meant that he has been able to get his own show together and travel the road.

Recommended:
Superbow (Mercury/–)
Hillbilly Jazz (Flying Fish/Sonet)
Bluegrass Session (Flying Fish/Sonet)
Grass Routes (Rounder/–)

Zeke Clements

'The Alabama Cowboy' was born near Empire, Alabama, on September 9, 1911, and has had one of the longest careers in country music, having appeared on radio shows in all sections of the country, as well as having the unusual distinction of having been a member of all three of the major barn dances at one time or another.

Zeke began on the National Barn Dance in 1928, toured for some years with Otto Gray's Oklahoma Cowboys, then joined the Grand Ole Opry in 1933 as a member of their first cowboy group, the Bronco Busters. After spending some time on the West Coast on radio and in films, he returned to the Opry in 1939, where he became one of the Opry's major stars throughout the '40s. He also became known as a songwriter during this era especially for **Blue Mexico Skies, There's Poison In Your Heart**, and as co-writer of **Smoke On The Water**, the top country record of 1945.

Clements later appeared on the Louisiana Hayride and on many other Deep South stations. He pursued a business career in Nashville in the late '50s and '60s, then moved to Miami, Florida, where he spent nearly a decade playing tenor banjo in a dixieland band before returning to the Nashville area.

Right: Grand Ole Opry and Hayride star Zeke Clements appeared on radio throughout his early career.

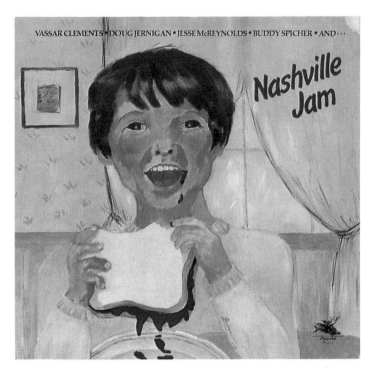

Nashville Jam, Vassar Clements. Courtesy Flying Fish Records.

Bill Clifton

Perennial globetrotter Clifton was born at Riderwood, Maryland, in 1931. A vocalist, guitarist and autoharp player, he became interested in the music of the Carter Family during the 1940s, later forming his own group, the Dixie Mountain Boys, which established a considerable reputation among bluegrass aficionados. In 1961, he recorded 22 Carter Family songs for a Starday album but some months later turned up in Britain where he became instrumental in setting up tours by Bill Monroe, the Stanley Brothers, the New Lost City Ramblers and others during the '60s. He also enhanced his own reputation as a bluegrass musician, embarking on tours of Europe and recording a programme of old-time music for transmission on Radio Moscow in 1966.

By 1967, Clifton was on the move once more, he, his wife and seven children sailing for the Philippines, where he became an active member of the Peace Corps. Still in the Pacific area at the commencement of the '70s, he arrived in New Zealand, playing at a banjo players' convention and cutting an album with

A Bluegrass Jam Session 1952, Bill Clifton. Courtesy Bear Family.

Hamilton County Bluegrass Band, a local outfit. Since that time, Clifton has been active in Europe, the States and Japan.

Recommended:
Happy Days (–/Golden Guinea)
Blue Ridge Mountain Blues (County/ Westwood)
Going Back To Dixie (–/Bear Family)
Mountain Folk Songs (Starday/–)

Patsy Cline

Patsy Cline (real name Virginia Patterson Hensley) was born in Winchester, Virginia, on September 8, 1932. Winner of an amateur tap-dancing contest at the age of four, she began learning piano at eight, and in her early teens became a singer at local clubs. In 1948, an audition won her a trip to Nashville, where she appeared in a few clubs before returning home – but her big break came in 1957 when she won an Arthur Godfrey Talent Scout show, singing **Walking After Midnight**. Her Decca single of the contest-winning song then entered the charts, both pop and country. In 1961 came **I Fall To Pieces**, one of Patsy's biggest hits, followed in quick succession by **Crazy**, **Who Can I Count On?**, **She's Got You**, **Strange** and **When I Get Through With You**, most of them being massive sellers.

During the same period she became a featured singer on the Opry, soon attaining the rank of top female country singer. Such hits as **Imagine That**, **So Wrong** and

Leavin' On Your Mind continued to proliferate until, on March 5, 1963, Patsy died in an air disaster at Camden, Tennessee. She had been returning home from a Kansas City benefit concert with Hawkshaw Hawkins and Cowboy Copas, both of whom were also killed in the crash.

But even after her death, Patsy's records continued to sell, **Sweet Dreams (Of You)** and **Faded Love** being top hits during '63, **When You Need A Laugh** and **He Called Me Baby** entering the country charts in 1964, and **Anytime** appearing in the latter as late as 1969.

Patsy has continued to be a major influence on singers like Loretta Lynn, who recorded a tribute album in 1977, Reba McEntire and Sylvia. In 1973 she was elected to the Country Music Hall Of Fame and her recordings and those of Jim Reeves were spliced together to produce a duet effect resulting in hits with **Have You Ever Been Lonely** and **I Fall To Pieces** during 1981. A film tracing her career, 'Sweet Dreams', was made in 1985 and led to Patsy's recordings making yet another comeback on the country charts.

This renewed interest and success has continued with two big-selling video programmes tracing her life and career through archive film and interviews. In 1992 a **Greatest Hits** compilation gained multi-platinum status with sales reaching 4 million copies, and all of her original albums were made available on CD in a massive promotional campaign. In Europe Patsy's success has been even more startling. A re-release of **Crazy** made the British pop charts at the end of 1990, and her albums also made the charts.

Recommended:
The Patsy Cline Story (MCA/–)
Always (MCA/MCA)
Sweet Dreams (MCA/MCA)
Live At The Opry (MCA/MCA)
Songwriters' Tribute (MCA/MCA)
Sentimentally Yours (MCA/MCA)

Jerry Clower

Country comedian Jerry Clower was born at Liberty, Mississippi, on September 28, 1926, and grew up in Amite County. After graduation in 1944 he joined the Navy.

The Heart Of Hank Cochran. Courtesy Monument.

Upon discharge came a football scholarship at Southwest Junior College, Summit, where he won a further scholarship to Mississippi State University.

After becoming a field representative with the Mississippi Chemical Company, Clower rose to become Director of Field Services with the company. Sales talks became part of his stock in trade and so his **Coon Hunt Story** and other routines were introduced to make such speeches more acceptable. A friend then suggested that Clower should record an album of his routines and, it was agreed that an album be cut on the Lemon label. Named **Jerry Clower From Yazoo City Talkin'** and advertised only by word of mouth, the album sold over 8,000 copies in a short period, gaining Clower a contract with MCA in 1971. His album later went into the 'Billboard' charts for a lengthy stay.

Following the release of other high-selling LPs, he became accepted as country

Ambassador Of Goodwill, Jerry Clower. Courtesy MCA Records.

music's funniest man, winning many spots on TV shows. The father of four children, Clower is a Yazoo City Baptist deacon, an active member of the Gideon Bible Society and author of the best-selling book, 'Ain't God Good'. For several years he was co-host of the syndicated TV show, Nashville On The Road.

Sweet Dreams – the soundtrack to the Patsy Cline biopic. Courtesy MCA.

Recommended:
Clower Power (MCA/–)
Country Ham (MCA/–)
Live in Picayune (MCA/–)
The Ambassador Of Goodwill (MCA/–)
Runaway Truck (MCA/–)

Hank Cochran

Singer-songwriter Henry 'Hank' Cochran was born in Greenville, Mississippi, on August 2, 1935. After completing school he moved to New Mexico, working in the oilfields during the mid-'50s, and eventually made his way to California, where he began entertaining in small clubs. In 1954, he and Eddie Cochran (no relation) formed a duo, the Cochran Brothers, initially recording country material but later switching to rock after watching Elvis Presley perform in Dallas.

After two years, the Cochrans went their separate ways, Hank going on to join the California Hayride TV show in Stockton, then in 1960 moving to Nashville in order to sell his songs. One such composition, entitled **I Fall To Pieces**, written with the aid of Harlan Howard, became a 1961 winner for Patsy Cline, after which came **Make The World Go Away** (a hit for both Ray Price and Eddy Arnold), **A Little Bitty Tear** and **Funny Way Of Laughing** (Burl Ives), **I Want To Go With You** (Eddy Arnold), and others. Signed by Liberty as a recording artist in 1961, Cochran's name appeared in the charts during '62 with **Sally Was A Good Old Girl** and **I'd Fight The World**. The singer later scored with **A Good Country Song** on Gaylord in 1963, and **All Of Me Belongs To You** on Monument in 1967.

Married for many years to Jeannie Seely, Hank re-emerged in the mid-'70s writing hit songs for Willie Nelson and Mel Tillis. He once again took up performing and recording, signing to Capitol Records in 1978 and making the album **With A Little Help From His Friends**, featuring Merle Haggard, Willie Nelson, Jack Greene and Jeannie Seely. Two years later he recorded an album for Elektra, **Make The World Go Away**.

Recommended:
Make The World Go Away (Elektra/–)
With A Little Help From His Friends
   (Capitol/–)
Going In Training (RCA/–)
Heart (Monument/–)

Commander Cody And His Lost Planet Airmen

This zany, modern western-swing outfit was named after space movie characters. Formed in 1967 by leader George 'Commander Cody' Frayne (born Boise, Idaho), previously Farfisa organ player with various small-time rock bands, it acquired a sizeable reputation in California. The Airmen signed to ABC-Paramount in 1969, recording the fine **Lost In The Ozone** album and subsequently gaining a Top 20 hit with a version of Johnny Bond's **Hot Rod Lincoln** (1972). In 1974 they moved to Warner Bros, releasing two studio albums and a live double, **We've Got A Live One Here**, after which the band split.

Line up changes have always affected Cody's unwieldy aggregation – among those who have worked with the band are Bobby Black (pedal steel), Lance Dickerson (drums), Bruce Barlow (bass), Norton Buffalo (harmonica, trombone) and vocalist Nicolette Larson – but somehow he has always managed to put something together. In the early '80s he logged a hit in Europe with **Two Triple Cheeseburgers (Side Order Of Fries)**, an MCA release.

Recommended:
Lost In The Ozone (Paramount/ABC)
Hot Licks, Cold Steel (Paramount/ABC)
Live – Deep In The Heart Of Texas
   (Paramount/ABC)
Tales From The Ozone (Warner Bros/
   Warner Bros)
We've Got A Live One Here (Warner
   Bros/Warner Bros)
Aces High (Relix/–)

We've Got A Live One Here, Commander Cody. Courtesy Warner.

David Allan Coe

This flamboyant and outrageous country star, born in Akron, Ohio, on September 6, 1939, made his initial impression in country music writing the hit songs, **Would You Lay With Me In A Field Of Stone** (Tanya Tucker) and **Take This Job And Shove It** (Johnny Paycheck). He spent most of his youth in various reform schools and prisons. Released from jail in 1967, Coe attempted a career as a singer and eventually went to Nashville. At that time, however, Coe was primarily a blues artist. He signed a recording contract with Shelby Singleton in Nashville and came up with **Penitentiary Blues**. He followed this with **Requiem For A Harlequin**.

Next came a switch to country music. He signed with Columbia Records in 1972 and with the album **The Mysterious Rhinestone Cowboy** he launched a successful career that saw him turning out top-selling albums such as **Once Upon A Rhyme**, **Longhaired Redneck**, **David Allan Coe Rides Again**, **Human Emotions** and **Family Album**. He finally made a big impression on the country singles chart with **The Ride**, the tale of a ghostly meeting with Hank Williams, which topped the charts in 1983. He had further success with the reflective **Mona Lisa's Lost Her Smile** in 1984, but has remained very much an album artist.

Recommended:
Once Upon A Rhyme (Columbia/CBS)
Family Album (Columbia/–)
Human Emotions (Columbia/–)
Rough Rider (Columbia/–)
Tennessee Whiskey (Columbia/–)
Castles In The Sand (Columbia/CBS)
A Matter Of Life And Death
   (Columbia/CD3)

Mark Collie

A rock'n'roll kid, Mark Collie was born on January 18, 1956, in Waynesboro, Tennessee, and spent the best part of 20 years perfecting his craft before making the commercial breakthrough in 1992 with **Even The Man In The Moon Is Cryin'**.

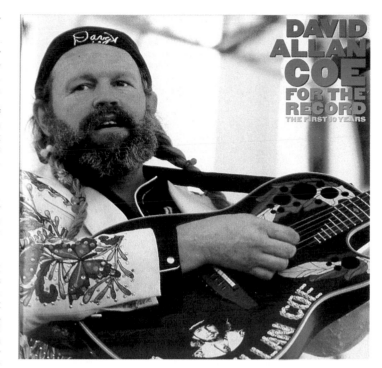

For The Record, David Allan Coe. Courtesy CBS Records.

Waynesboro, a small town near the Tennessee River, is where Mark cut his musical teeth. Playing piano and guitar as a child, music was his life, and during his high school days he was a DJ on local radio station WAAM. In his teens he played clubs around his hometown, then headed west to Memphis, where he formed a band and played local clubs. A few years later he took a vacation to Hawaii and spent the next 18 months singing country and rock'n'roll at a beach club.

When he returned home he decided to present his talent in Nashville. Moving to Music City in 1982, he signed as a writer with a large publisher, but, though he had a few album cuts, nothing much happened during the next five years. Looking for ways to gain recognition, he started doing showcases at Douglas Corner (a Nashville writers' venue) and was spotted by Tony Brown and Bruce Hinton, who offered him a contract with MCA Records. His first album, **Hardin County Line**, was an

Callin', Tommy Collins. Courtesy Gusto-Starday Records.

impressive mix of modern country and rockabilly, and Mark made his chart debut with **Something With A Ring To It** (1990). Gradually he built up a following, making Top 20 with **Let Her Go** (1991) and then into the Top 5 with **Even The Man In The Moon Is Cryin'** (1992).

Recommended:
Hardin County Line (MCA/–)
Born And Raised In Black & White (MCA/–)

Tommy Collins

Tommy Collins (real name Leonard Raymond Sipes) was born in Oklahoma City, Oklahoma, on September 20, 1930. A boyhood guitarist, he began performing at local clubs while at Oklahoma State College, also making appearances on radio stations. During the early '50s he became a resident of Bakersfield and a Capitol recording artist, his halcyon days being in 1954–55 when Collins followed **You Better Not Do That**, a half-million seller, with a quartet of other Top 20 discs. In 1966 he presented Columbia with a Top 10 item in **If You Can't Bite, Don't Growl**, but his later discs only achieved moderate chart placings.

As a songwriter, he provided Merle Haggard with some of his best numbers, including the chart-topping **Roots Of My Raising** in 1976.

Collins' past albums include **This Is Tommy Collins** (Capitol), **Dynamic** (Columbia), **On Tour** (Columbia) and two albums recorded in Britain during 1980, **Country Souvenir** and **Cowboys Get Lucky Some Of The Time**.

Jessi Colter

Writer and singer of the 1975 No.1, **I'm Not Lisa**, Jessi Colter (real name Miriam Johnson) was born in Phoenix, Arizona, on May 25, 1947, the sixth of seven children.

Jessi, Jessi Colter. Courtesy Capitol Records.

Jessi Colter

A church pianist at the age of 11, Jessi married guitarist Duane Eddy just five years later, touring England, Germany, South Africa and other countries as part of the Eddy show. A singer-songwriter, she was recorded by Eddy and Lee Hazelwood for the Jamie and RCA labels, meeting Waylon Jennings during some Phoenix-based sessions.

She split from Eddy in 1965 and, changing her name to Jessi Colter because her great, great uncle was a member of the Jesse James Gang, she moved to Nashville, signed a new contract with RCA and recorded the critically acclaimed album, **A Country Star Is Born**, in 1966.

By this time she had made an impression writing songs recorded by Eddy Arnold, Dottie West, Anita Carter, Patsy Sledd and Don Gibson. She teamed up with Waylon Jennings and the pair married in 1969, recording a series of duets including **Suspicious Minds** and **Under Your Spell Again**.

Jessi signed a solo contract with Capitol Records in 1974 and scored hits with **I'm Not Lisa**, which she wrote in five minutes, **What Happened To Blue Eyes** (1975), **It's Morning** (1976) and **Maybe You Should've Been Listening** (1978). She appeared on the best-selling RCA album titled **Outlaws** (1976) and has continued touring and recording with Waylon.

Recommended:
I'm Jessi Colter (Capitol/–)
Jessi (Capitol/Capitol)
Diamond In The Rough (Capitol/–)
That's The Way A Cowboy Rocks 'n' Rolls (Capitol/–)
Ridin' Shotgun (Capitol/–)
Leather & Lace – with Waylon Jennings (RCA/RCA)

Confederate Railroad

Mark DuFrene, drums; Michael Lamb, guitar; Chris McDaniel, keyboards; Gates Nichol, steel guitar; Wayne Secrest, bass; Danny Shirley, lead vocals and guitar.

Every now and then there is an act that draws a whole generation of rock'n'rollers to country music. Such an act is Confederate Railroad, a Georgia-based outfit that took a long, hard twelve-year ride to Nashville and a major record label deal in 1992. Their road-house mix of honky-tonk, rock, boogie and modern country has made them one of the fastest-rising new bands of the '90s.

Front-man Danny Shirley, born in Soddy Daisy, Tennessee, but raised in Chattanooga, Georgia, worked the club circuit with his own band and was in the back-up band for David Allan Coe for several years. The Danny Shirley Band had a regular stint at Miss Kitty's, Marietta, Georgia for six years, and Shirley also landed a deal with independent Amor Records, resulting in three albums and several minor country hits between 1984 and 1988.

The current band has been together the best part of eight years. Thousands of miles on the road have given these guys their rollicking approach on good-time songs, which conjures up vivid images of Southern manhood – aggressively independent, boisterous, self-opinionated, yet with a strong sense of decency shining through. It's all good ole whisky-drenched honky-tonk music.

The Danny Shirley Band changed its name to Confederate Railroad when they signed a record deal with Atlantic Nashville in the summer of 1991. The name refers to a Civil War locomotive, long associated with Chattanooga and Kennesaw, Georgia, where Shirley has lived since 1985. Their first self-titled album featured Nashville session players, and the initial single, **She Took It Like A Man**, helped by a tongue-in-cheek video, climbed into the Top 10. That was followed by the out-of-character ballad **Jesus And Mama** which reached No.3 (1992) and **The Queen Of Memphis** (1993), a raucous bar-room ditty.

Recommended:
Confederate Railroad (Atlantic/–)

John Conlee

The singer with the saddest voice in modern country music, Conlee was born on August 11, 1946 in Versailles, Kentucky and raised on a tobacco farm. By his early teens he was a member of a folk trio and later joined a rock group.

Following graduation he worked for six years as a mortician but finally landed himself a DJ stint on a Fort Knox Station. A move to Nashville in 1971, playing rock music, enabled him to make important music contacts, which led to signing with ABC Records.

His initial releases failed to make much impression but his fourth release, **Rose Colored Glasses**, a song he co-wrote with a newsreader at the radio station, made the country Top 5 in May 1978. That same year ABC Records were absorbed by MCA, for whom John scored more than a dozen Top 10 hits, including such chart-toppers as **Lady Lay Down** (1978), **Backside Of Thirty** (1979), **Common Man** (1983), **I'm Only In It For The Love** (1983), **In My Eyes** (1984), **As Long As**

Confederate Railroad's 1992 debut album. Courtesy Atlantic Records.

I'm Rockin' With You (1984). At the beginning of 1986, John signed with Columbia Records and continued to dominate the Top 10 with songs **Got My Heart Set On You** (1986), **The Carpenter** (1987) and **Domestic Life** (1987). This contract only lasted three years, then he joined 16th Avenue Records, but by 1990 was unable to make an impact.

Throughout his career Conlee has championed the ordinary working man.

This has been typified in such songs as **Busted**, **Common Man**, **Working Man** and **American Faces**, and for several years he was chairman of the Family Farm Defense Fund. He still continues to tour regularly and make TV appearances. When he joined the Grand Ole Opry in 1979, John was the first new member in five years.

Recommended:
Rose Colored Glasses (MCA/MCA)
Busted (MCA/–)
In My Eyes (MCA/–)
Blue Highway (MCA/–)
Harmony (Columbia/–)
Fellow Travelers (16th Avenue/–)
American Faces (Columbia/–)
Songs For The Working Man (MCA/–)

Earl Thomas Conley

Country music singer, songwriter and philosopher, Conley, who was born October 17, 1941, in Portsmouth, Ohio, made a major breakthrough in the 1980s with a string of chart-topping singles and acclaimed albums. His father was a railroad man, but with the advent of diesel locomotives was put out of work in the early '50s, which led to the large Conley family being on the breadline for many years. The young Earl took to carving, painting and drawing; in his teens he drifted around living off money earned from his artistic skills. During Army service in Germany he became interested in country music, and, following demob, he started singing in clubs around Huntsville, Alabama.

A move to Nashville led to songwriting. He provided Mel Street with **Smokey Mountain Memories**, a Top 10 hit in 1975, and Conway Twitty with the chart-topping **This Time I've Hurt Her More Than She Loves Me** the following year. Earl was then signed to GRT Records and had a few minor hits including **I Have Loved You Girl** (1975) and **High And Wild** (1976).

He added the Thomas to the middle of his name in 1978 to save confusion with John Conlee and Con Hunley and signed with Warner Brothers, scoring his biggest hit with **Dreamin's All I Do** (1979). A move to the small Sunbird label the following year and the release of his debut album, **Blue Pearl**, led to a Top 10 hit with **Silent Treatment** (1980) and a No.1 chart-placer with **Fire And Smoke** the following August.

Conley's contract with Sunbird was acquired by RCA and the next few years saw him emerge as the most successful country singer of the '80s. Using mainly self-written tunes, he's been hailed for his sensitive, introspective writing talents, blending traditional strains with elements of modern country and soul, bringing a fresh spirit to the country forms he celebrates

He hit the top of the charts with almost every release, the most notable being **Somewhere Between Right And Wrong** (1982), **Holding Her And Loving You** (1983), **Nobody Falls Like A Fool** (1985), **Once In A Blue Moon** (1986), **Right From The Start** (1987), **What She Is (Is A Woman In Love)** (1988), **We Believe In Happy Endings** (a duet with Emmylou Harris, 1988) and **Love Out Loud** (1989) Following the 1988 release of **The Heart Of It All** (Conley's most successful album, providing four No.1 singles), he had problems with his voice due to heavy smoking, and also a series of differences with RCA which held up further releases until the **Yours Truly** album in 1991. This album gave him the Top 10 hits **Shadow Of A Doubt** and **Brotherly Love**, the latter a duet with Keith Whitley. At the beginning of 1993, Conley, one of the most consistent country hit-makers of the previous twelve years, found himself without a record deal.

Recommended:
Blue Pearl (Sunbird/–)
Fire And Smoke (RCA/–)
Don't Make It Easy For Me (RCA/–)
Treadin' Water (RCA/–)
Somewhere Between Right And Wrong (RCA/–)
Greatest Hits (RCA/–)
The Heart Of It All (RCA/RCA)
Yours Truly (RCA/–)

Swinging The Devil's Dream, Spade Cooley. Courtesy Charly Records.

Above: Ry Cooder, the master of the guitar and American film music.

Ry Cooder

One-time Los Angeles session man, Cooder is of interest to country fans in that his music is soaked generally in southern folk styles. Born in Los Angeles, California, on March 15, 1947, he first came to public notice with his tasteful and well timed mandolin excursions on bluesman Taj Mahal's first CBS album and he played with Taj's band, the Rising Sons.

His solo career began in 1970 with the first in a series of highly acclaimed albums for Warner Brothers, which featured long forgotten or little known gospel, old-timey country, Cajun and blues tunes given a very distinctive treatment. He also became proficient on slide guitar and is now a rated exponent of that style. One of his finest albums is **Chicken Skin Music**, which introduced Tex-Mex music to a wide audience and featured accordionist Flaco Jiminez and his Conjuncto musicians from San Antonio.

Ry has also been in demand for writing and playing on film soundtracks such as 'The Long Riders', for which he created western music of a style played in saloons during the gunfighter era of Jesse James and Cole Younger, and the country blues used as the backcloth for the 1984 movie, 'Paris, Texas'.

Recommended:
Chicken Skin Music (Reprise/Reprise)
The Long Riders (Reprise/Reprise)
Into The Purple Valley (Reprise/Reprise)
Paradise And Lunch (Reprise/Reprise)

Spade Cooley

One-time King Of Western Swing, Donell C. Cooley had literally one of the biggest bands in country music, sometimes numbering round two dozen musicians.

Born in Grand, Oklahoma, on February 22, 1910, Cooley, of Scottish-Irish descent plus Cherokee Indian, acquired the nickname of Spade from an exceptional run of spades he once held during a poker game.

Both his father and his grandfather were fine fiddle players and Cooley, who was first taught cello, also became adept on fiddle, playing at square dances while still a boy. During the late '30s he became a Hollywood extra.

By 1942 Cooley was leading his own very successful band, in '46 leasing the Santa Monica ballroom for long-term use as the band's headquarters. A radio performer during the early '40s, he was signed for a Hollywood country TV show in 1948, shortly after returning from a lengthy tour with his band. Playing a mixture of jazz, country and pure dance music, the Cooley outfit gained further fame, but the fiddle-playing leader's career came to a dramatic end when he was jailed for wife-slaying. His death occurred shortly after his release from prison: Cooley suffered a heart attack on November 23, 1969 while playing a sheriff's benefit concert in Oakland, California.

During his career, his records were released on such labels as Okeh, Columbia, RCA Victor and Decca, Cooley's biggest hit being with the self-penned **Shame On You** in 1945.

Recommended:
The King Of Western Swing (Club Of Spade/–)
Swinging The Devil's Dream (–/Charly)
Rompin', Stompin', Singin', Swinging' (–/Bear Family)

Rita Coolidge

Nashville-born, on May 1, 1944, Rita Coolidge and her two sisters first began singing in a church choir. Rita later worked with a rock band, the Moonpies, playing at fraternity parties at the University of Florida and at Florida State. In college, she also sang with a folk rock unit, then, after leaving, went to Memphis and began working for Pepper Records, cutting some

The Lady's Not For Sale, Rita Coolidge. Courtesy A&M Records. Rita is known as the 'Delta Lady'.

sides with the label. Her sister Priscilla began working with and then married the popular R&B organist-bandleader Booker T. Jones, which brought Rita into further contact with the rock scene.

Following a tour with Joe Cocker's Mad Dogs And Englishmen in 1970, on which she was featured as a vocalist and pianist, Rita was signed to A&M as a solo artist, her first album, **Rita Coolidge**, being released in 1971. Forming a band known as the Dixie Flyers, she then began touring, playing engagements in Britain and Canada during 1971. Some time later she met Kris Kristofferson, whom she married in 1973.

The duo appeared on several tours and many TV shows, also recording together and scoring such hits as **A Song I'd Like To Sing** (1973) and **Loving Arms** (1974). Known as the Delta Lady (Leon Russell named the song in her honour), Rita is considered to be one of the leading performers in country rock with such solo hits as **Higher And Higher** and **We're All Alone** (1977), **The Way You Do The Things You Do** (1978) and **One Fine Day** (1980). Kris and Rita went their separate ways and were divorced in 1980.

Recommended:
Rita Coolidge (A&M/–)
Fall Into Spring (A&M/–)
The Lady's Not For Sale (A&M/A&M)
Breakaway – with Kris Kristofferson (Monument/Monument)
Natural Act – with Kris Kristofferson (A&M/A&M)
Very Best (A&M/A&M)

The Coon Creek Girls

Violet Koehler, vocals, guitar, mandolin; Daisy Lange, vocals, bass; Black Eyed Susan Ledford, bass; Lily Mae Ledford, vocals, banjo, fiddle; Rosie Ledford, vocals, guitar.

The Coon Creek Girls were an extremely popular all-girl string band of the '30s and '40s, led by the singer and multi-instrumentalist Lily Mae Ledford of Pinch-em-tight Holler, Kentucky.

Lily Mae began her career as a fiddler on the National Barn Dance in 1936, but it was John Lair who conceived the idea of an all-girl band built around Lily Mae. It first consisted of Daisy Lange and Violet Koehler as well as younger sister Rosie Ledford, but in later years the band consisted of the three Ledford sisters only. They spent their entire career on the Renfro Valley Barn Dance (1938–58), first over WLW and then over WHAS, and regrouped sporadically for events like the Newport Folk Festival.

Their most popular record was their theme song, **You're A Flower That Is Blooming There For Me** (Vocalion).

Wilma Lee And Stoney Cooper

Born at Harman, West Virginia, on October 16, 1918, singer-songwriter-fiddler Dale T. 'Stoney' Cooper came from a farming family of some considerable musical ability. By the time he was 12, he had become an accomplished musician and upon leaving school joined the Leary Family, a religious singing group, who were in need of a fiddle player. One member of the group was Wilma Lee Leary (born at Valley Head, West Virginia, on February 7, 1921), a singer-songwriter, guitarist and organist, whom Stoney courted and eventually married in 1939.

For several years the duo remained members of the Leary Family, appearing on radio shows and performing in churches and other venues. then, in the mid-'40s, the Coopers decided to go their own way and began playing dates on many radio stations throughout the country, in 1947 joining the WWVA Jamboree at Wheeling West Virginia, on a regular basis.

After a ten-year stay with WWVA, during which time they switched record labels from Columbia to Hickory (1955), the Coopers headed for Nashville, becoming members of the Opry in 1957. Soon after they scored hits with **Come Walk With Me, Big Midnight Special** and **There's A Big Wheel**, all three discs being Top 5 country hits during 1959. Further successes followed, including **Johnny My Love** (1960), **This Old House** (1960), and **Wreck On The Highway** (1961), then, though the duo left Hickory for Decca, the hit supply seemed to dry up. However, the Coopers continued to be a tremendous onstage attraction and in the mid '70s were still rated as one of the Opry's most popular acts. Stoney Cooper's death, caused by a heart attack, on March 22, 1977 put the future of the act in doubt, although Wilma Lee continued with daughter Carol Lee Snow (married to Hank Snow's son, Jimmie Rodgers Snow) and the Clinch Mountain Clan.

Recommended:
Satisfied (–/DJM)
Wilma Lee And Stoney Cooper (Rounder/–)
A Daisy A Day (Leather/–)
Early Recordings (County/–)
Wilma Lee Cooper (Rounder/–)

Cowboy Copas

A victim of the 1963 plane crash that also claimed the lives of Patsy Cline and Hawkshaw Hawkins, Copas' 1960 recording of **Alabam** had just placed him

Wilma Lee And Stoney Cooper. Courtesy Rounder Records.

back on top of the heap again, following his virtual disappearance from the country charts during the late '50s. Born in Muskogee, Oklahoma, on July 15, 1913, Lloyd 'Cowboy' Copas was brought up on a ranch, where his grandfather taught him Western folklore and songs. Learning guitar at the age of 16, Copas then formed a duo with an Indian fiddler, Natchee. After winning a talent contest, the twosome then played a series of dates throughout the country. Copas himself performed on 204 radio stations in North America between 1939 and 1950. When Natchee went his own way in 1940, Copas obtained a regular spot on a Knoxville station, eventually being featured on WLM's Boone County Jamboree and

signing for King Records, for whom he made a number of hits including **Filipino Baby, Tragic Romance, Gone And Left Me Blues** and **Signed, Sealed And Delivered**.

Becoming a featured vocalist with Pee Wee King's Golden West Cowboys on the Opry in 1946, he furthered his reputation with **Kentucky Waltz** and **Tennessee Waltz**, for a while he became a performer with an SRO reputation, but after the advent of **Strange Little Girl**, a 1951 chart-climber, Copas dropped from sight. Signed to Starday in 1959, his hit recording of **Alabam** seemed set to launch him on a new career. Then came the plane disaster.

Recommended:
The Best Of Cowboy Copas (Starday/ Starday-Midland)

Helen Cornelius

Finding fame in 1976 as Jim Ed Brown's singing partner and as a member of the Nashville On The Road TV Show, Helen Cornelius has also made a considerable impression as a songwriter, her compositions being recorded by Dottsy, LaCosta, Liz Anderson, Bonnie Guitar, Barbara Fairchild and many other artists.

Below: The married duo Wilma Lee and Stoney Cooper.

The Best Of Cowboy Copas. Courtesy Gusto Records.

Brought up on a farm in Hannibal, Missouri, where she was born on December 6, 1941, Helen was one of an eight-strong musical family, with her sisters Judy and Sharon combining with Helen to form a vocal trio, their father chauffeuring them from town to town in order to provide the threesome with opportunities to perform. As a solo act, Helen began obtaining work at various local gigs, playing some radio and TV dates, and won the Ted Mack Amateur Hour. But by 1970 she was songwriting as a profession, signing a contract with Columbia-Screen Gems and cutting some discs with Columbia Records.

Signing for RCA Records in September, 1975, her first release was **We Still Love**

Songs In Missouri, a well received single. However, being cast as the ideal vocal foil for Jim Ed Brown proved to be the real breakthrough, the duo's version of **I Don't Want To Have To Marry You** becoming both a controversial release – many radio stations banning the disc – and a country No.1. In early 1977, **Saying Hello, Saying I Love You, Saying Goodbye** found the Cornelius-Brown partnership chart-topping yet again. Further hits followed with **Born Believer** (1977), **If The World Ran Out Of Love Tonight** (1978) and **Lying in Love With You** (1979). Helen has been concentrating on a solo career since 1982, but has so far failed to score a major hit.

Recommended:
I Don't Want To Have To Marry You – with Jim Ed Brown (RCA/RCA)
Born Believer – with Jim Ed Brown (RCA/–)
Helen Cornelius (MCA-Dot/–)

Country Gazette

With the famous Flying Burrito Brothers now in abeyance, it was left to Country Gazette, the remains of the Burrito aggregation, to perpetuate the line. Byron Berline had originally been a championship-winning fiddle player and in-demand session man and he teamed up with Roger Bush (string bass), Kenny Wertz (guitar, vocals), Roland White (guitar, mandolin, vocals) and Alan Munde (banjo, vocals), to bring a souped-up, '70s-style bluegrass sound to the nation.

Since bluegrass was commonplace in America, their appeal there was rather limited, but in Britain and Europe they found themselves preaching to a new audience.

They have perhaps never bettered their first album for UA, **Traitor In Our Midst**, but in spite of personnel changes they have always maintained a standard of instrumental slickness and attractive vocal harmonies. On more than one occasion they have been voted Top Country Group in British award polls. Berline eventually left the band to form Sundance and was replaced for a time by Dave Ferguson. Far more popular abroad than at home, the band has continued regardless of numerous line-up changes.

Recommended:
All This And Money Too (Ridge Runner/–)
American And Clean (Flying Fish/–)
Traitor In Our Midst (UA/–)
Don't Give Up Your Day Job (UA/–)
From The Beginning (–/Sunset)

Country Gentlemen

One of the first progressive bluegrass groups, the Country Gentlemen played their first date on July 4, 1957.

During the group's embryonic days the personnel consisted of Charlie Waller, John Duffy, Bill Emerson and Eddy Adcock, though by the mid-'70s, lead singer and flat top guitarist Waller (born in Jointerville, Texas, on January 19, 1935) was the only remaining member of the original line-up.

Don't Give Up Your Day Job, Country Gazette. Courtesy UA Records.

Initially from the Washington DC area, the group played two nights a week for ten years at a Georgetown niterie known as the Shamrock Club – but during the '60s the Gentlemen gained a nationwide reputation, being featured on many networked TV shows, the group's popularity gaining ground along with the bluegrass explosion. Voted Best Band by 'Muleskinner News' in 1972 and 1973, they became the first Washington bluegrass band to play in Japan.

Eclectic in their choice of material – drawing equally from Bob Dylan, Charlie Poole, Lefty Frizzell and even Hollywood film composers – the Country Gentlemen have recorded for such labels as Folkways, Rebel, Mercury, Starday and Vanguard.

Recommended:
Country Songs Old And New (Folkways/–)
Folksongs and Bluegrass (Folkways/–)
Bringing Mary Home (Rebel/–)
Play It Like It Is (Rebel/–)
New Look, New Sound (Rebel/–)
The Award Winning Gentlemen (Rebel/–)
Live At Roanoke (Zap/–)
Sit Down Young Stranger (Sugar Hill/–)

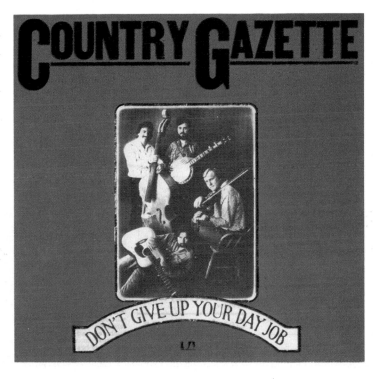

Above: Country Gazette in 1974 – Alan Munde, Byron Berline, Roger Bush and Kenny Wertz.

Cousin Jody

James Clell Summey began his career as a straight musician and was one of the fine early practitioners of the dobro. In fact, it was as a member of Roy Acuff's Smoky Mountain Boys that he recorded several of the early Acuff hits, including **Wabash Cannonball** and **The Great Speckled Bird**. It was he, as well, who first joined the Opry with Acuff in 1938.

He branched out as a musician, playing electric steel (one of the first to do so on the Opry stage) with Pee Wee King's Golden West Cowboys before delving into comedy with Oral Rhodes as Odie and Jody, then joining Lonzo and Oscar for a number of years prior to gaining his own solo Opry spot for over a decade.

Summey was born near Sevierville, Tennessee, on December 14, 1914. Plagued by ill health in his late years, he died of cancer in 1976.

Billy 'Crash' Craddock

Known as 'Mr Country Rock', Craddock was born on June 16, 1939 in Greensboro, North Carolina. Initially part of a group called the Four Rebels, along with his brother Clarence, Billy later signed to Columbia as a solo artist, scoring heavily with a 1959 single, **Don't Destroy Me**, which made a big impression in Australia. He claims he then quit the business because Columbia insisted on casting him in a pop role, while he saw his future in country music.

After taking many menial jobs, he eventually signed for Ron Chancey's Cartwheel label, coming up with a whole string of rock-oriented country hits, including **Ain't Nothin' Shakin'**, **Dream Lover** and **Knock Three Times**, a revamped version of Dawn's pop hit. Cartwheel was then absorbed into ABC-Dot and Craddock enjoyed further hits with **Rub It In** (1974), **Easy As Pie** (1976) and **Broken Down In Tiny Pieces** (1977). He joined Capitol Records in 1978 and continued with such hits as **I Cheated On A Good Woman's Love** (1978) and **I Just Had You On My Mind** (1980). Highly respected for his stunning in-concert antics, which recall the early days of Elvis Presley, he is regarded as one of the most exciting performers in country music.

Recommended:
Two Sides Of Crash (ABC/–)
The Country Side Of (–/MFP)
Greatest Hits Volume 1 (ABC/–)
The New Will Never Wear Off Of You (Capitol/–)
Laughing And Crying (Capitol/–)

Floyd Cramer

Pianist on a large proportion of Nashville hits during the late '50s – including Elvis Presley's **Heartbreak Hotel** – Cramer was born at Shreveport, Louisiana, on October 27, 1933, and grew up in Huttig, Arkansas, playing his first dates at local dances.

On completing high school in 1951 he returned to Shreveport where he appeared on KWKH's Louisiana Hayride show, played on sessions at the Abbott Record

Floyd Cramer

**20 Of The Best, Floyd Cramer.
Courtesy RCA Records.**

company and fitted in tours with Presley and other major acts.

Following various Nashville session dates, Chet Atkins advised Cramer to become a regular Music City sideman. This he did in 1955, quickly establishing himself as one of the city's most active musicians, helping to create the new Nashville Sound with his distinctive 'slipnote' piano style. He also toured and performed on radio and TV shows including Grand Ole Opry.

Signed to RCA, his first hit record was **Flip, Flop And Bop** in 1958, following this with two self-penned million sellers, **Last Date** (1960) and **On The Rebound** (1961).

Winner of countless polls and awards, Cramer has enjoyed many other high selling discs including **San Antonio Rose** (1961), **Chattanooga Choo Choo, Hot Pepper** (1962) and **Stood Up** (1967).

In 1977 Floyd emerged with **Keyboard Kick Band**, an album on which he played no less than eight keyboard instruments including various ARP synthesizers.

Recommended:
Super Hits (RCA/–)
Best Of Class Of (RCA/–)
Last Date (RCA/–)
Plays The Big Hits (Camden/–)
In Concert (RCA/–)
Piano Masterpieces (RCA/–)
This is Floyd (RCA/–)
Keyboard Kick Band (RCA/–)
Forever Floyd Cramer (Step One/–)

Rob Crosby

Blond singer-songwriter Rob Crosby, born on March 25, 1954, in Sumter, South Carolina, is one of the '90s most promising and formidable new voices. He received his first guitar when he was nine years old, and instead of hitting the college books he hit the college club circuit with his own band. Eventually he ended up in Nashville, making his mark as a writer, with Lee Greenwood, taking **Holding A Good Hand**

**Another Time And Place, Rob Crosby.
Courtesy Arista Records.**

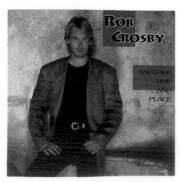

to No.2. Crosby signed with Arista Records and made Top 20 with **Love Will Bring Her Around** (1990). His strong voice with its expressive, gravelly edge helps him put his strong and vivid lyrics across. There have been further Top 20 successes with **She's A Natural** (1991) and **Still Burnin' For You** (1992).

Recommended:
Solid Ground (Arista/–)

Rodney Crowell

One of Nashville's most successful contemporary songwriters and producers, Rodney was born on August 7, 1950, in Houston, Texas and started his musical career in his teens playing in a high school band, the Arbitrators, in 1965. A few years later he was playing drums in his Kentucky-born father's band in Houston clubs. He dropped out of college and moved to Nashville in the early '70s, determined to become a songwriter. He was signed to Jerry Reed's publishing firm, but struggled to make a living. His luck changed when a chance meeting with Brian Ahern, husband of Emmylou Harris, led to a move to California where he joined Emmylou's Hot Band in 1975.

Rodney worked with Emmylou for just over two years, during which time he wrote several songs, such as **Bluebird Wine, 'Til I Gain Control Again** and **Leaving Louisiana In The Broad Daylight**, which Emmylou recorded. He embarked on a solo career towards the end of 1977, coming up with the critically-acclaimed **Ain't Living Long Like This** album. In 1979 he married Rosanne Cash.

Two further solo albums followed on Warners, though at the time he was having more success with rock fans than country. He scored a pop Top 40 hit with **Ashes By Now** (1980). A fourth album was recorded in 1984, but Warners rejected it, so Crowell changed four tracks and signed with Columbia, Rosanne Cash's label. **Street Language** (1986) was a superbly produced album, but it failed to produce any major country hits, and Rodney was now living in the shadow of his more famous wife. He decided to change direction, and moved away from his artistic, meaningful songs towards a more relaxed, country sound for **Diamonds & Dirt** (1988), an album that produced five No.1 country singles: **It's Such A Small World** (a duet with Rosanne Cash, 1988), **I Couldn't Leave You If I Tried, She's Crazy For Leavin'** (1988), **After All This Time** and **Above And Beyond** (both 1989). He received five nominations at the 1989 CMA Awards, but was still not fully accepted within country music.

His commercial success was not to last. The impressive **Keys To The Highway** (1989) album produced just two Top 10 hits, the excellent **Many A Long & Lonesome Highway** (1989) and **If Looks Could Kill** (1990). Another single, the superb **Things I Wish I'd Said**, a moving tribute to his late father, just managed to scrape to No.72 in 1991. By this time Rodney's marriage to Rosanne was going through rough times, leading to the pair filing for divorce in November 1991. Crowell has always tended to write from personal experiences and **Life Is Messy**, a 1992 album, reflected many of the pair's marriage problems in one of his strongest sets of songs. **What Kind Of Love** (a song he had written in partnership with Will

Jennings and the late Roy Orbison) made the country Top 20 (1992), but this album was not to be so readily accepted by the country fans or the critics as the more commercially slanted **Diamonds & Dirt**.

As a songwriter, Crowell has penned songs covered by Waylon Jennings, Crystal Gayle, the Oak Ridge Boys, Johnny Cash, Bob Seger, Nitty Gritty Dirt Band and others. He has produced albums for Guy Clark, Bobby Bare and Sissy Spacek. He seems to put others' musical endeavours in front of his own, and has not given his own career the commitment it has needed.

Recommended:
Ain't Living Long Like This (Warner Bros/ Warner Bros)
Rodney Crowell (Warner Bros/–)
Keys To The Highway (Columbia/CBS)
Life Is Messy (Columbia/Columbia)
Diamonds And Dirt (Columbia/CBS)

**Ramblin' Country, Dick Curless.
Courtesy Capitol Records.**

**Diamonds & Dirt, Rodney Crowell.
Courtesy CBS Records.**

The Cumberland Ridge Runners

Hugh Cross, banjo; Karl Davis, mandolin; Red Foley, bass; Doc Hopkins, guitar, vocals; John Lair, leader, announcer, harmonica; Slim Miller, fiddle; Linda Parker, vocals, guitar, banjo, dulcimer; Harty Taylor, guitar.

The Cumberland Ridge Runners were a popular string band brought to the National Barn Dance by John Lair in 1930. It had more or less dissolved in 1935, mainly because Karl and Harty, Doc Hopkins, and especially Red Foley had gone on to stardom in their own right. Hugh Cross had left WLS, and Linda Parker, 'The Sunbonnet Girl', who was the real star of the act, had met an early death.

As popular as they were for a time, their place in history is assured far more by their talented individual members than by the entire band itself.

Dick Curless

Born in Fort Fairfield, Maine, on March 17, 1932, Richard Curless joined the Trail Blazers soon after leaving high school. He had his own radio show as the 'Tumbleweed Kid' in Ware, Massachusetts in 1948, but, shortly after his marriage to wife Pauline in 1951, he was drafted into the army and sent to Korea. There he had his own programme on the Armed Forces Network, and achieved great popularity as the 'Rice Paddy Ranger'.

Discharged in 1954, Curless returned to his home in Bangor and worked as a vocalist in a local club. By 1957 he was playing Las Vegas and Hollywood clubs, having won first place on Arthur Godfrey's TV Talent Show. Then he faded from the scene, first involving himself in a logging business, then later playing small clubs in the Maine area.

His luck changed for the better in 1965 when he recorded **A Tombstone Every Mile** for Allagesh Records. It picked up national airplay, then Tower Records, a subsidiary of Capitol, bought the master, signed Curless to a contract and **Tombstone** became a Top 5 hit. Curless provided Tower with more high-selling singles before moving on to the parent Capitol label in 1970, scoring with **Big Wheel Cannonball** and **Drag 'Em Off The Interstate Sock It To 'Em J.P. Blues**.

Although he has always been – and still is – a true country singer, Curless, who wears a pirate-like patch over his right eye, has never been a Nashvillite, remaining a resident of New England to this day.

Recommended:
Hard Traveling Man (Capitol/–)
Last Blues Song (Capitol/–)
Keep On Truckin' (Capitol/–)
The Great Race (Rocade/–)

Billy Ray Cyrus

The overnight success of country hunk Billy Ray Cyrus in the summer of 1992 became known as the 'Cyrus Virus' as his popularity spread across America. The 30-year-old sex symbol turned country music upside-down with his debut single, the million-selling **Achy Breaky Heart**, the first country single in more than six years to make the American pop charts. It started a national dance craze with Melanie Greenwood, former wife of Lee Greenwood, choreographing the Achy-Breaky Dance, which became a massive hit on video and in dance clubs.

Cyrus was born August 25, 1962, in Flatwoods, Kentucky. His grandfather was a Pentecostal preacher, which is at odds with his sexy, sensual gyrations on stage, more blatantly sexual than Presley's were in the mid-'50s. Music didn't really feature in Billy Ray's plans as a child. His parents were divorced when he was six and he led an aimless type of life. He drifted through colleges without graduating. It wasn't until he turned twenty that he picked up a guitar and started to think about a music career.

His first band, Sly Dog, played its debut gig in Ironton, Ohio and played the club and bar circuit around the Kentucky-Ohio-West Virginia border for the next few years. By 1986 Cyrus was headlining five nights a week at the Ragtime Lounge in Huntington, West Virginia. A year later he was making the Nashville connection. Knocking on doors finally paid off when veteran Opry star Del Reeves listened to the young hopeful and produced a few demo tapes.

Reeves was impressed with Billy Ray's stage show, and after months of pitching Cyrus to different labels with no luck, he connected the singer with his present manager, Jack McFadden, who signed him in July 1989. It was to be another two years before McFadden gained Cyrus a record deal with Mercury. In the meantime Billy Ray and his band continued with the club dates and the occasional larger country package show. Del Reeves recorded Billy Ray's song **It Ain't Over 'Til It's Over**, and the singer had six of his own songs included on his debut album, **Some Gave All** (1992).

Released simultaneously with the **Achy Breaky Heart** single, **Some Gave All** was the fastest-rising debut album in any musical category in the history of the Billboard charts. Within weeks it went multi-platinum as it sat comfortably at the top of both the country and pop charts. In six months the album amassed sales in excess of five million and Cyrus was seriously challenging Garth Brooks as the biggest name in country music.

This sudden success led to the media and fellow country stars taking swipes at Billy Ray, calling him the 'Fabian of Country Music' and Nashville's quickest flash-in-the-pan. Travis Tritt, in a much publicized outburst, dismissed him as a one-hit wonder, but Billy Ray has enjoyed more tabloid press than any other country star.

Billy Ray did consolidate his position on the country charts with **Could've Been Me** (No.3, 1992) and **She's Not Cryin' Anymore** (No.6, 1993), though his self-penned **Where'm I Gonna Live** (1992), written after his ex-wife Cindy kicked him out of the house, failed to make the Top 20. His band, Sly Dog, is still the same outfit since those early club dates, but now they are more likely to be playing large stadiums. Billy Ray's stage presence has the female fans in ecstasy with his combination of romping energy, sex appeal and innocent country-boy good fun, all wrapped up into a muscle-rippling body. In a music not renowned for sex appeal, Billy Ray Cyrus has certainly made a major impact in a very short period. Only time will tell if he really does possess the talent and staying power to build a long-lasting country music career.

Recommended:
Some Gave All (Mercury/Mercury)
It Won't Be The Last (Mercury/Mercury)

Ted Daffan

Born in Beauregard County, Louisiana, on September 21, 1912, singer-songwriter-guitarist Theron Eugene Daffan spent his childhood in Texas, graduating from high school in 1930. During the early '30s he led

Left: Billy Ray Cyrus, 1992 Nashville Fan Fair's biggest success story. Billy Ray's Achy Breaky Heart catapulted him to fame and started a national dance craze.

the Blue Islanders, a Hawaiian band. In 1934 he moved on to become steel guitarist with the Blue Ridge Playboys, a unit featuring Floyd Tillman on lead guitar. He later worked with the Bar X Cowboys, a Houston band, and, after a long stay, formed a band of his own. In 1939 he wrote **Truck Driver's Blues**, reputed to be the first trucking song. This became such a high-selling disc that Daffan and his band, the Texans, were signed by Columbia, providing that label with a 1940 hit in **Worried Mind**, which sold about 350,000 copies.

The future seemed assured for Daffan, but, after cutting some two dozen of his own songs for Columbia (sometimes using the nom-de-plume of Frankie Brown), World War II intervened and the Texans were forced to disband. Within two years Daffan was recording once more, cutting **No Letter Today** and **Born To Lose**, a double-sided hit that won him a gold disc for a million sale. He also formed a new band to play at the Venice Ballroom, Los Angeles, California, during the mid-'40s heading back to Texas to organize bands in the Fort Worth-Dallas area. Throughout the '50s, many singers recorded Daffan's songs – including Faron Young and Hank Snow, the latter becoming a partner in a Daffan music publishing enterprise.

By 1961, Daffan was once more a resident of Houston, this time as general manager of a publishing house. And that same year yet another of his compositions ended up on a million-selling disc: Joe Barry won an award for his recording of Daffan's **I'm A Fool To Care**, which had been a hit nearly a decade earlier for Les Paul and Mary Ford. Other hits from the prolific Daffan pen include **Blue Steel Blues, Heading Down The Wrong Highway, I've Got Five Dollars And It's Saturday Night**, and **A Tangled Mind**.

Vernon Dalhart

A seminal figure in country music development, Vernon Dalhart (real name Marion Try Slaughter) was born in Jefferson, Texas, on April 6, 1883, the son of a ranch owner. While a teenager, he and his mother moved to Dallas. He began attending Dallas Conservatory of Music.

Next came a series of jobs in New York, during which time Dalhart sang in churches and vaudeville, auditioning for light opera. In 1912, he obtained a part in Puccini's 'Girl Of The Golden West' and later worked in other similar productions, though his first traceable recording, Edison cylinder **Can't Yo' Heah Me Callin' Caroline**, released June 1917, featured a 'coon' song. Following this came a deluge of Dalhart recordings on various labels, the singer tackling operatic arias, popular songs and patriotic World War I ditties. He recorded mountain musician Henry Whitter's **The Wreck Of The Old '97** for Edison in May 1924. He then cut the same song, backed with **The Prisoner's Song** (an adaptation of a traditional folk tune) for Victor, the disc having a November 1924 release. It promptly became a massive hit, encouraging Dalhart to record more hillbilly material, though more often than not he was content to re-record his hits. **The Wreck Of The Old '97**, sung by Dalhart in various guises, appears on more than 50 labels. Meanwhile, Victor sold over six million copies of the original version, making the disc their biggest seller of the pre-electric period.

Charlie Daniels

Once categorized as a southern boogie band, the Charlie Daniels Band has moved further and further into the pure country fold over the years. This was hardly surprising, considering Daniels' history as a bluegrass player and regular Nashville sessionman.

Born the son of a lumberjack in Wilmington, North Carolina, on October 28, 1937, the guitar- and fiddle-playing Daniels spent the years 1958–67 (except for a short period during which he found employment in a Denver junkyard) playing with a band known as the Jaguars. He claims that the band played every honky-

High Lonesome, Charlie Daniels Band. Courtesy Epic Records.

tonk, dive and low-life joint from Raleigh to Texas. It was in Texas that Daniels met producer Bob Johnston, who guided him to Nashville where he became a sessioneer with Flatt and Scruggs, Marty Robbins, Claude King, and Pete Seeger, also playing on Ringo Starr's country album and Bob Dylan's **Nashville Skyline**.

A classy songwriter, Daniels started pitching his songs in the late '50s and his first taste of success came with **It Hurts Me**, a tender ballad that became an Elvis Presley B-side in 1964. He's since had songs recorded by Tammy Wynette, Gary Stewart and many others. In the late '60s

Full Moon, Charlie Daniels Band. Courtesy Epic Records.

he produced two albums on Youngblood, **Elephant Mountain** and **Ride The Wind**. In 1970, **Charlie Daniels**, a self-titled album, was released on Capitol.

The Charlie Daniels Band was formed in 1970 and for the next four years recorded for Kama Sutra, gaining a gold album with **Fire On The Mountain** and hit singles in **Uneasy Rider** (1973) and **The South's Gonna Do It Again** (1975). During 1974, Daniels began his annual Volunteer Jam concerts, featuring some of the biggest names in country and rock. During the following year he signed the band to Epic Records in a contract worth a reported three million dollars. His first album for the new label, **Saddle Tramp**, was released in 1976 and went gold within a year. The CDB were blazing new territory as their records crossed boundaries with music that strained at country's fences.

The quality of the albums kept moving up and up – and so did their public acceptance. In 1979 the boundaries were forever re-defined when the multi-million-selling **Million Mile Reflections** provided a huge spin-off single in **The Devil Went Down To Georgia**, a Top 5 pop chart single that was full of country fiddling. Charlie took home a Grammy for Best Vocal Performance, wowing a primarily rock-oriented audience with his blazing performance. At the CMA Awards that year, Charlie not only picked up Single Of The Year, but the CDB was named Band Of The Year. The following year the band appeared in the film 'Urban Cowboy' and recorded another hit single, **In America**, which went Top 20 on both pop and country charts.

Since then Daniels has kept up a heavy road schedule and charted such singles as **The Legend Of Wooley Swamp** (1981), **Drinkin' My Baby Goodbye** (1985), **Boogie Woogie Fiddle Country Blues** (1986) and **Simple Man** (1989). There have also been several gold and platinum albums, such as **Full Moon** (1980), **Me And The Boys** (1985) and **Simple Man** (1989). In 1992 they signed a new contract with Liberty Records; the CDB's music still remaining raw, abandoned and frenetic with Daniels himself at the fore.

Recommended:
Nightrider (Kama Sutra/Kama Sutra)

Lacy J. Dalton

"A voice so unique it rises above the rest. Lacy J. Dalton possesses that exciting style and quality that make her special." So said Billy Sherrill about Lacy J. Dalton shortly before the release of her CBS debut album in 1980.

Born Jill Byrem, October 13, 1948, near Bloomsburg, Pennsylvania, Lacy J. has enjoyed mixed fortunes since Sherrill produced her debut album. She comes from a musical family, her father being a guitarist and mandolinist. She began her own musical career as a folk singer in her teens, performing protest songs in local clubs in Minnesota. In 1967 she moved to Los Angeles and, soon after, settled in Santa Cruz where she played the local club circuit for 12 years. At one point she became lead singer of a psychedelic rock group, Office, and accrued a hefty catalogue of self-penned songs. After a series of demo discs was recorded, one, **Crazy Blue Eyes**, found its way to CBS, who signed Lacy to a contract in May 1979. CBS immediately released a Sherrill-embellished version of **Crazy Blue Eyes** which went Top 20. Lacy, with her band the Dalton Gang, then began a heavy schedule of gigs, sometimes headlining, sometimes opening, for such country artists as Willie Nelson, Emmylou Harris, Christopher Cross and the Oak Ridge Boys. Her first two albums, **Lacy J. Dalton** and **Hard Times**, became Top 20 chart items in 1980.

Lacy J. enjoyed notable chart success with her singles, making Top 10 with **Hard Times** (1980), **Hillbilly Girl With The Blues, Whisper, Takin' It Easy** (all 1981), **Everybody Makes Mistakes** and **16th Avenue** (1982), and a revival of Roy Orbison's **Dream Baby** (1983). She's retained a solid country feel, yet also appeals to a rock audience with her gutsy blues/rock, passion-filled vocal style. Her 1986 album, **Highway Diner**, moved her into Bruce Springsteen territory, but there

Above: Lacy J. Dalton continues to output albums and singles in the '90s.

was still a definite country edge to such Top 20 hits as **If That Ain't Love** (1984), **You Can't Run Away From Your Heart** (1985), **Size 7 Round** (a duet with George Jones in 1985) and **Working Class Man** (1986).

In 1989 Dalton joined the new and ill-fated Universal Records, releasing the acclaimed **Survivor** album which contained Kristofferson's **The Heart** – another Top 20 hit. She moved to Capitol/Liberty when Jimmy Bowen closed Universal and took up an executive position there. She has maintained her high quality of output with the album **Crazy Love** (1991) and **Chains On The Wind** (1992), and with her most recent Top 20 single, **Black Coffee** (1990).

Hard Times, Lacy J. Dalton. Courtesy CBS Records. This album became a Top 20 chart item in 1980.

Recommended:
Hard Times (Columbia/CBS)
Takin' It Easy (Columbia /CBS)
Highway Diner (Columbia/CBS)
Blue Eyed Blues (Columbia/CBS)
Survivor (Universal/–)
Lacy J. (Capitol/–)
Crazy Love (Capitol/–)
Chains On The Wind (Capitol/–)

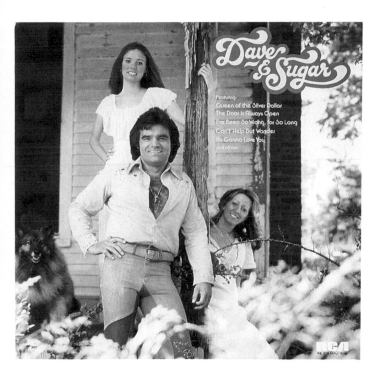

Dave And Sugar – the group's debut album. Courtesy RCA Records.

Volunteer Jam (Capricorn/Capricorn)
Saddle Tramp (Epic/Epic)
Fire On The Mountain (Epic/Epic)
High And Lonesome (Epic/Epic)
Full Moon (Epic/Epic)
Simple Man (Epic/Epic)

Dave And Sugar

Dave And Sugar were a one-man, two-girl vocal group that was momentarily hailed as Nashville's answer to Abba in the late '70s. Original members were Dave Rowland (born on January 26, 1942, in Los Angeles), a beefy, soulful singer, Vicki Hackman from Louisville, Kentucky and Jackie Franc (Frantz) from Sidney, Ohio.

Rowland started out as a dance band vocalist, becoming a trumpeter with the 75th Army Band after being drafted. Graduating from the Stamps School of Music in Texas he became a member of the Stamps Quartet, toured with Elvis Presley and eventually became a member of the Four Guys. While still a member of the Guys he backed Charley Pride and heard that Pride required a new backup group for vocal harmony work. So Rowland held auditions, signed ex-trumpeter Franc and Hackman (who later married Pride's guitarist) and had the group signed to Chardon, the company that so astutely masterminded Pride's own meteoric rise.

The trio had an immediate No.1 single with **The Door Is Always Open**, in mid-1976, following this with a second chart-topper, **I'm Gonna Love You**, just a few months later. Rowland then experienced some changes in partners but the hits – all Top 10s – continued to flow profusely. 1977 brought **Don't Throw It All Away**, **That's The Way Love Should Be** and **I'm Knee Deep In Loving You**; 1978 providing **Gotta Quit Lookin' At You Baby** and **Tear Time** (a No.1); and 1979 supplying **Golden Tears** (yet another No.1), **Stay With Me** and **My World Begins And Ends With You**, all RCA releases.

By 1980, the group, now labelled Dave Rowland And Sugar, began to slide in terms of record sales with only one single, **New York Wine And Tennessee Shine**, going Top 20. Then followed a label switch, to Elektra, where **Fool By Your Side** (1981) saw the group momentarily back in the Top 10 again, after which they joined MCA Records in 1985.

Below: Gail Davies became lead singer with Wild Choir in 1986, then went solo again.

By this time Dave Rowland had embarked on a solo career. Although he had label deals with MCA and Elektra, it seems that the glory days of the late '70s were just a faded memory.

Recommended:
Dave And Sugar (RCA/RCA)
New York Wine And Tennessee Shine (RCA/RCA)
Stay With Me (RCA/RCA)
Greatest Hits (RCA/–)

Gail Davies

A talented singer-songwriter, Davies was born in Broken Bow, Oklahoma on April 4, 1948, the daughter of a country musician who kept a home juke-box stacked with classic country singles. When her parents split up, Gail, her mother and her brother Ron relocated to Seattle. A one-time keypunch operator for Westinghouse, quitting after only two weeks, she opted for a singing career. Davies and her brother formed a folk-rock duo and recorded an unreleased album for A&M.

Gail, who had lost her voice and had been advised to stop singing for a while, turned to songwriting and headed for Nashville, scoring immediately as the writer of **Bucket To The South**, a 1978 Top 20 hit for Ava Barber. That same year Gail herself began logging country hits, signing for the Lifesong label and notching two Top 20 singles in **No Love Have I** and **Poison Love**. In the wake of one further Lifesong hit, **Someone Is Looking For Someone Like You** (1979), came a

Where Is A Woman To Go?, Gail Davies. Courtesy RCA Records. She recorded a Best Of compilation album in 1991.

Warner contract and Top 10 success with **Blue Heartache** (1979), **I'll Be There (If You Ever Want Me)** (1980), **It's A Lovely, Lovely World** (1981), **Grandma's Song** (1981) and **'Round The Clock Lovin'** (1982).

Two years later Gail switched labels again, signing with RCA, and immediately charted with **Jagged Edge Of A Broken Heart**, a single that had all the hallmarks of a high-grade pop cross-over, though one that ultimately did not gain the attention it deserved. RCA seemed unsure how to handle the headstrong Davies, who was the first woman in Nashville to produce her own recordings. Further singles like **Unwed Fathers** and **Break Away** in 1985 failed to match their potential in sales. Gail formed a band, Wild Choir, the following year, notching up two minor hits for RCA, then opting once again for a solo career. She signed with MCA in 1988, but, even with production by Jimmy Bowen, was unable to recapture her past glories. She followed Bowen to Capitol Records, and in 1991 re-recorded some of her past hits for **The Best Of Gail Davies**, artistically a great album, but, commercially, yet another flop. Gail continues to sing harmony on Nashville sessions, where she is held in high esteem by fellow singers and musicians but sadly not by the record-buying public.

Recommended:
What Can I Say? (Warner Bros/–)
Where Is A Woman To Go? (RCA/RCA)
The Game (Warner Bros/–)
The Other Side Of Love (Capitol/–)
Pretty Words (MCA/MCA)

Danny Davis

Davis, real name George Nowlan, was born in Randolph, Massachusetts, on April 29, 1925. He first played trumpet with high school bands during the '30s. At 17 he became a sideman with some of the best bands of the swing era, including those of Gene Krupa and Bob Crosby. Later, he recorded under his own name, having a hit with **Trumpet Cha Cha Cha**. In 1958 he became a record producer, first with Joy Records, then with MGM, where he helped Connie Francis on her way to several No.1 singles.

During a trip to Nashville, Davis – who terms himself 'a Yankee Irishman' – met publisher Wesley Rose and Chet Atkins and became the latter's production assistant at RCA in 1965. He then conceived the idea of adding a brass sound to a pop-oriented country rhythm section, recording under the name Nashville Brass.

The band proved a success right from the start with the Nashville-cum-Alpert sound of the Davis Outfit appealing to such a cross-section of the public that the band's first 14 albums all sold in excess of 100,000 copies. Such singles as **Wabash Cannonball** and **Columbus Stockade Blues** also made their way into the charts.

By the early '70s, Davis was living in a fabulous ranch house near Nashville, had a stake in several oil wells and a seaside motel, and was also the proud owner of a private airliner. For six straight years, from 1969 through to 1974, Davis and the Nashville Brass were voted Instrumental Band Of The Year at the CMA Awards. Davis also picked up a Grammy in 1969 for his **More Nashville Sounds** album.

Recommended:
Bluegrass (RCA/–)
The Best Of Danny Davis (RCA/RCA)
Moving On (RCA/–)
Danny Davis & Willie Nelson With The Nashville Brass (RCA/–)

Jimmie Davis

Elected Governor of Louisiana in both 1944 and 1960, James Houston Davis (born in Quitman, Louisiana, on September 11, 1902) is also an eminently successful recording artist and songwriter. His writing credits include such standards as **You Are My Sunshine**, **It Makes No Difference Now**, **Sweethearts Or Strangers** and **Nobody's Darlin' But Mine**.

Gaining a BA at Louisiana College and an MA at Louisiana State University, Davis became a professor of history at Dodd College in the later '20s. During the next decade he forwarded his musical career – recording for RCA, Victor and Decca – at the same time still managing to hold down various positions of public office. A popular performer by the end of the '30s, in 1944 he appeared in the movie 'Louisiana'. When his first term of office as State Governor came to an end in 1948, Davis returned to the entertainment industry once more. He concentrated much of his

Memories Coming Home, Jimmie Davis. Courtesy MCA Records.

activity within the sphere of gospel music where he won an award as Best Male Sacred Singer in 1957.

In 1960, Davis was asked to run in the primary, proving successful again. He also won against the might of the Huey Long machine in the election. During this second stint as Governor he had a hit in 1962, **Where The Old Red River Flows**.

Returning to active duty on the recording front in 1964, he provided Decca with an album, **Jimmie Davis Sings**, his other late '60s and early '70s releases including **At The Crossing**, **Still I Believe**, **Amazing Grace** and **Christ Is Sunshine**. In 1972, Davis was elected to the Country Music Hall Of Fame.

Recommended:
Greatest Hits (MCA/–)
You Are My Sunshine (MCA/–)
Christ Is Sunshine (Canaan/Canaan)
Country Side Of Jimmie Davis (MCA/–)
Barnyard Stomp (–/Bear Family)

Linda Davis

Davis, born on November 26, 1956, in Dotson, Texas, has been around the country music scene for a number of years without making a major breakthrough. She grew up in the small Texas town of Gary, and, prior to moving to Nashville in 1982, she was a regular on both the Louisiana Hayride in Shreveport and the Grapevine Opry. Linda teamed up with Skip Eaton, and, working as Skip & Linda, the duo signed to MDJ Records. They enjoyed chart success with **If You Could See Through My Eyes** (1982).

The next few years found Linda singing on demos and jingles. In 1988 she signed a recording contract with Epic Records and made her chart debut as a solo star with **All The Good Ones Are Taken** (1988). Two years later she joined Capitol Records and was back in the charts with **In A Different Light** (1991). In 1993 Linda duetted with Reba McEntire on **Does He Love You**.

Recommended:
In A Different Light (Capitol/–)
Linda Davis (Capitol/–)

In A Different Light, Linda Davis. Courtesy Capitol Records.

Mac Davis

Born at Lubbock, Texas, on January 21, 1941, Mac Davis's career has taken in rock'n'roll, songwriting, performing and record company work. He lived much of his early life in Atlanta, Georgia, and after attending high school he worked for the Georgia State Board of Probation. In his spare time he formed a band and toured in the south, playing mainly rock'n'roll. Later he took a job as a regional manager (in Atlanta) for Vee-Jay Records, then going to Liberty Records.

In 1968 Lou Rawls recorded one of Davis's songs, **You're Good For Me**, and Elvis Presley recorded his **In The Ghetto**. The latter was a funky departure for Presley at the time and it really brought Davis to prominence. At this point he was writing under noms-de-plume to avoid confusion with lyricist Mack David, although he finally switched back to using his own name.

He wrote some material for Presley's first TV spectacular and also provided some material for such films as 'Norwood', starring Glen Campbell. Additionally, he wrote hits for Kenny Rogers And The First Edition (**Something's Burning**) and Bobby Goldsboro (**Watching Scotty Grow**).

In 1970 he guested on TV shows with Johnny Cash and Glen Campbell. The following year he cut a debut album for CBS called **I Believe In Music**, the title track being covered by over 50 artists, the most successful version being that released by Gallery in 1972. That same year Davis came up with the big one, **Baby Don't Get Hooked On Me**, his first US pop chart-topper, following this with such hits as **One Hell Of A Woman**, **Stop And Smell The Roses** and **Rock'n'Roll (I Gave You The Best Years Of My Life)**, all in 1974. In 1974, too, he began hosting his own TV show.

After this period, the flood of pop chart hits began to ebb, but Davis's country audience stayed faithful and he continued to log country hits including **Forever Lovers** (1976). In 1979 he signed a new deal with Casablanca, scoring five Top 10 singles – **It's Hard To Be Humble**, **Let's Keep It That Way** and **Texas In My**

Rear View Mirror (all 1980) as well as **Hooked On Music** and **You're My Bestest Friend** (both 1981). His next Top 10 success came with **I Never Made Love ('Til I Made Love With You)** (1985), his first single for MCA Records. In the late '80s he worked closely with Dolly Parton and the pair co-wrote several songs including **White Limozeen** and duetted on the playful **Wait 'Til I Get You Home** (1989).

A brilliant live performer, always being able to ring the changes – which is why he has been able to command high fees at all the best Las Vegas night-spots – Davis has also developed a career as an actor, appearing in movies such as 'North Dallas Forty', 'Cheaper To Keep Her' and 'The Sting II'. Glen Campbell once said of him: "Mac Davis don't write songs, he paints them". Hence the album title, **Song Painter**.

Recommended:
Song Painter (Columbia/CBS)
Its Hard To Be Humble (Casablanca/ Casablanca)

Skeeter Davis

Suspended by the Opry in December 1973 for criticizing the Nashville Police Department on a WSM broadcast – following a week in which two Opry performers had been murdered and Tom T. Hall's house burned down – Skeeter Davis has always had an eventful career.

She began life (in Dry Ridge, Kentucky, on December 30, 1931) as Mary Frances Penick, the eldest of seven children. At high school, she and her friend Betty Jack Davis (born in Corbin, Kentucky, on March 3, 1932) formed a harmony vocal team, the Davis Sisters, that led to a regular programme on radio station WLEX, Lexington, Kentucky. This, in turn, led to other radio shows in Detroit and Cincinnati and, eventually, to a recording contract first with Fortune, then with RCA Victor. In 1953, their first RCA effort, **I Forgot More Than You'll Ever Know**, became a No.1 record, claiming a chart position for 26 weeks – and it appeared that the Davis Sisters were set for a long career. But while travelling to Cincinnati on August 2, 1953, the girls became involved in a car accident which killed Betty Jack and critically injured Skeeter.

It was some considerable time before she resumed work, but, after a brief spell working as a duo with Betty Jack's sister Georgia, Skeeter began a solo career. Her first real breakthrough occurred in 1959 when her recording of **Set Him Free** established her as a chart name. A 1962 release, **The End Of The World**, proved the real clincher, the disc earning Skeeter a gold record and worldwide reputation. Though she asked her agency not to book her into clubs where liquor was being

Song Painter, Mac Davis. Courtesy Columbia Records.

served (Skeeter claimed that she did not want her non-drinking fans drawn into a situation where they might be tempted to imbibe) her bookings became more and more prestigious. And her records continued to sell. **I'm Saving My Love** (1963), **Gonna Get Along Without You Now** (1964), **What Does It Take?** (1967) and **I'm A Lover, Not A Fighter** (1969) proved to be her biggest sellers. Along the way she also recorded two best-selling duets with Bobby Bare – **A Dear John Letter** (1965) and **Your Husband, Your Wife** (1971) – and appeared on disc with such artists as Porter Wagoner and George Hamilton IV.

Ever pop-connected – during the 1960s she toured with the Rolling Stones and in 1985 she did an album with nutty rock outfit NRBQ, one cut proving to be a version of **Someday My Prince Will Come** done in 4/4 time! – Skeeter has often been accused of betraying her country heritage. But she claims: "I've been with the Opry since joining in 1959 – which proves that my heart's in country."

Recommended:
The Hillbilly Singer (RCA/RCA)
She Sings They Play – with NRBQ (Rounder)
Tunes For Two – with Bobby Bare (RCA/RCA)

Billy Dean

In less than three years, Billy Dean, born on April 2, 1962, in Quincy, Florida, has become one of the top writer-performers in country music. The Academy Of Country Music named him Top New Male Vocalist and his self-titled No.1 hit, **Somewhere In My Broken Heart**, Song Of The Year for 1992. He also gained a Grammy nomination, and his first two albums, **Young Man** and **Billy Dean**, netted six Top 5 hits, including the No.1s **Billy The Kid** and **If There Hadn't Been You** (both 1992).

Billy was attracted to music at an early age. His father, an auto mechanic, moonlighted as a bandleader and encouraged his son's musical talents. Billy began playing guitar in grade school, making his first appearance with his father's band, the Country Rock, at the age of eight. By the time he was fifteen he was writing songs, and he spent much of his teenage years performing along the Gulf Coast of Florida. Following a year at college in Decatur, Mississippi, on a basketball scholarship, Billy became a national finalist in the Wrangler Star Search Competition, which resulted in an appearance at Nashville's Grand Ole Opry.

He then made a move to Nashville, where he found himself in demand as a jingle singer and back-up vocalist. He had songs recorded by the Oak Ridge Boys, Les Taylor, Ronnie Milsap, Shelly West and Randy Travis. He signed a publishing deal with EMI Music and a recording contract with SBK/Liberty Records in 1990. His first

Below: Newcomer to the '90s Billy Dean is making a big impact with Top 10 hits and his gold album.

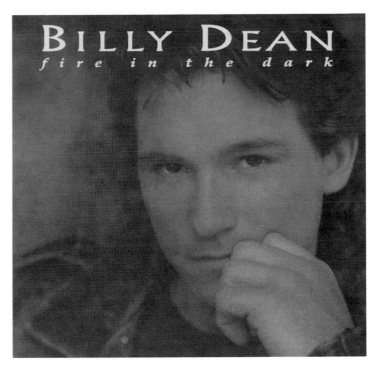

single, **Only Here For A Little While**, soared to No.3 (1991) and Dean enjoyed further Top 10 hits with **You Don't Count The Cost** (1991), **Only The Wind** (1992) and **Tryin' To Hide A Fire In The Dark** (1993). His second album, **Billy Dean**, gained a gold disc, and, along with Verlon Thompson, Dean has written and recorded the theme music for the ABC-TV series – Wild West C.O.W. Boys Of Moo Mesa.

Recommended:
Young Man (Capitol-SBK/–)
Billy Dean (Capitol-3DK/Capitol-SBK)
Fire In The Dark (Liberty/Liberty)

Jimmy Dean

The writer and performer of **Big Bad John**, a five-million-selling disc of semi-recitative nature, Jimmy Dean was born on a farm near Plainview, Texas, on August 10, 1928. He began his musical career at the age of ten, first learning piano and then mastering accordion, guitar and mouth harp. While in the Air Force during the '40s, he joined the Tennessee Haymakers, a country band comprised of service personnel who played off-duty gigs around Washington DC. Dean continued to play in that area after discharge in 1948.

Impresario Connie B. Gay hired him to perform for US Forces in the Caribbean during 1952 and, following this tour, Dean and his band, the Texas Wildcats, began playing on radio station WARL, Arlington, Virginia, obtaining a hit record on the Four Star label with **Bummin' Around** (1953). By 1957 he had his own CBS-TV show. Dean gained a CBS recording contract that same year. Initially he found hits hard to come by, but in 1961 he wrote **Big Bad John**, a somewhat dramatic tale of mineshaft heroism. He then supplied CBS with a run of Top 20 discs that included **Dear Ivan**, **Cajun Queen**, **PT109** (all 1962) and **The First Thing Every Morning**, the latter becoming a country No.1 in 1965.

A star of ABC-TV during the mid-1960s, Dean switched his record allegiance to RCA in 1966. But though this relationship began encouragingly with **Stand Beside Me**, a Top 10 record, Dean's country pop approach seemed to lose much of its

Fire In The Dark, Billy Dean. Courtesy Liberty Records. This 1993 album contains Billy's Top 10 hit, Tryin' To Hide A Fire In The Dark.

appeal as the '70s drew near – though such releases as **I'm A Swinger** (1967), **A Thing Called Love** (1968), **A Hammer And Nails** (1968) and **Slowly**, a duet with Dottie West (1971), all fared well.

After something of a lull, Dean was back in the Top 10 once more in 1976, with **I.O.U.**, a single which was re-released by the Churchill label in 1983. And though such records proved all too few at the start of the 1980s, Dean was hardly forgotten. On TV he had a syndicated music show, Jimmy Dean's Country Beat, while honours-wise he was still gaining nominations, becoming the 11th inductee into the Texas Hall Of Fame, his presentation being made by Roy Orbison and Buddy Holly's widow.

Recommended:
Greatest Hits (Columbia/–)
I.O.U. (GRT/–)
American Originals (Columbia/–)

Penny De Haven

From Winchester, Virginia (born on May 17, 1948), Penny De Haven was the first female country star to entertain the armed forces in Vietnam. A frequent Opry guest in the '60s and early '70s, she appeared in three films, 'Valley Of Blood', 'Traveling Light' and 'The Country Music Story' and had a number of minor hits on the Imperial and UA labels. Her highest chart placing came with **Land Mark Tavern**, a 1970 duet with Del Reeves.

Since that time her name has continued to pop up in the lower reaches of the country charts. De Haven achieved some success with **(The Great American) Classic Cowboy** on the Starcrest label in 1976, and, more recently, with such Main St releases as **Only The Names Have Been Changed** (1983) and **Friendly Game Of Hearts** (1984).

Recommended:
Penny De Haven (UA/–)

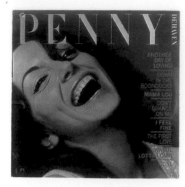

Penny De Haven. An excellent 1972 offering. Courtesy UA Records.

Delmore Brothers

Longtime Opry favourites and writers of a huge number of songs, including the oft-recorded **Blues Stay Away From Me**, the Delmore Brothers – Alton (born on December 25, 1908) and Rabon (born on December 3, 1910) – both hailed from Elkmont, Alabama. Farm raised, they were taught fiddle by their mother, Aunt Mollie Delmore, in 1930 winning an old-time fiddle contest in Athens, Alabama. Equally adept on guitar, the brothers soon won a contract with Columbia Records.

During the '40s came appearances on scores of radio stations, plus record dates for King. The duo's single of **Blues Stay Away From Me** became a Top 5 hit in 1949 and enjoyed a chart stay of no less than 23 weeks. Soon after, the Delmores became based in Houston, where Alton began drinking heavily due to the death of his daughter Sharon. Rabon became seriously ill with lung cancer, returning to Athens, where he died on December 4, 1952. Alton later moved to Huntsville, where his death occurred on June 9, 1964, the cause being diagnosed as a haemorrhage brought on by a liver disorder. The Delmores were posthumously honoured in October 1971, when they became elected to the Songwriters Hall Of Fame.

John Denver

Born John Henry Deutschendorf on December 31, 1943, John Denver grew up in an Air Force family. His father was a pilot and John also had flying ambitions until the music bug caught him. He took guitar lessons early as a boy on an old 1910 Gibson but it was during his time at Texas Tech that he felt he should try for a showbiz career, subsequently playing in West Coast clubs and eventually replacing Chad Mitchell in the trio of that name. Four years later, his own solo talents were sufficiently developed for RCA to sign him.

John has never been purely country. His albums tend to contain elements of country, folk, rock and ballads. However he has written one all-time country standard, **Take Me Home Country Roads**. He has also logged many country chart hits. He was back on the charts with **Some Days Are Diamonds**, **Wild Montana Skies** and **Dreamland Express** in the '80s.

Recommended:
Back Home Again (RCA/RCA)
Rocky Mountain High (RCA/RCA)
Some Days Are Diamonds (RCA/RCA)

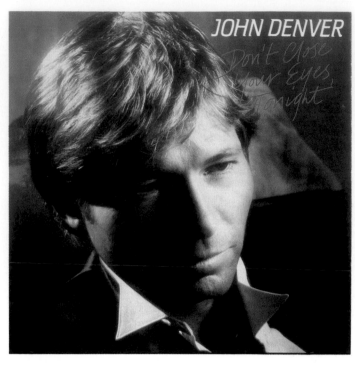

Desert Rose Band

Reviving glorious memories of the West Coast country-rock movement, the Desert Rose Band burst upon the country scene in the late '80s with a series of excellent albums and Top 10 country hits. Lead singer and main songwriter Chris Hillman made a couple of solo albums for Sugar Hill in the early '80s that laid the foundation for the formation of the Desert Rose Band in 1985.

Hillman brought in long-time music ally Herb Pedersen (lead and harmony vocals, and guitar), as well as John Jorgenson (background vocals, acoustic and electric guitars, mandolin), Jay Dee Maness (steel guitar), Bill Bryson (background vocals, bass) and Steve Duncan (drums). Hillman and the band signed with Curb Records. Their first self-titled album, produced by Paul Worley, included such Top 10 hits as

Don't Close Your Eyes Tonight, a 1985 RCA single from John Denver.

Love Reunited and **One Step Forward** (1987) as well as **He's Back And I'm Blue** (No.1, 1988).

A second album, **Running**, produced another No.1 single, **I Still Believe In You** (1988). The Top 10 hits continued, but the heavy touring schedule began to take its toll on musicians who had spent years on the road. In 1991 Maness left because he didn't want to be away from his family. A fourth album, **True Love**, featured session steel guitarist Paul Franklin. Later that year Tom Brumley was recruited, but then Jorgenson left in March 1992. An ideal replacement turned out to be Jeff Ross, but by the end of the year drummer Steve Duncan had also departed, with Tim Grogan becoming the newest DRB member.

Rocky Mountain High, a country-flavoured offering from John Denver. Courtesy RCA Records.

Back Home Again, John Denver. Courtesy RCA Records.

Recommended:
Desert Rose Band (MCA-Curb/RCA)
True Love (MCA-Curb/–)
Pages Of Life (MCA-Curb/–)
Running (MCA-Curb/–)

Al Dexter

Born in Jacksonville, Texas, on May 4, 1902, Dexter was the leader of a country outfit known as the Texas Troopers. The singer (real name Albert Poindexter) is best remembered for his self-penned **Pistol Packin' Mama**, a song that provided him and Bing Crosby with million-selling discs.

One of the first artists to use the term 'honky tonk' in a song (**Honky Tonk Blues**), Dexter died in Lewisville, Texas, on January 28, 1984. He was a prolific hitmaker in the '40s – he will also be remembered for **Too Late To Worry, Too Blue To Cry, Rosalita, Guitar Polka** and **So Long Pal**, all No.1 songs in that era.

Recommended:
Pistol Packin' Mama (Harmony/–)
Sings And Plays (–/Stetson)

De Zurich Sisters

Mary and Caroline DeZurich were a popular yodelling team on the WLS National Barn Dance for years, specializing in sky-high Alpine yodels. During their long career they were also known as the Cackle Sisters. Their career lasted from the mid-'30s to the early '50s.

Below: Al Dexter was best known for Pistol Packin' Mama.

Little Jimmy Dickens

The provider of **May The Bird Of Paradise Fly Up Your Nose**, a monster cross-over hit in 1965, the four-foot-eleven-inch Dickens had, at that time, already been hitmaking for some 16 years.

Born in Bolt, West Virginia, on December 19, 1925, Dickens was the youngest of 13 children. At 17, he won a spot on a Beckley, West Virginia, early morning radio show, moving on to appear on WIBC Indianapolis, WLW Cincinnati and WKNX Saginaw, Michigan, there meeting Roy Acuff, who invited him to appear on a duet spot on the Grand Ole Opry.

Signed to Columbia Records in the late '40s, Dickens' first Top 10 disc was **Take An Old Cold Tater And Wait** (1949). This diminutive showman followed with hits such as **Country Boy**, **Pennies For Papa** (1949), **A-Sleeping At The Foot Of The Bed**, **Hillbilly Fever** (1950), **The Violet And The Rose** (1962) and **May The Bird Of Paradise Fly Up Your Nose** (1965).

His TV credits are impressive, but the biggest night of his life came in 1982,

Roots And Branches, The Dillards. Courtesy UA Records.

when he climbed on stage at the Opry and made a short acceptance speech after being elected to the CMA Country Music Hall Of Fame. Dickens can be seen regularly at the Opryland Theme Park and on the Grand Ole Opry.

Recommended:
May The Bird Of Paradise (Columbia/–)
Little Jimmy Dickens Sings (Decca/–)
Straight From The Heart (Rounder/–)

Joe Diffie

A regular Joe, Diffie was born on December 28, 1958, in Tulsa, Oklahoma, and grew up in nearby Velma. He was in a high-school rock group called Blitz, then later joined Genesis II, a gospel outfit. After attending college, he married and moved to Texas. In 1977 he moved his family to Oklahoma where he worked in a foundry. In his spare time he continued with his music, joining another gospel group, Higher Purpose, and also a bluegrass group, Special Edition.

In 1986 Joe moved to Nashville. He had already had one of his songs, **Love On The Rocks**, recorded by Hank Thompson, but soon found it was quite difficult to break into the Nashville music scene. Eventually he signed a writer's contract with Forest Hills Publishing and for the next three years was busy co-writing and

Diamond Rio

This self-contained sextet is the first country band in history to reach No.1 with its debut single, **Meet Me In The Middle** (1991). The single paved the way for them to collect Vocal Group Of The Year from both the ACM (1991) and the CMA (1992), and see their self-titled debut album gain platinum status.

Diamond Rio won over country music fans with their superb harmonies and knack for picking commercial, but

appealing songs, anchored by Marty Roe's assertive lead vocals. The band's biggest strength is its ingenious hybrid of style. Marty Roe leans towards traditional country; lead guitarist and banjoist Jimmy Olander had played with Rodney Crowell and the Nitty Gritty Dirt Band; Gene Johnson, mandolin and vocals, spent many years on the bluegrass circuit; and keyboard player Dan Truman is classically trained and played in jazz groups. Drummer

Below: Little Jimmy Dickens was elected to the Country Music Hall Of Fame in 1982.

Above: The yodelling DeZurich Sisters, once stars of WLS.

Brian Prout played in rock bands before joining country group Heartbreak Mountain with Shenandoah vocalist Marty Raybon and he is married to Wild Rose drummer Nancy Given-Prout. Dana Williams, bass and vocals, is a nephew of bluegrass legends Bobby and Sonny Osborne, and has played with the likes of Vassar Clements and Jimmy C. Newman.

It was the chemistry and diverse musical history of this unlikely combination that jelled. The group originated as an entertainment attraction at the Opryland Theme Park. In the late '80s they started touring and changed their name to Diamond Rio (a trucking company based in Harrisburg, Pennsylvania), when they signed to Arista Records in 1990.

Though Diamond Rio are foremost a live band, they have chalked up impressive chart success with Top 10 hits such as: **Mirror, Mirror** (1991); **Mama Don't Forget To Pray For Me**, **Norma Jean Riley** and **Nowhere Bound** (all 1992); and **In A Week Or Two** and **Oh Me, Oh My Sweet Baby** (both 1993). Their second album, **Close To The Edge**, gained gold status within a few weeks of release, and there is little doubt that Diamond Rio are set to establish themselves as one of the most successful country bands of the '90s.

Recommended:
Close To The Edge (Arista/–)
Diamond Rio (Arista/–)

singing on demos while holding down a day-time job with Gibson Guitars. A recording contract with Epic in 1989 coincided with his first major success as a writer, with **There Goes My Heart**, a No.4 hit for Holly Dunn, on which he sang back-up harmonies.

Diffie became the only debut artist with his first single, **Home**, to go No.1 on all three major country charts and stay there for two weeks (1990). The follow-up, **If You Want Me To**, made No.2, then he was back at the top with **If The Devil Danced (In Empty Pockets)** (1991). Further Top 5 hits came in quick succession with **New Way (To Light Up An Old Flame)** (1991), **Is It Cold In Here** (1992) and **Ships That Don't Come In** (1992).

Destined for big things, Diffie has produced albums such as **A Thousand Winding Roads** and **Honky Tonk Attitude** with a mixture of down-home tear-jerkers and snappy up-tempo honky-tonk songs. He joined Mary-Chapin Carpenter on the Top 10 duet **Not Too Much To Ask** (1992), and has toured extensively during the past few years with his Heartbreak Highway band.

Recommended:
Honky Tonk Attitude (Epic/–)
A Thousand Winding Roads (Epic/–)
A Regular Joe (Epic/–)

The Dillards

Initially an ethnically rated bluegrass band who scored on cross-over appeal to a rock audience, Rodney (born on May 18, 1942) and Doug Dillard (born on March 6, 1937) from Salem, Missouri were the nucleus. They joined up with Mitch Jayne, a local radio announcer, and Dean Webb (from Independence, Missouri) and travelled to California where they were signed by Elektra Records.

The Dillards came from a strong blue-grass tradition but their novel, lighthearted approach, coupled with the fact that they themselves were a younger group, won them the plaudits of a wide public. They cut their **Back Porch Bluegrass** and **Live! Almost!** albums before meeting fiddler Byron Berline, with whom they made **Pickin' And Fiddlin'**, an album now much rated and sought after by fans of old-time music. Doug Dillard left to be replaced by Herb Pedersen and the Dillards then pursued a more commercial, rock direction. **Wheatstraw Suite** and **Copperfields** are albums from this period.

After recording albums for the Anthem and Poppy labels, the Dillards – then Rodney (vocals, guitar), Dean Webb (mandolin), Jeff Gilkinson (vocals, bass, cello), Paul York (drums) and Billy Ray Latham (banjo, guitar) – moved on to Flying Fish in 1977, releasing an album titled **The Dillards Vs The Incredible L.A. Time Machine**.

Since that time Rodney has continued to head the band, cutting such albums as **Decade Waltz** (1979), **Mountain Rock** (on Crystal Clear, 1980) and **Homecoming And Family Reunion** (1980), while Doug, who recorded solo in the early '70s, opted for a career as a studio musician.

Recommended:
Back Porch Bluegrass (Elektra/Elektra)
Pickin' And Fiddlin' (Elektra/Elektra)
Wheatstraw Suite (Elektra/Elektra)
I'll Fly Away (–/Edsel)

Dean Dillon

With his ponytailed hair, handlebar moustache and quiet drawl, Dillon (born Dean Rutherford on March 26, 1955, in Lake City, near Knoxville, Tennessee) looks and sounds more like a real cowboy on a time travel from the 1880s than one of Nashville's most successful songwriters. He first came to Music City in 1972, having already served a four-year apprenticeship on the Kathy Hill Show in Knoxville, and played in high school bands.

He landed a job at the Opryland Theme Park, impersonating Hank Williams, as a member of the Mac McGahey Quartet. Young and immature, Dillon tried to live out the role he was playing, becoming hooked on drugs and booze. He stayed at Opryland for four years, then turned to writing. He was signed to Pi-Gem Music,

**Hot, Country And Single, Dean Dillon.
Courtesy WEA Records.**

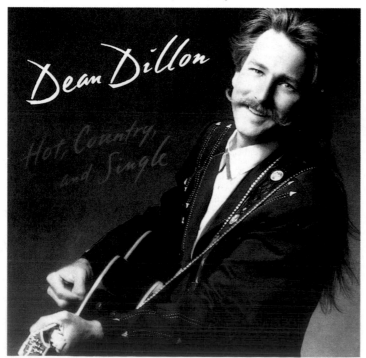

working a disciplined shift, perfecting his craft. The first song he had recorded was **She Called It Love** by Johnny Rodriguez in 1977. Two years later he provided Jim Ed Brown and Helen Cornelius with the chart-topping **Lying In Love With You**. While still in his early twenties, he became one of the hottest young writers around, providing George Strait with approximately 30 songs, several of them making No.1, such as **Ocean Front Property**, **The Chair** and **Famous Last Words Of A Fool**. He also wrote major hits for George Jones, Hank Williams Jr, Con Hunley, Vern Gosdin and Steve Wariner.

A recording contract with RCA in 1979 saw Dillon hit the country charts with several discs, the biggest two being **What Good Is A Heart** and **Nobody In His Right Mind (Would've Left Her)** (1980). RCA teamed him with fellow honky-tonker Gary Stewart. The pair made two albums and scored minor hits with **Brotherly Love** (1982) and **Those Were The Days** (1983). In retrospect, it was a big mistake, and Dillon started concentrating on his writing. By this time he was straightening out his hell-raising life; settling down to married life and raising kids. In November 1987 he was signed to Capitol Records and looked set to establish himself as a performer. Randy Scruggs produced two excellent albums, but the biggest chart-placing he achieved was with a revival of Peter & Gordon's **I Go To Pieces**.

Three years later he was on Atlantic Records. He produced a New-Traditionalist sound, laced with heartfelt singing and tough, melodic songs, as on **Friday's Night Woman** and **A Country Boy (Who Rolled The Rock Away)**, a tribute to Hank Williams, Elvis Presley and Buddy Holly. But Dillon was still unable to gain radio plays which could lead to public acceptance. He continues as a prolific tunesmith; his songs have a straight, no-nonsense approach to country music, and the lyrics are chock-full of wry humour, satire and lyrical sensitivity.

Recommended:
Hot, Country And Single (Atlantic/–)
Slick Nickel (Capitol/Capitol)
I've Learned To Live (Capitol/–)
Out Of Your Ever Lovin' Mind (Atlantic/–)

Peter Drake

Session man supreme, producer, owner of a studio and part-owner of a record company and music publishing firm, Pete Drake has played with everyone, from Jim Reeves to Bob Dylan, George Harrison and Ringo Starr. Born in Atlanta, Georgia, on October 8, 1932, Drake did not take up guitar until 1951 but rapidly became so proficient on the instrument that, within a year, he was leading his own band, the Sons Of The South.

After playing on radio station WLWA, Atlanta and WTJH, East Point, Georgia, he worked with Wilma Lee and Stoney Cooper, moving to Nashville with the duo in 1959.

He claims that he "starved for a year and a half" before catching the ears of Roy Drusky and George Hamilton IV, who both asked him to play on their sessions – after which he became one of the most sought-after sessioneers in Nashville. Drake also began cutting solo discs, his 1964 **Forever** becoming a Top 30 pop hit.

Recordings bearing Drake's name as an artist have also appeared on such labels as Starday, Stop, Hillside, Cumberland and Canaan, while he can be heard playing on the soundtracks of several Elvis movies.

As a producer, he is particularly proud of his **Amazing Grace** album for B. J. Thomas, a Grammy and Dove Award winner in 1982; as a music publisher he is equally proud of backing Linda Hargrove, who was named Writer Of The Year for providing Olivia Newton-John with **Let It Shine**. Pete Drake died in Nashville on July 29, 1988 from lung disease.

Recommended:
Forever (Smash/–)
Talking Steel Guitar (Smash/–)

Jimmie Driftwood

Singer-guitarist-fiddler-banjoist Driftwood (real name James Morris) was born in Mountain View, Arkansas, on June 20, 1917, and grew up in the Ozark Mountains, where he learned the songs and traditions of the early settlers. During high school he played at local dances, continuing his role as a part-time musician even after qualifying to become a teacher.

During the '50s he performed at various festivals and concerts and in 1958 signed for RCA producing **Newly Discovered Early Folk Songs**.

One song from the album, a revamped version of an old fiddle tune, **The 8th Of January**, recorded under the title of **The Battle Of New Orleans**, became a hit single for Johnny Horton during 1959, and was covered in Britain by skiffle star Lonnie Donegan. Other Driftwood songs, including **Sal's Got A Sugar Lip** and **Soldier's Joy**, also came into popular use. Another song, entitled **Tennessee Stud**, provided Eddy Arnold with a big hit.

Driftwood ceased recording in 1966 but still managed to devote much of his time to the cause of folk music, helping to run the Rackensack Folklore Society and assisting with some folk festivals. His **The Battle Of New Orleans** continues to be a much recorded number, Harpers Bizarre charting with the song yet again in 1968. The song proved popular again in 1975 with the Nitty Gritty Dirt Band and Buck Owens both cutting versions.

As well as being heavily involved in American folklore, Driftwood has gained a great deal of inspiration from the American Civil War.

Recommended:
Famous Country Music Makers (–/RCA)
Songs Of Billie Yank And Johnny Reb (–/RCA)
Americana (–/Bear Family)

Roy Drusky

Born in Atlanta, Georgia, on June 22, 1930, Roy Frank Drusky did not acquire an interest in country music until the late '40s, when he signed for a two-year term in the navy. While on ship, he met some C&W fans who had organized their own band – at which point Drusky bought a guitar and taught himself to play. Upon return to civilian life, he initially tried for a degree in veterinary medicine at Emory University. Then in 1951 he formed a band, the Southern Ranch Boys, who played a daily show on a Decatur radio station where Drusky subsequently became a DJ. Next came a three-year residency as a vocalist at a local venue, during which time Drusky made his TV debut and signed for Starday Records.

Following a later DJ stint on KEVE, Minneapolis, he took over another residency, this time at the city's Flame Club, where he began writing more of his own songs. These he began recording with Decca, one – **Alone with You** – was covered by Faron Young. However, after a move to Nashville, the Drusky hitmaking machine really went into action, his first solo successes coming with **Another** and **Anymore** in 1960, followed by five more winners before the singer opted for a switch to the Mercury label in 1963. With Mercury he maintained his supply of chart records right through to the early '70s, **Peel Me A Nanner** (1963), **From Now On All My Friends Are Going To Be Strangers** (1965), **Yes, Mr Peters** (a duet with Priscilla Mitchell that went to No.1 in 1965), **The World Is Round**, **If The Whole World Stopped Lovin'** (both 1966), **Where The Blue And The Lonely Go**, **Such A Fool** (both 1969), and **I'll Make Amends**, **Long Texas Road** and **All The Hard Times** (all 1970), being Top 10 entries.

Also during this period, Drusky appeared in two movies – 'The Golden Guitar' and 'Forty Acres Feud' – enjoying success with **White Lightning Express**.

In 1974, Drusky, still a consistent, if lower level hitmaker, joined Capitol. But after a brace of minor successes, he decided to label-hop to Scorpion, supplying two more mini-hits in **Night Flying** and **Betty's Song** (both 1977). Since that time, however, Drusky's name has been sadly absent from the charts, though, as the Como-like, smoothed-voiced singer proved during his Wembley Festival visits to the UK of the early 1980s, he remains very much a crowd-pleaser.

Recommended:
All My Hard Times (Mercury/–)
Country Special (Mercury/–)
Anymore (Decca/Stetson)
Night Flying (Scorpion/Big R)

Dave Dudley

One of the several country stars who could have made the grade in baseball, Dudley (born in Spencer, Wisconsin, on May 3, 1928) gained his first radio date after receiving an arm injury playing for the Gainsville Owls, Texas. While recuperating, he stopped by radio station WTWT and began playing along with the DJ's choice of discs. It was then suggested he should sing live, which he did, obtaining a positive reaction from listeners. Following stints on stations in the Idaho

Dave Dudley Sings. Courtesy Mercury Records.

Above: Roy Drusky, the Perry Como of country music.

region during 1951–52, Dudley moved on to lead a couple of small groups, his career taking a setback in the early '60s when he was hit by a car. However, this period proved kind to the near-rockabilly performer, hits coming on Vee, Jubilee and Golden Wing, the most important being the song **Six Days On The Road**, a release reputed to have commenced the whole truck song cycle.

In 1964 came a contract with Mercury Records and four Top 10 discs **in Last Day In The Mines** (1963), **Mad** (1964), **What We're Fighting For** and **Truck Drivin' Son-Of-A-Gun** (both 1965). The Nashville local branch of the truckers' union provided Dudley with a solid gold security card in appreciation of his musical efforts on behalf of their chosen profession. With his band, the Roadrunners, he has since continued on his truckstop way, switching labels and moving from Mercury to Rice, UA and Sun, providing each of them with hits of various sizes, including **The Pool Shark** (a No.1 in 1970), **Fireball Rolled A Seven** and **Me And Ole CB** (both 1975), **One A.M. Alone** (1978) and **Rolaids, Doan's Pills And Preparation H** (1980).

Recommended:
Truck Songs (–/Mercury)

Right: Whitey Ford, the Duke Of Paducah, died in Nashville in 1986.

Duke Of Paducah

A homespun comedian, always ready to close his routine with a rousing banjo solo, Benjamin Francis 'Whitey' Ford was born in DeSoto, Missouri, on May 12, 1901.

Brought up by his grandmother in Little Rock, Arkansas, he joined the navy in 1918, learning banjo while at sea. During the

'20s he toured with his own Dixieland band. Then, after some time in vaudeville and a stay with Otto Gray's Oklahoma Cowboys, he became MC on Gene Autry's WLS Chicago show, acquiring the title 'Duke Of Paducah'.

In 1937 he, John Lair, Red Foley and Red's brother Cotton Foley, founded the Renfro Valley Barn Dance. Ford gained his first date on the Grand Ole Opry in 1942, creating such an impression that he remained a member until 1959, thereafter becoming a constant visitor to the show.

Ford was a regular member of the Hank Williams Jr Road Show and a performer on countless TV shows originating out of Nashville. With his famous wind-up line – "I'm going to the wagon, these shoes are killin' me" – he toured for many years, often providing a serious lecture, 'You Can Lead A Happy Life', at colleges, sales functions and various conventions. Known as 'Mr Talent', Whitey Ford was elected to the Country Music Hall Of Fame in 1986, four months after his death on June 20, 1986, following a long fight against cancer.

Johnny Duncan

Born on a farm near Dublin, Texas, on October 5, 1938, Johnny Duncan came from a music-loving family. At first, Duncan thought of himself as an instrumentalist and Chet Atkins, Les Paul and Merle Travis were his idols. Then during his mid-teens, he realized that his singing ability was an equal asset. After attending high school in Dublin, he went on for a stay at Texas Christian University, meeting and marrying his wife Betty during this period. Shortly after their marriage, in 1959, the Duncans moved to Clovis, New Mexico, where John joined forces with Buddy Holly and producer Norman Petty with whom he worked for the next three years. Then in 1964, following a spell as a DJ in the Southwest, he headed for Nashville, where he applied his talents to a number of menial jobs while waiting to break into the music industry. After an appearance on WSM-TV Nashville, Don Law of Columbia Records signed Duncan.

His first hit came in 1967 with the release of **Hard Luck Joe**, after which Duncan, who for a while became a regular part of the Charley Pride band, began slotting two or three records into the country charts, going Top 10 with **Sweet**

Johnny Duncan

Country Woman (1973) and achieving No.1s with **Thinking Of A Rendezvous** (1976) and **It Couldn't Have Been Any Better** (1978). Several of his most successful records featured vocal assistance from Janie Fricke. It seemed that Duncan would have no difficulty extending his run of hits well into the '80s, but in the wake of an ill-titled and ill-received album, **The Best Is Yet To Come**, the Texan's luck ran out and the hits inexplicably began to dry up. In 1986 he turned up on the indie Pharoah label.

Recommended:
There's Something About A Lady
   (Columbia/–)
The Best Of Johnny Duncan (Columbia/–)
Johnny Duncan (–/CBS)
Nice 'n' Easy (Columbia/CBS)

Tommy Duncan

Although best known as Bob Wills' longtime lead singer, Tommy Duncan also had a long and significant solo career. Born January 11, 1911, in Hillsboro, Texas, he was steeped in the music of Jimmie Rodgers and loved both 'hillbilly' and the blues when he joined the Light Crust Doughboys in 1932. When their fiddler, Wills, split from the Doughboys, Duncan joined him in the newly formed Playboys, soon known as the Texas Playboys.

Duncan's years with Wills were great for both, his mellow, bluesy, high baritone appearing on hundreds of records, including **New San Antonio Rose**, the

Greatest Hits, Johnny Duncan. Courtesy CBS Records.

biggest of them all. He struck out on a career of his own in 1948 (taking a number of Texas Playboys with him) and, though many of his Capitol recordings were worthy enough, it was generally considered that neither Wills nor Duncan were as great apart as they had been together. He spent many years touring with his new band, the Western All Stars, but it was to everyone's delight when he and Bob Wills joined forces once more for a series of albums for Liberty in the '60s.

Although not to the inspired greatness of the '30s and '40s, these albums are tributes to the genius of two of country music's greats and now form part of the legacy of Duncan, who died from a heart attack on July 25, 1967.

Recommended:
Hall Of Fame – Bob Wills And Tommy
   Duncan (UA/–)

Right: One Of These Nights, the Eagles. Courtesy WEA Records. The title song of this album went to No. 1, although the group disbanded in 1980.

Holly Dunn

A multi-talented, radiant, singer-songwriter and a down-to-earth country girl, Holly Suzette Dunn was born on August 22, 1957, in San Antonio, Texas. Her father was a Church of Christ minister. Holly learned guitar while still a young girl and naturally sang in church. She was lead singer with the Freedom Folk Singers, representing Texas at the White House Bicentennial Celebrations in 1976. At university she took a degree in advertising and public relations and also became a member of the Hilltop Singers. Once studies were completed, Holly moved to Nashville to join her elder brother, Chris Waters Dunn, who had made his mark writing hit songs for Dr Hook and others.

She sang lead and harmony vocals on demo tapes and finally signed as a writer with CBS Songs. She co-wrote songs for Louise Mandrell, Cristy Lane, Terri Gibbs, Marie Osmond and others. In 1985 she gained a recording contract with MTM Records, making her chart debut with **Playing For Keeps** (1985). The next year she made Top 10 with the self-penned **Daddy's Hands**, and had further Top 10 hits with **A Face In The Crowd** (a duet with Michael Martin Murphey, 1987), **Love Someone Like Me** and **Only When I Love** (1987), **Strangers Again** and **That's What Your Love Does To Me** (both 1988). That year MTM went into liquidation, but Holly was able to secure a contract with Warner Brothers, scoring her first No.1 with **Are You Ever Gonna Love Me** (1989). She recorded a duet with Kenny Rogers, **Maybe**, that made No.25 in 1990. However, she was having more success with solo efforts such as **There Goes My Heart** (No.4) and **You Really Had Me Going** (No.1).

Holly still writes much of her own material, often working with her brother Chris. The pair also act as co-producers on her recordings. She caused controversy in 1991 with the song, **Maybe I Mean Yes**, which was lifted off her **Milestone** album. The lyrics put the onus on the woman not to give too many come-on signs to a man on a date, or face the consequences; it gained few radio plays. Since then Holly has failed to score a major hit, but still has excellent songs, as she showed with the album, **Getting It Dunn** (1992).

Recommended:
The Blue Rose Of Texas (Warner Bros/
   Warner Bros)
Getting It Dunn (Warner Bros/–)
Across The Rio Grande (MTM/–)
Milestones (Warner Bros/–)
Heart Full Of Love (Warner Bros/–)

Eagles

The Eagles is a now defunct West Coast country and soft rock band which featured lucid, flowing instrumental work and exquisite rough harmonies. They followed on from the Byrds and the Flying Burrito Brothers in bringing country to rock fans.

Founded by Randy Meisner (ex-Poco and Rick Nelson's Stone Canyon Band), Bernie Leadon (ex-Linda Ronstadt, Dillard & Clark and Flying Burrito Brothers), Glenn Frey (ex-Linda Ronstadt and John David Souther) and Don Henley (ex-Shiloh), they emanated from the ethically loose musical scene in Los Angeles but cut their first album in England under Rolling Stones' producer Glyn Johns. Later personnel changes saw guitarist and slide guitarist Don Felder boosting the line-up and Joe Walsh replacing Bernie Leadon.

The Eagles scored a No.1 single in the US with the memorable **The Best Of My Love**, and subsequent singles, **Lyin' Eyes** and **One Of These Nights**, notched up hit status in Britain.

In 1980 they disbanded to pursue solo careers, but many of their best-known songs have since been recorded by a number of established country acts. These include Conway Twitty, Tanya Tucker and Nat Stuckey.

Recommended:
Eagles (Asylum/Asylum)
Desperado (Asylum/Asylum)
On The Border (Asylum/Asylum)
One Of These Nights (Asylum/Asylum)
Hotel California (Asylum/Asylum)
Their Greatest Hits (Asylum/Asylum)

Steve Earle

The mid-'80s found Steve Earle, a young Texas country-rockabilly singer, poised to take country music by storm, but after making a big impact with **Guitar Town** in 1986, he rapidly turned his back on

country, heading towards modern rock and alienating himself from country music fans.

Earle was born on January 17, 1955, in Fort Monroe, Virginia, but grew up in San Antonio, Texas into a musical family. By the time he was eleven he had mastered guitar and was a wild tearaway, running away from home to make music when he was fourteen. He went to Austin, Dallas and Houston, working bars and coffee houses. In 1974 he followed other Texas writers Guy Clark and Townes Van Zandt to Nashville, and almost immediately landed a job as an 'extra' in the Robert Altman film 'Nashville'. For the next few years he performed in local Nashville bars, linking up with other singer-writers, such as Guy and Susanna Clark, Rodney Crowell and Townes Van Zandt.

In 1980, Steve relocated to Mexico for a while, then returned to San Antonio where he picked up a couple of musicians and took to the road as Steve Earle And The Dukes. A move back to Nashville in 1981 led to him being signed as a writer by Pat Carter and Roy Dea, and also being asked to run their music publishing company in Music Row. Carl Perkins cut his **Mustang Wine**, then Johnny Lee took **When You Fall In Love** into the Top 20 (1982). He cut demos of his songs, and, using his two-piece back-up group, he recorded a four-song EP which perfectly captured the excitement of 1950s rockabilly with a definite 1980s contemporary edge.

Consequently, Steve was offered a contract by Epic Records in early 1983, and his first single, **Nothin' But You**, was the first of a handful of minor country hits. Subsequently, other country stars such as

Right: Connie Eaton had her biggest success with Lonely Men, Lonely Women.

Johnny Cash, Waylon Jennings and Janie Fricke started cutting his songs. A move to MCA Records at the beginning of 1986 resulted in the acclaimed **Guitar Town** album, one of the most exciting records by a new Nashville-based artist in years. The title song became a Top country hit in 1986. Earle enjoyed further chart success with **Goodbye's All We've Got Left** (1987) and **Six Days On The Road** (1988), the latter featured in the film 'Planes, Trains and Automobiles'. At this time his style was fast, rockin' country, guitar-dominated and laden with heavy southern rock drumming. He became a major star in Europe, but with the album, **Copperhead Road**, he moved into heavy rock, and the Pogues featured on **Johnny Come Lately**. Struggling to become a country Bruce Springsteen, Earle has never fully

Above: The Eagles in 1974 – Bernie Leadon, Glenn Frey, Don Henley, Randy Meisner and Don Felder. The group brought a taste of country music to rock and pop fans throughout the '70s.

recaptured the freshness and vitality of his first two albums and now works outside of mainstream country music.

Recommended:
Guitar Town (MCA/–)
Copperhead Road (MCA/MCA)
Early Tracks (–/Epic)
Exit-0 (MCA/MCA)

Connie Eaton

A recording artist with Chart, GRC, Stax and ABC, Connie is the daughter of Bob Eaton, a one-time artist best known for his 1950 hit **Second Hand Heart**, and was born that same year, on March 1, in Nashville, Tennessee. Following an acting award in 1968, she met Chart Records' A&R man Cliff Williamson (whom she later married) who signed her to the label.

In 1970 Connie was voted Most Promising Female Artist by both Cashbox and Record World magazines, also having a fair-sized hit that year with her version of **Angel Of The Morning**. After providing several other minor hits (including two duets with Dave Peel) for Chart, Connie moved on briefly to GRC and Stax before signing to ABC in 1974 and having her most successful release in **Lonely Men, Lonely Women**, a Top 20 single in the spring of 1975. An album, **Connie Eaton**, was released later that year, but has since been deleted.

Stoney Edwards

Stoney, a soulful black country singer of Afro-Indian parents, was born Frenchy Edwards, on December 24, 1937 in Seminole, Oklahoma. He grew up listening to the country sounds of Hank Williams and Lefty Frizzell, as depicted in his 1973 hit, **Hank And Lefty Raised My Country Soul**.

Life was hard for Stoney who worked as a farm hand, truck driver, janitor, crane operator and dock worker before becoming a singer in small Texas clubs and finally in Oakland, California, where he made a minor breakthrough in 1970 when he signed with Capitol Records.

For the next decade or so, Stoney built up a cult following with his traditionally-styled honky-tonk sound that was firmly rooted in the 1950s. He scored minor country hits with **Poor Folks Stick Together** (1971), **She's My Rock** (1972), **Mississippi You're On My Mind** (1975) and **Blackbird (Hold Your Head High)** (1976). In his own modest way, he paved the way for the acceptance in the '80s of similarly styled singers, such as Con Hunley, John Anderson and John Conlee, but sadly Stoney has never really achieved the success he deserved. He was dropped by Capitol in 1977 and has since recorded for JMI Records and Music America. He lost a leg in a shooting accident and

Below: Joe Ely brought Texas music to a wider audience.

virtually retired from music in 1982, then unexpectedly returned in 1991 with a new album, **Just For Old Times' Sake**, which found him once again in top-notch form.

Recommended:
Mississippi You're On My Mind (Capitol/–)
Down Home In The Country (Capitol/–)
Just For Old Times' Sake (–/Ragged But Right)

Joe Ely

One of the most promising new singers to emerge from Texas in the late 1970s, Ely, born February 9, 1947, has never matched his cult following and rave reviews with commercial success.

Raised in Lubbock, a stone's throw away from where Buddy Holly lived, Joe never finished school, but instead hit the road playing bars and cafés, jamming with the likes of Johnny Winter. For a time he joined a theatre company and ended up on a European tour playing the arts circuit including shows in London and Edinburgh.

On his return to Texas in the early '70s, Joe teamed up with Butch Hancock and Jimmie Dale Gilmore to form the Flat-landers, an acoustic country group. They played throughout the South, and in 1972 the trio recorded an album for Shelby Singleton in Nashville. The record was not released at the time, though it did surface in the late '70s.

A move back to Lubbock in 1974 led to Joe forming a new band, an electric country-rock outfit designed to play up-tempo honky-tonk music for dancing audiences. A regular gig at the Cotton Club, a large honky-tonk on the outskirts of Lubbock, led to the Joe Ely Band gaining record company interest. An album cut at Chip Young's studio in Murfreesboro, Tennessee was released by MCA in 1977, and Joe Ely gained widespread acclaim but minimal sales.

Further albums like **Honky Tonk Masquerade** and **Down On The Drag** showed that the first album was no fluke. Each one was a mind-blowing celebration of Texas honky-tonk music, mixing rock sounds with the traditional to bring it slap-bang up-to-date. Ely and band proved to be a very popular live act in Texas and also Europe, where they toured several times in the late '70s and early '80s.

In 1984 he recorded **Hi-Res**, which was no more successful than his previous albums and he now found himself without a major label deal. Three years later, with a new band and a batch of new original songs, he was back in the studio recording **Lord Of The Highway** (1987) for Hightone Records, a strong mix of Texas honky-tonk. This gave Ely and his band a new lease of life; they were kept busy on the road building up a reputation with younger music fans. A dynamic **Live At Liberty Lunch**, recorded in 1990, gained Ely and the band a new contract with MCA, who immediately remastered four of his earlier albums – **Joe Ely**, **Honky Tonk Masquerade**, **Down On The Drag** and **Musta Notta Gotta Lotta** – and released them on CD. He was back in the Nashville studios in early 1992 working with producer Tony Brown on **Love And Danger**, his first studio album in four years. He also teamed up with musical colleagues John Mellancamp, John Prine, Dwight Yoakam and James McMurtry as the Buzzin' Cousins on the soundtrack to the Mellencamp movie, 'Falling From Grace'. Joe Ely continues to command a very large cult following, but sometimes his high-energy presentation falls between country and rock music, making radio programming in America very difficult.

Recommended:
Joe Ely (MCA/MCA)
Honky Tonk Masquerade (MCA/MCA)
Hi-Res (MCA/MCA)
Flatlanders – One Road More (–/Charly)
Down On The Drag (MCA/MCA)
Live At Liberty Lunch (MCA/MCA)
Lord Of The Highway (–/Demon)
Love And Danger (MCA/MCA)

Buddy Emmons

A multi-instrumentalist of exceptional ability – he is a first class pianist, an able bass player and not a bad singer, either – Emmons is generally considered in terms of his brilliantly inventive steel guitar work.

Born in Mishawaka, Indiana, on January 27, 1937, he was given a six-string 'lap' guitar at the age of 11 and subsequently studied at the Hawaiian Conservatory of Music, South Bend, Indiana. At 16 he appeared in Calumet City, Illinois, playing around the local clubs for most nights of the week and jamming in Chicago at weekends. By 1955 he had moved on to Detroit where, after deputizing for steelman Walter Haynes at a Little Jimmy Dickens gig, Emmons was awarded a permanent position with Dickens' band, which, in turn, led to dates on the Opry.

**Steel Guitar, Buddy Emmons.
Courtesy Flying Fish Records.**

During the years that followed came lengthy stints with Ernest Tubb and Ray Price, also the founding of the Sho-Bud company. He and his then partner Shot Jackson marketed the first steel guitar with push-rod pedals. In 1969 Emmons left Nashville, joined Roger Miller as a bassist, and became based in LA, playing West Coast sessions with Ray Charles, Linda Ronstadt, Henry Mancini and many others between tours with Miller.

When he and the King Of The Road parted company in December '73, Emmons returned to Nashville once more and since that time has involved himself in an incredible amount of session work, also spending some time in promoting his own Emmons Guitar Company, his association with Sho-Bud having terminated some years before.

Recommended:
Sings Bob Wills (Flying Fish/Sonet)
Steel Guitar (Flying Fish/Sonet)
Buddies – with Buddy Spicher (Flying Fish/Sonet)
Minors Aloud – with Lenny Breau (Flying Fish/Sonet)

Dale Evans

Wife of singing cowboy superstar Roy Rogers, Dale was born Frances Smith, at Ulvalda, Texas, on October 31, 1912.

Brought up in Texas and Arkansas, Dale married Thomas Fox in 1928, she and her husband parting two years later – at which time she began concentrating upon a career as a popular vocalist.

During the '30s she became a band singer with the Anson Weeks Orchestra, then became resident vocalist on the CBS News And Rhythm Show. Following many appearances on major radio shows, Dale moved into films, appearing in such productions as 'Orchestra Wives' (1942), 'Swing Your Partner' (1943), 'Casanova In Burlesque' (1944), 'Utah' (1945), 'Bells of Rosarita' (1945), 'My Pal Trigger' (1946), 'Apache Pass' (1947), 'Slippy McGee' (1948), 'Susanna Pass' (1949), 'Twilight In The Sierras' (1950), 'Pals Of The Golden West' (1951), many of these movies starring Roy Rogers whom she married in 1947.

With Rogers, she has recorded a number of albums for such labels as RCA, Capitol and Word, some of the these being in the gospel vein, and is also the author of an armful of small books of an inspirational/religious nature.

Recommended (with Roy Rogers):
In The Sweet Bye And Bye (Word/Word)
The Good Life (Word/Word)
The Bible Tells Me So (Capitol/–)

Leon Everette

In the space of a few short years, Leon Everette (born Leon Everette Baughman, June 21, 1948 in Aiken, South Carolina, but raised in Queens, New York), emerged as one of the most exciting and successful names on the country music scene. However, the transition from obscurity to overnight fame was not easy for the rugged, good-looking performer.

Rejection by the major labels in Nashville led to some frustrating years with labels like Dural Records and True Records, a company organized with the sole intention of establishing Leon as a major name in country music.

Carroll Fulmer, a Florida businessman, financed Orlando Records in the spring of 1978 and subsequent extensive recording sessions in Nashville were produced jointly by Jerry Foster, Bill Rice, Ronnie Dean and Leon himself. The first two singles, **We Let Love Fade Away** and **Giving Up Easy**, failed to make much impression, but the third release, **Don't Feel Like The Lone Ranger**, made the country Top 40 in the summer of 1979.

Further hits on Orlando, including **I Love That Woman (Like The Devil Loves Sin)**, **I Don't Want To Lose** and **Over You**, the latter his first entry into the Top 10, led to interest from major labels. In October 1980 Everette signed with RCA Records and was given creative freedom and control of his own recordings.

This Is Leon Everette – a British compilation. Courtesy RCA Records.

In The Sweet By And By, a 1973 release, Roy Rogers and Dale Evans. Courtesy Word.

He soon proved that RCA's faith in him was justified with such Top 5 country hits as **Giving Up Easy**, **If I Keep On Going Crazy**, **Hurricane** and **Don't Be Angry**. With his own five-piece band, initially called Tender Loving Care but changed to Hurricane in 1981, Leon has also made an impact as a dynamic stage performer with a fast-moving act that has gained rave reviews and praise from fellow performers Hank Williams Jr and Waylon Jennings.

Though he continued to chalk up Top 10 hits for RCA with **Soul Searchin'**, **Give Me What You Think Is Fair** and **Midnight Rodeo**, Leon was not entirely happy with the promotion he was receiving from the label, and at the end of 1984 he signed with Mercury Records. Bill Rice was engaged as producer and gave Everette a contemporary country styling that resulted in such hit singles as **Feels Like Forever**, **Too Good To Say No To** and **'Til A Tear Becomes A Rose**.

However, by 1986, Leon was back on his own Orlando Records, scoring minor hits with **Danger List (Give Me Someone I Can Love)** and **Still In The Picture**.

Recommended:
This Is Leon Everette (–/RCA)
Where's The Fire? (Mercury/–)

Everly Brothers

A mid-'50s teen heart-throb duo, the Everly Brothers came from a solid country music background, made rock'n'roll history, and then returned to country.

Born in Brownie, Kentucky, Don in 1937 and Phil in 1939, they were the sons of Ike and Margaret Everly, well-known local country stars (Ike was an influential guitar player). Early on the boys were joining their parents on tour and their first radio appearance with the show was on KMA, Shenandoah, Iowa.

After high school, Don and Phil procured a record contract with Cadence in 1957. They had previously made one unsuccessful Columbia single. At Acuff-Rose music publishers they were introduced to Felice and Boudleaux Bryant, the result of this liaison being their first hit, **Bye Bye Love**. The Everlys' sound was characterized by harmony singing which contrived to be velvety and whining at the same time, and which was matched with pounding, open-chord guitars and songs which perfectly caught the era's mood of teenage frustration. In no time at all they were causing riots at theatres, yet they were also acceptable to adults because of their clean-cut looks.

Bye Bye Love was a huge international hit for them, topping pop and country charts in America and becoming the most hummed international hit that year. With rock'n'roll losing some of its early steam the time was right for this distinctive and poignant teen sound. Subsequent hits included **Wake Up Little Susie**, **Bird Dog**, **Claudette** and **All I Have To Do Is Dream**, all huge sellers and the last-named making No. 1 in the American and British pop charts.

In 1960 they left Cadence for Warner Bros, thus losing the Nashville production team and the Bryant songwriting team.

However, the self-composed **Cathy's Clown** was an immediate hit for them and they followed up with **Ebony Eyes** and **Walk Right Back**. After a spell in the Marines they managed an excellent 1965 hit with **Price Of Love** but it was to be their last really big pop winner. Don had suffered a nervous breakdown on their 1963 tour of England and gradually the brothers began to go their separate ways.

The Everlys returned to their country roots with the albums **Great Country Hits**, **Roots** and **Pass The Chicken And Listen**, the latter album recorded in Nashville in 1972, reuniting them with producer Chet Atkins. Shortly after this Don and Phil split to pursue solo careers; Don based himself in Nashville and Phil in Los Angeles. Apart from a few spasmodic successes, they never really made a big impression as solo artists.

Pass The Chicken, Everly Brothers. Courtesy RCA Records.

In 1983, they reunited for a concert at London's Royal Albert Hall. It was such a huge success that they undertook a worldwide tour the following year, signed a new recording contract with Phonogram, and made a return to the charts with the Paul McCartney-penned **On The Wings Of A Nightingale** and **Born Yesterday** (1984), the latter became their first country Top 20 chart entry since 1959. Deservedly, the Everly Brothers were inducted into the Rock 'n' Roll Hall Of Fame in 1986.

Below: Phil and Don, the Everly Brothers, reunited for their famous Royal Albert Hall comeback concert in 1983.

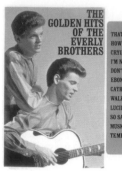

THE GOLDEN HITS OF THE EVERLY BROTHERS

THAT'S OLD FASHIONED
HOW CAN I MEET HER
CRYING IN THE RAIN
I'M NOT ANGRY
DON'T BLAME ME
EBONY EYES
CATHY'S CLOWN
WALK RIGHT BACK
LUCILLE
SO SAD
MUSKRAT
TEMPTATION

Recommended:
Born Yesterday (Mercury/Mercury)
1984 (Mercury/Mercury)
Very Best Of The Everly Brothers (Warner Bros/Warner Bros)
Great Country Hits (Warner Bros/Warner Bros)
Stories We Could Tell (RCA/RCA)
Pass The Chicken And Listen (RCA/RCA)

Don Everly solo:
Brother Jukebox (Hickory/DJM)
Sunset Towers (Ode/A&M)

Phil Everly solo:
Phil's Diner (Pye/Pye)
Star Spangled Springer (RCA/RCA)
Louise (–/Magnum Force)

Skip Ewing

Singer-songwriter Skip Ewing, born on March 6, 1965, in Redlands, California, has brought a fresh and dynamic voice to a traditional sound, and found himself in demand as a writer for such acts as George Jones, Charley Pride, Reba McEntire, George Strait, Sawyer Brown and many others.

Skip was hooked on country music since he first heard Merle Haggard as a youngster. It is reputed that he could play guitar before he could read. Having no funds for college, he headed out on the road with his music as soon as he graduated from high school. In 1984 he moved to Nashville and started out as a performer at Opryland; already a

Golden Hits, Everly Brothers. Courtesy WEA Records.

competent musician and budding songwriter, he landed a writer's contract. Jimmy Bowen heard Skip's demos and signed him to MCA Records in 1987. His first record, **Your Memory Wins Again**, made Top 20 in 1988. Other Top 10 hits followed, such as **I Didn't Have Far To Fall** and **Burning A Hole In My Heart** (both 1988), and **The Gospel According To Luke** and **It's You Again** (both 1989).

Possessing one of the most distinctive voices on the Nashville scene, Ewing is a multi-instrumentalist who has absorbed his musical influences – James Taylor, Dan Fogelberg and Jim Croce – into a modern-day country singer-songwriter with a soulful and energetic edge to his work. When Bowen moved to Liberty/Capitol, Skip followed in 1991 and produced two excellent albums for his new label.

Recommended:
The Will To Love (MCA/MCA)
Home Grown Love (Liberty/–)
A Healin' Fire (MCA/–)
Naturally (MCA/–)

Exile

Steve Goetzman, drums; Marlon Hargis, keyboards; Sonny Le Maire, bass, vocals; J. P. Pennington, guitar, vocals; Les Taylor, guitar, vocals.

This spirited five-piece band silenced any arguments about its rock'n'roll origins with a string of No.1 country singles throughout 1985. The band rivalled Alabama as the top country band of the mid-'80s.

Originally a pop group who scored with the chart-topping **Kiss You All Over** in 1978, Exile made their initial impact as a country group with **High Cost Of Leaving**, a country Top 10 entry in August 1983. Previously J. P. Pennington and Sonny Le Maire had made an impression as songwriters when Alabama, Kenny Rogers, Dave And Sugar, Janie Fricke and Bill Anderson all recorded their songs.

Hang On To Your Heart, Exile. Courtesy Epic Records.

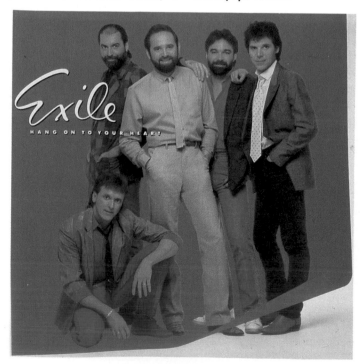

After their demise from the pop charts, they moved naturally towards country. The group had often played on country sessions long before they made it as a pop attraction. J. P. Pennington had a further connection with country music in his aunt, Lila May Ledford, who was one of the Coon Creek Girls.

Signed to Epic Records in Nashville, Exile enjoyed No. 1 hits with: **Woke Up In Love**, **I Don't Want To Be A Memory**,

Love's Old Song, Barbara Fairchild. Courtesy CBS Records.

Give Me One More Chance (all 1984); **Crazy For Your Love**, **She's A Miracle** and **Hang On To Your Heart** (all 1985); **I Could Get Used To You**, **It'll Be Me** (both 1986); **She's Too Good To Be True** and **I Can't Get Close Enough** (both 1987), In 1985 keyboard player Marlon Hargis left to be replaced by Lee Carroll. Problems within the band started to boil to the surface, and in 1988 the hit singles suddenly dried up. Founding members J. P. Pennington and Les Taylor left to pursue solo careers. With newcomers Mark Jones and Paul Martin, the new-look Exile signed with Arista Records in 1989. They were back in the Top 20 with **Nobody's**

Above: Barbara Fairchild, who signed to Capitol Records in 1986.

Talking, **Yet** (1980) and **Even Now** (1991) – all up-mood numbers with infectious country arrangements.

Recommended:
Kentucky Hearts (Epic/Epic)
Hang On To Your Heart (Epic/Epic)
I Love Country (–/Epic)

On The Move, Donna Fargo. Courtesy WEA Records.

Barbara Fairchild

A husky-voiced blonde, Barbara Fairchild was born in Knobel, Arkansas on November 12, 1950. Spending her high school years in St Louis, Missouri, at 15 she had recorded for a local station and had a regular spot on a weekly TV show. Later came the inevitable move to Nashville and a meeting with MCA staffman Jerry Crutchfield, who signed her to the company as a songwriter.

Still working primarily as a songwriter, she made some demos that came to the attention of Columbia's Billy Sherrill, the result was a new recording contract and a subsequent flow of minor hits with **Love Is A Gentle Thing** (1969), **A Girl Who'll Satisfy Her Man** (1970), **(Loving You Is) Sunshine** (1971), **Love's Old Song** (1971), **Thanks For The Memories** (1972) and others. Her real breakthrough came with **Teddy Bear Song** (1973), **Kid Stuff** (1973) and **Baby Doll** (1974), all three becoming Top 5 singles.

For a couple of years Barbara faltered on the charts, but made a minor comeback with the Top 20 hit **Cheatin' Is** towards the end of 1976 and **Let Me Love You Once Before You Go** the following year. Though she has faded from the scene in recent years, Barbara made an impression with British country fans following tours in 1978 and 1979 and recorded a successful duet with Billy Walker on **The Answer Game** in 1982.

Recommended:

Free And Easy (Columbia/CBS)
This Is (Columbia/CBS)
Mississippi (Columbia/CBS)
Greatest Hits (Columbia/CBS)
The Answer Game – with Billy Walker
   (–/RCA)

Donna Fargo

Born Yvonne Vaughn on November 10, 1949, the daughter of a Mount Airey, North Carolina tobacco farmer, Donna attended High Point, North Carolina, Teachers' College and also spent some time at the University of Southern California, her musical education consisting of just four piano lessons taken at the age of ten.

Nevertheless, she found herself torn between two careers, teaching, in the Corvin, California area, and singing, which she did under a stage name, in LA clubs.

After meeting record producer Stan Silver, whom she married in 1969, Donna set out for Phoenix where she cut some sides for Ramco Records. Her initial releases flopped so Donna continued with her teaching chores, later switching her recording activities to the Challenge label, also with little success.

Taught guitar by Silver, who also encouraged her to songwrite, Donna finally won a contract with a major company, ABC-Dot, repaying her belief in her talent via a self-penned No. 1 in **Happiest Girl In The Whole USA**, the CMA Single Of The Year for 1972. All possibilities of her being a one-hit wonder were soon dispelled when **Funny Face**, another 1972 Fargo original, climbed the charts, to be followed by **Super Man**, **You Were Always There**, **Little Girl Gone** (all 1973), **You Can't Be A Beacon** (1974), **It Do Feel Good** (1975) and **Don't Be Angry** (1976), all Top 10 entries that benefited from the distinctive, dry-throated, Fargo vocal style.

In 1977 she became part of the growing roster of Warner Bros Records' country artists, scoring such hits as **That Was Yesterday** (1977), **Do I Love You (Yes In Every Way)** (1978) and **Somebody Special** (1979). In 1979 she was stricken with Multiple Sclerosis, but has fought against the crippling disease and continued with her career, though on a

Left: Narvel Felts, who started out as a rocker in the 1950s.

Narvel The Marvel, Narvel Felts. Courtesy MCA/Dot Records.

lesser scale than previously. She has recorded for RCA, Cleveland, International and MCA-Songbird, as well as duetted with Billy Joe Royal on the **Members Only** single in 1988, and she hit the country charts with **Soldier Boy**.

Recommended:

The Happiest Girl In The Whole World
   (Dot/–)
All About A Feeling (Dot/–)
Country Sounds Of (–/MFP)
On The Move (Warner Bros/Warner Bros)
Dark Eyed Lady (Warner Bros/–)
Brotherly Love (MCA-Songbird/–)
Just For You (Warner Bros/–)
Shame On Me (Warner Bros/Warner Bros)

Narvel Felts

A native of Missouri, born on November 11, 1938, Felts grew up with country music, became known as a rock'n'roller in the mid-'50s and returned to country later in his career. The first singer he remembers hearing was Ernest Tubb: "I used to wonder what his girlfriend was doing on the floor and him walking over her."

In 1956 he won a high school talent contest by singing **Blue Suede Shoes** and in an effort to trace him and have him sing on the station, KDEX in Bernie, Missouri, put out a message for him. Narvel and his father drove the eight miles into Bernie in their pickup truck to find a telephone.

Performing on the station's Saturday show led to Narvel landing the bass guitar spot in Jerry Mercer's band. When Mercer left, Narvel became band leader. Felts worked with both Conway Twitty (then plain Harold Jenkins) and Charlie Rich at Sun Records in 1957.

He then signed first with Mercury and then with Pink Records where **Honey Love** and **3000 Miles** made the charts. In 1970, while contracted to Hi Records, he came to Nashville hoping to find a solid country label with good distribution. Then, discussing his problems with friend and DJ Johnny Morris, they decided to evolve a new label, Cinnamon Records. In 1973, **Drift Away** (written by Mentor Williams and a pop hit for Dobie Gray) was an impressive country hit for Narvel. Later that year he scored again with **All In The Name Of Love** and in 1974 with **When Your Good Love Was Mine**.

When Cinnamon folded in 1975, Narvel joined ABC-Dot Records, coming up with **Reconsider Baby**, which was a No. 1 hit and was chosen by 'Billboard' as No. 1 Song Of The Year and 'Cashbox' as No. 1 Country Song Of The Year. It also crossed over to the pop charts. **Somebody Hold Me (Until She Passes By)** (1975), **Lonely Teardrops** (1976) and **The Feeling's Right** (1977) have all been Top 20 country hits for Narvel. Since 1979 he has recorded for a variety of small labels, including College, GMC, Lobo, Compleat and Evergreen.

Recommended:
Drift Away (Cinnamon/–)
Inside Love (ABC-Dot/–)
Memphis Days (–/Bear Family)
Pink And Golden Days (Fox/–)

Below: Freddy Fender joined the Texas Tornados in 1990, and now has a solo contract with Warner Bros.

Freddy Fender

A maverick country artist, Fender (real name Baldermar Huerta) waited 20 years for record success. He was born on June 4, 1937, in South Benito, a South Texas border town. His family worked as casual farm labourers throughout the year, but made it back to the San Benito valley each Christmas. Fender remembers that music helped to make a hard life happy and that he always managed to persuade his mother to buy him a new guitar when the old one wore out.

He dropped out of high school at 16 and joined the Marines for three years. In the late '50s he was back in San Benito playing bars and Chicano dances. By 1958 his records, in which he utilized all-Spanish lyrics, were doing well in Texas and Mexico. Gradually he turned to the more commercial fields of R&B and country for inspiration. Local club owner Wayne Duncan formed Duncan Records, and the established Imperial Records took an interest in Fender's records. Imperial released **Wasted Days And Wasted Nights**, written by Fender and Duncan, and made it into a big pop hit in 1960.

In May 1960, Fender was arrested for possession of drugs, betrayed by a paroled informer. Fender served three years of his five-year sentence in the Angola State Penitentiary, Louisiana, cutting several titles for the Goldband and Powerpack labels while inside. The Governor of Louisiana, Jimmie Davis, himself something of a country singer, helped secure Fender's release. However, a condition of his parole was that Fender should leave the entertainment business.

Fender managed to pick up his career again though, forgoing record hits, but gigging steadily. He also worked as a

mechanic and even went to college for two years. In 1974 he was introduced to noted Louisiana R&B producer Huey Meaux, who put Fender's distinctive voice in a country setting. In Houston, Texas, they put down many tracks, among them a re-recording of **Wasted Days And Wasted Nights** and an update of **Before The Next Teardrop Falls**, performed partly in English and partly in Spanish. The latter was picked up by ABC-Dot and became a big pop and country hit, which led to the record being named CMA Single Of The Year in 1975, and Fender being named Top Male Vocalist by the ACM.

Further country and pop successes followed with **Secret Love** (1975), **You'll Lose A Good Thing** and **Vaya Con Dios** (both 1976), **The Day That The Rains Came** (1977) and **Talk To Me** (1978). He joined Starflite Records in 1979, then signed with Warner Brothers in 1982, but was unable to regain the enormous success he enjoyed in the late '70s: Fender was still indulging in drugs and hitting the bottle. In 1985 he entered a clinic, and recovered. He appeared in the 1987 film 'The Milagro Beanfield War', directed by Robert Redford. Three years later he became a member of the all-star Texas Tornados, with long-time friends Doug Sahm, Augie Meyers and Flaco Jimenez. This rekindled interest in Fender's older recordings and led to a new solo contract with Warner Brothers in 1991.

Recommended:
Before The Next Teardrop Falls (Dot/ABC)
Are You Ready For Freddy? (Dot/ABC)
If You're Ever In Texas (Dot/ABC)
Rock 'n' Country (Dot/ABC)
Swamp Gold (ABC-Dot/–)
The Texas Balladeer (Starflite/–)
Best Of (–/MCA)
Freddy Fender Collection (Reprise/Reprise)

Flatt And Scruggs

Lester Raymond Flatt, born on June 19, 1914 in Overton County, Tennessee, and Earl Eugene Scruggs, born on January 6, 1924, in Cleveland County, North Carolina, pioneered a particular type of bluegrass under Bill Monroe's leadership — especially Scruggs' 'three-finger banjo' technique — and thus helped to popularize bluegrass immensely.

Both came from highly musical families. Lester's parents both played the banjo (in the old 'frailing' style) and Lester practised on both guitar and banjo. He also sang in the church choir. Earl came from an area east of the Appalachians which was already using a three-finger style on the five-string banjo. The style was not new anyway (although the strict universal style then involved either two-finger picking or simply brushing or frailing the strings): a three-finger style had been used by Uncle Dave Macon and Charlie Poole, and Earl himself had heard such banjoists as Snuffy Jenkins use it locally. But Scruggs evolved a newer style, syncopated and rhythmic, blending in his three-finger banjo to make the bluegrass style sound fresh and alive.

Lester became a textile worker but still listened to a lot of 'hillbilly' music, while also continuing to play instruments. His wife could also play guitar and sing. He was a fan of Bill and Charlie Monroe who

were heard frequently on Carolina radio stations in the years before World War II. Lester was living in Covington, Virginia, and he got together with some old friends from Tennessee to play. By 1939 they had become pretty proficient and were to be hard on Radio WDBJ, Roanoke, as the Harmonizers. In 1943 Lester and his wife Gladys were hired by Charlie Monroe. Lester sang tenor harmony and played mandolin. He tired of the travelling and quit, then procured a position with a North Carolina radio station. It was there that he received a telegram from Bill Monroe asking Lester to come and play with him on the Grand Ole Opry.

Earl had played with his brothers from the age of six and by 15 he was playing on a North Carolina radio station with the Carolina Wildcats. He became a textile worker too (during the war years) but the end of the war saw him playing with 'Lost' John Miller in Knoxville. Shortly after, he began to be heard widely when Miller started broadcasting on Radio WSM from Nashville. Miller then stopped touring and Earl, out of work, was hired by Bill Monroe.

At this time Monroe was known mainly around the Southeast but the Opry was becoming more and more popular, and Bill's show rapidly gained a broader appeal. Monroe switched musical duties around and Lester Flatt's high tenor voice easily adapted to singing lead when necessary. Less easy was the pace Lester was required to keep on guitar. He sometimes shortcut his guitar part by developing a characteristic run to catch up and finish the lines. This became known as the 'Lester Flatt G Run' since it was usually played in that chord position.

Scruggs was given full rein by Monroe to develop his fluid banjo technique and helped popularize songs such as **Blue Grass Breakdown**, numbers which would remain associated with him after his departure from Monroe. Monroe even put the names of Flatt and Scruggs on some of his records. This precision and teamwork, which characterized Monroe's sound, was attracting many new listeners to the music and, by association, to the Opry itself.

In 1948, within weeks of each other, Earl and Lester resigned from Monroe to escape the constant travelling (Monroe has always been a dedicated touring man). Almost inevitably the two then decided to team up and do some radio work. They recruited ex-Monroe men Jim Shumate, on fiddle, and Howard Watts (stage name Cedric Rainwater), on bass, and then moved to Hickory, North Carolina, where they were joined by Mac Wiseman. That year, 1948, they made their first recordings for Mercury Records.

The band took its name from an old Carter Family tune, **Foggy Mountain Top**, calling themselves Foggy Mountain Boys. Wiseman left and was replaced by mandolin player Curly Seckler. Many of the fiddle players they used had previously worked with Bill Monroe. Earl's banjo was now more to the fore and the mandolin was used less often. In most other respects they promoted a harder, more driving music than that of Monroe, but Lester's vocals provided the mellowness.

They moved to Bristol on the Tennessee-Virginia border at the end of 1948 and while broadcasting on radio WCYB met the Stanley Brothers and Don Reno, both of whom developed this new sound into what we now know as 'bluegrass' and 'Scruggs-style banjo'.

In 1949 they recorded **Foggy Mountain Breakdown** and it was released the

following year. It has remained one of their most consistently popular numbers and was included in the film 'Bonnie And Clyde' as background to the famous car chase. In 1950 they were offered a lucrative contract by Columbia Records, a recording association that was to last for 20 years.

Earl introduced the 'Scruggs' peg', a device which allowed him to change the tuning of his banjo strings easily, for the number **Earl's Breakdown** (1951). That year a boost was given to their career when they appeared on a show headlined by the then fashionable Ernest Tubb and Lefty Frizzell. In 1953 the band began broadcasting 'Martha White Biscuit Time' on Nashville's Radio WSM, a show which not only ran for years, but which saw them coming well and truly into country music prominence. In 1955 their position was consolidated with an equivalent syndicated TV show and at this time they also became Grand Ole Opry members. They were travelling more than they had ever done with Bill Monroe, and they were also winning fan polls and industry awards.

The '60s folk revival also helped them, since by this time 'Scruggs picking' was already in instrument tutor terminology. Folkways released an album, compiled by Mike Seeger, titled **American Banjo Scruggs' Style** and both Mercury and Columbia released similar albums with the artist himself featured. Further recognition came in the shape of the CBS-TV series, The Beverly Hillbillies. The theme tune, **The Ballad Of Jed Clampett**, played by

Lester and Earl was No. 1 on the country charts for three months from December 1962. They became a household name and a symbol of this exciting, syncopated musical styling.

They consolidated their position as leaders of the bluegrass movement and sold a vast amount of records. Towards the end of the '60s (mainly pushed by Earl), they began experimenting with new folk songs, with drums and gospel-style harmonies in an effort to build on a younger audience. Some of their older fans were unhappy about these changes and in 1969 they split up. Lester returned to more traditional sounds and made reunion albums with his old buddy Mac Wiseman. He also formed the Nashville Grass, composed mainly of the Foggy Mountain Boys. Earl defiantly went off in new directions with his Earl Scruggs Revue, utilizing his own sons and later dobro player Josh Graves in a unit which could also appeal to young, rock audiences. Earl also played a big part in getting together the old stars for the 1971 Nitty Gritty Dirt Band album, **Will The Circle Be Unbroken**.

Lester Flatt died on May 11, 1979, and in recent years Earl Scruggs has cut back his activities, while his sons have made their mark as songwriters, producers and multi-instrumentalists in country music.

Recommended:
Foggy Mountain Breakdown (Hillside/–)
Carnegie Hall (Columbia/–)
Changin' Times (Columbia/–)

Blue Ridge Cabin Home (County/–)
The Golden Era (Rounder/–)
Mercury Sessions (Rounder/–)
Flatt & Scruggs Volume 1 & 2 (–/Bear Family)

Earl Scruggs:
Nashville's Rock (Columbia/–)
Duelling Banjos (Columbia/–)
Kansas State (Columbia/–)
I Saw The Light (Columbia/–)
Earl Scruggs Revue (Columbia/–)
Scruggs Revue Volume 2 (Columbia/–)
Rockin' Cross (Columbia/–)
Family Portrait (Columbia/–)
Live From Austin City Limits (Columbia/–)

Lester Flatt:
Before You Go (RCA/–)
Foggy Mountain Breakdown (RCA/RCA)
Over The Hills To The Poorhouse – with Mac Wiseman (RCA/–)
Best Of (RCA/RCA)
Flatt Gospel (Canaan/–)
Lester Raymond Flatt (Flying Fish/–)
Live Bluegrass Festival – with Bill Monroe (RCA/–)
Living Legend (CMH/–)
The One And Only (Nugget/–)

Rosie Flores

Rosie, another Texas-born singer-songwriter, came to the fore in the mid-'80s as part of the West Coast country movement. Born in San Antonio, Texas,

Above: Flatt And Scruggs with their band, the Foggy Mountain Boys, on the Grand Ole Opry in the mid-'50s.

Rosie's earliest musical influences were a mixture of Mexican, Tex-Mex and country music. At 12 her family moved to San Diego, California, where the guitar-playing youngster started to take music seriously. She joined Penelope's Children, an all-girl band playing country, rock and psychedelic music. Starting to write songs, Rosie also did some solo gigs, then teamed up with the Screamers, an all-male band that had made quite an impact in Los Angeles. A few years later she was in the Screamin' Sirens, an all-girl band that appeared in the movie 'The Running Kind'. By this time Rosie wanted to play country, so she put a four-track demo of her own songs together and eventually gained a record contract with Reprise (1986).

Dwight Yoakam produced her first album, and Rosie scored minor country hits with **Crying Over You** (1987) and **Somebody Loves, Somebody Wins** (1988). With her rock-tinged country music and raunchy vocal style, Rosie won over a younger audience for her music, but has been unable to break through to mainstream country acceptance. She continues to work the Californian club scene and at one time looked set to make an impact in Europe.

Recommended:
Rosie Flores (Warner Bros/Warner Bros)
After The Farm (Hightone/–)

Flying Burrito Brothers

The band was formed in 1968 by ex-Byrds Gram Parsons and Chris Hillman, to bring country music to the rock fans of California. A&M Records felt that the charismatic Parsons might help to generate some big sales with this new concept, and they subsequently put much promotional money behind the first album, **Gilded Palace Of Sin**. Bizarre photo sessions in the desert resulted in an album sleeve depicting the Burritos in extravagant Nudie suits. The marijuana leaves embroidered on the suits emphasized a new approach. **Gilded Palace** featured some of Parsons' best-ever songs and beefed up his sensitive but non-too-strong voice with a rock production, and Chris Hillman was also prominent on vocals. The line-up for this album was: Parsons, guitar, vocals; Chris Hillman, guitar, mandolin, vocals; Chris Ethridge, bass; Sneaky Pete Kleinow, pedal steel guitar; and Jon Corneal, drums.

In 1969, Corneal and Ethridge dropped out, and Bernie Leadon (guitar, vocals) and Mike Clarke (drums) joined. Hillman switched to bass. The next two albums, **Burrito De Luxe** and **Flying Burrito Brothers**, were straighter productions but still with a good dash of country included. Parsons left between the two albums (in 1970) and in 1971 Bernie Leadon also left, to subsequently form the highly successful Eagles. Sneaky Pete also left to undertake production and session work.

1971 saw a vastly expanded line-up in which Byron Berline (a top fiddle player who had recorded with the Rolling Stones), Al Perkins (pedal steel guitar), Kenny Wertz (guitar, banjo, vocals) and Roger Bush (string bass), all joined. This line-up saw the release of a good live album, **Last Of The Red Hot Burritos**.

The addition of Alan Munde (banjo) in 1971 completed a floating aggregation which rejoiced under the title, Hot Burrito Revue. The bluegrass-oriented members of this loose set-up who finally decided to stay became known as Country Gazette.

However, the Burritos were to re-form again in 1974. With a line-up of Sneaky

Flying Again, Flying Burrito Brothers. Courtesy Columbia/CBS Records.

Pete, Gib Guilbeau (a Cajun fiddle player), Gene Parsons (drums), Chris Ethridge and Joel Scott-Hill, they toured America and Europe, cutting albums for CBS.

By 1979, the Burritos were down to a two-piece, consisting of Guilbeau and John Beland. Known as the Burrito Brothers they moved from the West Coast to Nashville in 1981, determined to make an impression as a country act. They signed a recording contract with Curb Records, who were licensed through Columbia, and scored Top 20 country hits with **Does She Wish She Was Single Again** and **She Belongs To Everyone But Me** (1983). By 1985 had split. Beland concentrated on his songwriting skills and Guilbeau teamed up with Sneaky Pete Kleinow for yet another re-formed Flying Burrito Brothers line-up.

Recommended:
Gilded Palace Of Sin (A&M/Demon)
Last Of The Red Hot Burritos (A&M/–)
Flying Burrito Brothers (A&M/A&M)
Close Up The Honky Tonks (A&M/A&M)
Flying Again (Columbia/CBS)
Sleepless Nights – with Gram Parsons (A&M/A&M)
The Flying Burrito Brothers – Live From Tokyo (–/Sundown)
Cabin Fever (Relix Records/–)
Dim Lights, Thick Smoke And Loud Music (–/Edsel)
Hollywood Nights, 1979–1981 (–/Sundown)

Dan Fogelberg

Fogelberg grew up in the little town of Preoria, Illinois (where he was born on August 13, 1951), and attended the University of Illinois as an art student before settling on a musical career. He established himself in the mid-'70s as a pop-country singer-songwriter with a series of albums on Full Moon Records.

Although he has lived in Colorado for a number of years, most of his songs have a

Right: Red Foley on the Grand Ole Opry in the early '50s.

midwestern setting. His writings on freedom, lost love and women have proved to be decidedly effective and timely pieces. Dan showcased his country roots on the highly acclaimed 1985 album, **High Country Snows**.

Utilizing the talents of Ricky Skaggs, Herb Pedersen, Chris Hillman, Doc Watson, Al Perkins and Vince Gill, Dan produced a first-rate bluegrass-flavoured album, blending his own self-penned songs with those of Carter Stanley and Flatt And Scruggs. He made inroads on the country charts with **Go Down Easy** and **Down The Road (Mountain Pass)** during1985.

Recommended:
HIgh Country Snows (Full Moon/Full Moon)
The Wild Places (Full Moon/–)
Dan Fogelberg Live (Full Moon/–)

Red Foley

Elected to the CMA Hall Of Fame in 1967, Clyde Julian 'Red' Foley was born in Bluelick, Kentucky, on June 17, 1910.

A star athlete at high school and college, at the age of 17 he won the Atwater-Kent contest in Louisville. In 1930 he moved to Chicago to become a member of John Lair's Cumberland Ridge Runners on the WLS National Barn Dance Show.

Seven years later he helped to originate the Renfro Valley Show with Lair, by 1939 appearing on Avalon Time, a programme in which he co-starred with Red Skelton, thus becoming the first country star to have a network radio show.

His Decca records soon proved eminently popular. Foley's versions of **Tennessee Saturday Night**, **Candy Kisses**, **Tennessee Polka**, and **Sunday Down In Tennessee** all became Top 10 discs during 1949. In 1950 sales escalated even further, with no less than three Foley titles – **Chattanoogie Shoe Shine Boy** and the spirituals **Steal Away** and **Just A Closer Walk With Thee** – becoming million-sellers.

The following year, his success with religious material continued. Foley's recording of Thomas A. Dorsey's **Peace In The Valley** sold well enough to become an eventual gold disc winner. Meanwhile, his more commercial songs also accrued huge sales, **Birmingham Bounce** becoming a 1950 No.1, and **Mississippi** (1950), **Cincinatti Dancing Pig** (1950), **Hot Rod Race** (1951), **Alabama Jubilee** (1951), **Midnight** (1952), **Don't Let The Stars Get In Your Eyes** (1953), **Hot Toddy** (1953), **Shake A Hand** (1953), **Jilted** (1954), **Hearts of Stone** (1954) and **A Satisfied Mind** (with Betty Foley, 1955), all providing him with Top 10 placings.

The Red Foley Story. Courtesy MCA Records.

An Opry star during the '40s, in 1954 he moved to Springfield, Missouri, where he hosted the Ozark Jubilee –one of the first successful country TV series. During the early '60s, Foley co-starred with Fess Parker on an ABC-TV series Mr Smith Goes To Washington. He continued appearing on radio and TV, and making many personal appearances, right up to the time of his death on September 19, 1968, in Fort Wayne, Indiana.

Recommended:
Beyond The Sunset (MCA/–)
Red Foley Story (MCA/–)
Red & Ernie – with Ernest Tubb (–/Stetson)
Tennessee Saturday Night (–/Charly)
Company's Coming (Decca/Stetson)

Tennessee Ernie Ford

The singer who recorded **Sixteen Tons**, a mining song which sold over four million copies during the mid-'50s, Ernest Jennings Ford was born in Bristol, Tennessee, on February 13, 1919. At school he sang in the choir and played trombone in the school band – but he also spent much time at the local radio station, WOAI, where he began working as an announcer in 1937.

Four years later, following a period of study at the Cincinnati Conservatory of Music and further announcing stints with various radio stations, Ford enlisted in the Air Force, becoming first a bombadier on heavy bombers, then an instructor. After discharge, he returned to announcing, working on C&W station KXLA, Pasadena, where he met Cliffie Stone and appeared as a singer with Stone's quartet on the Hometown Jamboree show.

In 1948, Ford signed with Capitol Records, for whom his warm bass voice provided immediate hits in **Mule Train** and **Smokey Mountain Boogie** (1949). He subsequently scored with **Anticipation Blues** (1949), **I'll Never Be Free** (with Kay Starr, 1950), **The Cry Of The Wild**

Goose (1950) and **Shotgun Boogie**, a Ford original that became a million-seller in 1950.

His own radio shows over the CBS and ABC networks gained Ford further popularity, then, in 1955, following another handful of hits, he recorded **Sixteen Tons**, a superb Merle Travis song that was decked out in a fine Jack Marshall arrangement This became a massive hit, winning Ford his own NBC-TV show – which the singer hosted until 1961.

Since the early '60s Ford increasingly concentrated on religious music, the biggest seller being **Hymns**, reputed to be the first million-selling album in country music, and one which gained him a platinum-plated master in 1963. Gradually he cut down on his work, although he appeared on many TV shows and enjoyed some chart success with **Hicktown** (1965), **Honey-Eyed Girl** (1969) and **Happy Songs Of Love** (1971). Inducted

Ernie Sings & Glen Picks, Tennessee Ernie Ford. Courtesy Capitol Records.

into the Country Music Hall Of Fame in 1990, Tennessee Ernie died of liver disease, October 17, 1991 at HCA Hospital, Reston, Virginia, where he had been recuperating after being taken ill at a White House dinner on September 28.

Recommended:
Hymns (Capitol/–)
America The Beautiful (Capitol/–)
Civil War Songs (Capitol/–)
Country Hits Feelin' Blue (Capitol/–)
Ernie Sings And Glen Picks – with Glen Campbell (Capitol/–)
Precious Memories (Capitol/–)
Sixteen Tons (–/Bear Family)
Farmyard Boogie (–/See For Miles)

The Forester Sisters

Kathy (born January 4, 1955, Lookout Mountain), June (born September 25, 1956, Chattanooga), Kim (born December 4, 1960, Chattanooga) and Christy (born October 10, 1962, Chattanooga), four sisters from Georgia, burst upon the country scene at the beginning of 1985 when their very first single, **(That's What You Do) When You're In Love**, gave them a country Top 10 entry.

The girls, who count Bonnie Raitt, Linda Ronstadt and Emmylou Harris as being early influences and main inspiration, began by singing at weddings, funerals and community events around their Lookout Mountain home. Specializing in sweet harmonies, with Kim and eldest sister Kathy handling most of the lead vocals, they cut a demo tape in Muscle Shoals, Alabama, which eventually found its way to Warner Brothers Records in Nashville.

Jim Ed Norman signed the girls to the label at the end of 1984, and, under the guidance of Jerry Wallace and Terry Skinner, they recorded their debut album in Muscle Shoals. Their first single hit No.1 in the country charts, and two other No.1s followed, with **I Fell In Love Again Last Night** and **Just In Case** (both 1985). Further chart-toppers came with **Mama's Never Seen Those Eyes** (1986), a duet

with the Bellamy Brothers on **Too Much Is Not Enough** (1986), and **You Again** (1987).

In addition to Kathy's keyboards and Kim's guitar, the girls make use of a four-piece band, including Kathy's husband on bass, who also acts as the Foresters' road manager. The four sisters have five children between them, and they all travel on the road together. Unlike most other country stars, they have not moved to Nashville, preferring to live near their relatives in Lookout Mountain. With their roots in old-time country, they perfectly bridge the gap between traditional and contemporary country without edging too close to pop. The Forester Sisters have continued a consistent run of Top 10 hits, including **Lying In His Arms Again** (1987), **Letter Home** (1988), **Love Will** (1989) and **Men** (1991), plus several acclaimed albums that show they can be gutsy as well as sweet, serious and humorous, and, most importantly, musically entertaining.

Recommended:
The Forester Sisters (Warner Bros/–)
Talkin' 'Bout Men (Warner Bros/–)
Sincerely (Warner Bros/Warner Bros)
Come Hold Me (Warner Bros/–)
I Got A Date (Warner Bros/–)
Perfumes, Ribbons And Pearls (Warner Bros/Warner Bros)

Foster And Lloyd

This unlikely country duo first joined as songwriters in 1985 and went on to score several Top 10 country hits in the late '80s. They then went their separate ways, with Radney Foster emerging as a promising '90s solo performer.

Kentucky-born Bill Lloyd worked in New York, then put a band together in Kentucky before moving to Nashville in 1982, where he was signed as a writer with the MTM Music Group. Radney Foster, born on July 10, 1960, in Del Rio, Texas, played local clubs before moving to Nashville in 1981, where he waited on tables and pitched his songs. He signed with MTM, and soon after the pair started writing together. Their first success came in 1986 with **Since I Found You**, in a Top 10 hit for Sweethearts Of The Rodeo. Foster, the main writing force, co-wrote **Someone Like Me** with Holly Dunn, which gave the Texas lady a No.2 hit in 1987, the same year that Foster And Lloyd secured a record contract with RCA.

Their dynamic blend of '60s pop, country and R&B soon found them riding the charts with such Top 10 hits as **Crazy Over You** and **Sure Thing** (1987), **What Do You Want From Me This Time** (1988) and **Fair Shake** (1989), plus three superb albums, one of which, **Faster and Llouder**, crossed into the pop charts, gaining a gold disc. Both wanted to pull in different directions, so in 1991 they split.

Radney Foster signed with Arista Records and his first single, **Just Call Me Lonesome** (1992), went Top 20. His album, **Del Rio Tx 1959** contained all self-penned songs, his obvious strong point. The songs evoked memories of late '50s rock, pop and country dressed up in contemporary country arrangements. It proved to be a successful formula, with his second single, **Nobody Wins** (1993), climbing to No.2 on the country charts, and opening the doors for a highly successful solo career.

Recommended:
Version Of The Truth (RCA/RCA)
Faster And Llouder (RCA/–)

Radney Foster Solo:
Del Rio Tx, 1959 (Arista/–)

Curly Fox And Texas Ruby

Curly Fox, the fiddling son of a fiddler, was born Arnum LeRoy Fox in Graysville, Tennessee, on November 9, 1910. He joined a medicine show at the age of 13, and recorded as early as 1929, with the Roane County Ramblers. He also played with the Carolina Tarheels and headed his own band, the Tennessee Firecrackers, over WSB in Atlanta in 1932.

Texas Ruby was Tex Owen's sister, born on June 4, 1910 in Wise Country, Texas, who had come to the Grand Ole Opry as early as 1934 with Zeke Clements and his Bronco Buster. She and Clements worked for a while on WHO in Des Moines, before she and Curly Fox teamed up on WSM in 1937. Not long after this, they became one of the most popular acts on the Opry and in country music, with their winning combination of Ruby's deep, strong, sultry voice and Curly's masterful trick fiddling.

After marrying in 1939, their biggest years were on the Grand Ole Opry in the '40s, where they were stars of the Purina portion, and they recorded for Columbia (1945–46) and King (1947). In 1948 they journeyed to New York and then Houston, where they were to spend seven years on KPRC-TV before returning to the Grand Ole Opry.

They recorded an album for Starday during this second Nashville period, just prior to Texas Ruby's death in March 1963, when a fire raged through their house trailer. Curly went into virtual retirement afterwards, living in rural Illinois, but in the mid-'70s he began to appear at occasional bluegrass festivals and other gatherings.

My Baby Packed Up My Mind And Left Me, Dallas Frazier. Courtesy RCA Records.

Dallas Frazier

A respected singer-songwriter, Frazier is capable of penning country songs that 'cross-over' without losing too much individuality in the process (although it must be said that one big success in this area, **Alley Oop**, moulded into a novelty hit by Kim Fowley for the Hollywood Argyles, was pure gimmickry).

Born in Spiro, Oklahoma, in 1939, Frazier was a featured stage performer before he reached his teens and a best-selling songwriter by 21. Early on, his family moved to the country centre at Bakersfield, California. In a talent contest sponsored by Ferlin Husky he won first prize and Husky offered him a place on his show.

He was signed by Capitol Records and moved to Nashville to pitch his songs, and also starred on radio and TV there. Ferlin Husky had one of his most famous hits with Frazier's **Timber, I'm Falling** and there were other cross-overs with **There Goes My Everything** (Engelbert Humperdinck) and **Son Of Hickory Holler's Tramp** (O. C. Smith). But he could also pen a convincing dues-paying country song, as he showed with **California Cotton Fields**, a title recorded by Merle Haggard.

Frazier made a comeback as a writer in the last ten years with the Oak Ridge Boys' updated version of **Elvira**, a million seller in 1981, and several other singers raiding his vast catalogue of songs. He has been helped in his writing career by having a stronger voice than many composers and this has enabled him to succeed as a performer also. His albums have included **My Baby Packed Up My Mind And Left Me** and **Singin' My Song** (RCA).

Janie Fricke

Regarded as the most versatile female vocalist in country music, Janie, who was born December 19, 1947 on a farm near South Whitney, Indiana, came from a musical family. Her father was a guitarist and her mother taught piano and played organ at the local church.

Between study lessons at Indiana University, Bloomington, she broke into the thriving Memphis jingle scene. After completing her studies she tried her luck in Los Angeles as a background vocalist but failed to make any impression. Consequently, she returned to Memphis in the summer of 1972 and started building a first-rate reputation as a jingle singer and performed in the group Phase II.

In 1975 she moved to Nashville where she joined the Lea Jane Singers and Janie's natural vocal ability allowed her to stand out in the cut-throat Nashville session business. On a Johnny Duncan session she was asked to sing some solo

Above: Janie Fricke changed her name to Frickie in the '80s, then back again.

lines on **Jo And The Cowboy** and on subsequent Johnny Duncan recordings of **Stranger** and **Thinkin' Of A Rendezvous** (No.1s in 1976), **It Couldn't Have Been Any Better** and **Come A Little Bit Closer** (No.1s in 1977). During this period she contributed to more than 20 Top 10 country singles by Ronnie Milsap, Eddie Rabbitt, Crystal Gayle, Mel Tillis and Vern Gosdin.

Singer Of Songs, Janie Fricke. Courtesy CBS Records.

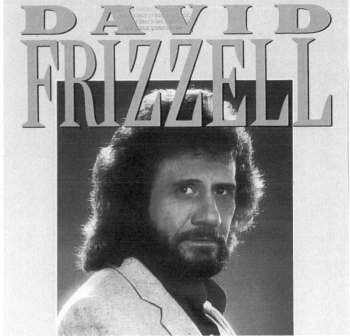

After being coaxed into a solo recording contract in 1977 with Columbia Records, where she was initially produced by Billy Sherrill, Janie enjoyed Top 20 hits with **What're You Doing Tonight**, **Baby It's You** and **Please Help Me I'm Falling** from her first album. Due to her reluctance to give up her session work to form a band and do show dates, she was dubbed 'the reluctant superstar'.

A duet with Charlie Rich, **On My Knees**, hit the top of the charts in 1978, then finally she made the breakthrough as a solo singer with **Down To My Last Broken Heart** (1980), which was followed by other Top 10 hits, such as **I'll Need Someone To Hold Me (When I Cry)** (1981), **Don't Worry 'Bout Me Baby** and **It Ain't Easy Bein' Easy** (both 1982).

By this time Janie had made the transition from secure anonymity as one of Nashville's most successful jingle and session singers to the forefront as a country star. She was named CMA Female Vocalist in both 1982 and 1983, and enjoyed further chart-toppers with **He's A Heartache (Looking For A Place To Happen)** (1983), **Let's Stop Talking About It** (1984) and **She's Single Again** (1985). Her recordings were now being produced by Bob Montgomery and her career was managed by her husband Randy Jackson. with her own Heart City Band, which she used on the acclaimed **It Ain't Easy** LP, Janie gained a reputation as one of country music's most dynamic female entertainers.

In 1986 she started spelling her name 'Frickie', and though she topped the charts with **Always Have, Always Will** that same year, suddenly her records stopped making such a big impact, though the quality of her albums were consistently high. By 1989 her contract with Columbia expired and the next two years found her without a record deal. Janie signed with the independent Intersound in 1991, reverting back to the original spelling of her name. She has continued to make good albums and tours regularly, but has failed to make a return to the charts – the standard by which all country music acts are gauged as far as star status is concerned.

Recommended:
Sleeping With Your Memory (Columbia/CBS)
Love Notes (Columbia/CBS)
The First Word In Memory (Columbia/CBS)
Janie Fricke (Intersound/–)
After Midnight (Columbia/CBS)
Black And White (Columbia/CBS)

Kinky Friedman

Leader of outlandish country rock band, the Texas Jewboys, Richard Friedman was born in Palestine, Texas, October 31, 1944, the son of a Texas University professor.

Brought up on a ranch, he later attended university in nearby Austin, in which town he formed his first band, King Arthur And The Carrots. Then came some time spent in Borneo, where he was a member of the Peace Corps.

In 1971 he headed for LA with his band, the Texas Jewboys, establishing a reputation as the Frank Zappa of country music in **Sold American**, for Vanguard.

He was signed to ABC Records during

Sold American, Kinky Friedman. Courtesy Vanguard Records.

1974, but by 1976 Friedman had moved on once more, to Epic, cutting **Lasso From El Paso**, an all-star album featuring such dignitaries as Bob Dylan and Eric Clapton. Although he has appeared on the Opry, Friedman's country is generally far-out and not really meant for mainstream fans. He has become a country music critic for 'Rolling Stone' magazine and something of a detective novelist with 'Greenwich Killin' Time', a story about a country singer turned detective. He still occasionally returns to the stage, but his live sets are mainly re-runs of his old songs.

Recommended:
Sold American (Vanguard/Vanguard)
Kinky Friedman (ABC/ABC)
Lasso From El Paso (Epic/Epic)
Old Testaments And New Revelations (Fruit Of The Tune/–)

David Frizzell

A younger brother of legendary Lefty Frizzell, David was born on September 26, 1941, in El Dorado, Texas. He spent 23 years recording for seven different labels

Solo, David Frizzell. Courtesy WEA/Viva Records.

under eight separate contracts before he made a major breakthrough in 1981, when he teamed up with Shelly West (daughter of singer Dottie West) on the chart-topping duet, **You're The Reason God Made Oklahoma**.

David hitch-hiked from his Texas home to California to be with Lefty in the late '50s, and his first recordings were made under the guidance of Don Law for Columbia Records in 1958. A handful of country-rockabilly singles were released, but all sank without trace. Following a stint in the US Army, he re-signed with Columbia in the late '60s, scoring a minor hit with **I Just Can't Help Believing** (1970). David spent a few years making regular appearances on Buck Owens' Ranch Show TV programme. A few recordings for Capitol were released, David scoring minor hits with **Words Don't Come Easy** (1973) and **She Loved Me Away From You** (1974).

Further recording stints followed without too much success. David invested in his own club in Concord, California, in 1977, and it was the following year that Shelly West, along with David's younger brother Allen Frizzell, joined him at the club. Shelly and David toyed with a few duets and did a demo tape of **We're Lovin' On Borrowed Time**. Producer Snuffy Garrett heard the tape and recorded an album. He set up a deal with Casablanca West, but it fell through, so he began shopping around for another one. He found no takers in Nashville. However, he played the tape to actor Clint Eastwood, his partner in Viva Records, who decided to use **You're The Reason God Made Oklahoma** on the soundtrack of his upcoming film, 'Any Which Way You Can'.

The rest was like a dream for David and Shelly. The song was put out as a single at the beginning of 1981, made it to the top of the country charts, and the pair walked off with a CMA Award for Top Country Duo for 1981, a feat they repeated the following year. More duet hits followed

Left: Friedman is an outlandish character who is a novelist, critic and singer.

with **A Texas State Of Mind** (1981), **Honky-Tonk Night On Broadway** (1982), **I Just Came Here To Dance** (1983) and **It's A Be Together Night** (1984).

Both were keen to follow solo careers, and David was first to record a solo album, **The Family's Fine, But This One's All Mine**. The album produced a No.1 country hit, **I'm Gonna Hire A Wino To Decorate Our Home**. He has continued to score solo hits with **Lost My Baby Blues** (1982), **A Million Light Beers Ago** (1983), **When We Get Back To The Farm** (1984) and **Country Music Love Affair** (1985). With changing trends in country, Frizzell's hits became harder to find, though he has continued to record for Viva, Nashville America and Compleat. He still tours regularly, preferring to play the club and cabaret circuit.

Recommended:
On My Own Again (Warner-Viva/–)
The David Frizzell & Shelly West Album (Warner-Viva/–)
Our Best To You – with Shelly West (Warner-Viva/–)
My Life Is Just A Bridge (BFE/–)

Lefty Frizzell

Acquiring the nickname 'Lefty' after disposing of several opponents with his left hand during an unsuccessful attempt to become a Golden Gloves boxing

Treasures Untold, Lefty Frizzell. Courtesy Bear Family Records.

The Legendary Lefty Frizzell. Courtesy MCA Records.

champion, the Texas-born (Corsicana, March 31, 1928) singer-songwriter-guitarist began life as William Orville Frizzell.

A childhood performer, at 17 he could be found playing the honky-tonks and dives of Dallas and Waco, moulding his early, Jimmie Rodgers-stylings to his environment, thus formulating a sound that was very much his own.

In 1950, Frizzell's Columbia recording of **If You've Got The Money, I've Got The Time** became a massive hit, claiming a chart position for some 20 weeks. The ex-pugilist followed this with two 1951 No.1s in **I Want To Be With You Always** and **Always Late**.

He became an Opry star, and throughout the rest of the decade he continued to supply a series of chart high-flyers, many of these in honky-tonk tradition. The '60s too found Frizzell obtaining more than a dozen hits, though only **Saginaw,**

Michigan – a 1964 No.1 – and **She's Gone, Gone, Gone** (1965) proved of any consequence. His last hit for Columbia was **Watermelon Time In Georgia** (1970).

He joined ABC Records in 1973 and was beginning to make a comeback with **I Never Go Around Mirrors** and **Lucky Arms** (both 1974) and **Falling** (1975), when he died on July 19, 1975 after suffering a stroke. Elected to the Country Music Hall Of Fame in 1982, Frizzell's influence has played a major role in much of the country music of the '90s. You can hear strains of his work in the style of Merle Haggard, which has been continued through George Strait, Keith Whitley and lately in the music of Clint Black and Doug Stone, among others.

Recommended:
The Classic Style (ABC/–)
The Legend Lives On (Columbia/–)
Songs Of Jimmie Rodgers (Columbia/–)
Lefty Goes To Nashville (Rounder/–)
American Originals (Columbia/–)
Treasures Untold (Rounder/Bear Family)
Life's Like Poetry (–/Bear Family)

Steve Fromholz

Purveyor of what he terms 'free-form, country-folk, science-fiction, gospel, cum existential bluegrass-opera music', the hirsute Fromholz (born June 8, 1945, Temple, Texas) once looked likely to become the most talented has-been in Austin, a situation later reflected in the title of his first solo album – **A Rumor In My Own Time**.

A Rumor In My Own Time, Steve Fromholz. Courtesy Capitol Records.

At 18, he attended North Texas State University, meeting singer-songwriter Michael Murphey, the duo becoming part of the Dallas County Jug Band. After an abbreviated stay in the navy, Fromholz befriended another singer-songwriter, Dan McCrimmon. The twosome formed Frummox and recorded an album **From Here To There** for Probe (1969), the disc featuring Fromholz's ambitious **Texas Trilogy**.

He moved to Austin (1974), and there became an accepted part of the outlaw community, providing material and singing on Willie Nelson's **Sound In Your Mind** LP. The first real Fromholz solo album, **A Rumour In My Own Time**, an all-star soirée featuring Red Rhodes, Willie Nelson, Doug Dillard, John Sebastian, B. W. Stevenson and the Lost Gonzo Band, found a Capitol release in 1976 and fulfilled all the hopes of his cult following. However, a later album, **Frolicking In The Myth**, proved him to be moving on in search of new frontiers to breach.

Recommended:
A Rumor In My Own Time (Capitol/–)
Frolicking In The Myth (Capitol/–)
Jus' Playin' Along (Lone Star/–)

Larry Gatlin

Born in Seminole, Texas, on May 28, 1948, but raised in nearby Odessa, clear-voiced Larry Wayne Gatlin is a singer-songwriter whose roots are in gospel music. When only five he could be found watching the Blackwood Brothers. At the same age he appeared in a talent contest as part of the Gatlins (along with his two brothers and one of his sisters), a gospel group that toured throughout the southern states. But his breakthrough came while he was working with the Imperials in Vegas, as part of the Jimmy Dean Show.

There Gatlin met Dottie West, one of Dean's guests, who offered to help him. In May 1971, he sent her eight songs – from which she selected and recorded two, **Once You Were Mine** and **You're The Other Half Of Me**. A few months later, when Dottie formed her own First Generation Music Company, Gatlin was the first writer to gain a contract. Following further songs for Dottie, including **My Mind's Gone Away**, Gatlin sang the verse plus harmony vocals on Kristofferson's **Why Me?** hit. Johnny Cash employed several Gatlin compositions for his 'Gospel Road' movie. Due to Kristofferson's insistence, Monument signed Gatlin in 1972, releasing singles by Gatlin and his band that year. Larry's first album, **The Pilgrim**, appeared in 1974. Also in 1974 he made his Top 20 debut

Treasures Untold:
The Early Recordings of
Lefty Frizzell

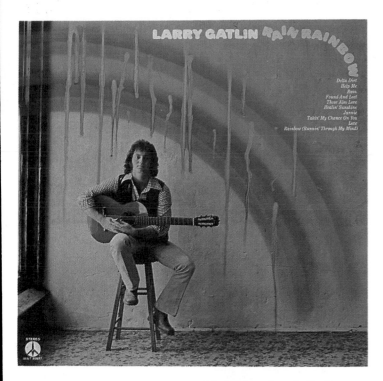

Crystal, Crystal Gayle. Courtesy UA Records.

with **Delta Dirt**, going Top 5 with a late 1975 release, **Broken Lady**, a song that won a Grammy in 1976.

During 1975, too, Gatlin produced some sides for Johnny Duncan, one of which, **Jo And The Cowboy**, provided Janie Fricke with her debut as a backup singer.

He also reunited with his brothers Rudy and Steve, forming a band and reshaping his whole musical approach once more. The next major hit, **Statues Without Hearts** (1976), was released under Larry Gatlin With Family And Friends. During 1977, in the wake of a flood of hits, he scored his first No.1 with **I Wish You Were Someone I Love**. There were three more Top 10 singles in 1978 along with two hit albums, **Oh Brother** and **Greatest**

Rain Rainbow, Larry Gatlin. Courtesy Monument Records.

Hits Volume 1, but the Monument label was slowly folding. In early 1979 Gatlin switched to Columbia, his act now billed as Larry Gatlin And The Gatlin Brothers Band. The result was another No.1, **All The Gold In California** (1979) as well as Top 10 singles **Take Me To Your Lovin' Place** (1980), **What Are We Doin' Lonesome** (1981), **Sure Feels Like Love** (1982), **Houston** (a No.1 in 1983), **Denver** and **The Lady Takes The Cowboy Everytime** (both 1984). But the strain of constant writing, recording and touring took its toll. On December 10, 1984 he voluntarily checked himself into a

California drug and alcohol abuse centre. Happily, he was soon back to full health once more, and he and his brothers cutting **Smile**, an album produced by jazz-funk guitarist Larry Carlton, in 1985.

Recommended:
The Pilgrim (Monument/–)
Rain, Rainbow (Monument/Monument)
Larry Gatlin With Family And Friends
   (Monument/Monument)
Straight Ahead (Columbia/CBS)
Live At 8pm (Capitol/–)
Alive And Well (Columbia/–)
Pure 'n' Simple (Universal/–)

Crystal Gayle

Loretta Lynn's younger sister (real name Brenda Gail Webb), Crystal was the last of eight children born to the Webbs and the only one who arrived in a hospital. Born in Paintsville, Kentucky, in 1951, she toured with Conway Twitty and Loretta at the age of 16. Her name change was inspired by the Krystal hamburger chain. In 1970, she placed her first Decca release, **I Cried (The Blue Right Out Of My Eyes)** on the country charts, but there was little other chart action during this period.

After the Decca deal ended, Crystal moved to UA Records, refusing to record any material associated with Loretta. There began an association with producer Allen Reynolds. Reynolds' own composition, **Wrong Road Again**, brought Crystal back into the country charts, this being followed by two other singles, all of them from her successful debut album **Crystal Gayle**. This 1975 comeback was the start of a consistent run of hitmaking. Crystal's **Somebody Loves You** single went Top 10 that year. The following year

Below: Larry Gatlin (centre) formed a band with his brothers in the late '70s.

saw the singer having two country chart-toppers, **I'll Get Over You** and **You Never Miss A Real Good Thing**, plus a best-selling third album, **Crystal**, all bearing the Reynolds' hallmark of quality. 1977 saw the advent of two further monster hits in **I'd Do It All Over Again** and the bluesy **Don't It Make My Brown Eyes Blue**, Crystal's first major cross-over single. 1978 saw her logging three No.1s in a row with **Ready For The Times To Get Better**, **Talking In Your Sleep** and **Why Have You Left The One You Left Me For**.

The flood of hits continued in 1979, the year that saw Crystal become the first country artist to tour China. Now with Columbia Records, she provided her new label with further No.1s: **It's Like We Never Said Goodbye** and **If You Ever Change Your Mind** (1980). There was another No.1, **Too Many Lovers**, for Columbia in 1981 before she signed for Elektra and carried on where she left off – logging yet another chart-topper with **'Til I Gain Control Again** (1982). The same year she duetted with Eddie Rabbitt on **You And I**, a country No.1 and pop Top 10 entry. Switching to Warner Brothers, further No.1s in the mid-'80s came with

These Days, Crystal Gayle. Courtesy CBS Records.

Our Love Is On The Faultline, **Baby, What About You**, **The Sound Of Goodbye**, **Turning Away** and a duet with Gary Morris on **Makin' Up For Lost Time**, the theme from the Dallas TV series.

Crystal has been devoted to charitable causes and received the Waterford 'Celebration Of Light' Award in 1988, in recognition of her involvement in such activities. Away from showbiz, she has her own fine gifts and jewellery business, 'Crystals', which is located in Nashville. But this did not interfere with her music and there were two more chart-topping hits for Warners, a revival of **Cry** (1986) and **Straight From The Heart** (1987). The late '80s saw a movement away from Crystal's smooth pop/country to more traditional-sounding music in Nashville,

and she found it more difficult to gain radio plays. In 1990 she moved over to Capitol Records and was reunited with Allen Reynolds, who produced the **Ain't Gonna Worry** LP, but this only resulted in one minor hit with a revival of **Never Ending Song Of Love** (1990). Two years later she was without a major label deal. Although there had been much talk of recording with her sisters Loretta Lynn and Peggy Sue Wright, this has not come to fruition, and Crystal has ended up re-recording several of her old hits for **Best Always** (1993).

Recommended:
Somebody Loves You (UA/UA)
Crystal (UA/UA)
When I Dream (UA/UA)
Ain't Gonna Worry (Capitol/Capitol)
Three Good Reasons (Capitol/Capitol)
Cage The Songbird (Warner Bros/Warner Bros)
Country Girl (–/Music For Pleasure)
True Love (Elektra/Elektra)

Bobbie Gentry

In July 1967, **Ode to Billy Joe**, a song about the suicide of a certain Billy Joe Macallister, was released. Bedecked in an imaginative, swamp-flavoured, Jimmy Haskell arrangement, it was one of the year's finest singles. Thus was the public introduced to the singing and songwriting talent of Bobbie Gentry.

Of Portuguese descent, Bobbie was born Roberta Streets, in Chickasaw County, Mississippi, on July 27, 1944, later changing her name to Gentry after seeing 'Ruby Gentry', a movie about swampland passion. A childhood singer and guitarist, Bobbie spent her early years in Greenwood, Mississippi, and then moved with her family to California, there attending high school in Palm Springs and UCLA, where she majored in philosophy. Already proficient on several instruments (she plays guitar, banjo, bass, piano and vibes) Bobbie attended the LA Conservatory of Music, studying theory.

Signed to Capitol Records in 1967, she cut **Ode To Billy Joe** at one half-hour session and became a star virtually overnight. Then followed a number of other cross-over hits including **Okolona River Bottom Band** (1967), **Fancy** (1969), **Let It Be Me** (1969) and **All I Have To Do Is Dream** (1970), the last two being duets with Glen Campbell.

Extremely popular in Britain where she had her own BBC-TV series and gained a No.1 with **I'll Never Fall In Love Again** (1970), Bobbie's sales waned as the '70s moved on. But in 1976 a film 'Ode To Billie Joe', based on the events documented in the Gentry song, reactivated some interest

Don't Stop Loving Me, Don Gibson. Courtesy Hickory Records.

in her Delta ditties. Her appeal was boosted on the Vegas-Reno circuit and at the Hughes hotel chain, her contract with the latter touted to be in the multi-million-dollar bracket.

Recommended:
Ode To Billy Joe (Capitol/Capitol)
Bobbie Gentry's Greatest (Capitol/Capitol)

Don Gibson

A rich-voiced singer-songwriter whose wares enabled him to move into the pop market of the 1960s, Don Gibson was born in Shelby, North Carolina, on April 3, 1928.

A competent guitarist before he left school, Gibson built up a regional following via live gigs and radio broadcasts. After finishing his education, he moved to Knoxville, where he was heard on the WNOX Tennessee Barn Dance. His first big writing success came from **Sweet Dreams**, a song which was a hit for Faron Young. In 1958 **I Can't Stop Loving You**, his best-known composition, became a hit for Kitty Wells. Later, Ray Charles was to have international success with the same song. Gibson himself recorded the number as a B-side of **Oh Lonesome Me**, but it broke through for him and gave him a name-making pop hit in the process. Total sales of **I Can't Stop Loving You** were not long in reaching the one million mark. Other songs that provided hit records for Don included: **Give Myself A Party**, **Blue Blue Day**, **Sea Of Heartbreak** and **Lonesome Number One**. The last three, and particularly **Sea Of Heartbreak**, showed that Gibson's deep voice and neatly novel songs could cross over into the pop charts.

Consistently successful in the country charts, Gibson has always kept his country image and has often been critical of the inroads rock has made into his chosen style of music. Though regarded mainly as

Above: Talented singer and multi-instrumentalist Vince Gill has had a steady climb to the top – from early years as a popular sessionman and singer to superstardom in the '90s.

a 1960s singer (because of his cross-over hits during that period), he was a fairly prolific hitmaker in the 1970s when, signed to Hickory and ABC-Hickory, he logged nearly 40 chart records, including a number of duets with Sue Thompson. One of his solo cuts, **Woman (Sensuous Woman)**, reached No.1 in 1972.

He recorded for MCA (1979) and Warner (1980), providing both with some chart action, but is now virtually retired form the music business. A purveyor of classic songs dealing with heartbreak and loneliness, Gibson once wrote: "If loneliness meant world acclaim, then everyone would know my name – I'd be a legend in my time." And he really is.

Recommended:
Don't Stop Loving Me (Hickory/DJM)
Rockin' Rollin' Gibson (–/Bear Family)
A Legend In My Time (–/Bear Family)
Sings Country Favorites (–/Pickwick)

Vince Gill

The son of an attorney who is now a federal appellate judge, Vincent Grant Gill (born on April 4, 1957, in Norman, Oklahoma) learned his craft in the bluegrass world before becoming a mainstream country star of the '80s and walking off with the CMA Male Vocalist award in 1991, 1992 and 1993.

Vince made his radio debut on a local radio station when he was eight. Two years later he had not only mastered guitar, but was leading his own band. While still in high school he was in a bluegrass outfit called Mountain Smoke. At the time he had to decide between being a musician or a professional golfer. A call from Sam Bush and Dan Crary asking him to join the Bluegrass Alliance solved the dilemma, and in 1974 he moved to Kentucky. A year later he was in Los Angeles, where he joined Byron Berline's Sundance for a two-year stint. It was at this time he met his future wife, Janis Oliver, who, with sister Kristine, was working the West Coast clubs as Sweethearts Of The Rodeo. Three years later they were married, and Vince was beginning to make his mark as lead singer with Pure Prairie League. He recorded three albums with the band and sang on their Top 10 pop hit, **Let Me Love You Tonight** (1980).

In 1982 Vince Gill lined up alongside Emory Gordy Jr and Tony Brown in Rodney Crowell's Cherry Bombs. This meant a move to Nashville, where Brown was also working at RCA. He signed Vince to the label in 1983, but before any sessions took

Pocket Full Of Gold, Vince Gill. Courtesy MCA Records.

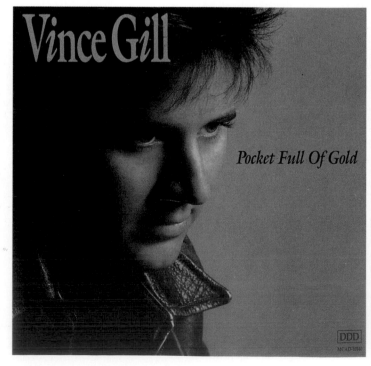

Above: Night-club owner Gilley became a star during the 'Urban Cowboy' craze.

place Brown left for greener pastures, joining MCA. Ironically, Gill's first solo sessions were produced by Gordy, and he made his country chart debut with **Victim Of Life's Circumstances** (1984). During the next four years Vince recorded three albums for RCA. Although he scored such Top 10 hits as **If It Weren't For Him** (1985), **Oklahoma Borderline** (1986), **Cinderella** (1987) and **Everybody's Sweetheart** (1988), and the Academy Of Country Music named him Best New Male Vocalist of 1984, it was hardly the successful solo career he had expected.

All this time Vince has been in demand as a session musician and singer, making guest appearances on recordings by Rosanne Cash, Rodney Crowell, Emmylou Harris, Dan Fogelberg, Vern Gosdin, Reba McEntire, Conway Twitty and many others. When his contract with RCA had run its course, Tony Brown signed Vince to MCA and produced the career-breaking album, **When I Call Your Name**. The title song, co-written by Gill and Tim DuBois, and featuring Patty Loveless on harmonies, became his first No.1. It was named Single Of The Year and Song Of The Year at the 1990 CMA Awards. The album crossed over onto the pop charts and gained a platinum award. The next album, **Pocket Full Of Gold**, contained Top 10 hits in the title song, the upbeat **Liza Jane** and **Look At Us** (Song Of The Year at the 1991 CMA Awards), plus another No.1 with **Take Your Memory With You**. It was another platinum album, and Gill made it a hat-trick for MCA with the album, **I Still Believe In You**. The title song, **Don't Let Our Love Start Slippin' Away**, and a duet with Reba McEntire on **The Heart Won't Lie** (1993) became chart-toppers.

One of Nashville's most talented performers, Gill can play guitar, banjo, mandolin and dobro. He teamed up with Steve Wariner, Ricky Skaggs, Mark O'Connor and the New Nashville Cats for a revival of Carl Perkins' **Restless** (1991), which won the CMA Instrumental Award. He also added harmonies to Dire Straits' album, **On Every Street**. Mark Knopfler invited him to join Dire Straits for their 1992 World Tour, but he turned it down,

preferring to concentrate on his own solo career. In 1993 Gill won five CMA awards, including Entertainer Of The Year. Now firmly established as one of country music's major stars, Vince Gill possesses the right temperament to handle the stardom and adulation now showered upon him.

Recommended:
Pocket Full Of Gold (MCA/MCA)
When I Call Your Name (MCA/MCA)
I Still Believe In You (MCA/MCA)
I Never Knew Lonely (RCA/–)
The Way Back Home (RCA/–)

Mickey Gilley

The piano-playing cousin of Jerry Lee Lewis and a performer in a similar vein, Mickey Gilley was born on March 9, 1936 in Ferriday, Louisiana. He moved to Houston at the age of 17 and began playing at local clubs, cutting the rock'n'roll songs **Tell Me Why** and **Oo-ee-baby** for the Minor label. This brought no rewards, so Gilley travelled on, recording for Dot, Rex and Khoury. In 1960 he recorded a Warner Mack song, **Is It Wrong**, for Potomac, and gained a regional best-seller – but the label folded and Gilley continued label-hopping.

In 1964, he formed his own record company, Astro. His second release, **Lonely Wine**, proved another regional hit. An album of the same name (later retitled **Down The Line** when reissued by Paula) was also released. However, 1965 found Gilley on 20th Century Fox. From there he moved to Paula, where he enjoyed a mid-1968 hit in **Now I Can Live Again**. It was not until 1974 and some reaction to his Astro version of George Morgan's old **Roomful Of Roses**, that things started coming together for Gilley. The single was picked up by Hugh Hefner's Playboy label and immediately went to No.1 in the charts. Chart-toppers followed in **I Overlooked An Orchid**, **City Lights** and **Window Up Above**. Two more No.1s came in 1976 – **Don't The Girls All Get Prettier At Closing Time** and **Bring It On Home To Me** – at which point he garnered the Entertainer Of The Year, Top Male Vocalist, Song Of The Year, Single Of The Year and Album Of The Year awards from the ACM.

After further hits for Playboy, including **She's Pulling Me Back Again**, a 1977 No.1, Gilley signed with Epic. His career gained an added fillip in 1980 when the movie 'Urban Cowboy', shot at Gilley's – the Houston club the singer bought in 1971 – provided him with international exposure and a pop hit in **Stand By Me**. The song was one of three country No.1s that year, the others being **True Love Ways** and **That's All That Matters To Me**. For the next few years the flow of hits continued, including **A Headache Tomorrow (Or A Heartache Tonight)**, **You Don't Know Me**, **Lonely Nights**, **Put Your Dreams Away**, **Paradise Tonight** (a duet with Charly McClain), **Fool For Your Love** and **You've Really Got A Hold On Me**. Based mainly in his thriving club, it appeared that Gilley was set up for life. It was not to be, though, and by 1986 he had scored his last Top 10 hit with **Doo-Wah Days** for Epic. The following year he signed with Airborne and only managed to place a few minor hits on the charts.

After Awhile, Jimmie Dale Gilmore. Courtesy Elektra Records.

Recommended:
At His Best (Paula/–)
Welcome To Gilley's (Playboy/Pye)
Down The Line (–/Charly)
That's All That Matters To Me (Epic/Epic)
Gilley's Smokin' (Epic/–)
It Takes Believers – with Charly McClain (Epic/–)
From Pasadena With Love (–/Sundown)

Jimmie Dale Gilmore

Texas singer-songwriter Jimmie Dale Gilmore's music is steeped in traditionalism, while maintaining a contemporary edge. This may help explain why it took him more than twenty years to gain any kind of following within mainstream country music. Jimmie was born in 1945 in the small Texas town of Tulia, into a family where country music was almost like a religion. Jimmie's father played electric guitar in an Ernest Tubb-inspired West Texas honky-tonk band. The family moved to Buddy Holly's nearby hometown of Lubbock in 1950, and his father stopped playing in the band to enrol in college. However, his father still maintained a keen interest in country music, and Jimmy can recall accompanying him to shows during the '50s.

Jimmie didn't get the music bug until the early '60s when the folk revival started. He picked up an acoustic guitar and hung out with Butch Hancock and Joe Ely. By the early '70s the three had teamed up as the Flatlanders, an acoustic band that also featured Steve Wesson and Tony Pearson. They played around Lubbock and Austin, and in 1971 travelled to Nashville to record an album. A single was released, Jimmie's lovely **Dallas**, and the other tracks were put out by Plantation Records.

Shortly after this the Flatlanders split. From 1974 to 1980 Jimmie lived in Denver at a spiritual community that followed teenage guru Maharaj Ji. In 1981 he moved back to Austin and started picking up the threads of his music career. Due to the success of Joe Ely, interest in the Flatlanders started to build, and Gilmore

found he had a cult following. A contract with Hightone Records led to **The Fair And Square** album, which produced minor country music hits **White Freight Liner Blues** (1988) and **Honky Tonk Song** (1989). A second album surfaced at this time and Gilmore teamed up with Butch Hancock for successful tours in England and Australia. His grainy, weather-beaten voice and timeless West Texas country songs gained a following among country music fans in these countries. Word of mouth praise for Gilmore and his music spread, and in 1991 he was signed to Elektra/Nonesuch's American Explorer series. He then released the acclaimed **After Awhile** album. For the first time Gilmore's music received recognition in the mainstream of country music. In early 1993 he was preparing a new album, to be released and marketed on Elektra itself, unlike its predecessor, which had been aimed squarely at the rootsy pop audience.

Recommended:
Fair And Square (–/Demon)
After Awhile (Elektra/Elektra)

Johnny Gimble

A brilliant session fiddle player and mandolinist, also the writer of **Fiddlin' Around**, a tune nominated for a 1974 Grammy Award, Johnny Gimble was born on May 30, 1926, in Tyler, Texas, and grew up on a farm nearby.

With his brothers Gene, Jerry, Jack and Bill, the 12-year-old Johnny began playing at local gigs. Gene, Jerry and Johnny combined with James Ivie during their high school days to form the Rose City Swingsters, a group that played on radio station KOKO. Leaving home in 1943, Gimble played fiddle and banjo with Bob and Joe Shelton at KWKH, Shreveport, Louisiana, also working as part of the Jimmie Davis band.

Gimble spent two or three stints with Bob Wills and his Texas Playboys. When western swing's popularity sagged, he left the music business and settled down.

A resident of Dallas for a while, he began working as a studio musician with Lefty Frizzell, Ray Price, Marty Robbins and

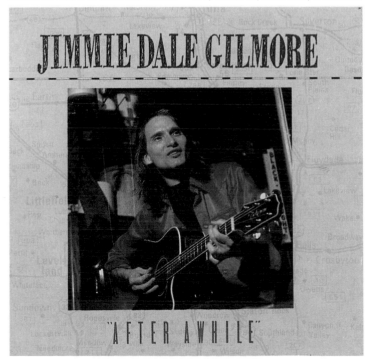

JIMMIE DALE GILMORE

"AFTER AWHILE"

others. He eventually moved to Nashville, where he gained more work, both in the studio and as a touring back-up man. He also played on such TV shows as Hee Haw and Austin City Limits. He won the CMA Instrumentalist Of The Year award in 1975, while the Academy Of Country Music adjudged him Top Fiddle Player in 1978 and 1979.

In the late '70s Johnny moved from Nashville to Austin, but he still turns up on countless Nashville sessions and tours with Merle Haggard, Asleep At The Wheel, Willie Nelson, and various all-star bands, playing both jazz and pure country with equal fluency.

Recommended:
Texas Dance Party (Columbia/–)
Still Swingin' – with the Texas Swing Pioneers (CMH/–)
The Texas Fiddle Collection (CMH/–)

Texas Dance Party, Johnny Gimble. Courtesy CBS Records.

Girls Next Door

Stretching the boundaries of country music with their close harmony singing, the Girls Next Door were specifically formed to fulfil a musical role in the early '80s, in much the same way that the Monkees had been created to perform pop music in the '60s.

Formed as Belle in 1982, they were the brainchild of record producer Tommy West and session singer Doris King (born February 13, 1957, Nashville, Tennessee), who thought it would be great to have an all-girl harmony group that could blend country with soul and big band swing music. King recruited the members: Cindy Nixon (born August 3, 1958, Nashville, Tennessee), whose father and uncle had worked in country music as the Nixon Brothers; Tammy Stephens (born April 13, 1961, Arlington, Texas), who had been singing with the Wills Family Gospel Group since the age of six, and was married to Hee Haw regular Jeff Smith; and Diane

Williams (born August 9, 1959, Hahn AFB, Germany). All four girls had performed on different shows at Opryland and worked sessions as back-up vocalists. They started playing small clubs, perfecting their repertoire and harmonies, then West took them to the studio to produce a demo tape. Eventually he gained the girls a contract with MTM Records in 1985 when Belle became the Girls Next Door. They made their chart debut in 1986 with **Love Will Get You Through Times With No Money**. The same year they made the Top 10 with a revival of **Slow Boat To China**. Another major hit came with **Walk Me In The Rain** (1987) before MTM Records folded. The Girls Next Door are still a popular touring act and signed with Atlantic Records, returning to the charts with **He's Gotta Have Me** (1989).

Recommended:
How About Us? (Atlantic/–)

Girls Of The Golden West

Authentic westerners, both from Muleshoe, Texas, Dorothy Laverne 'Dolly' Good (born December 11, 1915) and Mildred Fern 'Millie' Good (born April 11, 1913) were one of the most popular acts in early country music, and helped pave the way for other women singers. They were among the earliest to exploit the cowboy image in dress and song.

They began their career on WIL and KMOX in St Louis in 1930, then spent three years in Milford, Kansas, and on XER in Mexico, before coming to nationwide attention on the National Barn Dance from 1933 to 1937. The Goods, both of whom sang and played guitar, were even more popular on the Boone County Jamboree and the Midwestern Hayride (both over WLW) in Cincinnati, where they were voted the most popular act on WLW in 1945. Their appearances and performance tailed off in the '50s and they did not perform after about 1963. Dolly died on November 12, 1967, but Millie was still living in Cincinnati, Ohio at the start of the 1980s.

They never had any great success on record, but were among the most popular groups of their era – and one of the most influential.

Recommended:
The Girls Of The Golden West (Old Homestead/–)

Below: Johnny Gimble is a fine fiddle-player and superb mandolinist.

STILL SWINGIN'
Johnny Gimble & The TEXAS SWING PIONEERS

Still Swingin', Johnny Gimble. Courtesy CMH Country Classics.

Vern Gosdin

A singer whose success was a long time in coming, Vern Gosdin has played bluegrass, West Coast country-rock and rock'n'roll, but he is most at home with his impeccably pure honky-tonk country style, which finally gained him full recognition as a 50-year-old 'New Traditional' country star of the late '80s.

Born in Woodland, Alabama on August 5, 1936, Gosdin joined the Gosdin Family Gospel Radio Show on WKOK, Birmingham, Alabama, broadcast six days a week during the early '50s. In 1953 he moved to Atlanta where he worked as a singer in the evening. Three years later found him in Chicago, initially working as a welder, then later managing a country music night-club. He moved to California in 1960, where he formed the bluegrass outfit, Golden State Boys, with his younger brother, Rex. Two years later the Gosdin brothers were playing with Chris Hillman in the Hillmen, yet another bluegrass group. He was invited to join the Byrds in 1964, but declined and teamed up with Rex to work as the Gosdin Brothers. The pair recorded an album with Gene Clark in 1966, then a year later had a fair-sized hit with **Hangin' On** on the Bakersfield International label. This led to signing with Capitol Records, for whom they cut the album **Sounds Of Goodbye**, the title song an early Eddie Rabbitt composition.

By the early '70s they were finding it hard to make a good living from music. In 1972 Vern, his wife Cathy and two children moved back to Atlanta. He started selling glassware door-to-door, eventually operating his own successful glass and mirror business. Gary S. Paxton, who had produced the Capitol recordings, encouraged Vern to make a fresh start in music, this time in Nashville. Vern cut new versions of **Hangin' On** (1976), with Emmylou Harris singing harmony, and **Till The End** (1977), both these Elektra releases going Top 10, along with **Yesterday's Gone,** another Gosdin Top 10 entry in 1977. Vern was asked to make an entry on his revered Opry, following this with such major hits as **Never My Love**, **Break My Mind** and **You've Got**

Somebody, I've Got Somebody. He switched to the Ovation label in 1981 and had a couple of hits, including **Dream Of Me**.

A consistent label-hopper, he was back in the Top 10 with **Today My World Slipped Away** in 1982, this time on AMI. The following year he signed with Compleat, scoring Top 10 hits with: **If You're Gonna Do Me Wrong (Do It Right)**, **Way Down Deep**, **I Wonder Where We'd Be Tonight**, **I Can Tell By The Way You Dance (You're Gonna Love Me Tonight)** (his first No.1), **What Would Your Memories Do** and **Slow Burning Memories**. In 1987 he landed back on his feet on a major label, this time Columbia, who were looking for a 'New Traditional' country artist to cash in on the success of the back-to-basics country artists. 51-year-old Gosdin didn't let them down, going Top 10 with **Do You Believe Me Now** (1987) and right to the top with **Set 'Em Up Joe** (1988).

His first album for Columbia, **Chiseled in Stone** (the title song another Top 10 single), is one of the all-time classic honky-tonk albums. Further Top 10 entries followed with **Who You Gonna Blame It On This Time**, another No.1 with **I'm Still Crazy**, **That Just About Does It**, **Right In The Wrong Direction** and **Is It Raining At Your House**. Though held in high esteem by many of his contemporaries, and commanding a large and loyal fan following, Gosdin's age, looks and stature were alien to the country image of the early '90s. He has continued to produce classic albums for Columbia, but found it increasingly difficult to place his singles in the Top 10 in his future. He has invested in his future with his own music showplace, the Country Music Amphitheater in Ardmore, Alabama.

Recommended:
Till The End (Elektra/Elektra)
The Best Of (Elektra/–)
There Is A Season (Compleat/PRT Compleat)
Nickles & Dimes & Love (Columbia/–)
Chiseled In Stone (Columbia/–)
Alone (Columbia/–)

Above: Billy Grammer hit paydirt with his million-selling hit Gotta Travel On.

Billy Grammer

Originator of the Grammer guitar, a fine flat-top instrument, Billy Grammer's first guitar was installed in the Country Music Hall Of Fame in March, 1969.

One of 13 children fathered by an Illinois coalminer, Grammer (born Benton, Illinois, August 28, 1925) became a major star during the late '50s and early '60s. He performed on WRAL, Arlington in 1947 and by 1955 had earned a regular spot on the Washington-based Jimmy Dean TV Show, moving with Dean on to a CBS network programme later.

A popular bandleader, Grammer signed with Monument Records in 1958, having his first hit – a million seller – with **Gotta Travel On**, a song adapted by the Weavers from a traditional melody. Becoming an Opry regular in 1959 and obtaining a double-sided hit that year with **Bonaparte's Retreat/The Kissing Tree**, Grammer recorded for numerous labels throughout the '60s, with minor hits on most of them, via such titles as **I Wanna Go Home** (Decca, 1963), **The Real Thing** (Epic 1966), **Mabel** (Rice, 1967), **Ballad Of John Dillinger** (Mercury, 1968) and **Jesus Is A Soul Man** (Stop, 1969).

Recommended:
Country Guitar (Decca/–)
Favorites (Vocalion/–)

Dobie Gray

Dobie Gray (born Leonard Victor Ainsworth in Brookshire, Texas on July 26, 1942) is a much respected singer-songwriter in

That Feeling Inside, Mark Gray.
Courtesy CBS Records.

Nashville, who has never quite made that breakthrough to commercial acceptance that his talent has deserved.

A son of a Protestant minister, Dobie listened to country and blues music as a small boy. In 1960 he left his Texas home and headed for California to become a film star in Hollywood. Instead he landed a role as singer and was soon recording pop and soul records for a variety of West Coast labels, scoring a minor pop hit with **Look At Me** (1963). Two years later he made a bigger impact with **The In Crowd**, which made the Top 20 and led to work on the lucrative club circuit. In 1971 he became a member of rock band Pollution, then started recording demos for Paul Williams. Through Williams he met Mentor Williams (his brother), and established a partnership that saw Gray signed to MCA Records in

Nashville. Mentor wrote Dobie's biggest hit, **Drift Away** (1973). With MCA he recorded three albums that perfectly fused country simplicity and pop complexity. Utilizing the talents of David Briggs, Weldon Myrick and Buddy Spicher, Gray cut the original versions of such songs as **We Had It All**, **Lovin' Arms**, **I Never Had It So Good** and **There's A Honky Tonk Angel (Who'll Take Me Back In)**.

Three years later Dobie joined Capricorn Records, for whom he cut a couple of excellent southern-styled country-rock albums, achieving pop success with **If Love Must Go** and **Find 'Em, Fool 'Em And Forget 'Em** (both 1976). Shortly afterwards Capricorn folded, but Dobie continued writing and was also doing sessions in Nashville. He joined Infinity Records and had his last pop hit with **You**

Can Do It (1979). His next recordings came six years later when he signed with Capitol and made his debut on the country charts with **That's One To Grow On** (1986). His Capitol album, **From Where I Stand**, was a classic modern country album with Nashville pickers, singers and writers involved.

Recommended:
Drift Away (–/Cottage)
From Where I Stand (Capitol/–)
Love's Talkin' (Capitol/–)

Mark Gray

A one-time gospel singer, a composer of jingles for 17 years and a writer of pop hits, Mark Gray was born in Vicksburg, Mississippi, in 1952. His aunt was part of a gospel group and Gray toured with them for several years. At 19 he moved on to work with the Oak Ridge Boys' publishing company and appeared with them onstage. After seven years Gray returned to Mississippi and began concentrating on his songwriting career.

Eventually he made his way back to Nashville and became lead singer with Exile. But he continued to write songs, including **Take Me Down** and **The Closer You Get**, both No.1s for Alabama, and **It Ain't Easy Bein' Easy**, a chart-topper for Janie Fricke. One of his demo tapes for Fricke was heard by a Columbia Records executive and led to a contract as a solo act with the label in 1983. Gray made an immediate impact, notching a Top 20 single that year with **Wounded Hearts**. By 1984 he was up among the frontrunners, logging three Top 10 records. In 1985 Gray teamed with Tammy Wynette in a Top 10 duet, **Sometimes When We Touch**, returning to solo mode for **Please Be Love** (1986). His last Top 20 hit came with **Back When Love Was Enough** in 1987, after which he signed with the small 615 label, scoring two minor duet hits with Bobbi Lace in 1988.

Recommended:
Magic (Columbia/CBS)
This Ol' Piano (Columbia/CBS)
That Feeling Inside (Columbia/CBS)

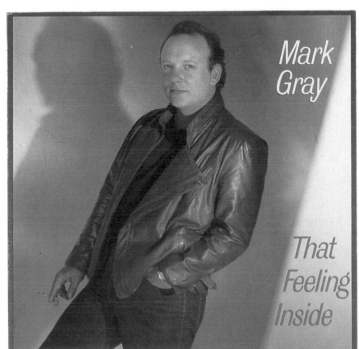

Lloyd Green And His Steel Guitar.
Courtesy M&M Records.

Lloyd Green

One of Nashville's top sessionmen, Mensa member Green was born in Mississippi. on October 4, 1937, and grew up in Mobile, Alabama. He began taking lessons on steel guitar at the age of seven, playing professionally three years later. During his high school days he played weekends at clubs and bars where 'real rough fights, shootings and stabbings were common', using material drawn mainly from the Eddy Arnold and Hank Williams songbooks. He attended the University of Southern Mississippi as a psychology major but left after two years to play in Nashville. He initially worked with Hawkshaw Hawkins and Jean Shepard, then toured with Faron Young and George Jones, his first recording session in Music City being on Jones' **Too Much Water Runs Under The Bridge** single in 1957. Though he has had hard times since, Green is now an in-demand steelie and plays on some 500 sessions a year. A recording artist in his own right, he has also had a few hit singles, the biggest of these being **I Can See Clearly Now**, on Monument in 1973.

Recommended:
Steel Rides (Monument/Monument)
Cool Steel Man (Chart/Chart)
Green Velvet (Little Darlin'/President)

Greenbriar Boys

A New York-based bluegrass group, Greenbriar Boys was formed in 1958 by Bob Yellin, John Herald and Eric Weissberg. Extremely popular at folk festivals in the 1960s, they recorded for Elektra and Vanguard and produced several well-regarded albums. The group has included among its personnel legendary mandolinist Frank Wakefield, fiddler Buddy Spicher and Ralph Rinzler, one-time manager of Bill Monroe and a leading authority on old-time country music. Original member Weissberg teamed with Steve Mandell in 1972 to provide **Dueling Banjos** – an instrumental from the film 'Deliverance' – which turned a million-selling single the following year.

Recommended:
Best Of (Vanguard/–)
Ragged But Right (Vanguard/–)
Better Late Than Never (Vanguard/–)

Jack Greene

Yet another of the long list of country entertainers who could play guitar at an early age, Jack Henry Greene (born Maryville, Tennessee, January 7, 1930), also a fine drummer, first became a full-time musician with the Cherokee Trio, an Atlanta GA group, moving on to become sticksman with the Rhythm Ranch Boys in 1950. Then came two years of Army service, followed by a stint with another Atlanta band, the Peachtree Cowboys.

Below: Talented Lee Greenwood was once a Las Vegas croupier.

Joining Ernest Tubb's Texas Troubadours in 1962, the amiable six-footer, dubbed 'the Jolly Giant', soon became a favourite. While still a member of Tubb's band, he began having solo discs released by Decca. One single, **Ever Since My Baby Went Away**, charted in mild fashion during 1965, this being followed by two No. 1s in **There Goes My Everything** (1966) and **All The Time** (1967). During 1967, Greene gained four CMA awards – Best Male Vocalist, Best Album, Best Song and Single Of The Year (for **There Goes My Everything**, a Dallas–Frazier composition). Thereafter he continued on his hit-making way, providing Decca with five more top singles during the late '60s.

In 1969, Greene and Jeannie Seely, his co-vocalist on the Ernest Tubb TV show, put together a roadshow and began touring with a band called the Green Giants. The twosome enjoyed immediate success with **Wish I Didn't Have To Miss You**. The first country act to play the Rooftop Lounge, King Of The Road, Nashville, in 1972, Greene and Seely received considerable acclaim for their 1974 Madison Square Garden concert. The duo played host and hostess at the Wembley Country Festival two years later. But at the beginning of 1981, they went their separate ways. Greene claimed the split gave him the opportunity to provide a less Vegas-styled presentation and a back-to-basics approach. Also, during the start of the '80s he began having hits again, for the first time since 1975. But his deal with the Frontline label fell through. However, his happy relationship with the country charts was resumed yet again in 1983 when he signed with EMH Records.

Recommended:
Greatest Hits (MCA/–)
Best Of (–/MCA)
Greene Country (MCA/–)
Two For The Show – with Jeannie Seely (MCA/–)
Jack Greene And Jeannie Seely (MCA/–)

Lee Greenwood

The son of half-Cherokee parents who split-up when he was just a year old, Lee Greenwood (born on October 27, 1942, in Los Angeles) was left in the care of his grandparents, who had a chicken farm near Sacramento. A sax-player and a pianist, he became a schoolboy member of a local band known as My Moonbeams. Later, reunited with his mother in Los Angeles, he played for various jazz and rock bands in the LA area. After returning to Sacramento in 1958, he moved into country music, joining a band headed by Capitol recording artist Chester Smith, and appearing on TV at the age of 15. Hired by Del Reeves for his sax expertise (he can also play guitar, bass and banjo), he learned the art of showmanship from Reeves. He then formed his own band, Apollo, which became based in Las Vegas in 1962. By 1965 Apollo had evolved into the Lee Greenwood Affair, a pop band signed to Paramount Records.

The band moved to the West Coast in an attempt to break into the pop market, but the Paramount label folded and so did the Affair. Greenwood returned to Vegas where he took up various jobs including bandleader, back-up singer, musical arranger, bar-room singer and casino card-dealer. In 1979 Mel Tillis' bandleader, Larry McFadden, heard Greenwood singing in a bar and arranged for him to fly to Nashville to record some demo discs. Once completed, Greenwood returned to jobs in Vegas and Reno, but started concentrating on his songwriting, switching from showbiz material to more country-oriented fare at McFadden's insistence. The latter took Greenwood's demos to various Nashville-based labels and eventually got MCA to sign a deal in June 1981.

A distinctive singer with a voice loaded with finely sifted gravel, Greenwood went Top 20 with his first MCA single in mid-'81, **It Turns Me Inside Out**. He followed this with three Top 10 hits during the following year – **Ring On Her Finger, Time On Her Hands, She's Lying, Ain't No Trick (It Takes Magic)** – all of which appeared on his debut album **Inside And Out**. But 1983 was really Greenwood's year, providing him with three hit singles – **IOU, Somebody's Gonna Love You** and **Going, Going, Going**, the last two being No.1s and all three crossing over into the pop charts. He also won the Male Vocalist Of The Year title at the 1983 CMA Awards.

Since that time he has had further hits with: **God Bless The USA, Fool's Gold, You've Got A Good Love Comin', To Me** (a duet with Barbara Mandrell) (all 1984); **Dixie Road, I Don't Mind The Thorns (If You're The Rose)** and **Don't Underestimate My Love For You** (1985); **Hearts Aren't Made To Break (They're Made To Love)** (1965) and **Mornin' Ride** (1987). During the Gulf War the patriotic **God Bless The USA** made a comeback, while Greenwood continued a consistent run of Top 10 hits with **Someone, If There's Any Justice** and **Touch And Go Crazy**. In 1989 he joined Capitol Records and immediately scored a Top 5 hit in 1990 with **Holdin' A Good Hand**. In 1991 he teamed up with Suzy Bogguss for the duet hit, **Hopelessly Yours**.

Greenwood is a talented songwriter who has had his material recorded by Kenny Rogers, Mel Tillis, Brenda Lee and others. He is also the voice on many commercials. In 1988 he starred in the CBS-TV series, High Mountain Rangers, in which he also performed the theme song. In Britain, however, Lee is best known for **The Wind Beneath My Wings**, a single which entered the UK pop charts in 1984.

Recommended:
Inside And Out (MCA/MCA)
Somebody's Gonna Love You (MCA/MCA)
Meant For Each Other – with Barbara Mandrell (MCA/–)
American Patriot (Liberty/–)
Streamline (MCA/MCA)
The Wind Beneath My Wings (–/MCA)
If Only For One Night (Capitol/–)

Ray Griff

The writer of many hundreds of songs, Ray Griff was born in Vancouver, British Columbia, Canada, on April 22, 1940, moving with his family to Calgary, Alberta, shortly before reaching his teens. A drummer in a band at the age of eight, Griff also mastered guitar and piano, becoming a bandleader on the night-club circuit at 18. His reputation as a songwriter was enhanced when Johnny Horton recorded **Mr Moonlight**, a Griff composition, during the late '50s. Jim Reeves cut **Where Do I Go?**, another Griff original, in 1962.

Encouraged by Reeves, he became Nashville-based in 1964, initially involving

Above: Lyle Lovett became an extra in Nanci Griffith's Last Of The True Believers 1986 album sleeve. Courtesy MCA.

himself in songwriting and music publishing, but later recording some sides for RCA's Groove label. An MGM release, **Your Lily White Hands**, provided him with his first hit (1967). Griff followed this with **Sugar From My Candy**, on Dot, a few months later. Label-switching again, he recorded Clarence Carter's **Patches** for Royal American, gaining a 1970 success. He climbed even higher with **The Morning After Baby Let Me Down**, in 1971, also enjoying Top 10 discs with **You Ring My Bell** (1975) and **If I Let Her Come In** (1976), both on Capitol.

Since that time, Griff has supplied a few mini-hits during the '80s for Vision and RCA but it is as a songwriter that he has

staked a claim to fame. His compositions include **Canadian Pacific** (recorded by George Hamilton IV), **Baby** (Wilma Burgess), **Better Move It On Home** (Porter Wagoner and Dolly Parton), **Step Aside** (Faron Young), **Who's Gonna Play This Old Piano** (Jerry Lee Lewis) and many others, the majority published by Griff's own Blue Echo company.

Recommended:
Ray Griff (Capitol/–)
The Last Of The Winfield Amateurs (Capitol/–)
Canada (Boot/–)

Nanci Griffith

Story-teller and 'folkabilly-poet' Nanci Griffith (born on July 6, 1953 in Seguin, Texas) is not, strictly speaking, a country artist, although country music does echo in her songs. Several of her songs have become mainstream country hits when

recorded by singers Kathy Mattea, Suzy Bogguss and Willie Nelson.

Griffith, the youngest of three children, had a middle-class upbringing; her mother was an amateur actress and her father sang in a barbershop quartet. They separated when Nanci was only six, and she absorbed herself in books and music. By her mid-teens she had already started performing as a solo singer in bars and honky-tonks in Austin. She attended the University of Texas where she majored in education. Although she became a kindergarten teacher, it was short-lived, and in 1977 she decided to pursue a career in music. By this time Nanci had married Texas singer-songwriter Eric Taylor. She made her first recordings in 1976 and they appeared on a folk sampler on B.F. Deal Records the following year. Her own debut album, **There's A Light Beyond These Woods**, was released by B.F. Deal in 1978. Shortly after this her marriage fell apart. Nanci took to handling her own career, driving up to 1,000 miles in her Toyota station wagon to play concerts in Minneapolis, New Mexico or San Francisco.

A second album, **Poet In My Window**, recorded in Kerrville, Texas, was released on Featherbed Records in 1982 and featured mainly self-penned songs. By this time Nanci's reputation was spreading, and in 1984 she met Jim Rooney, who produced her third album, **Once In A Very Blue Moon** for Philo/Rounder. Rooney also helped introduce Nanci and her music to a much wider audience. Recorded in Nashville, the title song from the album became a minor hit in 1986. The same year a fourth album was released, **Last Of The True Believers**, which started a European cult following for her music. Two songs, her own **Love At The Five And Dime** and Pat Alger's **Goin' Gone** became massive hits when later recorded by Kathy Mattea. Tony Brown, ex-keyboard player for the Oak Ridge Boys and Rodney Crowell's Cherry Bombs, was a young and dynamic A&R man for MCA Nashville, and he not only liked Nanci's music, but signed her to MCA in 1987. He produced her breakthrough album, **Lone Star State Of Mind**. The title song became her biggest country hit, but only peaked at No.37. In Europe her music was more readily accepted, with several songs from the album becoming standard fare among country music performers. This album also included the first recording of Julie Gold's **From A Distance**, a song which Griffith published and which was set to become a standard in the early '90s when covered by Cliff Richard, Bette Midler, Kathy Mattea and others.

Since then Nanci has maintained a high integrity on her recordings without in any way compromising her music for commercial gain. **Little Love Affairs** (1988) was a concept album filled with delicate little vignettes and tales of love. But, despite a high media profile, country radio failed to play her records, so MCA moved her promotion and publicity to Los Angeles in an effort to market her recordings more towards the rock and college market. This was borne out with **Storms** (1989), an album with a definite bias towards American radio, produced by Glyn Johns. It made both the American pop and country charts, but failed to attract American country fans towards Nanci and her music. By this time she had become a virtual superstar in Ireland, and in 1991 contributed to the Chieftains' Christmas album, **The Bells of Dublin**.

Above: Nanci Griffith broke through with Lone Star State Of Mind in 1987.

Though she has still not made a major impact on Nashville's mainstream country music, Nanci bought a 100-year-old farmhouse in Franklin on the outskirts of Music City in 1990, vowing, "I'm staying in Nashville and the music isn't going to change." With her band, the Blue Moon Orchestra, which sounds pure country, she has been a regular visitor to Britain where she is regarded as at the forefront of 'New Country', selling out major theatres, including London's Royal Albert Hall for four consecutive nights – a far cry from the Texas bars and honky-tonks where she used to play from 10pm until 2am. More of an album artist than a singles star, Nanci worked with the British team of Rod Argent and Peter Van Hook on **Late Night Grande Hotel** (1991). She reunited with Jim Rooney on **Other Voices, Other Rooms** (1993), a collection which took the Texas lady back to her roots as she performed songs by Bob Dylan, Tom Paxton, Gordon Lightfoot, John Prine and Woody Guthrie.

Recommended:
Other Voices, Other Rooms (MCA/MCA)
Last Of The True Believers (Philo/MCA)
Little Love Affairs (MCA/MCA)
Once In A Very Blue Moon (Philo/MCA)
There's A Light Beyond These Woods (Philo/MCA)

Below: Ray Griff, one of several Canadians who have enhanced country music.

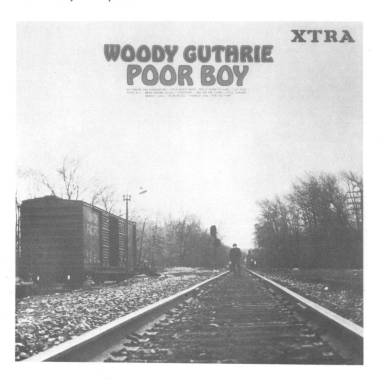

The Gully Jumpers

Charlie Arrington, fiddle; Roy Hardison, banjo; Burt Hutcherson, guitar; Paul Warmack, mandolin and guitar.

The Gully Jumpers were one of the early popular Opry string bands and participated in that early Nashville recording session for Victor in October 1928. Led by Paul Warmack, an auto mechanic by trade, they remained with basically the same personnel for well over two decades (they had joined the Opry about 1927) and in fact were one of the most popular and most used bands of the Opry's early years. The group was dissolved in the mid-'60s when four of the old-time Opry bands were accordioned into two.

Though few recordings of the Gully Jumpers are available on vinyl, the band can be heard on **Nashville – The Early String Bands Volume 1** (County) playing **Robertson County** and **Stone Rag**.

Woody Guthrie

An influential country folk singer, Guthrie's visual attitude and thin, fragmented vocal style have been copied by many, most notably Bob Dylan.

Born Woodrow Wilson Guthrie, in Okema, Oklahoma, in 1912, a hard rural upbringing amid a background of natural disasters set the tone for many of his songs. He championed the rural poor and the loser (as on **Dustbowl Ballads**) yet he was also capable of joyous hymns to the country itself (**This Land Is Your Land**).

He roamed the land extensively, incorporating what he found into songs. He later wrote that he saw things happen to oil people, cattle people and wheat folks, and detailed these happenings in songs which he broadcast over the LA station KFVD. He gave rise to what is sometimes called 'The Dustbowl Tradition', other exponents of which include Cisco Houston and Rambling Jack Elliot. The slogan on his guitar read 'this machine kills fascists' and as he roamed America during the

Poor Boy, Woody Guthrie. Courtesy Xtra Records. Guthrie found much of the material for his songs on the road.

Depression, singing in union halls and for picket lines, it was hardly surprising when the authorities, already scared by the crisis, tried to tag the 'red' label on him. In a parallel with the '60s decade, those who pointed the need for social change could find themselves ostracized or even in danger.

Guthrie's mother had died of Huntingdon's Chorea (a hereditary nerve disease) and Woody himself succumbed to it in 1967, having been in hospital since 1954. He was a country singer in the very widest sense, a drifting son of the earth, crafting his simple songs out of experience and his own perception. During 1976, the singer's autobiography 'Bound For Glory' became the subject of a film directed by Hal Ashby with David Carradine in the role of Guthrie.

Recommended:
Dust Bowl Ballads (Folkways/–)
Bound For Glory (Folkways/–)
This Land Is Your Land (Folkways/–)
Columbia River Collection (Rounder/Topic)

Merle Haggard

Country's most charismatic living legend, Merle Haggard is proof that you do not have to forsake your musical roots to achieve fame. The Haggard family had been driven from their farm in dustbowl East Oklahoma and were living in a converted boxcar in Bakersfield, California, when Merle was born on April 6, 1937. Merle was nine when his father, a competent fiddle player, died, and without his father's influence he began to run wild. He embarked on a series of petty thefts and frauds and was in and out of local prisons. Then, in 1957, he was charged with attempted burglary and sentenced to six to fifteen years in San Quentin.

While in prison Merle did some picking and songwriting, and was in San Quentin when Johnny Cash performed one of his prison concerts in 1958. This convinced him that music could help him to straighten

out his life, and when he left jail in 1960 he was determined to try and make a go of performing. He moved to Bakersfield, which was then growing into a respectable little country music centre. Helped initially by Bakersfield eminence gris, Buck Owens and his former wife Bonnie Owens, whom Merle eventually married, he started playing the local club scene. At this time Merle ran into Fuzzy Owen, an Arkansas musician who was also playing the Bakersfield clubs. Fuzzy, who is Merle's manager to this day, encouraged him and helped get Merle work locally.

In 1962 Fuzzy organized some recording sessions in a converted 'garage' studio and produced some singles, which were released on Tally, a label Owen had purchased from his cousin Lewis Tally. The next year Merle made his debut on the country charts with **Sing A Sad Song** which reached No.19. In 1964 **Sam Hill** made No.45. In 1965 they put out (**My Friends Are Gonna Be) Strangers**, which gave them a Top 10 hit. This led to Capitol acquiring Merle's contract, plus all the recordings made for Tally.

Merle's second Capitol single, the self-penned classic honky-tonker **Swinging Doors**, spent six months on the charts, reaching a Top 5 placing. Equally as impressive was **The Bottle Let Me Down**, which made No.3. This was followed by Haggard's first No.1, **I'm A Lonesome Fugitive**, which made 1966 a highly successful year for him. Merle had been trying to suppress the news of his prison record, but as the story emerged the hard-core country music public were fascinated by this man who had lived the songs he wrote. It appeared that his own life story was unfolding in such country No. 1s as **Branded Man** and **Sing Me Back Home** (1967); **Mama Tried**, which referred to his wild childhood and prison record (1968); and **Hungry Eyes** and **Workin' Man Blues** (1969). In reality it was closer to country romanticism, but Haggard was using his own background for the inspiration for many of his best songs. Few composers have had as much impact on country music as Merle Haggard, who has been referred to as 'the poet of the common man.'

Two other apparently innocent songs were committed to record in 1969: **Okie**

From Muskogee and **The Fightin' Side Of Me**. **Okie** re-stated redneck values in the face of then current campus disturbances and Vietnam marches, yet Merle had written it as a joke, picking up a remark one of his band members had made about the conservative habits of Oklahoma natives as they rolled through Muskogee one day. **Fightin' Side Of Me** was another apparent putdown of those who were so bold as to disparage America's image. When Haggard premiered **Okie** for a crowd of NCOs at the Fort Bragg, North Carolina camp, they went wilder than he had expected, and from then on the song became a silent majority legend.

Haggard had been gaining a reputation as the new Woody Guthrie before **Okie** and his hippy following was stunned yet intrigued by this new turn of events. Even President Nixon was said to have written to congratulate Haggard on the song. In 1972, the singer received a pardon for his prison sentence from Ronald Reagan, then governor of California.

Merle himself has admitted to feeling scared at the reaction the song provoked, and he backed away from further right-wing involvement, refusing a proposal to endorse George Wallace politically. Indeed, for his next single, he wanted to record a song about an inter-racial love affair (**Irma Jackson**), but Capitol advised against it.

After the **Okie** controversy had died down, Merle was able to settle into the straightforward country career with which he felt most comfortable. He has not appeared often on television, as he lacks the easy, flip manner which TV companies seem to want from a host, and he has not bothered to cultivate the medium. He once walked out on an Ed Sullivan show when they tried to tell him which songs to sing and how to sing them. However, this principled non-conforming attitude, which probably lost him lucrative work, only strengthened the bond between Merle and country fans.

Since **Okie**, hits have come consistently: **Daddy Frank (The Guitar Man)** (1971); **Carolyn**, **Grandma Harp** and **It's Not Love (But It's Not Bad)** (all

Kern River, Merle Haggard. Courtesy Epic Records.

Merle Haggard
KERN RIVER

Above: The legendary Merle Haggard opened shows for Clint Black in the early '90s, but still releases albums on Epic.

association. His tribute album, **My Farewell To Elvis** (1977), was slated by the critics, though it came across in typical Haggard fashion. In no way did he try to mimic the Elvis style, but his identifiable delivery captured the soul of Presley's music, creating an enjoyable encounter with past Presley hits.

By this time Merle and Bonnie Owens had divorced, though she did continue to run his business affairs. Leona Williams, a country singer in her own right, joined the Haggard group as a backing vocalist and soon a stormy relationship developed. The pair were married on October 7, 1978 and recorded several duets which failed to make much of an impression. Five years later they were separated, obtaining a divorce in 1984.

A move to Epic Records towards the end of 1981 led to duet recordings with George Jones (**A Taste Of Yesterday's Wine** album in 1982) and Willie Nelson (**Poncho & Lefty**, which was named CMA Album Of The Year in 1983). His solo hits continued with **Big City** (1982), **That's The Way Love Goes** (1983) and **Natural High** (1984), but as the '80s drew to a close, not so many Haggard singles hit the Top 10. The rather sentimental **Twinkle Twinkle Lucky Star** (1987) has been his last chart-topper, and **A Better Love Next Time** (1989) his last Top 10 entry. Merle Haggard has continued to release albums regularly for Epic, but by 1991 he was opening shows for Clint Black, one of the new, young country traditionalists, who had used the Haggard style as the basis for his own; it was a case of carrying on the country music of yesterday to make the country music of today and tomorrow.

Usually, legendary figures are larger than life, but somehow Merle Haggard has managed to become a legend in his own time without losing the reality of being a down-to-earth human being. Perhaps this is because his songs deal so closely with the reality of being human. A classic, uncompromising country artist, his voice is hurting, yet subtle, with no showbiz nuances. He gives the impression, with his sparsely instrumented band the Strangers, of being more comfortable before audiences of working men than in Las Vegas hotel lounges.

Recommended:

Same Train, A Different Time (Capitol/ Capitol)
Okie From Muskogee (Capitol/–)
The Fightin' Side Of Me (Capitol/Capitol)
I Love Dixie Blues (Capitol/Capitol)
It's All In The Movies (Capitol/Capitol)
My Love Affair With Trains (Capitol/ Capitol)
The Roots Of My Raising (Capitol/Capitol)
My Farewell To Elvis (MCA/MCA)
Back To The Barrooms (MCA/MCA)
Going Where The Lonely Go (Epic/Epic)
Amber Waves (Epic/Epic)
Out Among The Stars (Epic/–)
Chill Factor (Epic/Epic)
Blue Jungle (Curb/–)
Land Of Many Churches (Capitol/Stetson)

Bill Haley

Bill Haley was born William John Clifton Haley, in Highland Park, Michigan, on July 6, 1925. The leader of a series of good local country bands in the late '40s and '50s, Haley was undoubtedly more surprised than anyone when his creative mixture of R&B, boogie and country music

1972); **Everybody's Had The Blues** and **If We Make It Through December** (1973); and **Old Man From The Mountain** and **Kentucky Gambler** (1974); all have been No.1s. Albums have provided an area for experimentation, often paying tribute to his influences, as in **Same Train, A Different Time**, in which he performs the songs of Jimmie Rodgers, or one of his most auspicious projects, **A Tribute To The Best Damn Fiddle**

Player In The World, in which he teamed original members of Bob Wills' Band with his own.

Haggard had grown up with western swing, and Bob Wills returned the compliment by inviting him to appear on Wills' own album **For The Last Time**. This was a fateful occasion since Wills suffered a stroke during these sessions, from which he never recovered. Haggard has also made other concept albums including **The Land Of Many Churches**, recorded at various churches and featuring the Carter Family, Tommy Collins and other guest singers and musicians. On **Let Me Tell You About A Song**, a 1972 album, he

offers a selection of strong story songs, some self-penned, others written by country greats such as Red Foley, Tommy Collins and Red Simpson. Fascinated by the old American railroads, he recorded **My Love Affair With Trains** in 1976. Another concept album, **I Love Dixie Blues (So I Recorded Live In New Orleans)**, had his band the Strangers augmented by a Dixieland jazz band.

In 1977, he joined MCA Records. Although he enjoyed major hits with **If We're Not Back In Love By Monday** (1977), **I'm Always On A Mountain When I Fall** (1978) and **The Way I Am** (1980), it was not altogether a successful took off like a rocket in 1955, with the success of **Rock Around The Clock** and later **Shake, Rattle And Roll**, turning him into an international superstar overnight.

Haley had led bands which pretty much describe their musical approach – Bill Haley And The Four Acres Of Western Swing, Bill Haley And The Saddle Pals – before attempting to fuse the then all-black sound of R&B with that of swing, western and country music. The result met such a phenomenal reaction that it vaulted him out of the ranks of country into the ranks of rock, never to return.

It is more than significant, however, that until that turning point his roots and approach had been firmly – if experimentally – country, a trait he shared with many of rock's originators. Having become the first real star of rock'n'roll, Bill died in his sleep on February 9, 1981 at home in Harlingen, Texas.

Recommended:
Greatest Hits (MCA/MCA)
Rock The Joint (–/Roller Coaster)
Golden Country Origins (–/Australian Grass Roots)
Hillbilly Haley (–/Rollercoaster)

Tom T. Hall

The 'Mark Twain' of country music – even his band is called the Storytellers – Tom T. Hall's songs are full of colourful characters and intriguing or humorous situations. Born in Olive Hill, Kentucky, on May 25, 1936, the son of a preacher, he first learned to play on a broken Martin guitar, which his father, the Reverend Virgil L. Hall, restored to working order.

At the age of 14, Tom T. quit school and went to work in a clothing factory, two years later forming his first band, the Kentucky Travelers, playing local dates and appearing on radio station WMOR, Morehead, Kentucky. After the band broke up, Hall continued with WMOR as a DJ for a period of five years.

After enlistment in the US Army in 1957, Hall was posted to Germany, where he worked on the AFN radio network, taking the opportunity to try out a number of his own compositions – with some success. Discharged in 1961, he returned to WMOR, also working with the Technicians, another local band.

More stints as a DJ followed, during which time Hall penned **DJ For A Day**, a major hit for Jimmy Newman in 1963. Next, Dave Dudley scored with **Mad** (1964), another Hall composition, and Hall promptly moved to Nashville to begin supplying songs to such acts as Roy Drusky, Stonewall Jackson and Flatt And Scruggs, eventually having his own hit disc with **I Washed My Face In The Morning Dew**, a release on the Mercury label in 1967.

A year later, Jeannie C. Riley recorded **Harper Valley PTA** – a brilliant and highly commercial song about a fast-living woman and a band of small-town hypocrites – and Hall became the writer of a million-seller.

During the early '70s he became something of a star performer, sending the audience and press into raptures at his 1973 Carnegie Hall concert. Record buyers readily snapped up such Hall releases as: **The Ballad Of Forty Dollars** (1968); **A Week In A County Jail** (1969); **The Year That Clayton Delaney Died** (1971); **Old Dogs, Children And Watermelon Wine**,

Above: Tom T. Hall: "People who write songs are often as equally amazed by them as those who listen to them."

Ravishing Ruby (both 1973); **I Love, That Song Is Driving Me Crazy**, **Country Is** (all 1974); **I Care** (1975); and **Faster Horses** (1976), all chart-toppers from Nashville's prime yarn spinner.

His albums include **Songs Of Fox Hollow**, which Hall described as 'an LP of songs for children of all ages', and **The Magnificent Music Machine**, a bluegrass collection that spawned a popular single in **Fox On The Run** (a Tony Hazzard song which had been a 1969 pop chartbusters for Manfred Mann).

In 1977, Hall signed with RCA Records. Although he recorded some fine singles such as **What Have You Got To Lose** (1978), **The Old Side Of Town** (1979) and **Soldier Of Fortune** (1980), his record

sales slumped quite dramatically. At this point he took time off from performing to write books, resulting in the best-seller, 'The Storyteller's Nashville', and became host of the syndicated TV show 'Pop Goes The Country'.

On returning to the studio, a link-up with bluegrass musician Earl Scruggs led to the acclaimed album, **The Storyteller And The Banjoman** (1982). This stunning set mixed traditional country songs with contemporary tunes. Hall's laconic vocal style worked perfectly with Scruggs' fluid banjo work. the success of this album led to Hall rejoining Mercury Records, and his career took off again with the top-selling singles **Famous In Missouri** (1984) and **P.S. I Love You** (1985). Hall has also built a reputation as a novelist with the publication of 'The Laughing Man Of Woodmont Cove' and 'Spring Hill', while 'The Songwriter's Handbook' is of more interest to keen country music fans.

Recommended:
Homecoming (Mercury/Mercury)
I Witness Life (Mercury/Bear Family)
The Storyteller (Mercury/Mercury)
Songs Of Fox Hollow (Mercury/–)
Country Classics (–/Phillips)
The Magnificent Music Machine (Mercury/–)
Ol' T's In Town (RCA/RCA)
Places I've Done Time (RCA/RCA)
Everything From Jesus To Jack Daniels (Mercury/Mercury)
Music Man's Dreams (–/Range)

Wendell Hall

Although he was by no means a true country entertainer, it was Hall's hillbilly-like recording of **It Ain't Gonna Rain No Mo'**, a 1923 million-seller, that

We All Got Together And . . . , Tom T. Hall. Courtesy Mercury Records.

encouraged Victor to embark on a search for possible country hitmakers.

Born in St George, Kansas, on August 23, 1906, Hall attended the University of Chicago and, after military service during World War I, began touring in vaudeville, singing and playing ukelele. Known as the 'Red-Headed Music-Maker', Hall was a friend of Carson Robison. It was with Robison that he went to New York, where the pair recorded for Victor during the early '20s.

Director of many shows during the '30s, Hall was still active in the music business up to the time of his death in Alabama, on April 2, 1969.

The writer of such songs as **My Carolina Rose** and **My Dream Sweetheart**, he frequently guested on the WLS National Barn Dance show.

20 Of The Best, George Hamilton IV. Courtesy RCA Records.

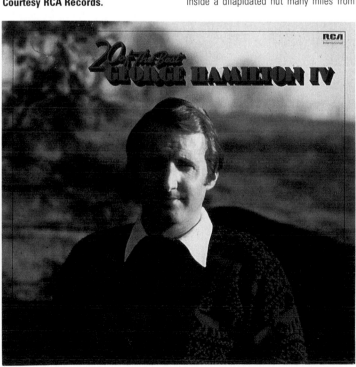

Stuart Hamblen

Born in Kellyville, Texas, on October 20, 1908, singer and bandleader Stuart Hamblen achieved considerable fame during the '50s as a songwriter. He attended the McMurray State Teachers College, Abilene, Texas in the '20s but later switched to a musical career, working and broadcasting in the California area, sometimes appearing in minor roles in western films.

In 1949, Hamblen had a Top 10 hit with a Columbia release, **But I'll Go Chasin' Women**, following this with **(Remember Me) I'm The One Who Loves You** a few months later.

An attempt to run for the Presidency of the United States, on a Prohibition Party ticket, proved a predictable failure in 1952, but in '54 he had more luck when his self-penned **This Ole House** (a song written after Hamblen had discovered a dead man inside a dilapidated hut many miles from the nearest habitation) became a country hit, prompting a million-selling cover version by Rosemary Clooney. This same song was later successfully revived by Shakin' Stevens, who topped the British charts with his updated rendition during the summer of 1981.

Hamblen, who was responsible for many other popular songs of the '50s, later turned increasingly to religious material, including the gospel standard **It Is No Secret (What God Can Do)**. Other Hamblen-penned classics include **My Mary** and **Texas Plains**, both of which first became popular in the early '30s. Stuart Hamblen died on March 8, 1989, following surgery on a brain tumor.

Canadian Pacific, George Hamilton IV. Courtesy RCA Records.

Recommended:
Cowboy Church (Word/Word)
A Man And His Music (Lamb & Lion/-)

George Hamilton IV

A pleasant-voiced vocalist who has gained tremendous popularity in Canada and England as well as his native country, George Hamilton IV was born on July 19, 1937 and raised in Winston Salem, North Carolina. Becoming a country music fan after watching Gene Autry and Tex Ritter films at Saturday matinees, he bought his first guitar at the age of 12, earning the necessary cash on a newspaper round.

He then began buying Hank Williams discs, and frequently caught the Greyhound bus out to Nashville, where he saw the Grand Ole Opry and met people like Chet Atkins, Eddy Arnold, Hank Snow and others. Later he began a high school band at Reynolds High, Winston Salem. In his senior year, he made a demo recording of Little Jimmy Dickens' **Out Behind The Barn**, and sent the results to talent scout Orville Campbell. Through Campbell, Hamilton met John D. Loudermilk and recorded his **A Rose And A Baby Ruth**, which sold over a million in 1956-57 when released by ABC-Paramount. A teen pop star, Hamilton found himself booked on Alan Freed's show during the autumn of 1956, also gaining a place on various package shows featuring Buddy Holly, Gene Vincent and the Everly Brothers.

Frustrated with his teeny-booper image, Hamilton moved to Nashville in 1959, scoring his first country Top 10 hit with **Before This Day Ends** (1960). He joined the Grand Ole Opry and signed to RCA Records in 1961, making it back into the Top 10 with the self-penned **If You Don't Know I Ain't Gonna Tell You** (1962). His first No.1 came with **Abilene** (1963), a John D. Loudermilk song, which also crossed over to pop. After scoring another Top 10 winner in **Fort Worth, Dallas Or Houston** (1964), Hamilton became influenced by the folk revival of the early '60s. Becoming friendly with Gordon Lightfoot in 1965, he began recording the Canadian's songs, making a Top 10 entry with **Early Morning Rain** (1966), and eventually recording more Lightfoot compositions than any other artist. Through this Canuck connection, he began to work more and more with Canadian writers and later signed with RCA's Canadian division. Prior to this he had more Nashville-produced Top 10 successes with **Urge For Going** (1967), **Break My Mind** (1968) and **She's A Little Bit Country** (1970), his last Top 20 entry coming with **Anyway** (1971).

He first visited England in 1967, en route to Nashville, following a tour of US bases in Germany. He did a guest spot on the BBC's Country Meets Folk programme, and later became a regular on many British programmes. He was booked several times for Mervyn Conn's Country Music Festival at Wembley. In Canada, Hamilton hosted his own TV show, North Country, for five years, while in 1977 he became signed to Anchor, a British record label, rejoining ABC-Dot for American releases only.

For several years he has been managed by Mervyn Conn in Britain, where George spends much of his time, and his recordings have been geared very much to the British market. However, he has

Bluegrass Gospel, George Hamilton IV. Courtesy Lamb & Lion Records.

remained a member of the Grand Ole Opry in Nashville. Known as the 'International Ambassador of Country Music', he was the first American country singer to perform in Russia and Czechoslovakia, where he recorded an album with Czech country group, Jiri Brabeck and Country Beat. He has also hosted successful country music festivals in Sweden, Finland, Norway, Holland and Germany.

A deeply religious person, in recent years George has undertaken several gospel tours throughout the British Isles. He has played mainly churches with 'themed' performances based on Thanksgiving, Easter or Christmas, all portrayed in an entertaining mix of music and bible readings. He has maintained a close association with country, touring with Slim Whitman and other country stars. He has participated in country music shows with his son, George Hege Hamilton V, who had a country hit with **She Says** (1988) and is popular around the British club circuit.

Recommended:
Bluegrass Gospel (Lamb & Lion/Lamb & Lion)
Canadian Pacific (RCA/RCA)
Country Music In My Soul (-/RCA)

Sunspots, and occasionally a host of distinguished Texas players. Some of these recordings have subsequently been reissued by Demon in England and Sugar Hill in America. An extensive traveller, Hancock has made a habit of touring Europe and Australia, playing his music and also indulging in his photography. He is an accomplished, published photographer, and, in addition to exhibiting shows of photographs and other visual arts, he spent much of his time as a video cameraman and producer of the regional show, 'Dixie Bar And Bus Stop' in the mid-80s. For four years he and associates taped some 150 episodes featuring over 100 artists and bands from Texas. In 1990 he recorded over 140 of his own original songs during a five-night run at Austin's Cactus Café. Then, during the following year, he started marketing the recordings on a 'No 2 Alike' tape on a tape-a-month mail-order basis. That year he also established his own gallery/retail outlet 'Lubbock Or Leave It', in Austin's downtown Brazos Street.

Music does play a major role in Hancock's life, but in the end it's all of a piece – his finely crafted songs, photos of faraway places, videos of honky-tonkers, displays of art. Like other idiosyncratic artists who don't fit into today's mass-marketing systems, Butch Hancock has figured out that he can do just as well by doing it all himself.

Recommended:
Own The Way Over Here (Sugar Hill/–)
Own And Own (Sugar Hill/Demon)
West Texas Waltzes And Dust Bowl
    Tractor Blues (Rainbow/Rainlight)

Arleen Harden

One-time secretary for an insurance company, Arleen Harden (born England, Arkansas, March 1, 1945) was part of the Harden Trio, a family group, whose **Tippy Toeing** charted for 21 weeks in 1966, gaining the trio Opry membership from 1966–68. During this time they supplied Columbia with other hits in **Seven Days Of Crying** (1966), **Sneakin' Across The Border** (1967) and **Everybody Wants To Be Somebody Else** (1968).

Arleen also became signed to the label as a solo artist, having a first hit with **Fairweather Lover** in 1967. Following the break up of the Harden Trio in '68 she enjoyed minor successes, **Lovin' Man** (1970) proving the most potent.

Following a stay with UA, Arleen later signed for Capitol, cutting a warm, easy-listening, Cam Mullins-arranged album, I **Could Almost Say Goodbye**, in 1975. She has since recorded for Elektra without too much success and spends much of her time working as a background vocalist on Nashville sessions.

Recommended:
Sings Roy Orbison (Columbia/–)
I Could Almost Say Goodbye (Capitol/–)

Linda Hargrove

A superior singer-songwriter and an outstanding guitarist (at least, Pete Drake and Mike Nesmith have said so), Linda

Famous Country Music Makers (–/RCA)
Travelin' Light (–/RCA)
Fine Lace And Homespun Cloth (Dot/
    Anchor)
Feel Like A Million (Dot/Anchor)
Songs For A Winter's Night (–/Ronco)
Music Man's Dream (–/Range)
George Hamilton IV (MCA-Dot/MCA)
American Country Gothic – with the Moody
    Brothers (Lamont/Conifer)
Easter In The Country (–/Word)

Butch Hancock

Born and raised in and around Lubbock, Texas, Butch Hancock is best known for his songwriting. Joe Ely, Emmylou Harris, Jerry Jeff Walker, the Texas Tornados, Alvin Crow and Jimmie Dale Gilmore are just a few who have recorded his songs. He has played a major role in the Texas music scene for more than twenty years. Although he was held in high esteem by other performers, gained write-ups in such

prestige publications as 'The New York Times', and released loads of recordings on various minor labels, no major record label has ever offered him a contract.

Butch started writing songs back in the heyday of the '60s folk movement. At the time he was driving a tractor for his father, an earth-moving contractor. He has favoured the Dylan/Guthrie guitar-and-harmonica set-up from the beginning, but it took a couple of false starts before he got serious about music. Even today music has to take its place alongside his many other projects. He attended architecture school at Texas Tech, studied arts and physics, and also pursued a photography course in San Francisco. In 1971 he joined up with Joe Ely, Jimmie Dale Gilmore, Steve Wesson and Tony Pearson in the Flatlanders, a short-lived folk-country outfit that recorded in Nashville and won a standing ovation at the 1972 Kerrville Folk Festival, then split up. A short stint doing construction work in Clarendon, Texas was followed by a move to Austin where he picked up on music and also undertook

other projects, including carpentry, photography and redesigning a train station in Seguin.

He formed his own Rainlight Records in 1978. Over the next ten years he released six albums and two cassettes, sometimes featuring his own simple guitar and harmonica, other times his band the

Great Country Hits, the Harden Trio. Courtesy Harmony.

Blue Kentucky Girl, Emmylou Harris. Courtesy WEA Records.

Gliding Bird, Emmylou Harris. A pirate version of Emmylou's debut album.

was born on February 3, 1950. She was raised in Tallahassee, Florida, where she took piano lessons at the age of five and moved on to become a French horn player in a high school band before getting bitten by the rock bug.

Influenced by Dylan's **Nashville Skyline**, she packed her bags and headed for Nashville in 1970. She hit hard times until Sandy Posey recorded one of her songs. Pete Drake, who sat in on the Posey session, then offered Linda a songwriting contract plus some session chores as a guitarist. Some time later, he taught her to handle the console at Drake's own studio.

An album featuring Linda was cut by Mike Nesmith for his ill-fated Countryside label but was never released. However, her songs met a better fate, Leon Russell employing two on his **Hank Wilson's Back** LP, Jan Howard, Billie Jo Spears, Melba Montgomery, David Rogers and many others also utilizing Linda's compositions on various recordings.

Since the abortive Nesmith dates, Linda has recorded for Elektra, cutting such albums as **Music Is Your Mistress** and **Blue Jean Country Queen**. After joining Capitol Records in 1975, she made a breakthrough to the singles chart with **Love Was (Once Around The Dance Floor)** (1975), and came up with the acclaimed album, **Love You're The Teacher**. Following a change of labels to RCA in 1978 and the release of two singles, Linda became a born-again Christian and no longer sings her secular material, devoting her life instead to her religious teachings.

Recommended:
Music Is Your Mistress (Elektra/–)
Impressions (Capitol/–)
Love You're The Teacher (Capitol/–)

Kelly Harrell

A country music pioneer who recorded as early as 1924 for Ralph Peer, then with Okeh Records, Crockett Kelly Harrell was born in Drapers Valley, Virginia, on September 13, 1899. A one-time rambler, he became a loom fixer in a mill around 1927, but also continued with a musical

career, making a number of important early records for Victor, including **Cuckoo, She's A Pretty Bird, New River Train, Rovin' Gambler, I Wish I Was Single Again, Charles Guiteau** and **The Butcher Boy**. Often accompanied by

banjo, fiddle and guitar, Harrell himself did not play an instrument.

Despite the success of his early records, and his songwriting efforts in two popular early songs, **Away Out On The Mountain** (as recorded by Jimmie Rodgers) and **The Story Of The Mighty Mississippi** (as recorded by Ernest Stoneman), his musical career was a brief one, and he ended his short life working in a Virginia factory. He died of a heart attack on July 9, 1942.

Recommended:
Kelly Harrell And The Virginia String Band (County/–)

Emmylou Harris

The 'First Lady' of contemporary country music, Emmylou was born in Birmingham, Alabama, on April 2, 1949. She turned country upside-down when she took the music back to its roots while still retaining a contemporary country-rock edge to her work. With the influence of Gram Parsons and his songs, she has been among those responsible for making country music acceptable to a wider audience.

Emmylou developed an early interest in country music. When her family moved to Washington DC in the mid-'60s she performed in local folk clubs and also in

Below: Through her Hot Band, Emmylou discovered and nurtured the careers of such stars as Rodney Crowell and Ricky Scaggs.

Greenwich Village, New York. Building up a reputation, she recorded a folksy album, **Gliding Bird**, for the Jubilee label in 1970, which featured some of her own songs plus others by Bob Dylan, Fred Neil and Hank Williams. The title song was penned by her first husband Tom Slocum. She was playing small clubs in Washington DC when Gram Parsons, who was looking for a female harmony singer, was urged to go and see her. Obviously impressed, he asked Emmylou to move to Los Angeles to work on his first solo album for Warner Brothers in 1972. After completing the recording of **GP**, Gram, Emmylou and the Fallen Angel Band embarked on a short tour. They then returned to the studio to start work on a second album. Parson's death occurred shortly after **Grievous Angel** was completed in 1973, the album becoming a

posthumous success and, in a way, paving the way for an Emmylou Harris solo career.

Emmylou had been close to Gram and was stunned by his death, and when she picked up the threads of her own career, it was to Gram's material that she turned. In 1975 she recorded **Pieces Of The Sky** for Reprise Records, an album which mixed country songs with some light rock'n'roll, and, although none of Gram's songs were included on this album, she was using his material in her act.

Pieces Of The Sky did not make a great impact, although her version of the Louvin Brothers' **If I Could Only Win Your Love** from the album did make the country Top 10 in 1975. But as Emmylou toured America and Europe her pure voice and impeccable backing band were to enchant listeners. She also has a fragile, Californian sort of beauty, and those who had admired her recorded work found that her stage act was everything they had hoped for. Over the years Emmylou's famous Hot Band, in all its various amalgamations has included such music greats as Ricky Skaggs, Tony Brown, Emory Gordy Jr, Glen D. Hardin, Albert Lee, Rodney Crowell and James Burton.

Her voice had a pure, innocent, classic quality and it lacked the nasal sound which so many non-country fans find hard to take. The second album, **Elite Hotel**, was released in 1976 and it featured three of Gram Parson's better compositions: **Wheels**, **Sin City** and **Ooh Las Vegas**. As usual, it was a well-balanced mix of country, ballads and rock. Emmylou's first No.1 came with **Together Again** in 1976, and further Top 10 entries followed with **One Of These Days** (1976), **Sweet Dreams** (a No.1 in 1976), **(You Never Can Tell) C'Est La Vie** (1977), **To Daddy** (1978) and **Two More Bottles Of Wine** (a No.1 in 1978).

Rodney Crowell proved himself a capable songwriter for her, having had a hand in **'Til I Gain Control Again**, **Leaving Louisiana In The Broad Daylight** and **Amarillo**. Ricky Skaggs, a fiddle player and mandolinist, brought a bluegrass influence to Emmylou's music and was largely responsible for the more traditional arrangements used on **Roses In The Snow**. This 1980 release finally brought recognition from a country audience and was to lead to Skaggs becoming a major country artist in his own right, and was also notable for being the first introduction many listeners had to the group the Whites, who, like Skaggs, became a top country act during the early '80s.

Always striving to vary her music, Emmylou had more Top 10 entries with **Save The Last Dance For Me** (1979) and **Beneath Still Waters** (No.1, 1980), as well as duet hits with Roy Orbison (**That Lovin' You Feelin' Again** in 1980) and Don Williams (**If I Needed You** in 1981). She almost certainly caught a lot of her fans unawares with her inventive re-workings of old pop songs like **Mister Sandman**, a pop and country hit in 1981. Throughout Emmylou's recordings, the greater the challenge the song provided the more inspired her performance became. She recorded such diverse material as Donna Summer's **On The Radio**, Jule Styne's **Diamonds Are A Girl's Best Friend**, Bruce Springsteen's **Racing In The Streets** and the early Presley classic, **Mystery Train**.

Up until the early '80s most of Emmylou's recordings were produced by Canadian Brian Ahern, her second husband. The final project they worked on was 1983's **White Shoes**, at which point Harris and Ahern separated, both personally and professionally. Emmylou had been working in the studio with British singer-songwriter Paul Kennerley on **The Legend Of Jesse James** concept album in 1982, and also recorded several of his songs. A relationship built, and, in 1985, Kennerley became Harris' third husband. Together they wrote and produced **The Ballad Of Sally Rose**, a superb, but commercially underrated concept album. Kennerley continued to produce her recordings and also provided some excellent song material, including **Born To Run** (Top 10 – 1982), **In My Dreams** (Top 10 – 1984) and **Heartbreak Hill**, which is, at the time of writing, Emmylou's last Top 10 entry, in 1989.

Emmylou and Kennerley separated in 1991, and around the same time the Hot Band ceased to exist. Emmylou formed a new band, the Nash Ramblers, an acoustic group comprising Sam Bush (fiddle, mandolin), Roy Huskey Jr (upright bass), Al Perkins (dobro, banjo, guitar), Jon Randall Stewart (mandolin, lead acoustic guitar) and Larry Mamaniuk (drums). She recorded a live album, **Emmylou Harris At The Ryman**, in 1991, which was also filmed for a TNN special in concert at the Ryman Auditorium in Nashville, the former home of the Grand Ole Opry. The album was not a commercial success and at the end of 1992 Emmylou was dropped by Reprise. The following year a new contract was signed with Asylum, which, like Reprise, is part of the large WEA group.

Emmylou Harris has discovered and nurtured some of the finest writers, singers and musicians of the past twenty years, and she exposed new audiences to standard songwriters. Emmylou Harris has always performed great music and continues singing and playing.

Recommended:
Pieces Of The Sky (Reprise/Reprise)
Elite Hotel (Reprise/Reprise)
Luxury Liner (Reprise/Reprise)
Quarter Moon In A Ten Cent Town (Warner Bros/Warner Bros)
Roses In The Snow (Warner Bros/Warner Bros)
Cimarron (Warner Bros/Warner Bros)
White Shoes (Warner Bros/Warner Bros)
The Ballad Of Sally Rose (Warner Bros/Warner Bros)
Thirteen (Warner Bros/–)
Blue Bird (Reprise/Reprise)
Brand New Dance (Reprise/Reprise)
Duets (Reprise/Reprise)
At The Ryman (Reprise/Reprise)

Freddie Hart

Born in Lockapoka, Alabama, on December 21, 1926, Hart is said to have run away from home at seven, becoming – amongst other things – a cotton picker, a sawmill worker, a pipeline layer in Texas and a dishwasher in New York.

By the age of 14, he had become a Marine, three years later helping to take Guam, having already been to Iwo Jima and Okinawa. A physical fitness expert and the possessor of a black belt in karate, he taught this form of self defence at the LA Police Academy in the '50s, eventually moving into the music business with the aid of Lefty Frizzell with whom he worked until 1953 when Hart signed a recording contract with Capitol.

Please Don't Tell Her, Freddie Hart. Courtesy Pickwick Records.

He subsequently recorded for Columbia (having his first hit in 1959 with **The Wall**), Monument and Kapp throughout the mid-'60s, logging around a dozen chart entries, becoming a major artist after re-signing for Capitol in 1969 and having a million-selling single, **Easy Loving** (1971), which won CMA Song Of The Year.

For the next few years Hart enjoyed a run of success, most of his singles claiming Top 5 status: **My Hang Up Is You**, **Bless Your Heart**, **Got The All Overs For You** (all 1972), **Super Kind Of Woman**, **Trip To Heaven** (1973), **If You Can't Feel It**, **Hang On In There Girl**, **The Want To's** (1974), **The First Time** (1975) and **Why Lovers Turn To Strangers** (1977) were just a few of his major hits.

In 1980 he joined the small Sunbird label and scored minor hits with **Roses**

Mark Twang, John Hartford. Courtesy Sonet Records.

Are Red (1980) and **You Were There** (1981). However, in recent years he has slipped in popularity. Now extremely wealthy, Hart owns many acres of plum trees, a trucking company and over 200 breeding bulls, and runs a school for handicapped children.

Recommended:
Easy Loving (Capitol/–)
That Look In Her Eyes (Capitol/–)
The Pleasure's Been All Mine (Capitol/Capitol)
Only You (Capitol/–)
The First Time (Capitol/–)
Greatest Hits (Capitol/–)
My Lady (Capitol/Capitol)

John Hartford

This banjoist, fiddler, guitarist, singer-songwriter is one of the most exciting solo entertainers in country music today. Born in New York, on December 30, 1937, but

Iron Mountain Depot, John Hartford. Courtesy RCA Records.

raised in St Louis by his doctor father and painter mother, he first learnt to play on a banjo which he claims was beaten-up and had no head. By the time he was 13 he had also mastered fiddle and played at local square dances; next he graduated to the dobro, then on to guitar.

Upon leaving school, he worked as a sign painter, a commercial artist, a deckhand on a Mississippi riverboat and as a disc jockey. After marriage and the birth of a son, Hartford headed for Nashville, becoming a session musician. His work on these sessions gained him a recording contract with RCA, for whom he cut eight albums and several singles, the first of which was **Tall Tall Grass**, a single released in 1966.

Soon many acts began recording Hartford's songs, and one, **Gentle On My Mind**, from his 1967 **Earthwords And Music** album, became a million-seller when covered by Glen Campbell. It entered the charts in both July 1967 and September 1969, winning three Grammies in the process and becoming the most recorded song of the period.

After appearances on the Smothers Brothers Comedy Hour and a regular spot on the Glen Campbell Goodtime Hour, Hartford toured with his own band for a while but eventually opted to become a solo performer. His 1976 **Mark Twang** album presents him in this role, unaccompanied by any rhythm section, Hartford providing all the percussive sounds with his mouth and feet!

An entertaining performer who utilizes his own songs and those drawn from the traditions of country music, he often performs at bluegrass festivals and plays and records with bluegrass musicians. Due to his keen sense of humour and natural entertaining skills he has been a regular guest on TV shows.

Recommended:
The Love Album (RCA/–)
Aero Plain (Warner Bros/Warner Bros)
Mark Twang (Flying Fish/Sonet)
Nobody Knows What You Do (Flying Fish/Sonet)
All In The Name Of Love (Flying Fish/Sonet)
Slumbering On The Cumberland (Flying Fish/–)
Down On The River (Flying Fish/–)

Hawkshaw Hawkins

Another victim of the plane crash that killed Patsy Cline and Cowboy Copas, Harold Hawkins was born in Huntingdon, West Virginia, on December 22, 1921. A

guitarist at the age of 15, he then won a local amateur talent show, the prize being a $15 a week spot on radio station WSAZ.

By the time of Pearl Harbor, Hawkins had established himself as a radio personality, but he then enlisted. By 1946 he was home again and singing on WWVA, Wheeling, West Virginia. Then came a recording contract with King and hit records in **I Wanted A Nickel** (1949) and **Slow Poke** (1951), plus a country classic in **Sunny Side Of The Mountain**.

Despite some recordings for RCA and a 1955 contract with the Grand Ole Opry, Hawkins enjoyed no further chart success until 1959, when Columbia single **Soldier's Joy** climbed high in the country list. Four years later – he was at this time married to Jean Shepard – his first country No.1 came with the release of **Lonesome 7-7203**. But on March 5, 1963, just two days after the disc had entered the charts, Hawkins was lying dead among the aircraft wreckage near Kansas.

Recommended:
16 Greatest Hits (Gusto/–)
Hawk 1953–1961 (–/Bear Family)

Below: Ronnie Hawkins' band the Hawks became Bob Dylan's backing band, and then evolved into the Band, but without Ronnie.

The All New Hawkshaw Hawkins. Courtesy London Records.

Ronnie Hawkins

Country rock'n'roller Ronnie was born on January 10, 1935 in Huntsville, Madison County, Arkansas and came from a country music background. He formed his first band while still in his teens, playing 'hopped-up hillbilly' music.

During the '50s he developed into a fully fledged rockabilly performer with his group the Hawks, who later went on to play with Bob Dylan and became the Band, the successful rock band of the late '60s.

Ronnie landed a contract with Roulette Records in 1958 and the following year enjoyed success on the American pop charts with **Mary Lou, 40 Days** and **Who Do You Love?**. Unlike most of the '50s rock'n'rollers, Ronnie has never changed his style to easy-listening pop or country music but has continued to perform genuine rock'n'roll, mainly in Canada, where he has lived since the early '60s.

Recommended:
Sings Songs Of Hank Williams (–/PRT)

George D. Hay

Founder of the Grand Ole Opry, George Dewey Hay (born Attica, Indiana, November 9, 1895) was once a reporter for the Memphis Commercial Appeal. Shortly after World War 1, while on an assignment in the Ozarks, he attended a mountain cabin hoedown, and conceived the idea of country music's most famous showcase.

When the Appeal moved into radio, setting up station WMC, Hay became radio editor. Later, in 1924, he took up an appointment on Chicago station WLS. With WLS he helped begin the National Barn Dance. This success led to the position of director with the new WSM, Nashville, in 1925.

By the end of the '60s Roy was very much a pop has-been and was finding his music more closely aligned with country. He signed to Mega Records in Nashville and scored a minor hit with Mickey Newbury's **Baby's Not Home** (1974). A move to Shannon Records led to his biggest hit, **The Most Wanted Woman In Town** (1975).

This resulted in a move to the major labels, beginning with ABC-Dot, for whom he had further hits with **The Door I Used To Close** (1976) and **Come To Me** (1977). Next came Elektra and success with **In Our Room** (1979) and **The Fire Of Two Old Flames** (1980). Since then Roy has recorded with a number of smaller labels including Churchill, NSD and Avion without exactly setting the charts on fire.

Recommended:
Ahead Of His Time (ABC-Dot/–)
The Many Sides Of Roy Head
   (Elektra/–)

Bobby Helms

A cross-over performer, Helms had a Top 10 pop hit with **Jingle Bell Rock** in 1957, the same year that he was adjudged the nation's leading country singer by Cashbox magazine.

Born in Bloomington, Indiana, on August 15, 1933, guitarist, singer-songwriter Helms appeared on radio at the age of 13, making his debut on the Grand Ole Opry four years later. In 1957, he achieved a No.1 country hit with **Fraulein**, the disc remaining in the charts for a whole year. His version of Jimmy Duncan's **My Special Angel** became both a country and pop hit, selling over a million copies.

The impetus was maintained throughout 1958, with **Jacqueline** (from the film 'A Case Against Brooklyn') and **Just A Little Lonesome** providing him with best-sellers.

But, despite constant seasonal reappearances by **Jingle Bell Rock** (which took five years to become a million-seller), Helms' recording career faded

All New Just For You, Bobby Helms. Courtesy Little Darlin' Records.

rapidly. Between 1960 and 1967 his name was absent from the charts, but later he achieved a series of mini hits on such labels as Little Darlin' and Certon, as he drifted in and out of the business.

Recommended:
My Special Angel (–/President)
Sings His Greatest Hits (Power Pak/–)
My Special Angel (Vocalion/–)
Fraulein – The Decca Years, 1956–1962
   (Harmony/Bear Family)

John Hiatt

Vocalist, guitarist and composer Hiatt was born in Indianapolis in 1952. Early albums **Hangin' Around The Observatory** and **Overcoats** were cut in Nashville where the artist maintains a steady workload with his writing and performing.

An unsuccessful stint in East Coast folk clubs was followed by employment with Ry Cooder's back-up band, where Hiatt played guitar and featured on a trio of Cooder albums, including **Borderline**, **Slide Area** and **The Border**.

His own recorded work was not commercially successful until Rosanne Cash cut Hiatt's **The Way We Make A Broken Heart** in 1987, which achieved prominence in the US country chart. Hiatt then formed a permanent band, the Goners, who cut **Slow Turning** and **Stolen Moments** for A&M Records.

Recommended:
Overcoats (Epic/–)
Two Bit Monsters (MCA/–)
All Of A Sudden (Geffen/–)
Warming Up The Ice Age (Geffen/–)
Bring The Family (A&M/Demon)
Slow Turning (A&M/–)
Y'All Caught (Geffen/–)
Stolen Moments (A&M/–)

Highway 101

A 'manufactured' group, Highway 101 gave country music a definite harder edge in the late '80s as they rose above the hype to produce some of the most refreshing

Again he instigated a similar Barn Dance programme, the first broadcast taking place on November 28, 1925, although it did not become a regularly scheduled programme until December of that year. The show rapidly grew in quality and popularity.

It was on December 10, 1927, that the WSM Barn Dance became officially retitled Grand Ole Opry. The show had been preceded by a programme featuring the NBC Symphony Orchestra and, after an introductory number by DeFord Bailey, Hay, who announced the show, declared: "For the past hour we have been listening to music taken from Grand Opera – but from now on we will present the Grand Ole Opry." And so the Opry it became.

Hay, known as the Solemn Old Judge, continued to expand and develop the Opry throughout the rest of his career, extending the range of WSM's broadcasts, encouraging the best country entertainers in the country to appear in Nashville, and recruiting new talent to keep the show both vital and fresh. However, he began to show some signs of mental instability, and in 1951 he retired to live with his daughter in Virginia and died at Virginia Beach,

Above: The man who named the Grand Ole Opry – George D. Hay.

Virginia on May 9, 1968, having been elected to the Country Music Hall Of Fame in 1966.

Roy Head

A rock'n'roll-based country singer, Roy was born on January 9, 1943, in Three Rivers, Texas. He started out in the early '60s with his own band, the Traits, reworking old rock'n'roll songs in clubs across Texas.

A recording contract with New York's Scepter Records in 1964 proved to be a failure, so Roy returned to Texas and joined the small Back Beat label, making a breakthrough with the R&B-styled **Treat Her Right**, which reached the Top 3 on the American pop charts towards the end of 1965.

Further pop success followed with **Apple Of My Eye** and **To Make A Big Man Cry** (both 1966), which led to Scepter re-releasing his singles from 1964 resulting in **Just A Little Bit** making the Top 40.

CHRIS HILLMAN CLEAR SAILIN'

順調航行

group also included Bernie Leadon and Kenny Wertz. Then came the Hillmen, which included Vern and Rex Gosdin. Later he had careers with several well-known bands where he was often underrated.

During a stint with the Byrds, Hillman (with Gram Parsons' support) urged the folk-rock group to make a country LP, **Sweetheart Of The Rodeo**, the pioneering country-rock album of 1968. Chris and Gram left the band soon afterwards, developing their country-rock ideas into the Flying Burrito Brothers.

Throughout the '70s, Chris worked with various country-rock outfits such as Manassas (with Steve Stills), the Souther-Hillman-Furay Band (with J.D. Souther and Richie Furay), Firefall (with Rick Roberts) and McGuinn, Clark And Hillman (with Roger McGuinn and Gene Clark).

In the early '80s Chris started to make his mark as a solo performer with a Sugar Hill Records contract. Two albums resulted, **Morning Sky** and **Desert Rose**, which neatly blended his country and bluegrass roots with rock. Scoring a minor country hit with **Somebody's Back In Town** (1984), he started building a bigger following and also worked regularly as a background vocalist and instrumentalist on recordings by Linda Ronstadt, Dan Fogelberg, John Denver and many other contemporary country acts. In 1989 he teamed up for a short period with former Byrds' members Dave Crosby and Roger McGuinn, and, with McGuinn, enjoyed a Top 10 country hit with a revival of the Byrds' **You Ain't Going Nowhere** (1989). However, Hillman remains totally committed to his highly successful Desert Rose Band, which he formed in 1986. This has finally given him the recognition he has worked towards so steadily for the past 30 years.

Recommended:
Desert Rose (Sugar Hill/Sundown)
Morning Star (Sugar Hill/Sundown)
Clear Sailin' (Asylum/Asylum)

Buddy Holly

One of rock's prime movers in its early years, Buddy Holly actually began his career as a country singer, and the sound

country-rock. They picked up a 1988 CMA award for Best Group.

The brainchild of respected band manager Chuck Morris, Highway 101 had been 'assembled' to fulfil a need for a group that could play 'traditional country with a rock'n'roll backbeat'. Two years in the planning stage, Morris initially recruited session-player Scott 'Cactus' Moser to play drums, who brought in bassist Curtis Stone (the son of the legendary Cliffie Stone) and lead guitarist Jack Daniels. The final piece of the jigsaw fell in place when Minnesota-born singer-songwriter Paulette Carlson was brought into the picture. Morris heard some demos that Paulette had made in Nashville, and knew he had found the right front-person for his fledgling outfit. He negotiated a singles deal with Warner Brothers, but without all the publicity in place, the initial single **Some Find Love** (released in late 1986) failed to make any impact.

A second single, **The Bed You Made For Me**, a Carlson original, hit the country Top 5, and Highway 101 were signed to a full contract by Warners. Then the hits really flowed, with: **Whiskey, If You Were A Woman, Somewhere Tonight** (No.1, 1988), **All The Reasons Why, Setting Me Up, Honky Tonk Heart** and **Who's Lonely Now** (No.1, 1989). The band definitely discovered a winning formula, initially creating their own unique sound, which other acts started to 'duplicate'. Acclaim and praise was heaped on them; they undertook extensive roadwork and even played the New York Ritz to a wildly enthusiastic sell-out audience! Discontent started to creep into

the group in 1990 when the three guys realized Paulette was attracting most of the attention and calling the shots. Paulette then left to pursue a solo career.

After listening to hundreds of demo tapes and sitting through extensive auditions, Nashville-based Nikki Nelson was chosen as new lead singer. She had performed in her father's band since the age of 12, and at the time was working as a waitress at the Nashville Palace. With Nikki upfront, the Highway 101 sound changed. There were more upbeat songs and fewer ballads devoted to the pain and heartache of lost love. They scored a Top 20 entry with **Bing, Bang, Boom**, the title song from the first album to feature Nikki in 1991, but have since failed to crack the Top 10. Obviously country music fans have been slow to accept change, and there is a strong possibility that Highway 101 may never regain the enthusiastic following and chart success they enjoyed for that three-year period at the end of the '80s.

Recommended:
Highway 101 (Warner Bros/–)
Highway 101 2 (Warner Bros/–)
Bing Bang Boom (Warner Bros/–)
Paint The Town (Warner Bros/–)

Chris Hillman

For most of his musical career, Chris Hillman, who was born on December 4,

Nashville, Tennessee, Buddy Holly. Part of MCA's wonderful boxed set.

Clear Sailin', Chris Hillman. Courtesy WEA Records.

1944, in San Diego, California, has chosen to take a back seat, leaving the spotlight on others. However, he has been recognized as the musical backbone of each band he's participated in.

He played mandolin in his first group, the bluegrass-oriented Scotsville Squirrel Barkers, while still in high school. This

NASHVILLE, TENNESSEE
Changing all those changes

was never to leave him during his short but brilliant life; nor has the power of his songwriting seemed to diminish, as **That'll Be The Day**, **Everyday** and **It's So Easy** have all been pop and country hits in recent years.

Charles Hardin Holley (the 'e' in his last name was dropped only after he signed his first record contract) was born on September 7, 1936, in Lubbock, Texas, and grew up listening to the blues and Tex-Mex music as well as to Hank Williams and Bill Monroe. His first band, with longtime friend Bob Montgomery, tells the story of their musical approach; they were called Buddy and Bob: Western and Bop.

Holly's first professional session was, in fact, a country session for Decca, produced in Nashville by Owen Bradley early in 1956, and featured not Holly's own band, the Crickets, but a group of Nashville sidemen. However, the combination of slick Nashville sound and raw Texas rockabilly did not mix well and the records were not successful. It is ironic that Holly's great success came on Coral Records, a Decca subsidiary, after the parent label had dropped him.

His career as a rock star – although many country stations continued to play his records and many country fans continued to buy them – was brief and hectic, filled with hit records **Oh Boy!**, **Peggy Sue**, **Rave On**, **Fool's Paradise** and **Raining In My Heart**. It was on one of his hectic tours that he died in a plane crash on February 3, 1959.

His songs, his style, and his sidemen – Waylon Jennings, Tommy Allsup, Bob Montgomery and Sonny Curtis – have all left great marks on country music, and Holly was a genuine influence on country at this pivotal point in its history.

Recommended:
The Complete Buddy Holly (6 LP Box Set) (–/MCA)

Homer And Jethro

Both from Knoxville, Tennessee, Henry D. Haynes (Homer) was born July 29, 1917 and Kenneth C. Burns (Jethro) was born March 10, 1923. They formed a duo in 1932, the two boys winning a regular stop on station WNOX, Knoxville.

Discovering that their parodies gained more attention than their 'straight' material, they opted to become country comics, holding down a residency at Renfro Valley, Kentucky, until war service caused a temporary halt to their career. With Japan defeated, the duo re-formed, for a decade appearing as cast members of the National Barn Dance on Chicago WLS, also guesting on the Opry and many networked radio and TV shows.

Signed to RCA Records in the late '40s, they cut **Baby It's Cold Outside** with June Carter in 1948, obtaining later hits with **That Hound Dog In The Window** (1953), **Hernando's Hideaway** (1954), **The Battle Of Kookamonga** (1959) and **I Want To Hold Your Hand** (1964). The duo also recorded a number of instrumental albums (Haynes on guitar, Burns on mandolin), at one time teaming with Chet Atkins to form a recording group known as the Nashville String Band.

The 39-year-old partnership terminated on August 7, 1971, with the death of Henry Haynes, but Burns continued with his musical career. A brilliant mandolinist, he became involved with country-jazz, playing almost in Django Reinhardt fashion. Following a short illness, Burns died on February 4, 1989.

Recommended:
Country Comedy (–/RCA)
The Far Out World Of Homer & Jethro (RCA/–)
Assault The Rock 'n' Roll Era (–/Bear Family)

Jethro Burns solo:
Jethro Burns (Flying Fish/–)
Back To Back – with Tiny Moore (Kaleidoscope/–)

The Hoosier Hot Shots

Frank Kettering, banjo, guitar, flute, piccolo, bass, piano; Hezzie Triesch, song whistle, washboard, drums, alto horn; Kenny Triesch, banjo, tenor guitar, bass horn; Gabe Ward, clarinet.

"Are you ready, Hezzie?" always signalled the arrival of the Hoosier Hot Shots on the National Barn Dance, a first-rate group of comedians and musicians who had one of the most popular novelty acts in the country before Spike Jones came along.

They started out as a small dance band but their flair for comedy and unusual instruments got the better of them. When they joined WLS in 1935 it was as a novelty group, and their success was immediate. They appeared in many films both with and without other Barn Dance cast members, and retired to California.

Their records (for the ARC complex of labels and Vocalion) did well, but they were primarily a visual comedy act.

Doc Hopkins

Doctor Howard Hopkins – yes, that is his real name – was born on January 26, 1899 in Harlan County, Kentucky. He was associated for a long time (1930–49) with station WLS and the National Barn Dance.

During that period he became well known as one of the best and most authentic of American folk singers.

Although he spent a great deal of time on WLS and has recorded for many labels (including Paramount, Decca and others), he has somehow never received the recognition as a a country music pioneer that he richly deserves.

Johnny Horton

With **Battle Of New Orleans**, a Jimmie Driftwood song said to be based on an old fiddle tune known as **The 8th Of January**, Horton achieved one of the biggest selling discs of 1959. A cover version by skiffle king Lonnie Donegan became a Top 5 record in Britain.

Born in Tyler, Texas, on April 3, 1925, Horton went to college in Jacksonville and Kilgore, Texas, later attending the University of Seattle in Washington. Spending some time in the fishing industry in Alaska and California, he then became a performer under the title of the Singing Fisherman, when he began starring on Shreveport's Louisiana Hayride during the mid-'50s.

Completing recording stints with both Mercury and Dot, he moved on to Columbia, his first hit being with **Honky Tonk Man** (1956) and his first country No.1 with **When It's Springtime In Alaska** (1959).

Following the runaway success of the million-selling **Battle Of New Orleans**, Horton became a nationwide star, having hits with **Johnny Reb/Sal's Got A Sugar Lip** (1959) and **Sink The Bismarck** (1960). He was also asked to sing Mike Phillips' **North To Alaska** in the John Wayne film of that title, the resulting record providing the Texan with yet another million-seller in 1960.

On November 5, 1960, Horton was killed in a car accident while travelling to Nashville, but his records continued to sell throughout the '60s and his songs have been recorded by Claude King, Dwight Yoakam and many other country stars over

The Spectacular Johnny Horton. Courtesy Columbia Records.

the years. In fact, Claude King recorded a tribute album to Johnny in the late '60s, and in 1983 a biography entitled 'Your Singing Fisherman' was published.

Recommended:
Honky Tonk Man (Columbia/–)
Makes History (Columbia/–)
On Stage (Columbia/–)
Spectacular (Columbia/–)
Greatest Hits (–/CBS)
Rockin' Rollin' (–/Bear Family)
America Remembers (CSP-Gusto/–)

David Houston

A direct descendant of Sam Houston and Robert E. Lee, Houston was born in Shreveport, Louisiana, on December 9, 1938.

Brought up in Bossier City, where he was taught guitar by his aunt, Houston was aided in his career by his godfather Gene Austin (a pop singer who had 1920s million-sellers with **My Blue Heaven** and **Ramona**).

By the age of 12, Houston had won a guest spot on Shreveport's famed Louisiana Hayride radio show, later joining the cast as a regular member. During his teens he had completed college, then, in the late '50s, began touring avidly, appearing on many TV and radio shows.

Signed to Epic in 1963, he gained an instant hit with **Mountain Of Love** which stayed in the charts for 18 weeks, winning Houston Most Promising Country Newcomer plaudits from magazines.

An accomplished yodeller and a talented guitarist-pianist, Houston went from strength to strength throughout the '60s, having No.1 hits with **Almost Persuaded** (1966), **With One Exception** (1967), **You Mean The World To Me** (1967), **My Elusive Dreams** (1968) and **Baby, Baby (I Know You're A Lady)** (1969), winning two Grammy awards for **Almost Persuaded** and earning a part in a 1967 film, 'Cottonpickin' Chickenpickers'.

During the early '70s, Houston's discs continued to chart regularly. Top 10 contenders were: **I Do My Swinging At Home** (1970), **After Closing Time** (with Barbara Mandrell, 1970), **Wonders Of The Wine** (1970), **A Woman Always Knows** (1971), **Soft Sweet And Warm** (1972), **Good Things** (1973) and **She's All Woman** (1973).

Since the mid-'70s David's decline has been rapid, as he has moved through a succession of labels, looking for the one song that might take him back into the Top 10. However, he has continued to work steadily, usually touring with his manager Tillman Franks, who also doubles as David's guitarist when he appears with a pick-up band.

Recommended:
Best Of Houston And Mandrell (Epic/–)
Day Love Walked In (Epic/–)
A Perfect Match – with Barbara Mandrell (Epic/–)
A Man Needs Love (Epic/–)
From The Heart Of Houston (Derrick/–)
From Houston To You (Excelsior/–)
American Originals (Columbia/–)

Harlan Howard

An outstanding performer, Howard (born Lexington, Kentucky, September 8, 1929) has generally preferred to remain a songwriter, picking up numerous awards, and running his Wilderness Music Publishing Company. Raised in Detroit, he began songwriting at the age of 12. Spending four years in the paratroops following high school, he became based in Fort Benning, Georgia, spending his weekends in Nashville.

Later, in Los Angeles, he met Tex Ritter and Johnny Bond who began publishing his songs, hits emerging with **Pick Me Up On Your Way Down** (Charlie Walker, 1958), **Mommy For A Day** (Kitty Wells, 1959) and **Heartaches By The Number** (Ray Price and Guy Mitchell, 1959). In 1960, Howard moved to Nashville with his wife, singer Jan Howard, where he became known as the 'king' of country songwriters, a title only challenged perhaps by Dallas Frazier and Bill Anderson.

His many songs have included: **I've Got A Tiger By The Tail**, **Under The Influence Of Love**, **A Guy Named Joe**, **Streets Of Baltimore**, **Heartbreak USA**, **Busted**, **No Charge**, **I Fall To Pieces** and **Three Steps To The Phone**.

As a recording artist, he has cut albums for Monument, RCA and Nugget.

Jan Howard

The daughter of a Cherokee maid and an Irish immigrant, Jan was born in West Plains, Missouri on March 13, 1932, acquiring her present surname after marriage to songwriter Harlan Howard.

An avid country music record collector early on, her first public performance came as a result of a meeting with Johnny Cash, a tour with Johnny Horton and Archie Campbell ensuing.

At the close of the 1950s, she began recording for the Challenge label, her first release being **Yankee Go Home**, a duet with Wynn Stewart. This followed with **The One You Slip Around With**, a 1960 hit that won her several awards in the Most Promising Newcomer category.

In the wake of recordings for such labels as Capitol and Wrangler, she moved to

Rock Me Back To Little Rock, Jan Howard. Courtesy MCA Records.

Nashville during the mid-'60s, there signing for Decca Records, and teaming with Bill Anderson as a featured part of his road and TV shows. With Anderson she cut a number of hit duets that included **I Know You're Married** (1966), **For Loving You** (a 1967 No.1), **If It's All The Same To You** (1969), **Someday We'll Be Together** (1960) and **Dissatisfied** (1971).

Proving similarly successful as a solo act, a score or so of her releases attained chart status, the most prominent of these being **Evil On Your Mind** (1966), **Bad Seeds** (1966), **Count Your Blessings, Woman** (1968) and **My Son** (1968), the last a self-penned tribute to her son Jim, who died in Vietnam just two weeks after the song had been recorded.

Following the tragic death of the second of her three sons, Jan opted for retirement during the early '70s. However, she later joined the Carter Family appearing on Johnny Cash's road show, and in 1985 she recorded her first album in many years when she signed with the reactivated MCA-Dot.

Recommended:
Rock Me Back To Little Rock (Decca/–)
Sincerely (GRT/–)
Jan Howard (MCA-Dot/–)

Paul Howard

Although hot western swing on the stage of the staid Grand Ole Opry sounds a little far-fetched, that was exactly Paul Howard's role in the 1940s, the height of western swing's popularity. Born July 10, 1908 in Midland, Arkansas, Howard drifted in and out of music until 1940 when he joined the Opry as a solo singer.

Always entranced by western swing, he began to build a bigger and bigger band, which grew to some nine or ten pieces, sometimes with multiple basses to make up for the lack of drums which were then still taboo on the Opry stage. His band, the Arkansas Cotton Pickers, was one of the hottest of the era, and he recorded for Columbia and King.

Frustrated by the lack of attention western swing got in the Southeast, Howard left the Opry in 1949 for a circuit of radio programmes and dances in Louisiana, Arkansas and Texas.

For many years, Paul lived in Shreveport where he led a band playing dances. He died on June 18, 1984 in Little Rock, Arkansas.

Con Hunley

Conrad Logan Hunley, born on April 9, 1946, Knoxville, Tennessee, the eldest of six children, found success in country music towards the end of the '70s with a run of Top 20 successes that started with **Week-end Friend**.

Country music's blue-eyed soul man grew up listening to the music of Lefty Frizzell and George Jones, but he switched to a soul-country sound modelled on Ray Charles' country-pop successes of the early '60s. He played with various local bands for a dozen years. In 1976 he put together his own group and landed a regular gig at the Village Barn in Knoxville.

Businessman Sam Kirkpatrick took an interest in Hunley's career, setting up a new record label, Prairie Dust, and paying for the singer to travel to Nashville and record. During 1976 and '77, Con enjoyed several minor hits on Prairie Dust including **Breaking Up Is Hard To Do** and **I'll Always Remember That Song**.

This led to the major record companies showing an interest and in 1978 he signed to Warner Bros with **Week-end Friend**

Above: Paul Howard and his Arkansas Cotton Pickers – a '40s western swing band.

(1978), beginning a run of Top 20 hits which included: **You've Still Got A Place In My Heart** (1978), **I've Been Waiting For You All My Life** (1979), **They Never Lost You** (1980), **She's Stepping Out** (1981) and **Oh Girl** (1982).

A short stint recording for MCA Records (1983–84) was followed by a contract with Capitol, which resulted in minor hits with **I'd Rather Be Crazy**, **All American Country Boy** (both 1985) and **What Am I Gonna Do About You** (1986).

Recommended:
As Any Woman (Warner Bros/–)
Oh Girl (Warner Bros/–)

Ferlin Husky

Born in Flat River, Missouri, on December 3, 1927, comedian-singer-songwriter-guitarist Husky grew up on a farm. It is claimed that his first attempt to own a guitar was foiled when the hen that he swopped it for failed to lay eggs, causing neighbours to cancel the deal.

He did, however, obtain a guitar at a later date. Following stints in the Merchant Marines and as a DJ, he began performing in the Bakersfield, California area using the name Terry Preston and eventually being discovered by Tennessee Ernie Ford's manager, Cliffie Stone, who asked Husky to deputize for Ford during a vacation period. About this time, Husky also created a character called Simon Crum, a kind of hick philosopher who became so popular that Capitol signed the singer to cut several sides as his alter ego.

Later, recording as Terry Preston, Husky had his first hit with **A Dear John Letter**, a duet recorded with Jean Shepard in 1953. Husky eventually obtained a minor hit under his own name with **I Feel Better all Over**. During 1957, he appeared on a Kraft TV theatre show playing a dramatic role. Also, in the same year, he recorded **Gone**, a remake of a Smokey Rogers' song originally cut by Husky in his Terry Preston era, this new version becoming a million-seller. By 1958 it was Crum's turn to become a chartbuster, a comedy song **Country Music Is Here To Stay** hitting the No.2 spot in the country listings. 1958 also saw Husky obtain a film role in

'Country Music Holiday', alongside Zsa Zsa Gabor and Rocky Graziano.

Since 1957 his long list of record hits has included **A Fallen Star**, **Wings Of A Dove** and **The Waltz You Saved For Me**, all cross-over successes, and **Once** and **Just For You**, both country Top 10 items. Father of seven children – the youngest being named Terry Preston in memory of Husky's earlier identity – the singer has made many radio, TV and film appearances and recorded for ABC during the early '70s. He tours with his group the Hush Puppies.

Recommended:
Ferlin Husky (MCA-Dot/–)
True True Lovin' (ABC/–)
Sings The Foster-Rice Songbook (ABC/–)
Country Sounds Of Ferlin Husky (–/Music For Pleasure)
Freckles And Polliwog Days (ABC/–)
Audiograph Live (Audiograph/–)

Alan Jackson

The most creatively consistent honky-tonker of the new breed of country performers, Alan Eugene Jackson was born October 17, 1959 in Newnan, Georgia.

Married by the time he was twenty, Jackson did everything from driving a forklift at K-Mart to waiting tables to fuel his addiction to cars and his love of country music. It was a chance meeting between his wife Denise (an airline stewardess) and

Above: Ferlin Husky's alter ego – Simon Crum, hick philosopher

Glen Campbell, who was waiting for a change of flights at Atlanta, that opened the first doors in Nashville. Campbell gave Jackson's wife a card and introduction to his music publishing company in Nashville. That encounter provided the impetus for Alan to move to Music City, where he

The Country Sounds Of Ferlin Husky. Courtesy MFP Records.

started making the right connections. He spent four years based in Nashville, writing songs and building a fan base by solid roadwork with his band, before the big break finally came.

New York-based rock label Arista Records decided to open a Nashville office and develop a country music roster. At the

same time Jackson, along with songwriter/producer Keith Stegall, completed some new demos, and, in 1989, Alan Jackson became the first country artist signed to Arista. His debut single, **Blue Blooded Woman**, made No.45 on the charts at the end of 1989. Jackson's career really took off the following year. **Here In The Real World**, a classic country love ballad, spent six months on the charts, reaching a peak of No.4. Further Top 10 entries came with **Wanted** and **Chasin' That Neon Rainbow**. His debut

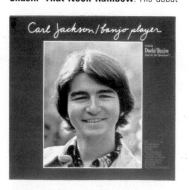

Banjo Player, Carl Jackson. Courtesy Capitol Records.

album, **Here In The Real World**, raced up both the country and pop charts, eventually reaching platinum status.

The hits have continued with amazing consistency, making No.1 with **I'd Love**

You All Over Again, **Don't Rock The Jukebox** and **Someday** (all 1991), **Dallas**, **Love's Got A Hold On You** and **Midnight In Montgomery** (all 1992). The latter, about a visit to Hank Williams' grave, is probably the best song he's written. His second album, **Don't Rock The Jukebox**, was more successful than his debut, rapidly going double platinum and leading to TV appearances.

A third album, **A Lot About Livin' (And A Little 'Bout Lovin')**, reached platinum status within seven weeks of release. It is now a certified double platinum, and total sales of Jackson's first three albums have exceeded six million in little more than three years. Another chart-topper came with **She's Got The Rhythm (And I Got The Blues)** and a Top 10 entry with **I Climbed The Wall** in 1993. Amazingly, Jackson has failed to pick up any of the major CMA awards. Writing and performing some of the most authentic-sounding country music around, Jackson's image is of a good-looking, straight-singing man who remains modest and unassuming. He has built his career gradually and sensibly, and is assured of being around for a long time, utilizing solid country values of the past, but with a fresh style and sound.

Recommended
Here In The Real World (Arista/Arista)
Don't Rock The Jukebox (Arista/–)
A Lot About Livin' And A Little 'Bout Love (Arista/–)

Carl Jackson

A fast-pickin' banjo and guitar player who was an integral part of the Glen Campbell Show, Jackson was born in Louisville, Kentucky, in 1953. He learned banjo at the age of five and at 13 began playing with a family bluegrass outfit. During his schooldays he toured as part of Jim And Jesse's band, cutting an album, **Bluegrass Festival**, for Prize Records during this period. In 1972, he learned that Larry McNeely, Campbell's banjoist, was leaving the group. McNeely then set up a meeting between Jackson and Campbell, the latter being so impressed by the 19-year-old's playing that he signed him as part of his touring show, producing Jackson's first solo album for Capitol, **Banjo Player** (1973).

Jackson stayed 12 years with Campbell, during this time cutting another album for Capitol and three for Sugar Hill. Then he split, opted for a true solo career, signed with Columbia, and in 1984 gained his first ever hit single with **She's Gone, Gone, Gone**, a Lefty Frizzell standard. He followed this with another mid-chart entry, **Dixie Train**, in 1985. In the late '80s, he teamed up with John Starling And The Nash Ramblers to produce the acclaimed **Spring Training** album for Sugar Hill.

Recommended:
Banjo Player (Capitol/Capitol)
Banjo Man – A Tribute To Earl Scruggs
   (Sugar Hill/–)
Banjo Hits (Sugar Hill/–)
Songs Of The South (Sugar Hill/-)

Stonewall Jackson's Greatest Hits. Courtesy CBS Records.

Stonewall Jackson

This is his real name; he was named after the Confederate general. Born in Tabor City, North Carolina, on November 6, 1932, Stonewall had an impoverished childhood and obtained his first guitar at the age of ten by trading an old bike. He figured out the chords by watching others and would listen to the radio, using what he heard as the basis for constructing his own songs.

By 1956, he had saved enough money to go to Nashville. Wesley Rose, head of Acuff Rose Publishing, heard him and signed him to a long-term contract. He was successful across the country via TV.

Up Against The Wall, Stonewall Jackson. Courtesy PRT Records.

Capitol Country Classics, Wanda Jackson. Courtesy Capitol Records.

In 1958 he had a big country hit with **Life To Go**. 1959 saw his monster cross-over smash **Waterloo**, an international pop hit in which a neat country backing was combined with novelty lyrics drawing military analogies to a love affair. As a result of the hit, he starred on Dick Clark's American Bandstand. Other Jackson-composed standards are **Don't Be Angry, Mary Don't You Weep** and **I Washed My Hands In Muddy Water**. In 1967 he came back strongly with **Stamp Out Loneliness** and also had a successful album based around the title.

Recommended:
At The Opry (Columbia/–)
Greatest Hits (Columbia/–)
American Originals (Columbia/–)

Wanda Jackson

Child prodigy Wanda Jackson was born Maud, in Oklahoma, on October 20, 1937, the daughter of a piano-playing barber. By the age of ten she could play both guitar and piano, three years later obtaining her own radio show. By 1954 she was cutting discs for Decca – charting with a Billy Gray-aided duet **You Can't Have My Love** – and she began touring with Hank Thompson's band. In 1955–56, Wanda toured with Elvis Presley, then became Capitol Records' leading female rocker, scoring heavily in the 1960 pop charts with **Let's Have A Party**. However, 1961 saw her return to more country-oriented fare – and her hits such as **Right Or Wrong** and **In The Middle Of A Heartache** went into both pop and country charts.

Throughout the '60s, Wanda racked up over a score of hits – even having a major success in Japan with the rocking **Fujiyama Mama** – and though her chart-

Make Me Like A Child, Wanda Jackson. Courtesy Myrrh Records.

busting continued into the '70s, in 1971 she asked for her release from Capitol. She switched to pure gospel music, cutting sides for the religious Word and Myrrh labels. Even so, Wanda can still easily be persuaded to revive her old rockabilly and country hits onstage.

Recommended:
The Best Of (Capitol/Capitol)
Capitol Country Classics (–/Capitol)
Early (–/Bear Family)

Sonny James

Sonny James is still thought of by many in terms of his pace-setting 1950s teen hit **Young Love** and there is no denying that his music has often been easily accessible to the MOR market.

Born in Hackleburg, Alabama, on May 1, 1929 (real name Jimmy Loden), into a showbiz family, he made his stage debut at the age of four, touring with his sisters after making his radio debut. He learned to play violin at seven, later becoming signed to a full-time contract with a Birmingham, Alabama, radio station. Following 15 months in Korea he returned home and pacted with Capitol Records, obtaining his first hit with **For Rent** in 1956, that same year recording **Young Love**, an eventual million-seller. After one more Top 10 entry, with the pop-slanted **First Date, First Kiss, First Love** (1957), he saw little chart action until 1963 when he scored with **The Minute You're Gone**. The song was successfully covered in Britain by Cliff Richard, which proves how suited James was to pop-oriented material.

During 1964, **Baltimore, Ask Marie** and **You're The Only World I Know** all charted for James, the last commencing an incredible run of Top 5 singles (most of them reaching the No.1 spot!) that extended well into the mid-'70s. After supplying one final No.1 hit, **That's Why I Love You Like I Do**, for Capitol in mid-1972, James switched to the rival Columbia label, claiming an immediate chart-topper with **When The Snow Is On The Roses**. He turned producer to fashion a hit record, **Paper Roses**, for Marie Osmond in 1973, and continued with his own flow of vinyl winners for a while, going to No.1 yet again with **Is It Wrong (For Loving You)** in 1974 and adding to his tally of Top 10 entries with **A Mi Esposa Con Amor** (1974), **A Little Bit South Of Saskatoon**, **Little Band Of Gold**, **What In The World's Come Over You** (1975), **When Something's Wrong With My Baby**, **Come On In** (1976), and **You're Free To Go** (1977). During this period he also made a couple of out-of-the-rut albums in **200 Years Of Country**

In Prison, In Person, Sonny James. Courtesy CBS Records.

Music (1976) and **In Prison, In Person** (1977), the latter produced by Tammy Wynette's husband George Richey inside Tennessee State Prison.

Since then, the career of the man known as the 'Southern Gentleman' has slowed right down, but he has been a remarkably consistent performer. He is capable of producing great licks on a number of instruments, and has even nudged his way into a number of minor films along the way, including 'Hillbilly In A Haunted House', a movie that also featured Lon Chaney and Basil Rathbone. In fact, the only thing he has missed out on is a CMA Award – which seems something of an oversight.

Recommended:
The Best Of (Capitol/Capitol)
Country Artist Of The Decade (Columbia/–)
200 Years Of Country Music (Columbia/CBS)
In Prison, In Person (Columbia/–)
American Originals (Columbia/–)

Waylon Jennings

A strong voice and a strong personality have enabled this charismatic man to aspire to country music's heights. From a modestly successful career as a mainstream country and folk-country artist, he became the definitive 'outlaw' figure, a man who, with Willie Nelson, spearheaded the movement away from orchestral blandness in country towards exciting, gritty, more personalized music.

Born in Littlefield, Texas, on June 15, 1937, the son of a truck-driver, Waylon could play guitar by this teens. He gained a DJ job on a Littlefield radio station at 12 and, although interested in pop in his teens, he had developed an interest in country by 21.

In 1958 he moved to Lubbock, working as a DJ there, and meeting Buddy Holly. In 1958–59 he toured as Holly's bassist. When Holly's plane crashed in 1959, killing the singer and two others, it was Waylon who, at the last moment, had given up his seat to J. P. Richardson, the 'Big Bopper' of **Chantilly Lace** fame.

In the early '60s, Waylon settled in Phoenix, Arizona, forming the Waylors to back him and becoming locally known at Phoenix's famous JD's club. Chet Atkins signed him to RCA in 1965 and the following year he moved to Nashville. He appeared on the Grand Ole Opry, made several TV appearances and also starred in the film 'Nashville Rebel'. But Waylon was to become more than just a celluloid rebel. Nashville was tightly business-minded, and artists had to work with certain staff producers. The label's own Nashville studios had to be used and so did an elite band of session musicians. Artists were not encouraged to record with their own bands and, consequently, much of the Nashville product sounded similar. Waylon, initially, conformed to this, chalking up an impressive list of Top 10 hits including **(That's What You Get) For Lovin' Me** (1966), **The Chokin' Kind** (1967), **Only Daddy That'll Walk The Line** (1968), **Yours Love** (1969), and **Brown Eyed Handsome Man** and **The Taker** (both 1970).

Waylon wanted to break out from this tight regime in order to direct his own material, musicians and production. He upset the RCA Nashville hierarchy by negotiating directly with the New York bosses.. He was guaranteed an

Will The Wolf Survive, Waylon Jennings. Courtesy MCA Records.

independent production package in which he would provide RCA with a number of sides each year for them to promote and sell. The big musical change for Waylon had already become apparent on the **Ladies Love Outlaws** album, where he at last succeeded in blending his own band, the Waylors, in with the regular session musicians, and picking some distinctive and evocative current song material. The Top 10 entries were now much more consistent, starting with **Good Hearted Woman** (1972) and continuing with **Sweet Dream Woman** and **Pretend I Never Happened** (also 1972), as well as **You Can Have Her** and **You Ask Me To** (both 1973).

Honky Tonk Heroes from 1973 proved an even bigger watershed. Waylon extensively plundered the repertoire of Billy Joe Shaver to come up with an album variously produced by himself, Tompall Glaser, Ronnie Light and Ken Mansfield, and featuring music sounding as hard and 'outlaw' as Waylon's reputation. His first No.1 came with **This Time** (1974), followed by **I'm A Ramblin' Man** (also 1974). He reached Top 10 with **Rainy Day Woman** and **Dreamin' My Dreams With You** in 1975. He made the pop charts with a double-sided single, **Are You Sure Hank Done It This Way/Bob Wills Is Still The King** in 1975. That same year he teamed up with Willie Nelson on a live version of **Good Hearted Woman**, which also hit No.1 in the country charts and crossed over to pop.

In 1976 he scored with **Suspicious Minds**, an evocative duet with his wife Jessi Colter. The previous year had seen him making an inroad into the CMA Awards by winning Male Vocalist Of The Year. But in 1976 **Suspicious Minds** involved Waylon in two awards, Duo Of The Year and Single Of The Year. He was also involved in Album Of The Year (**The Outlaws**), and it was evident that the new contemporary strain of country had finally gained official acceptance.

It was a period during which Jennings could do little wrong. In 1977, he had two No.1 singles in **Luckenbach, Texas (Back To The Basics Of Love)** and **The**

Wurlitzer Prize. In 1978 he came up with another chart-topping solo single, **I've Always Been Crazy**, and gained yet another by teaming with Willie Nelson for **Mammas, Don't Let Your Babies Grow Up To Be Cowboys**. Additionally the albums of identical titles also went to No.1 in their division, while a duet single with Johnny Cash, **There Ain't No Good Chain Gang** only just missed the top spot.

By 1979, grabbing No.1 singles had become almost routine. **Amanda** and **Come With Me** raised the total further, as did **I Ain't Living Long Like This** and **Good Ol' Boys**, Waylon's self-penned theme to the TV series The Dukes Of Hazzard in 1980. A **Greatest Hits** compilation also proved a popular seller. When the sales were added up they amounted to three million. There were no No.1s in 1981, although **Shine** climbed into the Top 5 and a couple of duets with Jessi Colter also sold well. Nevertheless, with the help of duet partner Willie Nelson, he returned to his chart-topping ways with **Just To Satisfy You** during 1982, following this with a solo effort, **Lucille (You Won't Do Your Daddy's Will)** in 1983.

Waylon provided further No.1 hits for RCA with **Never Could Toe The Mark** and **America** (both 1984), **Waltz Me To Heaven** and the superb **Drinkin' And Dreamin'** (1985), which came from the album called **Turn The Page**. The album also saw him quitting his label of 20 years. His next album, **Will The Wolf Survive,** came out on MCA and the hits continued with the title song and **Working Without A Net** (both 1986), the latter a reference to him kicking drugs. By this time he had formed a liaison with Willie Nelson, Johnny Cash and Kris Kristofferson, resulting in the best-selling album **Highwayman** in 1985, plus a No.1 single of that same title. Another chart-topper came with his fourth MCA single, **Rose In Paradise** (1987). He enjoyed further Top 10 entries with **Fallin' Out** and **My Rough And Rowdy Days** (both 1987).

In 1990 Waylon signed with Epic Records, scoring a Top 10 hit with **Wrong** (1990). Since then major chart success has eluded him, but he has continued to speak out through his music, as he showed with the album, **Too Dumb For New York**

City, Too Ugly For L.A. (1992). The title song is a tongue-in-cheek, self-penned ditty that pokes fun at the way those in high places think of country people and, more specifically, country music. Throughout his long career Jennings has always been patently country, but his use of a heavier instrumentation and his rock-star approach has tended to mislead people.

Recommended:
Ladies Love Outlaws (RCA/RCA)
Honky Tonk Heroes (RCA/RCA)
Leather And Lace – with Jessi Colter (RCA/RCA)
Waylon And Willie (RCA/RCA)
I've Always Been Crazy (RCA/RCA)
Wanted! The Outlaws – with Jessi Colter, Willie Nelson and Tompall Glaser (RCA/RCA)
Full Circle (MCA/–)
A Man Called Hoss (MCA/MCA)
Will The Wolf Survive (MCA/MCA)
The Eagle (Epic/Epic)
Files (–/Bear Family)
Too Dumb For New York City, Too Ugly For LA (Epic/–)

Jim And Jesse

Bluegrass-playing brothers Jim and Jesse McReynolds were both born in Coeburn, Virginia, Jim on February 13, 1927, Jesse on July 9, 1929. From a musical family – their grandfather was an old-time fiddler who recorded with Victor – the duo began playing at local get-togethers.

With Jim on guitar and Jesse on mandolin, they made their radio debut in 1947 and cut some records for the Kentucky label during the early '50s, later signing for Capitol. However, the duo's progress was terminated for a while during the Korean War when Jesse was called up for service. They reformed on Knoxville's WNOX Tennessee Barn Dance in 1954.

During the '60s, Jim and Jesse, with their band the Virginia Boys (which included such musicians as Bobby Thompson and Vassar Clements) signed for Epic Records. They began notching up a number of fair-sized chart entries with **Cotton Mill Man** (1964), **Diesel On My Tail, Ballad Of Thunder Road** (both 1967), **The Golden Rocket** (1968) and other titles before switching to Capitol for a 1971 success in **Freight Train**.

Regular on the Opry since 1964, Jim And Jesse are a fine, no-frills, bluegrass outfit, specializing in smooth, haunting, sky-high harmony vocals. They have played the Newport Folk Festival, have appeared at Britain's Wembley Festival many times and, in addition to their own TV show, have played on scores of TV shows throughout Europe and America. They have recorded well over 40 albums and in 1982 even made a return to the singles charts, having a mild hit with **North Wind**, a single that saw them teaming with Charlie Louvin.

Recommended:
We Like Trains/Diesel On My Tail (Epic/–)
The Jim And Jesse Show (Old Dominion/DJM)
All-Time Greatest Country Instrumentals (Columbia/–)
The Epic Bluegrass Years (Rounder/–)

Michael Johnson

A gifted songwriter, singer and acoustic guitarist, Michael Johnson was born in Alamosa, Colorado, on August 8, 1944. He first became involved in music while in his early teens in Denver and over the years he has covered the musical spectrum from rock'n'roll to the classics. Though he made his first recordings in Nashville in the early '70s, these were geared towards the pop market. It was not until 1985, when he teamed up with Sylvia for the duet country hit, **I Love You By Heart**, that he made a commitment to country that resulted in a highly successful chart run in the late '80s.

While attending Colorado State College in 1964, Johnson won a national amateur talent contest which earned him a recording contract with Epic Records. He took to the road as a folk singer touring the college and club circuit. Two years

The Jim And Jesse Show. Courtesy Old Dominion/DJM Records. Jim And Jesse provided classic bluegrass.

later he travelled to Spain where he spent a year in Barcelona studying classical guitar under Graciano Tarrego. On his return to Colorado he joined David Boise and John Denver in the 'new' Chad Mitchell Trio. This was a short-lived association, as Denver embarked on a solo career and Johnson became an actor in a touring production of 'Jacques Brel Is Alive And Well And Living In Paris'.

In 1971 he recorded his first solo album, **There Is A Breeze**, for Atlantic. He formed his own Sanskrit label and continued working as a folk singer, mainly recording and performing his own self-penned songs. Two of his songs attracted the attention of Gene Cotton, resulting in a move to Nashville, where he worked sessions and teamed up with Brent Maher. This led to a contract with EMI-America, for whom he scored significant pop chart success with **Bluer Than Blue** and **Almost Like Being In Love** in 1978. Dropped by EMI in 1981, Johnson started all over again, writing songs and making demos. In 1984, his old friend Brent Maher (by this time producing the Judds and Sylvia), signed him to RCA, resulting in his duet with Sylvia on **I Love You By Heart** (1985), and solo success with **Give Me Wings** (No.1, 1986), **The Moon Is Still Over My Shoulder** (No.1, 1987), **Crying Shame** (1987), **I Will Whisper Your Name** and **That's That** (both 1988).

By 1990 Johnson's record sales had dropped off. He also had a lengthy period of ill-health and was subsequently dropped by RCA. By 1992 he had gained a new contract with Atlantic Records and was beginning to build a new career with his delicate, folk-country style of music.

Recommended:
That's That (RCA/RCA)
Life's A Bitch (RCA/RCA)
Michael Johnson (Atlantic/–)

David Lynn Jones

A performer who leans more towards the rock and blues side of country music, David Lynn Jones, from Bexar, Arkansas, is a singer-songwriter who has never slotted into the Nashville mainstream. He has been performing since the early '70s, where his uncompromising style of country with its Springsteen and Dylan overtones won him a cult following. He made his initial impact in Nashville as a writer, but his reputation as a dynamic performer led to a recording contract with Mercury in 1986 and a Top 10 entry with **Bonnie Jean (Little Sister)** the following year.

His debut album, **Hard Times On Easy Street**, received rave reviews, grabbing him some attention from outside of country

Mixed Emotions, David Lynn Jones. Courtesy Liberty Records.

music. Waylon Jennings added harmonies to **High Ridin' Heroes** (Top 20, 1988). Becoming disillusioned with Nashville, Jones maintained a base in Bexar where he had built his own studio and continued working with musicians who had played with him since the beginning. A second album for Mercury failed to gain any commercial acceptance, so he returned to his musical beginnings of playing honky-tonks and clubs. Another shot at the big time was offered when Jimmy Bowen signed him to Liberty Records in 1992. This time the performer was determined to do it his way, and his third album, **Mixed Emotions**, was recorded in his own studios. The project was a joint production between the singer and Richie Albright, who had produced some of Waylon Jennings' edgier work. For once Jones' highly charged blend of country, rock, gospel and soul had finally been allowed to fly free. From spicy rock'n'roll to blues-tingling numbers, this was a roots-oriented collage of every emotion that encapsulates the essence of country.

Recommended:
Hard Times On Easy Street (Mercury/Mercury)

George Jones

Known as the 'Rolls Royce Of Country Singers', George Glenn Jones' nasal, blues filled, vocal styling has influenced a host of country performers.

Born in Saratoga, Texas, on September 12, 1931, Jones grew up against a musical background. His mother played piano at the local church and his father was an amateur guitarist. He got his first guitar at the age of nine and was soon performing at local events. In his late teens he served with the Marines in Korea, and upon discharge began working as a house painter while also playing evening gigs. By 1954 he had gained a sufficiently good reputation to attract the interest of industry executive H.W. 'Pappy' Dailey at Starday Records in Houston.

Jones saw his first big country hit, **Why Baby Why**, in 1955. He stayed with Starday until 1957, cutting both country and rockabilly sides, before moving on to Mercury. His first No.1 for his new label was **White Lightning**, an uptempo song with a novelty chorus, in 1959.

After 18 hits including another No.1, **Tender Years** (1961), he landed at UA Records, where he hit a fertile period, turning out songs that have become country standards. He proved particularly strong with the anguished, two-timing women type of song, singing in a manner that suggested he had lived the lyric.

So he hit big with **Window Up Above** (1961), **She Thinks I Still Care,** an archetypal Jones song and one covered by countless other artists (1962), **We Must Have Been Out Of Our Minds**, performed with his travelling co-star Melba Montgomery (1963), and the classic **Race Is On** (1964).

In 1965 he renewed acquaintance with Pappy Dailey. Dailey had left Starday to form Musicor, and Jones was an obvious target for him. This proved a successful liaison and Jones' tally of hits continued to grow via such singles as **Things Have Gone To Pieces, Love Bug, Take Me** (1965), **I'm A People, 4033** (1966), **Walk Through This World With Me, I Can't Get There From Here, If My Heart Had**

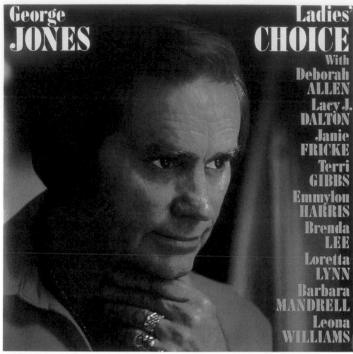

Ladies' Choice, George Jones.
Courtesy Epic Records.

Windows and **Say It's Not You** (1967). But the singer became increasingly unhappy with the way he was being recorded and began a fight to shake off the Musicor contract. At this period of his life he went through a rough patch, having become divorced from his wife. He began drinking heavily as he undertook endless overseas tours. He seemed to be increasingly living out his honky-tonk songs and became associated with stories of wild and destructive living, sometimes having to be helped onstage. During 1967 he met Tammy Wynette, when the two played the same package tour. Tammy was having problems with her marriage and she and George became romantically entwined. When, in the wake of his 1968 hits, **Say It's Not You**, **As Long As I Live** and **When The Grass Grows Over Me**, he released **I'll Share My World With You** (1969), the fans knew it was Tammy he was singing about. The record went to

Below: George Jones shows up for a rare photo call.

No.2 – kept out of the No.1 spot by Tammy's **Stand By Your Man**. That year, both George and Tammy joined the Opry. They also got married, being hailed as 'Mr And Mrs Country Music'.

Though Jones continued having hits with Musicor, he still wished to quit the label and eventually did so in 1971, joining Tammy and producer Billy Sherrill on Epic. Tammy was a huge star during this period (she had five chart-toppers during 1972–73) and though George had his share of hits, it was only when the twosome worked together that he really hit the heights. The duo's **We're Gonna Hold On** (1973) provided him with a half-share in his first No.1 since 1967. In 1974, things began to swing around. Tammy has only one hit, while George had two No.1s with

We Love To Sing About Jesus,
George Jones and Tammy Wynette.
Courtesy Epic Records.

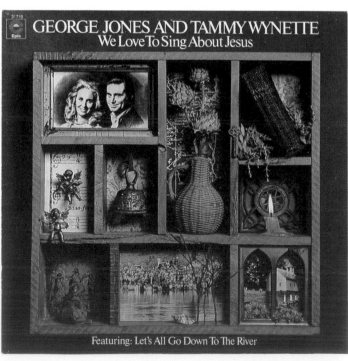

The Grand Tour and **The Door**. Also that year, the stars swung apart, Tammy filing for a legal separation. And in 1976 she remarried – in the same year that her and George's duets, **Golden Ring** and **Near You,** went top of the charts.

Though Jones was named Country Singer Of The Year by 'Rolling Stone' in 1976, the hits stopped flowing as regularly as they once did. He had one solo Top 10 record in 1978 with **Bartender's Blues** and duetted to good effect with Johnny Paycheck on **Mabellene**.

During 1980, he released three chart albums (one with Tammy, another with Johnny Paycheck) and five Top 20s. One, **He Stopped Loving Her Today**, reached No.1 and helped George win a Grammy Award for the Best Male Country Vocal Performance. Also in 1980 he was adjudged Male Vocalist Of The Year by the CMA, a title he claimed again in 1981.

Jones continued to create his own problems. He frequently failed to turn up at events and sometimes appeared to be living through a permanent nightmare. Nevertheless, he kept on supplying hits, such as: **If Drinkin' Don't Kill Me (Her Memory Will)**; **Still Doin' Time** (1981); **Same Ole Me** (1982); **Yesterday's Wine** and **C.C. Waterback** – both with Merle Haggard (1982); **Shine On**; **I Always Get Lucky With You**; **Tennessee Whiskey** (1983); **We Didn't See a Thing** – with Ray Charles (1983); **You've Still Got A Place In My Heart**; **She's My Rock** (1984); **Who's Gonna Fill Her Shoes** (1985); **The One I Loved Back Then** (1986) and **The Right Left Hand** (1987).

By the mid-'80s Jones had settled down, with his career being guided by divorcee Nancy Sepulveda, whom he married in 1983. Idolized by many of the young New Traditionalists, he had settled into a comfortable career as a legendary country veteran, but still maintained that high quality in his recordings. He teamed up with beautiful newcomer Shelby Lynne, the pair scoring a duet hit with **If I Could Bottle This Up** (1988). He made the Top 10 with his own distinctive revival of Johnny Horton's **I'm A One-Woman Man** (1989) and duetted with Randy Travis on **A Few Ole Country Boys** (1990). In 1991 Jones joined MCA Records, gaining minor hits with **You Couldn't Get The Picture**,

I Don't Need Your Rockin' Chair and **Wrong's What I Do Best**.

George Jones is more than a classic country singer. He is *the* classic country singer – a product of honky-tonks and heartaches, hard living and hard loving. He finally received the recognition he deserved in 1992 when he was inducted into the Country Music Hall Of Fame.

Recommended:
White Lightning (–/Ace)
The King Of Country Music (–/Liberty)
My Very Special Guests – with various guests (Epic/Epic)
Burn The Honky Tonk Down (Rounder/–)
Alone Again (Epic/Epic)
I Am What I Am (Epic/Epic)
George Jones And Tammy Wynette – Greatest Hits (Epic/Epic)
George Jones Meets Hank Williams and Bob Wills (–/EMI)
Too Wild Too Long (Epic/Epic)
Don't Stop The Music (–/Ace)
You Ought To Be Here With Me (Epic/Epic)
Walls Can Fall (MCA/–)
A Good Year For The Roses (–/Castle)
Who's Gonna Fill Their Shoes (Epic/–)
Friends In High Places (Epic/–)

Grandpa Jones

A long-time regular on both the Opry and Hee Haw, high-kicking, joke-cracking, story-telling, foot-stomping vaudevillian Grandpa Jones is one of the most colourful figures in country music.

Born Louis Marshall Jones, in Niagara, Kentucky, on October 20, 1913, he began playing guitar on an instrument costing only 75 cents. At 16 he had become so proficient that he won a talent contest promoted by Wendell Hall, while 1935 found him with Bradley Kincaid's band.

Jones began disguising himself as an old-timer while only in his twenties. By 1937 he was leading an outfit known as Grandpa Jones And His Grandchildren, this unit becoming regulars on WWVA's Wheeling Jamboree, and then Cincinnati WLW, during the late '30s and early '40s. It was here that he began recording for King Records, by himself, with Merle Travis, and with the Delmore Brothers as Brown's Ferry Four. In 1944 Jones joined the US Army and was posted to Germany, where he played on AFN Radio until his discharge in 1946. Almost immediately he became a member of the Opry, remaining so for many years. Elected to the Country Music Hall Of Fame in 1984, he published an autobiography 'Grandpa: 50 Years Behind The Mike'.

Recommended:
The Grandpa Jones Story (CMH/–)
Everybody's Grandpa – Hits From Hee Haw (Monument/–)
20 Of The Best (–/RCA)

Jordanaires

A vocal group that has appeared on hundreds of Nashville recordings, the Jordanaires were formed in Springfield, Missouri during 1948. Initially a male barbershop quartet, performing mainly gospel material, they gained their first Opry appearance in 1949.

A year later they were featured on Red Foley's million-selling version of **Just A Closer Walk With Thee**, and in 1956

The Man From Kentucky, Grandpa Jones. Courtesy Bulldog Records.

Recommended:
Sing Elvis' Gospel Favorites (–/Magnum Force)

sprang to even wider fame by commencing a long and successful association with Elvis Presley. Grammy award winners in 1965 (for best religious album), the Jordanaires have appeared on many TV and radio shows, also lending their talents to an impressive number of movie scores.

Sarah Jory

The 'Queen of British Country Music', Sarah Elizabeth Jory was born on November 20, 1969 in Exeter, Devon, England. A multi-instrumentalist, Sarah can play banjo, mandolin, acoustic, rhythm and steel guitar and keyboards. Her ability to hold a tune is natural. It all started with a toy drum, then a small guitar, and most amazingly a steel guitar with a local band, Colorado Country. Within three years she was travelling all over southern England, playing country clubs, social evenings, fêtes and barbecues.

By this time Sarah had started making an impression in America. At only eleven she appeared at the annual Steel Guitar Convention in St Louis, Missouri. Recognized steel guitarists like Lloyd Green, Weldon Myrick and Pete Drake accepted this young girl as their equal. She returned to the States a dozen times, on a number of occasions as a guest at the Steel Guitar Convention and, at other times, to Nashville where she sat in on sessions, jammed at nightspots and guested on television, including Ralph Emery's Nashville Now. At 15 Sarah had become possibly Britain's finest steel guitarist. Sarah brings a feminine touch to her work that has made her much more than just another steel guitarist. There is a passion in her playing that, added to a considerable technique, makes her country

themes an especially moving experience.

A precocious child prodigy, Sarah began developing an interest in expanding her talents to include singing and entertaining. At 18 Sarah formed her own band and started making inroads into Europe. In 1989 she gained a standing ovation at Holland's famed Floralia Festival, and less than two years later was the invited guest of Eric Clapton, when the 'king of blues-rock' appeared at The Point, Dublin. Since then she has toured the UK theatre circuit as an opening act for Glen Campbell and Charley Pride, played all the major festivals throughout Britain and Europe and undertaken her own headlining concert tours.

Sarah is a remarkably mature and sophisticated entertainer. With a powerful and versatile voice, and instrumental skills that would leave most musicians in awe, this lady really has little to worry about. Since the early '80s Sarah has recorded regularly, mainly with steel guitar instrumental albums, then later adding vocals. In 1992 she signed with the London-based Irish Ritz Records, and her first album for them, **New Horizons**, was named Country Album Of The Year by the British Country Music Association. On the threshold of a highly successful international career, Sarah Jory, a pure, natural and complete musician, a brilliant singer and all-round entertainer, was named European Country Music Artist Of The Year in April 1993 for the second consecutive year.

Why Not Me?, The Judds. Courtesy RCA Records.

Recommended:
New Horizons (–/Ritz)

The Judds

This mother (Naomi, born Diana Ellen Judd on January 11, 1946, Ashland, Kentucky) and daughter (Wynonna, born Christina Criminella on May 30, 1964, Ashland, Kentucky) vocal duo managed to go 'New Country' while retaining links with traditional roots. Naomi moved her one-parent family to Hollywood in 1968. During the next seven years Wynonna and her younger sister, Ashley, attended public school, while Naomi worked at various jobs, among them a model, a secretary for the pop group the Fifth Dimension, and Girl Friday to an Oriental millionaire.

In 1976 the family moved back to Morrill, Kentucky, close to their hometown, where Naomi pursued a career in nursing. Because they had no TV, they began singing duets at home and realized they

Left: The Jordanaires team up with their most famous client – Elvis.

were good enough to embark on a musical career. They began singing at local functions, bought a 30-dollar tape deck and began making demo tapes, all the time honing their harmonies to perfection. Following a move back to California, Naomi completed her nursing training in San Francisco, then decided to push for a career in music. She and her daughters headed for Nashville in 1979, where Wynonna finished high school, winning a talent contest in the 10th grade

As a duo they worked on WSM's Ralph Emery Show, but their big break came when Naomi met producer Brent Maher while nursing his daughter, taking the opportunity to pass on one of her demo tapes. Eventually with the help of Maher, Woody Bowles (a veteran Nashville manager and publicist) and manager Ken Stilts, they landed an RCA recording contract after an unprecedented live audition before the company's executives.

Immediate Top 20 chart-jumpers with **Had A Dream (For The Heart)**, a late 1983 release, the twosome's career really took off in 1984 when they gained two No.1s with **Mama He's Crazy** and **Why Not Me**, also netting a Grammy for Best Country Performance for the former title and Single Of The Year for the latter at the CMA Awards, a ceremony that also saw them win Best Vocal Group. Since that time, the Judds have logged further massive hits with **Love Is Alive, Girls Night Out, Have Mercy** (1985), **Grandpa (Tell Me About The Good Old Days)** and **Rockin' With The Rhythm Of The Rain** (1986).

The most glamorous duo in country music, Naomi and Wynonna won the CMA Duo Of The Year for six consecutive years and helped bring a new youth audience to country music. All of their albums have attained multi-platinum status, and they achieved further single hits with: **Cry Myself To Sleep, I Know Where I'm Going** and **Maybe Your Baby's Got The Blues** (all No.1s in 1987); **Turn It Loose, Give A Little Love** and **Change Of Heart** (1988); **Young Love, Let Me Tell You About Love** (1990); **Born To Be Blue** and **Love Can Build A Bridge** (1990). In 1988 the pair became the first female country act to form their own booking agency (Pro-Tours), but there was speculation that Wynonna (definitely the lead singer) would embark on a solo career. In the end, unforseen circumstances forced a decision. On October 17, 1990 it was announced that Naomi Judd was to retire at the end of the duo's 'Love Can Build A Bridge' 1990–91 concert tour. Having been diagnosed with hepatitis ten months earlier, the 44-year-old entertainer admitted her health condition had prompted her retirement.

The tour became one of the most successful in country music history. The show was simultaneously televised across America and set new records as the most watched musical event in pay-per-view cable history. The concert's gross revenues were estimated in excess of 4.4 million dollars. A tearful tribute to Naomi and Wynonna's career, the Judds' farewell concert can be considered one of the most memorable country shows of all time.

In 1992, Wynonna, having dropped the surname Judd, set out on a solo career, which is likely to see her emerge as one of country music's most successful ground-breaking female entertainers of the '90s.

Recommended:
The Judds (RCA mini-LP/–)
Why Not Me? (RCA/RCA)

Rockin' With The Rhythm (RCA/RCA)
Give A Little Love (–/RCA)
Love Can Build A Bridge (RCA/RCA)
River Of Time (RCA/RCA)

Karl And Harty

Karl Victor Davis (born December 17, 1905) and Hartford Connecticut Taylor (born April 11, 1905, died October, 1963), both of Mt Vernon, Kentucky, composed one of the earliest and most influential of the mandolin-guitar duets. They were brought to the WLS National Barn Dance by John Lair in 1930 as members of the Cumberland Ridge Runners and remained on the show for some 20 years.

Their records for the ARC complex of labels (and, later, Capitol) were popular in their era, especially **I'm Just Here To Get My Baby Out Of Jail** (1934), **The Prisoner's Dream** (1936) and **Kentucky** (1938), all written by Karl. They both left the recording and performing field in the '50s, Karl continuing to work at WLS as a record turner for many years.

Best known as a songwriter (all the above have been recorded and have been hits by several groups at different times), Davis was also able to write a hit song as late as the '60s – Hank Locklin's **Country Music Hall Of Fame** (1967) being one of Karl's compositions.

Wayne Kemp

Born in Greenwood, Arkansas on June 1, 1941, honky-tonk-style vocalist Kemp, the son of a motor mechanic, naturally enough became interested in automobile racing in his early teens.

He grew up in Oklahoma and, after forming his own band and touring throughout the Southwest, he met Buddy Killen, who signed him to a writer's contract with Free Music and a recording deal with the Dial label in 1963. He's made the biggest impact as a writer, with George Jones taking **Love Bug** into the Top 10 in 1965. Conway Twitty was next to pick up on Wayne's songs, recording **The Image Of Me, Next In Line, Darling, You Know I Wouldn't Lie** and **That's When She Started To Stop Loving You**, all No.1s between 1968 and 1970.

The association with Twitty enabled Kemp to gain a contract with Decca Records in 1969, for whom he supplied several minor hits, leading up to **Honky Tonk Wine**, which went Top 20 in 1973. He has consistently charted the lower reaches for MCA, UA, Mercury and Door Knob, with his **I'll Leave This World Loving You** hit of 1980 being revived by Ricky Van Shelton in 1988.

Recommended:
Wayne Kemp (MCA/–)
Kentucky Sunshine (MCA/–)

The Kendalls

A father and daughter team, Royce Kendall was born in St Louis, Missouri, on 25 September, 1934, while Jeannie hails from the same town, born on 30 November, 1954. Royce began guitar-picking at five and by the age of eight was on radio with his brother Floyce, the twosome forming an act called the Austin Brothers and touring.

After serving in the US Army, Royce worked in various jobs, eventually settling in St Louis.

When the Kendall's only child, Jeannie, began singing duets with her father for fun, Royce realized that he and his daughter had an outstanding harmony sound. In 1969 Royce and Jeannie took a trip to Nashville, cutting a demo that caught the ear of Peter Drake, who signed the couple to his Stop label. The Kendalls' debut single **Leavin' On A Jet Plane**, climbed to 52 in the country charts in 1970. Encouraged, Royce moved the family to Nashville, where the Kendalls began recording for Dot. During this three-year period they made numerous appearances on TV shows and played the Opry, while Jeannie notched a Beatle connection, singing harmony on Ringo Starr's **Beaucoup Of Blues** album.

After Dot, they signed to UA for a year, but still could not make the desired breakthrough, at which point the duo took a six-month hiatus from recording to reassess. In 1977 they returned to the studio once more, this time working for the Ovation label. Their first release, a version of an old country standard **Making Believe**, nudged into the lower regions of the charts. The follow-up **Live And Let Live** was well received but looked no chart-buster until some country stations reported interest in the single's B-side and Ovation flipped the release and began plugging **Heaven's Just A Sin Away**, which soared to No.1. At the next CMA Awards ceremony in 1978 the Kendalls romped away with the Single Of The Year plaudit after being nominated in three categories. They were also judged Best Country Group at the Grammy Awards.

The Kendalls stuck with Ovation until 1982, having hits with **It Don't Feel Like Sinnin' To Me, Sweet Desire** (No.1, 1978), **I Had A Lovely Time, Put It Off Until Tomorrow** (1980) and **Heart Of The Matter** (1981), among others. The duo then began charting with Mercury and 1983 saw them go to the Top 20 with **Precious Love** and **Movin' Train**, and chart-top with **Thank God For The Radio**.

During the late '80s, the Kendalls did some label-hopping from MCA/Curb to Step One and Epic, scoring minor hits with each one, but failing to return to the Top 10. An unlikely pair in some ways – the idea of father and daughter swopping choruses on cheatin' songs has often led to the duo being asked if they are married to each other – they have stayed country and paid the price by never seeing their records cross over into the more lucrative pop market. It could be argued that Jeannie Kendall should have embarked upon a solo career in the early '80s. She has possibly left it too late in life, especially now that country music is dominated by new, younger stars, making it very difficult for veteran stars to make an impact.

Recommended:
Heaven's Just A Sin Away (Ovation/ Polydor)
Hearts Of The Matter (Ovation/Ovation)
Movin' Train (Mercury/–)
Fire At First Sight (MCA/MCA)
Break The Routine (Step One/–)

Ray Kennedy

Known as the 'High-Tech Hillbilly', singer-guitarist Ray Kennedy (born in Buffalo, New York) is one of country music's more versatile and creative personalities. Prior to becoming a 'naturalized' Nashvillian in the early '80s, Kennedy rode the drifter's trail, living in Massachusetts, on the Virginia shore, in the Oregon mountains and in Vermont. He rode motorcycle escort for funerals by day, while working the club circuit by night. His father, Ray Sr, was a vice-president with Sears, and was responsible for creating the Discover Card.

In 1980 Ray Jr arrived in Nashville with plans to become a top songwriter. Within six months he had a song, **The Same Old Girl**, cut by John Anderson. He signed a

Below: New York-born Ray Kennedy debuted for Atlantic in 1990 with his Top 10 hit What A Way To Go.

writer's contract with Tree Music and had more cuts by Charley Pride, David Allan Coe and T. Graham Brown. This enabled him to build his own studio, where he churned out radio and TV jingles as well as demos of his own songs, while also working as a session musician and singer. His studio has also been used by many diverse artists, including Kevin Welch, T. Graham Brown, Stevie Nicks, Diamond Rio, Dude Mowery and Michelle Wright.

With his black leather jackets and rockabilly look, Ray Kennedy doesn't quite fit the standard image of a country singer. But, in 1989 he signed a recording contract with Atlantic, his debut album, **What A Way To Go**, being an almost totally solo affair with Kennedy arranging, producing and playing all instruments, except steel guitar and dobro. He also wrote, or co-wrote, all the songs. The title track became a Top 10 single in 1990. Since then Kennedy has scored minor hits with **Scars** (1991) and **No Way Jose** (1992).

Recommended:
Guitar Man (Atlantic/–)
What A Way To Go (Atlantic/–)

The Kentucky HeadHunters

A real modern 'hillbilly' band, the Kentucky HeadHunters, a rock quintet from Edmonton, Kentucky, brought a heavy metal and blues influence to country music in the late '80s. Their first album, **Pickin' On Nashville**, went multi-platinum as it raced up both the country and pop charts. After 20 years of struggling, the band had found 'instant success' with major awards, and hit following hit, then within three years the band was torn apart. Both their lead singer and bass player decided to leave and pursue their own careers.

The history of the Kentucky HeadHunters is intertwined with another group, Itchy Brother, formed in the late '60s when two brothers, Richard and Fred Young, and two of their cousins, Anthony Kenney and Greg Martin, got together to play a raunchy brand of blues, rock'n'roll and country. The name Itchy Brother came from a cartoon character and the foursome worked the club circuit for the next decade. In 1980 they added lead vocalist Mark Orr and pursued a recording contract with Led Zeppelin's Swan Song label. When it didn't materialize, the five split up.

In 1986 the Young brothers decided to re-form Itchy Brother. Kenney opted out, so Greg Martin suggested recruiting Doug Phelp, who was playing with him in Ronnie McDowell's band. They also needed a lead vocalist, so Doug's brother, Ricky Lee Phelps came into the line-up, alongside the three original members. The five-piece opted for a new name, taking their cue from Muddy Waters' band, the Headchoppers. In 1987 the Kentucky HeadHunters were born.

The following year they made an eight-song demo tape that set the Nashville community buzzing and led to a contract with Mercury Records. Several of the tracks from the demo were used on the debut album, **Pickin' On Nashville**, including their first country hit, a revival of Bill Monroe's **Walk Softly On This Heart Of Mine** (1989). The HeadHunters enjoyed further hits with **Dumas Walker** and **Oh Lonesome Me** (1990), but it's as album artists and a live act that they have really

Above: The Kentucky HeadHunters rockin' it up in their inimitable way.

scored. They have a boisterous, fun-packed, rockin' country show; a southern outfit that specializes in head-banging party music. In 1991 their second album, **Electric Barnyard**, again featured revivals of old country classics, and soon went gold. Then, as they prepared to start a third album, the brothers Doug and Ricky Lee Phelps announced their departure. It was on June 2, 1992, when they sent a fax to the others, notifying them of their intention. On the very same day a filmed segment of their announcement was shown on the TNN Crook & Chase Show.

The remaining members re-grouped, bringing in 'new' members Mark Orr (lead vocals) and Anthony Kenney (bass), who had played with them in the old days of Itchy Brother. The change has brought about a more bluesy edge to the HeadHunters' music, which might well alienate them from mainstream country. Meanwhile the Phelpses have claimed that their music will be a return to the country roots and geared more towards mainstream country radio. Both sides emphasize that the split was due to different musical directions.

Recommended:
Rave On! (Mercury/Mercury)
Pickin' On Nashville (Mercury/Mercury)
Electric Barnyard (Mercury/Mercury)

Doug Kershaw

Cajun fiddler Douglas James Kershaw, born at Tiel Ridge, Louisiana, on January 24, 1936, first appeared onstage as a child, accompanying his mother (singer-guitarist-fiddler Mama Rita) at the Bucket Of Blood, Lake Arthur. In 1948, together with his brothers Russell Lee ('Rusty') and Nelson ('Pee Wee') Kershaw, he formed the Continental Playboys, gaining a spot on Lake Charles KPLC-TV in 1953. Rusty and Doug then began recording as a duo for the Feature label, later obtaining a contract with Hickory.

With an Everly-like treatment of a Boudleaux Bryant song, **Hey Sheriff**, the Kershaws made an indent on the country charts in October 1958 and even briefly joined the Opry. After Doug completed his military service, the duo resumed their joint career, scoring with country classics **Louisiana Man** and **Diggy Diggy Lo**.

After cutting sides for Victor and Princess, the twosome parted in 1964,

Doug moving on to record for Mercury, MGM, Warner Bros, Starflyte and Scotti Bros. He has also guested on scores of sessions, appearing on albums with Longbranch Pennywhistle, Bob Dylan, Johnny Cash, John Stewart and even Grand Funk Railroad. After playing a cameo role in the film 'Zachariah' (1971), he also appeared in 'Medicine Ball Caravan' (1971) and 'Days Of Heaven' (1978).

Recommended
The Cajun Country Rockers – Rusty And Doug (–/Bear Family)
The Cajun Way (Warner Bros/–)
Devil's Elbow (Warner Bros/Warner Bros)
Douglas James Kershaw (Warner Bros/Warner Bros)
Hot Diggity Doug (–/Sundown)

Sammy Kershaw

A self taught Cajun chef, Sammy Kershaw was born in 1958, in Kaplan, Louisiana, a third cousin of Cajun fiddler Doug Kershaw. Before making a breakthrough with **Cadillac Style** in 1991, Sammy paid his dues, starting out in music when he was only 12, and coming through two divorces, a brace of bankruptcies and numerous jobs, including a stint as a professional baseball player. A man of many talents, he's a terrific story-teller (having worked as a stand-up comedian) and a soulful singer, with more than a hint of George Jones in his voice.

He played the Louisiana club scene for 20 years, and at one point quit music. Years on the road playing clubs six nights a week had taken its toll with heavy drinking and cocaine, and Sammy headed down a dead-end street. In 1988 he married for a third time and settled down. Two years later he got a call to head for Nashville for an audition with Mercury Records. Once safely in Nashville, Sammy recorded the album, **Don't Go Near The Water**, a collection of hard-country ballads and saloon songs which garnered a gold disc and spawned such big hits as **Cadillac Style** (1991), **Don't Go Near The Water** and **Anywhere But Here** (1992).

A self-named 'ballad singing fool', Sammy's warm, emotional vocal style with its country-to-the-core phrasing frequently elicits comparisons to George Jones. "I've been singing like this since I was a kid", Sammy's quick to point out. "So many times I was compared to George Jones, but it wasn't my fault. It's just natural harmonics." Sammy's management decided to cash in on the sweet smell of

success with Starclone, a new fragrance for women made from Kershaw's natural 'body essences'. The sweat of his back and chest is distilled with flowers, herbs and oils. Slickly packaged with cassettes and photos of the Cajun star, you have 'Spray On Sammy'. This is a long way from the old days of country music when stars would sweat it out all day behind a plough, then drive into town in the evening to sing at the local school gym or church.

Recommended:
Haunted Heart (Mercury/–)
Don't Go Near The Water (Mercury/–)

Hal Ketchum

One of country music's fastest-rising stars, success for Hal Ketchum (born Michael Ketchum, April 12, 1953 in Greenwich, New York) came later in life than most.

His father was a linotype operator for Gannett Press, and also a keen country music fan. His mother, who suffered from multiple sclerosis, enjoyed crooners. Because of his mother's illness, he spent much of his childhood at his grandparents' home where his grandfather listened to jazz and classical music. A carpenter by trade, Hal absorbed all these musical influences, and was encouraged by his father who played banjo and can also boast to being a member of the Buck Owens Fan Club. Hal started out as a teenage drummer in a New York R&B outfit before relocating south. He first moved to Florida, where he played in a blues band, then to Texas, where he became a singer-songwriter on the Austin music scene.

By this time, Ketchum was married with two young children, and really had no idea in which direction to take his music. He

Past the Point Of Rescue, Hal Ketchum. Courtesy Curb.

Hal Ketchum

maintained a day-time job as a carpenter, working the bars night after night searching for some kind of musical recognition. This lifestyle put a heavy strain on his marriage and led to divorce. In 1987 he produced his own album, **Threadbare Alibis**, which was no more than a gig cassette for Watermelon Records. Two years later it was picked up by Line Records in Germany and put out on CD. It was an appearance at the Kerrville Folk Festival in 1990 that led to him signing a major record deal with Curb Records the following year. Noted producer Jim Rooney brought him to Nashville where he started writing and doing demos for Forerunner Music.

His first single, **Small Town Saturday Night**, helped by a video which was directed by photographer Jim McGuire, hit No.2 in the charts in 1991. His debut album, **Past The Point Of Rescue**, raced to gold status. That same year he married Terrell Tye, president of Forerunner Music, and also put together his four-piece band, the Alibis, consisting of musicians who had worked with him in Texas. Ketchum consolidated this initial success with such chart singles as **I Know Where Love Lives** (1991), **Past The Point Of Rescue**, **Five O'Clock World** and **Sure Love** (1992), and **Hearts Are Gonna Roll** (1993).

An unabashed fan of country music, Hal is more than just a songwriter. He's also a writer of short stories and plans to write children's books some day. At this time, though, it is his music that is bringing him fame and fortune. All his musical influences are united in a style that is totally his own, yet represents the eclectic traditions of the Texas song poets.

Recommended:
Sure Love (Curb/–)
Past The Point Of Rescue (Curb/–)
Threadbare Alibis (–/Sawdust)

Merle Kilgore

Born Wyatt Merle Kilgore, in Chickasha, Oklahoma, on September 8, 1934, Merle's family moved to Shreveport, Louisiana, when he was still young. He learned guitar as a boy and got a job as a DJ on Shreveport's KENT when he was just 16. At this time he was already attracting attention as a performer and writer, and by the age of 18 Kilgore had his first hit composition, **More, More, More**. Invited to join the Louisiana Hayride, he became the principal guitarist on the show. In 1952 he appeared on the Opry and in that same year attended Louisiana Tech. The following year saw him working at the American Optical Company but performing at night. He appeared on the Hayride throughout the '50s, initially recording for the Imperial and D labels, but his first big hit came in 1959 with **Dear Mama**, a Starday release. Johnny Horton scored with **Johnny Reb**, a Kilgore composition, around the same time.

Another of Kilgore's Starday releases, **Love Has Made You Beautiful**, charted in 1960, as did **Gettin' Old Before My Time**, while in 1962 he co-wrote **Wolverton Mountain** with Claude King and **Ring Of Fire** with June Carter, the later composition providing Johnny Cash with a million-selling single in 1963.

Though his record sales fared less successfully as the '60s wore on, Kilgore became established as an impressive Western actor, appearing in such movies

Above: Pee Wee King, co-writer of Slowpoke and You Belong To Me.

as 'Nevada Smith' (1966), 'Five Card Stud' (1968) and a number of others. For many years Kilgore has acted as Hank Williams Jr's manager and masterminded his transition into a major country music superstar.

Recommended:
Merle Kilgore (Mercury/–)
Teenager's Holiday (–/Bear Family)

Bradley Kincaid

A pioneer broadcaster of traditional Kentucky mountain music, Kincaid (born Point Leavell, Kentucky, July 13, 1895) began singing folk songs on WLS, Chicago, in August, 1925, while still attending that city's George Williams College. By 1926 he had become a regular on the WLS Chicago Barn Dance, remaining with the show (later to be known as the National Barn Dance) until 1930. Following graduation in June, 1928, Kincaid began touring, at the same time collecting folk songs from a variety of sources, publishing these in a series of songbooks.

His recording career also began in 1928, when he made a number of sides for Gennett, these discs appearing on myriad labels, sometimes under a pseudonym. Throughout the '30s and '40s, Kincaid continued to record for many different labels.

A banjo picker at the age of five, Kincaid, who became known as the 'Kentucky Mountain Boy', purveyed such materials as **I Gave My Love A Cherry**, **The Letter Edged In Black** and **Barbara Allen**, singing the latter over WLS every Saturday night for four successive years. An ever-active radio performer, he bought his own station (WWSO, Springfield, Ohio) in 1949 but sold it again in 1953. His more recent recordings include albums for Bluebonnet and McMonigle.

Besides appearing on nearly every major barn dance, Kincaid played for years in the Northeast, introducing folk and country music to a whole new area before retiring in Springfield.

Recommended:
Mountain Ballads And Old Time Songs (Old Homestead/–)

Claude King

Wolverton Mountain – a distinctive and menacing country-styled 'Jack And The Beanstalk' saga – was a 1962 million-seller for King and co-writer Merle Kilgore.

Born in Shreveport, Louisiana, on February 5, 1933, King attended the University of Idaho and then returned to

Shreveport, to business college. He had been interested in music, having bought his first guitar from a farmer for 50 cents when he was 12.

During the '50s he began writing and performing, playing clubs, radio and TV. He was signed to Columbia in 1961, gaining country hits with, among others: **Big River**, **Big Man** (1961), **The Comancheros** (1961), **Burning Of Atlanta** (1962), **I've Got The World By The Tail** (1962), **Building A Bridge** (1963), **Hey Lucille** (1963), **Sam Hill** (1963), **All For The Love Of A Girl** (1969), **Friend, Lover, Woman, Wife** (1969). **Big River, The Comancheros, Wolverton Mountain** and **Burning Of Atlanta** also crossed over into the pop charts.

During the early '60s, Nashville expected King to become a superstar, but it was not to be. Public taste seemed to move away from butch sagas of the great outdoors and, as a result, the '70s failed to prove kind to the singer, though he did see some chart action with **Montgomery Mabel** (1974) and **Cotton Dan** (1977).

Recommended:
Claude King's Best (Gusto/Gusto)
Meet Claude King (Columbia/–)

Pee Wee King

The leader of what was claimed to be the first band to use an electric guitar and drums on the Opry, King is also a noted songwriter, being writer or co-writer of such hits as **Slow Poke**, **Bonaparte's Retreat**, **You Belong To Me** and **Tennessee Waltz**, the last named being declared the State song of Tennessee in February 1965.

Born in Abrams, Wisconsin, on February 18, 1914, of Polish descent, Frank 'Pee Wee' King learned a harmonica, accordion and fiddle while still a boy, broadcasting over radio stations in Racine and Green Bay at the age of 14.

After stints with the WLS (Chicago) Barn Dance during the early '30s, he joined the

Don't Say Aloha, Bashful Brother Oswald (Pete Kirby). Courtesy Rounder Records.

Gene Autry Show, taking over the band in 1934 when Autry headed for Hollywood. Renamed the Golden West Cowboys, the band – which featured such stars as Eddy Arnold, Redd Stewart, Cowboy Copas, Ernest Tubb and guitarist Clem Sumney at various points in its history – first graced the Opry in the mid-'30s. In 1938 the band followed Autry to Hollywood to make 'Gold Mine In The Sky' for Republic Pictures, the first in a series of cowboy movies.

From 1947 to 1957 King hosted his own radio and TV show on Louisville WAVE, also in 1947 signing a record deal with RCA-Victor. Additionally, he did a weekly television circuit.

Success as a composer came when **Tennessee Waltz**, penned by King and Stewart, became a hit record for Cowboy Copas in 1948. Around the same time, King himself began logging a tally of hits. **Tennessee Tears** (1949), **Slow Poke** (a 1951 million-seller), **Silver And Gold** (1952) and **Bimbo** (1954) all became Top 10 entries.

The Golden West Cowboys were hit by the rise of rock'n'roll during the late '50s, King adding horns in an effort to compete with the all-conquering rockers. However, by 1959 the financial struggle had become uneven and King disbanded the Cowboys, forming another unit several months later when Minnie Pearl asked him to accompany her on a roadshow. When Minnie ceased touring in 1963, King kept the unit – which included Redd Stewart and the Collins Sisters – together until 1968. Then he disbanded once again, relying on local musicians to support him.

Though King's records have failed to sell in any tremendous quantities since he terminated his contract with RCA in 1959, he remains a popular and highly respected member of the country music profession, worthily being elected to the Country Music Hall Of Fame in 1974.

Recommended:
Ballroom King (–/Detour)
The Legendary Pee Wee King (Longhorn/–)
The Best Of Pee Wee King And Redd Stewart (Starday/–)
Rompin, Stompin', Singin', Swingin' (–/Bear Family)
Hog Wild Too (–/Zu Zazz)

Pete Kirby (Bashful Brother Oswald)

Real name Beecher Kirby, born in Sevier County, Tennessee, this guitarist, banjoist and dobro player was one of eight brothers and two sisters, all of whom played instruments, their father being proficient on fiddle, banjo and guitar. As a young man, Kirby worked in a sawmill, a cotton mill and on a farm before becoming a guitarist in an Illinois club.

During the World's Fair in Chicago, he played in local beer joints, passing the hat around, also working part-time in a restaurant in order to survive. Then came a move to Knoxville, Tennessee, where he joined Ray Acuff's Crazy Tennesseans on radio station WRL. As Bashful Brother Oswald, the bib-overall-clad Kirby sang and duetted with Acuff, playing the banjo for most solo work, and reverting to dobro whenever Acuff's distinctive band sound was required. A member of the Smoky Mountain Boys for many years, Kirby

Above: Kristofferson as Billy The Kid in 'Pat Garrett And Billy The Kid'.

looked after Acuff's Nashville museum in the '70s, often indulging in good-time pickin' in order to attract extra customers.

One of the stars to appear on the Nitty Gritty Dirt Band's **Will The Circle Be Unbroken** (1971), Kirby cut a fine series of albums for the Rounder label during the '70s, some of the sessions lining him up alongside fellow Smoky Mountain Boy Charlie Collins.

Recommended:
Brother Oswald (Rounder/–)
That's Country – with Charlie Collins (Rounder/–)

Alison Krauss

A fiddle prodigy for most of her young life, Alison Krauss (born in 1971 in Champaign, Illinois) has taken bluegrass into the country charts and country radio.

Alison began to play fiddle at five, formed her first band at 12, and signed with Rounder Records to make her first album at 14. She began entering fiddle contests while still a young child, and was seven times a fiddle champion in five Midwestern states by the time she was 16. By this time she had made a big impact at the Newport Folk Festival and was recording with some of the top session players in Nashville, including Jerry Douglas and Sam Bush for the album **Too Late To Cry** (1987). Putting together her own bluegrass band, Union Station, she began touring, playing coffee houses,

Me And Bobby McGee, Kris Kristofferson. Courtesy Monument Records.

Jesus Was A Capricorn, Kris Kristofferson. Courtesy Monument Records.

made her music accessible to fans of country and other types of music.

Recommended:
I've Got That Old Feeling (Rounder/–)
Two Highways – with Union Station (Rounder/–)
Too Late To Cry (Rounder/–)

Kris Kristofferson

Born in Brownsville, Texas, on June 22, 1936, the son of a retired Air Force Major-General, Kristofferson's family moved to California during his high school days. Living in San Mateo, he went to Pomona College. In 1958, he won a Rhodes Scholarship to Oxford University, England, where he began writing his second novel, becoming a songwriter as a sideline, using the name of Kris Carson.

His novels rejected by publishers, he became disenchanted with a literary career and left Oxford after a year, first getting married, then joining the Army and becoming a helicopter pilot in Germany. He began singing at service clubs in Germany, also sending his songs to a Nashville publisher. Upon discharge in 1965, Kristofferson headed for Nashville, initially becoming a janitor in Columbia Records' studio. Broke and with his marriage in tatters, he was about to take a construction job when Roger Miller recorded one of his songs, **Me And Bobby**

McGee, the composition also being covered by Janis Joplin, whose version became a million-seller in 1971. During 1970, Johnny Cash waxed **Sunday Morning Coming Down**, another Kristofferson original, and the Texan cut his first album for Monument, Cash writing a poem documenting the singer-songwriter's lean years, for use as a sleeve note.

Appearances on Cash's TV show and other triumphs followed, including a debut engagement at a name club (The Troubadour, L.A.) and another hit via Sammi Smith's version of his **Help Me Make It Through The Night** – a million-seller in 1971. During the following year, Kristofferson's **Silver Tongued Devil And I** single went gold, while in November, 1973, another single, **Why Me?** also qualified as a gold disc. Additionally, in 1973, the year that he married singer Rita Coolidge, two albums, **The Silver Tongued Devil And I** and **Jesus Was A Capricorn**, provided the Texan with further gold awards.

He and Rita merged bands and began recording together, though still continuing with their solo careers. But Kris's recording career was burning out and sales started to dip. However, he had made his debut as an actor in 'Cisco Pike' (1972) and from there on gained role after role. He and Rita appeared in 'Pat Garrett And Billy The Kid' (1973), the real breakthrough coming with 'Alice Doesn't Live Here Anymore' (1974), after which came major roles in movies such as 'The Sailor Who Fell From Grace With The Sea' (1976), 'A Star Is Born' (1976), 'Convoy' (1978), 'Heaven's Gate' (1980), 'Rollover' (1981), etc.

He kicked a 20-year drinking problem at the end of the '70s (too late to save his marriage to Rita Coolidge, which ended in 1979), and was singing better than at any time in his life. He even got his name on a No.1 album in 1985 when he joined with Willie Nelson, Johnny Cash and Waylon Jennings to create the **Highwayman** LP and hit single. Shortly after this he signed with Mercury Records. His songwriting returned to the biting edge of his earlier work, with a hard-hitting political stance to the fore on **Third World Warrior**, a 1990 album. He also undertook more concert work, both as a member of the Highwaymen and with his own band, or with just a couple of back-up musicians.

Recommended:
Kristofferson (Monument/Monument)
Me And Bobby McGee (Monument/ Monument)
Jesus Was A Capricorn (Monument/ Monument)
Full Moon – with Rita Coolidge (A&M/A&M)
The Legendary Years (–/Connoisseur)
Third World Warrior (Mercury/Mercury)

k.d. lang

Farmer's daughter k.d. lang (born Kathy Dawn Lang in 1962 in Consort, Alberta, Canada) requests that her name is always printed in lowercase type, because she believes that you have to be different to stand out, and this young lady certainly is different. She dresses differently, and her whole lifestyle is different from any other country music performer. She has her own uncompromising musical style. As a child she heard a lot of country music, and by the time she reached her teens she had mastered piano and guitar, and had started writing songs. In the early '80s she began working with local bands, singing and writing country-influenced songs. By 1983 she had formed her own band, the Reclines (a nod towards her idol, the late Patsy Cline). In 1984 the group produced **A Truly Western Experience**, an independent Canadian release on Bumstead Records. This eventually led to a contract with Sire Records who brought in Dave Edmunds to produce **Angel With A Lariat** (1987), a rock-influenced country album that gained rave reviews in the rock press, but little mainstream country radio play. That same year lang duetted with Roy Orbison on **Cryin'**, which was used in the movie soundtrack for the comedy 'Hiding Out'. The duet introduced her to the country charts for the first time.

In October 1987, k.d. coaxed veteran producer Owen Bradley out of semi-retirement to produce **Shadowlands**, a kind of quirky tribute to Patsy Cline, but also an album that had a little bit of everything, from '50s country to pop and big band. One track, **The Honky Tonk Angels Medley**, featured Kitty Wells, Loretta Lynn and Brenda Lee, and the whole project brought k.d. closer to country. She scored on the country charts with **I'm Down To My Last Cigarette** and **Lock, Stock And Teardrops** in 1988, and was also included in the CMA's Route 88 European country music promotion. **Absolute Torch And Twang**, which she co-produced with band members Ben Pink and Greg Penny, hit both the pop and country charts in 1989 on its way to platinum status. k.d. won several major music awards in Canada, and was also nominated by the ACM in the New Female Vocalist category.

It was to be another three years before k.d. produced her next album, **Ingenue** (1992), a brilliant artistic and commercially successful record that gained platinum status in America and gold in Britain, where she made a big impact on the pop charts. This took her a long way from country, a style of music that k.d. has probably left behind her.

Recommended:
Ingenue (Sire/Sire)
Absolute Torch And Twang (Sire/Sire)
Angel With A Lariat (Sire/Sire)
Shadowland (Sire/Sire)

Jim Lauderdale

Singer-songwriter Jim Lauderdale (born April 11, 1957 in Statesville, North Carolina) draws from a wealth of American musical styles and fashions to produce a quirky combination of progressive country-rock, bar-room ballads and soul-searching

Absolute Torch And Twang, k.d. lang. Courtesy Sire Records.

Above: Canadian k.d. lang, who brought a fresh approach to modern country music.

blues. He has built a cult following in the early '90s that could break through to the mainstream of country music.

He grew up in various towns in the Carolinas, where his father was an Associate Reformed Presbyterian Minister and his mother served as a music teacher and choir director. Lauderdale began his own musical pursuits playing drums in the school band. He then delved into country, bluegrass and folk, music, learning banjo and guitar. Throughout his college years at the North Carolina School of the Arts, he was active as a solo performer. Once studies were completed and he had gained a degree in theatre, he moved to New York, where he played the country/folk scene with his own band, mixing country, swing and blues. Later landing a part in the off-Broadway show 'Cotton Patch Gospel', he joined several touring productions. One, 'Diamond Studs', found him playing Jesse James. He was in Los Angeles with the 'Pump Boys And Dinettes' show when he came to the attention of Pete Anderson, the well-known producer of Dwight Yoakam. Impressed by Lauderdale's songs and singing, Anderson produced the singer-songwriter for the second volume of **A Town South Of Bakersfield** compilation. This led to Lauderdale singing back-up on recordings by Carlene Carter, Dwight Yoakam, Darden Smith and Jann Browne, and also having his songs cut by Vince Gill, Shelby Lynne, Kelly Willis, Jann Browne and George Strait.

His own record deal came in 1991 when he signed with Reprise and teamed up with John Leventhal and Rodney Crowell. They co-produced his debut album, **Planet Of Love**, which combined a healthy roots reverence with some flat-out blues, honky-tonk and even a yodel.

Recommended:
Planet Of Love (Reprise/–)

Tracy Lawrence

One of the young 'hunks' of country music, Tracy Lawrence (born January 27, 1968 in Atlanta, Texas) is determined to make his career in country music a long and successful one. Lawrence is still young enough to look boyish – he has long, curling, blondish-brown hair, a starter moustache, and, at six feet tall, he makes a big impact with the female fans. His blossoming career was almost cut short before it had a chance to get started. In May 1991, he was celebrating the completion of his first album with an old friend in Nashville when they were confronted by three men with two guns. The trio robbed the couple, and when Tracy put up a fight to protect his female friend, he was shot four times, resulting in several weeks in hospital and his album release put on hold until he had recovered.

Tracy had dreamt of being a singing star from quite a young age. In 1972 his family moved to Foreman, Arkansas. His stepfather was a banker, while his mother raised six kids, with Tracy being more trouble than the other five put together. Even so, he faithfully attended the Methodist church and sang in the choir. He learned to play guitar and was performing at jamborees by the time he was 15. Two years later he was gigging in honky-tonks and night-clubs. As soon as he graduated from high school, he moved around Louisiana, Arkansas, Texas and Oklahoma with bands. He studied at Southern Arkansas University, then moved to Louisiana to join a band as lead singer. When the group's routine of three-day weekend gigs seemed to be leading nowhere, he packed up and moved to Nashville, arriving in September of 1990. Seven months later he signed a record deal. Prior to that he had earned his living entering and winning singing contests at open-mike nights in Tennessee and Kentucky. The youngster also landed a regular gig on the Nashville radio show, 'Live At Libbys', and one night was spotted at the club in Kentucky by the man who would become his manager.

Definitely one of the hottest acts on the country music scene, his debut album, **Sticks And Stones**, has sold in excess of 800,000 copies, gaining a gold disc. Lawrence became the first country artist on Atlantic to score a No.1 single, with **Sticks And Stones** in 1992. Since then he has had more No.1s with **Today's Lonely Fool** and **Runnin' Behind** (also 1992). A fourth single from the album, **Somebody Paints The Wall**, was a Top 5 entry. His follow-up album, **Alibis**, is proving just as successful and hit-laden, with the title song making No.1 in 1993. Tracy and his band undertook more than 280 show dates during 1992, and he picked up ACM's New Male Vocalist award in 1993. He is now regarded as one of the finest and youngest new breed honky-tonkers to hit country music in the '90s.

Recommended:
Sticks And Stones (Atlantic/–)
Alibis (Atlantic/–)

Chris LeDoux

While many modern country stars like to think of themselves as cowboys, only Chris LeDoux (born on October 2, 1948 in Biloxi, Mississippi) can lay claim to being the real McCoy. Amazingly adept at bringing the rodeo life into vivid colour, he's not just blowing smoke. The singer is a world champion rodeo star, and since the early '80s has run his own 500-acre ranch in Wyoming

His family settled in Texas after his father retired from the Air Force. Chris began his musical odyssey at 14 when he started playing guitar and writing songs. He was also heavily involved in youth rodeo, and his songs reflected his love of the sport. After the family relocated to Wyoming, LeDoux began to actively pursue a rodeo career. He had twice won the state's bareback title while still attending high school in Cheyenne. After graduation he won a rodeo scholarship and received a national title in his third year. Chris started singing his songs to fellow rodeo contestants, and they reacted favourably to early works such as **Bareback Jack**, **Rodeo Life** and **Hometown Cowboy**. Shortly after getting married in 1972, LeDoux made his first independent recordings in Sheridan, Wyoming, resulting in **Rodeo Songs Old And New** and **Songs Of Rodeo And Country** (on cassette). He made his first Nashville recordings after his parents moved to Tennessee, and over the next few years recorded 15 albums in Nashville for his own American Cowboy label. In those days, LeDoux supposedly regarded the music as just a sideline to being a cowboy. But he apparently took the music seriously enough to sell 14 million dollars' worth of cassettes, most of them manufactured by his parents in their own home tape-duplicating room.

By 1976, Chris was becoming known as a singer-songwriter of note and his rodeo career was riding high. He won the Bareback Bronc World Title, and also picked up awards in Wyoming and Nevada for his bronze sculptures of a Bull Rider and Bronc Rider.

Something of a cult figure, LeDoux continued to rodeo until 1984, when

Above: Chris LeDoux is known for a rodeo as well as for a music career.

accumulated injuries made him hang up his spurs. Once he had his Wyoming ranch operational, he began working on his musical career. He was now booking himself and his Saddle Boogie Band. Finally his recording career bolted out of the chute when a mention from Garth Brooks, who sang about listening to 'a worn-out tape of Chris LeDoux' in his 1989 hit **Much Too Young (To Feel This Damn Old)** was enough to kick up new interest in Wyoming's singing cowboy.

In early 1991 Chris LeDoux was signed to Capitol Records. With his recordings released on Liberty, his first album, **Western Underground**, co-produced by Jimmy Bowen and Jerry Crutchfield, sold in excess of 100,000 units and included a minor country hit in **This Cowboy's Hat** (1991). Impressed by these sales, Capitol took over all of the singer's entire 22 independent cassettes, and re-released them on CD during 1991 and 1992. Chris teamed up with Garth Brooks for the title song of his 1992 album **Whatcha Gonna Do With A Cowboy**, and saw the single race up the country charts with the album attaining gold status. Another single, **Cadillac Ranch** (1992), went Top 20 and the cowboy singer co-starred with Suzy Bogguss in a TNN special, 'Ropin' And Rockin'' in early 1993.

LeDoux describes his music as 'a combination of western soul, sagebrush blues, cowboy folk and rodeo rock 'n' roll; and captures a piece of modern-day Americana in his songs. An 18-year overnight sensation, he is now playing to

**Planet Of Love, Jim Lauderdale.
Courtesy Reprise Records.**

packed audiences and attracting younger fans with his Western Underground Band.

Recommended:
Whatcha Gonna Do With A Cowboy (Capitol/Capitol)
Life As A Rodeo Man (Capitol/Capitol)
Rodeo's Singing Bronco Rider (–/Westwood)
Western Underground (Capitol/–)
Under This Old Hat (Liberty/)

Brenda Lee

Once known as 'Little Miss Dynamite' – she is only 4 feet 11 inches tall – Brenda Lee was born Brenda Mae Tarpley, in Lithonia, Georgia, on December 11, 1944. She won a talent contest at the age of six and in 1956 she was heard by Red Foley who asked her to appear on his Ozark Jubilee Show. Her success on that show led to further TV stints and a Decca record contract in May, 1956. After her initial record release – a version of Hank Williams' **Jambalaya** –she began chalking up an impressive tally of chart entries, commencing with **One Step At A Time**, which became both a country and pop hit in 1957. Later came a series of hard-headed rockers like **Dynamite** (1957) and **Sweet Nuthin's** (1959), Brenda proving equally adept at scoring with such ballads as **I'm Sorry** (1960) and **As Usual** (1963). For a while she was undoubtedly one of the world's most popular singers; but after a major hit with **Coming On Strong** in 1966, her record sales tapered off considerably.

After a few years in an easy-listening wilderness, Brenda made a return to the country Top 10 in 1973 with a version of Kris Kristofferson's **Nobody Wins**. She followed this with other major records such as **Sunday Sunrise** (1973), **Wrong Ideas**, **Big Four Poster Bed**, **Rock On Baby** (1974), **He's My Rock** (1975), **Tell Me What It's Like** (1979), **The Cowgirl And The Dandy**, **Broken Trust** (1980), and a joyous version of **Hallelujah I Love You So**, a 1984 duet with George Jones. At this time, Brenda had disagreements with MCA, her label for 30 years, and for a time she made no new recordings. In 1990 she signed with Warner Brothers, but has so far failed to make a return to the best-sellers' lists.

Still an energetic onstage performer, Brenda has appeared in the movie 'Smokey And The Bandit 2' and has her own syndicated radio show. She has also contributed her time on behalf of country music as a director of the CMA.

Recommended:
The Brenda Lee Story (MCA/MCA)
The Golden Decade (–/Charly)
L.A. Sessions (MCA/MCA)
Brenda Lee (Warner Bros/–)
Even Better (MCA/MCA)

Johnny Lee

East-Texan John Lee Ham was born in Texas City, Texas on July 3, 1946. Raised on a farm at Alta Loma, he formed a high school band called Johnny Lee And Roadrunners, winning various talent contests. After high school he joined the US Navy, becoming a bosun's mate. Upon discharge he lived for a while in California, but later returned to Texas, working in honky-tonks and gaining a job as a singer and trumpet-player with Mickey Gilley's band.

By 1971 he was heading Mickey's band at Gilley's Houston club. He also signed a number of short-lived record deals, grabbing a place in the country charts with **Sometimes**, a 1975 ABC-Dot release.

National fame really began heading his way in 1979. When the TV movie 'The Girls In The Office', starring Barbara Eden and Susan St James, was shot in Houston, Lee and his band being given a spot in the film. The following year, the John Travolta movie 'Urban Cowboy' used Gilley's band as a focal point. Travolta heard Johnny Lee sing **Looking For Love**, a pop song penned by two Gulfport, Mississippi, schoolteachers, and insisted it went on to the film soundtrack. Released as a single by Full Moon/Asylum Records, it proved a massive cross-over hit, reaching No.1 in the country charts, and Top 5 in the US pop listings. He recorded a best-selling album of the same title and three singles from this, **One In A Million** (No.1, 1980), **Pickin' Up Strangers** and **Prisoner Of Hope** (1981), all charted high, along with **Bet Your Heart On Me** (No.1, 1981) the title track of Lee's next album.

He became an in-demand act, working with the Urban Cowboy Band, either headlining or co-headlining with former boss Mickey Gilley. He also gained much publicity when he began dating Charlene Tilton (Lucy Ewing of TV's Dallas series), the couple getting married on St Valentine's Day, 1982. That same year he logged two further Top 10 singles. **Be There For Me Baby** and **Cherokee Fiddle**. Other notable hits were **Sounds Like Love**, **Hey Bartender** (1983), **The Yellow Rose**, with Lane Brody, **You Could Have A Heart Break** (both 1984 No.1s) and **Rollin' Lonely** (1985). During 1985 he also contributed a track called **Lucy's Eyes** to an album of songs by the stars of Dallas. He and Charlene were divorced in 1984 and Lee's recording career started a rapid downward spiral. He only managed a few minor hits for Warner Brothers and Curb, making his last chart entry in 1989 with **You Can't Fly Like An Eagle**.

Recommended:
Lookin' For Love (Asylum/–)
Bet Your Heart On Me (Full Moon/–)
Hey Bartender (Warner Bros/–)

Bobby Lewis

Born in Hodgerville, Kentucky, Bobby Lewis appeared on the Hi-Varieties TV show at the age of 13, later working on the Old Kentucky Barn Dance radio show, CBS's Saturday Night Country Style and the highly rated Hayloft Hoedown.

Only 5-feet 4-inches tall, Lewis had problems handling his heavy and bulky Gibson J-200 guitar and eventually bought a 'funny-shaped small guitar' in a Kentucky music shop. This 'guitar' proved to be a lute, which he fitted with steel strings and adopted as his main instrument.

Signed to UA Records during the mid-'60s, Lewis' first Top 10 hit came in 1964 with **How Long Has It Been**, which he followed with such other sellers as **Love Me And Make It Better** (1967), **From**

Below: Bobby Lewis, who turned lute into loot, was a frequent Opry guest. He last made the charts in 1985 with Love Is An Overload.

Heaven To Heartache (1968), **Things For You and I** (1969), and **Hello Mary Lou** (1970) **From Heaven To Heartache**, a cross-over hit, earned him a Grammy nomination as Best Male Performer in 1969. In 1973, after supplying UA with 14 hits, he moved on to Ace Of Hearts and added three more, the biggest of these being **Too Many Memories**. Since then Lewis had had minor hits on GRT Records (1974), Ace Of Hearts (1975) and the ill-fated Capricorn label (1979). In 1985 he charted with **Love Is An Overload**.

Recommended:
The Best Of (UCA/–)
Tossin' And Turnin' (–/Line)

Jerry Lee Lewis

Yet another example of the 1950s' interplay between country and rock 'n' roll, this pianist-singer with the wild stage manner was originally influenced by the pumping, honky-tonk piano style of Moon

Odd Man In, Jerry Lee Lewis. Courtesy Mercury Records. The album includes the classics Shake, Rattle And Roll and Your Cheatin' Heart.

Mullican. Vocally he incorporated the delivery of black singers into his routine and, finally, Jerry Lee returned to this country roots splitting his programmes into half rock, half country affairs.

Born in Ferriday, Louisiana, on September 29, 1935, Lewis was exposed to a wide range of music and particularly church music – his parents sang and played at the Assembly of God church. Jerry learned piano and played his first public gig in 1948 at Ferriday's Ford car agency, where to introduce a new model he sang **Drinkin' Wine Spo Dee O Dee**. Like many of his generation, Lewis spent time in the local black clubs and when he cut his first sides for Sam Phillips' Sun label in Memphis, they proved to be some of the wildest rock'n'roll sounds of their time. But amid the frantic rockers Jerry Lee also snuck in an array of pure country cuts, his first Sun release being a cover of the Ray Price hit **Crazy Arms** that made the country charts.

His career went through a traumatic period after he married his 13-year-old cousin. He was booed off the stage in Britain and the UK press crucified him. However, by the late '60s he was making a comeback. Jerry Lee was back making more country records this time. He scored big on the US country charts of the period with out and out honky-tonkers like **Another Place, Another Time** and **What Made Milwaukee Famous** (both 1968) and other hits for the Smash label, such as **To Make Love Sweeter For You** (No.1, 1968), **One Has My Name**, **She Even Woke Me Up To Say Goodbye** (1969) and **Once More With Feeling** (1970).

Ever controversial – in 1976, 'The Killer' was picked up by the police for waving a gun around and demanding entry to Elvis Presley's Memphis mansion – he continued accruing both publicity and hits for the Mercury label throughout the '70s, the latter including **Touching Home**, **Would You Take Another Chance On Me** (1971), **Chantilly Lace** (1972), **Sometimes A Memory Ain't Enough** (1973), **He Can't Fill My Shoes** (1974), **Let's Put It Back Together Again** (1976), **Middle Aged Crazy** (1977), **Come On In** and **I'll Find It Where I Can** (1978).

By 1979 Jerry Lee had moved over to Elektra, his first Top 10 record for his new

label being a bluesy version of the Yip Harburg standard **Over The Rainbow** (1980). During 1981 he played London's Wembley Festival and jammed with Carl Perkins, the duo becoming a Sun rock trio when they were joined onstage by Johnny Cash in Germany later that same tour. Also in 1981 Jerry Lee went Top 10 yet again with **Thirty Nine and Holding**. Then he quit Elektra and joined the MCA roster. Unfortunately his health has been poor – a couple of times he has reportedly been on the point of death. He fought the law (or rather the income tax authorities) and happily managed to win through but he also lost his fifth wife, Shawn, who died from an overdose of methadone in 1983. Sometimes Jerry Lee's biography seems no less than a horror story – two of his sons have died in accidents, two of his wives have met untimely deaths, – but Lewis himself carried on, often making magnificent music, earthy, gutsy, the sort that is the very roots of both country and rock music.

A strange personality, combining arrogance and boastfulness with an apparent respect for religion and traditional Southern values, Jerry Lee is the ultimate country music enigma. He was one of the first performers to be inducted into the Rock'n'Roll Hall Of Fame, in 1986. Three years later, a bio-pic of his early career, 'Great Balls Of Fire', starring Dennis Quaid, brought him back into the pubic eye, with the soundtrack album making an appearance on the US pop charts.

Recommended:
The Sun Years (–/Charly)
Odd Man In (Mercury/–)
Country Class (Mercury/–)
The Best Of (Mercury/Mercury)
Southern Roots (Mercury/Mercury)
Killer Country (Elektra/Elektra)
I Am What I Am (MCA/–)
Classic Jerry Lee Lewis (–/Bear Family)
Pretty Much Country (–/Ace)
When Two Worlds Collide (Elektra/Elektra)
The Country Sound Of (–/Pickwick)

COUNTRY CLASS
Jerry Lee Lewis

Featuring
LET'S PUT IT BACK
TOGETHER AGAIN
JERRY LEE'S ROCK & ROLL
REVIVAL SHOW
YOU BELONG TO ME
NO ONE WILL EVER KNOW

Country Class, Jerry Lee Lewis. Courtesy Mercury Records.

Light Crust Doughboys

The Doughboys, basically a western swing outfit, first came to life when Bob Wills and Herman Arnspiger began playing as Wills' Fiddle Band. With the addition of vocalist Milton Brown they became the Aladdin Laddies in 1931 and later gained a job advertising Light Crust Flour on Fort Worth radio station KFJZ, at which point they became the Fort Worth Doughboys, then in 1932 the Light Crust Doughboys.

The personnel of the Doughboys changed frequently during the band's career and even by 1933 – the year that

Below: An odd individual, Jerry Lee Lewis makes fine country music.

the band switched to another Fort Worth station, WBAP – all the original members had departed. O'Daniel restocked the outfit with new members (including his sons).

But despite the changes, the band continued their long association with Burrus Mills until 1942, when they became the Coffee Grinders for a while under the sponsorship of the Duncan Coffee Co. Later, the Doughboys – who in various forms had recorded for Victor and Vocation – reverted to their former and better-known title, but never again achieved the fame that was theirs during the '30s.

Recommended:
The Light Crust Doughboys (Texas Rose/–)
String Band Swing Volume 2 (Longhorn/–)
Live 1936 (–/Flyright)

Little Texas

One of Nashville's 'long hair' acts, Little Texas have brought a fresh, high-energy approach to traditional country, highlighted by soaring vocal harmonies and versatile instrumental work. The band's beginnings can be traced back to 1984, when lead vocalist Tim Rushlow (son of Tom Rushlow, lead singer with '60s band Moby Dick And The Whales) and guitarist Dwayne O'Brien, both originally from Oklahoma, got together in Arlington, Texas to play local clubs. A year later the pair teamed up with two native Texans, lead guitarist Porter Powell and bass player Duane Propes. The foursome took to the road, honing their skills and learning their craft. At a fair in Massachusetts they met up with keyboard player Brady Seals (nephew of songwriter Troy Seals and cousin to Dan Seals) and drummer Del Gray.

At this time the six-man band didn't have a name, but, having cut some demos as Band X, they signed a development and record deal with Warner Brothers in 1988. After passing on the name Possum Flat, they came up with Little Texas, a hollow 35 miles south of Nashville where the band had their first rehearsals. The area was named for its tough characters; in the 1920s it was a lawless place where people on the run would hide out. Warners sent the band out on the road for two years, then took them in the studio at the end of 1990 to cut their first single, **Some Guys Have All The Love**, which started a steady ascent up the country charts the following summer and peaked at No.8.

Little Texas were then packed off to Memphis' legendary Ardent Studios to record an album, **First Time For Everything**, on which they sing all the vocals, play all basic instruments and have written all the songs. The title song became their second Top 10 single in early 1992, with the album also providing three more major hits in **You And Forever And Me** and **What Were You Thinkin'** (both 1992) and **I'd Rather Miss You** (1993). The album went on to reach gold status as

The Era Of Hank Locklin. Courtesy Ember Records, a British release.

Little Texas picked up nominations for both Top New Vocal Group and Top Vocal Group Of The Year at the 1993 ACM Awards. What makes their sound so unique is the combination of five voices representing a whole new generation of country bands. "I feel like we're the first country band that was influenced by young country," says Tim Rushlow. "Sure, we love bands like the Eagles and Poco, but our real influences were Alabama and Restless Heart – country's new sound."

Recommended:
First Time For Everything (Warner Bros/–)
Big Time (Warner Bros/–)

Hank Locklin

Elected mayor of his hometown during the 1960s, Locklin is the possessor of a vocal style that somehow endears him to audiences of Irish extraction.

Born in McLellan, Florida, on February 15, 1918, Lawrence Hankins Locklin played guitar in amateur talent shows at the age of ten. During the Depression years he did almost any job that came his way, gaining his first radio exposure on station WCOA, Pensacola.

At the age of 20 he made his first professional appearance in Whistler, Alabama, and then embarked on a series

of tours and broadcasts throughout the South, becoming a member of Shreveport's Louisiana Hayride during the late '40s. Record contracts with Decca and Four Star were proffered and duly signed, Locklin gaining two hits with Four Star in **The Same Sweet Girl** (1949) and **Let Me Be The One** (1953). The success of the latter helped him obtain Opry bookings and become an RCA recording artist.

With RCA he began to accrue a number of best-sellers – **Geisha Girl** (1957), **Send Me The Pillow You Dream On** and **It's A Little More Like Heaven** (both 1959), all being Top 10 items. but he surpassed these in sales with the self-penned **Please Help Me I'm Falling**, a 1960 No.1 that provided Locklin with a gold disc – the composer again recording the song in 1970, with Danny Davis' Nashville Brass.

A habitual tourer, Locklin, whose many other hits have included **Happy Birthday To Me** (1961), **Happy Journey** (1962) and **Country Hall Of Fame** (1967), was among the artists who, as part of the 'Concert In Country Music' made the first country music tour of Europe, in 1957. During the '70s, the singer based himself in Houston, appearing on KTR-TV and also on Dallas' KRID Big D Jamboree and by 1975 had become signed to MGM Records.

Recommended:
The First 15 Years (RCA/RCA)
Famous Country Music Makers (–/RCA)
Hank Locklin (MGM/MGM)
Irish Songs Country Style (RCA/RCA)

Josh Logan

A native of Kentucky, Josh Logan worked in an auto wrecking yard in Richmond, Kentucky during the week, and on weekends he performed at local clubs and private parties. That was in the mid-'70s when Nashville was not ready for the pure honky-tonk country style that has always been the Logan trademark. In the early '80s Josh decided to make music a full-time occupation. He recorded for several independent labels. One release, **I Made You A Woman For Somebody Else** (NSD, 1981), started to gain extensive radio plays, only for Conway Twitty to put the song on the B-side to his **Tight-Fittin' Jeans** hit.

Logan signed with Charley Pride's booking agency Chardon and undertook several major tours as Earl Thomas Conley's opening act. Following this, he worked several club dates with Sandy Powell (sister of Sue Powell – a member of Dave And Sugar). In 1987 he came to the attention of producer Nelson Larkin, who recorded some sides in the hope of setting up a deal with RCA. They liked what they heard, but were only signing girl acts, so Josh signed with Curb and made his debut on the country charts with **Everytime I Get To Dreamin'** (1988). The following year he gained another chart entry with **Somebody Paints The Wall**, the title song to what is, so far, his only album.

Recommended:
Somebody Paints The Wall (Curb/–)

Lone Justice

A West Coast rock band formed in 1984, Lone Justice was always a vehicle for lead singer Maria McKee, a talented songwriter, vocalist and guitarist, who was born on August 17, 1964 in Los Angeles. She started performing in local L.A. clubs from the age of 16 with her half-brother Bryan MacLean, who had cut his musical teeth playing in the rock band Love. Lone Justice landed supporting roles on tours with both U2 and the Alarm during 1984. Bob Dylan caught the band doing a couple of his songs, and, suitably impressed, he paved the way for them to sign with Geffen Records in 1985. Their debut album, **Lone Justice**, was aimed at country-rock fans with McKee's strident vocals having that edge to appeal to both markets. Most songs were penned by McKee, with **Sweet, Sweet Baby (I'm Falling)** and Tom Petty's **Ways To Be Wicked**, both hitting the pop singles chart, while the album also climbed the pop charts, earning the band a gold disc. Developing as a writer, McKee wrote **A Good Heart**, a No.1 British pop hit for Feargal Sharkey. She also duetted with Dwight Yoakam on **Bury Me**, a track included on **Guitars, Cadillacs**, Yoakam's debut album in 1985. Lone Justice topped the British pop charts

Below: Maria McKee of Lone Justice flavours her music with country.

in 1988 with **I Found Love**, while they continued to straddle a fine line between country and rock stylings. Maria McKee embarked on a solo career in 1991, but has remained close to that hard-edged country rock sound.

Recommended:
Lone Justice (Geffen/–)

Lonzo And Oscar

Really the Sullivan brothers, John (Lonzo) was born in Edmonton, Kentucky, on July 7, 1917, and Rollin (Oscar) was born in Edmonton, Kentucky, on January 19, 1919. Lonzo And Oscar were the top comedy act on the Opry, their 20-year stint being terminated by the death of Johnny Sullivan on June 5, 1967. Originally there was another Lonzo, a performer named Ken Marvin (real name Lloyd George) teaming with Rollin in pre-World War II days and recording a nationwide comedy hit, **I'm My Own Grandpa**, a song penned by the Sullivans. The act went into store while the brothers became part of the armed forces. Shortly after their return to civilian life, Ken Marvin retired. John assumed the guise of Oscar, the duo touring with Eddy Arnold until 1947 – in which year the Sullivans became Opry regulars.

Some time after the death of John, Rollin Sullivan again resurrected Lonzo And Oscar using a new partner Dave Hooten. In its various permutations over the years, the act recorded for RCA, Decca, Starday, Nugget, Columbia and GRC.

Recommended:
Traces Of Life (GRC/–)

John D. Loudermilk

The writer of such hits as **Talk Back Trembling Lips**, **Tobacco Road**, **Abilene**, **Ebony Eyes**, **Indian Reservation**, **Language Of Love**, **Norman**, **Angela Jones**, **Sad Movies** and **A Rose And A Baby Ruth**, also co-writer (with Marijohn Wilkin) of **Waterloo**, Loudermilk was once a Salvation Army bandsman. Born in Durham, North Carolina, on March 31, 1934, he learned to play trumpet, saxophone, trombone and bass drum at Salvationist meetings, later learning to play a homemade ukelele which he took to square dances. Although he made his TV debut at the age of 12 – with Tex Ritter, no less – his big break came in the mid-'50s, when he set a poem to music and performed it on TV. George Hamilton heard Loudermilk's composition and recorded it, the result – **A Rose And Baby Ruth** – released in 1956, selling more than a million copies.

After penning **Sittin' In The Balcony**, a 1958 smash hit for Eddie Cochran, Loudermilk married Gwen Cooke, a university student and headed for Nashville, there meeting Jim Denny and Chet Atkins. His own recording of **Language Of Love** became a huge hit on both sides of the Atlantic during the winter of 1961–62 but all his subsequent releases have made but slight chart indentations. He is, nevertheless, an onstage performer of considerable talent and charm and has always been a great favourite in Britain.

Recommended:
A Bizarre Collection Of The Most Unusual Songs (RCA/–)
Country Love Songs (RCA/–)
Encores (RCA/RCA)
Blue Train (–/Bear Family)
It's My Time (–/Bear Family)
Elloree (Warner Bros/–)

Louvin Brothers

The Louvin Brothers, Ira and Charlie, formed one of the finest duos in country music, offering superb close harmony vocals that often displayed their gospel roots.

Born in Rainesville, Alabama (Ira on April 21, 1924; Charlie on July 7, 1927), the Louvins (real name Loudermilk) were raised on a farm where they first learned to play guitar. Drafted into the forces during World War II, they returned to music at the cessation of their active service, gaining dates on Knoxville's KNOX Mid-Day Merry-Go-Round. However, just when the brothers seemed to be making the grade, Charlie was recalled for duty during the Korean crisis.

Once more, the Louvins had to re-establish themselves. Following some appearances on a radio show in Memphis, they signed a recording contract with MGM Records, followed by a signing with Capitol Records. By 1955 they had become Opry regulars, also having a hit record with their self-penned **When I Stop Dreaming**, a disc which sparked off a run of similarly successful singles by the Louvins during the period 1955–62. Then, after one last duo hit via **Must You Throw Dirt In My Face?**, the Louvins decided to go their separate ways. Charlie proved the more popular of the two, with three 1964 chart records, **I Don't Love You Anymore**, **See The Big Man Cry** and **Less And Less**. Just a few months later, Ira was dead, the victim of a head-on car accident near Jefferson City, Missouri (June 20, 1965). His wife Florence, who sang under the name of Anne Young, was also killed in the crash.

Since that time, Charlie Louvin has continued as a top flight country entertainer. He also provided Capitol with a number of chart entries before leaving the label to join United Artists in the fall of 1973 and immediately scoring with **You're My Wife, She's My Woman** (1974). He has still notched the odd hit or two in recent times – he and Emmylou Harris charted with **Love Don't Care**, a Little D release, in 1979, while in 1982 he teamed with Jim And Jesse for **North Wind**, a mid-chart entry for the Soundwaves label – and at the beginning of the '80s claimed to be averaging 100,000 miles a year playing concert dates.

Recommended:
Great Gospel Singing Of The Louvin Brothers (Capitol/–)
Tragic Songs Of Life (Rounder/–)
The Louvin Brothers (Rounder/–)
Running Wild (–/Sundown)
Close Harmony (–/Bear Family)
Live At New River Ranch (Copper Creek/–)
Sing Their Hearts Out (–/See For Miles)

Charlie Louvin:
Somethin' To Brag About – with Melba Montgomery (Capitol/–)
50 Years Of Making Music (Playback/Cottage)
I Forgot To Cry (Capitol/Stetson)

Patty Loveless

A genuine coal miner's daughter, Patty Loveless (born Patricia Ramey on January 4, 1957 in Pikeville, Kentucky) spent her younger years in the tiny eastern Kentucky community of Beecher Holler. She was one of eight children who watched their father's health ebb away to black lung disease. When Patty was ten the family moved north to Louisville so her father could receive medical treatment. Her brother, Roger Ramey, introduced her to local country music shows, and by 1971 they were working together as a duo. Patty had already started writing songs and the pair drove to Nashville armed with around 30 songs and high ambitions. The Wilburn Brothers heard her sing and invited her on their show to replace Loretta Lynn. They signed Patty to their publishing company, and featured her in their weekly TV series and as a member of their road show from 1973 to 1975.

In 1976 she married Terry Lovelace, the Wilburns' drummer, and moved to Charlotte, North Carolina, where she continued her singing, mainly with rock and pop bands. When the marriage didn't work out, she decided to pursue a country career again. With help from her brother, Roger, who became her manager, and using the name Patty Loveless, she worked local clubs and opened shows for such major acts as Jerry Reed, Pure Prairie League and Hank Williams Jr. In early 1985 Patty again travelled to Nashville and recorded some of her own tunes as demo tapes. She became a staff writer with Acuff-Rose and Tony Brown signed her to MCA Records later that year. After scoring several minor hits, Patty finally made a breakthrough with a Top 10 entry of **If My Heart Had Windows** (1988). Her soulful voice with its high lonesome mountain edge evoked real emotion, and for the next few years she seldom scored outside the Top 10. Her hits included **A Little Bit In Love** and **Blue Side Of Town** (1988), **Don't Toss Us Away**, **The Lonely Side Of Love**, and her first No.1 – **Timber I'm Falling In Love** (all 1989). Patty scored another chart-topper with **Chains** in 1990, plus further Top 10 entries with **On Down The Line** (1990), **I'm Not That Kind Of Girl** and **Hurt Me Bad (In A Real Good Way)** (1991).

By this time, Patty had married again. New husband Emory Gordy Jr, one-time member of Emmylou Harris' Hot Band, had co-produced her first two albums with Tony Brown. The pair were living in Georgia, though they also had an apartment in Nashville, and by early 1993 they had bought a townhouse in Music City, obviously anticipating a move. Alongside her own recordings, Patty built a reputation for the soulful, ethereal harmonies she provided for Vince Gill's hits, such as **When I Call Your Name**. She gained a gold disc for her impeccable **Honky Tonk Angel** album, but has yet to break through to superstar status. Feeling that there were too many female singers with MCA (Trisha Yearwood, Reba McEntire and Wynonna), Patty joined Epic Records in 1992.

In the midst of recording her first album for the new label (produced by Emory Gordy Jr) she had to undergo voice-saving laser surgery on one of her vocal chords, which proved a successful operation. With her winning combination of wholesome beauty, shy, sweet nature and powerful,

emotional voice, Patty Loveless is a singer yet to reach her peak of achievements and accolades.

Recommended:
Only What I Feel (Epic/–)
If My Heart Had Windows (MCA/–)
Honky Tonk Angel (MCA/MCA)
On Down The Line (MCA/MCA)

Lyle Lovett

Lyle Lovett isn't your typical country singer – his music is as different as his distinctive high hair, exploring not only country, but jazz, gospel and blues. He was born on November 1, 1957 in Houston, Texas, but grew up in the rural Klein community, an area populated by farmers of German extraction. After graduating from Klein high school, Lovett attended Texas A&M University, where he received a degree in journalism in 1980 and a year later one in German. It was at this time that he first started writing songs and performing in the songwriter showcase clubs of Houston, Dallas and Austin. He visited Europe in 1979, to improve his German, and became friendly with a local country musician named Buffalo Wayne. When he completed his university studies, Lovett started playing further afield, from New Mexico to New York. In 1983 Wayne was involved in Luxembourg's annual fair, the Schueberfouer, and invited Lovett to appear. Also on the bill was a Texan outfit, J. David Sloan And The Rogues, whose members included Matt Rollings and Ray Herndon; both were later involved with Lovett's first recordings, made in Phoenix in the summer of 1984.

The tape was taken to Nashville by Guy Clark, who passed it to Tony Brown, who in turn wasted no time in signing Lyle to MCA/Curb Records in 1985. His songs started to be picked up by other performers including Nanci Griffith and Lacy J. Dalton.

Above. This honky-tonk angel with an edge is Patty Loveless.

Lyle made an impact on the country charts with **Cowboy Man** (1986), **Why I Don't Know** and **Give Me Back My Heart** (1987) and **She's No Lady** (1988). His albums, which combined elements of western swing, '70s singer-songwriter and contemporary country, gained rave reviews

Below: Cult country singer and film extra, Lyle Lovett.

outside mainstream country music, and it was obvious that Lovett could never be constrained by the confines of country.

He writes most of his music, which leans towards dark humour and satire. His first albums featured such guests as Vince Gill, Rosanne Cash, Emmylou Harris and members of the Phoenix band that played on the original demo tape. In 1989 he won a Grammy for Best Vocal Performance By A Male Artist, but by this time was far removed from country music. He moved from Nashville and started recording in Los Angeles. In 1992 Lyle was chosen as the opening act for Dire Straits' first world tour of the '90s. In June of 1993 Lyle married Hollywood actress Julia Roberts in a highly secretive, surprise wedding.

Recommended:
Joshua Judges Ruth (MCA-Curb/MCA-Curb)
Cowboy Man (MCA/MCA)
Pontiac (MCA/MCA)
Lyle Lovett And His Large Band (MCA/MCA)

Lulu Belle And Scotty

Husband-wife teams have long been a staple of country music performance but one of the earliest and most popular was Lulu Belle And Scotty, mainstays of the National Barn Dance from 1933 to 1958.

Lulu Belle was born Myrtle Eleanor Cooper in Boone, North Carolina, on December 24, 1913. Active musically as a teenager, she auditioned for the National Barn Dance in 1932 and was hired, immediately becoming one of the stars of the show. She often teamed with Red Foley (then bass player with the Cumberland Ridge Runners) in duets.

In 1933 another cast member was added to the National Barn Dance: a guitarist, banjoist, singer and songwriter

Above: Husband and wife team Lulu Belle and Scotty were regulars on the National Barn Dance for 25 years.

named Scott Wiseman, known professionally as Skyland Scotty. Born near Spruce Pine, North Carolina, on November 8, 1909, Scotty had appeared on radio over WVRA in Richmond as early as 1927, and on WMMN, Fairport, West Virginia, while attending Fairport Teachers College.

The two hit it off and became a very popular team (although some listeners wrote angry letters to WLS, thinking Scotty had 'stolen' Red Foley's girl), largely on the basis of their smooth duet sound and on Scotty's prolific songwriting, which produced such country standards as **Mountain Dew** (co-written with Bascomb Lamar Lunsford), **Remember Me**, the folk

favourite **Brown Mountain Light**, and their biggest hit, **Have I Told You Lately That I Love You?**

They also appeared as stars of several films based around the National Barn Dance cast, including 'Village Barn Dance', 'Hi Neighbor', 'Country Fair', 'Sing, Neighbor, Sing' and 'National Barn Dance'. They spent a brief time away from the Barn Dance at the Boone County Jamboree in Cincinnati (1938–41), but were closely associated with Chicago, where they had a daily TV show over WNBQ from 1949–57.

Scotty began working towards a masters degree in education during the '50s and when the act bowed out of the performing limelight in 1958 he and Lulu Belle retired to their native North Carolina, where Scotty finally fulfilled his early ambition to teach, Lulu Belle spending a

couple of terms in state legislature. Scotty died of a heart attack in 1981, in Florida.

Recommended:
Have I Told You Lately That I Love You? (Old Homestead/–)
Lulu Belle And Scotty (Starday/–)
Sweethearts Still (Starday/–)

Bob Luman

Once a teenage rockabilly, Luman became an Opry regular in August 1969. Born in Nachogdoches, Texas, on April 15, 1937, Robert Glynn Luman spent much of his boyhood listening to various country and R&B shows on the radio. Encouraged to pursue a musical career by this father, he

learned guitar but was torn between continuing as a musician or as a baseball player. But after being offered a trial with the Pittsburgh Pirates during the mid-'50s, he flunked it and from then on concentrated his energies on becoming a rock star in the Presley mould.

In 1955, Luman recorded tracks for a small Dallas company. A short time later he won an amateur talent contest that resulted in a spot on Shreveport's Louisiana Hayride. Record dates with Imperial and Capitol followed, plus Las Vegas bookings and a part in the rock movie 'Carnival' (1957) but it was not until 1960 and the Warner release of a Luman single called **Let's Think About Livin'** that the real breakthrough came. The Boudleaux Bryant song provided the singer with a residency in both the pop and

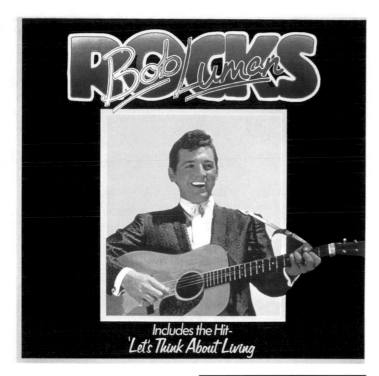

Bob Luman Rocks. A British compilation. Courtesy DJM Records.

country Top 10. He was, however, unable to capitalize on this position. A reservist, Luman was called up for active duty, Jim Reeves taking over his band during Luman's army stay.

With the advent of the Beatles, Luman once more turned to country, signing for Hickory and Epic and logging over three dozen hits, the biggest being: **The File** (1964), **Ain't Got The Time To Be Unhappy** (1968), **When You Say Love**, **Lonely Women Make Good Lovers** (1972), **Neither One Of Us**, **Still Loving You** (1973) and **The Pay Phone** (1977). From 1976 he suffered health problems which affected his career but in 1977 he made an album, produced by Johnny Cash, that proclaimed he was **Alive And Well**. But well he was not. He died in December 1978.

Recommended:
Alive And Well (Epic/–)
The Rocker (–/Bear Family)
Let's Think About Livin' (–/Sundown)
Loretta (–/Sundown)

Robert Lunn

As the 'Talking Blues Boy' (or the 'Talking Blues Man'), Robert Lunn brought an unusual form of both comedy and blues to the Grand Ole Opry for two decades and was long the country's foremost exponent of the talking blues, a style which was to become a staple of folk song revival.

Lunn was born in Franklin, Tennessee, on November 28, 1912. He apprenticed in vaudeville before joining Opry in 1938, and he stayed with the show, except for service in World War II, until 1958. A left-handed guitar player, he rarely sang, relying instead on his droll, dry, talking blues recitations, most of which he wrote himself. His only recording was a long out-of-print Starday album called **The Original Talking Blues Man**. Lunn died of a heart attack on March 8, 1966.

Right: Robert Lunn's forte, the talking blues, was popularized on the Opry. This style was brought to a greater prominence by the great Woody Guthrie.

Frank Luther

Often remembered best for his children's records, Frank Luther actually had a long career in country music as well as some success in the pop field. Born Frank Crow in Kansas, on August 5, 1905, he grew up in Bakersfield, California, and his early musical experience was as a singer and pianist with gospel quartets.

He moved to New York in the late '20s, where he teamed up with Carson J. Robison as a recording act (frequently called on record Bud and Joe Billings) and as songwriters, collaborating on **Barnacle Bill The Sailor** and **What Good Will It Do?** He and his wife Zora Layman also did extensive recording, some of it with Ray Whitley.

He recorded a wide variety of country material in the '20s and '30s, for such labels as Victor, Conqueror and Decca. He moved into the field of children's recording in the late '30s and '40s, recording stories, ballads and cowboy songs, largely for the Decca label.

In addition, he lectured on American music and even wrote a book on the subject: 'Americans And Their Songs'.

Other achievements include early country music films (c.1933), authorship of some 500 songs and a good bit of popular recording as well as country. In the '50s he moved into an executive role before finally retiring in the New York area.

Few of his country recordings are available, but he can be heard on Carson J. Robison's **Just A Melody**, an Old Homestead album.

Loretta Lynn

CMA Female Vocalist Of The Year in 1967, 1972, 1973 and, with Conway Twitty, three times winner of the Association's Vocal Duo Of The Year section, Loretta, the daughter of Melvin Webb, a worker in the Van Lear coal mines, was born in Butcher's Hollow, Kentucky, on April 14, 1935.

Part of a musical family, she sang at local functions in her early years, marrying Oliver 'Moonshine' Lynn (known as Mooney) immediately prior to her fourteenth birthday. In the '50s, the Lynns moved to Custer, Washington, where Loretta formed a band that included her brother Jay Lee Webb on guitar. Later, signed to Zero Records, the diminutive vocalist hit the charts with **Honky Tonk Girl**, a 1960 best-seller. She and Mooney toured in a 1955 Ford in order to promote the record.

The Wilburn Brothers were impressed enough to ask Loretta to come to Nashville, where Mooney took a job in a garage to support his four daughters, while Loretta and the Wilburns tried to negotiate a record deal – the singer eventually signing for Decca.

With a song appropriately titled **Success**, she broke into the charts in 1962, at the same time winning the first of her numerous awards. And for the rest of the '60s and all of the '70s, Loretta became the most prolific female country hit-maker

in Nashville. Virtually every one of her releases made the Top 10 during this period, many of them, including **Don't Come Home A-Drinkin'** (1966), **Fist City** (1968), **Woman Of The World** (1969), **Coal Miner's Daughter** (1970), **One's On The Way** (1971), **Rated X** (1972), **Love Is The Foundation** (1973), **Trouble In Paradise** (1974), **Somebody Somewhere (Don't Know What He's Missin' Tonight)** (1976), **She's Got You** (1977) and **Out Of My Head And Back In My Bed** (1977), reaching the premier position. And her series of duets with Conway Twitty claimed impressive sales figures, the duo enjoying joint No.1s with **After The Fire Is Gone**, **Lead Me On** (1971), **Louisiana Woman, Mississippi Man** (1973), **As Soon As I Hang Up The Phone** (1974), and **Feelin's** (1975).

A grandmother at 32, Loretta has six children. The owner of various business interests, she also owns the whole town of Hurricane Mills, Tennessee, where she resides. Ever-popular – even in the '80s she continued to notch up more than a dozen chart records including such Top 10 singles as **It's True Love** (1980) and **I Still Believe In Waltzes** (1981), both duets with Conway Twitty, and a solo effort with **I Lie** (1982) – the singer suddenly found herself with a whole new host of fans in 1980 when her autobiography, 'Coal Miner's Daughter', was turned into a much-hailed movie, with Sissy Spacek portraying Loretta and Tommy Jones playing Mooney. The first female artist to win the CMA's coveted Entertainer Of The Year award (1972), Loretta has never been above a bit of controversy when acting as a spokesperson on behalf of downtrodden womanhood. Her songs included such feminist banner-wavers as **The Pill**, a 1975 hit that endorsed birth control.

A very wealthy woman, Loretta owns property in Mexico and Hawaii, and is a popular guest on American chat shows. Still active on the touring circuit, her magnificent soprano is the very voice of rural heart and heartache. In 1988 she became one of the most popular stars to be inducted into the Country Music Hall Of Fame.

Recommended:
I Remember Patsy (MCA/MCA)
Greatest Hits Volumes 1 & 2 (MCA/–)

The Very Best Of Conway And Loretta (MCA/MCA)
Coal Miner's Daughter (MCA/MCA)
Just A Woman (MCA/MCA)
Don't Come Home A-Drinkin' (MCA/–)
Loretta Lynn Story (–/Music For Pleasure)
Sings Country (–/Music For Pleasure)
Country Partners – with Conway Twitty (MCA/–)

Shelby Lynne

A young lady with a distinctive blues-flavoured vocal style, Shelby Lynne (born on October 22, 1969 in Quantico, Virginia) made her initial impact in Nashville in 1987, when she appeared on TNN's Nashville Now series. The very next day she had four record label executives all eager to sign her. A tough young lady with a determined attitude, she decided to wait so that she could sign with Billy Sherrill at Epic Records. For this lady, no other label would do, she wanted what she considered to be the best.

Shelby had been around music for a number of years, previously working clubs in Alabama. She had grown up in Jackson, Alabama, where her father was a local bandleader. Along with younger sister, Alison, she would often add vocal harmony support at her father's night-club and Holiday Inn gigs. Music played a major role in the Lynne household. As a child she grew up on a rich diet that ranged from the Mills Brothers to Barbra Streisand, Bob Wills to Les Paul and Mary Ford. In 1986 the Lynne family was torn apart when their heavy-drinking father killed himself and their mother in a shooting tragedy in the driveway of their home. To overcome her grief, Shelby immersed herself in music, and entered singing contests. Following an unsuccessful Opryland audition, she was asked to demo some songs for a local songwriter. It was this demo tape that led to the appearance on Nashville Now.

Her first single, a duet with George Jones on **If I Could Bottle This Up**, made the country charts in 1988, and Shelby has since charted on a regular basis with such

Below: Loretta Lynn's biography was made into the Oscar-winning film, 'Coal Miner's Daughter', in 1980.

Above: The diminutive, Virginia-born Shelby Lynne is a powder keg vocalist ready to explode.

songs as **The Hurtin' Side** (1989), **I'll Lie Myself To Sleep** and **Things Are Tough All Over** (1990) and **What About The Love We Made** (1991), without making the breakthrough to the Top 10. In 1991 she gained the ACM's Horizon Award and has produced three albums for Epic.

Recommended:
Temptation (Morgan Creek/–)
Soft Talk (Columbia/–)
Tough All Over (Columbia/–)

Mac And Bob

Lester McFarland (mandolin and vocals), born on February 2, 1902, in Gray, Kentucky, and Robert Alexander Gardner (guitar and vocals) born on March 16, 1897, in Olive Springs, Tennessee, met each other at the Kentucky School for the Blind in their middle teens and became one of the first of the mandolin-guitar duet teams that became so popular in America in the middle 1930s.

They spent several long stints with the National Barn Dance (1931–34, 1939–50) as well as on KNOX, Knoxville (1925–31) and KDKA, Pittsburgh and KMA, Shenandoah, Iowa. They began recording with Brunswick in 1926 and also recorded for the American Record Company complex of labels, Conqueror, Columbia, Dixie, Irene and others. They were best known for **When The Roses Bloom Again**, but introduced many old-time songs and ballads to the repertoires of the duet teams that followed. Although they were long favourites, their sound was rather stiff and they were superseded by later duos.

Bob retired in 1951, while Mac went on as a solo until 1953. A talented musician, he also played piano, trumpet, cornet and trombone.

Mac McAnally

Singer-songwriter Mac McAnally (born on July 1, 1959 in Belmont, Mississippi) first tasted success while still a teenager, when his self-penned song, **It's A Crazy World**, became a Top 40 pop hit in 1977. Musically, McAnally cut his teeth on his mother's gospel piano-playing. His first gig, when he was only 13, was as a piano player at 'state-line' clubs north of the Tennessee–Mississippi border. Alcohol sales were, and still are, illegal in Belmont.

In search of another place to play, Mac took his tasteful finger-pickin guitar style to Muscle Shoals, Alabama, where he still lives. Working in the famous studios as a guitar player, he played some of his own songs when a session was cancelled. Before he knew it, his first album had been completed. It's A Crazy World went to No.2 on the Adult-Contemporary charts and broke into the pop Top 40. The song was later revived by country star Steve Wariner.

The song established McAnally as a singer-songwriter with a unique artistic voice, but he maintained his session work and blossomed as a songwriter, penning hits for Jimmy Buffett (**It's My Job**), Alabama (**Old Flame**), Shenandoah (**Two Dozen Roses**), Steve Wariner (**Precious Thing**) and Ricky Van Shelton (**Crime Of Passion**). He also became involved in production, co-producing Ricky Skaggs' album **My Father's Son**. All this behind-the-scenes work not only keeps the bills paid and his record-making skills intact, but allows Mac to spend time with friends, who are otherwise on the road.

In 1989, he signed with Warner Brothers Records, producing the album, **Simple Life**, a brilliant collection of his own songs that featured contributions from Ricky Skaggs, Vince Gill, Tammy Wynette, Mark Gray and Mark O'Connor. He made a Top 20 entry on the country charts with the autobiographical **Back Where I Came From** (1990). Two years later he landed on MCA, with Tony Brown producing yet another superb collection of vignettes from real life, under the title **Live And Learn**. Mac specializes in compelling stories told with sensitive lyrics, seasoned with a dash of wry humour, a style that is perhaps at odds with '90s honky-tonk.

Recommended:
Live And Learn (MCA/–)
Simple Life (Warner Bros/Warner Bros)

Leon McAuliffe

"Take it away, Leon", was Bob Wills' famous cry which made Leon McAuliffe's name a household word in the Southwest during the heyday of western swing. Although he rose to prominence with the Texas Playboys, he actually had a long career of his own as well.

Born William Leon McAuliffe on January 3, 1917, in Houston, Texas, he joined the Light Crust Doughboys in 1933, at the age of 16, and began his famous association with Wills in 1935. One of the first to electrify his steel, he popularized the sound for many years with Wills.

After his return from World War II, Leon set up his own band, the Cimarron Boys, in Tulsa. He recorded for Columbia through to 1955, then with Dot, ABC, Starday, Capitol, his own label Cimarron, and also Stoneway, before leading the newly revived Texas Playboys on Capitol. His biggest hits were **Blacksmith Blues** and **Cozy Inn**, though he wrote and performed many western swing and steel guitar classics while a Texas Playboy. These included the following notables: **Steel Guitar Rag**, **Panhandle Rag**, **Bluebonnet Rag**.

As western swing faded in popularity in the late '50s, Leon developed other business interests including two Arkansas radio stations. But by the late '70s Leon was back in the band business once more, leading a revitalized version of the Original

Texas Playboys, and recording for Capitol and Delta. He died on August 20, 1988, in Tulsa, Oklahoma.

Recommended:
Bob Wills' Original Texas Playboys Today (Capitol/–)
Cozy Inn (ABC/–)
Everybody Dance, Everybody Swing (–/Stetson)

McBride And The Ride

McBride And The Ride's electrifying three-part harmony vocal blend saw Billy Thomas, Terry McBride and Ray Herndon riding the crest of a wave of success. The trio came together in 1989, but the members brought to the band three lifetimes of country music experience.

Lead singer and bassist Terry McBride was born in Austin, Texas, and grew up 60 miles down the road in the small ranching community of Lampasas. He started playing guitar at the age of nine and by his early teens had already played with his father's band. After high school he spent three years on the road with his father, Dale McBride, who had eleven country chart hits on independent labels. Terry followed with a two-year stint in Delbert McClinton's band, then moved to Austin. Guitarist Ray Herndon also grew up with music. In his early teens he played in his father's band in Scottsdale, Arizona. Later, as a member of J. David Sloan And The Rogues, he played on some demos for the then unknown Lyle Lovett. The demos became the basis of Lovett's first MCA album and the band became the core ensemble of Lovett's Large Band. Drummer Billy Thomas started playing the kit in sixth grade and grew up working in rock bands around Fort Myers, Florida. In 1973 he moved to Los Angeles, where he toured with Rick Nelson, Mac Davis and the Hudson Brothers. After moving to Nashville in 1987, he toured and recorded with Vince Gill and Emmylou Harris.

MCA Nashville President Tony Brown brought the three together in 1989 and produced the debut album, **Burnin' Up The Road**, which didn't even get off the starting grid. The first two singles, **Every**

Below: Martina McBride went from t-shirt saleswoman to major star in a year.

Step Of The Way and **Felicia**, failed to chart, so the three veteran musicians loaded up a van and took to the road for a heavy schedule of live appearances. Slowly building a fan base, they made the Top 20 with **Can I Count On You** (1991). Another, **Same Old Star** (1991), also charted, but it was **Sacred Ground**, their first No.1 in 1992, which really established the strong, modern driving sound of McBride And The Ride. The album of the same title gained them a gold disc and provided further Top 10 hits in **Going Out Of My Mind** and **Just One Night** (1992).

Recommended:
Sacred Ground (MCA/–)
Hurry Sundown (MCA/–)
Burnin' Up The Road (MCA/–)

Martina McBride

One of the many young female singers to hit Nashville in the early '90s, Martina McBride (born Martina Schiff on her family's Kansas farm in 1969) was raised on the traditional country music of Merle Haggard, Buck Owens and Hank Williams. Growing up in a small Texas town, she sang at various VFW and barn dances in her father's band, the Schiffters, in which she also played keyboards. Following graduation from high school, Martina toured Kansas with several bands and ended up marrying soundman John McBride. In 1990 the couple moved to Nashville. John handled sound for Charlie Daniels, Ricky Van Shelton and other stars, while Martina waitressed and sang songwriter demos. Eventually John produced a five-song demo of his wife and they took it door-to-door around the Nashville record labels.

Eventually the foot-slogging paid off and Martina was offered a recording contract with RCA. By this time John had also moved up the ladder and was Garth Brooks' production manager, planning and organizing equipment for the superstar's tours. Martina took to the road with the Brooks' entourage, selling T-shirts and other merchandise throughout 1991. Her love for country music's traditionalism was an obvious accent on her first album, **The Time Has Come**. She had a minor hit single with the title song in 1992, and with the controversial **Cheap Whiskey** (with Garth Brooks adding harmonies, 1992) and **That's Me** (1993).

The association with Brooks paid dividends when she was selected as the opening act for his 1992 tour dates. Standing up for modern women, Martina says, "I try to portray women with dignity and respect. I don't want to do any songs about women getting walked on, treated badly and putting up with it all."

Recommended:
The Time Has Come (RCA/–)

C. W. McCall

McCall (real name William Fries, born Audubon, Iowa, November 15, 1928) worked his way up the ladder in the advertising industry, and won a 1973 Cleo award for a TV campaign he masterminded on behalf of the Metz Bread Company. Creating a fictional Old Home Bread truckdriver called C. W. McCall as lead character in this series of commercials, he

began using his own voice on the soundtracks, later recording a single based on the commercials.

Adopting his McCall guise he cut **The Old Home Filler-Up and Keep On A-Truckin' Café** (1974), the result eventually becoming a national hit. With truckers fast becoming the folk heroes of the '70s, Fries aimed further narrative-type singles at this market, scoring with such releases as **Wolf Creek Pass**, **Classified**, **Black Bear Road** and **Convoy**, the last named becoming a worldwide multi-million seller in early 1976.

That same year, Fries/McCall left MGM Records and signed for Polydor, entering the country music charts with **There Won't Be No Country Music**. During 1977 he went Top 10 once more with **Roses For Mama**, but when his Polydor contract ended a few months later he decided to quit music and return to advertising, gaining some added income when Sam Peckinpah decided to make a 1978 film based on Fries' **Convoy** hit..

In 1982 Fries and his family moved to Ouray, Colorado, where the former performer became involved in local politics.

Recommended:
Black Bear Road (MGM/MGM)
Wilderness (Polydor/–)

The McCarters

A traditional-sounding trio from Sevierville in the Smoky Mountains of Tennessee, the McCarters, comprising Jennifer McCarter and her younger twin sisters, Lisa and Teresa, brought refreshing mountain harmonies to mainstream country music for an all-too-brief period in the late '80s.

The sisters grew up surrounded by country music. Their father, Gerald McCarter, a factory foreman, played banjo in local bands, while his wife was a popular gospel singer at the local Baptist church. Watching clog dancing on TV, the three girls learned the routines and appeared with their father's band. Soon their skills landed them a spot on local TV. Three years later, when Jennifer was 14, she made a move into music, learning guitar and singing, with the twins adding harmonies. During the next three years, they played local shows, gaining experience working with Opry performer Stu Phillips and comedian Archie Campbell. In 1986, the girls made a big push for the big time. Jennifer started contacting Nashville record companies, and eventually gained the attention of producer Kyle Lehning, who arranged an

Above: McBride And The Ride are possessors of a trio of smooth voices.

impromptu audition in his office. Suitably impressed, he signed the McCarters to Warner Brothers. With the help of top Nashville pickers, they produced **The Gift**, a beautiful debut album, which contained their two Top 10 hits **Timeless And True Love** and **The Gift** in 1988.

The McCarters toured extensively, initially as a opening act for Randy Travis. Their mountain harmonies were laced with energy and power, and expressed with infectious enthusiasm. By the time they released their second album, **Better Be Home Soon**, in 1990, they had become known as Jennifer McCarter And The McCarter Sisters. Failing to score any more major hits, the sisters were dropped by Warner Brothers in 1992, a prime example of a major label unable to promote and build a traditional-flavoured country act.

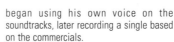

The Gift, the McCarters. Courtesy Warner Bros Records.

Recommended:
The Gift (Warner Bros/Warner Bros)
Better Be Home Soon (Warner Bros/–)

Charly McClain

Born Charlotte Denise McClain in Memphis, Tennessee, on March 26, 1956, Charly sang and played bass in her brother's band at the age of nine. At 17 she became a regular on Memphis' Mid-South Jamboree. Urged by Ray Pillow, she went onstage with Shylo at a fair, after which Shylo's producer Larry Rogers cut a demo, which he handed on to Billy Sherrill. By 1976 she had been signed to Epic, her first single being **Lay Down**. In 1978 Charly went Top 20 with **Let Me Be Your Baby**, climbing even higher with **That's What You Do To Me**.

Live At Randy's Rodeo, O.B. McClinton. Courtesy Enterprise.

Harpin' The Blues, Charlie McCoy. Courtesy Monument.

She kept up the flow with four more major singles in 1979 – including **I Hate The Way I Love It**, a duet with Johnny Rodriguez – and an additional quartet during 1980, the year that she gained her first chart-topper with **Who's Cheatin' Who?** Awards were showered on her. She responded by placing three singles in the Top 10 during 1981 (**Surround Me With Love, Sleepin' With The Radio On, The Very Best Is You**) and also going Top 10 in the album charts.

The girl George Jones dubbed the 'Princess of Country Music' has added to her toll of Top 10 singles with: **Dancing With Your Memory, With You** (1982), **Sentimental Ol' You** (1983), **Paradise Tonight** (a duet with Mickey Gilley that went to No.1 in 1983), **Candy Man** (another Gilley–McClain duet, 1984) and **Radio Heart** (No.1 in 1985). Charly married singer/actor Wayne Massey in 1984 and the pair enjoyed two Top 10 duet hits, **With Just One Look In Your Eyes** (1985) and **You Are My Music, You Are My Song** (1986). Her most recent solo success came with **Don't Touch Me There**, which spent six months on the charts in 1986. In 1988 Charly signed with Mercury and scored a few minor hits.

Recommended:
Paradise (Epic/–)
Women Get Lonely (Epic/Epic)
Surround Me With Love (Epic/–)
Who's Cheatin' Who? (Epic/–)
I Love Country (–/Epic)
Still I Stay (Epic/–)
Ten Years Anniversary (Epic/–)

Obie McClinton

McClinton was one of the few black country stars who began carving a fairly impressive career in country music during the early '70s.

Right: Hip harmonica man Charlie McCoy has played sessions and solo in his career.

Born May 25, 1940 in Senatobia, Mississippi, Obie Burnett McClinton was raised on country music, though in his early days he tried to move into R&B as a singer. After completing high school, he headed for Memphis, and ended up as a dishwasher. Next came a choir scholarship

to Rust College, Holly Springs, Mississippi, where he graduated in 1966. At the end of the year he volunteered for the Air Force and began singing on service talent shows. During this period he formed a songwriting relationship with the Stax label, contributing songs waxed by Otis Redding, Clarence Carter and others.

In 1971 he became a Stax-Enterprise artist himself, cutting several hits singles including **Don't Let The Green Grass Fool You** (1972) and **My Whole World Is Falling Down** (1973) before the label folded. Afterwards he moved on to Mercury, Epic and Sunbird, supplying all three with chart records before surfacing on Moonshine Records during 1984 with a wonderfully titled hit, **Honky Tonk Tan**. Following a lengthy illness, Obie died of abdominal cancer on September 23, 1987.

Recommended:
Country (Enterprise/–)
Obie From Senatobie (Enterprise/–)

Charlie McCoy

One of the finest harmonica players ever to grace the Nashville scene, McCoy was born at Oak Ridge, West Virginia, on March 28, 1941. Once a member of Stonewall Jackson's touring band, he opted for session work during the '60s, gaining a wide audience through his appearances on various Bob Dylan albums. He became a member of Area Code 615 in 1969 and was featured on the Code's **Stone Fox Chase**, a theme to BBC-TV's Whistle Test rock show.

Signed to Monument since 1963, McCoy had a minor pop hit with **Cherry Berry Wine** while recording for Cadence in 1961. Since then he has had a fairly active chart career, his biggest solo records being **I Started Loving You Again, I'm So Lonesome I Could Cry, I Really Don't Want To Know, Orange Blossom Special** (all 1972), **Boogie Woogie** (with Barefoot Jerry, 1974), and **Fair And Tender Ladies** (1978). He formed a music-making partnership with Laney Hicks and charted with **Until The Nights** (1981) and **The State Of Our Union** (1983). A brilliant all-round musician, McCoy was adjudged CMA Instrumentalist Of The Year in both 1972 and 1973.

Stand Up, Mel McDaniel. Courtesy Capitol Records.

Recommended:
Goodtime Charlie's Got The Blues (Monument/–)
Nashville Hit Man (Monument/Monument)
Harpin' The Blues (Monument/–)
Stone Fox Chase (–/Monument)
Appalachian Fever (Monument/Monument)
Beam Me Up Charlie (Step One/–)

Neal McCoy

A long-haired, half-Filipino, half-Irish country singer, McCoy was born Neal McGaughey on July 30, 1963 in Jacksonville, Texas. By his mid-teens Neal had started playing clubs and singing at private functions. His parents divorced and his mother, Virginia, remarried, moving to Houston with her second husband, Don McCoy. When Neal took to the clubs, he adopted the name Neal McGoy, and in the early '80s entered a country music talent contest in Dallas, walking away with the first prize. He gained the attention of Charley Pride, who signed him to a management contract.

He joined the Pride road show and toured the world with Pride for seven years. In 1987 he landed a record deal with 16th Avenue Records in Nashville, making his country chart debut with **That's How Much I Love You** (1988). Two years later he changed his name to Neal McCoy, gained a new contract with Atlantic Records and has gradually been building a healthy following for his modern honky-tonk music. With his band, Justice, he has toured regularly, opening shows for Tracy Lawrence, Alan Jackson and Clint Black. He made an impression on the charts with **If I Built You A Fire** (1991), **There Ain't Nothin' I Don't Like About You** (1992) and **Now I Pray For Rain** (1993).

Recommended:
Where Forever Begins (Atlantic/–)

Mel McDaniel

A rugged but amiable singer, McDaniel was born on September 6, 1942 in the Creek Indian area of Checotah, Oklahoma. During his high school days he became a trumpet player but, influenced by Elvis Presley, he switched to guitar. He joined a band that played local gigs and cut some singles. One, **Lazy Me**, on the Galway label, was produced by J. J. Cale. After graduation from high school, he headed for Alaska where he found he could make a living as an entertainer. Two more years on and he was in Nashville, working at the Holiday Inn. He began selling his songs and also became a demo singer, recording songs for writers who lacked the vocal equipment to do the jobs themselves.

One of this own songs, **Roll Your Own** was recorded by Hoyt Axton, Commander Cody and Arlo Guthrie but it was not until 1976 that McDaniel gained a record contract of his own. His debut single for Capitol was a version of a Bob Morrison song, **Have A Dream On Me**, which went Top 50. Throughout the rest of the '70s, his singles charted regularly but modestly. Among the most successful were **Gentle To Your Senses** (1977), **God Made Love** (1977) and **Play Her Back To Yesterday** (1979). McDaniel was proficient in songwriting, providing hits for Bobby Goldsboro and Johnny Rodriguez.

As the '80s moved in, Mel McDaniel suddenly became fashionable. In 1981, two of his singles, **Louisiana Saturday Night** and **Right In The Palm Of Your Hand**, went Top 10, while **Preachin' Up A Storm** also sold well. Since then he has gone Top 20 in almost routine fashion, notching hit after hit.

In 1986 he joined the Grand Ole Opry. The same year he charted with Bruce Springsteen's **Stand On It**. Mel's most recent Top 10 entry came with **Real Good Feel Good Song** in 1988. Three years later, he was recording for the independent DPI Records, and like so many of the veteran country stars, made the Branson connection, signing a recording contract with Branson Records in 1993.

Recommended:
I'm Countryfied (Capitol/–)
Stand Up (Capitol/–)
Naturally Country (Capitol/–)
Mel McDaniel With Oklahoma Wind (Capitol/–)
Take Me To The Country (Capitol/–)
Country Pride (DPI/–)

Ronnie McDowell

A singer who favours the dramatic, sensual style of country crooning, Ronnie McDowell (born in Fountain Head, Tennessee) initially found fame through his ability to imitate the voice of Elvis Presley. He first started singing publicly while in the US Navy in the late '60s. After completing his service, he moved to Nashville working as a sign painter while building his reputation as a songwriter. His self-penned tribute to Elvis Presley, **The King Is Gone** (1977), became a major pop/country hit peaking at No.13 on both charts. Later that year he made the country Top 10 with **I Love You, I Love You, I Love You**, setting the tone for McDowell's later sexy love-song hits.

He continued to score minor hits for Scorpion during the next two years. Then, in 1979, he signed with Epic Records, making a Top 20 entry with **World's Most Perfect Woman** (1979), but his next few releases were only minor successes. In early 1981 he made it to No.2 with **Wandering Eyes**. This was followed by the chart-topping **Older Women** (1981) and **You're Gonna Ruin My Bad Reputation** (1983). He had provided the voice of Presley for the the soundtrack of the film 'Elvis' in 1979, otherwise all traces of Presley had been erased from his repertoire. He built up a reputation as a

Below: Red River Dave McEnery onstage with Bill Fenner and Roy Huxton.

country sex symbol, concentrating on 'women' songs. Ronnie scored two more massive hits for Epic with **In A New York Minute** and **Love Talks** (1985). He then switched labels to MCA/Curb and had Top 10 winners in **All Tied Up** (1986) and **It's Only Make Believe** (1987), the latter featuring a guest vocal by Conway Twitty. By this time he was using his own band, the Rhythm Kings, on his recordings, including future Kentucky HeadHunters Doug Phelps and Greg Martin. Phelps also played a major role in the vocal arrangements, which evoked memories of late '50s teen-beat vocal groups. McDowell teamed up with Jerry Lee Lewis for **Never Too Old To Rock'n'Roll**, a minor chart entry in 1989. A revival of **Unchained Melody** in 1990 has been his last major country hit, though with his slick, choreographed show, he is still a popular live entertainer.

Recommended:
All Tied Up In Love (MCA/MCA)
Unchained Melody (Curb/–)
I'm Still Missing You (Curb/–)

Red River Dave McEnery

Although saga songs have long been a tradition in country music – dating back to broadside sheets – the foremost exponent of the style has been a tall, blue-eyed Texan named Red River Dave McEnery.

Born in San Antonio, on December 15, 1914, he began a professional career in 1935, playing a host of radio stations all

across the country but finding success in New York from 1938 through to 1941. Dave returned to Texas in the early '40s, playing the Mexican border stations and then basing himself in San Antonio. Though he found time to record for Decca, Sanora, MGM, Confidential and a whole host of smaller labels, he also appeared in a film for Columbia ('Swing In The Saddle', 1948) and a couple for Universal ('Hidden Valley' and 'Echo Ranch', both 1949).

He really found his niche when he wrote **Amelia Earhart's Last Flight**. Although he was long popular as a singer of country songs, it was these modern-day event songs which were to become his forte. Using the course of current events, he has written **The Ballad Of Francis Gary Powers**, **The Flight Of Apollo Eleven**, and **The Ballad Of Patty Hearst**.

In the early '70s Red River Dave moved to Nashville, where he became a well-known sight, with his gold boots, lariat strapped to his side, big hat and leonine white hair and goatee. He later moved back to Texas and makes occasional appearances at folk festivals.

Reba McEntire

Adjudged Female Vocalist Of The Year at the CMA awards in 1984 (and for the next three years), Reba McEntire was born in Chockie, Oklahoma, on March 28, 1954. Daughter of a world champion steer-roper, she became part of a country band while still in the ninth grade, sometimes playing at clubs until the early hours of the morning. A promising rodeo performer, she intended to become a school teacher and enrolled at Southeastern Oklahoma State University as an elementary education major. But in 1974 she was offered the opportunity to sing the national anthem at the National Rodeo Finals, where she met

It's Your Call, Reba McEntire. Courtesy MCA Records.

Red Steagall. Impressed by her voice, Steagall arranged for her to cut a demo tape in Nashville. The results gained her a contract with Mercury Records.

Her first chart record, **I Don't Want To Be A One Night Stand**, came in mid-1976, coinciding with her marriage to rodeo champion Charlie Battles on June 21. For the first couple of years, her records sold well enough, but only a duet with Jacky Ward (**Three Sheets In The Wind**, 1978) pierced the barrier into the Top 20. By 1979 she had a Top 20 single of her own with **Sweet Dreams**, while 1980 saw her in the Top 10 with **(You Lift Me) Up To Heaven**. The next few years saw her chart with such singles as: **I Don't Think Love Ought To Be That Way**, **Today All Over Again** (1981), **I'm Not That Lonely Yet** (1982), **Can't Even Get The Blues** (No.1, 1982), **You're The First Time I've Thought About Leaving** (No.1, 1983), **Why Do We Want (What We Know We Can't Have)** and **There's No Future In This** (1983).

Below: Reba is a determined soprano who wraps her songs around woman-to-woman themes.

Then, as Mercury boasted about having the next Nashville superstar, she switched her affiliation to MCA. At the same time, she found a new booking agency, tried new producers, ditched her long-time manager and played her first dates in Las Vegas. But she did not intend to move into cross-over country. She told 'Billboard' magazine, "We're wanting to go traditional country – no, I'll take that back – we want to go new country. We're wanting to go new Loretta Lynn – to get new pickers, young pickers who are like me and want to stay country."

So she stayed real country but threw in little bits of business dreamed up by choreographers, lighting directors and others who could help her act stay imaginative. And the results paid off in record sales. Her first three singles for MCA, **Just A Little Love**, **He Broke Your Mem'ry Last Night** and **How Blue** all went Top 20 in 1984, the last named reaching the top of the charts.

During 1985 she logged yet another No.1 with **Somebody Should Leave** and clambered twice more into the Top 10 via **Have I Got A Deal For You** and **Only In My Mind**. The following year she had a trio of No.1s with **Whoever's In New England**, **Little Rock** and **What Am I Gonna Do About You**. She also walked off with the CMA's Entertainer Of The Year award, as well as being a third-time Female Vocalist Of The Year winner. **Whoever's In New England**, a tear-stained ballad, became her first music video. It led to her first million-selling album and in 1987 gained her a Grammy. The No.1s continued in 1987 with **One Promise Too Late** and **The Last One To Know** as her album sales took off. **My Kind Of Country**, **Whoever's In New England**, **What Am I Gonna Do About You** and **The Last One To Know**, all became gold albums. Turning the emphasis of her music to female themes, Reba succeeded in reaching the women record-buyers like no other female country singer. This has been reflected in her huge album sales and sell-out concert appearances. She is one of the few country music entertainers who can draw huge crowds just as easily in New England and New York as she can in the southern states.

Top-of-the-chart singles continued with **Love Will Find Its Way To You**, **I Know How He Feels** (1988), **New Fool At An Old Game** and **Cathy's Clown** (1989). In 1988 Reba was listed in a Gallup Youth Survey as one of the Top 10 Female Vocalists of any kind of music, the same year People magazine named her in the Top 3 female vocalists. Four years later she did even better in the People's Choice when she was named favourite female vocalist. These awards mirrored Reba's skyrocketing record sales. Her **Greatest Hits** album went platinum in 1990, as did **Rumor Has It**. The following year, **For My Broken Heart** climbed high on the pop charts and chalked up sales in excess of two million copies. Reba's success continued on the country charts with such Top 10 high climbers as: **Walk On**, **You Lie** (1990), **Fallin' Out Of Love**, **For My Broken Heart** (1991), **The Greatest Man I Never Knew** (1992), **Take It Back** and **The Heart Won't Lie** (1993), the last a chart-topping duet with Vince Gill.

In 1987, Reba separated from Charlie Battles, her husband of eleven years, and immersed herself in her career. On June 3, 1989, she took everyone by surprise when she married Narvel Blackstock, her one-time steel guitarist and, at the time, her

road manager. With all the success, there was also tragedy, and in March 1991 Reba was devastated when eight members of her band were killed in a plane crash in California. One week after the accident, she braved her fears and faced the world at the Academy Of Country Music awards.

Since making her first video in 1986 for **Whoever's In New England**, Reba has used the format to explore the ambiguities of songs. No other artist in country music remotely matches Reba when it comes to chronicling the ups and downs of life for modern women.

Recommended:
Unlimited (Mercury/–)
Behind The Scene (Mercury/–)
My Kind Of Country (MCA/MCA)
Just A Little Love (MCA/MCA)
Whoever's In New England (MCA/MCA)
It's Your Call (MCA/MCA)
For My Broken Heart (MCA/MCA)
Live (MCA/–)
The Last One To Know (MCA/–)
Reba Nell McEntire (Mercury/–)
Reba (MCA/MCA)

Reba Live, Reba McEntire. Courtesy MCA Records.

Sam And Kirk McGee

The McGee brothers were both born in Franklin, Tennessee, Sam on May 1, 1894, Kirk on November 4, 1899. They were influenced by their father, an old-time street fiddle player, and the black street musicians of Perry, Tennessee, where the McGees spent part of their boyhood. With Sam on banjo and Kirk on guitar and fiddle, they joined Uncle Dave Macon's band in 1924, joining him on the Opry two years later. In 1930 they worked with fiddler Arthur Smith, forming the Dixieliners. Smith left in the early '40s, at which time the brothers occasionally joined a popular Opry act, Sara And Sally.

Occasional members of several of the Opry's old-time bands in ensuing years, the duo eventually opted to go their own way again, becoming favourites at many folk festivals in the '60s.

Sam, who claimed to be the first musician to play electric guitar on the Opry (a claim disputed by others), was killed on his farm on August 21, 1975 when his tractor fell on him. But Kirk soldiered on and was still appearing on the Opry up to his death on October 24, 1983.

Recommended:
Sam McGee – Grand Dad Of Country
  Guitar Pickers (Arhoolie/–)
The McGee Brothers With Arthur Smith
  (Folkways/–)

Warner Mack

Nashville-born, on April 2, 1938, singer-songwriter Warner McPherson was raised in Vicksburg, Mississippi. While at Vicksburg's Jett School he played guitar at various events, from there moving on to perform in local clubs. During the '50s, McPherson became a regular on KWHH's Louisiana Hayride and was also featured on Red Foley's Ozark Jubilee. His record career made progress in 1957 when his recording of **Is It Wrong?** charted in fairly spectacular manner. In the wake of this initial success, McPherson – who had become Warner Mack after his nickname had inadvertently been placed on a record label – decided to return to Music City. But there was a lull in his record-selling fortunes until 1964 when, following a moderate hit with **Surely**, Mack suddenly hit top gear, providing Decca with 14 successive Top 20 entries between 1964 and 1970. One of these, **The Bridge Washed Out**, was the best-selling country disc for a lengthy period of 23 weeks during 1965.

An ever-busy songwriter, Mack has written over 250 songs. Several of his other chart climbers include **Talkin' To The Wall** (1966) and **How Long Will It Take?** (1967).

During the early '70s, Mack continued on his chart-filling way with such singles as **Draggin The River**, **You're Burnin' My House Down** (1972), **Some Roads Have No Ending**, **Goodbyes** and **Don't Come Easy** (1973), all for Decca/MCA. Mack's last chart appearance came on Pageboy in late 1977 with **These Crazy Thoughts**, but still he continues playing successful tours. In recent times, Mack has completed two, well-received jaunts around Europe.

Uncle Dave Macon

Known variously as the 'Dixie Dewdrop', the 'King Of The Hillbillies' and the 'King Of Banjo Players', David Harrison Macon was the first real star of the Grand Ole Opry.

Born in Smart Station, Tennessee, on October 7, 1870, he grew up in a theatrical environment, his parents running a Nashville boarding house catering for travelling showbiz folk.

Following his marriage to Mathilda Richardson, Macon moved to a farm near Readyville, Tennessee, there establishing a mule and wagon transport company which operated for around 20 years. A natural entertainer and a fine five-string banjoist, David Macon played at local functions for many years but remained unpaid until 1918 when, wishing to decline an offer to play at a pompous farmer's party, he asked what he thought was the exorbitant fee of 15 dollars, expecting to be turned down. But the fee was paid and Uncle Dave played his first paid function, being spotted there by a Loew's talent scout who offered him a spot at a Birmingham, Alabama, theatre.

In 1923, while playing in a Nashville barber's shop, he met fiddler and guitarist Sid Harkreader, the two of them, teaming to perform at the local Loew's Theatre, then moving on to tour the South as part of a vaudeville show. A year later, while

The Gayest Old Dude In Town, Uncle Dave Macon. Courtesy Bear Family Records. Uncle Dave was the first real star of the Grand Ole Opry.

playing at a furniture convention, the duo were approached by C. C. Rutherford of the Sterchi Brothers Furniture Company, who offered to finance a New York recording date with Vocalion. Macon and Harkreader accepted, cutting 14 sides at the initial sessions, returning in 1925 to produce another 28 titles. Macon's next New York sessions (1926) found him playing alongside guitarist Sam McGee, cutting such sides as **The Death Of John Henry** and **Whoop 'Em Up Cindy** – and that same year he first appeared on the Opry, where the jovial, exuberant Macon, clad in his waistcoat, winged collar and plug hat, soon became a firm favourite.

An Opry performer almost up to the time of his death, the fun-loving banjoist cut many records during his lifetime, sometimes recording solo, sometimes as part of the Fruit Jar Drinkers Band (not the same as the Opry band of the same name) or, on more religious sessions, as a member of the Dixie Sacred Singers, usually employing fiddler Mazy Todd and the McGee Brothers as supporting musicians. He appeared in the 1940 film 'Grand Ole Opry'.

He died aged 82 on March 22, 1952, in Readyville, just three weeks after his final appearance on the Opry, his burial taking place in Coleman County, Murfreesboro, Tennessee. Uncle Dave had never learned to drive a car, and even said in one song, "I'd rather ride a wagon to heaven than to hell in an automobile."

In October 1966, he was elected to the Country Music Hall Of Fame, his plaque recalling that the man known as the 'Dixie Dewdrop' was "a proficient banjoist and singer of old-time ballads who was, during his time, the most popular country music artist in America."

Recommended:
Gayest Old Dude in Town (–/Bear Family)
Uncle Dave Macon 1926–1939 (Historical/–)
Early Recordings (County/–)
Laugh Your Blues Away (Rounder/–)
At Home In 1950 (–/Bear Family)

Rose Maddox

Born in Boaz, Alabama, on December 15, 1926, Rose Maddox began her show business as part of a family band, an outfit justifiably known as 'the most colourful hillbilly band in the land'. With Cal on guitar and harmonica, Henry on mandolin, Fred on bass, Don providing the comedy and Rose handling the lead vocals in her full-throated, emotional style, the Maddox Brothers and Rose established a reputation first in California then on to the Louisiana Hayride in Shreveport.

During the '50s, the Maddoxes produced several fine records, also putting in appearances on the Grand Ole Opry and other leading country music shows, moving back to California as the decade came to a close. Shortly after the group disbanded and Rose became a solo act, recording for Capitol and supplying the label with such successful records as **Gambler's Love** (1959), **Kissing My Pillow** (1961), **Sing A Little Song Of Heartache** (1962), **Lonely Teardrops** (1963), **Somebody Told Somebody** (1963) and **Bluebird, Let Me Tag Along** (1964).

During this period she also recorded a number of duets with Buck Owens – one of which **Loose Talk/Mental Cruelty** proved a double-sided hit in 1961. She cut an album called **Bluegrass**, a disc made at the suggestion of Bill Monroe, who played mandolin on the sessions.

After being in semi-retirement for a while, she began working again, often in partnership with Vern Williams and his band. This unit played many benefits for Rose in order to pay her hospital bills when she became gravely ill in the late '70s. During 1983 Rose and Vern Williams again joined forces to record **A Beautiful Bouquet**, an album of gospel music, recorded in honour of Rose's son Donnie, who died in August 1982.

Recommended:
The Maddox Brothers And Rose – On The Air (Arhoolie/–)
Rockin' Rollin' Maddox Brothers And Rose (–/Bear Family)
Maddox Brothers And Rose 1946–1951 Volumes 1 and 2 (Arhoolie/–)

This Is Rose Maddox (Arhoolie/–)
A Beautiful Bouquet (Arhoolie/–)
Family Folks (–/Bear Family)

J. E. Mainer

The leader of the Mountaineers, one of the first string bands on record, banjoist and fiddler J. E. Mainer was born in Weaversville, North Carolina, on July 20, 1898.

A banjo player at the age of nine, by his early teens he had become a cotton mill hand, working alongside his father at a Glendale, South Carolina mill. In 1913, he moved to Knoxville, Tennessee, there witnessing an accident in which a fiddler was killed by a railroad train. He then claimed the musician's broken instrument as his own, had it repaired and learned to play it, soon becoming one of the finest fiddlers in his area.

By 1922, Mainer had hoboed his way to Concord, North Carolina, there marrying Sarah Gertrude McDaniel, and, later, forming a band with his brother Wade (banjo), Papa John Love (guitar) and Zeke Morris (mandolin/guitar). The band gained a fair degree of fame locally. But in the early '30s came a change of fortune, when Mainer's unit, adopting the title of the Crazy Mountaineers, began a series of broadcasts from Charlottesville, sponsored by the Crazy Water Crystal Company. Record dates for RCA Bluebird followed, the Mountaineers cutting such tracks as **John Henry**, **Lights In The Valley**, **Ol' Number 9** and **Maple On The Hill**.

The band's popularity continued throughout the '30s and '40s. Mainer and the Mountaineers recorded over 200 sides for RCA and broadcast over WPTF, Raleigh, North Carolina. And by the late '60s J.E. was still performing and recording – one of his releases being a single featuring unaccompanied jew's-harp – but the grim reaper eventually caught up with him in 1971.

Recommended:
J. E. Mainer's Mountaineers Volumes 1 and 2 (Old Timey/–)
Good Old Mountain Music (King/–)

Wade Mainer

The banjo-playing younger brother of J. E. Mainer, Wade had a long and influential career of his own. Born on April 21, 1907, near Weaverville, North Carolina, Wade developed an advanced two-finger banjo picking style which led to a distinctive sound on his records as well as those he made with his brother.

After splitting from Mainer's Mountaineers, Wade formed his own group (which at times included Clyde Moody and Wade Morris of the Morris Brothers) called Wade Mainer And The Sons Of The Mountaineers.

Possessed of a strong clear voice, his **Sparkling Blue Eyes** was a major hit in 1939, one of the last commercial releases by a string band. Wade recorded for Bluebird until 1941, and after the war spent years with King but without much commercial success. After a brief retirement in North Carolina, he moved to Flint, Michigan, where he worked for Chevrolet until his retirement. In later years he recorded for Old Homestead and proved that his strong, pure country voice

and unique banjo style had not been affected by his advanced years.

Recommended:
Sacred Songs Of Mother And Home (Old Homestead/–)
Wade Mainer And The Mainer's Mountaineers (Old Homestead/–)

Barbara Mandrell

Barbara is the singer who, probably more than anyone else, has managed to weld Las Vegas glitz to the relatively more down-homey sounds of Nashville. She picks but she is slick, she sings songs like **I Was Country When Country Wasn't Cool** yet still manages to make them sound as though they had originally been penned for some Hollywood disco-flick. She is beautiful and glossy, but has brains, business-sense and enough talent to win the CMA Entertainer Of The Year award in 1980 and 1981, along with several other major plaudits.

Born in Houston, Texas, in 1948, but raised in L.A., she became part of the family band, headed by her father. At the age of 11 she could play pedal-steel, demonstrating her prowess at Las Vegas' Showboat Hotel that same year. Also before hitting her teens she could find her way around a piano, bass, guitar, banjo and saxophone. At 13 she toured with Johnny Cash and in 1966–67 played at military bases in Korea and Vietnam.

During the late '60s she began recording for the minor Mosrite label, cutting titles that included **Queen For A Day**. But following a family move to Tennessee, she set her sights on a Nashville contract, eventually signing for Columbia in March 1969, and gaining her first hit that year with her version of Otis Redding's **I've Been Loving You Too Long**, establishing a successful country-meets-soul format that saw her achieving further chart status with such R&B material as **Do Right Woman – Do Right Man** (1971), **Treat Him Right** (1971) and Joe Tex's **Show Me** (1972). During 1971 she had her first Top 10 record with **Tonight My Baby's Coming Home**, following this with **Midnight Oil** (1973). In 1975 she signed to ABC/Dot and immediately went Top 5 with **Standing Room Only**, providing the label with many other major hits, including the No.1s **Sleeping Single In A Double Bed** (1978) and **(If Loving You Is Wrong) I Don't Want To Be Right** (1979).

When ABC/Dot sold out to MCA, Barbara went on hitmaking. **Fooled By A Feeling** (1979) was succeeded by such hits as **Years** (No.1, 1979), **The Best Of Strangers** (1980), **I Was Country When Country Wasn't Cool** (No.1 1981), **Till You're Gone** (No.1, 1982), **In Times Like These** (1983), **One Of A Kind Pair Of Fools** (No.1, 1983), **Only A Lonely Heart Knows** (1984) and **To Me**, a duet with Lee Greenwood (1984).

In 1984 the Mandrell luck momentarily changed and Barbara narrowly escaped death when her car was hit head-on. Barbara and her two children were badly injured. Hospitalized for 19 days, she was unable to work for nearly a year. The singer lost much of her credibility when she sued,

Left: Mainer's Mountaineers, circa 1936. J.E. is top left, and brother Wade is bottom right.

Left: Barbara Mandrell wrote her best-selling biography and now has her own museum on Nashville's Division Street.

the troupe headed by Opry star Stu Phillips. Next came a musical liaison with Merle Haggard, Louise singing both lead and back-ups on Haggard live dates and recordings, after which she decided to go it alone, signing a deal as a solo act with Epic. The label also signed R. C. Bannon, whom Louise married in 1979.

The first hit, a minor one, was **Put It On Me**, in 1978. But the following year her career took off. Louise garnered no less than five successful singles, including a Top 20 shot with **Reunited**, a duet with Bannon. By 1981, the couple had signed to RCA, immediately making some impression with **Where There's Smoke, There's Fire.** Louise was given considerable exposure by her weekly appearances on her sister's TV show, and during 1983 she increased her solo fortunes. Two singles, **Save Me** and **Too Hot To Sleep,** both reached Top 10, while a third, **Runaway Heart**, reached Top 20, During 1984 she again had a Top 10 record with **I'm Not Through Loving You Yet**, and the following year two more with **Maybe My Baby** and **I Wanna Say Yes**. By this time Louise had her own TV series and continued charting minor hits for RCA through 1988 and **As Long As We Got Each Other**, a duet with Eric Carmen.

Recommended:
Inseparable – with R. C. Bannon (Epic/–)
Too Hot To Sleep (RCA/–)
I'm Not Through Loving You Yet (RCA/–)
Louise Mandrell (Epic/Epic)

Zeke Manners

An accordion player, singer and songwriter, Zeke Manners is best known as a co-founder of the Beverly Hillbillies and for his association with Elton Britt.

Manners befriended Britt when he joined the Hillbillies in 1932. In 1935 the two of them headed for New York, where they proved popular for many years – sometimes playing together, sometimes as solo acts.

Aside from his Brunswick recordings with the Beverly Hillbillies, Manners recorded on his own for Variety, Bluebird and RCA, collaborating with Elton Britt in the late '50s for the **Wandering Cowboy** album on ABC-Paramount.

Joe And Rose Lee Maphis

A husband and wife team whose popularity peaked during the '50s and '60s, Otis W. 'Joe' Maphis (born Suffolk, Virginia, May 12, 1921) and Rose Lee (born Baltimore, Maryland, December 29, 1922) met on Richmond, Virginia's WRVA Old Dominion Barn Dance in 1948. Shortly after meeting, they married and moved out to the West Coast, there playing on Cliffie Stone's Hometown Jamboree and Crompton's Town Hall Party for several years, also performing vocally and instrumentally. Joe played fiddle, guitar, banjo, mandolin and bass, while Rose Lee played guitar on various recording sessions. Joe, who is Barbara Mandrell's

on her insurance company's advice, the late driver's family for 10 million dollars. Back in the studios, she continued her hit-making mode with **There's No Love in Tennessee**, **Angel In Your Arms** (1985),

**Clean Cut, Barbara Mandrell.
Courtesy MCA Records.**

Fast Lanes And Country Roads and **No One Mends A Broken Heart Like You** (both 1986). In 1987 she signed with EMI–America/Capitol, and returned to a more solid country style with a Top 10

revival of **I Wish That I Could Fall In Love Today** (1988).

Barbara was a guest on many of the top chat shows, and her autobiography, 'Get To The Heart', became a best-seller. Following her accident, she was seen in many TV public service announcements, telling viewers to buckle-up. By the end of the '80s, the hit singles started tapering off, and a last Top 20 entry came in 1989, with **My Train Of Thought**.

Recommended:
The Best Of (Columbia/–)
Live (MCA/MCA)
The Key's In The Mailbox (Capitol/–)
Sure Feels Good (EMI-America/EMI-America)
Get To The Heart (MCA/MCA)
I'll Be Your Jukebox (Capitol/–)

Louise Mandrell

Born in Corpus Christi, Texas, on July 13, 1954, Louise is the fiddle and bass playing member of the Mandrell girls. A member of Barbara's Do-Rites at 15, mainly playing bass, she toured with the group for several years, but during the '70s became part of

uncle, is possibly best known for the time be spent on the road and in the studio with Rick Nelson. He died in June 1986.

Recommended:
Honky Tonk Cowboy (CMH/–)
Joe And Rose Maphis With The Blue
   Ridge Mountain Boys (–/Stetson)

Jimmy Martin

Born in Sneedville, Tennessee, in 1927, James Henry Martin rose to prominence as a member of Bill Monroe's Bluegrass Boys. He was lead vocalist, guitarist and front-man for the group for much of 1949–53, his last session with the band taking place in January 1954. Next came some fine sides for Victor, which found Martin in the company of the Osborne Brothers, fiddler Red Taylor and bassist Howard Watts, a

luminary of both Monroe's band and Hank Williams' Drifting Cowboys.

Some time later, Martin formed his own regular outfit, the Sunny Mountain Boys, and began recording for Decca. He sometimes employed material of a novelty nature but always used musicians of quality. J. D. Crowe, Vic Jordan (later with Lester Flatt), Bill Emerson (with Country Gentlemen) and Allan Munde (of Country Gazette) were among those who worked with the band.

Maligned for his use of drums – thus horrifying some purists – Martin is perhaps one of the more unsung heroes of the bluegrass scene, though his contribution, both vocally and instrumentally, has been of inestimable value.

Recommended:
Big Instrumentals (MCA/–)
Jimmy Martin (MCA/–)
Good'n'Country (MCA/–)

Fly Me To Frisco, Jimmy Martin And The Sunny Mountain Boys. Courtesy MCA Records.

Jimmy Martin And The Sunny Mountain Boys (MCA/–)

Frankie Marvin

Following in the footsteps of his elder brother Johnny, Frankie Marvin (born Butler, Oklahoma, 1905) journeyed to New York and joined him at the peak of his popularity, doing comedy as well as playing steel guitar and ukelele. He also worked with the Duke Of Paducah in a comedy team known as Ralph And Elmer, and cut numerous records for a host of companies, being among the earliest country sides recorded in New York.

He joined Gene Autry – whom he had befriended in New York in 1929 – in Chicago in the early '30s, as Autry's popularity began to grow. Frank toured, broadcast and recorded with Autry for the next two decades, adding the distinctive steel guitar styling that was so much part of the Autry sound. He left the Autry show in 1955 and later retired in the mountains near Frazier Park, California.

Johnny Marvin

Born in Butler, Oklahoma, in 1898, young Johnny ran away from home at the age of 12 to pursue a career as a musician, singer and entertainer. His quest eventually took him to New York City where he became popular on Broadway, also logging a couple of hit records on Victor: **Just Another Day Wasted Away** and **Wait For Me At the Close Of A Long, Long Day**, which was his theme song.

He also became popular in the country field as the 'Lonesome Singer Of The Air' and used his steel guitar playing alongside brother Frankie both as a comedian and as a musician. The two befriended Gene Autry in 1929, and, after the Depression, he went

Above: Jimmy Martin and his Sunny Mountain Boys. The girl is Lois Johnson.

to work for Gene as songwriter and producer on the Melody Ranch radio show. He contracted an illness while entertaining GIs in the South Seas during World War II and died in 1945 at the age of 47.

Louise Massey And The Westerners

Milt Mable, vocals and various instruments; Allen Massey, vocals and various instruments; Curt Massey, fiddle, trumpet, piano, vocals; Dad Massey, vocals and various instruments; Louise Massey, vocals; Larry Wellington, vocals and various instruments.

One of the earliest, most popular and most professional western bands in country music was known as the Musical Massey Family, then as the Westerners and, finally, as Louise Massey And The Westerners. Natives of Texas, they were the first to dress in flashy cowboy outfits and exploit a western image. They appeared for several years on Plantation Party and other popular radio shows.

The main vocals were by Louise Massey, whose growth in popularity is reflected in the changing band name, with many other solos by her brother Curt. Curt had an active and successful career in popular music both before and after his association with the Westerners, ultimately working as musical director and writer of the theme songs for the Beverly Hillbillies and Petticoat Junction TV shows.

Supporting vocals were done by all the band members, most notably the third sibling Allen, and Louise's husband Milt Mable. They recorded for Vocalion, Okeh and Conqueror. Their biggest hit was probably **The Honey Song**, although they are best known for Louise's composition **My Adobe Hacienda**.

peak of her career. She was named CMA Vocalist Of The Year in 1989 and 1990, and continued with amazing consistency placing her records in the Top 10 – **She Came From Fort Worth** (1990), a duet with Tim O'Brien on **The Battle Hymn Of Love** (1990), **A Few Good Things Remain** and **Time Passes By** (1991).

In 1990, she completed work on her seventh album, **Time Passes By**, a radical departure from her past albums and her most ambitious project so far. The album, an eclectic blend of folk, country, Scottish and a touch of classical, could hardly be termed radio-friendly, with one cut five minutes long, and another five about four minutes long. In country, three minutes is the absolute maximum length for a country hit. The following year, Kathy suffered serious throat problems and it was discovered she had ruptured a blood vessel on her vocal chords. This meant several months off the road. But she still succeeded in hitting the charts with **Lonesome Standard Time** (1992) and **Standing Knee Deep In A River (Dying Of Thirst)** (1993).

Recommended:
Lonesome Standard Time
    (Mercury/Mercury)
Time Passes By (Mercury/Mercury)
Untasted Honey (Mercury/Mercury)
Walk The Way The Wind Blows
    (Mercury/Mercury)
Willow In The Wind (Mercury/Mercury)

Ken Maynard

Ken Maynard (born July 21, 1895, Vevay, Indiana) was a major cowboy film star in both the silent and sound era, making and losing several screen fortunes in his many years on the screen. His place in country music was assured firstly by his being the first cowboy to sing on film, in 'The Wagon Master' in 1930; secondly by being the first to use a western song as a film title (**The Strawberry Roan**, 1933); thirdly by introducing Gene Autry to films, as a singer in 'In Old Sante Fe' in 1934; and lastly by his 1930 recording session for Columbia at which he cut eight cowboy songs.

A fiddler, banjoist, guitarist and rough but appealing singer, as well as a stunt man, rodeo star and film hero of over two decades (1922–45), Ken Maynard died in California on March 23, 1973.

Kathy Mattea

A country song stylist who leans more towards the traditional strains of the music, Kathleen Alice Mattea was born on June 21, 1959 in South Charleston, West Virginia, and grew up in nearby rural Cross Lanes. Her musical career began when she was given her first guitar at the age of ten. She sang in the local choir and community theatre throughout high school. At West Virginia University she joined a bluegrass group, Pennsboro, but dropped out of college in 1978 to go to Nashville with the leader of the band. Initially she was waitressing at TGI Friday's, then came a stint as a tour guide in the Country Music Hall Of Fame Museum. By this time she was recording demos, jingles and commercials, and for a time worked as a secretary at a music publishers. In 1982, she became part of Bobby Goldsboro's road show. The following year she signed a recording contract with Mercury Records.

Kathy's first single, **Street Talk** (1983), made the country charts. Over the next three years she had several more minor hits, eventually cracking the Top 10 with **Love At The Five And Dime** (1986). This was followed by **Walk The Way The Wind Blows** (1986), **You're The Power**, **Train Of Memories**, and her first No.1, **Goin' Gone** (all 1987). When Kathy first arrived in Nashville, she wrote the hauntingly beautiful **Leaving West Virginia**, which has since been used by the West Virginia Department of Tourism as the centrepiece of a million-dollar advertising campaign encouraging tourism

Above: Kathy Mattea hit the charts in 1993 with Standing Knee Deep In A River.

in her home state. Kathy's talent as a song interpreter was recognized early in her Nashville career and she gained nominations as Best Female Vocalist before she had made the Top 20.

A major breakthrough came with **Eighteen Wheels And A Dozen Roses**, her second No.1 in 1988, which also won the CMA Single Of The Year. The hit singles continued with **Untold Stories** (1988), **Life As We Knew It**, **Come From The Heart** and **Burnin' Old Memories** (all 1989). On February 12, 1988 Kathy married Nashville songwriter Jon Vezner, who was to provide his wife with one of her finest songs a year later. **Where've You Been**, written about his grandparents, was only an album track when it was named 1989 Song Of The Year by the Academy Of Country Music. Released as a single, it made the Top 10, and was also named the 1990 Song Of The Year by the CMA. Kathy was now at the

Below: Ken Maynard fiddles his way through the movie 'Strawberry Roan'.

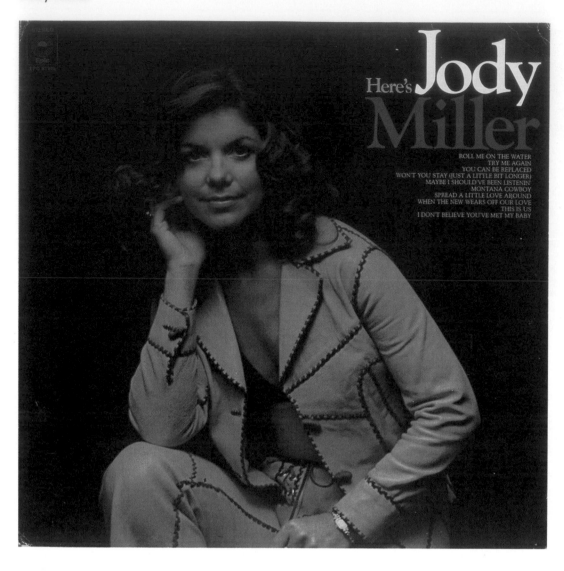

Here's Jody Miller. Courtesy Epic Records.

Jody Miller

The complete cross-over singer, Jody Miller is equally at home in pop, country or folk, a trait that leads to most articles on her talents commencing with the words: "Jody Miller is difficult to classify".

Born in Phoenix, Arizona, on November 29, 1941, the daughter of a country fiddle player, Jody grew up in Oklahoma, where she and school friends formed a trio known as the Melodies. Upon graduation she decided on a solo singing career and began establishing herself locally, joining the Tom Paxton TV Show, and gained a reputation as a folk singer. Through actor Dale Robertson she became signed to Capitol Records in 1963, making a fairly commercial folk album in **Wednesday's Child**, later cutting a hit single, **He Walks Like A Man** (1964), and obtaining a place in the Italian San Remo Song Festival. A year later, Jody's version of **Queen Of The House** – Mary Taylor's sequel to Roger Miller's **King Of The Road** – became a monster country and pop hit. But, despite some enjoyable pop–country albums that included **Jody Miller Sings The Hits Of Buck Owens** and **The Nashville Sound Of Jody Miller**, there were no further hit singles for Capitol.

Following a short retirement, during which Jody spent her time on her Oklahoma ranch raising her daughter Robin, she returned to performing once more, cutting sides for Epic. An association with producer Billy Sherrill provided her with a 1970 chart entry called **Look At**

Mine, a Tony Hatch song. Her other Top 10 hits have included **He's So Fine, Baby I'm Yours** (1971), **There's A Party Goin' On, Darling, You Can Always Come Back, Good News** (1972), while another 1972 single, **Let's All Go Down The River**, a duet with Johnny Paycheck, also sold well.

A popular act at such diverse venues as the Wembley Country Music Festival and the Riviera and Frontier in Las Vegas, Jody spends most of her spare time on the family farm in Oklahoma, where she breeds and raises quarter horses.

Recommended:
There's A Party Going On (Epic/Epic)
He's So Fine (Epic/Epic)
Here's Jody Miller (Epic/Epic)

Roger Miller

The voice and songs of Roger Miller have been heard in films ranging from 'Waterhole 3' through to the Disney version of 'Robin Hood'. He has also paid some dues as a TV actor while his records made him one of the most original and successful pop stars during the '60s.

Born in Fort Worth, Texas, on January 2, 1936, Roger Dean Miller was raised by his uncle in Erick, Oklahoma. Influenced by the singing of Hank Williams, Miller saved enough money to buy a guitar, later also acquiring a fiddle.

Following a period spent as a ranch hand, Miller spent three years in the US Army in Korea. Upon discharge, he made his way to Nashville. In the sleeve notes to his **Trip In The Country** album, Miller describes himself at this period as being "a young ambitious songwriter, walking the streets of Nashville, trying to get anybody and everybody to record my songs. All in all, I wrote about 150 songs for George

Jones, Ray Price, Ernest Tubb and others. Some were hits and some were not. In the beginning I created heavenly, earthy songs."

Ray Price was one of the first to benefit from the Miller songwriting skill, having a 1958 hit with **Invitation To The Blues**. And signed to RCA in 1960, Miller began accruing his own country winners with **You Don't Want My Love** (1960) and **When Two Worlds Collide** (1961). In 1962 he joined Faron Young's band as drummer, also guesting on the Tennessee Ernie TV Show. After one last hit for RCA in **Lock, Stock And Teardrops**, Miller moved to Smash, having an immediate million-seller with **Dang Me**, following this with other gold disc winners in the infectious **Chug-A-Lug** (1964) and the lightly swinging **King Of The Road** (1965). His endearing mixture of humour, musicianship and pure corn continued to pay dividends throughout the '60s, with many of his songs becoming Top 40 US pop hits.

The '70s, which saw Miller switch labels first to Mercury then to Columbia, brought less success to the then California-based singer-songwriter and hotel chain owner, though he kept up a steady flow of moderately sized hits. Contracts with Mercury Records (1979) and Elektra (1981) did not change the situation and it was not until 1982 and a liaison with Willie Nelson and Ray Price on **Old Friends**, a Columbia release, that Miller climbed back into the Top 10 for the first time since 1973.

But by 1985 he had moved on to a new stage in his career as 'Big River', a Miller musical based on the writings of Mark Twain, opened on Broadway. He won a coveted Tony Award for scoring the hit show. At the same time, MCA recorded an original cast album, the first album of its type to use a Nashville-based producer (Jimmy Bowen). He also signed an album deal with MCA, not that Miller really worried too much about records at the time. He had accumulated a haul of gold records and numerous industry awards, including an astonishing feat of 11 Grammies in two years, an achievement which has not yet been repeated by

Supersongs, Roger Miller. Courtesy CBS Records.

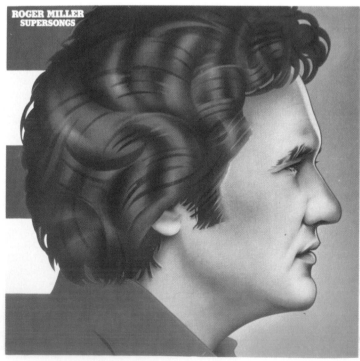

anyone. Roger Miller died on October 25, 1992 at Los Angeles' Century Hill Hospital. He had been diagnosed with cancer less than a year earlier.

Recommended:
Spotlight On (–/Philips)
Supersongs (Columbia/CBS)
King Of The Road (–/Bear Family)
Country Tunesmith (Mercury/–)
Roger Miller (MCA/MCA)

Ronnie Milsap

The winner of the CMA Male Vocalist Of The Year award in 1974 and Entertainer Of The Year 1977, Milsap is equally at home with the blues as with country ballads.

Born blind in Robbinsville, North Carolina (1944), he learned the violin at the age of seven and could play piano just a year later. By 12 he had mastered the guitar. Attending the State School for the Blind in Raleigh, he became interested in classical music but formed a rock group, the Apparitions. Upon completing high school, Milsap attended Young Harris Junior College, Atlanta, studying pre-law and planning to go on to law school at Emory College, where he had been granted a scholarship.

However, he quit studies to play with J. J. Cale and in 1965 formed his own band, playing blues, country and jazz, also signing with Scepter and cutting **Never Had It So Good/Let's Go Get Stoned**, two R&B tracks for his first single release.

By 1969, he and his band had moved to Memphis, becoming resident group at a club called TJ's, Milsap recording for the Chips label and coming up with a hit disc in **Loving You Is A Natural Thing** (1970). After a stint with Warner Brothers Records, Milsap, who had always featured some country material in his act, decided to devote his career to becoming a country entertainer. At that point he moved to Nashville, there gaining a residency at Roger Miller's King Of The Road motel and signing a management deal with Jack D. Johnson, the Svengali behind the rise of Charley Pride. In April 1973 he became an RCA recording artist, his first release on the label being **I Hate You**, a Top 10 single.

His hits since then are too numerous to list but some of his chart-toppers were: **Pure Love, (I'd Be) A Legend In My Time** (1974), **Daydreams About Night Things** (1975), **(I'm A) Stand By My Woman Man** (1976), **It Was Almost Like A Song** (1977), **Only One Love In My Life** (1978), **Nobody Likes Sad Songs** (1979), **Why Don't You Spend The Night, My Heart, Cowboys And Clowns, Smokey Mountain Rain** (1980), **Am I Losing You, (There's) No Getting Over Me, I Wouldn't Have Missed It For The World** (1981), **Any Day Now, He Got You, Inside** (1982), **Don't You Know How Much I Love You, Show Her** (1983) and **Still Losing You** (1984).

By this time Milsap had his own highly successful 'state of the art' GroundStar recording studios in Nashville and had also become heavily involved in video production. His 1985 album, **Lost In The Fifties Tonight**, had a doo-wop flavour captured in the title song and **Happy, Happy Birthday Baby**. Milsap kept edging further towards pop than he had previously, and though he ditched his

There's No Getting Over Me, Ronnie Milsap. Courtesy RCA Records.

honky-tonk approach, he remains one of the most potent performers on the scene.

Some of his more notable recent successes include: **In Love, How Do I Turn You On** (1986), **Snap Your Fingers** (1987), **Make No Mistakes She's Mine** (a duet with Kenny Rogers, 1987), **Don't You Ever Get Tired (Of Hurtin' Me)** (1989) and **A Woman In Love** (1990). In 1992, still regularly scoring Top 10 hits, after nearly 20 years of amazing pop and country success, a disgruntled Milsap announced that he had left RCA for Liberty Records: "You got to have a reason to do

this sort of thing, so I gotta say it will be a revitalization of my career. For one thing, we'll have a record company behind us for a change."

Recommended:
A Legend In My Time (RCA/RCA)
Images (RCA/RCA)
Pure Love (RCA/RCA)
Live (RCA/RCA)
Night Things (RCA/RCA)
Vocalist Of The Year (Crazy Cajun/–)
Milsap Magic (RCA/RCA)
Lost In The Fifties Tonight (RCA/RCA)

Lost In The Fifties Tonight, Ronnie Milsap. Courtesy RCA Records.

Stranger Things Have Happened (RCA/–)
True Believer (Liberty/–)
There's No Getting Over Me (RCA/RCA)

Hugh Moffatt

Long-haired, folk baritone Hugh Moffatt (born on November 10, 1948 in Fort Worth, Texas) has been providing Nashville stars such as Ronnie Milsap, Dolly Parton, Bobby Bare, Lacy J. Dalton, Rex Allen Jr, Johnny Rodriguez and Alabama with hit songs since 1974. With a keen interest in music from a young age, he played trumpet in his high school band and developed a liking for big band jazz. He learned guitar and started performing at local clubs while obtaining a degree in English at Houston's Rice University. After a stint on the Austin music scene, Moffatt headed for Washington DC, but stopped off en-route in Nashville. He decided that Music City would be a better environment for his delicate song-poetry.

In 1974 Ronnie Milsap recorded Moffatt's **Just In Case**. The following year it became a Top 5 country hit. By this time the singer-writer had married Pebe Sebert, and the couple wrote **Old Flames (Can't Hold A Candle To You)**, which Joe Sun took into the Top 20 in 1978. The most recorded of Moffatt's songs, it became a chart topper for Dolly Parton two years later. Irish duo Foster And Allen converted the song into a British easy-listening pop hit. Also in 1978, Hugh signed a recording contract with Mercury Records, scoring a minor hit with a cover version of Don Schlitz's **The Gambler** (1978). In the early '80s he formed the

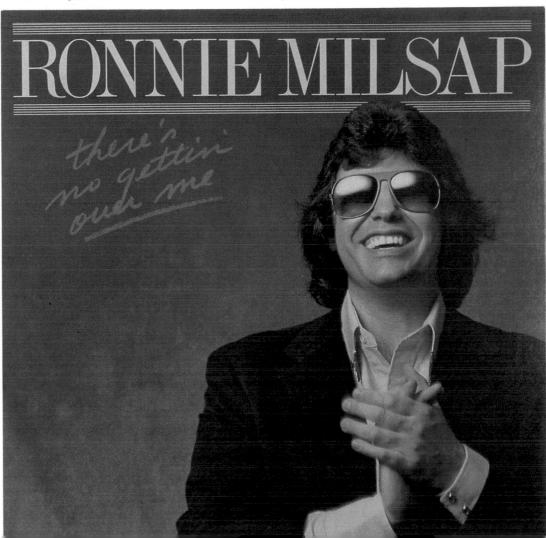

band Ratz, which included his wife, and produced a self-marketed five-track EP, **Putting On The Ratz**. Throughout the '80s Moffatt continued writing and performing at Nashville's songwriting bars and showcase stages. In 1987 he signed with Philco Records and produced the exquisite **Loving You** album. Very much a modern troubadour, Moffatt packs his guitar and takes his songs and music on the road, when the fancy takes him. He plays small clubs in America and Europe, where he has built a cult following for his invigorating and deeply enriching musical style.

Recommended:
Hugh And Katy – Dance Me Outside
   (Philo/–)
Live And Alone (Brambus/–)
Loving You (Philo/–)
Troubadour (Philo/–)

Katy Moffatt

Often referred to as a country-rocker, Katy, sister of singer-songwriter Hugh Moffatt, was born on November 19, 1950 in Fort Worth, Texas. Her musical style is as varied and large as the Lone Star State. Although her parents were not musical, Katy started piano lessons at five and continued regularly until she was 11. Like most teenagers in the '60s she was influenced by the Beatles. She bought her first guitar at 14 and two years later was performing songs from songwriters as diverse as Lennon and McCartney, and Leonard Cohen. Blues and folk music played a major role in her musical development and she began writing her own songs and singing in small coffee houses in and around Fort Worth.

During the '70s she recorded a couple of country-rock albums for Columbia. Since then she has gradually edged closer to country, with all of the elements of her past musical loves filtering through to her current style. Many years on the club circuit, sometimes performing solo, others working with her own band, has made Katy equally at ease on acoustic and hard-rocking material. In the late '80s she started a song partnership with Tom Russell and has recorded a number of

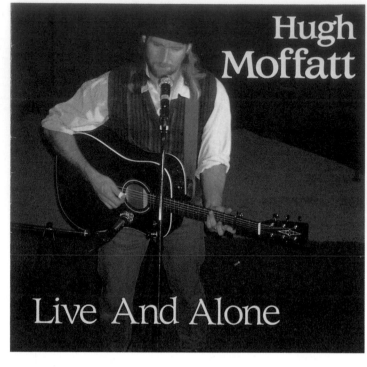

Live And Alone

**Live And Alone, Hugh Moffatt.
Courtesy Brambus Records.**

independent albums. Now living in Los Angeles, she has built up a sizeable following in Europe, mainly with the younger 'New Country' fans who enjoy her diverse, contemporary-slanted approach to country music.

Recommended:
The Greatest Show On Earth (–/Round
   Tower)
Child Bride (Philo/Heartland)
Walking On The Moon (Philo/Heartland)

Bill Monroe

The virtual base on which the whole of bluegrass music rests, William Smith (Bill) Monroe was born at Rosine, Kentucky, on September 13, 1911, the youngest of eight children. Brother Charlie was next youngest, having been born eight years previously on July 4, 1903. This gap, coupled with Bill's poor eyesight, inhibited

**The High, Lonesome Sound Of Bill
Monroe And His Blue Grass Boys.
Courtesy MCA Records.**

the youngest son from many of the usual play activities and gave him an introverted nature which carried though into later life. However, this sense of isolation did allow him to develop his musical talents with great alacrity. Church was a major formative influence. Bill could not see to read the shape note hymnals too well and so learned the music by ear. The shaped notes were to appear later in Bill's bluegrass music and the ear training was also important since it has obviously contributed to the man's fine sense of harmony in high vocal ranges.

The Monroe family was musical on both sides. Brother Charlie could play guitar by 11 and Birch could play fiddle. Bill's mother's side, the Vandivers, were the more musical and Uncle Pendleton Vandiver (later immortalized in Bill's most famous composition, **Uncle Pen**) would often stay overnight at the household, occasions of great musical festivity. Uncle Pen was a rated fiddler locally and Bill was playing publicly with him by 13, backing Pen's fiddle with guitar.

Another influence was a black musician from Rosine, Arnold Shultz. Bill would gig with him and rated him a fine musician with an unrivalled feel for the blues. At this time he also started to hear gramophone records featuring such performers as Charlie Poole and the North Carolina Ramblers.

Birch and Charlie left to seek work in Indiana and Bill joined them in 1929, when he was 18. Until 1934, in East Chicago, Indiana, they worked manual jobs by day and played dances and parties at night. For a while they went on tour with the Chicago WLS station Barn Dance, doing exhibition dancing. In 1934, Radio WLS, for whom the three brothers (Birch on fiddle, Charlie on guitar and Bill on mandolin) had been working on a semi-professional basis, offered them full-time employment. Birch decided to give up music but Charlie and Bill reformed as a duet, the Monroe

Brothers. In 1935 they were sponsored on Carolina radio by Texas Crystals. In that same year Bill married Caroline Brown – their children, Melissa (born 1936) and James (1941) have both performed with Bill. James eventually formed his own band, the Midnight Ramblers.

The Monroe Brothers were engaged on radio work in Greenville, South Carolina, and Charlotte, North Carolina. They were then persuaded forcefully (by Eli Oberstein of Victor Records) to cut some records in 1936. That year, in the Radio Building at Charlotte, they cut ten sides during February, including an early best-seller **What Would You Give (In Exchange For Your Soul)**. At first they did not feel interested in the idea of recording since they were already doing well via radio and live broadcasts, but sales of the early sides were impressive enough to warrant five more such sessions during the next 12 months. Besides, featuring popular traditional material (the Monroes did not write their own songs at the time), they had pioneered a distinctive style in which then-advanced mandolin and guitar techniques were coupled with a high clear, recognizable vocal sound.

In 1938 they went their separate ways. Bill formed the Kentuckians in Little Rock, Arkansas and then moved on to Radio KARK, Atlanta, Georgia, where the first of the Blue Grass Boys line-ups was evolved. At this time, Bill began to sing lead and to take mandolin solos rather than just remaining part of the general sound. In 1939 he auditioned for the Opry and George D. Hay was impressed enough to sign him. The following Saturday Bill played his first Opry number, the famous **Mule Skinner Blues**.

Bill Monroe's music then started to undergo subtle changes. He added accordion and banjo (played by Sally Ann Forester and Stringbean respectively) in 1945 when he joined Columbia Records and this period saw the evolution of a fuller sound with the musicians taking more solos. But in 1945 the accordion was dispensed with never to return, and in that year the addition of Earl Scruggs, with a banjo style that was more driving and syncopated than anything heard previously, put the final, distinctive seal on Monroe's bluegrass sound. Flatt and Scruggs remained with Bill until 1948.

Songs from this period include **Blue Moon Of Kentucky**, **I Hear A Sweet Voice Calling**, **I'm Going Back To Old Kentucky** and **Will You Be Loving Another Man**? Other musicians with Bill at this time were Chubby Wise (fiddle) and Howard Watts – also known as Cedric Rainwater – (bass).

Bill left Columbia in 1949 because he objected to them signing the Stanley Brothers, a rival bluegrass group. With his next label, Decca, his main man was Jimmy Martin, a musician with a strong thin, highish voice, whose talents enabled Monroe to fill in more subtle vocal harmonies alongside. This was Monroe's golden age for compositions. He wrote **Uncle Pen**, **Roanoke**, **Scotland** (a nod towards the original source of string band jigs and reels) **My Little Georgia Rose**, **Walking In Jerusalem** and **I'm Working On A Building**, the last two being religious 'message' songs, always part of the Monroe tradition from the earlier days.

By the end of the decade, bluegrass, though it had added a new dimension to country, was in decline due to the onset of rock'n'roll (it is interesting to remember that when Elvis Presley released his **Blue**

Moon Of Kentucky in 1954, Bill's record company rushed out a re-release of Monroe's (very different) original). But the '60s saw a folk revival and Bill now found hordes of students eager to embrace indigenous rural white folk music. In 1963 Bill made his first college appearance at the University of Chicago; later that same year he played to 15,000 people at the Newport Folk Festival.

Bill Monroe was elected to the Country Music Hall Of Fame in 1970. In 1985 his record company, MCA, went through several major changes, culminating in a new regime. Emory Gordy Jr, former bass player with Emmylou Harris and Rodney Crowell, was brought in as Bill's producer, which resulted in three albums that are among the most important recordings he has ever made. Stars Of The Bluegrass Hall Of Fame (1986) brought Bill together with Jim and Jesse McReynolds, Ralph Stanley, Mac Wiseman, the Osborne Brothers, Del McCoury, Carl Story, and members of Country Gentlemen and Seldom Scene. Bluegrass '87 added greatly to the bluegrass repertoire with the inclusion of six newly written songs, four of them instrumentals. Southern Flavor included five new tunes and featured Blue Grass Boys' guitarist Tom Ewing on all but one of the lead vocal parts. The album won the first Grammy ever awarded for bluegrass in 1989.

Monroe has always trodden his own musical path, never bowing to commercial pressure, and his contribution to country music is inestimable. On August 13, 1986, one month to the day before his 75th birthday, the US Senate passed a resolution recognizing "his many contributions to American culture and his many ways of helping American people enjoy themselves". It also said, "As a musician, showman, composer and teacher, Mr Monroe has been a cultural figure and force of signal importance in our time."

As for Charlie, he had a long and successful career – though not nearly as spectacular as Bill's – with his own band, the Kentucky Pardners, well into the '50s. He returned from retirement in the early '70s to appear on the bluegrass circuit – displaying great grace and charm – before dying of cancer in 1975.

16 All-Time Greatest Hits, Bill Monroe. Courtesy CBS Records. The album contains the classic Blue Moon Of Kentucky.

Recommended:
The Original Bluegrass Band (Rounder/–)
Best Of Bill Monroe And The Bluegrass Boys (–/MCA)
Bluegrass Instrumentals (MCA/–)
Bluegrass Ramble (MCA/–)
Blue Moon Of Kentucky 1950–1958 (–/Bear Family)
Bluegrass, 1959–1969 (–/Bear Family)
'87 (MCA/–)
Country Music Hall Of Fame (MCA/–)

Monroe Brothers:
Early Blue Grass Music (Camden/–)

Charlie Monroe:
Who's Calling You Sweetheart Tonight (Camden/–)
Charlie Monroe On The Noonday Jamboree (County/County)

Patsy Montana

Patsy Montana, born Rubye Blevins, on October 30, 1914, in Hot Springs, Arkansas, became the first woman in country music to have a million-selling record when **I Want To Be A Cowboy's Sweetheart** was released in 1935. She began her early career with silent film cowboy star Monte Montana (no relation), but was long associated with the Prairie Ramblers on the National Barn Dance radio show (1934–52). The Ramblers backed her on **Cowboy's Sweetheart** and most of her other hits. She recorded with them on the ARC complex of labels (1935–42) and then Decca (1942–49) and RCA (1949–51) before leaving them and Chicago for the West Coast in 1952.

She has been in and out of retirement ever since, occasionally appearing with her daughter Judy Rose, and recording in later years on Surf and Starday.

Recommended:
Early Country Favorites (Old Homestead/–)

John Michael Montgomery

Country's latest hunk, John Michael Montogemery, was born on January 20, 1965, in Nicholasville, Kentucky. His parents, Harold and Carol Montgomery, raised their three children to make music. Harold had his own country band, playing clubs in central Kentucky, with his wife on drums. All three children, Eddie, also on drums, John Michael on guitar and vocals, and daughter Becky on vocals, performed with the band.

When John was 17 his parents divorced. This marked the end of the band, so the youngster started solo stints. In 1984 he started a rock band called Erly Tymz (Early Times), playing the music of Bob Seger, Jimmy Buffett and Lynyrd Skynyrd. A couple of years later he returned to country, and by 1988 was performing at Lexington's Austin Saloon, where he played five nights a week over a four-year period. The gig paid off. Executives from Atlantic Records, tipped off by songwriter Steve Clark, saw him, and signed him to a contract in 1991. Not happy with the way his first album was shaping up, Montogemery took his career in his hands and phoned Atlantic–Nashville executive Rick Blackburn. Blackburn brought in Doug Johnson to complete the production, and the result was an immediate Top 5 country single in late 1992 with the album's title song, **Life's A Dance**. A second single, **I Love The Way You Love Me**, soared to No.1 in 1993.

Montgomery's powerful voice and compelling charisma jump out from an album that runs the gamut from laid-back country balladry to rowdy honky-tonk tunes. Instead of just working the honky-tonk bars of central Kentucky, John Michael now takes his music to a much wider audience, including opening shows for Reba McEntire and Alabama.

Recommended:
Life's A Dance (Atlantic/–)

Below: Melba Montgomery's eponymous album. Courtesy Elektra Records.

Melba Montgomery

Born in Iron City, Tennessee, on October 14, 1938, Melba was raised in Florence, Alabama. She began her singing at the local Methodist church where her fiddle- and guitar-playing father taught singing.

Melba moved to Nashville, there catching the attention of Roy Acuff, whose show she stayed with for four years. In 1962 she went solo and released her first singles, her initial Top 10 entry coming with **We Must Have Been Out Of Our Minds**, a duet with George Jones released by UA in 1963. Further duet hits with Jones followed, and she also made duets with pop singer Gene Pitney, placing **Baby, Ain't That Fine** into the Top 20 in 1966.

She continued recording for UA and Musicor in moderately successful fashion through to 1967, when her musical partnership with George Jones ended. Melba moved on to Capitol and a series of duets with Charlie Louvin, the most successful being **Something To Brag About** (1970).

Her time at Capitol saw the start of a liaison with Pete Drake that carried over fruitfully into her stint at Elektra. She began at Elektra in 1973 with **Wrap Your Love Around Me** (1973).

By 1974 she had a No.1 record with **No Charge**, a sentimental 'talkover' song penned by Harlan Howard that provided J. J. Barrie with a British pop hit in 1976. She also went Top 20 with **Don't Let The Good Times Fool You** (1975), but, by 1977, was back on UA once more, doing pretty well with a version of **Angel Of The Morning**. After this her name became absent from the annual list of chart contenders, although she has since recorded for Kari and Compass.

Recommended:
Baby You've Got What It Takes – with Charlie Louvin (Capitol/–)
Don't Let The Good Times Fool You (Elektra/–)
No Charge (Elektra/–)
We Must Have Been Out Of Our Minds – with George Jones (RCA/RCA)

Clyde Moody

Born on a Cherokee Reservation in North Carolina on September 19, 1915, Clyde Moody rose to prominence in the '40s as the 'Hillbilly Waltz King', largely on the strength of his gold record for **Shenandoah Waltz** for King Records, which sold some three million copies.

Moody apprenticed with Mainer's Mountaineers, spent several successful years with Bill Monroe, with whom he recorded the classic **Six White Horses**, and spent a bit of time with Roy Acuff before joining the Opry on his own in the mid-'40s. He left the Opry in the late '40s to pioneer television in the Washington DC area, then returned to his native North Carolina, where he had a long-running TV show and several business interests. But he resumed his musical career in Nashville, annually appearing at bluegrass festivals (those fans did not forget his years as a Blue Grass Boy) and touring over 300 days a year with Ramblin' Tommy Scott's Show. He passed away on April 7, 1989.

Recommended:
Moody's Blue (Old Homestead/–)

George Morgan

The writer and singer of **Candy Kisses**, the biggest country song of 1949, Morgan, for a brief period, looked capable of usurping Eddy Arnold's position as the 'king of country pop'.

Born in Waverly, Tennessee, on June 28, 1925, he spent his teen years in Barberton, Ohio. On completing high school, Morgan worked as a part-time performer. Obtaining a regular singing spot on WWWA Jamboree, Wheeling, West Virginia, he established something of a reputation there and became signed to Columbia Records. His first release was

Above: Clyde Moody – North Carolina's Hillbilly Waltz King.

Candy Kisses, which reached No.1 in the country charts (subsequently selling a million) while Elton Britt's cover version reached No.3. Invited to join WSM in 1948 in the dual role of DJ and vocalist, he soon became an Opry regular, scoring with further 1949 hits in **Rainbow In My Heart**, **Room Full Of Roses** and **Cry-Baby Heart**.

Establishing a smooth, easy style that came replete with fiddle and steel guitar, Morgan became a popular radio and concert artist. but, despite major successes with **Almost** (1952), **I'm In Love Again** (1959) and **You're The Only Good Thing** (1960), his record sales remained little more than steady.

In 1966 he joined Starday, who provided him with elaborate orchestral trappings, a ploy which gained Morgan a quintet of mini-hits during 1967–68. But soon he was on the move again, recording with Stop, Decca and Four Star, but only twice attaining Top 20 status, with **Lilacs And Rain**, a 1970 Stop release, and **Red Rose From The Blue Side Of Town**, a 1973 MCA item.

Morgan's death occurred in July 1975, following a heart attack sustained while on the roof of his house, fixing a TV aerial.

Sounds Of Goodbye, George Morgan. Courtesy Starday Records.

Recommended:
Remembering (Greatest Hits) (Columbia/–)
The Best Of (Starday/–)
American Originals (Columbia/–)

Lorrie Morgan

Lorrie Morgan is one of country music's most attractive women, and her life story is as dramatic and tragic as the words to many country songs. The youngest daughter of country star George Morgan, Loretta Lynn Morgan was born on June 27, 1959 in Nashville, Tennessee. A consummate professional reared in a country-star family, she has performed publicly since she was five. Lorrie made her debut on the Grand Ole Opry at 13, and for some years toured with her father. Having more than her fair share of heartache, her father died when she was 16, then came pregnancy and marriage at 20, followed by divorce at 21. She struggled for acceptance as a country singer for 15 years, and just when she began to taste success, that happiness was overshadowed by the death of her second husband, singer Keith Whitley, of alcohol poisoning on May 9, 1989.

She had married Whitley in November 1986, and the couple had a son, Jesse (Lorrie had a daughter, Morgan, from her previous marriage). The pair were ecstatically in love, and the marriage had given a boost to both their careers. Lorrie had previously recorded for Hickory Records in 1979 and MCA in the early '80s

Above: George Morgan's Candy Kisses was the biggest country song of 1949.

without too much success. She signed with RCA in 1986 and immediately made the Top 20 with her first single, **Trainwreck Of Emotion** (1988). This was followed by her Top 10 debut with **Dear Me**, a song she demoed ten years earlier.

"I always swore that when I got to do a record I was going to record **Dear Me**," Lorrie explained, "But every producer I had said, 'Naw, that doesn't sound like you, we're not doing that,' but when I played it for Barry Beckett [her producer at RCA], he just flipped over it. I knew he was the right producer then, because I knew it was a great song."

Astute at choosing the right material, Lorrie portrays a masterful combination of vocal emotion and vocal beauty. Her voice has a contagious feeling and sincerity. A third RCA single, **Out Of Your Shoes**, spent three weeks at No.2 on the country charts in 1989, while her first album, **Leave The Light On**, went gold. A chart-topper with **Five Minutes** (1990) lay the foundation for further Top 10 entries with **He Talks To Me** (1990), **We Both Walk** and **A Picture Of Me (Without You)** (1991). A posthumously released duet with Keith Whitley, **'Til A Tear Becomes A Rose**, went Top 20 in 1990. A second album, **Something In Red**, also gained a gold disc, and the title song and **Except For Monday** presented her with Top 10 hits in 1992. That same year she moved to the affiliated BNA label, scoring with **Watch Me** (1992) and a chart-topper with **What Part Of No** (1993).

Life was still no bed of roses for the determined Lorrie Morgan. In January 1992 she was forced to file Chapter 11 bankruptcy, though by the end of the year, she had paid all her creditors in full. A third marriage in October 1991 to Brad Johnson, a former bus driver for Clint Black, was reportedly on the rocks, and a routine operation in the summer of 1992 turned out to be major surgery. But despite all her setbacks, Lorrie has not stood still licking wounds. She has pushed her career forward, and, following acclaimed music videos, she is beginning to make her mark as an actress, with a role in a TV movie in production during 1993.

Recommended:
Watch Me (BNA/–)
Leave The Light On (RCA/RCA)
Something In Red (RCA/RCA)

Gary Morris

Like country pioneer Vernon Dalhart, Gary Morris is able to sing both country and opera. He was born on December 7, 1948 in Fort Worth, Texas. A junior high school guitarist who sang in the church choir, Morris formed a trio during the late '60s. After the trio played a Hank Williams' medley at a live, audience-attended audition, they were booked into a Denver night-club.

After several years at the club, Morris went solo and headed back to Texas, there meeting Lawton Williams, writer of **Fraulein**, a massive hit for Bobby Helms. Williams introduced Morris to various

Above: Gary Morris has rebuilt his career during the '90s via minor country hits.

music-biz people and in 1978 he was invited to play at a White House party hosted by President Carter, after which he was asked to record a number of sides for MCA Nashville. For a while Morris went back to Colorado, forming a band called Breakaway. But in 1980 he flew to Nashville once more, meeting producer Norro Wilson, who had seen him at the White House gig. He cut **Sweet Red Wine** and **Fire In Your Eyes**, both going Top 40 on Warner.

Late in 1981 he had his first Top 10 single in **Headed For A Heartache**. The following year he had three major singles, the biggest of these being **Velvet Chains**. By 1983 he had become a fully fledged Top 10 act, logging three solo hit records – **The Love She Found In Me**, **The Wind Beneath My Wings**, **Why, Lady, Why?** – and **You're Welcome Tonight**, a high-selling duet with Lynn Anderson, recorded for the Permian label. The next year saw Gary netting three further Top 10 records, **Between Two Fires**, **Second Hand Heart** and **Baby Bye Bye** (the latter becoming his first No.1) and being acclaimed as country music's premier male sex symbol.

After that, everything headed his way. He was chosen to star opposite Linda Ronstadt in the New York Shakespeare Festival production of the opera 'La Bohème'. This led to regular guest appearances on the TV soap Dynasty II – The Colbys, in which he played Wayne Masterson, a blind musician. In 1987 Gary

headed back to New York to star in Broadway's 'Les Misérables', and reprised the role in London for the complete symphonic recording in 1988.

Alongside all this activity, his country hit-making continued with **Lasso The Moon**, **Making Up For Lost Time** (a duet with Crystal Gayle), **I'll Never Stop Loving You** (all 1985), **100% Chance Of Rain** (1986), and a No.1 with **Leave Me Lonely**, as well as another duet with Crystal Gayle on **Another World** (both 1987). In 1988 he signed with the short-lived Universal Records, finally landing on Capitol in 1990 and slowly rebuilding his career via minor hits, such as **Miles Across The Bedroom** (1991) and **Love Hurts** (1992).

Recommended:
Faded Blue (Warner Bros/–)
Second Hand Love (Warner Bros/Warner Bros)
Full Moon, Empty Heart (Capitol/–)
Stones (Universal/–)
These Days (Capitol/–)

Michael Martin Murphey

A pioneer of the Texas 'cosmic' cowboy scene of the early '70s, Michael Martin Murphey was born in 1946 in Dallas, Texas, and was raised on the music of Hank Williams, Bob Wills and Woody Guthrie. He had sang in a folksy outfit, the Texas Twosome, while still at high school in Dallas. After graduation he attended the University of California in Los Angeles, where he started to take his songwriting more seriously. He signed a writer's contract with Screen Gems Music in 1965, and wrote mainly theme tunes and soundtrack material for television, though he did provide the Monkees with one of their better songs – **What Am I Doin' Hangin' Around**. In 1967 he toured as Travis Lewis of the pop outfit the Lewis And Clarke Expedition. He then embarked on a solo career, basing himself in Austin

Danny's Song, Anne Murray. Courtesy Capitol Records.

where he joined the thriving Texas music scene. Murphey worked with producer Bob Johnston, and signed to A&M Records, achieving a Top 40 pop placing for the self-penned **Geronimo's Cadillac**.

Building a career as a major singer-songwriter, Murphey moved to Colorado in 1974 and signed to Epic Records. He made his debut on the country charts with **A Mansion On The Hill** in 1976. Three years later, he moved again, this time to Taos, New Mexico. Gradually enlarging his country following, he appeared in the films 'Hard Country', 'Take This Job And Shove It' and 'Urban Cowboy', and made it to No.1 on the country charts for Liberty with **What's Forever For** (1982), a record that also made the pop Top 20. Further country success came with: **Still Taking Chances**, **Don't Count The Rainy Days** (1983), **Will It Be Loving By Morning** (1984), and **What She Wants** and **Carolina In The Pines** (1985). By this time his records were appearing on EMI-America.

In 1986 he signed with Warner Brothers Records, that year going Top 20 with **Rolling Nowhere**. The following year he was back in the Top 10 with **A Face In The Crowd** (a duet with Holly Dunn), and at No.1 with **A Long Line Of Love**. The Top 10 hits continued with **Talkin' To The Wrong Man** (1988) featuring his son, Ryan Murphey. Getting closer to his musical roots, in 1990 Murphey released **Cowboy Songs**, a collection of traditional campfire and trail songs that made an impact on the charts and helped to re-kindle interest in cowboys and their music.

Recommended:
Land Of Enchantment (Warner Bros/–)
Cowboy Songs (Warner Bros/–)
River Of Time (Warner Bros/–)
Michael Martin Murphey (Liberty/Liberty)

Anne Murray

A deceptively light-voiced Canadian singer, Anne Murray packed enough punch on her **Snowbird** hit in the '60s to score a major international pop hit.

Born in Spring Hill, Nova Scotia, on June 20, 1946, Anne was the only girl in a

Anne Murray

family of five brothers. She obtained a bachelor's degree at the University of New Brunswick and taught physical education. Eventually, finding that singing was taking more of her time, she quit and moved entirely into show-biz when offered a contract by Capitol Records.

Snowbird was one of her first releases and its light airy melody was soon on everyone's lips. It scored in both the pop and country charts in 1970 and provided Anne with two potential markets which she proceeded to tightrope-walk.

She made some high-selling singles during 1972, including **Cotton Jenny**, **Danny's Song** and **Love Song** but had to wait until 1974 and **He Thinks I Still Care** before gaining her second No.1. After this she had Top 10 singles with **Son Of A Rotten Gambler** (1974), **Walk Right Back**, **You Needed Me** (1978), hitting a winning streak in 1979 when **I Just Fall In Love Again**, **Shadows In The Moonlight** and **Broken Hearted Me** all went to No.1. Then came such hits as **Daydream Believer**, **Could I Have This Dance?** (1980), **Blessed Are The Believers**, **It's All I Can Do** (1981), **Another Sleepless Night**, **Hey! Baby!**, **Somebody's Always Saying Goodbye** (1982) and **A Little Good News** (No.1, 1983). The last named is, lyrically at least, the finest song that Murray has ever

Above: Feed This Fire proved a Top 10 entry for Anne Murray in 1990, getting her back in the limelight after a turbulent few years in the late '80s.

recorded and one that won her a Grammy award as Best Country Female Singer, helping her accrue a tally of major awards that includes four Grammys, three CMA awards and no less than 22 Canadian Juno plaudits.

During 1984 she logged two further country No.1s with **Just Another Woman In Love** and **Nobody Loves Me Like You Do**, a duet with Dave Loggins. The following year had a further hit **Time Don't Run Out On Me**. Another No.1 came with **Now And Forever (You And Me)** in 1986. Anne, completely confused by her continuing country success, claimed her album, **Something To Talk About**, was her first real pop album in six years. The late '80s saw her records struggling to make a major impact on the country charts. Then in 1990 she was back in the Top 10 with **Feed This Fire**. A regular presenter and host on the country music award shows, retirement is not in the cards: "This business of retirement and getting old and all that is garbage," says Anne. "There is no such thing. People work 'til they drop now. That's the way it should be, heading for new challenges when you're 70–75."

Recommended:
Anne Murray's Greatest Hits
   (Capitol/Capitol)
A Little Good News (Capitol/Capitol)
Something To Talk About (Capitol/Capitol)
Heart Over Mind (Capitol/Capitol)
Songs Of The Heart (Capitol/Capitol)

Jerry Naylor

Once front-man with the Crickets, Naylor won 'Billboard' awards in 1973 and 1974 for providing the best syndicated country radio show.

Born in Stephenville, Texas, on March 6, 1939, he formed his own group at the age of 14 and soon proved able enough to perform on the Louisiana Hayride show, touring alongside such acts as Johnny Cash, Elvis Presley and Johnny Horton. A DJ during his high school days, he later enrolled at the Elkins Electronic Institute, employing his radio know-how for AFRS in Germany during 1957.

Following discharge from the army after a spinal injury, he returned home and recorded for Sklya Records, also befriending Glen Campbell. The duo moved to L.A. where Naylor worked for KRLA and KDAY. In 1961 he became a member of the Crickets, replacing bassist Joe B. Maudlin

(although both musicians are depicted on the sleeve of the **Bobby Vee Meets The Crickets** album!). But he suffered a heart attack in 1964 and left the group, taking up a solo career in country music, recording first for Tower, then for Columbia and MGM before signing for Melodyland — for which label he provided a hit in **Is That All There Is To A Honky Tonk?** in 1975.

Along the way, Naylor, who once recorded for Raystar under the name of Jackie Garrard, has notched hits for Hitsville, MC and Oak, also working for Hoyt Axton's Jeremiah without much success. He now concentrates on DJ work and lives in Angoura, California with his wife Pamela and three children.

Recommended:
Love Away Her Memory (MCA/–)

Rick Nelson

The child of a showbusiness family (his parents Ozzie and Harriet had a radio and later a TV show), Nelson made the transition from teenage idol to modern country artist.

Below: The late Rick Nelson, who crashed in a plane once owned by Jerry Lee Lewis.

Born on May 8, 1940, in Teaneck, New Jersey, he signed as Ricky Nelson first for Verve and then Imperial; his lonesome teenthrob voice was allied to light, country-influenced backings on songs such as **Poor Little Fool**, **It's Late** and **Lonesome Town**, sagas of jilted love and dating frustrations, and perfectly in tune with the softening tone of rock'n'roll.

This was the major record companies' answer to the more raw, sharper music of Memphis. Since Nelson was also blessed with archetypal boy-next-door looks, his appeal was further propagated via concerts and TV.

The coming of the British Invasion swept away many of these clean-cut American teen rockers, although Nelson was by then signed to MCA and had shortened his name to Rick. Although he had James Burton in his band, he failed to make a real impression. However, two country albums, **Country Fever** and **Bright Lights And Country Music**, found favour with some people.

The formation of the Stone Canyon Band in the '70s saw Nelson being accepted as a viable country rocker. This band included, at one point, Randy Meisner, also known from Poco and the Eagles, and Tom Brumley, Buck Owens' rated steel player for five years). **Garden Party**, a poignant auto-biographical piece of country-rock, made the American pop Top 10 in 1972 and won Nelson yet another gold record. Although he recorded some outstanding country-rock albums during the '70s for MCA, Epic and Capitol, he failed to make any further inroads into the charts.

During the early '80s, Rick and his excellent Stone Canyon Band were mainly working rock'n'roll revival shows, but his musical integrity was always maintained by his insistence on giving many of his old songs fresh, new arrangements. He successfully toured Britain during November 1985 with Bo Diddley, Bobby Vee and Frankie Ford. Two months later, on December 31, 1985, Rick, along with his fiancée, Helen Blair, and members of his band were in a fatal air crash while en route to a show in Dallas, Texas.

Recommended:
Country (MCA/–)
Garden Party (MCA/MCA)
Rudy The 5th (MCA/MCA)
Sings Rick Nelson (MCA/MCA)
String Along with Rick (–/Charly)
Playing To Win (Capitol/Capitol)
Country Fever/Bright Lights And Country Music (–/See For Miles)

Willie Nelson

Willie Nelson has run a long, hard race in country music but has won through as a premier stylist. Born in Abbott, Texas, on April 30, 1933, Nelson was raised by his

Help Me Make It Through The Night, Willie Nelson. Courtesy RCA Records.

grandparents after his own parents separated.

His grandparents taught him some chords and by his teens he was becoming proficient on guitar. In 1950, he joined the Air Force and on his subsequent discharge married a Cherokee Indian girl by whom he had a daughter, Lana. Living in Waco, Texas, Nelson took various salesman jobs. But, anxious to gain a proper intro into music, he talked his way into an announcing job on a local station.

Soon after, he was hosting country shows on a Fort Worth station, doubling at night as a musician in some rough local honky-tonks and, whenever he could, he was jotting down songs. It was during this period that he wrote **Family Bible** and **Night Life**, songs which have become standards.

When he finally made his way to Nashville and found a job in Ray Price's band as a bass player, he found that he was finally placing his songs. Price, a huge name of that era, made **Night Life** his theme tune. Faron Young cut **Hello Walls**, Patsy Cline **Crazy** and Willie himself recorded **The Party's Over**. They were sombre but haunting melodies, true 'white man's blues', and Willie has since incorporated them tellingly into his sparse, bluesy act. More than 70 artists have recorded **Night Life**.

After poaching most of Ray Price's band from him, Nelson went on the road. At this time his first marriage broke up and he went off with the wife of a DJ Association president and married again, settling in Fort Worth, Los Angeles and Nashville.

Besides recording 18 albums in three years, he also helped the career of Charley Pride, featuring him on his show in the deepest South during the racially sensitive years of civil rights.

During the '60s the smooth Nashville Sound was in its ascendant and Willie found himself becoming increasingly disillusioned with big business methods, hankering to make his mark as a singer rather than as a songwriter and preferably on his own terms. By the early '70s he was determined to get out of his RCA contract, and with the help of Neil Reshen (afterwards Nelson's manager) he landed a contract from the new Nashville offices of Atlantic. However country music was new to Atlantic, who had built their reputation on black music. But with Atlantic's Jerry Wexler producing in New York, Willie came up with **Shotgun Willie** and **Phases And Stages**, the second had a new, intense country sound and made no concessions to modern Nashville.

Nelson had by now settled in Austin with his third wife, Connie. By this time Atlantic's Nashville operation had folded and Willie signed with Columbia, for whom he made **Red Headed Stranger** and **The Sound In Your Mind**. Like **Phases And**

Above: Tax problems gave Willie Nelson a major headache in 1991, but his Across The Borderline in 1993 put him back in pocket.

Stages, Red Headed Stranger was a concept album, but even more personal. It threw up the national cross-over hit single **Blue Eyes Cryin' in The Rain** and established Willie Nelson as a nationally known figure.

Willie, recognized as the unofficial Mayor of Austin, reconciled hip and redneck musical interests and helped lead a new explosion of interest in country music. Teaming up with Waylon Jennings, they topped the country charts in 1976 with **Good Hearted Woman** and were both featured on the compilation album, **Wanted: The Outlaws**, the first certified platinum album in country music, and so started the Outlaw Movement. The two were voted into top positions in the annual Country Music Association awards, a sure sign of industry acceptance.

Refusing to be tied down to commercial considerations, Nelson has recorded such diverse album projects as **Stardust** (popular standards), **The Troublemaker** (a gospel set), **To Lefty From Willie** (a tribute to Lefty Frizzell) and **Angel Eyes** (featuring jazz guitarist Jackie King).

Willie also instigated the now legendary Fourth Of July Picnics, massive outdoor festivals in Texas which have featured stars such as Leon Russell, Kris

Kristofferson, Roy Acuff, Waylon Jennings, Tex Ritter and Asleep At The Wheel.

During the early '80s, Willie became acknowledged as the 'king' of the country duets. Alongside his highly successful duets with Waylon Jennings, which resulted in the chart-topping **Mammas Don't Let Your Babies Grow Up To Be Cowboys** winning a Grammy in 1978, he has recorded duet albums with Roger Miller, Ray Price, Faron Young, Webb Pierce and Merle Haggard, as well as guesting on albums and singles by Emmylou Harris, Pam Rose, Rattlesnake Annie and many others.

Poncho And Lefty, a duet album recorded with Merle Haggard, was named CMA Album Of The Year (1983) with the title song topping the country charts. Nelson achieved even more success the following year when he teamed up with Julio Iglesias for the pop and country hit, **To All The Girls I've Loved Before**, which also won CMA and Grammy awards.

Nelson continued to chalk up hits throughout the '80s and '90s, with such songs as **Always On My Mind** (1982), **Highwayman** (1986), **Ain't Necessarily So** (1990). He has also organized several Farm Aid benefits. In early 1991 his tax shelter was exposed as a scam and the singer was left owing 17 million dollars in unpaid taxes. In co-operation with the IRS Nelson released a two-record set, **Who'll Buy My Memories aka The IRS Tapes**, with the proceeds paying his tax bill.

A return to the commercial mainstream came with **Across The Borderline**, a 1993 album produced by Don Was and featuring collaborations with Paul Simon, Bob Dylan, Sinead O'Connor, Mark O'Connor, David Crosby, Mose Allison and others. A rich mixture of musical styles, it took Nelson a long way from his well-established country sounds, but once again put him in touch with a mass audience.

Recommended:
Phases And Stages (Atlantic/–)
Shotgun Willie (Atlantic/–)
Live (RCA/RCA)
Red Headed Stranger (Columbia/CBS)
Famous Country Music Makers (–/RCA)
The Sound In Your Mind (Columbia/CBS)
Tougher Than Leather (Columbia/CBS)

Me And Paul (Columbia/–)
Always On My Mind (Columbia/CBS)
Across The Borderline (Columbia/Columbia)
Beautiful Texas, 1936–1986 (–/Bear Family)
City Of New Orleans (Columbia/CBS)
I Love Country (–/CBS)

Michael Nesmith

One of the fabulously successful Monkees, a teenybopper quartet whose main claim to artistic fame was that they were usually given good commercial song material, Nesmith left in 1969 to carve a modestly notable career as a sort of freewheeling cosmic cowboy.

Although he claimed to be only nominally into country, his songs have provided good country fodder, and Nesmith's records with the First and Second National Bands have their own cult audience.

Born in Houston, Texas, on December 30, 1942, Nesmith only learned to play guitar after his Air Force discharge in 1962. However, he was writing songs and his **Different Drum** was covered by Linda Ronstadt.

Becoming increasingly disenchanted by the big business surrounding the Monkees,

The Troublemaker, Willie Nelson. Courtesy CBS Records.

Above: Willie Nelson set up Farm Aid concerts in 1985 and 1986.

he had, by 1968, produced an album of self-composed instrumentals, **The Wichita Train Whistle Sings**.

Nesmith was the creator of the First National Band, which included pedal steel player Red Rhodes, and was signed to RCA. In 1970 they put out the album **Magnetic South**, a Nesmith composition from his album, **Joanne**, being covered by Andy Williams among others. Another album that year was **Loose Salute**.

The First National Band split in 1971 and James Burton and Glen D. Hardin were brought in to help complete the album then being recorded, **Nevada Fighter**. Another line-up (again including Red Rhodes) recorded **Tantamount To Treason Volume 1**, and in 1972 only Nesmith and Rhodes made **And The Hits Just Keep On Comin'**.

Nesmith founded his own label, Countryside, a subsidiary of Elektra, with the intention of milking some of the country music talent that was going to waste in Los Angeles. But a change of leadership at Elektra, where David Geffen replaced Jac Holzman, saw Countryside closed down.

However, Nesmith had formed another band during this time, the Countryside Band (again including Rhodes) and 1973 saw them releasing **Pretty Much Your Standard Ranch Stash**. He then moved from RCA and formed Pacific Arts, which has seen him involved in mixed media projects, notably 'The Prison', a book with a soundtrack.

One of the first to recognize the importance of video in music promotion, Nesmith became an innovative director performer in the video field. His 1977 album, **From A Radio Engine To The Photon Wing**, was possibly the first record to utilize video images for effect, and resulted in a British hit single for the self-penned **Rio**.

It is generally agreed that Nesmith has written some very good country, or country-influenced songs, one of the most famous being **Some Of Shelley's Blues**.

Recommended:
And The Hits Just Keep On Comin' (RCA/ Island)
Pretty Much Your Standard Ranch Stash (–/Island)
The Prison (Pacific Arts/Island)
From A Radio Engine To The Photon Wing (Pacific Arts/Island)
The Newer Stuff (–/Awareness)
The Older Stuff (Rhino/–)

New Grass Revival

A young, electric, bluegrass band, New Grass Revival evolved a distinctive hard-edged picking sound during the early '70s and helped to spread the appeal of bluegrass to a youth audience.

Based around the jazz-tinged fiddle of Sam Bush (who also plays guitar and sings, and is now regarded as one of the world's foremost mandolin players) the four-piece

Nevada Fighter, Mike Nesmith. Courtesy RCA Records.

group had some success with the single **Prince Of Peace**, an evocative reworking of a Leon Russell song. The number subsequently appeared on **New Grass Revival** (Starday), the band's debut album. Later, the Revival moved on to Flying Fish, cutting several albums before touring with Leon Russell. One of those gigs, at Pasadena's Perkin's Palace, was recorded, the results appearing on the Paradise Records album, titled **Leon Russell And The New Grass Revival**.

As the '80s moved on, the Revival signed to the Sugar Hill label, in 1984 cutting **On The Boulevard**, an album that featured the foursome playing material that ranged from Bob Marley's **One Love** and Curtis Mayfield's **People Get Ready**, through to **County Clare**, an original on which bluegrass renewed acquaintance with Irish folk music. In 1986 interest in New Grass Revival soared as they signed a major label deal with EMI-America. At this

Too Late To Turn Back Now, New Grass Revival. Courtesy Flying Fish.

time the line-up comprised Bush and long-time member John Cowan (bass, vocals), plus Pat Flynn (guitars, vocals) and banjoist Bela Fleck, who has been credited with virtually re-inventing the banjo, playing every conceivable type of music on an instrument traditionally scorned by sophisticates. The Revival scored minor country hits with **Ain't That Peculiar** (1986), **Unconditional Love** (1987) and **Can't Stop Now** (1988), making it into the country Top 40 with **Callin' Baton Rouge** (1989). Regarded as one of the finest live bands on the circuit, with their richly textured harmonies and dazzling instrumental work, New Grass Revival succeeded in taking acoustic music into the mainstream of country music. In 1991, Emmylou Harris formed the Nash Ramblers, an acoustic band led by Sam Bush, which could signal the end of one of country music's finest acoustic outfits of recent times.

Recommended:
New Grass Revival (Starday/–)
Fly Through The Country (Flying Fish/–)
Barren Country (Flying Fish/–)
Live Album – with Leon Russell (Paradise/Paradise)
Too Late To Turn Back Now (Flying Fish/Sonet)
On The Boulevard (Sugar Hill/–)
Friday Night In America (Capitol/Capitol)
Hold On To A Dream (Capitol/Capitol)

New Riders Of The Purple Sage

Originally formed as a splinter group from San Francisco's leading acid rock band the Grateful Dead, the New Riders eventually became a name in their own right.

The album **Workingman's Dead** saw the Grateful Dead moving from rock towards a more earthy, sometimes country sound, and the New Riders were the natural off-shoot of this movement.

The New Riders at first played gigs with the Dead and were able to utilize Dead guitarist Jerry Garcia's latent talents on pedal steel guitar. Garcia was eventually replaced by Buddy Cage. Famed West Coast rock artists who have been in NRPS include Mickey Hart and Phil Lesh (Grateful Dead), Spencer Dryden (Jefferson Airplane) and Skip Battin (Byrds).

The band originally recorded for Columbia, but in the mid-'70s they changed labels and recorded for MCA. However, they appeared to lose direction. To their credit, though, in their hey-day the NRPS were a fine country-rock band.

Recommended:
New Riders Of The Purple Sage (Columbia/CBS)
Powerglide (Columbia/–)
Gypsy Cowboy (Columbia/CBS)
The Adventures Of Panama Red (Columbia/CBS)
Home, Home On The Road (Columbia/CBS
New Riders (MCA/MCA)

New Riders Of The Purple Sage. Courtesy CBS Records.

Mickey Newbury

Called 'a poet' by Johnny Cash, Newbury's often ultra sad songs have been recorded by Elvis Presley, Jerry Lee Lewis, Ray Charles, Lynn Anderson, Andy Williams, Kenny Rogers and countless others.

Born in Houston, Texas, on May 19, 1940, Newbury travelled around in earlier years, eventually joining the Air Force for four years, during which time he was based in England.

"After that", he says, "I worked on the shrimp boats in the Gulf, diddled around, did a little writing and lots of other things. I started playing guitar when I was a kid, just enough to be able to go through three or four chords and sing something with it. But when I went into the Air Force, I ditched it all. One day I wound up at a place where they served snacks and had a piano. I began playing it because I just had to get my hands on something that made music. Later I borrowed a guitar from a guy because I didn't have enough money to buy one of my own – but I didn't really start trying to write until I was 24."

Moving to Nashville in the mid-'60s, Newbury began writing songs of many different styles, at one time having four songs simultaneously in the R&B, country, easy-listening and pop charts.

As a recording artist he began cutting albums for RCA and Mercury, without making much impact, though his Mercury release **It Looks Like Rain** became a collectors' item hauling in high bids before it became repackaged as part of a double album set following Newbury's signing with Elektra in 1971.

His biggest hit to date has been **American Trilogy** (1972), a composition formed from three Civil War era songs, which also became an international hit for Elvis Presley.

Throughout the '70s Newbury recorded a series of albums, carefully crafted works that won him high critical praise, but no large sales. He has continued to provide country acts with hit songs, including Tompall And The Glaser Brothers (**I Still Love You, After All These Years**), Marie

Osmond (**Blue Sky Shinin'**), Johnny Rodriguez (**Makes Me Wonder If I Ever Said Goodbye**) and Don Gibson (**When Do We Stop Starting Over**). Since that time Newbury has released few new songs, although still performs in the USA.

Recommended:
Frisco Mabel Joy (Elektra/Elektra)
Heaven Help The Child (Elektra/Elektra)
Live At Montezuma/It Looks Like Rain (Elektra/Elektra)
I Came To Hear The Music (Elektra/ Elektra)
Rusty Tracks (ABC/ABC)
After All These Years (Mercury/–)
His Eye Is On The Sparrow (ABC/–)
Sweet Memories (MCA/–)
In A New Age (Airborne/–)

Mickey Newbury Sings His Own. Courtesy RCA Records.

Jimmy C. Newman

Born of part-French ancestry, in Big Mamou, Louisiana, on August 27, 1927, Jimmy began singing in the Lake Charles area, his style employing many Cajun characteristics. During the early '50s, he became a regular on Shreveport's Louisiana Hayride and signed with the major Dot label, obtaining a Top 10 disc with **Cry, Cry, Darling** in 1954. An Opry regular by 1956, he celebrated by cutting **A Fallen Star**, his most successful record, during the following year.

Next came an MGM contract and such winners as **You're Making A Fool Out Of Me** (1958), **Grin And Bear It** (1959), and **Lovely Work Of Art** (1960), before Newman became a long-term Decca artist. His run of hits continued with the chat-

Above: Mickey Newbury formed his American Trilogy from Civil War songs.

filled **Bayou Talk** (1962), **Artificial Rose** (1965), **Back Pocket Money** (1966), **Blue Lonely Winter** (1967), **Born To Love You** (1968) and others.

Proficient on virtually any type of country material, it was with the formation of his band, Cajun Country, in the mid-'70s and a return to his Cajun roots that Jimmy made a big impact. With a musical style that mixed traditional Cajun with contemporary country, he built up a sizeable following in Europe, especially Britain, and recorded some fine modern Cajun albums.

Recommended:
Cajun Country (–/RCA)
Alligator Man (Rounder/Charly)
Progressive C.C. (–/Charly)
The Happy Cajun (–/Charly)
Bop-A-Hula (–/Bear Family)
Wild'n'Cajun (–/RCA)

Juice Newton

Country-rock singer Juice was born Judy Kaye Cohen on February 18, 1952 in Lakehurst, New Jersey. The daughter of a Navy man, she grew up in Virginia Beach, Virginia. The only musical person in a family of five, she started to play guitar and sing folk songs in her early teens. At college in North Carolina, she started working in local bars, some nights waiting on tables, and others taking to the stage with her guitar and entertaining.

In the late '60s, Juice moved to northern California where she attended Foothill College and first met her longtime boyfriend and partner Otha Young. At first she performed in local folk clubs then, combining her folk interest with rock'n'roll, formed an electric band with Young called Dixie Peach.

A move to Los Angeles in 1975 led to Juice and Otha forming a new band called Juice Newton And Silver Spur. They signed a recording deal with RCA and released their debut self-titled album, a mixture of country, rock and pop which spawned a minor country hit in **Love Is A Word** in 1976.

Two years later Juice and the band moved on to a new deal with Capitol Records. That same year she provided the Carpenters with **Sweet, Sweet Smile**, a Top 10 country hit. After **Come To Me**, the first album for the new label, was completed, Juice disbanded Silver Spur, opting to work as a solo artist. By the beginning of 1980 she was making inroads into the country charts with **Sunshine** and **Let's Keep It That Way**. A year later her major breakthrough came with the album simply titled **Juice**, which produced two big pop hits in **Angel Of The Morning** and **Queen Of Hearts**, both singles also making it into the country Top 20. Juice started picking up several awards, including a Grammy for **Angel Of The Morning** and several gold discs.

Her next single, **The Sweetest Thing (I've Ever Known)**, written by Otha Young back in the mid-'70s, also made the pop Top 10 and shot to No.1 on the country charts. Juice enjoyed another major pop and country hit with Capitol in her dramatic revival of Brenda Lee's **Break It To Me Gently** (1982). She then moved back to RCA, and hit No.1 in the country charts with her third single for the label, **You Make Me Want To Make You Mine** (1985). An accomplished equestrian, Juice married polo star Tom Goodspeed in 1986. That same year she dominated the country charts with: a revival of **Hurt** that went to No.1; **Old Flame**, a Top 10 entry; **Both To**

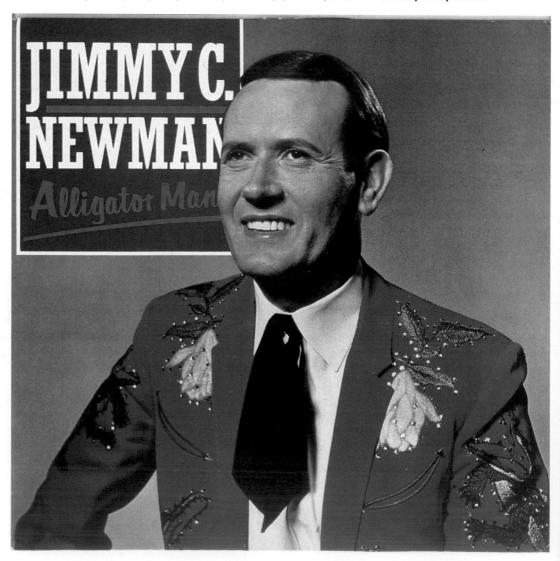

Alligator Man, Jimmy C. Newman. Courtesy Charly Records.

Each Other (Friends And Lovers), a No.1 with Eddie Rabbit; and Cheap Love, a Top 10 entry.

After all that activity, Juice took time off the following year to give birth to a daughter, Jessica Ann. She still scored two more Top 10 hits with What Can I Do With My Heart and Tell Me True. These have been her most recent major hits, though she has recorded some quality albums and still makes regular TV and concert appearances.

Recommended:
Juice (Capitol/Capitol)
Quiet Lies (Capitol/Capitol)
Can't Wait All Night (RCA/RCA)
Ain't Gonna Cry (RCA/–)

The Nitty Gritty Dirt Band

A Californian country-rock band, the Nitty Gritty Dirt Band finally gained country acceptance in the early '80s with country chart-toppers Sharecroppers' Dream (A Long Hard Road), I Love Only You and High Horse, following 17 years of releasing critically acclaimed albums covering a sort of all-American eclecticism with strands of a whole musical range: blues, hillbilly, Cajun, folk, boogie, traditional and modern country.

Formed in Long Beach in 1966 by Bruce Kunkel and Jeff Hanna as the Illegitimate

Jug Band (Jackson Browne was a one-time member), they engaged other like-minded local students: Jimmie Fadden, Leslie Thompson, Ralph Barr and John McEuen. Then, changing their name to the Nitty Gritty Dirt Band, John's elder brother, Bill, became their manager and producer.

Left: Juice Newton's most recent hits have included What Can I Do With My Heart and Tell Me True.

They signed with Liberty Records in 1967 and made the American pop charts with Buy For Me The Rain (1967), Mr Bojangles, House At Pooh Corner and Some Of Shelly's Blues (all 1971). Good musicians and fine songwriters, they made an impression with their albums. However, it was the historic recording sessions they undertook at Woodland Sound Studio, Nashville in 1971 which really put the NGDB on the musical map.

A three-record set entitled Will The Circle Be Unbroken, conceived by the NGDB but in no way dominated by them, was an ambitious project. It was the first of its kind and required total co-operation between contemporary and old country artists as the NGDB shared the studio with Doc Watson, Mother Maybelle Carter, Roy Acuff, Merle Travis, Jimmy Martin and the Scruggs Family. Even more astounding is the fact that the whole thing was mixed live on a two-track tape machine.

Despite the presence of all these greats of traditional country music, the Nitty Gritties kept their cool splendidly, with John McEuen's banjo and Jimmie Fadden's mouth harp proving particularly outstanding. It is probably the highest-energy acoustic music ever recorded (not a single electric instrument on the whole thing) and a testimonial to both the musicians involved and the music they play. When finally released in 1973 in a lavish booklet sleeve, it became one of the most discussed albums of the time and gave old-time country music a big boost.

Throughout the mid-'70s the NGDB continued to release albums which showed they were not to be tied down by musical labels, as they mixed old rock'n'roll songs, country tunes, folk numbers, self-penned songs and material by contemporary writers Michael Murphey, J. D. Souther and Jackson Browne. Sadly they failed to achieve any kind of commercial success on record, though they were in continuous demand as an exciting stage act.

In 1976 they shortened their name to the Dirt Band and began to formulate a more straightforward country-rock sound,

making a brief return to the American pop charts in 1978 with In For The Night. After reverting to the name the Nitty Gritty Dirt Band at the end of 1982, the group had their first taste of success on the country charts with Shot Full Of Love and Dance Little Jean, which rose to Nos.19 and 9 respectively in 1983. The following year the band changed labels for the first time in 17 years, joining Warner Brothers Records and so beginning a series of country No.1s.

Their initial album for Warner Bros, Plain Dirt Fashion, established a fine modern country sound and set the pattern for the next few years, with hits: Long Hard Road (No.1, 1984), I Love Only You (1984), High Horse, Modern Day Romance, Home Again In My Heart (1985) and Partners, Brothers And Friends (1986), which paid tribute to their illustrious, sometimes disappointing, but always fun career. The following year, John McEuen left to pursue a solo career, and for a time ex-Eagle Bernie Leadon joined them. Due to various other commitments, and the heavy road schedule of the band, Leadon eventually declined full membership, opting to play on their recordings and undertake the occasional live show. Now down to a leaner, meaner four-piece, Workin' Band, their 1988 album, perfectly summed up how the band saw themselves. They had another No.1 with Fishin' In The Dark (1987) and Top 10 entries with Baby's Got A Hold On Me, Oh What A Love (1987), Workin' Man (Nowhere To Go), I've Been Lookin' (1988) and Down That Road Tonight (1989).

In late 1988 the NGDB signed with the new Universal Records, and set out on a major recording project to produce Will The Circle Be Unbroken, Volume 2. The collective band members drew on the finest talent contemporary American music had to offer. Johnny Cash, the Carter Family, Emmylou Harris, Roy Acuff, Bruce Hornsby, John Prine, Jimmy Martin, John Denver, Michael Martin Murphey, John Hiatt, Rosanne Cash, and members of

Below: After 25 years together, the Nitty Gritty Dirt Band recorded their Not Fade Away album.

Above: In 1986, the Nitty Gritty Dirt Band performed at London's Wembley Festival.

Highway 101 and New Grass Revival, were among the artists who joined in the sessions. The album became a big seller and produced Top 20 country hits with **And So It Goes** (with John Denver) and **When It's Gone** in 1989.

With the demise of Universal Records in 1990, the NGDB found themselves on MCA for their next album, **The Rest Of The Dream**. Though in the same style as previous band albums, it failed to produce any major country hits, but this was due to record company changes and politics, rather than the quality of the music. That same year, Jimmy Ibbotson took some time off to work some dates with Jim Salestom and Jim Ratts as the Wild Jimbos, and produce a neat little off-the-wall country album for MCA.

The NGDB celebrated their 25th year together by signing with Capitol/Liberty (their first label, in 1967), releasing **Live Two Five**, a live album recorded in Red Deer, Alberta, Canada. Still true to their original music, the first studio album for their new label was appropriately titled **Not Fade Away**; fading away is certainly unlikely for a band that has become an American institution.

Recommended:
Will The Circle Be Unbroken (UA/UA)
Plain Dirt Fashion (Warner Bros/–)
Partners, Brothers and Friends (Warner Bros/–)
Let's Go (UA/UA)
Dirt, Silver And Gold (UA/–)
Workin' Band (Warner Bros/Warner Bros)
The Rest Of The Dream (MCA/MCA)
Live Two Five (Capitol/–)
Not Fade Away (Liberty/–)

All The Good Times (UA/Beat Goes On)
Uncle Charlie And His Dog Teddy (UA/Beat Goes On)

The Notting Hillbillies

It was only to be expected that one day Mark Knopfler, leader of rock band Dire Straits, would turn his hand to country music. From the beginning, Dire Straits' music and, more especially, Knopfler's

Pure Dirt, the Nitty Gritty Dirt Band's first album. Courtesy UA Records.

writing leaned heavily towards country at times. Several Dire Straits' songs had been covered by American country stars Waylon Jennings, Gail Davies and Highway 101, and by the late '80s Knopfler was no stranger to the Nashville studios, having played alongside Chet Atkins, and guested on recordings by Wynonna Judd, Vince Gill and John Anderson.

The Notting Hillbillies came together in 1989 when two of Knopfler's old musical buddies, Steve Phillips and Brendan

Croker, decided to make an album. They called in Knopfler to assist. He in turn recruited Dire Straits' keyboardist Guy Fletcher. The recordings took place in Knopfler's small home studio in Notting Hill, London, hence the name. Always planned as a one-off project, the sessions (that also featured Nashville steel guitarist Paul Franklin) resulted in the album, **Missing ... Presumed Having A Good Time**. The album was a mixture of country-blues, gospel and traditional country that harked back more to the old-timey country sounds of the '30s and '40s than the electrified music of the '50s and '60s.

Due to Knopfler's involvement, the album sold in excess of one million copies. The four musicians took to the road, playing a spring tour in 1990 that saw them performing sell-out shows at civic halls and university campuses. For Knopfler, it was a unique opportunity to get back to his roots: a tour of small, accessible venues. Knopfler had previously played with Steve Phillips in the early '60s in Leeds, Yorkshire as a duo known as the Duolian String Pickers, a name taken from a brand of National guitar. Crocker, also from Leeds, is a singer, songwriter and guitarist with his own band, the Five O'Clock Shadows. In recent years Crocker has had his songs recorded in Nashville by Wynonna Judd and others.

Oak Ridge Boys

Duane Allen, lead; Joe Bonsall, tenor; Steve Sanders, baritone; Richard Sterban, bass.

For many years, the Oaks (as they now prefer to be called) were one of the top groups in Gospel music, winning 14 Dove Awards from the Gospel Music Association and four Grammies. Then in 1975 they decided to make a move towards country music and within three years they won the first of many Country Music Association awards, as Best Vocal Group of 1978.

The Oaks were originally known as the Country Cut-Ups and were formed shortly after World War II. They performed at the atomic energy plant in Oak Ridge, Tennessee. The group was reformed in 1957 by Smitty Gatlin as the Oak Ridge Quartet and became fully professional in April 1961.

Their initial appeal lay with their high quality sacred material in an infectious, foot-stomping fashion. In 1971 they received a Grammy for their recording of **Talk About The Good Times** and in 1976 did the same thing for **Where The Soul Never Dies**.

William Lee Golden (born January 12, 1939, Brewton, Alabama) was the longest serving member of the group, having joined in 1964. Lead singer Duane Allen (born April 29, 1944, Taylortown, Texas), formerly a member of the Southernaires Quartet, joined in 1966 and is generally regarded as the Oaks' spokesman. Newer members are Richard Sterban (born April 24, 1944, Camden, New Jersey), who joined in 1972, and Joe Bonsall (born May 18, 1944, Philadelphia, Pennsylvania), who joined in 1973.

The foursome made a move towards country acceptance in 1975, scoring a minor hit with their secular recording of **Family Reunion** for Columbia the following year. Soon after, they provided the back-up on Paul Simon's **Slip Sliding Away**, which became a million-seller.

Encouraged by Johnny Cash, who asked them to open for him in Las Vegas, and signed by booking agent Jim Halsey, the Oaks began recording for ABC-Dot, and shortly had their first Top 5 country hit with **Y'all Come Back Saloon**.

Since then the Oaks have been red-hot with their gospel-flavoured country-pop songs, scoring hits with **I'll Be True To You** (1978), **Sail Away** (1979), **Leaving Louisiana In The Broad Daylight** (1979), **Trying To Love Two Women** (1980) and **Beautiful You** (1980).

The inevitable pop chart breakthrough came with the multi-million selling **Elvira** (1981) and **Bobbie Sue** (1982), each album achieving platinum status within weeks of release. They have continued to dominate the country charts with **American Made** (1983), **Love Song** (1983), **I Guess It Never Hurts To Hurt Sometimes** (1984), **Make My Life With You** (1985) and **Come On In (You Did The Best You Could)** (1986).

In March, 1987, Golden was dismissed from the group due to 'continual musical and personal differences', and set out on a solo career. He filed a $40 million suit against the three remaining members, which was eventually settled out of court. His replacement was the band's rhythm guitarist Steve Sanders (born September 17, 1952, Richland, Georgia), who had a long musical career in gospel music starting when he was five. By the time he was 12 Steve had appeared on Broadway, and two years later starred as Faye Dunaway's son in the film 'Hurry Sundown'. He had joined the Oaks' band in 1982, and took over the baritone vocal chores on their 1987 **Heartbeat** album and their '87 Fast Lane concert tour. The change didn't seem to make any considerable difference to the Oaks' ability as hitmakers, and they scored such No.1s as **This Crazy Love** (1987), **Gonna Take**

Above: Bill, Joe, Richard and Duane – the Oak Ridge Boys.

A Lot Of River (1988) and **No Matter How High** (1990). The following year the Oak Ridge Boys left MCA to sign with RCA, immediately scoring yet another Top 10 hit with **Lucky Moon** (1991).

With their own six-piece Oak Ridge Boys Band, the Oaks have gained a reputation for their exciting live performances, a fast-paced showcase with dynamic presentations.

Recommended:
Room Service (MCA/–)
Deliver (MCA/MCA)
American Made (MCA/MCA)
Step On Out (MCA/MCA)
Heartbeat (MCA/–)
Where The Fast Lane Ends (MCA/–)
The Long Haul (RCA/–)
American Dreams (MCA/MCA)

Mark O'Connor

For many years Nashville's most in-demand session musician, Mark O'Connor was born on August 5, 1961 in Seattle, Washington. A virtuoso on the guitar and mandolin, and a varied and accomplished composer, it is as a violinist that he is recognized as a true master. He has done remarkable work in jazz, country, pop, fusion and the classics, combining them in ways that have re-defined both the instrument and its audience.

At age six, Mark began guitar lessons, winning his first contest at ten in a classical/flamenco competition at the

Seasons, the Oak Ridge Boys. Courtesy MCA Records.

University of Washington. By the time he was 11, he could play mandolin, banjo, steel-string guitar and dobro. Seven months after picking up a violin he entered the National Old-Time Fiddle Championship and won second place in the 12-and-under division. By the time he was a senior in high school, he had won every major fiddle contest in the country. He had been introduced to Roy Acuff when he was 12, and he so impressed the father of country music that he was given a spot in Acuff's Grand Ole Opry set that same night. At this time he was signed to Rounder Records and the label put out six

releases covering Mark's astonishing teenage career development.

After graduation in 1979, he played the bluegrass festival circuit, then toured with David Grisman and Stephane Grappelli as guitarist, and can be heard on several of Grisman's albums. In 1981 he joined country-fusion band, the Dregs, appearing on the album **Industry Standard**. Moving to Nashville in 1983, he soon became a popular session player. Devoting his time to studio work, he appeared on nearly 500 recordings in just over six years. He also continued with his own recordings, with Michael Brecker and James Taylor

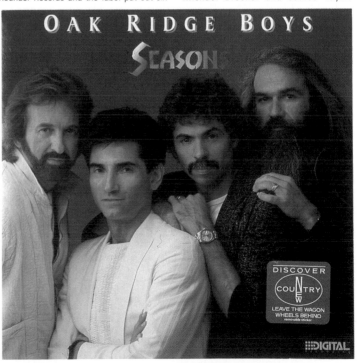

The New Nashville Cats, Mark O'Connor. Courtesy Warner Brothers Records.

guesting on his 1989 album, **On The Mark**. By this time he was beginning to follow a more independent career and writing much of his own material. In 1990, with an assemblage of 53 prominent Nashville studio musicians, he recorded **The New Nashville Cats** album, which won a Grammy in 1991 for Best Country Instrumental Performance. A revival of Carl Perkins' **Restless** from the album, with vocals by country stars Vince Gill, Steve Wariner and Ricky Skaggs, was a Top 30 country hit and won the CMA Vocal Event. O'Connor picked up the Musician Of The Year in 1992.

An accomplished composer of contemporary classical music, he has composed for the Sante Fe Music Festival, appeared as a guest soloist with the Boston Pops Orchestra and is musical director of TNN's American Music Shop. His latest project is the production of **Violin Heroes**, which will pair him with Stephane Grappelli, Vassar Clements, Charlie Daniels, Jean-Luc Ponty, Buddy Spicher, Byron Berline, Johnny Gimble and Doug Kershaw.

Recommended:
Markology (Rounder/–)
Pickin' In The Wind (Rounder/–)
Soppin' The Gravy (Rounder/–)

Molly O'Day

Molly O'Day had an earnest exhortative style – not unlike that of Roy Acuff and Wilma Lee Cooper – which was the epitome of a style and brand of old-time music not found today.

She was born LaVerne Williamson in Pike County, Kentucky, on July 9, 1923, and embarked on a professional career in the summer of 1939, when she joined her fiddling brother Skeets in a band which also included Johnny Bailes. Here she went by the first of her many stage names, Mountain Fern, which she changed to Dixie Lee in the autumn of 1940. She married her longtime husband – and, at the time, fellow bandmember – Lynn Davis on April 5, 1941.

Molly and Lynn made the rounds of a number of Southeastern radio stations for the next few years – Beckley, West Virginia; Birmingham, Alabama; Louisville (where she finally chose the name Molly O'Day), Beckley again and then Dallas and finally Knoxville, where they were heard by Fred Rose who interested Satherley in recording them.

Their first Columbia session (December 16, 1946) produced many of her classics: **Tramp On The Street** (written by Hank Williams), **Six More Miles, Black Sheep Returned To The Fold** and others.

The session also marked the recording debut of Mac Wiseman, who played bass on the recordings.

The records were minor hits, and they resumed the circuit of radio stations, also doing more Columbia recordings: **Poor Ellen Smith** (with Molly on the banjo), **The First Fall Of Snow**, **Matthew Twenty-four** and others.

In 1950 they began recording only sacred material for Columbia, and when Molly contracted tuberculosis in 1952, she and Lynn both left musical careers to become ministers in the Church of God, careers which they followed through to the mid-'80s. Molly occasionally broadcast over a Christian station based in Huntingdon, West Virginia. After several months of illness, Molly died of cancer on December 5, 1987.

There is no question that Molly O'Day quit performing and recording well before her prime; she certainly had all the talent and appeal to become country music's first really great and popular woman singer.

Recommended:
Molly O'Day And The Cumberland Mountain Folks (Old Homestead/–)
The Heart And Soul Of Molly O'Day (Queen City/–)
Living Legend Of Country Music (Starday/–)

Kenny O'Dell

One of Nashville's most successful songwriters, Kenny was born in Oklahoma, raised in California, and began writing songs in his early teens. After graduating from Santa Maria High School in California, he formed his own record label, Mar-Kay Records, and recorded his own song, **Old-Time Love**, which received only minimal attention from the public.

Success finally came his way with the self-penned **Beautiful People**, a release on the small Vegas Records which made Top 40 in the American pop charts in 1967, only to be overtaken by a cover version by Bobby Vee. Another of Kenny's songs, **Next Plane To London**, as recorded by Rose Garden, made the Top 20 at the end of that year.

Kenny made a move to Nashville in 1971 to write songs and take over the running of House of Gold, Bobby Goldsboro's publishing firm. With **Why Don't We Go Somewhere And Love** by Sandy Posey and **I Take It On Home** by Charlie Rich, his songs began appearing on the country charts.

In 1973 Kenny came up with **Behind Closed Doors**, a song that made Charlie Rich a major country-pop cross-over star and was named Song Of The Year by the CMA and ACM. This success led to Kenny signing a recording contract with Capricorn Records and scoring minor country hits with **You Bet Your Sweet Love** (1974) and **Soulful Woman** (1975), before scoring Top 10 hits with **Let's Shake Hands And Come Out Lovin'** and **As Long As I Can Wake Up In Your Arms** (both 1978).

Kenny, who has served on the Board of Directors of the CMA and the Board of the Nashville Songwriters Association, has continued to pen hits for such artists as Billie Jo Spears (**Never Did Like Whiskey**), Tanya Tucker (**Lizzie And The Railman**) and the Judds (**Mama He's Crazy**), though his own recording career seems to have come to a halt with no further releases since 1979.

Recommended:
Kenny O'Dell (Capricorn/Capricorn)
Let's Shake Hands And Come Out Lovin' (Capricorn/–)

Daniel O'Donnell

The most popular 'Country'n'Irish' entertainer, Daniel O'Donnell (born on December 12, 1961 in Kincasslagh, Co. Donegal, Eire) was out-selling all American country stars and most MOR acts in the British Isles during the late '80s and early '90s. Adding to this huge record success, he also undertook sell-out concert tours.

He came from a musical family and his elder sister, Margo, was a popular Irish country singer in the late '60s and throughout the '70s. During school days Daniel sang in local variety concerts staged in the Kincasslagh parish hall, and would also occasionally perform with his sister. After completion of his school education, he undertook several jobs, then attended Galway Regional College on a business studies course in 1980. He dropped out in December and joined Margo's band on a full-time basis, making his first professional appearance at The Rag, Thurles, Co. Tipperaray, on January 28, 1981. Daniel stayed with Margo's band for two years, then opted for a solo career. He made his first record, **My Donegal Shore**, in early 1983, and in July formed his first band, Daniel O'Donnell And Country Fever. Selling the record at his gigs, he gradually built up a following for his easy-listening, Irish-flavoured country music. The summer of 1984 found him organizing a new band, Grassroots, at the same time completing more recordings, which would later surface on **The Boy From Donegal**.

It was at his appearance at the Irish Festival in London in 1985 that O'Donnell received his first breakthrough. Michael Clerkin, the owner of the independent Ritz Records, an Irish label based in London, saw the young Irish singer's performance and immediately offered him a recording

The O'Kanes, their debut album. Courtesy CBS Records.

contract. His first album for Ritz, **The Two Sides Of Daniel O'Donnell**, was released at the end of 1985. In early 1986 he signed a management contract with Clerkin. A second album, **I Need You**, released in late 1986, was the first to reach the UK country charts. Like the first, it featured a blend of Irish favourites and country standards, all performed in an effortless and undemanding manner. With his youthful good looks, O'Donnell was gaining a female following, and a third album, **Don't Forget To Remember**, entered the UK country chart at No.1, as did all his subsequent albums.

By now, O'Donnell's concert tours were selling out. He was undertaking two tours each year, usually of three months' duration. In 1988 Ritz licensed his next album, **From The Heart**, to TV marketing company Telstar Records. As well as entering the UK country chart at No.1, the album also crossed over to the UK pop chart, gaining the singer his first gold disc. The following year brought **Thoughts Of Home**, an album and video. The album made the UK pop album chart and the video reached No.1 on the UK music video chart. Slowly broadening his scope, in 1990 O'Donnell went to Nashville to record with producer Allen Reynolds, and the subsequent album, **The Last Waltz**, was his most country offering so far.

O'Donnell was inadvertently involved in controversy when the UK CMA and the Chart Committee decided to remove most of his albums (plus those of contemporary acts like Steve Earle) from the UK country chart as 'not being country'. This produced an uproar in British country music, not just from O'Donnell fans, but also from noted country music experts, who could see British country music was being dismissed in favour of 'the real thing' from the USA. After a few months there was a change of heart. All of his albums were reinstated, and O'Donnell continued as the most successful country act in Britain. He has also started building a following in Australia and New Zealand, and has played selected concerts in America, including Carnegie Hall, but performing mainly in cities with a large Irish immigrant population. In 1992 he made further strides in the UK when his single, **I Just Want To Dance With You**, made the UK pop Top

20, the first British country act to achieve this, leading to appearances on the BBC-TV show Top Of The Pops.

Recommended:
Follow Your Dream (–/Ritz)
From The Heart (–/Ritz)
The Last Waltz (–/Ritz)
Thoughts Of Home (–/Telstar)
Don't Forget To Remember (–/Telstar)

The O'Kanes

A pair of Nashville-based songwriters, Jamie O'Hara (born, Toledo, Ohio) and Kieran Kane (born Queens, New York), teamed up in 1986 to produce an exciting fusion of traditional country harmony singing, with a rock'n'roll backbeat and bluegrass-flavoured instrumentation. Several big-selling singles resulted, along with a Grammy nomination and write-ups in 'Time', 'Newsweek', 'USA Today' and 'Rolling Stone'.

O'Hara seemed destined for a career in professional sport until a knee injury changed his plans. A birthday gift of a guitar created an interest in songs and songwriting, and, after working clubs and honky-tonks in the Midwest, he arrived in Nashville in 1979 and signed a songwriter's contract with Cross-Keys. He gained his first cut with **Old Fashioned Love**, a John Conlee album track, in 1980.

Kieran Kane was raised in Mount Vernon, just outside New York City, and started playing drums in his brother's rock'n'roll band when he was nine. Later he turned to folk and bluegrass music. In the early '70s he was living in Los Angeles, where he worked as a lead guitarist, playing the club scene, writing songs and trying to land a record deal. Befriended by songwriter Kate Van Hoy, who urged him to try Nashville, Kieran moved to Music City in 1979 and signed with Tree Music. Two years later he landed a recording contract with Elektra Records, making the country Top 20 with **You're The Best** (1981) and **It's Who You Love** (1982).

Throughout the early '80s both O'Hara and Kane built up a reputation for their writing, penning hits, individually, for Janie Fricke, T.G. Sheppard, the Judds and many others. In 1984 they started writing together and recorded a demo in Kane's attic studio. Producer Bob Montgomery thought the demos were good enough for a recording contract, so, adopting the name the O'Kanes, they signed to Columbia Records in 1986. The acoustic demo recordings (two guitars, bass, fiddle, banjo, accordion, drums) made up most of their debut album. The first single, **Oh Darlin'**, made the Top 10 in 1986, followed by **Can't Stop My Heart From Loving You**, a No.1 the following year. Further Top 10 entries came with **Daddies Need To Grow Up Too**, **Just Lovin' You** (1987), **One True Love** and **Blue Love** (1988). They took their music on the road with a fast-paced and exciting stage show. A second album, **Tired Of The Runnin'**, was released hot on the heels of their debut, but appealed more to a cult audience.

The O'Kanes had become part of the 'New Traditionalists'. In 1989 they recorded a third album, but it was scrapped because both they and Columbia were unhappy with it. Jamie and Kieran returned to the studios, this time with ace producer Allen Reynolds, and emerged with **Imagine That**, a masterpiece album that successfully blended all the best

Tired Of The Runnin', the O'Kanes. Courtesy CBS Records.

elements from their first two albums to create the definitive 'O'Kanes sound'. Unfortunately by the time the album hit the stores in 1990, the O'Kanes' career had lost momentum. Though the album made a brief appearance on the country charts, the singles failed to gain radio plays and Columbia didn't renew their contract in 1991. The pair returned to songwriting and playing sessions, with country music losing one of the finest acts that it had produced during the '80s.

Recommended:
The O'Kanes (Columbia/CBS)
Imagine That (Columbia/CBS)
Tired Of The Runnin' (Columbia/CBS)

Roy Orbison

Born in Vernon, Texas, on April 23, 1936, Orbison's roots were deep country. His first band, the Wink Westerners, were named after the town of Wink, where he was raised. He was one of the many youngsters who fell under the spell of rockabilly, and under the guidance of Sam Phillips, had his first hit on Sun Records, **Ooby Dooby**, in 1956. However, his totally unique voice owes nothing to any particular genre and he moved into popular music, where he became an international star.

A victim of tragedy since leaving Monument Records in 1965 – his career immediately plummeted, his wife Claudette was killed in a motorcycle accident and two of his children died in a fire during 1968 – Orbison resumed his relationship with Monument in 1977. A subsequent album, **Regeneration**, proved to be his strongest since the early '60s.

In 1980 he made his debut on the country charts with **That Lovin' You Feelin' Again**, a stylish duet with Emmylou Harris that was featured in the film 'Urban Cowboy' and won a Grammy award. During 1985, Orbison took part in the Sun reunion – with Johnny Cash, Jerry Lee Lewis and Carl Perkins – that produced the **Class Of '55** album. That same year he

re-recorded several of his old hits and started to rebuild his career. Two years later he recorded **A Black And White Night**, a live concert at Coconut Grove that featured guest spots by Bruce Springsteen, Elvis Costello and Bonnie Raitt. Also in 1987 he became a member of the Travelling Wilburys. Orbison also joined k.d. lang on a new version of his pop classic **Cryin'**, which became a minor country hit. A new solo contract was signed with Virgin Records and he had just completed the **Mystery Girl** album, when he died of a heart attack on December 6, 1988 in Madison, Tennessee. Released the following year, the album made the country chart, with a single, **You Got It**, becoming a Top 10 entry in 1989.

Recommended:
All Time Greatest Hits (Monument/Monument)
Regeneration (Monument/Monument)
The Sun Years (–/Charly)
Big O Country (–/Decca)
In Dreams (Virgin/Virgin)
Mystery Girl (Virgin/Virgin)
A Black And White Night (Virgin/Virgin)
Laminar Flow (Asylum/Asylum)

Osborne Brothers

Among the first of the so-called progressive bluegrass outfits, the Osborne Brothers (both born at Hyden, Kentucky, Bob on December 7, 1931, Sonny on October 29, 1937) made their radio debut on station WROL, Knoxville, Tennessee, in the early '50s.

After teaming for a time with Jimmy Martin, they signed for MGM Records in 1956. They became regulars on WWVA's Wheeling Jamboree show, where they specialized in precise, sky-high three-part harmony with guitarist Benny Birchfield.

Their gig at Antioch College in 1959 was a milestone, sparking off a series of campus dates, while they also found themselves accepted on the Opry.

Constantly dismaying purists with their electric sounds and their use of steel guitar, drums and piano, the Osbornes became Decca artists in 1963, terminating their seven-year relationship with MGM. As electric bluegrass began to prosper, the group (later featuring Ronnie Reno or Dale Sledd as the third vocalist) began accumulating a number of low chart singles: **The Kind Of Woman I Got** (1966), **Rocky Top** (1968), **Tennessee Hound Dog** (1969) and **Georgia Pinewoods** (1971).

In 1976 they cut their first album for the new CMH label, featuring accompaniment more sparse than in past years, focusing as always on Bob's awesome tenor voice and impressive harmony singing. They have since recorded more albums for CMH.

Recommended:
Voices In Bluegrass (MCA/Stetson)
Ru-bee (MCA/–)
Pickin' Grass And Singin' Country (MCA/–)
Number One (CMH/–)
From Rocky Top To Muddy Bottom (CMH/–)

The Classic Roy Orbison. Courtesy London Records.

THE CLASSIC ROY ORBISON

Some Things I Want To Sing About, Bob and Sonny – The Osborne Brothers. Courtesy Sugar Hill.

K.T. Oslin

Kay Toinette Oslin was born in Crossitt, Arkansas in 1943. She emerged as a major country star in the late '80s; well over 40, a little overweight, yet a hip dresser. It was just the right image needed to give a voice to older women. Musically a diverse artist, K.T. provided a view of love in the '80s from the perspective of a woman in her 40s, through her mainly self-penned songs. Her **'80s Ladies** album and single became best-sellers in 1987, and the lady won a Grammy and was named both CMA and ACM Female Vocalist in 1988.

Raised mainly in Mobile, Alabama, her Southern upbringing exposed her to honky-tonk music, blues, rock'n'roll and soul. By the early '60s she was living in Houston, Texas, where she made her professional debut as a folk singer. She teamed up with school friend David Jones and songwriter Guy Clark in a folk trio.

She moved to Nashville, sang harmony on Clark's 1978 album, and landed both a writer's contract and a record deal, signing with Elektra Records. She made her debut on the country charts as Kay T. Oslin with Chip Taylor's **Clean Your Own Tables** in 1981. She also cut an early version of **Younger Men**, but lack of radio plays led to her being dropped. Gail Davies recorded her **'Round The Clock Lovin'** and **Where Is A Woman To Go**, which gave Oslin the incentive to continue. She borrowed

$7,000 from an aunt and hired a band for a Nashville showcase. RCA producer Harold Shedd was suitably impressed, and signed her to a new recording contract in 1986. The first single, **Walls Of Tears**, made the country Top 40 in 1987, but it was the title song of her debut album, **'80s Ladies**, that made K.T. Oslin into a major star. The single went into the country Top 10, while the album gained a platinum award.

K.T. made No.1 with **Do Ya** (1987), **I'll Always Come Back** and **Hold Me**

(1988), while a second album, **This Woman**, gained her another platinum award. Her songs were felt to be too feminist for Nashville, but with her wry good humour and solid sense she broke down the barriers. Touring with Alabama in 1989, she guested on their chart-topping single, **Face To Face**, meanwhile enjoying

Below: Tommy Overstreet began work on TV, as Tommy Dean from Abilene.

further solo success with **Hey Bobby** and **This Woman** (1989), before starting work on a third album, **Love In A Small Town**. A single, **Come Next Monday**, was a No.1 in 1990, and the album gained a gold disc. There has not been a new studio album, but in 1993 she did release a **Greatest Hits** set.

Recommended:
Love In A Small Town (RCA/RCA)
'80s Ladies (RCA/RCA)
This Woman (RCA/RCA)

Paul Overstreet

A multi-award-winning songwriter, Paul Overstreet (born on March 17, 1955, in Newton, Mississippi) is a country tunesmith who prefers to write with an optimistic outlook on love and happiness. It is obviously a successful ploy as he has been named BMI's Songwriter Of The Year for five straight years, 1987–1992. In addition, Paul has also managed to carve out his own comfortable niche as a performer, with several self-penned country hits to his credit.

Just Between The Two Of Us, Bonnie Owens with Merle Haggard. Courtesy Capitol Records.

The son of a Baptist minister, Paul came to Nashville after finishing high school in Newton. He had his years of struggle, and played the clubs. He started songwriting because he wanted his own material, but, recording briefly for RCA in 1982, he soon found it would be more profitable to let others cut his songs. In 1983 George Jones turned **Same Ol' Me** into a Top 10 hit and doors started opening. But Paul had already fallen prey to self-destructive tendencies. Briefly married to Dolly Parton's younger sister Frieda Parton, Overstreet came to rely on drugs and alcohol to fuel his writing inspiration. Finally, in 1984, he stopped drinking, kicked the drug habit, and in early 1985 married Julie, a make-up artist for a TV show in which he was appearing.

A steadying influence, Julie helped her husband find his feet. In 1986 he teamed up with fellow songwriters Thom Schuyler and Fred Knobloch as the country trio SKO. They signed to MTM Records, and charted Top 10 with **You Can't Stop Love** (1986), then a No.1 with **Baby's Got A New Baby** (1987). However, Paul soon left the group, intent on pursuing his own solo career. His first – and last – single for MTM was **Love Helps Those**, which rose to No.3 in 1988. Shortly after MTM closed down, so Overstreet took his material to his old label RCA. He scored two Top 10 hits with **Sowin' Love** and **All The Fun** in 1989. His RCA debut album, also titled **Sowin' Love**, was full of catchy melodies

Best Of Buck Owens – a compilation of hits. Courtesy Capitol Records.

and traditional country swing. Further hits followed with **Seeing My Father In Me**, **Richest Man On Earth** and **Daddy's Come Around** (all 1990), the latter making No.1. He joined Tanya Tucker and Paul Davis on the chart-topping **I Won't Take Less Than Your Love** in 1987, and picked up two Grammies for Best Country Song with **Forever And Ever Amen** (1988) and **Love Can Build A Bridge** (1991).

His optimistic lyrics brought Overstreet close to gospel music, though he is not a gospel performer. This came through strongly on his second album, **Heroes**, with the title song going Top 10 in 1991. More hits have come his way as a singer with **Ball And Chain** (1991), **Still Out There Swinging** (1992) and the infectious **Take Another Run** (1993).

Recommended:
Heroes (RCA/RCA)
Love Is Strong (RCA/–)
Sowin' Love (RCA/RCA)

Tommy Overstreet

Born in Oklahoma, on September 10, 1937, Overstreet began his career in Houston, Texas, working on a Saturday morning TV show in the guise of Tommy Dean from Abilene.

In 1956–57 he studied radio and TV production at the University of Texas. After a short stint as a touring performer and a spell in the Army, he claims to have just 'coasted' for a few years. His fortunes changed in 1967 when, following a move to Nashville, he became manager of Dot Records' Nashville office, at the same time becoming a Dot recording artist.

His initial singles failed to make much impression, but following the Top 5 success of **Gwen (Congratulations)** (1971), virtually every release made the Top 20. These hits include **Ann (Don't Go Running)**, **Heaven Is My Woman's Love** (1972), **Jeannie Marie (You Were A Lady)** (1974) and **Don't Go City Girl On Me** (1977).

Recommended:
Heaven Is My Woman's Love (Dot/–)
This Is Tommy Overstreet (Dot/–)
Welcome To My World Of Love (–/Ember)
I'll Never Let You Down (Elektra/–)

Bonnie Owens

The ex-wife of Merle Haggard and mother of Buddy Allan from a marriage to Buck Owens, Bonnie Campbell Owens was born in Blanchard, Oklahoma, on October 1, 1932.

In her early years she sang at clubs throughout Arizona, working with Buck Owens as part of the Buck And Britt Show on a Mesa radio station, later joining him in Mac's Skillet Lickers. During the '60s, Bonnie moved to Bakersfield, California, there meeting Merle Haggard, whom she married in 1965.

The twosome became signed to Capitol Records, cutting an album of duets entitled **Just Between The Two Of Us**, which led to them being voted Best Vocal Group of 1966 by the ACM. Prior to this, the duo had cut a single of the same name for Tally, which had become a 1964 hit. Bonnie also achieved two solo successes with Tally via **Daddy Don't Live Here Anymore** and **Don't Take Advantage Of Me**.

Following a small clutch of other minor chart entries, including **Number One Heel** (1965) and **Lead Me On** (1969), Bonnie officially retired from performing in 1975.

Recommended:
That Makes Two Of Us – with Merle Haggard (Hilltop/–)
Lead Me On (Capitol/–)
Just Between The Two Of Us – with Merle Haggard (Capitol/Stetson)

Buck Owens

Main man behind the 'California Sound' and the establishment of Bakersfield, Alvis Edgar 'Buck' Owens was born in Sherman, Texas, on August 12, 1929.

While Buck was still young, the Owens family moved to Arizona in search of a better standard of living but they failed to find prosperity. Buck left school while in his ninth grade to work in farm labouring. A fine guitarist and mandolin player, he began playing with a band over radio station KTYL, Mesa, Arizona when he was barely 17. At the same age he got married – by 18 he was a father.

In 1951 he moved to Bakersfield, forming a band, the Schoolhouse Playboys, with whom he played sax and trumpet. He also established himself as a first-class session man on guitar. Following a stint as a lead guitarist with Tommy Collins' band, he became signed as a Capitol recording artist on March 1, 1957.

His first chart entry was with **Second Fiddle** (1959), then followed a long sojourn in the Top 5 via such releases as **Under Your Spell Again** (1959), **Excuse Me, It Think I've Got A Heartache** (1960), **Fooling Around** and **Under The Influence Of Love** (1961).

With his band the Buckaroos – an outfit that has featured Don Rich, Doyle Holly and Tom Brumley – Owens began playing to sell-out crowds. Owens registered no less than 17 No.1 hits between 1963–69.

During the early '60s, the band leader had recorded a series of extremely successful duets with Rose Maddox. At the onset of the '70s Owens revived this practice, employing Susan Raye as a partner and logging up hits with **We're Gonna Get Together, Togetherness** and **The Great White Horse**. Although some had begun to suggest that Owens had

Below: Vernon Oxford now makes religion a part of his shows.

become **Too Old To Cut The Mustard** – a 1971 single featuring his son Buddy Alan – the Baron of Bakersfield continued to supply Capitol with major discs.

However, in 1976 he terminated his long association with Capitol, signing with Warner Brothers and releasing **Buck 'Em!**. This marked the end of his days as a Top 10 regular, though he did make Top 10 with **Play Together Again, Again**, a duet with Emmylou Harris in 1979.

He continued as a regular on the TV show Hee-Haw until the early '80s, but had retired to run his many business interests. In 1987 Dwight Yoakam prised Owens out of retirement to join him on a remake of an Owens' oldie, **Streets Of Bakersfield**. It hit No.1 on the charts in 1988 and gave Owens a new lease of life. He signed a new contract with Capitol and scored two minor hits with **Hot Dog** (1988) and **Act Naturally** (1989), the latter featuring Ringo Starr. Owens also took to the road but he announced his retirement from performing in 1992.

Recommended:
Buck 'Em (Warner Bros/–)
Our Old Mansion (Warner Bros/–)
Kickin' In (Capitol/–)
Blue Love (–/Sundown)

Vernon Oxford

Highly regarded in Europe, Oxford was born on June 8, 1941, in Benton County, Arkansas, one of seven children of one of the area's leading fiddle players. Like his

father, he became a fiddler, entering the well-known Cowtown contest and also the Kansas State championship.

After forming his own band and touring throughout the Midwest, Oxford then moved on to Nashville, where he was turned down by several record companies as being 'too country'. Eventually, in 1965, he became signed to RCA, who released seven singles and an album before dropping him. He also signed for Stop, with continued lack of real recognition.

In 1971, fans in Britain and Sweden organized a petition urging RCA to release Oxford's discs once more and, two years later, British RCA duly obliged with a double album in their **Famous Country Music Makers** series, a release which accrued impressive sales figures.

This encouraged RCA Nashville to re-sign Oxford in 1974, the singer immediately responding by providing a minor hit in **Shadows Of My Mind** (1975), then a major hit with **Redneck** (1975). Remaining a major star in Europe, Oxford turned increasingly to religion, often preaching about hell and damnation during his country performances. In 1989 he was filmed for a BBC documentary, Power In The Blood, in which he took his cowboy hat, guitar and his Hank Williams' voice to the sinners of Northern Ireland, performing in drinking dens, mission halls and the Maze Prison.

Recommended:
Famous Country Music Makers (–/RCA)
I Just Want To Be A Country Singer (RCA/RCA)
Keepin' It Country (Rounder/Sundown)
Tribute To Hank Williams (–/Meteor)
A Better Way Of Life (–/Sundown)
His And Hers (Rounder/–)

Ozark Mountain Daredevils

A country-rock band from Springfield, Missouri, the Daredevils sprang from an outfit known as Cosmic Corncob And His Amazing Mountain Daredevils.

Their first album for A&M Records came out in 1973 and was well received. By 1974 they had a pop hit single with **If You Want To Get To Heaven**. Their next album, **It'll Shine When It Shines** – generally considered to be their best – spawned yet another hit in **Jackie Blue**, penned by band members Steve Cash (vocals, harmonica) and Larry Lee (drums). Mixing pure rock'n'roll with slick country picking, the Daredevils pushed ahead for a while, heading for Nashville to cut their third LP, **The Car Over The Lake Album**.

But interest began to wane and by 1977 members Randle Chowning (guitar, vocals) and Buddy Brayfield (piano) had quit. Original members Steve Cash and John Dillon (vocals, guitar, keyboard, fiddle) appeared on Paul Kennerley's all-star **White Mansions** album in 1978, but they were not destined to stay with A&M much longer. In the wake of a live double, they moved on, signing with Columbia, for whom they cut an eponymously titled album in 1980. But by that time only Dillon, Cash and Mike Granda (bass) remained from the line-up that cut their first sides at a ranch in Missouri.

The band were back in the studios in 1988 working with producer Wendy Waldman on the **Modern History** album, an exciting blend of American heartland

THE CAR OVER THE LAKE ALBUM

The Car Over The Lake Album, the Ozark Mountain Daredevils' third album. Courtesy A&M Records.

roots and a powerful contemporary sound, which is still popular at their live dates throughout North America.

Recommended:
Ozark Mountain Daredevils (A&M/A&M)
It'll Shine When It Shines (A&M/A&M)
The Car Over The Lake Album (A&M/A&M)
Modern History (–/Conifer)
Heart Of The County (–/Dixie Frog)

Lee Roy Parnell

With his musical and lyrical mix of blues, country, rock, heartache and hope, Lee Roy Parnell (born on December 21, 1957, in Stevenville, Texas) brought a harder, rocking edge to country in the early '90s. His music flaunted the gritty vocals and jagged rhythm licks more akin to R&B than country.

He started performing after high school, spending more than a decade plying his trade in Texas clubs before descending on Nashville in 1987. Life on the road had been hard, leading to a divorce in 1986 and drinking. The most difficult part of moving to Nashville was leaving his children behind, but he found the means to visit them at regular intervals, due to his increasing success as a songwriter.

Parnell's demos, which featured his own electric lead and slide guitar work, led to a recording contract with Arista Records in 1989. This coincided with a second marriage to a fellow Texan, Kim, who worked for Polygram Music in Nashville. Parnell scored minor hits with **Crocodile Tears** and **Oughta Be A Law** in 1990. However, his music, with elements of blues, old rock'n'roll and western swing, was at odds with the trend of traditional country. His next few singles all failed to chart, but Arista had faith in him, and **What Kind Of Fool Do You Think I Am** soared to No.2 on the charts in the summer of 1992. The title track of his second album, **Love Without Mercy**, reached the Top 10 and **Tender Moment** reached No.2 in 1993.

Recommended:
Love Without Mercy (Arista/–)
Lee Roy Parnell (Arista/–)

Gram Parsons

A seminal figure in the country-rock movement of the late '60s, Gram was born Cecil Connor in Winterhaven, Florida, on November 5, 1946. His father 'Coon Dog' Connor owned a packing plant in Waycross, Georgia. Coon Dog shot himself when Gram was 13 and Gram's mother married again, to Robert Parsons, a rich New Orleans businessman, Parsons formally adopted Cecil and changed the boy's name to Gram Parsons.

With much drinking in both real and adopted families, and a hitherto uprooted life, Gram ran away at 14 and two years

Love Without Mercy, Lee Roy Parnell. Courtesy Arista Records.

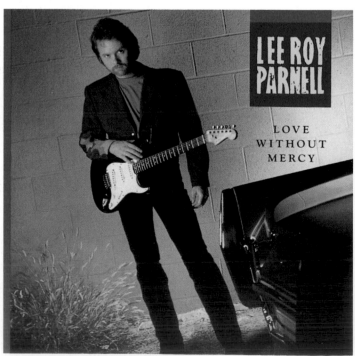

later was in New York's Greenwich Village singing folk songs. At one point he formed a folk band with Jim Stafford, and with a later band, Shiloh, Gram specialized in a commercial brand of folk.

Studying theology at Harvard in 1965, Gram formed the International Submarine Band. After he dropped out of university, the band reformed and an album, on Lee Hazelwood's label, showed them to be following a fairly purist country path.

By the time that album came out, Gram had joined the Byrds. Meeting Chris Hillman of that band in L.A. in 1968, he convinced Hillman that the hitherto rock-oriented Byrds should experiment with country. The result was **Sweetheart Of The Rodeo**, the first real country-rock album. Although much of Gram's contribution was mixed out, the album set a new style among rock groups and reminded many a southern-bred rocker just where his roots lay. The Byrds appeared on the Grand Ole Opry and sang Gram's own composition **Hickory Wind**.

Gram's fantasy about marrying country with rock was nurtured by his association with the Rolling Stones. He quit the Byrds on the eve of a South African tour, causing a welter of ill feeling. However, he reunited with Chris Hillman in 1969 when his country aspirations were more fully realized in the Flying Burrito Brothers, that band's **Gilded Palace Of Sin** album being hailed as a country-rock classic, showcasing compositions that have since become standards via the talents of Emmylou Harris.

But Parsons was getting into the West Coast drug lifestyle and by the recording of the band's second album, **Burrito Deluxe**, he seemed more interested in hanging out with Jagger and Richard in Europe. With his trust fund providing him extensive monies to indulge his lifestyle and a fantasy about getting to rock superstar level, Gram's preoccupations were tending more towards drugs and drink than productive musical output. However, Warner Reprise came up with a contract and, better still, was the possibility of Merle Haggard producing his next album. Parsons went to visit Haggard but Merle appeared to have a change of heart at the last moment. Even so, the session went ahead using Haggard's engineer Hugh

Sleepless Nights, Gram Parsons. Courtesy A&M Records.

Davis. Also booked were Glen D. Hardin, James Burton and a new girl singer from Baltimore, Emmylou Harris.

Gram was evidently drunk to the point of falling down for the first sessions. Nevertheless, the album showed that his writing ability was still there. **GP** was not a big commercial success on its release in 1972, and it was followed by **Grievous Angel**, which featured a similar line-up and more classic Parsons' songs. A tour around that time, with Emmylou Harris and the Fallen Angels Band gave hints of what might have been for Gram had he lived. It has been left to Emmylou to perpetuate the songs and the legend.

Parsons probably did not expect to live long and on September 19, 1973, he died of a heart attack at Joshua Tree, in the California desert. The causes were apparently a heavy mix of drink and drugs, followed by (according to Byrd Roger McGuinn) a lovemaking bout with his wife. Later, at L.A.'s International Airport, his body was snatched and instead of ending up in New Orleans for a family funeral, was driven to the desert at Joshua Tree and unofficially cremated, the result of a pact between Gram and manager Phil Kaufman that whoever died first would be taken to the desert and cremated.

Because of this bizarre incident no autopsy was possible and no official cause of death established. Parsons has since become a cult figure, following one of his country idols, Hank Williams, to an early and mysterious death. But, unlike Williams, Parsons had to wait until after his demise for recognition.

Recommended:
Sleepless Nights – with the Flying Burrito Brothers (A&M/A&M)
Live 1973 – with the Fallen Angels (Sierra/ Sundown)
The International Submarine Band (LHI or Shiloh/Edsel)
GP/Grievous Angel (Warner Bros/Warner Bros)

Dolly Parton

Born on a farm in Locust Ridge, Seiver County, Tennessee, on January 19, 1946, Dolly Rebecca Parton was the fourth of 12 children born to a mountain family. At the age of ten, she was already an accomplished performer, her first regular radio and TV dates being on the shows of Cas Walker, in Knoxville. At 13 she was cutting sides for a small Louisiana record company, the same year making an appearance on Grand Ole Opry.

Graduating from Seiver County High School in June 1964, she immediately left for Nashville, where she, at first, scraped

by as part of a songwriting team (with her uncle, Bill Owens). Her first success came in 1967, with two hit records on Monument (**Dumb Blonde** and **Something Fishy**) and a contract to join the Porter Wagoner TV and road show. Also that year, Dolly began recording for RCA, her duet with Wagoner on Tom Paxton's **Last Thing On My Mind** entering the charts in December 1967, and rapidly climbing into the Top 10.

For the next six years, the Parton–Wagoner partnership continued to flourish, over a dozen of their duets becoming RCA best-sellers. However, it seemed that Dolly was gradually becoming the major attraction on disc, obtaining a No.1 with her recording of **Joshua** in 1970. By 1974, she had branched out as a true solo act , though continuing to record duets with Wagoner and utilize his talents on some of her sessions. The result was a move away from mainstream country in an attempt to gain a wider audience. And the bid proved profitable. Dolly's recording of **Jolene** (1974) became a world-wide hit, this being followed by such other '70s winners as **The Bargain Store**, **We Used To** (1975), **Hey Lucky Lady**, **All I Can Do** (1976)**, Light Of A Clear Blue Morning** (1977) and then five No.1s in a row with **Here You Come Again** (1977), **It's All Wrong But It's All Right**, **Heartbreaker**, **I Really Got The Feeling**, **Baby I'm Burnin'** (1978) and **You're The Only One** (1979).

During this period Dolly began exploring every pop avenue, from bluegrass through to disco. Her albums ranged from **Great Balls Of Fire**, on which she provided her own versions of earlier pop and rock hits, to **New Harvest, First Gathering**, a release which featured half of Nashville providing back-up assistance on **Applejack**, one of Dolly's own songs.

By this time Dolly had become a pop personality and the best-known country performer in the world. Unfortunately much of this was down to her cheesecake poses rather than her unquestioned singing ability, and her outstanding talent as a songwriter. A major film career was

Below: Dolly – she once claimed she lost a Dolly Parton lookalike contest.

sparked by a starring role in the comedy '9 to 5', and this was followed by 'The Best Little Whorehouse In Texas' (1982), 'Rhinestone' (1984) and 'Steel Magnolias' (1990), by which time she had invested in her own film production company.

She continued to accrue an imposing array of awards, including CMA Female Vocalist Of The Year (1975 and 1976) and the coveted CMA Entertainer Of The Year (1978). There were further country No.1s with **Starting Over Again**, **Old Flames Can't Hold A Candle To You**, **9 To 5** – also one of her pop hits (1980), **But You Know I Love You** (1981), **I Will Always Love You** (1982), **Islands In The Stream** (a duet with Kenny Rogers that went to No.1 in many countries, 1983), **Tennessee Homesick Blues** (1984), **Real Love** (another Parton–Rogers duet, 1985) and **Think About Love** (1986).

Dolly saw another dream come true in 1986 with the opening of her Dollywood Theme Park in Pigeon Forge, Tennessee. The following year she hosted her own TV variety series, left RCA Records to sign with Columbia, and also completed the long-awaited **Trio** album with Emmylou Harris and Linda Ronstadt. It produced a No.1 country hit with a revival of **To Know Him Is To Love Him** (1987), won a Grammy for Best Country Album and also went on to gain a platinum award. Dolly's first Columbia album, **Rainbow**, was a pure pop record. Superbly produced, Dolly was in great voice, but it was slated by the critics and failed to sell. Unperturbed, she teamed up with Ricky Skaggs who produced **White Limozeen**, which saw her score No.1s with **Why'd You Come In Here Lookin' Like That** and **Yellow Roses** (1989). Further major country hits came with **Rockin' Years** (a No.1 duet with Ricky Van Shelton, 1991), **Silver And Gold** (1991), **Country Road** (1992) and **Romeo** (1993).

Her phenomenal success continued as both writer and performer. Soul singer Whitney Houston had the biggest-selling single in 1992 with Parton's composition, **I Will Always Love You**, a No.1 in Britain and America, which was featured in the film, 'The Bodyguard'. Meanwhile Dolly's own **Eagle When She Flies** album

Jolene, Dolly Parton. Courtesy RCA Records.

gained a platinum award. The following year she released **Slow Dancing With The Moon**, a subtle mix of country and pop themes that featured an all-star guest list. Unable to stand still for too long, and always moving on to new projects, Dolly Parton teamed with Loretta Lynn and Tammy Wynette for the 1993 album **Honky Tonk Angels**.

Recommended:
Coat Of Many Colors (RCA/RCA)
My Tennessee Mountain Home (RCA/RCA)
Jolene (RCA/RCA)
New Harvest, First Gathering (RCA/RCA)
Burlap And Satin (RCA/RCA)
White Limozeen (Columbia/CBS)
Eagle When She Flies (Columbia/CBS)
Slow Dancing With The Moon (Columbia/Columbia)
Golden Streets Of Glory (RCA/–)

Stella Parton

The sister of Dolly Parton and the sixth of 12 children, Stella Parton (born Seiver County, Tennessee, May 4, 1949) married while still at high school and was pregnant by the time she graduated. A TV performer in Knoxville at the age of nine, she recorded early on for some minor Nashville labels and formed a gospel group the Stella Parton Singers, working as performer, manager and booking agent.

High The Moon and **The World Is Waiting For The Sunrise**.

Les had experimented with electric guitars as early as the late '30s – in fact he had never stopped being fascinated by electronics since his first crystal set in 1927 – and in 1952 Gibson began putting out their fabulously successful series of Les Paul guitars, designed by Les himself.

After he and Mary Ford divorced in 1962, Les retired from performing, turning to inventing in his New Jersey home. The boom in interest in the Les Paul guitar, however, made his name a household word among musicians, and in 1973 he began performing again on a limited scale. Using a guitar called a Les Pulveriser which was light years ahead of the standard Gibson production model, he recorded a number of albums with Chet Atkins. One – **Chester And Lester** – won a Grammy for the Best Country Instrumental Performance of 1976.

Recommended:
Chester And Lester – with Chet Atkins (RCA/RCA)
Guitar Monsters – with Chet Atkins RCA/RCA)

Johnny Paycheck

A one-time Nashville renegade who, during the mid-'70s, temporarily adopted the name of John 'Austin' Paycheck in honour of the Music City's greatest rivals. This singer-songwriter (born Don Lytle, Greenfield, Ohio, May 31, 1941) began his career as a Nashville sideman, enjoying a brief stay as bass-guitarist with Porter Wagoner's Wagonmasters. Later he became a member of Faron Young's Deputies before moving on to play with both George Jones and Ray Price. During this period he switched to steel guitar, rejoining Jones' band as a guitarist during 1959–60.

As a rockabilly he cut some sides for Decca using the pseudonym Donny Young – then came sessions for Mercury and Hilltop, Paycheck having two fair-sized hits on the latter label with **A-11** (1965) and **Heartbreak, Tennessee** (1966). He then helped to form Little Darlin'

Records, providing the label with several good sellers during the '60s, the biggest of these being **The Lovin' Machine**, a Top 10 entry during 1966. It was around this time that Paycheck also made the grade as a writer, his **Apartment No. 9** affording Tammy Wynette her first hit. **Touch My Heart**, another of his compositions, went Top 10 via a version cut by Ray Price.

Little Darlin' folded at the end of the '60s, a period during which Paycheck virtually hit rock bottom, becoming a self-confessed alcoholic. However, he proved not to be a quitter. He took the cure and fought back with considerable determination, teaming up with producer Billy Sherrill to cut some sides for Epic. His first release on the label was **She's All I Got,** which reached the top of the country charts in 1971.

For the next couple of years, he was rarely out of the Top 20, thanks to singles such as **Someone To Give My Love To**, **Love Is A Good Thing** (1972), **Something About You I Love**, **Mr Lovemaker** and **Song And Dance Man** (1973). And though the hits continued, for a while they came at lower-order level. Even so, it was surprising when in 1976 Paycheck was reported to be bankrupt. Once again he bounced back and in 1977 notched three major hits, **Slide Off Your Satin Sheets**, **I'm The Only Hell (Mama Ever Raised)** and **Take This Job And Shove It**. The latter, one of David Allan Coe's anti-establishment anthems, became one of the year's biggest records. He teamed up with George Jones for a session that produced hits in **Maybellene** (1978), **You Can Have Her** (1979), and **You Better Move On** (1980), the duo adopting a gruesome twosome guise for the sleeve of **Double Trouble**, a rock'n'fun album that came out in 1980.

By 1981 he was working with Merle Haggard, Hag turning up on Paycheck's album **Mr Hag Told My Story**, which provided a spin-off single in **I Can't Hold Myself In Line**. But, despite fine records, Paycheck's popularity seemed to be waning again. By 1983 he had slipped his Epic/Columbia connection and was on AMI, charting with **I Never Got Over You**. Three years later he joined Mercury Records, returning to the Top 20 with **Old Violin** (1986). Paycheck was making the headlines, with stories of his drunken behaviour and bankruptcy doing nothing for his already rock-bottom reputation. In 1988 he started a nine-year prison sentence for aggravated assault relating to a bar-room shooting incident in 1985. While in jail he studied and received his General Education Diploma and, having served less than three years, was released for model behaviour. Known for years as a renegade and a victim of drugs and booze, Paycheck came

Heartbreak, Tenn. An early Paycheck release on Hilltop Records which became a fair-sized hit in 1966.

She formed her own label Soul, Country And Blues Records, in the early '70s and in 1975 released **Ode To Olivia**, supporting Olivia Newton-John's right to be acclaimed Top Female Vocalist by the CMA. Also that same year she recorded a song of her own called **I Want To Hold You In My Dreams**, which provided her with her first Top 10 single.

By 1976 she was with Elektra-Asylum, her records being produced by Jim Malloy. The partnership proved successful and resulted in twin major records in 1977, **The Danger Of A Stranger** and **Standard Lie Number One**, the former becoming a pop hit in Britain, where she made a promotional tour.

1978 was another good year for Stella, bringing three sizable hits including **Four Little Letters**, a Top 20 entry. Two more chart entries followed in 1979 but since then it has been all quiet on the vinyl front for a lady who has valiantly fought a battle to be accepted for her own ability, generally steering clear of any situation that might make it seem that she owed anything to Dolly's influence.

Recommended:
Stella Parton (Elektra/Elektra)
Country Sweet (Elektra/Elektra)

Les Paul

One of the most influential guitarists in popular music history. Les Paul (born Lester William Polfus, Waukseha, Wisconsin, June 9, 1915) began his career as a country musician-comedian named Hot Rod, later becoming Rhubarb Red. He toured for some time with a popular Chicago group, Rube Tronson And His Texas Cowboys, but his growing interest in jazz led him to play with big bands and small combos for a time. At one point, from 1934 to 1935, he had a country show as Rhubarb Red over WJJD, Chicago, in the morning and an afternoon jazz show as Les Paul on WIND.

In 1936, he, plus vocalist and rhythm guitarist Jim Atkins (Chet's half-brother)

Everybody's Got A Family, Johnny Paycheck. Courtesy Epic Records.

Stella Parton, Dolly's sister's eponymous album. Courtesy WEA Records.

and bassist Ernie Newton (a longtime Opry and Nashville session bassist in the '40s and '50s) auditioned in New York as the Les Paul Trio and spent the next five years with Fred Waring.

Les moved to L.A. late in 1941, where he spent much of his time in the studios as well as a stint in the services. In 1947 he teamed up with an ex-Gene Autry band member named Colleen Summers, who was such a fine guitarist she played lead guitar in Jimmy Wakely's band, singing harmony with him on **One Has My Name, The Other Has My Heart**.

Colleen, whom Paul later married, became Mary Ford, and the combination of her singing, his extraordinary playing and his then unique use of multiple track recording for guitar and voice made the team immensely popular in the '40s and early '50s, producing eleven No.1 pop hits for Capitol, including **Nola**, **Lover**, **How**

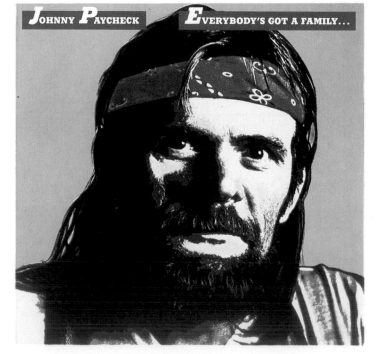

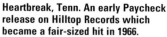

Hank Penny

Hank Penny was one of the few East Coast musicians who tried to bring Western swing sound to country music in the '40s. He was born in Birmingham, Alabama, on August 18, 1918.

He began his career as early as 1933, and later founded the Radio Cowboys with stints on WWL in New Orleans and the Midwestern Hayride WLW in Cincinnati, before departing for the West Coast in the mid-'40s. An influential country comedian, he was a regular on Spade Cooley's LA TV show in the late '40s. In 1949 he co-founded the legendary Palomino night-club, then in the late '50s sold the club and took up residency in Vegas. He performed regularly in Vegas until 1972, when he moved back to Los Angeles and semi-retirement. Hank died of a heart attack on April 17, 1992, in California.

Recommended:
Rompin', Stompin', Singin', Swingin'
(–/Bear Family)

Carl Perkins

Although Perkins is known as one of the seminal figures of Memphis rock'n'roll, he came from a solid country background and his albums have always been dotted with pure country songs

Born in Lake City, Tennessee, on April 9, 1932, in a poor farming community, he started his career performing at local country dances and honky-tonks, along with brothers Jay and Clayton. Independently of Elvis Presley, Carl realized that country was moving in new directions. But, when he first approached Sam Phillips at Sun Studios in Memphis, Phillips insisted that he cut country music only since Elvis had the other scene tied up. The result was three country singles, **Turn Around, Let The Jukebox Keep On Playing** and **Gone, Gone, Gone.** But Perkins persuaded Phillips to let him do

Stars Of The Grand Ole Opry (RCA).
Minnie performs Jealous Hearted Me.

out of jail 'clean', and by 1993 was headlining in Branson, Missouri.

As Epic once claimed in a press handout: "With a life story that fits impeccably into the 'rags to riches to rags to riches' stereotype, the only truly amazing thing about Johnny Paycheck is that no-one has yet seen fit to put his biography on the silver screen. Change a couple of names to protect the guilty and avoid lawsuits and you'd have an instant smash."

Recommended:
Double Trouble – with George Jones (Epic/Epic)
Take This Job And Shove It (Epic/Epic)
Armed And Crazy (Epic/Epic)
Everybody's Got A Family (Epic/Epic)

Leon Payne

A smooth-voiced singer and multi-instrumentalist, Payne was blind from childhood. Born in Alba, Texas, on June 15, 1917, he attended the Texas School for the Blind between 1924 and 1935 learning to play guitar, piano, organ, drums, trombone and other instruments.

During the mid-'30s he began playing with various Texas bands, occasionally joining Bob Wills and his Texas Playboys. In the late '40s, he became a member of Jack Rhodes' Rhythm Boys, in 1949 forming his own outfit, The Lone Star Buddies, and playing on Grand Ole Opry. A prolific songwriter, Payne penned a great number of much-covered songs including

Above: Opry favourite from Grinder's Switch, Minnie Pearl – "Howdy. I'm jest so proud to be here!"

Lost Highway, Blue Side Of Lonesome, They'll Never Take Her Love From Me and **I Love You Because**, the latter providing him with his own hit in late 1949.

Payne, who recorded with such labels as MGM, Bullet, Decca, Capitol and Starday, suffered a heart attack in 1965 and had to curtail many of his performing activities. He died on September 11, 1969.

Minnie Pearl

Born Sarah Ophelia Colley in Centerville, Tennessee, on October 25, 1912, she majored in stage technique at Nashville's Ward-Belmont College during the '20s, then taught dancing for a while before joining an Atlanta production company as a drama coach in 1934. By 1940, Sarah had become Minnie Pearl from Grinder's Switch (Grinder's Switch is a railroad switching station just outside Centerville) and made her debut on the Grand Ole Opry in this guise. She became an instant Opry favourite and appeared on numerous tours, radio and TV shows, also appearing on the first country music show ever to play New York's Carnegie Hall (1947).

Much honoured by the music industry, Minnie – Nashville's Woman Of The Year in 1965 – was elected to the Country Music Hall Of Fame in 1975. Though she has recorded for such labels as Everest, Starday and RCA, her only chart success

came with the Top 10 hit, **Giddyup Go – Answer** (1966), the woman's reply to Red Sovine's country No.1. Minnie continued with her stage and TV career right up until 1991 when she suffered a severe stroke and was forced into semi-retirement.

Recommended:
Stars Of The Grand Ole Opry – one track only (RCA/RCA)

Carl Perkins

and Jerry Lee Lewis (forming three-quarters of Sun's legendary million-dollar quartet) and was the subject of a magnificent Charly Records boxed set, **The Sun Years**. In 1985 he signed with MCA Records, the same year that he starred in a television special, 'Blue Suede Shoes: A Rockabilly Session' to mark the 30th anniversary of **Blue Suede Shoes**. He also appeared with Johnny Cash, Jerry Lee Lewis and Roy Orbison on the **Class Of '55** album in 1986, the same year that his **Birth Of Rock And Roll** became his biggest country hit since **Restless** in 1969.

In 1987 Carl Perkins was inducted into the Rock'n'Roll Hall Of Fame, and two years later he released a new album, **Born To Rock**, a collection of inspired performances blending rockabilly, lazy low-down blues and soulful country ballads. Perkins was still writing, providing the Judds with **Let Me Tell You About Love**, a country No.1 in 1989, while his **Restless** was revived by the Nashville Cats in 1991, gaining a CMA award.

Recommended:

Long Tall Sally (–/CBS Embassy)
The Sun Years – boxed set (–/Charly)
Classics (–/Bear Family)
Country Boy's Dream (–/Bear Family)
Friends, Family And Friends (–/Magnum Force)
Carl Perkins (MCA/Dot/MCA)

Webb Pierce

Born in West Monroe, Louisiana, on August 8, 1926, Webb Pierce became a distinctive stylist in the heavily electric country of the '50s. Early in his youth he learned to play good guitar and was soon gaining notice playing at local events. After regular stints on Radio KMLB, Monroe, Pierce moved to Shreveport, home of the Louisiana Hayride. He was noticed by Horace Logan, programme director of KWKH, the sponsoring station of the Hayride, and subsequently joined the Hayride. During this period, the early '50s, his band included many who were themselves to find fame: Faron Young, Jimmy Day, Floyd Cramer.

Early '50s hits with Decca included **Wondering**, **That Heart Belongs To Me** and **Back Street Affair**, while Pierce also co-wrote his **The Last Waltz**. By 1953 he had become popular enough to win the No.1 singer award given by the American Juke Box Operators. Soon after he moved to Nashville and joined the Grand Ole Opry. In 1954 he recorded **Slowly**, a No.1 single that featured a ground-breaking pedal steel solo (by Bud Isaacs), while during 1955 he had three No.1 hits: **In The Jailhouse Now**, **Love, Love, Love** and **I**

Carl Perkins – The Man Behind Johnny Cash. Courtesy CBS Records.

some faster material. This plea resulted in **Blue Suede Shoes**, a Perkins original which topped the pop, country and R&B charts simultaneously in 1956. Perkins looked set to be the next superstar from the Sun stable, but late that year he was on his way to do the Perry Como and Ed Sullivan shows in New York when a car crash left Perkins with multiple injuries and a broken career. His brother Jay later died as a result of that same crash. However, Elvis had recorded **Blue Suede Shoes** and Perkins was assured of a place in the rock'n'roll honours list.

Nevertheless, Carl's solo career seemed to be at a standstill. Elvis had overtaken him as a rock star and Perkins began drinking heavily. But a tour of Britain in 1964, and another as a headliner in 1965, convinced him that he was a star in some countries. Also the Beatles had recorded his **Honey Don't, Matchbox** and **Everybody's Trying To Be My Baby**.

After this, Perkins was approached by Johnny Cash to become part of his road show and for many years remained a mainstay of the Cash package. He began cutting country records and also recorded

Above: Carl Perkins is a country singer who is also one of rock's seminal figures.

an album with the eclectic NRBQ in 1970. In 1978 he released a UK album titled **Ol' Blue Suede's Back**, which saw him rockin' once more. He also began touring with his sons on drums and bass.

A frequent visitor to Britain, where he has appeared on several Wembley Festival bills, he turned up on Paul McCartney's **Tug Of War** album in 1981. He also recorded live in Germany with Johnny Cash

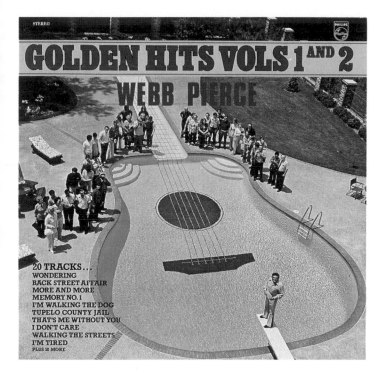

Golden Hits, Volumes 1 & 2, Webb Pierce. Courtesy Phonogram Records.

Don't Care. 1956 saw him scoring duet hits with Red Sovine – **Why, Baby, Why?** and **Little Rosa.** He recorded **Teenage Boogie,** an item now much sought after by rockabilly collectors. He followed up with more Top 10 hits including **Bye Bye Love, Honky Tonk Song** and **Tupelo County Jail.**

Below: A distinctive stylist of '50s country, Webb Pierce died in 1991.

His voice had the authentic, nasal, modern country ring and his songs had a bar-room edge, uncluttered by the excessive orchestration later to dominate Nashville recording.

He became extensively involved in the business side of music – a record company, radio stations and a publishing company or two. He was also the first star actually to own the Nashville cliché, the guitar-shaped swimming pool. However, though Webb had the occasional mini-hit during the '70s and even charted as recently as 1902 (when he teamed up with

Willie Nelson on a revival of **In The Jailhouse Now**), he semi-retired from music in 1975. In later years his health caused many hospital visits, initially for heart problems, but in 1990 he was diagnosed with cancer. He died on February 24, 1991, in Nashville.

Recommended:
I Ain't Never (–/Charly)
The Wondering Boy, 1951–1958 (–/Bear Family)
Cross Country (Decca/Stetson)

Ray Pillow

Voted Most Promising Male Country Artist Of The Year by 'Billboard' and 'Cashbox' in 1966, singer-guitarist Pillow was born in Lynchburg, Virginia, on July 4, 1937. Following four years in the forces during the late '50s, he completed a stay at college, then opted for a singing career.

Later signed to Capitol Records, he gained his first sizeable hit with **Take Your Hands Off My Heart** in 1965 and obtained a Top 20 entry that same year with **Thank You Ma'am.** During 1966 came four more chart-fillers, including **I'll Take The Dog,** a duet with Jean Shepherd that was to become Pillow's most successful record. On April 30, 1966, he became a member of the Grand Ole Opry.

Still an Opry regular, Pillow has not had the best of luck with his records since the '60s; he has moved through such labels as Dot, Mega, Hilltop, MCA and First Generation.

Recommended:
Slippin' Around (Mega/–)
Countryfied (Dot/–)
One Too Many Memories (–/Allegiance)

Poco

A country-slanted rock band, Poco formed in 1969 when ex-Buffalo Springfield cohorts Richie Furay (guitar and vocals) and

Poco. Courtesy CBS Records. The band was originally named Pogo.

Jim Messina (guitar and vocals) linked with Rusty Young (pedal steel, banjo, guitar, vocals), George Grantham (drums) and Randy Meisner (bass).

Three desertions took place during the band's nine-album stay with the Epic label – Messina moving out to join Kenny Loggins as half of a hit-making duo; Meisner becoming part of Rick Nelson's Stone Canyon Band before joining the Eagles; and Furay eventually helping to form the Souther-Hillman-Furay Band. In the wake of some commercially unsuccessful but musically interesting attempts to create an 'orchestral country' style – as exemplified by the title track of their **Crazy Eyes** album (1973) – Poco completed their obligations to Epic and signed a deal with ABC Records. The immediate result was **Head Over Heels** (1975), one of their best-received albums. Though it had been rumoured the band would fold in 1973, a version of Poco still existed in 1982, cutting an album called **Ghost Town** for Atlantic, after cutting three albums for MCA.

In 1984 the band disbanded, but five years later reformed with the original line-up from 1968. They signed to RCA Records and released **Legacy,** an album that produced the Top 20 single **Call It Love,** while the album went gold. This marked the first time that the original line-up had ever recorded; so, 21 years after they were formed, Poco finally made what was, in a sense, its first album.

Recommended:
Poco (Epic/CBS)
Deliverin' (Epic/Epic)
Crazy Eyes (Epic/Epic)
Cantamos (Epic/Epic)
Rose Of Cimarron (ABC/MCA)
Legacy (RCA/RCA)
The Forgotten Trail – 1969–1974 (Epic/–)

Charlie Poole

Leader of the North Carolina Ramblers, one of the most popular bands to emerge from that area in the '20s, five-string banjo player, singer and hard drinker Charlie Poole was born in Alamance County, North Carolina, on March 22, 1892.

Charlie Poole

HLP 8005   HISTORICAL

CHARLIE POOLE

1926·1930

A textile worker for most of his life, in 1917 he met Posey Rorer, a crippled miner who played fiddle. They teamed up and played together in the West Virginia–North Carolina area, eventually adding guitarist Norman Woodlieff and recording for Columbia on July 27, 1925. Among their first sides was **Don't Let Your Deal Go Down**, one of the band's most requested numbers.

Personnel changes followed throughout the ensuing years, Roy Harvey replacing Woodlieff on the band's Columbia sessions of September 1926 and Posey Rorer leaving in 1928 to be succeeded first by Lonnie Austin, and later by Odell Smith.

Invited to provide background music for a Hollywood movie in 1931, Poole readied himself for a move to California. But later that same year, on May 21, he suffered a heart attack and died having reached the age of 39.

Recommended:

Charlie Poole And The North Carolina
    Ramblers Volumes 1–3 (County/–)
Charlie Poole (Historical/–)

The Prairie Ramblers

The Prairie Ramblers, long associated with WLS and the National Barn Dance, were one of the most influential of the early string bands, although their style progressed through the years from South-east string band to western swing in their National Barn Dance tenure of 1932–56.

There were numerous personnel changes in the band throughout its life but the nucleus of the Ramblers was formed by Chick Hurt (mandolin, tenor, banjo) and three of his neighbours in western Kentucky, Jack Taylor (string bass), Tex Atchison (fiddle) and Salty Holmes (guitar, harmonica, jug).

Originally called the Kentucky Ramblers, they began on radio on WOC, Davenport, Iowa, but within a few months were members of the National Barn Dance, where they teamed with Patsy Montana, backing her on her records and live. They introduced many important songs like

Charlie Poole 1926–1930. Courtesy Historical Records.

Feast Here Tonight, **Shady Grove** and **Rolling On**.

As time went on, however, their style became increasingly swingy. An interesting aside – they also recorded a number of risqué songs under the name Sweet Violet Boys.

Atchison left the band in 1937, heading for California, where he appeared in many films and with the bands of Jimmy Wakely, Ray Whitley, Merle Travis and others. Holmes left and returned, then went on to a career that took him to the Opry with his wife Maddie (Martha Carson's sister) as Salty and Maddie. Atchison was replaced by Alan Crockett, who shot himself in 1947, and he was replaced in turn by Wade Ray, later to lead his own swing band and record for RCA. Wally Moore was his replacement, and when the band finally ground to a halt in 1956, Hurt and Taylor (the original members) were playing with a polka band, Stan Wallowick And His Polka Chips, which they continued to do for nearly another decade.

They recorded for the ARC complex of labels, Conqueror, Vocalion, Okeh, Mercury, Victor and Bluebird.

Elvis Presley

When Elvis Presley took country music into undreamed-of realms in 1955, many thought that he had killed it for all time. For there was no doubt that Presley was a country singer up until then. In fact, until the term rock'n'roll was coined, the new music was believed to be just country with an extra hard backbeat.

Elvis Aaron Presley was born in Tupelo, Mississippi, on January 8, 1935, and brought up in a religious family atmosphere. He sang with his parents at revival meetings, at concerts and in church, also learning to play some guitar. The

family moved to Memphis when he was 13 and he began to sing at local dances. After graduating from high school, he was employed as a truck driver, playing with local groups at night.

That year he cut his first record, a private recording of **My Happiness**, to give his mother as a birthday present. The people at Sam Phillips' Memphis studio became interested in the country boy with the strange inflections in his voice and, later that year, they set up some experiments in the studio with Presley, Scotty Moore and Bill Black, to find a sound that suited Elvis. Country songs were not quite suitable, but when Elvis started a wild version of blues singer Arthur Crudup's **That's All Right, Mama**, they knew it was the missing piece of the puzzle, a piece that linked fast, almost breathless, country backups with Presley's frantic, uninhibited vocals. However, he was to keep his country connections, backing each single he released with a country title. Indeed, Charlie Feathers has described Presley's version of **Blue Moon Of Kentucky** as classic rockabilly – bluegrass, speeded up and with a black music feel. Presley was particularly influenced by the blues and by black musicians generally. He tended to dress in the extravagantly coloured suits of the black street hipsters.

That's All Right Mama was doing well locally, where DJ Dewey Phillips had plugged it. A local country agent, Bob Neal, Presley's manager for a while, got

Roustabout, Elvis Presley. Courtesy RCA Records.

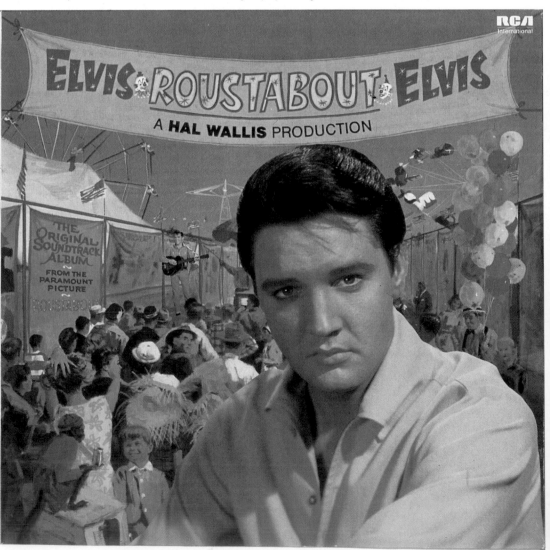

"Elvis Country", Elvis Presley. Courtesy RCA Records.

him some bookings on local country shows. But it was his next manager, 'Colonel' Tom Parker, a hustling wheeler-dealer who undoubtedly would have been running a medicine show in earlier days, who procured him vital exposure on the prestigious Louisiana Hayride on March 3, 1955. The Hayride was the next most important radio show to the Saturday night Grand Ole Opry from Nashville, which the then 'Hillbilly Cat' was also to play.

He toured on country bills with people like Hank Snow and Johnny Cash and the receptions got wilder, girls trying to get at him and tear his clothes. Parker eventually negotiated a deal for him to join the major RCA label and Presley's days as a country-styled rock'n'roller were over as RCA smoothed him gradually into a singer acceptable to both kids and parents.

Although the biggest of superstars, Presley would never again reach those primitive but exciting heights as he settled into a career of Las Vegas concerts and second-rate films. He had taken country music to the limit, making even honky-tonk country seem tame by comparison. But in so doing, he badly bruised country music for many years. Conversely, however, it is as well to remember country's contribution to rock'n'roll. When archivists rediscovered the roots of rock years later, they were led to a whole wealth of half-forgotten '50s music and were able to bring it from the

Elvis At Madison Square Garden. Courtesy RCA Records.

shadow of the then prevailing 'Nashville Sound'. Elvis Presley may have utilized black music to launch rock'n'roll but country enthusiasts might argue that he sounded like the fashionable bar-room wailers of the day, taken to their wild, bopping conclusion.

Elvis was found dead at his Gracelands home in Memphis on August 16, 1977, his death attributed to 'acute respiratory distress' (though later investigation revealed that drugs may have been a factor). He amassed well over 100 US Top 40 hits during his lifetime, though he was outsold on the country chart.

Gracelands, where Elvis laid in state prior to being buried in a mausoleum at Forest Hill Cemetery, in Memphis, was opened to the public in late 1982. The singer's ex-wife claimed that funds were needed to maintain the property.

Recommended:
The Sun Sessions (–/RCA)
I'm 10,000 Years Old – Elvis Country (RCA/RCA)
World Wide 50 Gold Award Hits – four album set (RCA/RCA)
The Complete '50s Masters (–/RCA)
Promised Land (RCA/RCA)
Welcome To My World (RCA/RCA)

Kenny Price

Known as the 'Round Mound Of Sound', Price, a chunky singer-multi-instrumentalist and Hee Haw regular, was born in Florence, Kentucky on May 27, 1931. Raised on a farm in Boone County, Kentucky, he learned to play a guitar bought from Sears Roebuck and began playing country music at local functions.

During his service career in Korea he entertained the troops, and, upon discharge, he enrolled at the Cincinnati Conservatory of Music. He became a regular on Cincinnati's WLW Midwestern Hayride in 1954 as lead singer with the Hometowners. He then moved to Nashville and signed with the new Boone Records as a solo act, registering an immediate hit with **Walking On New Grass** in 1966. That same year he obtained a second Top

10 record with **Happy Tracks**. Further hits for Boone flowed, the biggest of these being **My Goal For Today** (1967). In 1969 Price took his happy sound to RCA – two of his 1970 releases, **Biloxi** and **Sheriff Of Boone County** becoming Top 10 hits. Price became a regular member of Hee Haw and continued to chalk up minor hits throughout the '70s for RCA, MRC and Dimension, his last chart entry being with **She's Leavin' (And I'm Almost Gone)** in 1980. He died of a heart attack on August 4, 1987.

Recommended:
Turn On Your Love Light (RCA/–)
Supersideman (RCA/–)
The Red Foley Songbook (RCA/–)
North East Arkansas Mississippi County Bootlegger (RCA/–)

Ray Price

Born on a farm in Perrybille, East Texas, on January 12, 1926, Ray Noble Price, the 'Cherokee Cowboy', was brought up in Dallas. After high school, he spent several years in the forces, returning to civilian life in 1946 and attending college to study veterinary surgery. However, an able singer-songwriter-guitarist, he began performing at college events and local clubs, eventually making his radio debut as an entertainer in 1948, on station KRBC, Abilene. Later came further exposure on Big D Jamboree, a Dallas show.

Below: Hee Haw regular and 'Round Mound Of Sound' Kenny Price.

Price began recording for Bullet during the early '50s, his first release being a song called **Jealous Lies**. Then in 1951 came a contract with Columbia. Many of his early records for the label reflected the influence of Hank Williams – Price's band, the Cherokee Cowboys, was formed from the remnants of Williams' outfit, the Drifting Cowboys.

By the end of 1952 Price was an Opry regular with two hit singles to his credit – **Talk To Your Heart** and **Don't Let The Stars Get In Your Eyes**, both charting during the year. And though his name was absent from the charts for the next 14 months, in February 1954 he began a run of major hits that continued to 1973. The most prominent of these were **Crazy Arms** (a 1956 million-seller), **I've Got A New Heartache** (1956), **My Shoes Keep Walking Back To You** (1957), **City Lights** (another million-seller, 1958), **Heartaches By The Number**, **The Same Old Me** (1959), **One More Time** (1960), **Soft Rain** (1961), **Make The World Go Away** (1963), **Burnin' Memories** (1964), **The Other Woman** (1965), **Touch My Heart** (1966), **For The Good Times**, **I Won't Mention It Again** (1970), **I'd Rather Be Sorry** (1971), **Lonesomest Lonesome**, **She's Got To Be A Saint** (1972), and **You're The Best Thing That Ever Happened To Me** (1973), all Columbia releases.

An astute judge of current trends and possessing an ear for up and coming songwriters – he was one of the first to recognize Kris Kristofferson's potential – Price realized that country had to appeal to a wider audience in order to forge ahead. Accordingly he began using large back-up units, often employing full string sections, in his plan to take country to a non-country audience. He ditched any pretensions to a cowboy image and began appearing onstage in a dress suit. Yet the ballads still sounded as though they came out of Texas and the ploy worked.

In 1974 Ray began recording for Myrrh, obtaining a Top 10 single for this mainly gospel label with **Like Old Times Again** and following it with another in **Roses And Love Songs** (1975). He then signed with ABC/Dot, and during 1975 had hits on three different labels, Columbia still cashing in on his back catalogue material. His records still sold better than most and the ABC/Dot hits continued, albeit at a lower level, through to 1978, when Ray decided to make a comeback. He signed to Monument Records and gained an immediate Top 20 single with **Feet**. During 1979 he provided three more hits, reaching the Top 20 again with **That's The Only Way To Say Goodbye**, while in 1980 he teamed with Willie Nelson to cut an excellent duet album that spawned the hit single **Faded Love**. By 1981 Ray had switched to the Dimension label, cutting three hits, including such Top 10 entries as **It Don't Hurt Me Half So Bad** and **Diamonds In The Stars**. His 1982 haul contained **Old Friends**, a single made with Roger Miller and Willie Nelson. The following year he had label-jumped yet again, this time to Warner, scoring with two tracks recorded for the soundtrack of the movie 'Honkytonk Man'. He continued label-hopping, scoring minor hits through to 1989 and recording albums, mainly in his old '50s country style. In 1992 he cut an album for Columbia titled **Sometimes A Rose**. But, despite such a long and distinguished career, Ray has only landed one CMA award: Album Of The Year in 1971 for **I Won't Mention It Again**.

Recommended:

For The Good Times (Columbia/CBS)
Willie Nelson And Ray Price (Columbia/CBS)
Like Old Times Again (Myrrh/–)
Hank 'n' Me (ABC/–)
The Heart Of Country Music (Step One/–)
Sometimes A Rose (Columbia/–)
Essential (Columbia/–)

Charley Pride

Easily the most successful black entertainer to emerge from the country music scene, Charley Pride was born on a Delta cotton farm in Sledge, Mississippi, March 18, 1938. One of 11 children, Pride picked cotton alongside his parents during his boyhood days, eventually saving enough cash to purchase a $10 silvertone guitar from Sears Roebuck. Despite being born in blues territory, Pride preferred playing country music. However, he initially turned to baseball, not show business – playing for the Memphis Red Sox as a pitcher and outfield player in 1954. Two years later, he was drafted into the forces, during this period marrying Rozene, a girl he met in Memphis. Returning to civilian life in 1959, he quit baseball following a wage disagreement. Several jobs later he settled down in Helena, Montana, working at a zinc smelting plant, also playing semi-pro ball in the Pioneer League. And though he continued his efforts to break into major league ball, he was turned down by the California Angels in 1961 and by the New York Mets a year later.

However, his secondary career reaped rewards when, in 1963, Pride sang a song on a local show headed by Red Sovine and Red Foley, earning praise from Sovine, who urged him to try his luck in Nashville. Taking this advice, Pride made the move. Chet Atkins eventually heard some of his demo tapes and signed him to RCA.

Above: The first black country superstar, Charley Pride.

Pride's first RCA single, **Snakes Crawl At Night**, was released with little in the way of accompanying publicity in December 1965. Few of the DJs who played the disc realized that the singer was black. But, by the following spring, the Mississippian was nationally known after coming up with **Just Between You And Me**, his performance gaining him a Grammy nomination. A couple of hits later, in January 1967, and he was on the Opry. His introduction, by Ernest Tubb, received a warm reception.

As the '70s rolled in, Pride reached superstar status. Having logged five No.1s in a row with **All I Have To Offer Is Me**, **I'm So Afraid Of Losing You** (1969), **Is Anybody Goin' To San Antone?**, **Wonder Could I Live There Anymore** and **I Can't Believe That You've Stopped Loving Me** (1970), he was adjudged Entertainer Of The Year in 1971, by the CMA, also winning the association's Male Vocalist Of The Year award, a title he retained in 1972.

Basically a honky-tonk singer who, like many others, moved towards a smoother, more pop-oriented country sound, Pride proved one of the most consistent record sellers on the RCA roster. Some of his No.1s have been: **I'd Rather Love You**, **Kiss An Angel Good Mornin'** (1971); **It's Gonna Take A Little Bit Longer**, **She's Too Good To Be True** (1972); **A Shoulder To Cry On**, **Amazing Love** (1973); **Then Who Am I?** (1974); **Hope You're Feelin' Me** (1975); **My Eyes Can Only See As Far As You** (1976); **She's Just An Old Love Turned Memory**, **I'll Be Leaving Alone**, **More To Me** (1977); **Someone Loves You Honey** (1978); **Where Do I Put Her Memory?**, **You're My Jamaica** (1979); **Honky Tonk Blues**, **You Win Again** (1980); **Never Been So Loved (In All My Life)**, **Mountain Of Love** (1981); **You're So Good When You're Bad**, **Why Baby Why?** (1982); and **Night Games** (1983).

The possessor of a warm baritone voice, Charley Pride sounds as pure country as Hank Williams, a hero whom he honoured in 1980 via **There's A Little Bit Of Hank In Me**, a No.1 album. Paradoxically, he had become RCA's biggest-selling country act since Elvis Presley – a country boy who tried his hardest to sound black.

In 1984, he scored his last Top 10 hit on RCA with **The Power Of Love**. Disillusioned with RCA's inability to market his recordings, he signed with 16th Avenue Records in 1987. After a three-year absence he was back in the Top 20 with **Have I Got Some Blues For You** (1987), soaring into the Top 10 with **Shouldn't It Be Better Than This** (1988). Having built a European fan base in the early '70s, Pride was able to capitalize on this career investment with annual sell-out tours, which have seen him more popular than the new superstars of the '80s and '90s.

Everybody's Choice, Charley Pride. Courtesy RCA Records.

Recommended:
(Country) Charley Pride (RCA/RCA)
There's A Little Bit Of Hank In Me (RCA/RCA)
Amy's Eyes (16th Avenue/Ritz)
In Person (RCA/RCA)
Classics With Pride (16th Avenue/Ritz)

John Prine

One of the most acclaimed singer-songwriters to come out of the '70s, John Prine was born on October 10, 1946 in Maywood, Illinois. He spent much of his childhood in Kentucky, where his grandparents lived, but he had his musical beginnings in Chicago, where he started writing songs as a teenager. Following a stint in the army, he worked as a postman, but, discovering he could make more money playing at local folk clubs, he took up music as a full-time profession. Prine's big break came through his close friend, singer-songwriter Steve Goodman, who introduced him to Paul Anka and Kris Kristofferson, who in turn introduced him to Jerry Wexler. Wexler signed Prine to an Atlantic record contract in 1971.

Prine made a series of critically acclaimed albums throughout the '70s, along the way writing such classic songs as **Hello In There, Paradise, Sam Stone** and **Angel From Montgomery**. In 1979 he recorded **Pink Cadillac**, a rockabilly-flavoured album at Sam Phillips' Sun Studios in Memphis. By the early '80s he was based in Nashville, writing country hits for everyone from Don Williams to Tammy Wynette, Johnny Cash to Gail Davies. Without a major label deal, Prine decided to form his own label, Oh Boy Records, with his long-time manager, Al Bunetta. He released three low-key albums. Two of them, the acoustic-flavoured **German Afternoons** and the two-record set, **John Prine Live**, gained Grammy nominations. Turning his hand to various projects, Prine spent time working with John Mellencamp on the soundtrack of his movie 'Falling From Grace', also making his screen debut in the film. He recorded a duet, **If You Were The Woman And I Was The Man**, with Margo Timmins and the Cowboy Junkies, and visited Britain to perform and act as compère for the Channel 4 TV series Town & Country.

A major turnaround came in Prine's career with **The Missing Years** album, which was produced by Howie Epstein, bassist for Tom Petty And The Heartbreakers. Whereas his previous studio albums had been completed in about a week with a limited budget, this one took almost ten months. Alongside fellow Heartbreakers Mike Campbell and Benmont Tench, noted Prine fans Tom Petty, Bruce Springsteen and Bonnie Raitt all dropped by to add background vocals. Again, released on Prine's own Oh Boy Records, **The Missing Years** was something of a sleeper. It eventually sold over 500,000 copies and won John a Grammy at the 1992 awards. This led to tours with Bonnie Raitt and the Cowboy Junkies, and recognition, at long last, for performing, rather than just songwriting.

Recommended:
Aimless Love (Oh Boy/This Way Up)
German Afternoons (Oh Boy/This Way Up)

Ronnie Prophet. The all-rounder's debut RCA album.

John Prine Live (Oh Boy/This Way Up)
The Missing Years (Oh Boy/This Way Up)
Diamonds In The Rough (Atlantic/Atlantic)
Pink Cadillac (Asylum/Asylum)

Ronnie Prophet

Described by Chet Atkins as 'the greatest one-man show I've seen', singer-guitarist Prophet was born near Montreal, Canada, on December 26, 1937, and was raised on a farm at Calumet. He began playing at square dances in his early teens and soon moved to Montreal, later playing club dates in Fort Lauderdale. He first appeared in Nashville in 1969.

He obtained a residency at Nashville's Carousel Club. His drawing power proved such that the venue became renamed Ronnie Prophet's Carousel Club. His first American album was released on RCA in 1976, and the LP contained such tracks as **Shine On, Sanctuary** and **It's Enough**, all minor country hits. He played the British Wembley Festival of 1978 and broke the place up, looning around with compère George Hamilton IV and regaling the audience with his 'Harold The Horny Toad'. This led to further appearances at Wembley, regular tours and his own TV series, but over-exposure of his rather 'samey' act, without any major hits to back him up, led to fans tiring of Ronnie Prophet.

Recommended:
Ronnie Prophet Country (RCA/RCA)

Jeanne Pruett

Jeanne, a singer-songwriter, was born Norma Jean Bowman on January 30, 1937 in Pell City, Alabama. One of 10 children, she used to listen to the Grand Ole Opry as a youngster. She first headed for Nashville in 1956 along with her husband Jack Pruett, a guitarist who played lead guitar with Marty Robbins for almost 14 years.

It was Robbins who was responsible for her signing to RCA Records in 1963, at which time she cut six titles. And though there was little reaction, the following year found her making her debut on the Grand Ole Opry. Jeanne continued writing and performing, eventually securing a new record contract with Decca in 1969 and enjoying a minor hit in 1971 with **Hold On To My Unchanging Love**.

The real breakthrough came in 1973 when her recording of **Satin Sheets** became a phenomenal seller, crossing over to enter the pop charts. Throughout the

Left: A talented writer, John Prine is finally making an impact onstage.

Pure Prairie League. Courtesy RCA Records. Norman Rockwell provided the sleeve.

Riley Puckett (Old Homestead/–)
Red Sails In The Sunset (–/Bear Family)

Pure Prairie League

Formed in Cincinnati in 1971, this country-rock band took their name from a Women's Temperance Society that appeared in an Errol Flynn movie. Their trademark, which decorated all of their album covers, was 'Luke', an old-timer originally created by

Pure Prairie Collection. Courtesy RCA Records.

'Saturday Evening Post' artist Norman Rockwell.

League signed for RCA, the line-up then being Craig Fuller (guitars, vocals), George Ed Powell (guitars, vocals), Jim Lanham (bass, vocals), Jim Caughlan (drums) and John David Call (steel guitar). By the time their second album, **Bustin' Out**, appeared, only Fuller and Powell remained from the original band.

In 1973, after further personnel problems, PPL ceased recording and their record company thought they had broken

up. But the group continued playing live dates and caused such a response by these appearances that RCA were forced to reissue **Bustin' Out**, plus **Amie**, a single taken from the album, the latter going into the US pop charts during 1975.

That year, the group, then comprising original members Fuller and Call plus Larry Goshorn (lead guitar), Michael Connor (keyboards), Mike Reilly (bass) and William Frank Hinds (drums), cut **Two Lane Highway**, an album that featured such guests as Chet Atkins, Emmylou Harris, Johnny Gimble and Don Felder. But, despite further albums and the odd hit like **That'll Be The Way** (1976), the line-up continued to fluctuate. Powell quit in 1977 along with Larry Goshorn and brother Timmy Goshorn, who had earlier replaced Call. The band, by then West Coast-based, regrouped yet again, one of the new members being Vince Gill, who had earlier worked with Boone Creek and Byron Berline's band.

By 1980, still unable to make the breakthrough that would take them up a notch on the concert circuits, PPL moved to the Casablanca label. The switch brought

rest of the '70s, Jeanne graced the country charts with such MCA singles as **I'm Your Woman** (1973), **You Don't Need To Move A Mountain** (1974), **A Poor Man's Woman** (1975) and **I'm Living A Lie** (1977). She switched to Mercury for a while, then made something of a comeback with **Back To Back** (1979), **Temporarily Yours** and **It's Too Late** (both 1980), three IBC releases that all went Top 10. Since then there's been no major hits, but Jeanne still appears on the Opry, though she tends to spend much of her spare time cooking or gardening.

Recommended:
Encore (IBC/RCA)
Introducing Jeanne Pruett (–/MCA)

Riley Puckett

One of the pioneers of recorded old-time music, George Riley Puckett was born in Alpharetta, Georgia, on May 7, 1884. When only three months old he suffered an eye infection, and following incorrect treatment of the ailment lost his sight. Educated at a school for the blind in Macon, Georgia, he learned to play five-string banjo, later moving on to guitar. During the early '20s, Puckett worked with a band led by fiddle player Clayton McMichen. He then joined Gid Tanner's Skillet Lickers in 1924, remaining featured vocalist with the outfit until its disbandment some 10 years later. Puckett's many solo recordings include **Rock All Our Babies to Sleep**, reputed to be one of the first discs to feature a country yodeller, cut three years prior to Jimmie Rodgers' initial session.

From 1934 to 1941, Puckett recorded for RCA Victor – also cutting a few sides for Decca in 1937 – and worked on radio stations in Georgia, West Virginia, Kentucky and Tennessee up to his death in East Point Georgia, on July 13, 1946. At the time of his death, caused by blood

Welcome To The Sunshine, Jeanne Pruett. Courtesy MCA Records.

poisoning from an infected boil on his neck, Puckett was working with a band called the Stone Mountain Cowboys, on radio station WACA, Atlanta.

His exuberant – sometimes even wild – bass-run guitar style was very influential on country guitarists of his day, the forerunner of the pulsing style which characterizes bluegrass.

Recommended:
The Skillet Lickers Volumes 1 & 2 (Country/–)

Right: Pure Prairie League – John David Call, Mike Reilly, William Frank Hinds, Larry Goshorn, George Ed Powell and Michael O'Connor.

the band immediate benefits. By the middle of the year they had gone Top 10 in the pop charts with **Let Me Love You Tonight**, following this with other major pop hits in **I'm Almost Ready** (1980) and **Still Right Here In My Heart** (1981). But Gill left, first to work with Rodney Crowell and Rosanne Cash and then to pursue a solo career with RCA, and soon PPL were having problems once more and searching for a label deal.

Recommended:
Pure Prairie League (RCA/RCA)
Bustin' Out (RCA/RCA)
Two Lane Highway (RCA/RCA)
Dance (RCA/RCA)
Just Fly (RCA/RCA)

Eddie Rabbitt

Considered by many pundits to be pure MOR, singer Eddie Rabbitt (real name Edward Thomas, born in Brooklyn, New York on November 27, 1944) has, nevertheless, won many friends among country music buyers.

A one-time truck driver, soda jerk, boat helper and fruit picker, Rabbitt recorded for 20th Century Fox and Columbia during the 1960s. He achieved little until, as a staff writer with music publishers Hill and Range, he wrote **Kentucky Rain**, which Elvis Presley recorded and turned into a hit (1970) In 1973, Ronnie Milsap waxed Rabbitt's **Pure Love** and grabbed a No.1, this leading to the New Yorker gaining an Elektra recording contract of his own and getting his chart career underway with **You Get To Me**, a middle-order hit.

By 1975, his records were hitting the Top 20, the first No.1 being with **Drinkin' My Baby (Off My Mind)** in 1976, a year in which Rabbitt also went Top 10 with **Rocky Mountain Music** and **Two**

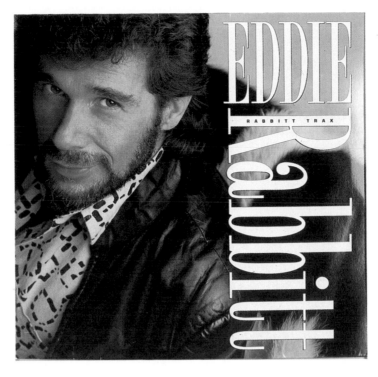

Rabbitt Trax, Eddie Rabbitt. Courtesy RCA Records.

Dollars In The Jukebox. But the best was yet to come for, in the wake of three more Top 10 singles, he provided Elektra with three chart-toppers in a row during 1978 – **You Don't Love Me Anymore, I Just Want To Love You** and **Every Which Way But Loose**, the latter being the title track of a Clint Eastwood movie. There was another No.1 in 1979, **Suspicions**, then three in 1980: **Gone**

Below: Eddie Rabbitt once wrote hits for Elvis Presley and Ronnie Milsap.

Too Far, Drivin' My Life Away and **I Love A Rainy Day**. Two more in 1981 were **Step By Step** and **Someone Could Lose A Heart Tonight**. Rabbitt's **Step By Step** album became the best-selling album in the country market.

He became guest host on the late TV show The Midnight Special and even had a TV special of his own. But CMA award nominations never came his way.

Not that the lack of acclaim in Music City meant much to Rabbitt. He just kept on doing the thing he was good at, notching hits. And in 1982 he notched a couple more; one, a duet with Crystal Gayle (**You And I**), provided the singer with yet another chart-topper that crossed over into the pop listings. Throughout the rest of the '80s he has hardly faltered. He supplied another No.1 in 1983, **You Can't Run From Love**, and yet another in 1984, **The Best Year Of My Life**. During 1985 Rabbitt notched two Top 10 records with **Warning Sign** and **She's Coming Back To Say Goodbye**. That same year he joined RCA Records, making a Top 10 entry with **Repetitive Regret** early in 1986, and going all the way with Juice Newton to No.1 with **Both To Each Other (Friends And Lovers)**. Two more No.1s came his way in 1988 with the self-penned **I Wanna Dance With You** and a revival of Dion's rock'n'roll classic, **The Wanderer**. The following year he moved to Universal Records, immediately hitting No.1 with **On Second Thought**, before the label was absorbed into Capitol/Liberty with Rabbitt back in the Top 10 with **Runnin' With The Wind** (1990). But even still (gold records apart), his awards cupboard stays somewhat bare.

Recommended:
Rabbitt (Elektra/Elektra)
Loveline (Elektra/Elektra)
Radio Romance (Elektra/Mercury)
Step By Step (Elektra/Elektra)
Horizon (Elektra/Elektra)
Jersey Boy (Capitol/–)
Rocky Mountain Music (Elektra/Elektra)
Ten Rounds (Capitol/–)

Especially For You, Marvin Rainwater. Courtesy Westwood Records.

Gonna Find Me A Bluebird, Marvin Rainwater. Courtesy MGM Records.

Marvin Rainwater

Of Indian ancestry, Rainwater – a singer and prolific songwriter, who also plays guitar and piano – became a star during the 1950s when several of his records sold well over a million each. Born in Wichita, Kansas on July 2, 1925, his real name was Marvin Percy. Rainwater was his mother's maiden name, which he later adopted for his stage work. He trained as a veterinary surgeon, becoming a pharmacist's mate in the Navy during World War II. Upon discharge, he opted for a career in the music business. His first breakthrough came in 1946 when he debuted on Red Foley's Ozark Jubilee Radio Show, the station receiving so many enquiries about 'that singer with the Indian name' that Rainwater was signed to a regular spot on the programme.

During the early '50s he began touring and cutting records for Four Star and Coral. In 1955 he entered the Arthur Godfrey CBS Talent Scout TV Show, and was brought back for four consecutive wins. The following January he signed with MGM Records. With his second release, the self-penned **Gonna Find Me A Bluebird**, he won his first gold disc. Promoted by MGM as a full-blooded Cherokee brave, Rainwater usually appeared bedecked in Indian head-dress and similar paraphernalia. The idea seemed to work, for in 1958 his rocking **Whole Lotta Woman** became a world-wide hit, reaching the top of the British charts and ensuring Rainwater a season at the London Palladium. However, the USA reaction to the disc was mixed and some radio stations banned the song as being 'too suggestive'.

Soon after – following another million-seller with his version of John D. Loudermilk's **Half-Breed** (1959) – Rainwater and MGM parted company, the singer moving on to record for such labels as Warner Brothers, UA, Warwick and his own Brave Records. In the mid-'60s came a serious throat ailment that resulted in an operation, after which Rainwater was not

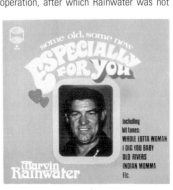

to record for four years. Throughout the '70s he toured Britain, and, like George Hamilton IV and Vernon Oxford, he has enjoyed a higher reputation in Europe than in his homeland.

Recommended:
Rockin' Rolling Rainwater (–/Bear Family)
With A Heart With A Beat (–/Bear Family)

Bonnie Raitt

A white blues singer, songwriter and guitarist with a country-rock feel in her work, Bonnie Raitt was born on November 8, 1949 in Burbank, California. She grew up in a musical family; her father, John Raitt, starred in musicals during the '40s and '50s. Bonnie attended college in Boston in 1967, then two years later moved to the East Coast where she played blues in an acoustic duo with Freebo. Later she joined Paul Barrere in the Bluebusters.

Her gravelly, emotionally mature voice and dynamic slide guitar work resulted in a recording contract with Warner Bros in 1971. Throughout the '70s she produced excellent albums, many of which sold well, while her **Don't It Make Ya Wanna Dance**, featured in 'Urban Cowboy', made the US country charts in 1980.

Raitt finally broke through to superstar status with her **Nick Of Time** album on Capitol in 1989, which sold in excess of two million and gained a Grammy award as Album Of The Year. She has worked in Nashville on many occasions, playing sessions and concerts with Emmylou Harris and Wynonna Judd. The Judd youngster cites Bonnie Raitt as a major influence on her own music.

Recommended:
Sweet Forgiveness (Warner Bros/–)
The Glow (Warner Bros/–)
Nine Lives (Warner Bros/–)
Nick Of Time (Capitol/–)
Luck Of The Draw (Capitol/Capitol)

Boots Randolph

A premier Nashville session man, Homer Louis 'Boots' Randolph III was born in Paducah, Kentucky. He first learned to play trombone but later switched to saxophone, playing first in a high school unit then in bands throughout the Midwest.

Eventually he was spotted by Homer And Jethro, who saw him at a Decatur, Illinois club and promptly relayed their enthusiasm to Chet Atkins. Later, Atkins was to hear a tape of Randolph playing **Chicken Reel** in his good-timey, slap-tongued style, and was similarly impressed. He invited Randolph to Nashville and enthused about the sax-man's talents to his friends. Within a few days, Owen Bradley hired him for a Brenda Lee session. From then on he became a much-sought-after sessioner and an established part of the 'Nashville Sound', recording as a solo act for both RCA and Monument.

In 1963 he obtained a major hit with **Yakety Sax**, following this with such other pop successes as **Mr Sax Man** (1964), **The Shadow Of Your Smile** (1966) and **Temptation** (1967). But perhaps the most interesting Randolph disc, at least to country fans, is **Country Boots,** a 1974 album made in the company of Maybelle Carter, Chet Atkins, Uncle

Josh Graves and a host of other pickers. The majority of his other album releases fall outside the scope of this book.

Recommended:
Yakety Sax (–/Bear Family)

Rattlesnake Annie

A singer whose stage name comes from the habit of wearing a rattlesnake's rattler on her ear, her real name is Annie McGowan and she was born Ann Gallimore on December 26, 1941 in Puryear, Tennessee, of Cherokee Indian heritage. From a poor family who worked in the tobacco and cotton fields near Puryear, she grew up in a music-making home environment, Annie singing and playing piano at the local church. At the age of 12, she and two cousins formed the Gallimore Sisters and appeared as regulars on the Junior Grand Ole Opry in 1954, but when she married Max McGowan her musical ambitions had to take a back seat.

Later, Annie headed for Memphis where she sang the blues on Beale Street, travelling through the South and ending up in Austin, where she befriended Willie Nelson, Billy Joe Shaver and David Allan Coe. Coe co-wrote **Texas Lullaby** with Annie and recorded it on his 1976 **Long Haired Redneck** album.

The first woman from the West to record a country album in Czechoslovakia, she has a cult following in Europe and has made a brace of highly acclaimed appearances at the UK's Wembley Festival. She released a brilliantly conceived album, **Rattlesnakes And Rusty Water**, on her own Rattlesnake label during 1980. Featuring such guests as

Below: During the '60s, Eddy Raven played in blues bands headed by Edgar and Johnny Winter.

John Hartford, Josh Graves, Vassar Clements and Charlie McCoy, the album merged blues and traditional country in a fashion Jimmie Rodgers would have approved of. Signed to Columbia Records in 1987, Annie scored some minor country hits, then returned to doing things her own way, marketing her own recordings, which include the albums **Indian Dream** and **Rattlesnake Annie Sings Hank Williams**. For several years she and her husband have lived in Spain, and more recently she has taken her traditional country-blues music to Japan.

Recommended:
Rattlesnakes And Rusty Water
(Rattlesnake/–)
Country Livin' (Rattlesnake/–)
Sings Hank Williams (Montana/–)
Rattlesnake Annie (Columbia/CBS)

Eddy Raven

Eddy was born Edward Garvin Futch on August 19, 1944 in the bayou country of Lafayette, Louisiana, one of nine children whose father travelled all over the South as a musician and trucker. At seven Eddy had his first guitar and at 13 his first band. Although his father geared him towards country music, Eddy followed the prevailing rock'n'roll path, even though he was concerned about lyrics.

He lived in Georgia and had his own radio slot on WHAB, even gaining a local hit on the Cosmo label. Then his father moved the family back to Lafayette, Louisiana, where Eddy met Lake Charles record entrepreneur, Bobby Charles, and wrote a country-blues hit for him which sold 60,000 on Charles' label.

After an experimental period in the 1960s when Eddy performed all around the Gulf Coast (at one time playing with albino brothers Edgar and Johnny Winter), he

All I Can Be, Collin Raye. Courtesy Epic Records.

tired of travelling and, in 1970, went to Nashville where fellow Cajun Jimmy 'C' Newman put him on to Acuff-Rose.

Eddy's first writing success was **Country Green**, which provided a hit for Don Gibson. He did likewise for Jeannie C. Riley (**Good Morning Country Rain**) and Don Gibson again (**Touch The Morning**). A one-time lounge performer at Nashville's King Of The Road Inn, he became a headliner and grabbed the attention of ABC Records, a label for whom he began providing hits in 1974 (starting with **The Last Of The Sunshine Cowboys**), continuing in a moderately successful way through to 1976.

In an effort to get his own recording career into higher gear, Eddy signed for Monument in 1978, gaining just one mini-hit with **You're A Dancer**. He switched again, this time to Dimension, and at last began really chart-climbing. One 1980 single, **Dealin' With The Devil**, gained him access to the Top 25 for the first time. A year later he was on Elektra and reaching even higher through releases such as **I Should Have Called** and **Who Do You Know in California?**.

By 1982, 12 years after making the trip to Nashville, he made his Top 10 debut with **She's Playing Hard To Forget**. But the long hard climb to the very top was not achieved until 1984, when Raven, now with yet another record company, RCA, got to No.1 with **I Got Mexico**.

Raven continued his hit-making formula throughout the '80s and into the '90s with many Top 10 hits and a trio of No.1s with **Shine, Shine, Shine** (1987), **I'm Gonna Get You** and **Joe Knows How To Love** (1988). He then joined Universal Records, chalking up two more No.1s with **In A Letter To You** and **Bayou Boys** (1989). Universal was then absorbed by Capitol/Liberty, and Raven continued with **Sooner Or Later** and **Island**, two more Top 10 entries in 1990.

Recommended:
I Could Use Another You (RCA/–)
That Cajun Country Sound (La Louisianne/–)
This Is Eddie Raven (Dot/–)
Eyes (Dimension/–)
Desperate Dreams (Elektra/–)
Right For The Flight (Capitol/–)
Temporary Sanity (Universal/–)
Right Hand Man (RCA/–)

Collin Raye

The sweetest high-flying tenor to hit country music in years, Collin Raye (born in 1961 in Texarkana, Arkansas) had country music in the blood. Raised in Texas, his mother Lois was a regional star in the '50s, sharing bills on the back of flat-bed trucks with artists like Elvis Presley, Johnny Cash, Jerry Lee Lewis and Carl Perkins. His father played guitar and an uncle was a professional musician. Collin started singing harmony on stage when he was seven. He spent his teenage years in a band with brother Scott, playing in the clubs in Oregon in the Pacific Northwest. When he was 20 he married and briefly moved back to Texas. Then he put together a show band, playing a wide mixture of music in the casinos in Las Vegas and Reno. His band landed a recording contract with Mercury Records in 1985, released several singles, and completed an unreleased album. At this time his personal life was turned upside-down when in 1985 his wife Connie developed complications during pregnancy with the couple's second child and she lapsed into a two-month coma. The child, Jacob, was born with cerebral palsy, and Connie had to re-learn many basic skills. Collin was trying to hold down a seven-night-a-week club date in Reno. The couple later divorced, but have remained friends and the singer is very close to his two children, Britanny and Jacob, who live with their mother in Greenville, Texas.

A move to Nashville in 1989 eventually led to a recording contract with Epic Records. His first single, **All I Can Be (Is A Sweet Memory)**, made No.29 on the country charts in 1991. His debut album, also titled **All I Can Be**, was released virtually simultaneously with the single, rare for a new name in country music. Initially, the album was a sleeper, but the single's video spent weeks at the top of CMT's Chart, and the album was named one of the ten best of 1991 by 'USA Today'. Early the next year a second single, **Love Me**, a heart-rending tale of enduring romance, raced up the charts, spending three weeks at No.1. The song, again

accompanied by a superb video, struck a chord with music fans. Collin Raye's 'career song', **Love Me** boosted the sales of his album, eventually gaining the singer a gold disc. A dynamic stage performer, Raye tears up his audience with a powerful mix of soaring rockers, dramatic ballads and, harking back to his Las Vegas days, a few Eagles' songs. He has continued with the country hits with **Every Second** (1992), **In This Life** (No.1 1992), and further Top 10 entries in **I Want You Bad (And That Ain't Good)** and **Somebody Else's Moon** (1993).

Recommended:
In This Life (Epic/Epic)
All I Can Be (Epic/Epic)

Susan Raye

A long-time regular on Hee Haw and the Buck Owens Show, singer Susan Raye had a number of hit singles during the late 1960s and early 1970s. Once a member of a rock group, Raye (born in Eugene, Oregon in 1944) switched to country after winning a regular spot with a radio station that was looking for a country singer. Later, after stints as a DJ and night-club singer, she was invited to Bakersfield to meet Buck Owens, whose show she joined. She also gained a contract with Capitol. Her first release, **Maybe If I Closed My Eyes** (1969), was an Owens original.

Her other hits have included a series of duets with Owens, plus such Top 20 solo efforts as: **L.A. International Airport**,

Below: Collin Raye and his second wife Tammie. Raye burst on the scene in the early '90s with such hits as Love Me.

Above: Susan Raye had a number of hit singles in the '70s.

Pitty, Pitty, Patter (1971), **My Heart Has A Mind Of Its Own**, **Wheel Of Fortune**, **Love Sure Feels Good In My Heart** (1972), **Cheating Game** (1973), **Stop The World (And Let Me Off)** and **Whatcha Gonna Do With A Dog Like That** (1974), all on Capitol. Later she signed with UA, without much success. But by 1984, her name still appeared in the charts, aboard **Put Another Notch In Your Belt**, a Westexas release.

Recommended:
Best Of (Capitol/–)
Whatcha Gonna Do With A Dog Like That (Capitol/–)

Jerry Reed

One of Nashville's most remarkable guitarmen, Reed was born Jerry Hubbard in Atlanta, Georgia on March 20, 1937. A cotton mill worker in his early days, he began playing at local Atlanta clubs, obtaining a record contract with Capitol in 1955 and cutting some rockabilly tracks. However, these made little impact, Reed's first claim to fame arising through his songwriting ability, predominantly with **Crazy Legs**, which Gene Vincent waxed in 1956. Following a two-year stint in the forces, Reed then settled in Nashville, there providing Columbia with two minor 1962 hits in **Goodnight Irene** and **Hully Gully Guitars**.

Establishing himself as a superior session man, Reed was signed to RCA as a solo act in 1965, his first hit for the label being the rocking **Guitar Man** (1967), which Elvis Presley covered in 1968. That same year, Presley also scored with **US Male**, another Reed composition. The Georgian's own records all sold increasingly well, **Tupelo Mississippi Flash** (1967), **Remembering** (1968), **Are You From Dixie?** (1969), **Talk About The Good Times** (1970) and **Georgia Sunshine** (1970) all reaching high chart positions. Then, late in 1970, came **Amos Moses**, one of Reed's swamp-rock specials. The song proved to be a Top 10 pop hit and resulted in Reed being

nominated CMA Instrumentalist Of The Year. He also won a Grammy for Best Country Male Vocal Performance of 1970.

A maker of somewhat erratic albums, his guitar duet LPs with Chet Atkins, cut during the mid-1970s, resulted in some fine music. Additionally, he has become much acclaimed as an actor, an appearance in 'WW And The Dixie Dance Kings' (1974) resulting in an association with Burt Reynolds that has since seen the duo pairing in 'Gator' (1976), 'Smokey And The Bandit' (1977) and 'Smokey And The Bandit II' (1980). A performer with a larger-than-life personality, Reed has also starred alongside Claude Akins in a TV series 'Nashville 99' and has continued his hit single way with such Top 10 records as **When You're Hot, You're Hot** (No.1, 1971), **Lord Mr Ford** (No.1, 1973), **(I Love You) What Can I Say?** (1978), **She Got The Goldmine (I Got The Shaft)** (No.1, 1982) and **The Birds** (1982). 1984 proved to be the first year since 1967 that failed to provide Reed with chart action of any kind.

Reed concentrated more on his acting than music during the mid-'80s, making several film appearances and starring in his own TV series, Concrete Cowboys. After a long absence he returned to the studios in 1992 to cut **Sneakin' Around**, a guitar duet album with Chet Atkins.

Recommended:
Me And Chet – with Chet Atkins (RCA/RCA)
20 Of The Best (–/RCA)
Sneakin' Around – with Chet Atkins (Columbia/–)

Ko-Ko Joe, Jerry Reed. Courtesy RCA Records.

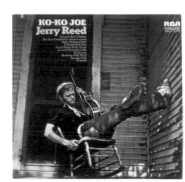

Live At The Palomino Club, Del Reeves' 1974 album. Courtesy UA Records. Del was with United Artists from his first No.1 in 1965 until 1978.

The Abbott Recordings, Jim Reeves. Courtesy RCA Records.

Del Reeves

Singer-songwriter, multi-instrumentalist Franklin Delano Reeves was born in Sparta, North Carolina on July 14, 1934. At the age of 12 he had his own radio show in North Carolina. Then, after attending Appalachian State College and spending four years in the Air Force, he became a regular on the Chester Smith TV show in California.

By the late 1950s, Reeves had his own TV show which he fronted for four years before moving to Nashville, signing for Frank Sinatra's Reprise label and writing songs with his wife Ellen Schiell Reeves – these being recorded by Carl Smith, Sheb Wooley, Roy Drusky and others. Reeves' own initial hit single came with **Be Quiet Mind**, a 1961 Decca release. But, despite label changes and a couple of minor chart entries, it was not until 1965 and a contract with UA that he obtained his first No.1 with **Girl On The Billboard**.

In October 1966, just four hits later, Reeves became a member of the Grand Ole Opry. His reputation as a hit artist was maintained by a stream of chart singles that included such Top 10 records as **Looking At The World Through a Windshield**, **Good Time Charlies** (1968), **Be Glad** (1969) and **The Philadelphia Fillies** (1971). Del continued supplying such hits for UA right through to 1978, cutting duets with Penny DeHaven and Billie Jo Spears.

By 1980 he was on the Koala label and back in the charts once more, logging minor hits – the biggest of these being **Slow Hand** (1981) – through to 1982.

Del Reeves has often been tagged the 'Dean Martin of Country Music' because of his laid-back stage manner. The multi-talented Reeves has appeared in such movies as 'Second Fiddle To A Steel Guitar', 'Sam Whiskey', 'Cottonpickin' Chickenpickers' and 'Forty Acre Feud'. He also has managed Billy Ray Cyrus.

Recommended:
Live At The Palamino (UA/–)
10th Anniversary (UA/–)
By Request – with Billie Joe Spears (UA/–)
Baby I Love You (–/Bear Family)

Below: Jim Reeves' posthumous hits outnumbered those during his life. A duet with Patsy Cline was recorded in 1981, long after they had both died.

Goebel Reeves

An early-century Woody Guthrie figure, Reeves, known as the 'Texas Drifter', specialized in songs of hobos and hard times, writing from his own experience on the road.

Born in Sherman, Texas, on October 9, 1899, he came from a solid middle-class background but chose to live a rough travelling life. After a stint in the US Army, during which time he saw front-line action in World War I, he wandered around the USA, noting the things he saw and eventually turning his thoughts into songs, some of which he recorded for the Okeh and Brunswick labels. He played in vaudeville, the main outlet for music at that time, and also did some radio work. He claimed to have taught Jimmie Rodgers his yodelling style. His songs include **Hobo's Lullaby**, **Hobo And The Cop**, **Railroad Boomer**, **Bright Sherman Valley** and **Cowboy's Prayer**. A one-time member of the Workers Of The World Organization, Goebel Reeves died in California in 1959.

Jim Reeves

Originally a stone country singer, smooth-toned Jim Reeves from Texas reached amazing heights as a pop ballad singer and since his death in an air crash his fame has burgeoned into cult proportions.

James Travis Reeves was born on August 20, 1923, in Galloway, Panola County, Texas. His father died when he was young and his mother supported a large family by working in the fields. Early in his life he heard the sound of Jimmie Rodgers. He acquired a guitar at the age of

DISTANT DRUMS
JIM REEVES

I Missed Me / Is It Really Over / This Is It / Good Morning Self / Losing Your Love
Not Until the Next Time / Where Does a Broken Heart Go / Snow Flake / Distant Drums
A Letter to My Heart / Overnight*/ The Gods Were Angry with Me*
*Stereo Electronically Reprocessed

Distant Drums, Jim Reeves. Courtesy RCA Records.

five; it had strings missing but an oil construction worker fitted it up for him and taught him some basic chords. At nine he made his first radio broadcast, a 15-minute programme on a Shreveport station.

At high school in Cathage, Texas, he was just as interested in sport as in music and became star of the school baseball team, although he still performed at local events. He entered the University of Texas in Austin, and his baseball prowess as a pitcher soon attracted the attention of the St Louis Cardinals scouts who signed him up. But an unlucky slip gave him an ankle injury that was to halt his career.

In 1947 he met and married school-teacher Mary White, who encouraged his musical interest. Jim had studied phonetics and pronunciation and now sought a job in radio, becoming a DJ and newsreader at station KGRI in Henderson, Texas. (He later bought the station.)

Jim then made a momentous journey. He and Mary, having decided to make a determined effort to further Jim's career, drove to the crossroads of Highway 80 in Texas. They tossed a coin to determine whether to proceed to Dallas or Shreveport. Shreveport won and Jim moved there, ending up with a job as announcer on KWKH, the station that owned the Louisiana Hayride.

It was one of Reeves' jobs to announce the Saturday night Hayride show and he was even allowed to sing occasionally. One night in 1952, Hank Williams failed to arrive and Jim was asked to fill in. In the audience was Fabor Robinson, owner of

20 Of The Best, Jim Reeves. Courtesy RCA Records.

Abbott Records, who immediately signed Reeves to a contract. Jim had already made four obscure sides for the Macy label – these records only coming to light in 1966. However, his Abbott deal soon began bearing fruit, via **Mexican Joe**, his second release, which went to No.1 in the country charts during 1953. That same year he also released **Bimbo**, one of the 36 tracks he recorded for Abbott. This too sold well and attracted the attention of RCA

who signed him in 1955 amid considerable competition. That same year, he joined the Grand Ole Opry at the recommendation of Ernest Tubb and Hank Snow.

A string of country hits followed and from the release of **Yonder Comes A Sucker** in 1955 through to 1969, Reeves' name was never absent from the country

chart. The February, 1957 release of **Four Walls** proved the real turning point. That year, Reeves had undertaken a European tour in the company of the Browns, Del Wood and Hank Locklin and was unaware the song had hit both pop and country fields, earning him his third gold disc. He returned to find radio and TV offers in abundance, including a spot on NBC-TV's prestigious Bandstand Show. He also gained his own daily show on ABC-TV.

In the wake of **Billy Bayou**, a 1958 No.1, Reeves recorded his all-time greatest hit, **He'll Have To Go**, a 1959 chart-buster. The theme was familiar enough. Some years earlier it might have been called a honky-tonk song. But the treatment, with Reeves' dark, intimate, velvet tones gliding over a muted backing, was something different again. The result brought him international stardom.

Over the next few years, Jim travelled to every state in America and to most parts of the world. He toured South Africa with Chet Atkins and Floyd Cramer.

During 1963 he returned to South Africa to star in his only film, 'Kimberley Jim', the story of a con man in South Africa's diamond strike era. He had not toured British venues in these years because of Musicians' Union restrictions, but in 1964 he arrived in Britain for some TV dates and to promote his current single, **I Love You Because**. During the early 1960s, he also continued to dominate the US country charts; some of his many hits during this period include: **I'm Getting Better** (1960), **Losing Your Love** (1961), **Adios Amigo** (1962), **I'm Gonna Change Everything** (1962), **Is This Me?** (1963), **Guilty** (1963) and **Welcome To My World** (1964). But on a flight back to Nashville from Arkansas on July 31, 1964, following the negotiation of a property deal, Jim and his manager Dean Manuel reported that their single engine plane had run into heavy rain while crossing remote hills just a few miles from Nashville's Beery Field airport. The plane was making its approach to land when it disappeared from the airport radar screen. A search was instigated involving 12 planes, two helicopters and a ground party of 400. But it was not until two days later that the wreckage and the bodies were discovered amid thick foliage.

On August 2, 1964, services were held for Reeves and Manuel, most of the country music fraternity being present. Jim's body was flown back to Cathage where hundreds filed past the coffin. Honorary pall bearers included Chet Atkins and Steve Sholes, the man who had signed him to RCA.

But the legend lived on and Reeves' records continued to hit the charts, his after-death No.1s out-numbering those made while he was alive. Voted into the Country Music Hall Of Fame in 1967, Reeves continued to log hits posthumously as 1970s moved in. And even in the 1980s, Reeves' name has cropped up in the Top 10 via electronically created duets with Deborah Allen (**Take Me In Your Arms And Hold Me** – 1980) and Patsy Cline (**Have You Ever Been Lonely?** – 1981).

Recommended:
The Abbott Recordings Volumes 1 & 2 (–/RCA)
50 All-Time Worldwide Favourites – four album set (RCA/RCA)
Gentleman Jim, 1955–1959 (–/Bear Family)
Good 'n' Country (Camden/Camden)
Jim Reeves On Stage (RCA/RCA)
Songs From The Heart (RCA/Pickwick)

Mike Reid

A former All-American football player for Penn State University, Mike Reid (born 1948, Altoona, Pennsylvania) initially made an impact in country music as a songwriter. He was the recipient of ASCAP's Songwriter Of The Year award in 1985, and two of his songs Ronnie Milsap recorded – **Stranger In My House** and **Lost In The Fifties Tonight** – earned Grammy awards. Other successes as a writer include **One Good Well** (Don Williams), **Love Without Mercy** (Lee Roy Parnell), **Born To Be Blue** (the Judds), **There You Are** (Willie Nelson) and **He Talks To Me** (Lorrie Morgan).

Reid received his degree in music in 1970, but he was a star football player, winning the Outland Trophy as outstanding college football player in 1969, and he was a first-round draft pick for the Cincinnati Bengals, being named Rookie Of The Year in 1971. In between playing pro ball, he had made some off-season appearances with symphony orchestras in Cincinnati, Dallas and San Antonio. This whetted his appetite, and in 1975 he quit the Bengals and began touring as a keyboard player for the Apple Butter Band. A few months later he formed his own group, but after a year on the road, Reid split away and continued touring as a solo act. He worked the listening-room circuit up and down the East Coast.

In concentrating on his performing, Reid also worked more diligently on his songwriting. One of his demos caught the ear of a Nashville publisher, who offered him a job as a staff writer. So, in 1980, Reid and his family moved to Music City. Initially, he played the clubs, but as more of his songs were recorded the financial pressure was lifted and he settled in as a professional writer, working closely with Ronnie Milsap, providing him with one hit song after another. Reid sang a duet with Milsap on **Old Folks**, which went Top 5 on the country charts in 1988, but, ultimately, he and Milsap parted company. After taking stock, Reid decided to return once more to performing, and in 1990 signed a recording contract with Columbia, producing the album, **Turning For Home**, with a first single, **Walk On Faith**, hitting No.1 on the country charts in 1991.

With his songs concerning love and romance, many fueled by his love for his wife Susan, Reid scored further country hits with **Till You Were Gone**, **As Simple As That** (1991), **I'll Stop Loving You**, **Keep On Walkin'** and **Call Home** (1992), while providing songs for Bonnie Raitt, Gene Watson, Glen Campbell and Barbara Mandrell. Reid also found time to make his mark in the theatrical world with 'A House Divided', a musical saga he co-wrote, which debuted at Nashville's Performing Arts Center in January 1991.

Recommended:
Turning For Home (Columbia/–)
Twilight Town (Columbia/–)

The Remingtons

With their mature vocals and slick instrumentation, the Remingtons have made a big impression on the country scene of the early '90s with their carefully crafted albums and hit singles. Both individually and in various artistic configurations, the three members, Jimmy Griffin, Richard Mainegra and Rick Yancey, have weather the ups and downs of the music business for more than two decades.

Griffin was a founder member of '70s pop group Bread, which scored such hits as **Everything I Own**, **Make It With You**, **If**, plus six gold albums. He also won an Academy Award for co-writing **For All We Know**, from the 1971 film 'Lovers And Strangers'. When Bread split he embarked on a solo career, then in the mid-'80s he linked up with Randy Meisner and Billy Swan to form Black Tie, who produced a sleeper album **When The Night Falls** for Bench Records in 1988. The album's lushly romantic **Learning The Game** became a country hit in 1990.

At the time Bread were knocking out the hits, Mainegra and Yancey were in Memphis putting together a band called Cymarron. While it would prove to be a short-lived act, their first single, **Rings**, went to the pop Top 20 in 1971, while Tompall And The Glaser Brothers turned the song into a Top 10 country hit that same year. Mainegra relocated to Nashville to write songs and sing jingles, penning hits for Elvis Presley, Tanya Tucker, Reba McEntire and others. Yancey also maintained a Nashville connection, working as a session musician.

As the story goes, producer Josh Leo went out to a friend's home one Sunday afternoon, to listen to three songwriters who were in the process of working up some new material. The three were sitting in a circle, each picking acoustic guitars and harmonizing. Leo phoned RCA Nashville President Joe Galante and called him in to see the trio. After hearing the first song, Galante declared, "You got a deal – play another one."

The Remingtons' authentic blend, with its multiple chimes of lead, alto and high tenor wrapped snugly around alluring self-written material, was immediately radio-friendly, with the debut single, **Long Time Ago**, making the country Top 10 in 1991. Further hits have followed with **I Could Love You (With My Eyes Closed)**, **Two-Timin' Me** (1992) and **Nobody Loves You When You're Free** (1993).

Aim For The Heart, the Remingtons. Courtesy RCA Records.

Recommended:
Blue Frontier (RCA/–)
Aim For The Heart (RCA/–)

Restless Heart

Creating a sound which is a cross between contemporary music and the traditional country, Restless Heart's blending of lush country harmonies, folk-pop melodies and rock guitar resulted in a string of chart-topping country singles, five gold albums and being named the ACM's Vocal Group Of The Year in 1990.

Formed in 1984 when producer Tim DuBois brought together five studio musicians, John Dittrich, Paul Gregg, Dave Innis, Greg Jennings and Larry Stewart, to form a new country-rock band. Restless Heart's name was chosen after each

Above: Restless Heart was reduced to a trio in 1993.

member submitted 50 possible names, which were all discarded in favour of the title of a song they had previously recorded. Signed to RCA Records, the first single, **Let The Heartache Ride**, went to No.23 on the country charts in 1985. All subsequent releases have gone Top 10 with seven hitting No.1, including: **That Rock Won't Roll** (1986); **I'll Still Be Loving You** (which also crossed into the pop charts), **Why Does It Have To Be (Wrong Or Right)**, and **Wheels** (all 1987); **The Bluest Eyes In Texas**, **A Tender Lie** (1988); and **Fast Moving Train** (1990). Alongside these successes, Restless Heart have also been a major album act with **Wheels**, **Big Dreams In A Small Town** and **Fast Moving Train** going gold, while **The Best Of Restless Heart** gained them a platinum award.

From the very beginning the distinctive sound of Restless Heart has revolved around the forceful, sad-tinged lead vocals of Larry Stewart. The other four members always provided two, three and four-part harmonies behind Stewart, but never took the lead. At the beginning of 1992 Stewart announced that he would be leaving the band to pursue a solo career. Initially the remaining members started looking for a new lead singer, then decided to share the vocal honours among themselves. They produced a new studio album, **Big Iron Horses**, immediately scoring a Top 10 country hit with **When She Cries**, which also gained a Grammy nomination. The band were then dealt a double blow when keyboardist Dave Innis departed at the beginning of 1993. Now down to a three-piece, with only drummer John Dittrich, lead guitarist Greg Jennings and bassist Paul Gregg remaining from the original five members, Restless Heart scored another Top 20 country hit with **Mending Fences**, while **Big Iron Horses** crossed into the pop charts, earning them another gold disc. The three partners hired keyboardist Dwain Rowe and guitarist Chris Hicks to flesh out the Restless Heart sound, and they have maintained a gruelling road schedule.

C L A S S I C   R I C H

CHARLIE RICH

Recommended:
Big Iron Horses (RCA/RCA)
Fast Movin' Train (RCA/RCA)
Big Dreams In A Small Town (RCA/RCA)

Charlie Rich

Born in Forrest City, Arkansas on December 14, 1932, the 'Silver Fox' (his hair turned prematurely white at 23) was the son of a hard-drinking father and a Bible-thumping mother. Rich's high school and University of Arkansas era saw him heavily influenced by jazz and blues. He studied music formally at college and when the USAF posted him to Oklahoma in the early 1950s, one of his first groups, the Velvetones, secured a spot on local TV. Upon his discharge, Rich moved to West Memphis, Arkansas, to work on his father's cotton farm. After sitting in one night with Bill Justis' band, Rich was invited to Sam Phillips' Memphis studio to lay down some trial tracks, but was told he was too jazzy.

After playing sessions with Warren Smith, Ray Smith and Billy Lee Riley, Rich landed his own rockabilly hit in 1959 – **Lonely Weekends**. The demise of Sun saw Rich without a record label and Bill Justis persuaded him to sign for Groove, an RCA subsidiary, in 1963. From this period came a foot-stomping hit single, **Big Boss Man**.

In 1965 Rich moved to Smash, where Shelby Singleton encouraged Rich to utilize both rock and country influences. That year he scored another hit with **Mohair Sam**.

After an unproductive stint with Hi, Epic signed him in 1968 and made him part of their modern country push under producer Billy Sherrill. However, even Sherrill had trouble stimulating more than average sales with Rich, though local critical acclaim was voiced for **Raggedy Ann** and **I Almost Lost My Mind**.

But in 1972, the smoothly soulful country **I Take It On Home**, backed with **Peace On You**, proved a country and pop hit and was nominated for a Grammy award. The album **The Best Of Charlie Rich** swept up many of the earlier Epic titles, re-presented them to the public and

Classic Rich, Charlie Rich. Courtesy UA Records.

suddenly Rich was a big country name. But success really came with the next album, **Behind Closed Doors**. By this time, Sherrill and Rich had become a winning combination and the new urbane country sound known as 'countrypolitan' became the talk of the 1973 CMA awards. Rich was topping the country charts with such singles as **Behind Closed Doors** and **The Most Beautiful Girl** (both 1973 No.1s). Rich was so big that, when RCA released his old **There Won't Be Anymore** single, it also went to No.1 (1973).

In 1974, Charlie had four chart-toppers in a row, two (**A Very Special Love Song, I Love My Friend**) stemming from Epic, and two (**I Don't See Me In Your Eyes Anymore, She Called Me Baby**) from RCA. He also won CMA's Entertainer Of The Year in 1974.

There were further Top 10 records in 1975, but gradually interest waned. It looked as though Rich might be running out of time, but in 1977, following a Top 20 record in **Easy Look**, he returned to the top of the charts with **Rollin' With The Flow**. By 1978 he was as massive a seller as ever, with four hits on two different labels (Epic and UA) – his No.1 that year, **On My Knees**, achieved with the vocal aid of Janice Fricke. By 1979 Charlie had signed with Elektra and had a Top 10 record in **I'll Wake You Up When I Get Home**. But it was difficult to ascertain exactly who he was working for. He had five other hits that same year, four for UA and one for Epic. Perhaps there were just too many Rich records around, but by the mid-'80s the fans had tired of buying his records, so he just stopped making them.

In 1992 a new Charlie Rich album, **Pictures And Paintings**, a mixture of jazzy original and new versions of songs from his past, suddenly surfaced.

Recommended:
Behind Closed Doors (Epic/Epic)
Boss Man (Epic/Epic)
Classic Rich (Epic/–)
Nobody But You (UA/UA)
Silver Linings (Epic/–)
Pictures And Paintings (Warner Bros/Warner Bros)

American Originals (Columbia/–)
Original Hits And Midnight Demos (–/Charly)

Jeannie C. Riley

An international star on the strength of just one record – a multi-million-selling version of Tom T. Hall's **Harper Valley PTA** (1968) – Jeannie (born in Anson, Texas, on October 19, 1945) had only minimal experience in the entertainment industry prior to her arrival in Nashville.

In Music City she worked as a secretary for some time, cutting a few demo discs, but generally had little success until Shelby Singleton signed her to launch his new Plantation label with **Harper Valley PTA**, an ably constructed song dealing with small town hypocrisy. An immediate hit which sold four million copies in the US alone, the single sparked off an album which qualified for a gold disc, while Jeannie C. was awarded a Grammy as Best Female Country Vocalist of 1968.

The Girl Most Likely (1968), **There Never Was A Time** (1969), **Country Girl** (1970), **Oh Singer** (1971) and **Good Enough To Be Your Wife** (1971) were other Plantation releases that achieved Top 10 status. But, following a switch to MGM in 1971, sales of her discs began to taper off and it's now been a long time since she had a major record, although her name appeared on the charts in 1974 with **Plain Vanilla** and in 1976 with **The Best I've Ever Had**. A born-again Christian, these days she exclusively records gospel songs and only plays dates where the sale of alcohol is banned.

Recommended:
Harper Valley PTA (Plantation/Polydor)
Jeannie (Plantation/Polydor)
Total Woman (–/Sundown)
Here's Jeannie C. (Playback/Cottage)

Tex Ritter

Born near Murval, in Panola County, Texas on January 12, 1905, Woodward Maurice Ritter aspired to a career in law at the

University of Texas and at Northwestern before heading for a career on the Broadway stage, where he appeared in five plays in the early 1930s, including 'Green Grow The Lilacs' in 1930. During his New York years, he also appeared as a dramatic actor on radio's popular Cowboy Tom's Round-Up and co-hosted the WHN Barn Dance with Ray Whitley, making his first records for ARC in 1934. One of the first to follow Gene Autry into films as a singing cowboy, Tex moved to Hollywood in 1936, where he was to star in some 60 films for Grand National, Monogram, Columbia, Universal and PRC up to 1945. And, after several unsuccessful years as a Decca recording artist, he was the first singer to sign with the new Capitol label in 1942, providing a long string of hits for them, thus becoming one of country music's biggest sellers of the 1940s.

When his film career declined, he turned to touring. In addition, he and Johnny Bond co-hosted 'Town Hall Party' from 1953 to 1960, during which time his rendition of the theme-song for the film 'High Noon' won an Academy Award (1953).

Ritter moved to Nashville in 1965, where he joined the Grand Ole Opry and took over a late night radio programme on WSM. He acted on a long-standing desire to run for political office, when he stood (unsuccessfully) for the US Senate in 1970.

A lifelong student of western history, he was instrumental in setting up the Country Music Foundation and the Country Music Hall Of Fame, to which he was elected in 1964. He did not have a great voice, but his unusual accent, odd slurs and phrasing, allied to a strong feeling of genuine honesty, made his voice one of the most appealing in country music history. His long string of hits included: **Jingle Jangle Jingle** (1942), **Jealous Heart** (1944), **There's A New Moon Over My Shoulder** (1944), **I'm Wasting My Tears On You** (1945), **You Two Timed Me Once Too Often** (1945), **Rye Whiskey** (1945), **Green Grow The Lilacs** (1945), **High Noon** (1952), **The Wayward Mind** (1956) and **I Dreamed Of A Hillbilly Heaven** (1961). Tex died on January 2,

Fall Away, Tex Ritter. Courtesy Capitol Records.

many years, following up by recording the hummable **Singing The Blues**, **Knee Deep In The Blues**, **The Story Of My Life**, **White Sport Coat** and **Teenage Dream**. Robbins was a convincing rock'n'roller, a fact not lost on the British Teddy Boy fraternity, who tended to shout "You gotta rock, Marty" at Wembley Festivals when it became apparent that the singer was bent on providing an exclusively country set.

The cross-over hits continued, at least in America, where Robbins had success in 1958 with **She Was Only Seventeen** and **Stairway Of Love**. In 1959 came his biggest ever, **El Paso**, the lyrics of which would have made a convincing Western film and the rhythm of which slipped insistently along, tinged with Mexican nuances. This was the archetypal Robbins, purveying a mixture of macho western feel and melodic sentiment in a dramatically powerful but held-back voice.

Following **Don't Worry**, a 1961 country No.1, **Devil Woman** brought the same response as **El Paso** among pop fans and again they brought Robbins into the pop charts on both sides of the Atlantic. That same year (1962) he again climbed high on the pop charts with **Ruby Ann**. From then on, his wares were to be found in the country charts only, where he logged hits from 1956 through to his death, topping the chart with **Begging To You** (1963), **Ribbon Of Darkness** (1965), **Tonight Carmen** (1967), **I Walk Alone** (1968), **My Woman, My Woman, My Wife** (1970) during his first stay with Columbia.

He signed with Decca/MCA in 1972 and stayed with the label for three years, having minor hits. In 1976 he returned to Columbia and moved back into the area of former glories with **El Paso City**. A neatly crooned version of the old standard **Among My Souvenirs** provided him with his second No.1 of the year.

An actor of some substance – Robbins appeared in such films as 'The Gun And The Gavel', 'The Badge Of Marshal Brennan' and 'Buffalo Gun' – he was also a successful album artist and maintained a fairly prolific presence in this area, showing an ability in later years to appeal to the MOR market with his releases. He also appeared on most major American TV

shows and toured heavily. An Opry favourite, the one-time desert rat held the distinction of being the last person to perform at the Ryman Auditorium. He survived major heart surgery in 1970 and made a return to the Opry where he was forced to remain on stage for 45 minutes by his appreciative fans.

With the irony that so often besets singers (Hank Williams releasing **You'll Never Get Out Of This World Alive** just prior to his death), Marty went Top 10 in 1982 with **Some Memories Just Won't Die**. But on December 8, 1982, just after the song had drifted out of the chart and two months after his induction to the Country Music Hall Of Fame, Marty himself died, the victim of a heart attack. The name Robbins, however, still crops up in the charts these days, Marty's son Ronnie taking over where his father left off and logging hits for such labels as Artic, Columbia and Epic, though his singles are often outsold by Marty's re-releases.

Recommended:
Gunfighter Ballads And Trail Songs (Columbia/CBS)
Rock'n'Rolling Robbins (–/Bear Family)
A Lifetime Of Song 1951–1982 (Columbia/ CBS)
El Paso City (Columbia/CBS)
All Around Cowboy (Columbia/Pickwick)
Marty Robbins, 1951–1958 (–/Bear Family)
Just Me And My Guitar (–/Bear Family)

Eck Robertson

Born in Delaney, Madison County, Arkansas on November 20, 1887, old-time fiddler Alexander 'Eck' Robertson grew up in Texas and was probably the first country musician to make records.

Following a Confederate reunion held in Virginia in 1922, he and fiddler Henry Gilliland dressed as western plainsmen and travelled to New York where they persuaded Victor to let them record. On June 30 and July 1, 1922, they cut six titles, the first of these – including Robertson's

**Devil Woman, Marty Robbins.
Courtesy CBS Records.**

1973, after a heart attack at the Metro Jail, Nashville (where he was arranging bail for one of his band) and was dead on arrival at Baptist Hospital.

Recommended:
An American Legend (Capitol/–)
Blood On The Saddle (Capitol/Capitol)
Songs Of The Golden West (Capitol/MFP)
High Noon (–/Bear Family)
Capitol Collectors Series (Capitol/Capitol)
Songs From The Western Screen (Capitol/Stetson)
Country Music Hall Of Fame (MCA/–)

Marty Robbins

In a music where 'western' has often been considered a misnomer, Marty Robbins emphasized the Western of C&W through a series of memorable cowboy/Mexican-style ballads, many of them crossing over to the pop fields.

Born in Glendale, Arizona, on September 26, 1925, he grew up in a desert area. His earliest musical recollections involved his harmonica-playing father and the songs and stories of his grandfather, Texas Bob Heckle, a travelling medicine man. Many of

Above: In 1982, after releasing Some Memories Just Won't Die, Marty Robbins died of a heart attack.

Robbins' own songs, such as **Big Iron**, owed much to his grandfather's tales.

Influenced by the films of Gene Autry, Robbins developed an ambition to become a singing cowboy. Following a three-year term of service in the Navy, he began playing clubs in the Phoenix area, also appearing on radio station KPHO. Soon he gained his own TV show, Western Caravan, at one time having Little Jimmy Dickens as guest. Dickens was so impressed by Robbins' performance that he contacted Columbia Records who immediately signed him, releasing **Love Me Or Leave Me Alone**, in 1952.

With his third Columbia release, **I'll Go On Alone**, Robbins hit the country music Top 10 in 1953, followed by another, **I Couldn't Keep From Crying**. He had already guested on the Grand Ole Opry and in 1953 became a regular on the show, celebrating his signing with two 1954 hits in **Pretty Words** and **That's All Right**, the latter being the same Arthur Crudup up-tempo blues with which Elvis Presley made his name. Robbins thus established a rock'n'roll connection that haunted him for

version of **Sally Goodin** – being released in April 1923. A month earlier, Robertson had played **Sally Goodin** and **Arkansas Traveler** – the latter also being among the recorded tracks – over radio station WBAP, thus becoming the first country performer to promote his own discs over the air. The duo's **Arkansas Traveler** can be heard on the RCA release, **60 Years Of Country Music**.

Carson J. Robison

Composer of such songs as **Barnacle Bill The Sailor**, **Open Up Them Pearly Gates**, **Carry Me Back To the Lone Prairie**, **Little Green Valley**, **Blue Ridge Mountain Home**, **Left My Gal In the Mountains** and the hit monologue, **Life Gets Teejus Don't It?**, Robison's formula of vaudeville, new songs and pure hillbilly made him one of the most popular country songwriters of his era.

Born in Oswego, Kansas on August 4, 1890, he first sang at local functions in the Oswego area, moving to Kansas City in 1920, where he became one of the first country singers ever to appear on a radio show. In New York during 1924 he recorded as a whistler for Victor, teaming (as guitarist and co-vocalist) with ex-opera singer Vernon Dalhart to form a formidable hit-making partnership that lasted for four years.

After the termination of this association, Robison formed another duo – with Frank Luther (Francis Luther Crowe) whose voice resembled Dalhart's, also moving on to lead such bands as the Pioneers, the

Buckaroos, the Carson Robison Trio and the Pleasant Valley Boys.

Based in Pleasant Valley, New York, during the 1940s and 1950s, Robison remained an active performer and writer right up to his death on March 24, 1957, one of his final MGM recordings being a rockabilly track, **Rockin' And Rollin' With Grandmaw!** Known as the Kansas Jayhawk, he recorded many hundreds of songs during his career, working for RCA, Conqueror, Supertone and a host of others.

Recommended:
Just A Melody (Homestead/–)

Jimmie Rodgers

Known as the 'Father Of Country Music', James Charles Rodgers was born in Meridan, Mississippi on September 8, 1897, the son of a section foreman on the Mobile and Ohio Railroad. Always in ill health (his mother died of TB when Rodgers was four), he left school in 1911, becoming a water carrier on the M&O.

He later moved on to perform other tasks on the railroad until ill health caught up with him once more and he was forced to seek a less strenuous occupation. An amateur entertainer for many years, he became a serious performer in 1925. In 1926 he appeared in Johnson City, Tennessee, as a yodeller, assisted by guitarist Ernest Helton. Also in 1926, Rodgers and his wife Carrie – whom he married in 1920 – moved to Ashville, North Carolina, there organizing the Jimmie Rodgers' Entertainers, a hillbilly band

comprising Jack Pierce (guitar), Jack Grant (mandolin/banjo), Claude Grant (banjo) and Rodgers himself (banjo).

Together they broadcast on station WWNC, Ashville, in 1927 for a period of six weeks, then set out to play a series of dates throughout the Southeast. Upon hearing that Ralph Peer of Victor Records was setting up a portable recording studio in Bristol, on the Virginia–Tennessee border, the entertainers headed in that direction. But due to a dispute within their ranks, Rodgers eventually recorded as a solo artist, selecting a sentimental ballad, **The Soldier's Sweetheart**, and a lullaby, **Sleep, Baby, Sleep**, as his first offerings. These tracks were released in October 1927, alongside the first release by the Carter Family. The record met with instant acclaim, thus causing Victor to record further Rodgers' sides throughout 1927. These included **Ben Dewberry's Run**, **Mother Was A Lady** and **T For Texas**, the latter originally issued as **Blue Yodel** and becoming a million-seller.

By the middle of 1928, two more **Blue Yodels** (the series was eventually to include 13 such titles) were in the catalogue and Rodgers had become America's 'Blue Yodeller'. His amalgam of blues, country, folk music and down-to-earth songs had worldwide appeal, and made him the first true country superstar. Victor began to provide Rodgers with various backing groups, jazzmen accompanying him on some tracks, Hawaiian musicians being drafted in to assist on others, even a whistler named

Famous Country Music Makers, Jimmie Rodgers. Courtesy RCA.

My Time Ain't Long, Jimmie Rodgers. Courtesy RCA Records.

Bob McGimsey being signed to accompany on **Tuck Away My Lonesome Blues**.

Rodgers' popularity grew daily. **Brakeman's Blues** became his third million-selling disc. And even though the Depression had hit America, his fans still bought his records by the tens of thousands. But Rodgers was gradually wasting away. The illness that he sang about in songs such as **TB Blues** often forced him to cancel performances. In 1931 he joined humourist Will Rodgers in a series of concerts in aid of the drought sufferers in the southeastern regions, while in 1932 he began a twice-weekly radio show from station KMAC, San Antonio, Texas, but quit when he became hospitalized in early 1933. However, later that year, though critically ill, he returned to Victor's New York recording studios on 24th Street, there cutting 12 sides over a period of eight days, a special cot being erected in which Rodgers rested between takes. The final song, **Fifteen Years Ago Today**, was completed on May 24, but during the following day Rodgers began to haemorrhage and then lapsed into a coma from which he never regained consciousness. He died on May 26, 1933.

Rodgers never appeared on any major radio show or even played the Grand Ole Opry during his lifetime. But he, Fred Rose and Hank Williams were the first persons to be elected to the Country Music Hall Of Fame in 1961, which is indicative of his importance in the history of country music.

Recommended:
Famous Country Music Makers Volumes 1 & 2 (–/RCA)
My Rough And Rowdy Ways (RCA/–)
Train Whistle Blues (RCA/–)
You And My Old Guitar (–/Conifer)
The Singing Brakeman (–/Bear Family)
Never No Mo' Blues (RCA/RCA)
My Old Pal (–/Living Era)

Judy Rodman

A singer who enjoyed brief success in the mid-'80s, Judy Rodman was born on May 23, 1951, in Riverside, California, into a musical family. She travelled extensively as a child, living in England, Mississippi, Tennessee and Alaska, but was raised mainly in Miami and Jacksonville, Florida, where she completed her college education. In the late '60s she moved to Memphis, becoming a roommate to Janie Fricke. The pair were both trying to make it as professional singers and they found work singing jingles. Later they teamed up with Karen Taylor to form Phase II and started working local clubs. This came to an end in 1975 when Judy married John Rodman and became a mother.

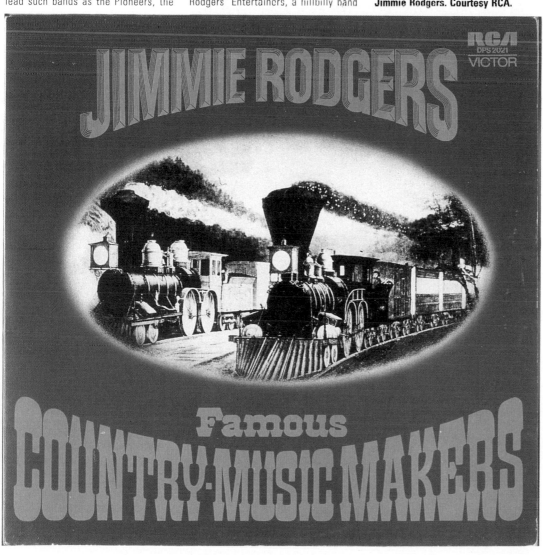

There followed another quiet period and in 1986 he was without a recording contract. He signed with Capitol Records in December 1987, and returned to the Top 20 with **I Didn't (Every Chance I Had)** the next year. Not heeding that song title's advice, Rodriguez backslid again with stories of cocaine use, a failing marriage, financial hardship and loss of his voice. In early 1993 he was back in Nashville. He had, supposedly, yet again kicked his drug habit and was looking for a new record deal. In his early 40s, Rodriguez still has many good opportunities to resurrect his career.

Recommended:
Rodriguez (Epic/Epic)
For Every Rose (Epic/–)
All I Ever Meant To Do Was Sing (Mercury/Mercury)
My Third Album (Mercury/Mercury)
Country Classics (–/Phillips)
Gracias (Capitol/–)

David Rogers

Rogers grew up in a country music environment, listening to the Grand Ole Opry every Saturday night of his boyhood. Born in Atlanta, Georgia, on March 27, 1936, the singer set his sights on becoming an entertainer at an early stage. In 1956 he was auditioned by Roger Miller, then part of the Third Army Special Services Division, but he failed to become a forces entertainer, merely being drafted in the normal manner. On his return to civilian life in 1958, he began working at various venues in the Atlanta area, in 1962 singing for the city's Egyptian Ballroom, where he continued to work for nearly six years.

In October 1967, he became a full member of Wheeling WWVA's Jamboree

In 1980 the Rodmans moved to Nashville where Judy worked on jingles and also landed studio work as a back-up vocalist for Crystal Gayle, Dolly Parton, George Jones and many others. When the new MTM Records was set up in 1985, Judy Rodman was the first act signed. After scoring a trio of Top 40 country hits, she shot to No.1 with **Until I Met You** (1986). That was followed by further Top 10 successes in **She Thinks That She'll Marry** (1986), **Girls Ride Horses Too** and **I'll Be Your Baby Tonight** (1987). When MTM closed down the following year, Judy was unable to find her way back into the Top 10, though she still keeps busy as a session singer and performs the odd concert and club date.

Recommended:
Judy Rodman (MTM/–)

Johnny Rodriguez

Chicano country star Juan Raul Davis Rodriguez was born in Sabinal, Texas, on December 10, 1952, the second youngest of nine children born to André and Isabel Rodriguez. He was given a guitar by his brother Andres at the age of seven, and, during his high school days he became vocalist and lead guitarist with a rock outfit. At 17 he recorded a demo disc in San Antonio but a possible record deal fell through. Then, following a couple of minor offences (including the barbecuing of a goat he and some friends had stolen),

Rodriguez was taken by a friendly Texas Ranger to see Happy Shahan, the owner of the Alamo Village resort in Bracketville – the belief being that if he obtained a regular job in music he would be more likely to stay out of trouble. Employed by Shahan (who became Rodriguez's co-manager) he spent the summers of 1970 and 1971 at the village driving a stagecoach, riding horses and singing for the tourists. It was during 1971 that Tom T. Hall and Bobby Bare heard Rodriguez in Bracketville and urged him to come to Nashville.

This he did a few months later when, following the deaths of his father and his brother Andres, he headed for Music City to become a guitarist with Tom T. Hall's band, the Storytellers. Hall, signed to Mercury Records, obtained Johnny an audition with the label, Rodriguez gaining an immediate contract.

His first release, **Pass Me By**, became a Top 10 hit before the end of the 1972. His next three singles, **You Always Come Back (To Hurting Me)**, **Riding My Thumb To Mexico** and **That's The Way Love Goes** all hit the No.1 spot. In 1975 he logged three more No.1s with **I Just Can't Get Her Out Of My Mind**, **Just Get Up And Close The Door** and **Love Put A Song In My Heart**. His flood of winners (mostly Top 20) for Mercury continued through to 1979, when he signed to Epic Records. That year he had four further Top 20 records, the biggest of which was **Down On The Rio Grande**. One, **I Hate the Way I Love It**, was a duet with Charly McClain.

Above: Rodriguez is braced for a comeback career after an absence of several years.

One of the better-looking of the younger singers on the scene in the early '80s, Rodriguez possessed both teen-appeal and the ability to sell to older audiences. But during 1981 his appeal started to ebb and his releases charted in lowly positions. Later, he admitted that a long stint with drugs had led to a careless attitude to his career. In late 1983 he sacked his band, quit drugs, formed a new band and took a more serious approach to his work. His record sales showed an almost immediate response. Johnny climbed back into the Top 10 with **Foolin'** and **How Could I Love Her So Much?** during 1984, also notching four more hits, including a Top 20 entry in **Too Late To Go Home**.

Reflecting, Johnny Rodriguez. Courtesy Mercury Records.

Farewell To The Ryman, David Rogers. Courtesy WEA Records.

show, his first strong disc coming in 1968 via **I'd Be Your Fool Again**, a Columbia release.

After further success that year with **I'm In Love With My Wife**, Rogers decided on a move to Nashville. It was here that he began appearing on various package shows, also receiving bookings for top-flight clubs and a number of syndicated TV programmes.

Following a run of money-spinning discs including **A World Called You** (1969), **I Wake Up In Heaven** (1970), **She Don't Make Me Cry**, **Ruby You're Warm** (both 1971) and **Need You** (1972), Rogers signed for Atlantic, becoming the label's first country act. Immediately he provided a Top 20 hit in **Just Thank Me** (1973), following this with **Loving You Has Changed My Life**, a Top 10 hit during 1974. After a hit album with **Farewell To**

The Ryman, Rogers switched to the Republic label and continued with his flow of chart contenders through to 1979. The biggest of these was **Darlin'** (1979). Since that time his name has appeared on releases from Kari (1981), Music Master (1982), Mr Music (1983) and Hal Kat (1984). David Rogers died on August 10, 1993, after a long illness.

Recommended:
Farewell To The Ryman (Atlantic)

Kenny Rogers

One of the real superstars of country music, Kenneth Donald Rogers was born in Houston, Texas on August 21, 1938, the son of a dock worker who played fiddle. A member of a high school band, the Scholars, who had a pop hit with **Crazy Feeling** in 1958, 'Rogers later attended the University of Houston where he studied music and commercial art. After working with the Bobby Doyle Trio, a harmony quartet called the Lively Ones, plus the New Christy Minstrels, he and other ex-Minstrels formed the First Edition in 1967. The group signed for Reprise Records and had a Top 10 pop hit in 1968 with a version of Mickey Newbury's **Just Dropped In (To See What Condition My Condition Was In)**. Other monster discs followed including **But You Know I Love You** (1969), **Ruby, Don't Take Your Love To Town**, an outstanding Mel Tillis song (1969), **Reuben James** (1969), **Something's Burning, Tell It All, Brother** and **Heed The Call** (1970). The group's popularity gradually tapered off following the success of **Someone Who Cares** in 1971.

Later becoming a solo artist — it had always been his grainy voice that had helped sell the Edition's mixture of folk, country and pop — Rogers gained a recording contract with UA, making some headway on the country scene with **Love Lifted Me**, a chart single in early 1976. By 1977 he was really on his way. UA released his version of **Lucille**, a pure country saga regarding an unfaithful wife, which reached No.1 in the country charts. It also crossed over to become the first of many of his pop Top 10 singles, and gained the bearded six-footer a Grammy award for Best Country Vocal Performance. Additionally, **Lucille** provided Rogers with Single Of The Year and Song Of The Year at the CMA awards ceremony.

From there on, it became difficult deciding just what CMA award he was not going to win. In 1978 and 1979, he and Dottie West claimed the Vocal Duo title. During 1979, too, Kenny was declared Male Vocalist Of The Year, while **The Gambler**, another Rogers' million-seller, was Song Of The Year. In the interim Rogers notched further No.1s with **Daytime Friends** (1977), **Love Or Something Like It** (1978) and **Every Time Two Fools Collide** (with Dottie West – 1978). 1979 provided four further chart-toppers in **All I Ever Need Is You** (with Dottie West), **She Believes In Me, You Decorated My Life** and **Coward Of The County**.

The 1980s saw little let-up in Rogers' career, though purists may knock him for being too pop, and rock fans may consider him pure MOR. He has also made further inroads into TV, in 1980 starring in 'The Gambler', a TV movie based on Don Schlitz's outstanding song, since when he

Above: The ever-popular Kenny Rogers has recently duetted with Travis Tritt on his 1993 album, If Only My Heart Had A Voice.

has also appeared in 'Coward Of The County' (1981) and 'The Gambler II' (1983).

But it is his records that continue to provide Rogers with an entry into most homes. His 1980 album **Kenny** was reputed to have sold five million copies worldwide, while **Lady**, a song penned for him by Lionel Richie, not only topped the country charts but also provided Rogers with his first US pop No.1, hanging onto that position for six straight weeks in 1981. In the wake of further No.1s with **I Don't Need You** (1981), **Love Will Turn You Around** (1982) and **We've Got Tonight** (with Sheena Easton, 1983), after five years with UA/Liberty – during which time he sold some 35 million albums – Kenny signed to RCA for a reported 20 million dollars. He immediately provided them

with one of his biggest ever hits, **Islands In The Stream**, a duet with Dolly Parton that again went to No.1 in both the US country and pop charts.

Since then there have been further chart-toppers with **Crazy** (1984), **Real Love** (another duet with Dolly Parton, 1985), **Morning Desire** (1985) and **Tombstone Of The Unknown Love** (1986). Kenny and Dolly also lit up the end of 1984 with a TV Christmas Special. In 1987 he teamed up with Ronnie Milsap for another country No.1 with **Make No Mistake She's Mine**, while his solo offerings of **Twenty Years Ago** and **I Prefer The Moonlight** made No.2. He joined Reprise Records in 1989, immediately scoring with **The Vows Go Unbroken (Always True to You)**, another Top 10 entry. The following year he duetted with Holly Dunn on **Maybe** and Dolly Parton on **Love Is Strange**, but was now finding it difficult to gain country radio plays with his pop-flavoured records. In a

concerted effort to win his mainstream country support back, he cut **Back Home Again** in 1991, his first 'real country' album in nearly ten years.

In 1993 he signed with Giant Records. His first album for his new label, **If Only My Heart Had A Voice**, took him closer to the 'New Traditional' country of the '90s, including a duet with Travis Tritt. Not that Rogers really needed to compete with the younger stars. One of the richest men in country music, he has homes in Beverly Hills, Malibu, Bel Air and Georgia, and in 1991 started his own restaurant business.

Recommended:
Daytime Friends (UA/UA)
The Gambler (UA/UA)
Eyes That See In The Dark (RCA/RCA)
Duets (EMI-America/EMI-America)
Back Home Again (Reprise/–)
I Prefer The Moonlight (RCA/RCA)
The Heart Of The Matter (RCA/RCA)
If Only My Heart Had A Voice (Giant/–)

Roy Rogers

A major western movie star between 1938 and 1953 and known as the 'King Of The Cowboys', Rogers started out as Leonard Slye, born in Cincinnati, Ohio on November 5, 1911. His biggest early musical influence was his father, who played mandolin and guitar. He grew up on a farm in the Portsmouth, Ohio, area and, following high school, became employed in a Cincinnati shoe factory. During the 1920s he began playing and singing at local functions, and in 1930 hitched a ride to California, initially becoming a peach picker then a truck driver.

After stints with such groups as the Rocky Mountaineers and the Hollywood Hillbillies, he formed his own band, the International Cowboys later – with the aid of Tim Spencer and Bob Nolan – he formed the Sons Of The Pioneers.

Though this outfit established a considerable reputation, Slye set his sights higher and began playing bit parts in films, first under the name of Dick Weston and then assuming his guise as Roy Rogers, eventually winning a starring role in 'Under Western Skies', a 1938 production. With his horse Trigger and frequent female partner, Dale Evans (whom he married in 1947), and occasional help from such people as the Sons Of The Pioneers and Spade Cooley, Rogers became Gene Autry's only real rival, starring in over 100 movies and heading his own TV show in the mid-1950s. His films include 'Carson City Kid' (1940), 'Robin Hood Of The Pecos' (1942), 'The Man From Music Mountain' (1944), 'Along The Navajo Trail' (1946), 'Son Of Paleface' (1952). 'Pals Of The Golden West' (1953) and 'Mackintosh And TJ' (1975).

Seen on TV guesting on series such as The Fall Guy, Rogers was a recording artist with RCA-Victor for many years. He later recorded for Capitol, Word and 20th Century, gaining a Top 20 single **Hoppy, Gene And Me** (1974) with 20th Century. Even in 1980, then signed to MCA, Rogers was still charting. He and the Sons Of The Pioneers teamed up once more for **Ride Concrete Cowboy, Ride**, a song stemming from the movie 'Smokey And The Bandit II'. Inducted into the Country Music Hall of Fame in 1988, three years later he was back in the country charts with **Hold On Partner**, a duet with Clint Black from Rogers' **Tribute** album. This

Roy Rogers

album had the 80-year-old cowboy duetting with such youngsters as Lorrie Morgan, Kathy Mattea, Ricky Van Shelton, Randy Travis, Restless Heart and the Kentucky HeadHunters. The owner of a chain of restaurants, Rogers is estimated to be worth something over 100 million dollars.

Recommended:
Best Of Roy Rogers (Camden/–)
Happy Trails To You (20th Century/–)
The King Of The Cowboys (–/Bear Family)

Linda Ronstadt

These days, Linda is a rocker who has notched some of her biggest albums with Sinatra-styled standards and made an onstage impact by singing Gilbert And Sullivan on Broadway. But once she sang plenty of country and employed some of the best country-rockers in the business.

Born on July 16, 1946, in Tucson, Arizona, she arrived in L.A. in 1964 and formed the folksy Stone Poneys. After kicking around for a year, they signed to Capitol. 1967 saw the release of two albums, **Stone Poneys** and **Evergreen**, **Stone Poneys** yielding a hit single in Linda's version of Mike Nesmith's **Different Drum**.

Linda next went out as a solo act and made two more albums, **Hand Sown, Home Grown** (1969) and **Silk Purse** (1970), the first featuring the talents of such musicians as Clarence White, Red Rhodes and Doug Dillard, while the latter was made with the aid of Nashville pickers. By 1971, however, she made the first move in a new direction, forming a backing band consisting of future Eagles members Glenn Frey, Don Henley and Randy Meisner, and releasing an album called **Linda Ronstadt**.

Since that time Linda has moved further and further away from her original country-oriented sound, though every now and then she has cut a track to remind country fans of days gone by. Her hit singles include **Silver Threads And Golden Needles, I Can't Help It (If I'm Still In Love With You)** (both 1974), **When Will I Be Loved** (No.1, 1975), **Crazy** (1976) and **Blue**

Bayou (1977). Ringing the changes in her musical output, the finishing touches were put to the **Trio** album in 1987. The project saw Ronstadt teamed with Dolly Parton and Emmylou Harris on traditional country music. The album also won a Grammy for

Hasten Down The Wind, Linda Ronstadt. Courtesy WEA Records.

Above: Roy Rogers with Bob Hope in the 1952 movie 'Son Of Paleface'.

Best Country Album and produced four Top 10 country singles – **To Know Him Is To Love Him** hitting No.1. That same year she also returned to her childhood memories in Arizona when she recorded **Canciones De Mi Padre**, a Mexican album that was so successful that she released another one four years later, **Más Canciones**. She made a return to pop success with the superlative album **Cry Like A Rainstorm – Howl Like The Wind**; her haunting duet with Aaron Neville on **Don't Know Much** became a Top 10 pop hit in Britain and America.

Recommended:
Linda Ronstadt – A Retrospective (Capitol/Capitol)
Don't Cry Now (Asylum/Asylum)
Prisoner In Disguise (Asylum/Asylum)
Más Canciones (Asylum/Asylum)

Billy Joe Royal

A singer who first found fame as a pop idol in the '60s before moving over to country music, Royal was born on April 3, 1942 in Valdosta, Georgia, and spent most of his childhood in Marietta, Georgia. His father owned a trucking company and in 1952 moved his family and business to Atlanta. Music played a role in the Royal household, with country at the top of the agenda. Billy Joe got his first taste of

entertaining in school concerts, and during high school formed his own band, the Corvettes. After graduation he worked in a Savannah night-club, already a talented guitarist, pianist and drummer. In the early '60s he recorded several unsuccessful singles, and in 1964 teamed up with Joe South, a local singer-songwriter. A year later they produced **Down In The Boondocks**, which made the pop Top 20 when released by Columbia. Billy Joe had several more pop hits in the '60s before ending up on the cabaret circuit.

Eventually he returned, musically, to his Georgia country roots. While recording in Nashville and Memphis, he landed a record deal with Atlantic America in 1985. Mixing up an R&B beat, a country attitude, heart-felt vocals and a touch of rock'n'roll, he started to make an impact on the country charts with: **Burned Like A Rocket** (No.10, 1985), **I Miss You Already** (No.14, 1986), **Old Bridges Burn Slow** (No.11, 1987) and **I'll Pin A Note On Your Pillow** (No.5, 1987). With his dynamic stage show and his varied mixture of material and styles, Royal built up a big following in country. Several more Top 10 hits resulted, including: **Out Of Sight And On My Mind** (1988), **Tell It Like It Is, Love Has No Right** and **Till I Can't Take It Anymore** (all 1989). Then he mysteriously stopped hitting the charts, though he still continues to tour regularly, mixing pop and country into a slick act.

Recommended:
Royal Treatment (Atlantic/Atlantic)
Out Of The Shadows (Warner Bros/–)

150

Johnny Russell

John Bright Russell was born in Sunflower City, Mississippi on January 23, 1940, his family moving to California when he was 12. A singer-songwriter and guitarist, he got a job plugging for the Wilburn Brothers' music publishing company and also pushed his own songs. One, **Act Naturally**, became a chart-topper for Buck Owens in 1963, the song providing a favourite for the Beatles, who also recorded it.

A Burl Ives-type character himself, he wrote songs for Burl plus Loretta Lynn, Del Reeves, Patti Page, Dolly Parton and Porter Wagoner. Eventually, he got his own recording career underway with RCA in 1971. By 1972 he had Top 20 hits with **Catfish John**, **Rednecks, White Socks And Blue Ribbon Beer** and **Baptism Of Jesse Tylor**. But despite such singles as **She's In Love With A Rodeo Man** and **Obscene Phone Call**, Russell's only other major hit for the label came with **Hello I Love** (1975) and in 1978 he turned up on Mercury.

His onstage act simply gets better and better, while his songs continue to bring in an abundant supply of royalties. Russell's **You'll Be Back (Every Night In My Dreams)** went Top 5 for the Statlers in 1982, while **Let's Fall To Pieces Together** made it to No.1 in the charts for George Strait in 1984.

Recommended:
Rednecks, White Socks And Blue Ribbon Beer (RCA/RCA)
She's In Love With A Rodeo Man (RCA/RCA)
Mr Entertainer (–/RCA)

Tom Russell

Singer-songwriter Tom Russell, who since the late '60s has played the clubs and bars in North America and Europe, and had his songs recorded by Johnny Cash, Jerry Jeff Walker, Nanci Griffith, Ian Tyson, Suzy Bogguss and many others, has remained an under-appreciated artist.

He was born in California and grew up in Los Angeles, but has spent much of his life travelling. While living in Canada, he wrote **End Of The Trail**, a song that secured him a great deal of acclaim. His own version of the song was included on a compilation album for Buddha Records. Russell moved on through Boston to Austin, Texas. At this period he recorded two albums with pianist Patricia Hardin, but was soon on the move again, working as a performer in Puerto Rico.

He teamed up with guitarist Andrew Hardin, the pair touring Europe together, eventually travelling to Norway, where they settled. Also, during the mid-'80s he developed his songwriting, often co-writing with Steve Young, Tom Pacheco and Katy Moffatt. One of his songs, **Navajo Rug**, was recorded by Canadian Ian Tyson. The song became the Canadian Country Music Association's Single Of The Year in 1987, and was recorded as the title track for Jerry Jeff Walker's 1992 album.

In the meantime, Russell assembled a band to play his unique mixture of country, rock, Tex-Mex, blues and folk. The Tom Russell Band is capable of playing in wide-ranging styles, but with the freedom to really cook, which provides the ideal backdrop for Russell's grainy baritone.

Recommended:
Heart On A Sleeve (–/Bear Family)
Beyond St Olav's Gate (Rounder/Round Tower)
Hurricane Season (Philo/–)
Poor Man's Dreams (–/Sonet)

Doug Sahm

Although Doug Sahm became known originally through his teeny-bop hits and then moved on to utilize blues, Mexican music, rock and country in his recordings, it is his involvement in the so-called 'Outlaw' community of Austin, Texas that won him his large and loyal cult following.

Born on November 6, 1941, and raised in San Antonio, he was subject to the varied root musical influences of that area, but nevertheless found himself part of the mid-'60s garage band movement.

She's About A Mover featured a pumping 4/4 beat, Sahm's strange whining vocal and the amateurish sounding organ dabs of Augie Meyers. It is a sound that has since become Sahm's trademark, with various refinements. The Sir Douglas Quintet, as his band was known, then moved to the San Francisco scene.

But Sahm was still a native Texan (a sentiment he has expressed in the song **I'm Just A Country Boy In This Great Big Freaky City**). His country-orientated albums, **Doug Sahm And Band** and **Texas Rock For Country Rollers**, have shown his natural flair for the music. Sahm recorded and toured throughout the '80s and in 1990 joined forces with long-time musical buddies Freddy Fender, Flaco Jimenez and Augie Meyers to form the Texas Tornadoes.

Recommended:
Texas Rock For The Country Rollers (ABC/ABC)
Wanted – Very Much Alive (Texas Records/Sonet)
Doug Sahm And Band (–/Edsel)
Back To The Dillo (–/Sonet)

Buffy Sainte-Marie

Hardly a pure country singer – she began as a folk singer and has since headed every which way – Buffy has nevertheless made several recordings of interest to country music enthusiasts.

Below: Buffy Sainte-Marie's I'm Gonna Be A Country Girl Again album was pure country.

Her birthplace is clouded in mystery though Sebago Lake, Maine (February 20, 1941), is the location most generally accepted. Born to Cree Indian parents, she was adopted at an early age and raised mainly in Massachusetts.

She broke into the folk scene in Greenwich Village during the early '60s, learning to play Indian mouth-bow from singer-songwriter and fellow Cree, Patrick Sky. A codeine addict at one point in her career, she wrote a classic song, **Cod'ine**, about her experiences, though it proved to be Donovan's version of her **Universal Soldier** that brought her songwriting into perspective.

Achieving considerable kudos through her appearances at the Newport Folk Festivals during the '60s, Buffy signed to Vanguard Records, cutting her first album, **It's My Way** (containing both **Cod'ine** and **Universal Soldier**) for the label in 1964.

By 1968, Buffy's intense vibrato was to be heard in a Nashville studio where she cut a pure country album **I'm Gonna Be A Country Girl Again**, achieving a mild pop hit with the title track, but having even more success with **Soldier Blue** (1971), the theme song from a film dealing with the massacre of the Indians during the last century.

Leaving Vanguard in 1973, she signed for MCA but after only two albums moved on to ABC, making a strong album, **Sweet America**, in 1976.

One Sainte-Marie composition, **Until It's Time For You To Go**, recorded by Buffy in 1965, later became a 1972 million-seller for Elvis Presley and she was also co-writer of the 1982 Grammy award-winning **Up Where We Belong**. Much of Buffy's recorded work lies outside the scope of this book but **I'm Gonna Be A Country Girl Again** and **A Native North-American Child** (both Vanguard), the latter album being a plea on behalf of the North-American Indians, should be heard.

Recommended:
I'm Gonna Be A Country Girl Again
   (Vanguard/Vanguard)
Sweet America (ABC/ABC)

Sawyer Brown

Duncan Cameron, lead guitar; Gregg (Hobie) Hubbard, keyboards; Mark Miller, lead guitar; Jim Scholten, bass; Joe Smyth, drums.

Country-rock band Sawyer Brown made their breakthrough in 1984 when they won Star Search, an American syndicated television talent contest. This led to a recording contract with Capitol and tours with such stars as Kenny Rogers, Dolly Parton, Crystal Gayle, the Oak Ridge Boys and Eddie Rabbitt.

Prior to their long run on Star Search, Sawyer Brown had been together for two years, working the American club circuit and building a reputation as one of the most musically proficient acts to have emerged in country music.

Their first single, **Leona**, made the country Top 20 at the end of 1984, and the self-contained five-piece outfit hit No.1 with **Step That Step** in 1985, followed by such Top 10 entries as **Used To Blue** and **Betty's Bein' Bad**, also in 1985. Flamboyant performers, Sawyer Brown appeal to both country and rock fans with their exciting live shows, but have not always been consistent on the charts. They made Top 20 entries in 1986 with **Heart**

Don't Fall Now and **Shakin'**, then seemed to slip in popularity. They made a comeback with **This Missin' Heart Of Mine** in 1988 and a revival of George Jones' **The Race Is On** in 1989. The following year there were a couple of minor hits, coinciding with the first line-up change in ten years. Lead guitarist Bobby Randall left, to be replaced by Duncan Cameron, who had previously been in the Amazing Rhythm Aces.

This change seemed to breathe new life into the band. They signed with Curb (their records still being released through Capitol), and made a big impact with their 8th album, **Buick**, and a single, **The Walk**, which took them back into the Top 10 in 1991. The following year they had a trio of big hits with **The Dirt Road**, **Some Girls Do** and **Cafe On The Corner**, continuing into 1993 with **All These Years**. And after all these years, Sawyer Brown show no signs of slowing down, playing over 225 shows annually. 'Amusement Business', in its 1991 year-end issue, lists the band as the 9th ranked top-grossing country act.

Recommended:
Shakin' (Capitol/Capitol)
Dirt Road (Capitol-Curb/–)
Buick (Capitol-Curb/–)

John Schneider

Actor turned singer, John was born on April 8, 1954 in New York, and came to prominence as Bo Duke in the TV series The Dukes Of Hazzard. He then found success in country music, scoring his first hit in 1981 with **It's Now Or Never**.

John first demonstrated an inclination towards a career in showbusiness during his early schooldays, landing a part in 'L'il

Abner', which was being staged by a community theatre group. Following his parents' divorce in 1968, John moved to Atlanta, Georgia with his mother.

While in high school he became active in the drama club and played the lead roles in many musicals and dramas. Following graduation he appeared in several community theatre productions, sang in Atlanta's clubs and co-wrote the musical score for a play called 'Under Odin's Eye'.

His big break came in 1978 when he won the coveted role of Bo Duke, the youngest Duke of Hazzard. John signed a recording contract with Scotti Brothers Records in 1981 and scored a Top 5 country hit with his update of the Elvis Presley classic **It's Now Or Never**.

In 1984 Schneider signed with MCA Records, and his first single, **I've Been Around Enough To Know**, was sent out to radio stations as an unmarked promo copy. Because it was on the same label as George Strait, many thought it was the Texan. Slowly the record climbed the country charts, eventually becoming Schneider's first No.1. The following year came another No.1 with **Country Girls**, while **It's A Short Walk From Heaven To Hell** and **I'm Going To Leave You Tomorrow** were both Top 10 entries. Alongside his singing career, Schneider continued with his acting, appearing in films 'Eddie Macon's Run', 'Dream House', 'Happy Endings' and 'Gus Brown And Midnight Brewster'. In 1986 he placed two more singles, **What's A Memory Like You (Doing In A Love Like This)** and **You're The Last Thing I Needed Tonight**, at No.1 on the charts. More Top 10 entries followed in: **At The Sound Of The Tone** (1986), **Take The Long Way Home** and **Love, You Ain't Seen The Last Of Me** (1987). Dividing his time between music and acting was not really working out, so finally he decided to

concentrate on acting. He appeared in a remake of 'Stagecoach', also took up scriptwriting and directing, and in 1990 starred in the TV series The Grand Slam.

Recommended:
Tryin' To Outrun The Wind (MCA/–)
Now Or Never (Scotti Bros/–)
Take The Long Way Home (MCA/MCA)
You Ain't Seen The Last Of Me
   (MCA/MCA)

Dan Seals

Born on February 8, 1948 in McCamey, Texas, and raised in Dallas, singer-songwriter Dan Seals' background is steeped in country music. His family were originally settlers in mid-Tennessee, who moved to Texas in the 1920s. Here, Dan's father gained a reputation as an accomplished guitar player, and with his son Jimmy (Dan's older brother, who later became part of Seals And Crofts) on fiddle, he played backup for many of the country music stars who toured in the Midland-Odessa area of Texas.

Jimmy eventually joined the Champs (along with Glen Campbell) and played on such pop hits as **Tequila** and **Limbo Rock** in the late '50s and early '60. Dan started playing in bands while at high school and joined up with John Ford Coley and Shane Keister to form Southwest F.O.B. (Freight On Board), scoring a minor pop hit in 1968 with **Smell Of Incense**.

Moving to Los Angeles, Coley and Dan landed a recording contract with Atlantic, by this time working as a duo called England Dan And John Ford Coley. During the '70s they released a string of pop hits,

Below: Sawyer Brown, who took their name from a Nashville street.

including **I'd Really Love To See You Tonight**, **We'll Never Have To Say Goodbye Again** and **Nights Are Forever Without You**.

The act split in 1979, with Dan retaining the band's name and a mountain of unpaid tax bills. He recorded a couple of solo albums, **Stones** and **Harbinger**, for Atlantic without any success. Kyle Lehning, who had produced the duo's hits, suggested he make a move to Nashville. In 1982 he uprooted his family from L.A., determined to make his mark in country music, but arriving in Music City bankrupt. Separated from his wife and children, who were living with friends, he started his career again. With Lehning's help, Seals recorded a demo and landed a contract with Capitol, scoring a Top 20 hit with **Everybody's Dream Girl** in 1983. A couple of minor hits followed, then he hit the Top 10 with **God Must Be A Cowboy**, **(You Bring Out) The Wild Side Of Me** (1984), **My Baby's Got Good Timing** and **My Old Yellow Car** (1985).

A big breakthrough came when he teamed up with Marie Osmond for **Meet Me In Montana** in 1985, the first of an incredible run of nine consecutive country No.1s, many of them self-penned. The infectious **Bop** crossed over to the pop charts in 1986, but all the others were straight country – **Everything That Glitters (Is Not Gold)**, **You Still Move Me** (1986), **I Will Be There**, **Three Time Loser**, **One Friend** (1987), **Addicted** and **Big Wheels In The Moonlight** (1988). With his meticulous choice of song material and musical presentation, Seals became a big star. His albums **Won't Be Blue Anymore** and **On The Front Line** went gold. He scored a Top 5 hit with the superb **They Rage On** in 1989, and was back at No.1 the following year with **Love On Arrival** and **Good Times**.

In 1991 he signed with Warner Brothers, and though he has continued to produce impeccable recordings, he has only managed a few minor hits for his new label, the best being **Sweet Little Shoe** (1991), **When Love Comes Around The Bend** and **We Are One** (1992).

Recommended:
Won't Be Blue Anymore (EMI-America/–)
San Antone (EMI-America/–)
On Arrival (Capitol/Capitol)
Rage On (Capitol/Capitol)
On The Front Line (Capitol/Capitol)
Walking The Wire (Warner Bros/–)

Jeannie Seely

An Opry member since 1966, Jeannie was born in Pennsylvania on July 16, 1940, and grew up in the Titusville area. She began singing on local radio in Meadville, Pennsylvania at the age of 11, and during her high school era appeared on the prestigious Midwest Hayride show.

Although she studied banking and associated subjects at the American Institute of Banking, Jeannie preferred the trappings of showbiz and moved to L.A., signing with Four Star Music as a writer and cutting a couple of unsuccessful discs for Challenge Records.

With encouragement from Hank Cochran, who later became her husband, she moved to Nashville in 1965, becoming a writer for Tree International Music. She also signed for Monument Records and had an instant hit with Cochran's **Don't Touch Me** (1966), a release which won

her a Grammy award for the Best Female C&W Vocal Performance.

In the wake of eight chart singles for Monument – these including **It's Only Love** (1966), **A Wanderin' Man** (1966) and **I'll Love You More** (1967) – Jeannie became a part of the Jack Greene Show in 1969. Joining Greene on the Decca label, the duo impressed record buyers via **I Wish I Didn't Have To Miss You**, a Top 5 disc in 1969. Jeannie's biggest solo hits arrived with **Can I Sleep In Your Arms?** in 1973 and **Lucky Ladies** (1974).

Recommended:
Greatest Hits On Monument (Sony/–)

Ronnie Sessions

A singer who looked set for the big time in the late '70s, Ronnie (born on December 7, 1948, in Henrietta, Oklahoma) had faded from the limelight by the mid-'80s, though he continues to work the club and honky-tonk circuit where his driving country music is best appreciated.

Something of a child prodigy, he made his first records for the small Pike Records in Bakersfield, California when he was nine, and was a regular on the Herb Henson Trading Post TV show. He continued his television career on the West Coast with an array of popular performers including Billy Mize, Wes Sanders and the Melody Ranch Show. In the mid-'60s he started recording for such small labels as Starview and Mosrite, then signed to Gene Autry's Republic Records in 1968. He notched up regional hits with **Life Of Riley** and **More Than Satisfied**.

A move to Nashville in 1972 saw him signed as a writer to Tree Publishing and he started recording at MGM, making his debut on the country charts with **Never Been To Spain** (1972). Then he joined MCA Records, achieving success with **Makin' Love** (1975) and his first Top 20 entry **Wiggle Wiggle** (1976). Finally establishing himself with his rocking country music, more hits came with **Me And Millie**, **Ambush** (both 1977) and **Juliet And Romeo** (1978). Then, with his records only just making the country Top

Above: Successful singer Ricky Van Shelton is a farmer who still ploughs and cultivates his own land.

100, he was dropped by MCA in 1980 and has hardly recorded since.

Recommended:
Ronnie Sessions (MCA/MCA)

Billy Joe Shaver

A 'New Wave' singer-songwriter who rose to prominence while in his mid-'30s, Shaver was a part-time poet who set his sights on Nashville after hearing Waylon Jennings sing.

Born in Corsicana, Texas, on September 15, 1941, he moved to Waco at the age of 12, spending his early life employed at a sawmill, punching cattle, working as a carpenter and performing various menial tasks as a farmhand. His ambitions as a songwriter later led him to Nashville where he was rejected by every publisher. Shaver, on the brink of starvation, was forced to return to Texas. However, on a later trip to the Music City he sold a song to Bobby Bare that became the B-side of a hit and also signed as a writer to Bare's own Return Music Publishing Company, achieving something of a breakthrough when Kristofferson recorded his **Good Christian Soldier** (1971).

Next, Tom T. Hall latched on to Shaver's songs, as did Dottie West, Jan Howard, Jerry Reed, Tex Ritter and Jim Ed Brown. His reputation as one of the most potent new writers in Nashville was established when Waylon Jennings cut **Honky Tonk Heroes** (1973), an album of songs nearly all penned by Shaver.

An often controversial writer – one of his songs **Black Rose** deals with the subjects of inter-racial marriage – he became a fully fledged recording artist when Kris Kristofferson produced **Old Five And Dimers Like Me**, Shaver's first album for the Monument label. Further recordings for Capricorn and Columbia received critical acclaim but were commercial failures, though he has continued to score as a writer, providing

John Anderson with his first chart-topper, **I'm Just An Old Chunk Of Coal** (1981), as well as providing hits for Johnny Cash, George Jones and Conway Twitty.

Recommended:
Gypsy Boy (Capricorn/–)
I'm Just an Old Chunk Of Coal ... But I'm Gonna Be A Diamond Someday (Columbia/–)
Salt Of The Earth (Columbia/–)

Ricky Van Shelton

With his silky-smooth baritone, Ricky Van Shelton (born on January 12, 1952, in Danville, Virginia) has displayed an innate ability to pick great songs. He has amassed 13 No.1 singles since hitting the country charts in 1987, from the rollicking **Crime Of Passion** to **Keep It Between The Lines** four years later. He grew up in the small town of Grit, Virginia, with southern gospel all around him. His father played guitar and sang in a gospel quartet, but as a teenager Ricky was more interested in the music of the Beatles and the Rolling Stones. Displaying a vocal ability at a young age, country music was not an interest of young Shelton, until the intervention of an older brother in need of a lead singer for his country band. Ricky slotted in neatly, so he was working as a gas jockey and pipe fitter by day and playing honky-tonks by night in Virginia.

In the mid-'80s Ricky's wife Bettye landed a job in Nashville, and this enabled him to start working on a country music career. He continued working club dates and a demo tape led to a showcase for CBS executives. A contract with Columbia Records resulted in 1986. His first single, **Wild-Eyed Dream**, made the country Top 30 in 1987, followed by a Top 10 entry with **Crime Of Passion**. This started a consistent run of No.1s with: **Somebody Lied** (1987), **Life Turned Her That Way**, **Don't We All Have The Right**, **I'll Leave This World Loving You** (1988), **From A Jack To A King**, **Living Proof** (1989), **Statue Of A Fool**, **I've Cried My Last Tear For You** (1990), **Rockin' Years** (a duet with Dolly Parton, 1991), **I Am A Simple Man** and **Keep It Between The Lines** (1991).

Shelton made a success out of finding little-known songs from the past and making them into modern hits. It was a winning formula, because by the end of 1991 his first four albums, **Wild-Eyed Dream**, **Living Proof**, **RVS III** and **Backroads**, had all earned platinum awards. He won the CMA Horizon award in 1988, while winning as CMA Male Vocalist in 1989. Fans also voted him both Entertainer and Male Artist Of The Year in the MCN 1991 awards. The following year he remembered the gospel music he heard as a child, and, specially for his parents, he recorded **Don't Overlook Salvation**, a gospel album, which became a commercial success. Demonstrating that he is multi-talented, he wrote a children's book, 'Tales From A Duck Named Quacker'. Unable to get a publisher interested in it, he set up his own RVS Book Publishers, and the first of a proposed six-book series had sold 60,000 copies by the end of 1992. Meanwhile, hit singles continued with **Backroads** and **Wild Man** (1992), and Shelton participated in the 'Honeymoon In Las Vegas' soundtrack. His version of the

Presley classic, **Wear My Ring Around Your Neck**, provided him with a Top 20 country hit in 1992.

Recommended:
RVS (Columbia/–)
Don't Overlook Salvation (Columbia/–)
Loving Proof (Columbia/Columbia)
Wild-Eyed Dream (Columbia/Columbia)
Backroads (Columbia/–)

Shenandoah

Ralph Ezell, bass; Mike McGuire, drums; Marty Raybon, lead vocals; Jimmy Seales, lead guitar; Stan Thorn, keyboards.

A quintet formed in Muscle Shoals, Alabama, Shenandoah started out in the early '80s as the MGM Band, so named because they were the house band at the MGM Club in Muscle Shoals. The name change to Shenandoah came in 1986, when some demos they made at the legendary Fame studios with Rick Hall landed them a recording contract with Columbia Records.

All southern boys, lead singer Marty Raybon was raised in Florida. Heavily into bluegrass music, he joined his father and brothers in the American Bluegrass Band for nine years. He then moved to Nashville, where he worked as a songwriter, having material recorded by George Jones and Johnny Duncan. Marty was invited to Muscle Shoals when the MGM Band had a vacancy for a lead singer. At the same time they were looking for a bass player, so in stepped Ralph Ezell from Jackson, Mississippi, who had played recording sessions for David Allan Coe, Mac Davis and others. The three founder members of the MGM Band were Jimmy Seales, a session-man and songwriter from Illinois, Mike McGuire, from Alabama and who penned T. Graham Brown's 1987 Top 10 hit **She Couldn't Love Me Anymore**, and Stan Thorn, who started out in the family gospel group, then joined '70s group Funkadelic.

This line-up has stayed together as Shenandoah, emerging as one of the top

I'm A Believer, Jean Shepard. Courtesy UA Records.

Right: T.G. Sheppard was most successful in the '80s for his country-pop music.

country bands of the late '80s and early '90s. They scored minor country hits during 1987, then the following year hit the Top 10 with **She Doesn't Cry Anymore** and **Mama Knows**. Their gritty sound with a soulful edge behind Raybon's raspy, sawdust and splinters vocal style is just right for the mainly southern themes of their songs. It resulted in a trio of No.1s in 1989 – **The Church On Cumberland Road**, **Sunday In The South** and **Two Dozen Roses**. There was another chart-topper with **Next To You, Next To Me** the following year, while **See If I Care** and **Ghost In This House** were Top 10 entries. Two of their albums, **The Road Not Taken** and **Next To You**, went gold. At this time a dispute arose over the group name Shenandoah, and a tough legal battle ensued. The band had a couple more Top 10 hits with **I Got You** and **The Moon Over Georgia** in 1991, but for almost a year all their earnings were frozen while lawyers battled over the ownership of their name. Eventually it was decided in the band's favour. They left Columbia Records and signed with RCA Records, immediately returning to the charts with **Hey Mister (I Need This Job)** (1992), and **Leavin's Been A Long Time Comin'** (1993).

Recommended:
Long Time Comin' (RCA/–)
The Road Not Taken (Columbia/–)
Extra Mile (Columbia/–)

Jean Shepard

Born in Pauls Valley, Oklahoma, on November 21, 1933, Jean originally sang and played bass with an all-girl western swing outfit known as the Melody Ranch Girls.

After impressing Hank Thompson via a Melody Ranch Girls–Brazos Valley Boys joint gig, Jean became signed to Capitol Records in 1953, that same year gaining her first No.1 with **Dear John Letter**, a duet recorded with Ferlin Husky. Next came a sequel, **Forgive Me, John** (1953),

then a brace of 1955 solo winners with **Satisfied Mind** and **Beautiful Lies**.

Jean became a regular on the Red Foley Show over KWTO, two years later moving to Nashville and attaining Opry status. But her hits remained infrequent until 1964 (shortly after the death of husband Hawkshaw Hawkins) when her recording of **Second Fiddle (To An Old Guitar)** sparked off a long flow of successes.

During the mid-'70s, Jean made a big impact with British country audiences through her outspoken insistence on keeping country free from pop contamination. Her repertoire of pure '50s-type country, full of hard-sob ballads and full-throttle honky-tonk won her standing ovations at the Wembley Festivals in 1977, 1978, and subsequent concert tours.

Solitary Man, T.G. Sheppard. Courtesy Hitsville Records.

Recommended:
I'm A Believer (UA/Music For Pleasure)
Mercy Ain't Love Good (UA/UA)
I'll Do Anything It Takes (–/Sunset)
Lonesome Love (Capitol/Stetson)

T. G. Sheppard

T. G. (real name Bill Browder) was born on July 20, 1944, in Humboldt, Tennessee, and moved to Memphis in 1960 where he became a guitarist and backup singer in Travis Wammack's band.

Securing a contract with Atlantic Records and using the name Brian Stacy, he had a number of pop-styled singles released in the early '60s, including **High School Days**. In 1965 he got married and took a hard look at his modest singing

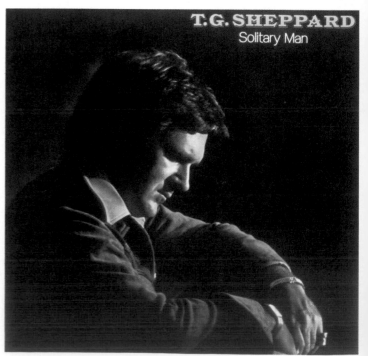

career, but he wanted to stay in records so became a promotion man.

After a stint as RCA's Memphis promotion man, he formed his own independent company, Umbrella Productions. He picked up **Devil In The Bottle** from writer Bobby David and demoed it himself, eventually finding an unlikely outlet in Tamla Motown.

Since the name Bill Browder would coincide with his promotional activities, he called himself T. G. Sheppard, after spotting a bunch of German shepherd dogs through an office window. The record was released on Motown's Melodyland label in 1974 and rapidly climbed to the top of the country charts, crossing over to the pop charts the following spring.

Further hits followed with **Tryin' To Beat The Morning Home**, **Motel And Memories** (both 1975), **Solitary Man** and **Show Me A Man** (both 1976), by which time the record label Melodyland had become Hitsville.

Finally, Motown closed down its country division and T. G. signed with Warner Brothers, making a return to the Top 20 with **Mr DJ** in 1977. Following Top 10 hits **When Can We Do This Again** and **Daylight** (both 1978), he changed producers and, under the guidance of Buddy Killen, scored No.1s with **Last Cheater's Waltz**, **I'll Be Coming Back For More** (both 1979), **Smooth Sailin'** and **Do You Wanna Go To Heaven** (both 1980), and crossed over to the pop charts in 1981 with the million-selling **I Loved 'Em Every One**.

With his good looks, slightly sexy song lyrics and dynamic stage act, T.G. has appealed mainly to women, creating mob scenes that are usually associated with pop stars rather than mature country singers. His success on record has been maintained with such songs as **Finally**, **War Is Hell (On The Homefront Too)** (1982), **Faking Love** (a duet with Karen Brooks, 1982), **Slow Burn** (1983), **One Owner Heart** (1984) and **You're Going Out Of My Mind** (1985).

He changed labels in 1985, moving over to Columbia. His run of hits continued with **Doncha?** (1985), **Strong Heart**, **Half Past Forever (Till I'm Blue In The Heart)** (1986), **You're My First Lady** and **One For The Money** (1987). He only managed a few minor hits in the late '80s, though his concert tours have still proved highly successful. In 1991, he signed with Curb Records, but his **Born In A High Wind** never really took off.

Recommended:
3/4 Lonely (Warner Bros/–)
I Love 'Em All (Warner Bros/–)
Livin' On The Edge (Columbia/–)
Crossroads (Columbia/–)

Billy Sherrill

An ex-R&B producer who developed a smooth line in modern country production during the 1960s, Sherrill sparked off success for Tammy Wynette and Tanya Tucker. In early '70s he helped revitalize the career of ex-rock'n'roller Charlie Rich, the seductive, soporific sound being dubbed 'countrypolitan' by the critics.

Working for Columbia and Epic, Sherrill evolved a masterly way of balancing steel guitars and orthodox country instruments against orchestras. Such was the success of this fine balance, with all the rough edges knocked off, that records made by

Above: A mid-1970's shot of Billy Sherrill, Nashville's leading producer.

Sherrill sold in spectacular quantities and helped identify the 'Nashville Sound' as mainstream country to most people, when in fact it was just part of a larger whole.

He also worked in the studio with such singers as Johnny Paycheck, Elvis Costello, George Jones, Marty Robbins, Lacy J. Dalton and David Allan Coe, illustrating the scope of his musical styles. Over the years he has co-written dozens of country hits, including **Too Far Gone**, **Stand By Your Man** and **Almost Persuaded**.

The Shooters

Walt Aldridge, lead vocals; Gary Baker, lead vocals, bass; Barry Billings, guitar; Chalmers Davis, keyboards; Michael Dillon, drums.

A contemporary studio band, the Shooters were based around the multi-talented Walt Aldridge, a prolific sessionman, songwriter and producer at the Muscle Shoals' Fame studios. Aldridge had already started recording the band's first album in 1986 before the band was actually formed. Once he had a few ideas down on tape with studio musicians, he then brought in the other musicians. That first album, simply titled **The Shooters** and released by Epic, produced such country hits as **They Only Come Out At Night** and **Tell It To Your Teddy Bear** (1987) as well as **I Taught Her Everything She Knows About Love** (1988).

Aldridge was raised in the Muscle Shoals area and graduated from the commercial music programme at the University of North Alabama. He started working at the Fame studios and made a big impact in country music penning hits such as **There's No Getting Over Me** (Ronnie Milsap), **Holding Her And Loving You** (Earl Thomas Conley) and **Crime Of Passion** (Ricky Van Shelton). Gary Baker, who shares lead vocals with Aldridge, is a

former member of pop groups Boatz, LeBlanc and Carr, and has penned country hits for Steve Wariner, Gary Morris and Alabama. Chalmers Davis began his session work in Jackson, Mississippi for Malaco Records and worked on the road and in the studios with the Gatlins, Tammy Wynette, T.G. Sheppard and Mac Davis. Barry Billings has played guitar since fourth grade. Based in Huntsville, Alabama, he went on the road with the Cornelius Brothers And Sister Rose, before moving to Muscle Shoals and joining the Shooters. Michael Dillon, from Florida, came to Muscle Shoals in the early '80s as a member of a revue band. He was part of the line-up of the Allman Brothers reunion tour before joining the Shooters.

The Great Conch Train Robbery, Shel Silverstein. Courtesy Flying Fish.

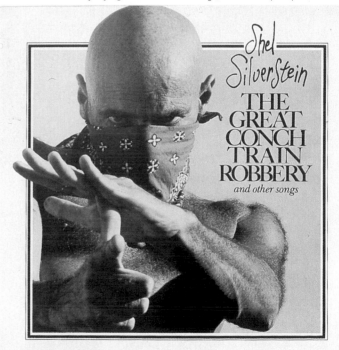

A second album, **Solid As A Rock**, produced their first Top 20 records in **Borderline** (1988) and **If I Ever Go Crazy** (1989). Strictly into contemporary country, the Shooters had a hard-cutting edge in a style that was a rich mix of Eagles-sounding West Coast country and the more rootsy southern country-rock. Not willing to tour, their career was short lived.

Recommended:
Solid As A Rock (Columbia/–)

Shel Silverstein

Cartoonist with Playboy magazine for over 20 years, Silverstein is the most eccentric figure in popular music. A bald hipster from Chicago, who writes poetry and children's books, he has made a number of bizarre solo albums, and is a highly professional country songwriter.

Silverstein's musical past does not suggest much affinity with country music. He grew up with Chicago jazz, blues and folk music. On his own records his humour comes from hipster tradition – he uses black language like Leiber and Stoller did with the Coasters. A highly sophisticated lyricist, it is hard to believe that he could approach country without cynicism, derision or calculation, but he does! His best songs use a conventional form to tell pointed stories, and he has kept faith with the popularity and reality that still underlie country sentiment.

Songs such as **One More On The Way** (a hit for Loretta Lynn) make their humorous point through self-commentary. He also wrote **A Boy Named Sue**, a Grammy award winner for Johnny Cash in 1969, and is best known in the wider pop world for his work with Dr Hook, for whom he wrote **Syvia's Mother** and such comic songs as **The Cover Of Rolling Stone** and **Freaker's Ball**.

In country circles, he is best known for his work with Bobby Bare, who enjoyed hits with **Daddy What If**, **Marie Laveau** and **Alimony**, and a series of concept albums including **Hard Times Hungrys**, **Lullabys**, **Legends And Lies** and **Drinkin' From The Bottle, Singin' From**

The Heart, which were all penned by Silverstein.

Although as a songwriter he specializes in the catchy and clever, occasionally he proves himself capable of the sincerity and sensitivity inherent in country song-writings, as with his **Here I Am Again** (recorded by Loretta Lynn).

Recommended:
The Great Conch Train Robbery (Flying Fish/–)

Asher And Little Jimmy Sizemore

One of the early professional bands on the Grand Ole Opry consisted of Asher Sizemore (born on June 6, 1906, in Manchester, Kentucky) and his young son Jimmy (born on January 29, 1928), who specialized in sentimental hearth-and-home-type ballads and songs, and were one of the first Opry acts to put out a very successful songbook.

Asher put little Jimmy on the radio as early as the age of three, and the Opry's Harry Stone, having heard them on WHAS in Louisville, brought them to the Opry where they stayed for some ten years (1932–1942), recording for Bluebird

Records as well, although no big hits emerged.

After World War II they appeared on KXEL, Waterloo, Iowa, SMOX, St. Louis, WHO in Des Moines, and WSB in Atlanta, often with Asher's younger son Buddy Boy, who was killed in Korea late in 1950. Jimmy Sizemore worked into the '80s as a radio executive, while Asher died some years ago, in the '70s.

Ricky Skaggs

Ricky Skaggs' roots and sound are pure bluegrass, western swing and traditional country, and his vocals mountain-flavoured, yet he dominated the country charts in the early 1980s with No.1 singles and gold albums. He won CMA awards as Male Vocalist Of The Year (1982) and Entertainer Of The Year (1985).

Born on July 18, 1954, near Cordell, Kentucky, Ricky had an old-fashioned, mountain upbringing, traditional music and religion being a vital part of family life. A child prodigy, in bluegrass terms, he appeared on TV with Flatt And Scruggs when he was seven and joined Ralph Stanley's band when he was just 15.

Below: Ricky Skaggs' traditional country didn't gain sales in the '90s.

His reputation as a tenor vocalist adept at high harmonies, and his skill on mandolin, fiddle, acoustic guitar and banjo, landed him a job with the bluegrass group Country Gentlemen in Washington D.C. Ricky later formed his own band, Boone Creek, and recorded two very good albums.

When Rodney Crowell left Emmylou Harris' Hot Band in 1977, Ricky filled the vacancy as acoustic guitarist, fiddle player, mandolinist and, above all, second voice to Emmylou. In his three years with the band, he played a big part in influencing her musical direction and had a key role in her **Roses In The Snow**, an LP widely acclaimed as a bluegrass masterpiece.

In 1980, Ricky decided to branch out on a solo career and recorded for the small North Carolina label Sugar Hill. With the help of Emmylou, Albert Lee, Jerry Douglas and Bobby Hicks, he came up with the acclaimed **Sweet Temptation** album and hit the country charts with **I'll Take The Blame**. This led to signing to Epic in Nashville in 1981, where he made the Top 20 with a fine update of Flatt And Scruggs' **Don't Get Above Your Raising**.

The album that followed, **Waitin' For The Sun To Shine**, resulted in the chart-topping singles **Crying My Heart Out Over You** and **I Don't Care** and his CMA award as Male Vocalist Of The Year (1982). Ricky's pure country styling and the sharp instrumentation of his band brought a breath of fresh air to the country charts and also won him a following by pop and rock audiences.

Ricky has cut an enviable number of country chart-toppers, including: **Heartbroke** (1982), **Don't Cheat In Our Hometown** (1983), **Honey (Open That Door)** (1984), **Country Boy** (1985), **Cajun Moon** (1986) and **Lovin' Only Me** (1989). In 1981 he married Sharon White of the Whites family group. The pair have recorded several duets, one of which, **Love Can't Ever Get Better Than This**, made the country Top 10 in 1987, the same year they won the CMA Vocal Duo award. Ricky also gained a Grammy for Best Country Instrumental for **Wheel Hoss**, using it later as the theme for his BBC Radio 2 series Hit It Boys. Ricky has shown that traditional country music can be commercially successful, having achieved his own worldwide success simply by being himself and playing and singing the music he loves. His hit singles continued into the '90s with such Top 20 entries as **Hummingbird** (1990) and **Same Ol' Love** (1992), but generally Skaggs' record sales had started to dip quite considerably and Epic did not renew his contract at the end of 1992.

Recommended:
Sweet Temptation (Sugar Hill/Ritz)
Country Boy (Epic/Epic)

Live In London, Ricky Skaggs. Courtesy Epic Records.

Highways And Heartaches (Epic/Epic)
Favorite Country Songs (Epic/Epic)
Kentucky Thunder (Epic/Epic)
Comin' Home To Stay (Epic/Epic)
My Father's Son (Epic/Epic)

The Skillet Lickers

Ted Hawkins, mandolin, fiddle; Bert Layne, fiddle; Clayton McMichen, fiddle; Fate Norris, banjo, harmonica; Riley Puckett, guitar; Hoke Rice, guitar; Lowe Stokes, fiddle; Arthur Tanner, banjo, guitar; Gid Tanner, fiddle; Gordon Tanner, fiddle; Mike Whitten, guitar.

An extremely popular and influential Atlanta-based string band of the 1920s and 1930s, the Skillet Lickers was led by Gid Tanner. The band included two other country music figures of great importance in their own right: Clayton McMichen and Riley Puckett.

Tanner (1885–1960), a Georgian like all the band-members through the years, first recorded with Puckett (1894–1945), the blind guitarist, for Columbia in 1924. He continued to record with various permutations of the Skillet Lickers for Columbia and Victor for the next decade, although the band name did not actually exist until McMichen (1900–1970) joined Tanner, Puckett and Norris in 1926.

Their material, for the most part, was composed of fiddle breakdowns, minstrel songs and a bizarre and hilarious series of eighteen spoken comedy records called **A Corn Likker Still In Georgia**, although the fiddle breakdown **Down Yonder** is most closely associated with them.

Their sound together was rough and wild, typically featuring the fine twin fiddling of McMichen and Layne, falsetto

Above: Songwriter Paul Overstreet left SKO in the late '80s to begin a successful solo career.

shouts and snatches of verses by Tanner, and often Puckett's bluesy singing. All three mainstays went their separate ways after 1934, Tanner dying on May 13, 1960, but the legacy of the Skillet Lickers is one of humorous, extremely good-natured, old-time music played in the most spirited of styles. They were unique, but their sound was in many ways the sound of an old-time sub-style of country music already on the way out as they were recording it.

Recommended:
The Skillet Lickers Volumes 1 and 2 (County/–)
Gid Tanner And His Skillet Lickers (Rounder/–)

SKO/SKB

The group with the unusual name, Schuyler, Knobloch and Overstreet (SKO) was formed in 1986 and, less than a year later, had changed its name to Schuyler, Knobloch and Bickhardt (SKB), throwing country fans and DJs into total confusion. the original SKO came together when three of Nashville's most successful songwriters, Thom Schuyler, Fred Knobloch and Paul Overstreet, decided to work as a recording unit and touring band. Prior to that, all three individual songwriters had penned dozens of country hits and also recorded as solo acts.

Thom Schuyler, born in 1952 in Bethlehem, Pennsylvania, was a carpenter by trade, who moved to Nashville in 1978. He was doing carpentry work on Eddie Rabbitt's recording studio, and this enabled him to demonstrate some of his songs. This opened doors, and he initially

penned hits for Lacy J. Dalton, Leon Everette and Eddie Rabbitt, then in 1983 Schuyler signed with Capitol Records. An album, **Brave Heart**, spawned the country hit, **A Little At A Time** (1983). Fred Knobloch was born in Jackson, Mississippi and started out with a rock band, Let's Eat, in the late '70s in Atlanta, Georgia. In 1980 a move to Los Angeles led to him signing with Scotti Bros Records, scoring on both the pop and country charts with **Why Not Me** (1980), a duet with Susan Anton on **Killin' Time** and a revival of Chuck Berry's **Memphis** (1981). Due to the country success of these records, he moved to Nashville in 1983. Paul Overstreet, from Newton, Mississippi, is a more traditional country songwriter, who moved to Nashville straight from high school. Originally working the clubs, he made his mark penning hits for George Jones, Michael Martin Murphey, the Judds and Randy Travis.

Signing to the new MTM Records, SKO immediately hit the Top 10 with **You Can't Stop Love** (1986), followed by the chart-topping **Baby's Got A New Baby** (1987) and **American Me**, which was a Top 20 entry. The trio cut an album, then Overstreet opted for a solo career, which has seen him achieving notable success on RCA. Rather than disband, Schuyler and Knobloch brought in another writer, Craig Bickhardt, the group now becoming SKB. Bickhardt was from Pennsylvania, where he was leader of Wire And Wood in 1972, a band that had opened for Bruce Springsteen, Stephen Stills and Harry Chapin. A few years later he formed the Craig Bickhardt Band and gained a sizeable following. He signed a writer's contract with Screen Gems in New York and had songs recorded by Art Garfunkel, B.B. King and Randy Meisner, who had a Top 40 pop hit with **Never Been In Love**. He moved to Nashville in 1984. One of his first projects was writing songs for the film 'Tender Mercies', which saw Bickhardt make the country charts with **You Are What Love Means To Me** (1984).

Like SKO, SKB recorded an album, **No Easy Horses**. the title song became a Top 20 hit in 1987, followed by **Givers And Takers**, which made the Top 10 the following year. MTM Records closed its doors at the end of 1988, and that, more or less, marked the end of SKB.

Recommended:
S-K-O (MTM/–)
SKB – No Easy Horses (MTM/–)

Arthur 'Guitar Boogie' Smith

Leader of an outfit known as the Crackerjacks, guitarist-banjoist-mandolin player Arthur Smith was born on April 1, 1921, in Clinton, South Carolina. One of the state's most popular performers, he played on radio station WBT, Charlotte, for over 20 years, achieving national fame when his recording of **Guitar Boogie**, originally issued by the Superdisc label, was subsequently released on MGM, providing Smith with a 1947 million-seller.

After several years of hits for MGM, many of which were of the eight-to-a-bar genre, Smith moved on to other labels. Smith signed to Starday and Dot during the '60s and has since recorded for Monument and CMH. His **Feudin' Banjos** (frequently called **Duellin' Banjos**) became

internationally well known as a result of its prominent part in the film 'Deliverance'. He has copywrited over 500 songs and written a book, 'Apply It To Life', in 1991.

Recommended:
Battling Banjos (Monument/–)
Feudin' Again – with Don Reno (CMH/–)

Fiddlin' Arthur Smith

Born in 1898 in Dixon County, Tennessee, Smith was a railroad worker who, during the early '30s, joined Sam and Kirk McGee in a trio known as the Dixieliners. Becoming an Opry favourite, Smith toured under the auspices of WSM for several years, sometimes playing with the McGees, at other times working with his own trio. His trio acquired a national reputation with their recording of **There's More Pretty Girls Than One** in 1936.

Later, Smith moved on to play with the Delmore Brothers, and throughout the '40s and '50s worked variously as a sideman or with units of his own, much of it on the West Coast, where he appeared in western films.

The 1960s brought him a new lease of life, thanks to the advent of the folk festivals and the rediscovery of many folk heroes by a new and youthful audience. This period was marked by **Fiddlin' Arthur Smith**, an album for Starday in 1963, and a Mike Seeger-masterminded Smith–McGee Brothers set for Folkways. Smith died in 1973.

Recommended:
The McGee Brothers With Arthur Smith (Folkways/–)

Cal Smith

Born Calvin Grant Shofner on April 7, 1932, in Gans, Oklahoma, Smith was raised in Oakland, California. He became a regular on the California Hayride TV show, gaining his first regular club job in San Jose, California, during the early 1950s.

Later, after engagements that included a spell as a DJ, Smith became MC and vocalist with Ernest Tubb's Texas Troubadours. Through Tubb, Smith became signed to Kapp Records, initially charting with **The Only Thing I Want** in 1967, then continuing to keep the label supplied with a number of lower-level hits (**Drinking Champagne, It Takes All Night Long, Heaven Is Just A Touch Away**, etc.) through to 1971. From this time, his discs began appearing on Decca.

Around the same time, his chart placings began to rise. **I've Found Someone Of My Own** became a Top 5 hit in 1972. In 1973, he joined the MCA label and earned yet another top placing with **The Lord Knows I'm Drinking**, capping even this success with that of **Country Bumpkin**, a release that won him his first CMA award – for Single Of The Year in 1974.

Further hits followed with **Jason's Farm** (1975), **MacArthur's Hand** (1976) and **I Just Came Home To Count The Memories** (1977). Then, mysteriously, Cal faded from the country charts, though he continued to record for MCA until early 1980 and has since had recordings released on the small Soundwaves label.

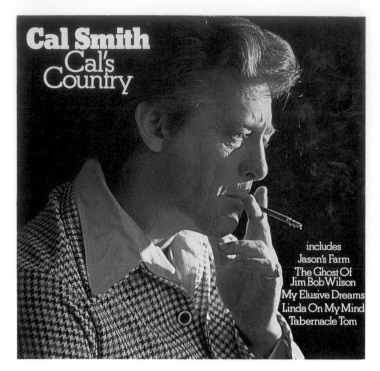

Recommended:
Cal's Country (MCA/MCA)
Introducing (MCA/MCA)
I Just Came Home To Count The
Memories (MCA/–)

Carl Smith

Born in Maynardsville, Tennessee, on March 15, 1927, Carl Smith sold flower seeds to pay for his first guitar, then cut grass to pay for lessons.

His first break in show business came a few years later, with radio station WROL, Knoxville, Tennessee. Then in 1950, Jack Stapp, at that time programme director of WSM, asked Smith to come to Nashville and work on the WSM morning show.

Soon after, he won a place on the Opry, signed a contract with Columbia Records and, with his second release, **Let's Live A Little**, had a smash hit. That same year (1951), he was voted No.1 country singer by several polls and accrued three further chart-busters via **If Teardrops Were Pennies**, **Mr Moon** and **Let Old Mother Nature Have Her Way**.

During the '50s and '60s he was rarely out of the charts, averaging around three hits per year, the biggest of these being **Don't Just Stand There**, **Are You Teasing Me?** (1952); **Trademark**, **Hey, Joe** (1953); **Loose Talk**, **Go, Boy, Go** (1954), **Kisses Don't Lie** (1955) and **Ten Thousand Drums** (1959).

Following his success on radio, Smith moved on to TV, working for such shows as Four Star Jubilee (ABC/TV) and Carl Smith's Country Music Hall, a weekly networked show in Canada, syndicated to several US stations. He has also been featured in two films – 'The Badge Of Marshall Brennan' and 'Buffalo Guns'.

In 1957, Smith married country singer Goldie Hill (his second wife; the first having been June Carter) and moved to a ranch near Franklin, Tennessee.

Early in 1974, the singer left Columbia Records after a 24-year stay with the label and moved on to Hickory Records, for whom he had some minor successes. In recent years, however, Carl has preferred to spend most of his time on his ranch,

Cal's Country, Cal Smith. Courtesy MCA Records.

though he has re-recorded his older hits for a successful TV-advertised album.

Recommended:
Sings Bluegrass (Columbia/–)
Legendary (Gusto-Lakeshore/–)
This Lady Loving Me (Hickory/DJM)
The Essential (Columbia/–)
Old Lonesome Times, 1951–1956
(Rounder/–)

Connie Smith

In 1963, Connie Smith won an amateur talent contest in Ohio, and was heard by Bill Anderson. The result was an offer to sing with Anderson and an opportunity to embark on a recording career which allowed her to accrue a tally of nearly 30 Top 10 hits.

Born in Elkhart, Indiana, on August 14, 1941, one of a family of 16, Connie learned

A Way With Words, Carl Smith. Courtesy DJM Records.

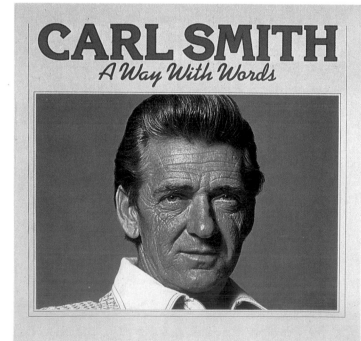

to play guitar while hospitalized with a serious leg injury. A performer at local events, she later married and settled down. But following her discovery by Anderson, she became signed to RCA Records, creating a tremendous impact with her initial release **Once A Day**, an Anderson-penned song that became a country No.1 in 1964.

An overnight success, Connie was signed to make her TV debut on the Jimmy Dean Show, won the Most Promising Singer of 1964 from 'Billboard' and – in the wake of three early '65 hits with **Then And Only Then**, **Tiny Blue Transistor Radio** and **I Can't Remember** – she became an Opry star on June 13, 1965.

Since that time, Connie has appeared on scores of TV and radio shows and has featured in country-oriented films. Also, recording mainly Bill Anderson and Dallas Frazier numbers, she has had hits with **Ain't Had No Lovin'**, **The Hurtin's All Over** (both 1966), **Cincinnati, Ohio**,

Famous Country Music Makers, Connie Smith. Courtesy RCA Records.

Burning A Hole In My Mind (both 1967), **I Never Once Stopped Loving You** (1970), **Just One Time** (1971), **If It Ain't Love**, **Just For What I Am** (both 1972), **Love Is What You're Looking For** (1973), **Till (I Kissed You)** and **I Don't Wanna Talk About It Anymore** (1976).

One of the many country artists with deep religious convictions, the diminutive Connie toured Australia, New Zealand and Japan during 1972, raising funds for the children of Bangladesh. She often plays on radio and TV shows, and appeared in Britain in 1990.

Recommended:
Famous Country Music Makers (–/RCA)
Songs We Fell In Love To (Columbia/CBS)
If It Ain't Love (RCA/RCA)
Live in Branson (Branson/–)

Darden Smith

Singer-songwriter Darden Smith was born on March 11, 1962 in Blenham, Texas. A modern troubadour, Smith's music has rich traces of rockabilly, blues, country and rock'n'roll, yet he neatly fits into the Texas singer-songwriter genre with his poetic lyrics and heart-tugging melodies. He grew up on a farm between Austin and Houston and was writing his first embryonic songs before he was ten. His family moved to Houston in 1975 and Darden played in his older brother's band during his high school days while pursuing his songwriting. When he started college in San Marcos, he put playing aside for some months, but, discovering the thriving Austin club scene, Smith soon strapped his guitar on and played three nights a week to earn a bit of money. He graduated from the University of Texas and immediately set out to put his own songs on record.

The self-produced **Native Soil**, put out on his own RediMix label in 1986, was a low-key collection of captivating vignettes of real people in real life situations. Working regularly on the Texas music scene with his own 'band', the Big Guns, comprised of himself on guitar, Roland

Denney on stand-up bass and Paul Pearcy on drums, Smith's reputation spread throughout country music circles. He signed with Epic Records in Nashville, and his debut, simply titled **Darden Smith**, was produced by Ray Benson of Asleep At The Wheel and featured guest appearances from Lyle Lovett, Nanci Griffith, C.J. Chenier, Sonny Landreth and various Asleep At The Wheelers.

Not fitting into the accepted confines of mainstream country, Darden only made a brief appearance on the country charts with **Little Maggie**, a track from his debut Epic album in 1988. Realizing that he was unlikely to gain country radio plays, Darden Smith's contract was moved away from Nashville and his career was handled from New York which gave him a better springboard for both an international breakthrough, and building a bigger following in America. He has succeeded in developing a cult following, and, now on the main Columbia label, has produced some very fine albums, which typify his wide-ranging, country-tinged music.

Recommended:
Little Victories (Columbia/Columbia)
Trouble No More (Columbia/Columbia)
Native Soil (Redimix/–)
Darden Smith (Columbia/CBS)

Margo Smith

A petite, ex-school teacher, born Betty Lou Miller on April 9, 1942 in Dayton, Ohio, Margo initially used her vocal talents singing country and folk songs as a teaching aid in her kindergarten classes.

Margo started writing songs in her spare time and cut a demo tape which she took to Nashville and promptly signed a recording contract with Chart Records.

A few singles were released, but they made little impression. However, in 1975 she signed a new contract with 20th Century Records and made her debut on the country charts with the self-penned **There I Said It**, which slowly headed towards the Top 10. At this point, Margo gave up teaching.

Shortly after this, 20th Century closed their Nashville offices and Margo was without a label. Eventually she signed with Warner Brothers and was soon back in the Top 10 with **Save Your Kisses For Me**, **Take My Breath Away** (both 1976) and **Love's Explosion** (1977), before making the coveted top spot with **Don't Break The Heart That Loves You** (1978).

For the next couple of years Margo was rarely out of the charts, scoring another No.1 with **It Only Hurts A Little While** (1978), a Top 5 hit with her update of **Little Things Mean A Lot** (1978) and Top 10 entries with **Still A Woman** and **If I Give My Heart To You**. She also recorded duets with Rex Allen Jr of **Cup O' Tea** and **While The Feeling's Good** (1980 and 1981 respectively), with plans for an album to follow.

Changes at Warner Brothers during 1981 meant that Margo was dropped by the label, but she has since recorded for AMI, Moonshine and Bermuda Dunes, achieving minor hits but failing to make a return to the Top 10. In 1986 she began her climb back to the top once more by signing with Dot/MCA and cutting an album, simply titled **Margo Smith**. A tremendously talented lady and exciting stage performer, Margo is one of the few country ladies who yodel on stage.

Recommended:
Margo Smith (MCA–Dot/–)
Diamonds And Chills (Warner Bros/–)
Just Margo (Warner Bros/–)
Song Bird (Warner Bros/–)

Below: Connie Smith had her heyday in the late '60s and the '70s, and now works for charity and makes guest appearances on television and radio.

As Long As There's A Sunday, Sammi Smith. Courtesy WEA Records.

Sammi Smith

Considered a country rebel, to be mentioned alongside Jennings and Nelson, Sammi originally made her mark as a cross-over artist of some potential. Her version of Kristofferson's **Help Me Make It Through The Night** (which gained CMA Single Of The Year in 1971) sold over two million copies.

Born in Orange, California on August 5, 1943, she grew up in Oklahoma, playing clubs in that area at the age of 12. Encouraged in her career by Oklahoma City songwriter/recording studio owner Gene Sullivan, she was heard by Tennessee Three bassist Marshall Grant, who persuaded her to make the inevitable trip to Nashville where she became a Columbia recording act.

Some moderate hits followed including **So Long, Charlie Brown** (1968) and **Brownsville Lumberyard** (1969), after which Sammi moved on to the Mega label in 1970, recording **He's Everywhere**, the title track becoming a chart single. A second track from the same album was then selected as a follow-up. The amazingly successful **Help Me Make It Through The Night** prompted Mega to title the parent album in line with the single and to embark on a re-promotion campaign.

However, Sammi found it hard to hit the charts consistently, though she has enjoyed Top 20 hits with **I've Got To Have You** (1972), **Today I Started Loving You Again** (1975), **Sunday School To Broadway** (1976), **Loving Arms** (1977) and **What A Lie** (1979) as she has moved through such labels as Elektra, Zodiac, Cyclone and Sound Factory.

One of the most soulful singers in country music, Sammi has the ability to transform even the most banal lyrics into a charged, emotional experience.

Recommended:
Girl Hero (Cyclone/–)
New Winds, All Quadrants (Elektra/–)
Mixed Emotions (Elektra/–)

Hank Snow

The most revered of all Canadian country performers, Clarence Eugene Snow was born in Liverpool, Nova Scotia, on May 9, 1914. Leaving home at 12, he became a cabin boy on a freighter for four years, but began singing in Nova Scotia clubs, obtaining his first radio show in 1934, on CHNS, Halifax, Nova Scotia.

Known initially as the 'Yodelling Ranger' and later as the 'Singing Ranger', he

COUNTRY MUSIC
HALL OF FAME
ELECTED 1979

HANK SNOW

MAY 9, 1914

CANADA'S HANK SNOW IS ONE OF COUNTRY MUSIC'S MOST PROMINENT AND INFLUENTIAL ENTERTAINERS. HIS DETERMINED MOTIVATION AND TALENT AS A SINGER, SONGWRITER AND GUITAR PLAYER HAVE EARNED HIM INNUMERABLE HITS AND AWARDS. CAREER MILESTONES FOR THE SINGING RANGER INCLUDE JOINING RCA VICTOR IN 1936, MAKING HIM THE LONGEST-TERM ARTIST ON ANY LABEL; HOLDING BILLBOARD'S #1 CHART POSITION FOR AN UNEQUALLED 49 CONSECUTIVE WEEKS FOR SELF-PENNED "I'M MOVIN ON"; JOINING THE GRAND OLE OPRY IN 1950; AND FOUNDING THE HANK SNOW CHILD ABUSE FOUNDATION.

COUNTRY MUSIC ASSOCIATION

became signed to RCA-Victor in 1934, his first sides being **Lonesome Blue Yodel** and **Prisoned Cowboy**.

Despite a move to the US during the mid-'40s and appearances on such shows as the WWVA Jamboree, Snow remained virtually unknown south of the Canadian border until 1949, when, following a disappointing Opry performance on January 7, his recording of **Marriage Vows** became a Top 10 hit.

In 1950 he became an Opry regular, that same year seeing the release of **I'm Moving On**, a self-penned hit that became a US No.1. Throughout the '50s and early '60s, Snow continued to provide RCA with a huge number of Top 10 singles – several of them being train songs, revealing his debt to Jimmie Rodgers.

Too numerous to list, Snow's hits include **Golden Rocket** (1950), **Rhumba Boogie** (1951), **I Don't Hurt Anymore** (1954) and the tongue-twisting **I've Been Everywhere** (1962), all country No.1s. **I'm Moving On** and **I Don't Hurt Anymore** both became million-sellers.

Snow, who has consistently fought against what he believes to be over-commercialization of country music, has proved to be one of country's most travelled ambassadors, appearing in his somewhat stagey cowboy attire at venues all over the world.

His eldest son, Jimmie Rodgers Snow, is both a country performer and a travelling evangelist. Hank still appears on the Opry, though he rarely tours nowadays, and he has had no inclination to record since being dropped by RCA after a record-breaking 45 years with the same company. He was elected to the Country Music Hall Of Fame in 1979.

Recommended:
Famous Country Music Makers (–/RCA)
Award Winners (RCA/RCA)
Grand Ole Opry Favorites (RCA/RCA)
Best Of (RCA/RCA)
The Yodeling Ranger, 1936–1947 (–/Bear Family)
The Singing Ranger – I'm Movin' On (–/Bear Family)
The Singing Ranger – Volume 2 (–/Bear Family)
The Singing Ranger – Volume 3 (–/Bear Family)

Country Music Hall Of Fame (–/RCA)
Hits Covered By Snow (RCA/RCA)

Jo-El Sonnier

Acclaimed French-Cajun accordionist, Jo-El Sonnier was born on October 2, 1946, in Rayne, a rural area of Louisiana. Something of a child prodigy, at only six he was singing and playing accordion on his own 15-minute radio spot in nearby Crowley, and recorded his first single, **Tes Yeux Bleus (Your Blue Eyes)** when he was 13. Working the Louisiana club circuit, he recorded prolifically for the local Swallow and Goldband records and won first prize in the Mamou Mardi Gras competition in 1968, but found that his strong French accent was proving something of a handicap. In 1972 he moved to Los Angeles, where he built up a reputation as accordion player in the bars and honky-tonks. Two years later he relocated to Nashville, where, as well as making an impression as a songwriter and studio musician, he landed a contract with Mercury Records, scoring a few minor country hits during 1975–76 under the name Joel Sonnier. In 1980 he returned to Louisiana and recorded **Cajun Life**, performed entirely in French and released by Rounder Records. Renewing friendships he'd built up in Nashville, Sonnier moved back to Los Angeles in 1982 and formed an all-star band, Jo-El Sonnier And Friends, with Sneaky Pete Kleinow, Albert Lee, Garth Hudson and David Lindley. Elvis Costello saw his show and recruited Sonnier for his **King Of America** album.

Commuting between the West Coast, Nashville and Louisiana, Sonnier eventually landed a recording contract with RCA in Nashville in 1987. His first single, **Come On Joe**, a song written for and about him by a New York songwriter in 1974, made the country Top 40 in 1987. The following year he made the Top 10 with **No More One More Time** and **Tear-Stained Letter**. With his exciting mixture of Louisiana swamp-rock, French-Cajun tunes, infectious country-rock and blues, and a tight-knit powerhouse band, Sonnier built up a reputation as one of the best live acts around. He has never really

Country Music Hall Of Fame, Hank Snow. Courtesy RCA Records.

successfully duplicated the raw magic of his live shows on to record. He had further minor hits with **Rainin' In My Heart** (1988) and **If Your Heart Should Ever Roll This Way Again** (1989), and in 1991 took his rootsy Cajun music to Capitol.

Recommended:
Come On Joe (RCA/RCA)
Have A Little Faith (RCA/RCA)
Tears Of Joy (Capitol/–)
Cajun Life (Rounder/–)
The Complete Mercury Sessions (Mercury/–)

Sons Of The Pioneers

Originally a guitarist/vocals trio when formed by Roy Rogers, Bob Nolan and Tim Spencer in 1934 as the Pioneer Trio, the name changed to Sons Of The Pioneers in deference to the American Indian heritage of members Karl and Hugh Farr.

They did much radio work during the '30s and recorded variously for Decca, Columbia and RCA. Films also figured large for them and they appeared in many of those featuring Rogers.

Other members of the group have included Lloyd Perryman, Ken Carson, Ken Curtis, Pat Brady, Doye O'Dell, Dale Warren, Deuce Spriggins, Tommy Doss, Shug Fisher and Rusty Richards.

Bob Nolan composed the group's biggest hits, **Tumbling Tumbleweeds** and **Cool Water**, and Spencer, who left in 1950 but managed the Sons until 1955, composed **Cigarettes, Whiskey And Wild Wild Women, Careless Kisses** and **Roomful Of Roses**. Spencer died on April 26, 1974 aged 65, in California. However, the Sons were still performing at that time, led by Perryman who had originally joined the group back in 1936 and passed away on May 3, 1977, aged 60.

A word should be said about Bob Nolan, whose songwriting may be the finest ever to appear in country music. A brilliant poet with an inventive ear for melody and

harmony, he virtually invented the sound and style of western harmony singing single-handedly. He supplied the once thriving field with the great majority of its classic songs, which, in addition to the above, include **Trail Herding Cowboy, A Cowboy Has To Sing, One More Ride, Way Out There** and **Song Of The Bandit**.

Nolan himself recorded an acclaimed solo album, **Sound Of A Pioneer**, for Elektra in 1979. The following year he died at his home in California on June 15, aged 72, and the Sons Of The Pioneers were elected to the Country Music Hall Of Fame the following October.

Recommended:
Cowboy Country (–/Bear Family)
Riders In The Sky (Camden/–)
Sons Of The Pioneers (Columbia/CBS)
Country Music Hall Of Fame (MCA/–)

Southern Pacific

Stu Cook, bass; Kurt Howell, keyboards; David Jenkins, lead singer; Keith Knudsen, drums; John McKee, guitar, fiddle.

A modern country-rock band, Southern Pacific are a 'supergroup' formed in Los Angeles in 1985, comprising ex-Doobie Brothers Keith Knudsen and John McKee, plus Stu Cook (formerly of Creedence Clearwater Revival), Kurt Howell (who had previously played with Waylon Jennings and Crystal Gayle) and Tim Goodman. They signed to Warner Brothers and made their debut on the charts with **Someone's Gonna Love Me Tonight** (1985).

Their self-titled album showed a strong resemblance to early Eagles, with Southern Pacific playing with all the energy of a blaring rock band but also free gliding and as poetic and graceful as classic country-rock outfits. Emmylou Harris added vocals to **Thing About You**, which became the band's first Top 20 country hit. This was followed by **Perfect Stranger**, but, just as the band was really beginning to take off, lead singer Goodman departed. He was replaced by David

Jo-El Sonnier's 1987 eponymous album. Courtesy RCA Records.

jo-El

TUMBLING TUMBLEWEEDS
COOL WATER
RIDERS IN THE SKY
RINGO
RED RIVER VALLEY

Jenkins, a former member of rock band Pablo Cruise, who also sang back-up vocals on the Huey Lewis album, **Fore**. The change didn't slow the band down as they scored a series of Top 10 hits with **Reno Bound** (1986), **New Shade Of Blue** (1988), **Honey, I Dare You** and **Anyway The Wind Blows** (1989), the latter from the film 'Pink Cadillac.'

Recommended:
Southern Pacific (Warner Bros/Warner Bros)
Zuma (Warner Bros/Warner Bros)
Country Line (Warner Bros/-)

Red Sovine

King of the truck-driving songs and narrations, Woodrow Wilson Sovine was born in Charleston, West Virginia on July 17, 1918. He learned guitar at an early age and tuned in to C&W radio stations, obtaining his own first radio job with Jim Pike's Carolina Tar Heels on WCHS, Charleston, West Virginia, in 1935. Later the unit moved on to play the WWVA Jamboree, Wheeling, West Virginia.

During the late 1940s, Sovine formed his own band, the Echo Valley Boys. He and the group gained their own show on WCHS. Then on June 3, 1949, Hank Williams left the Louisiana Hayride to become an Opry regular and Sovine's band was drafted in as a replacement, the Echo Valley Boys also taking over Williams' daily Johnny Fair Syrup Show stint.

Teddy Bear, Red Sovine. Courtesy RCA Records.

20 Of The Best, Sons Of The Pioneers. Courtesy RCA Records.

From 1949 until 1954, Sovine remained a star attraction on the Hayride, during that period striking up a friendship with Webb Pierce. The twosome performed duets on the show, combining to write songs and, in turn, both became Opry regulars. On disc they joined up for **Why, Baby Why?**, a country No.1 in 1956, following this with **Little Rosa**, a Top 10 hit that same year.

Though Sovine remained a top-rated performer throughout the late '50s and early '60s, his name disappeared from the charts until 1964, when a Starday release, **Dream House For Sale**, climbed into the listings. This was followed a few months later by **Giddyup Go**, which provided the singer with yet another No.1.

From that time on, Sovine continued adding to his list of chart honours, making a major impression in 1967 with **Phantom 309**. Then, in the mid-'70s, following a flood of recordings based on tales of CB radio, Sovine came into his own, achieving one of his biggest-ever successes with **Teddy Bear**, a highly sentimental tale regarding a crippled boy, his CB radio and a number of friendly truckers. He had, at the age of 58, finally earned a million-selling record.

Red was killed in a motor accident in Nashville on April 4, 1980, but had a posthumous British pop hit with **Teddy Bear** when it was re-released and reached No.2 in the charts in 1981, selling more than half-a-million copies.

Recommended:
Little Rosa (-/Release)
Teddy Bear (Starday/RCA)
Woodrow Wilson Sovine (Starday/-)
Classic Narrations (Starday/-)

Billie Jo Spears

Though she has a voice that is hardly in Opry tradition — take away the country backings and you are left with a bluesy sound befitting an uppercrust torch singer — Billie Jo was country-raised (born on January 14, 1937, Beaumont, Texas) and appeared on the Louisiana Hayride in her early teens. She performed **Too Old For Toys, Too Young For Boys**, a ditty which she recorded on the reverse of a Mel Blanc Bugs Bunny-type disc at the age of 13.

In 1964, country songwriter Jack Rhodes heard her sing and talked her into a trip to Nashville where she became signed to UA Records. However, her first country hit came with **He's Got More Love in His Little Finger**, a Capitol release of 1968. Billie Jo reached the Top 5 during the following year with **Mr Walker It's All Over**. Apart from an elongated chart stay with **Marty Gray** (1970), her other Capitol sides, though fair sellers, failed to emulate the success of **Mr Walker**.

A change of fortune occurred following a switch to UA in 1974. **Blanket On The Ground** (1975), a Roger Bowling song dealing with the delights of alfresco lovemaking, established Billie Jo with an international reputation.

Since then she has scored with **What I've Got In Mind**, **Misty Blue** (both 1976), **If You Want Me** (1977), **Lonely Hearts Club**, **'57 Chevrolet** (both 1978) and **I Will Survive** (1979). She has maintained her successes with **What I've Got In Mind** and **Sing Me An Old-Fashioned Song**, though in America she has failed to gain a contract with a major label for a number of years.

Recommended:
We Just Came Apart At The Dreams (-/Premier)
For The Good Times (-/Music For Pleasure)
Special Songs (Liberty/Liberty)
50 Original Tracks (-/EMI)
Ode To Billie Jo (-/Capitol)

Carl T. Sprague

Known as the 'Original Singing Cowboy', Sprague was born near Houston, Texas, in 1895. A cowboy music enthusiast in his college days, he led a band while at Texas A&M, playing on the campus radio station.

In August, 1925, inspired by Vernon Dalhart's hit record, **The Prisoner's Song**, he recorded ten songs for Victor. His initial release — **When The Work's All Done This Fall** — sold nine hundred thousand copies. Further sessions (in 1926, 1927 and 1929) ensued, at which Sprague recorded mainly traditional cowboy material from the late nineteenth century.

A man of many talents — including insurance salesman, Army officer, coach, garage operator, etc — Sprague, who settled in Bryan, Texas, performed at various folk festivals during the 1960s and recorded for the German Folk Variety label in 1972. Following a short illness, he died at his home in 1978.

Recommended:
Carl T. Sprague (-/Bear Family)
Classic Cowboy Songs (-/Bear Family)

Joe Stampley

Born on June 6, 1943, in Springhill, Louisiana, Stampley was influenced by both country entertainers and rock'n'rollers like the Everly Brothers and Jerry Lee Lewis. His first forays into recordings were made in 1959 when he cut some rock'n'roll records for Imperial and Chess.

Becoming a member of the Uniques, a pop outfit that had hits in the late '60s

with **Not Too Long Ago** and **All These Things**, Stampley started making a name for himself as a songwriter, signing with Gallico Music in Nashville. This led to a move towards country music and signing a contract with Dot Records in 1969.

He achieved a minor country hit via **Take Time To Know Her** (1971), finally making the Top 10 with **If You Touch Me (You've Got To Love Me)** in 1972 and achieving his first No.1 with **Soul Song** the following year. He achieved an impressive tally of major hits with such releases as **I'm Still Loving You** (1974), **Roll On Big Mama** (1975) — his first for Epic Records, **All These Things** (1976), **Everyday I Have To Cry Some** (1977), **Do You Ever Fool Around** (1978) and **Put Your Clothes Back On** (1979).

In 1979 Stampley teamed up with Moe Bandy, resulting in a No.1 hit with **Just Good Ole Boys** and the Top Vocal Duo award by the ACM (1979) and CMA (1980). Stampley consolidated his position in the '80s with such hits as **There's Another Woman** (1980), **Whiskey Chasin'** (1981), **Back Slidin'** (1982) and **Double Shot Of My Baby's Love** (1983), plus more duets with Moe Bandy, including the 1984 chart-topper **Where's The Dress**.

Recommended:
Soul Song (-/Ember)
Saturday Nite Dance (Epic/-)
Ten Songs About Her (Epic/-)
After Hours (Epic/-)
I'm Goin' Hurtin' (Epic/-)

Stanley Brothers

Responsible for some of the most beautiful harmony vocals ever to emerge from the bluegrass scene, guitarist and lead vocalist Carter Glen Stanley (born in McClure, Virginia, on August 27, 1925) and his brother, banjoist and vocalist Ralph Edmond Stanley (born in Stratton, Virginia, on February 25, 1927) formed an old-time band, the Stanley Brothers And The Clinch Mountain Boys, in 1946, and began broadcasting on radio station WCYB, Bristol, Virginia.

Recording for the small Rich-R-Tone label in 1948, they cut **Molly And Tenbrooks**. The band switched direction and played in the bluegrass style of Bill Monroe with Ralph Stanley utilizing the three-finger method of banjo playing popularized by Earl Scruggs.

In March 1949, the Stanleys signed for Columbia Records and began cutting a series of classic bluegrass sides (all vocals), retaining mandolin player and vocalist Pee Wee Lambert from their previous band and adding various fiddle and bass players at different sessions. George Shuffler replaced Lambert and became part of the Stanley Brothers' sound just prior to the band's last Columbia session in April 1952.

Throughout the '50s and '60s, the Stanleys recorded for such labels as Mercury, Starday and King, often cutting purely religious material. They also engaged on many tours, playing a prestigious date at London's Albert Hall as part of their European tour in March, 1966. But it was to be the Stanley Brothers' only British appearance. Carter Stanley died in a Bristol, Virginia hospital on December 1 that same year.

Since his brother's death, Ralph Stanley has kept the tradition of the Clinch Mountain Boys alive — though his music

Above: Bluegrass harmony vocal duo Carter (left) and Ralph Stanley.

has become increasingly traditional in character.

The music of the Stanleys has been reactivated by younger artists like Emmylou Harris, Dan Fogelberg and Chris Hillman, who have used many of the brothers' classics in their repertoires.

Recommended:
Recorded Live Volumes 1 & 2 (Rebel/–)
The Best Of (Starday/–)

Left: Kenny Starr started his career by appearing with Loretta Lynn.

Saturday Night And Sunday Morning (Freeland/–)

Ralph Stanley:
Ralph Stanley, A Man And His Music (Rebel/–)
Old Country Church (Rebel/–)

Kenny Starr

Loretta Lynn protégé Kenny Starr was born in Topeka, Kansas on September 21, 1953, his family later moving to Burlingame, Kansas, where Starr grew up.

At an early age he began visiting the local Veterans Of Foreign Wars hall, where he would unplug the jukebox and sing for nickles and dimes. By the age of nine he was leading his first band, the Rockin' Rebels. This was quickly superseded by another group, Kenny And The Imperials, which toured the area, earning Starr 10 to 15 dollars a night.

At 16 he became a country entertainer, initially leading a band called the Country Showman, later winning a talent contest held in Wichita after singing his version of Ray Price's **I Won't Mention It Again**.

Local promoter Hap Peebles saw Starr's performance on the show and asked if he would appear on a forthcoming Loretta Lynn and Conway Twitty concert, which Starr did, winning a standing ovation. After the concert, Loretta offered him a job in her own road show. She also helped him obtain a recording contract with MCA.

A singer-songwriter-guitarist, Starr had a No.1 country hit with his own **The Blind Man In The Bleachers** in January, 1976. He followed this with minor successes **Tonight I Face The Man Who Made It Happen** (1976), **Hold Tight** (1977) and **Slow Drivin'** (1978), before mysteriously fading from the limelight.

Recommended:
The Blind Man In The Bleachers (MCA/–)

The Statler Brothers

The Statlers vocal group originally consisted of Philip Balsley (born Augusta County, Virginia, August 8, 1939), Don Reid (born Staunton, Virginia, June 5, 1945), Harold Reid (born Augusta County, Virginia, August 21, 1939) and Lew DeWitt (born Roanoke County, Virginia, March 8, 1938). The Statlers – first Harold (bass), Lew (tenor) and Phil (baritone) – began singing together in 1955 at Lyndhurst Methodist Church in Staunton, Virginia. In 1960, Harold's younger brother Don joined the group – then known as the Kingsmen – and became front-man. The quartet passed an audition to become part of the Johnny Cash Show some three years later. At this point, they changed their name to the Statler Brothers after espying the name Statler on a box of tissues in a hotel room.

In 1965 they went further up the ladder after recording **Flowers On The Wall**, a song penned by DeWitt. This Columbia release became a Top 5 pop hit, also gaining a high place on the country charts. The group won two Grammy awards as a consequence.

Further hits followed – **Ruthless** and **You Can't Have Your Kate And Edith Too** (both 1967) proving among the most popular – but it was not until 1970 and a new recording contract with Mercury that the Statlers moved into top gear, immediately gaining a second cross-over hit with **Bed Of Roses**.

They became the undisputed kings of country vocal groups, winning a Grammy in 1972 for Best Vocal Performance for **Class Of '57** and scoring such major country hits as **I'll Go To My Grave Loving You** (1975), **Do You Know You Are My Sunshine**, **Who Am I To Say** (1978), **Charlotte's Web** (1980), **Don't Wait On Me** (1981) and **You'll Be Back (Every Night In My Dreams)** (1982). They were voted CMA Vocal Group Of The Year every year from 1972 to 1977, and then again in 1979 and 1980.

Due to ill-health, Lew DeWitt retired from the group in July 1982, though he did briefly pursue a solo career, releasing the album **On My Own** in 1985. He died from Crohn's disease in Waynesboro, Virginia on August 15, 1990. His place in the group was taken by Jimmy Fortune, who not only brought a high, clear tenor singing voice to the Statlers, but also a songwriting talent, penning several of their subsequent country hits. These continued with **Oh Baby Mine (I Get So Lonely)** and the chart-topping **Elizabeth** (1983), **Atlanta Blue** (1984), two more No.1s with **My Only Love** and **Too Much On My Heart**, plus a revival of **Hello Mary Lou** (all 1985), **Count On Me** (1986) and **Forever**

Left: The Statler Brothers have their own TV show on TNN.

Sing Country Symphonies In E Major (Mercury/–)
The Originals (Mercury/–)
Pardners In Rhyme (Mercury/Mercury)
10th Anniversary (Mercury/–)
Music Memories And You (Mercury/–)
Four For The Show (Mercury/Mercury)
Radio Gospel Favorites (Mercury/–)
Words And Music (Mercury/–)

Red Steagall

Russell 'Red' Steagall was born on December 22, 1937 in Gainesville, Texas. Polio struck when he was 15, leaving Steagall without the use of his left hand and arm. He used months of therapy and recuperation to master the guitar and mandolin, and later began playing in coffee houses during his stay at West Texas State University. His first job found him working for an oil company as a soil chemistry expert, with performing remaining a sideline until 1967 when **Here We Go**

If You've Got The Time, I've Got The Song, Red Steagall. Courtesy Capitol Records.

Again, a Steagall original penned with the aid of co-writer Don Lanier, provided Ray Charles with a chart record.

Other Steagall songs subsequently found their way on to disc, and the Texan became involved on the song publishing side of the industry, eventually signing a recording contract with Dot in 1969.

He joined Capitol Records in 1972, coming up with such hit singles as **Party Dolls And Wine**, **Somewhere My Love** (both 1972) and **Someone Cares For You** (1974). He then rejoined ABC-Dot, finally making the Top 10 with **Lone Star Beer And Bob Wills Music** (1976). That success was short-lived, though he has recorded some fine albums, mainly with a western swing or cowboy feel.

In 1974, he helped Reba McEntire get started. He produced her first demo recordings in Nashville, which resulted in her being signed to Mercury Records. An in-demand rodeo performer, Red has become a real singing cowboy. He has his own ranch just outside Fort Worth, Texas, and plays a major role in keeping alive the music of the cowboy. In 1991 he was named 'Cowboy Poet of Texas' by the State Legislature, and is also responsible for organizing the annual Cowboy Gathering and Western Swing Festival in Fort Worth, Texas. Early 1993 saw Red gain a contract with Warner Brothers Records' spin-off label, Warner Western.

Nashville, Ray Stevens. A self-produced album for Barnaby Records.

Recommended:
Red Steagall (MCA-Dot/–)
Cowboy Favorites (Delta/Silver Dollar)
Party Dolls And Wine (Capitol/–)
Lone Star Beer And Bob Wills Music (ABC-Dot/–)

Keith Stegall

A talented Nashville-based songwriter, Keith (born in 1955 in Wichita Falls, Texas, the son of Bob Stegall who played steel guitar for Johnny Horton) has seen his songs score on the country, pop, R&B, adult contemporary and jazz charts.

At the age of eight he made his stage debut on a country music show in Tyler, Texas, and before he reached his teens he had formed his own four-piece combo called the Pacesetters. Keith's family moved to Shreveport, Louisiana and he joined a folk group, the Cheerful Givers.

By this time he was busy writing songs while holding down a job as a night-club singer. Urged to make a move to Nashville, Stegall became a staff writer for CBS Songs (then called April/Blackwood) in 1978. He rapidly distinguished himself as a writer for the likes of Al Jarreau (**We're In This Love Together**), Leon Everette (**Hurricane**), Dr Hook (**Sexy Eyes**), Mickey Gilley (**Lonely Nights**) and the Commodores (**The Woman In My Life**).

After a brilliant start as a songwriter, Keith made a dismal recording artist, signing with Capitol in 1980 and making the lower rungs of the charts with **The Fool Who Fooled Around**. Never able to score higher than the mid-'50s with Capitol (and subsequently with its sister label EMI America), Keith signed with Epic in 1984 and made No.25 with **I Want To Go Somewhere**, followed by **Whatever Turns You On** (No.19), **California** (No.13) and cracked the Top 10 in 1985 with the self-penned **Pretty Lady**.

He has continued to concentrate on his writing, coming up with hits for such varied artists as Kenny Rogers, Juice Newton, Charley Pride, Johnny Mathis, Reba McEntire and Glen Campbell. Increasingly Stegall has turned to production, and has been responsible for all three of Alan Jackson's platinum albums.

Recommended:
Keith Stegall (Epic/–)

Ray Stevens

A talented singer-songwriter, arranger, producer and multi-instrumentalist, Stevens (born Ray Ragsdale in Clarkdale, Georgia, 1939) studied music at Georgia State University. He then moved to Nashville where he began recording such

(1987). While the hits started to become less frequent, the Statlers have maintained a very strong fan base, and, apart from 1983, have won the MCN fan-voted award as Top Vocal Group every year from 1971 through to 1992. Since 1991 they have hosted their own TV variety series on TNN, one of the most popular country shows of all time. The Statlers' name is associated with a certain meticulous attention to detail, an immediately recognizable sound and an almost unflagging compositional quality. Their most recent country hit came with **More Than A Name On A Wall**, a Top 10 entry in 1989, although they continue to produce excellent albums.

Recommended:
Today (Mercury/Mercury)

Oh Happy Day, Statler Brothers. Courtesy CBS Records.

novelty hits as **Jeremiah Peabody's Poly Unsaturated Quick Dissolving Fast Acting Pleasant Tasting Green And Purple Pills** (1961), **Ahab The Arab** (1962), **Harry The Hairy Ape** (1963), **Mr Businessman** (1968) and **Gitarzan** (1969).

Since the end of the '60s Stevens, who has recorded for such labels as Judd, Mercury, Monument, Barnaby, Janus, Warner, RCA and MCA, has turned increasingly to country music, scoring with such discs as **Turn Your Radio On** (1971), **Nashville** (1973) and a semi-bluegrass version of **Misty** (1975), for which he was awarded a Grammy for Best Arrangement Accompanying A Vocalist.

From time to time he still produces pieces of sheer lunacy like **The Streak** (a pop No.1 in 1974), **Shriner's Convention** (1980), **Mississippi Squirrel Revival** (1984) and **It's Me Again, Margaret** (1985). In 1990 he opened his own theatre in Branson, Missouri, but, following the success of his 1992 Greatest Hits Comedy Video, which sold 1.6 million copies and topped the 'Billboard' video chart for months, Stevens was looking to expand his career in 1993 by working on a TV series and making a sideways step into movies.

Recommended:
Misty (Barnaby/Janus)
He Thinks He's Ray Stevens (MCA/MCA)
Beside Myself (MCA/MCA)

Gary Stewart

An exciting honky-tonk singer-songwriter whose vibrato-filled voice places him in a love or hate category, Stewart was born on May 28, 1945, in Letcher County, Kentucky, moving to Florida with his family when he was 12.

His recording career began in 1964 with **I Loved You Truly**. Stewart then went on the road, playing bass with the Amps, a rock outfit, eventually returning home to work for an aircraft firm.

In 1967 he met Bill Eldridge, an ex-rocker who had contacts in Nashville. Together they began writing songs, one becoming a minor hit for Stonewall Jackson. Others included: **Sweet Thang And Cisco**, a 1969 hit for Nat Stuckey; **When A Man Loves A Woman** and **She Goes Walking Through My Mind**, both 1970 Top 5 discs for Billy Walker; and other material for such artists as Kenny Price, Jack Greene, Johnny Paycheck, Cal Smith, Hank Snow and Warner Mack.

But, with his own recording contract with Kapp petering out, Stewart returned to Fort Pierce, Florida, leaving behind some demo sessions he had made of Motown material.

These demos were later heard by Roy Dea, a Mercury producer who was subsequently signed to RCA by Jerry Bradley. He immediately signed Stewart for his new label, his belief in the singer paying off when Stewart's **Drinkin' Thing**, a second-time-around release, became a Top 10 hit in 1974.

Since that time, Stewart has had other major chart discs with **Out Of Hand** (1975), **She's Actin' Single (I'm Drinkin' Doubles)** (1975), **In Some Room Above The Street** (1976), **Ten Years Of This** (1977) and **Whiskey Trip** (1978).

In 1982, Gary teamed up with singer-songwriter Dean Dillon, and the two wild honky-tonkers came up with some dynamic numbers, like **Brotherly Love** (1982) and

Smokin' In The Rockies (1983), but failed to make their mark with the record-buying public.

A reputation for heavy drinking mixed with drug addiction saw Stewart's career fall apart. His wife left him and his son committed suicide as Stewart retreated to the Florida honky-tonk circuit, where he felt most at home. He recorded briefly for the local Red Ash Records in 1984, then resurfaced to national prominence at the end of the '80s, when he signed with the California-based Hightone Records. There was a handful of minor country hits, including **Brand New Whiskey** and **An Empty Glass** (1988), while the album **Brand New** made the charts in 1989.

Recommended:
Little Junior (RCA/–)
Brotherly Love – with Dean Dillon (RCA/–)
Battlefield (Hightone/–)
Brand New (Hightone/–)
Gary's Greatest (Hightone/–)

John Stewart

With over a dozen albums to his name as a solo performer, singer-songwriter John Stewart (born on September 5, 1939 in San Diego, California) has been a major influence on the American country and rock scene for more than 20 years.

He played rock'n'roll in his youth, but soon turned to folk music. A prolific writer, he performed a couple of his songs for the Kingston Trio backstage after one of their concerts. The Trio liked the songs **Green**

Above: Hard-drinking honky-tonker Gary Stewart lives out the lyrics to his songs in real life.

Grasses and **Molly Dee**, which led to John being asked to form a similar folk trio by Roulette Records. the result was the Cumberland Three, who recorded three albums for the New York-based label between 1959 and 1961.

When founder member Dave Guard left the Kingston Trio at the end of 1961, John was asked to join them. This was after the days of **Tom Dooley**, but before the beat explosion, and the Trio were big news. However, despite appearing before mass audiences and playing an important part in the Trio, John never felt a real part of the Trio, or happy with the 'college fraternity' lifestyle they led. Indeed, for the whole six years he was with them, until the break-up in 1967, he was on a salary.

Cannons In The Rain, John Stewart. Courtesy RCA Records.

Judging by his subsequent music, the split must have been a welcome relief. He was far more in touch with other artists and once before nearly left the Trio to form a new group with John Phillips (of the Mamas And Papas) and Scott McKenzie. For a while he hung out with John Denver and, though they never went out as a duo, they recorded demos of **Leaving On A Jet Plane** and **Daydream Believer**. The latter song became a multi-million seller for the Monkees in 1967, Stewart surviving for years on the revenue from the song.

Stewart next found himself with Buffy Ford, and together they recorded **Signals Through The Glass**, an album based around the paintings of Andrew Wyeth. In the late '60s he worked on the Bobby Kennedy election campaign and utilized some of his experiences in the song **Omaha Rainbow**.

Throughout the '70s John recorded a series of albums as he moved through such labels as Capitol, Warners and RCA. **California Bloodlines**, recorded for Capitol in 1969 and produced by Nick Venet in Nashville, is counted as something of a milestone. Further albums featured the talents of such musicians and singers as James Taylor, Carole King, Doug Kershaw, Chris Darrow, James Burton, Glen D. Hardin, Buddy Emmons, Fred Carter Jr, Pete Drake and Charlie McCoy. But at the centre were John's songs.

He built up a sizeable cult following, especially in Britain, where a magazine, Omaha Rainbow, is named after one of his songs. Finally he achieved the commercial success he deserved when his second album for RSO Records, **Bombs Away**

Dream Babies, made the Top 10 album charts and his single Gold reached Top 5 and won John a gold disc in 1979.

This, however, turned out to be a short-lived success, and during the '80s John Stewart was once again relegated to cult hero status, a singer-songwriter who appeals to the more discerning music lovers. He penned Rosanne Cash's chart-topping Runaway Train, and she has worked closely with Stewart, even borrowing from his sound and style for some of her own recordings. He continues to please dedicated fans with regular album releases, which are now issued on small independent labels.

Recommended:

California Bloodlines (Capitol/Capitol)
The Phoenix Concerts (RCA/RCA)
Forgotten Songs Of Some Old Yesterday (RCA/RCA)
Bombs Away Dream Babies (RSO/RSO)
Blondes (Allegiance/Line)
Bullets In The Hourglass (Shanachie/–)
Cannons In The Rain/Wingless Angels (–/Bear Family)
Lonesome Picker Rides Again (Warner Bros/Line)

Redd Stewart

Henry Redd Stewart, born in Ashland City, Tennessee, on May 27, 1921, began his career by writing a song for a car dealer's commercial at the age of 14. He then formed and played in bands around the Louisville, Kentucky area until 1937, when Pee Wee King came to Louisville to play on radio station WHAS and signed Stewart as a musician. Eddy Arnold was the band's vocalist at the time, although Redd was Eddy's replacement when Arnold went solo. Then came Pearl Harbor, and Stewart was drafted for Army service in the South Pacific, during which period he wrote A Soldier's Last Letter, a major hit for Ernest Tubb.

After the war he rejoined King and began taking a serious interest in songwriting, teaming with King to write Tennessee Waltz (a hit for both King and Cowboy Copas but a 1950 six-million-seller for Patti Page), following this with Slow Poke (a 1951 gold disc for King), You Belong To Me (which, in the Joe Stafford version, topped the US charts for five

weeks during 1952), and the reworked old fiddle tune, Bonaparte's Retreat.

Stewart's own career on disc has been less successful – despite stints with such labels as RCA, Starday, King and Hickory – and it seems that he will generally be remembered for his songwriting and his 30-year association with Pee Wee King.

Recommended:

The Best Of Pee Wee King And Redd Stewart (Starday/–)

Wynn Stewart

Born in Morrisville, Missouri on June 7, 1934, singer-songwriter Stewart received early singing experience in church, and at 13 appeared on KWTO, Springfield, Missouri. A year or so later his family moved to California and this was where he made his first recording at the age of 15.

During the mid-'50s, Stewart became signed to Capitol Records, later switching to Jackpot Records, a subsidiary of Challenge. His song Above And Beyond provided a big hit for Buck Owens in 1960,

while some of Stewart's own Jackpot sides featured the voice of Jan Howard. For Challenge itself, Stewart provided such hits as Wishful Thinking (1959), Big Big Day (1961) and Another Day, Another Dollar (1962), around that period opening up his club in Las Vegas and appearing on his own TV show.

Some two and a half years later he sold the club and moved to California, signing once more for Capitol and promoting his discs by touring with a new band, the Tourists. Purveying his California style of honky-tonk and beer-stained ballads, Stewart made friends and influenced record buyers. The result was a flow of country chart entries that has included: It's Such A Pretty World Today (a No.1 in 1967), 'Cause I Have You (1967), Love's Gonna Happen To Me (1967), Something Pretty (1968), In Love (1968), World-Wide Travelin' Man (1969) and It's A Beautiful Day (1970).

Moving through a succession of labels, he made a chart comeback with After The

Below: Redd Stewart, a songwriter whose Tennessee Waltz was a hit for Patti Page (1950) and others.

Love (1993). Stone's first three albums, all produced by Doug Johnson, have gone gold.

Recommended:
From The Heart (Epic/Epic)
The First Christmas (Epic/–)
I Thought It Was You (Epic/–)
Doug Stone (Epic/–)

Stoneman Family

One of the most famous groups in country music, the Stonemans revolved around Ernest V. 'Pop' Stoneman (born in Monorat, Carroll County, Virginia, on May 25, 1893), a carpenter who wrote to Okeh and Columbia seeking an audition in 1924.

A jew's-harp and harmonica player by the age of ten, and a banjoist and autoharp player in his teens, Pop was eventually heard by Okeh's Ralph Peer, who recorded some test sides in September, 1924, cutting a number of sides the following January. These included **The Sinking Of The Titanic**, one of the biggest-selling records of the '20s.

Between 1925 and 1929 Pop, sometimes with his wife or other members of his family, cut well over 200 titles for Okeh, Gennett, Paramount, Victor and other companies, also playing on dates with such acts as Riley Puckett and Uncle Dave Macon.

Having spent their royalties on cars and other luxuries, the Depression of 1929 hit

Ernest V. Stoneman And The Blue Ridge Corn Shuckers. Courtesy Rounder Records.

the Stonemans hard. Only one recording date, featuring Pop and his son Eddie, emanated from this period, and Pop had to resume his former occupation as a carpenter in a Washington DC naval gun factory. Meanwhile, his wife Hattie struggled to bring up her family – which eventually numbered 13 children.

Several of the children became musicians and Pop formed a family band during the late '40s, playing in the Washington area and recording an album for Folkways in 1957 that helped spark off a whole new career.

Proving popular at the major folk festivals and on college dates, the Stonemans became an in-demand outfit, making their debut on the Grand Ole Opry and recording for Starday in 1962.

During the mid '60s the family moved to Nashville, appeared on the Jimmy Dean ABC-TV show, and were signed to appear in their own TV show, Those Stonemans, in 1966. A year later, they won the CMA award for the Best Vocal Group. The band then consisted of Pop (guitar, autoharp),

Above: Singer-songwriter Wynn Stewart was singing in his hometown church at five and was appearing regularly on radio at 13. He scored masses of hits in the '60s.

Storm, which reached the Top 10 in 1976. Subsequent releases failed to bring him the chart success he deserved, and Wynn continued recording for small labels up until shortly before his death at his home in Hendersonville, Tennessee, on July 17, 1985.

Recommended:
After The Storm (Playboy/–)
Baby It's Yours (Capitol/–)
Wishful Thinking (–/Bear Family)

Doug Stone

The man with one of the saddest voices in country music, Stone was born Doug Brooks in 1957, in Newnan, Georgia. He changed his name to avoid confusion with Garth Brooks, and, as he had just written a song **Heart Of Stone**, decided that Stone was a natural choice. Before arriving in

Nashville in 1989, Doug had spent years playing the clubs of Georgia. A multi-instrumentalist who can play guitar, keyboards, fiddle and drums, he made his professional debut at 11, playing drums with the Country Rhythm Playboys. Prior to this, he had a moment of glory when he was seven, being invited by Loretta Lynn to get up onstage and play guitar with her. His mother used to sing around the house and encouraged young Doug, but, when he was 12, his parents separated, and he went to live with his father. After dropping out of high school, Doug had many jobs, mainly as an auto mechanic, but also worked as a carpenter, a lawn-mower mechanic and in a hamburger joint. He married in his early 20s, but family life and playing in dead-end bar bands was not easy, and later he divorced.

Doug built a little studio in his house, and also started his own dump truck business, as he chased a dream of being a singing star. In 1987 he lost everything, but his fortunes were revived when he was signed to an artist management contract by Phyllis Bennett. A demo reached producer Doug Johnson, and that was followed by a recording deal with Epic Records in Nashville in 1989.

His debut record, **I'd Be Better Off (In A Pine Box)**, a classic country weeper, rose to No.4 on the country charts in 1990. Further Top 10 success came with **Fourteen Minutes Old** and **These Lips Don't Know How To Say Goodbye**, then he hit the top with **In A Different Light** (1991). With his Stone Age Band, Doug took to the road. A hyperactive person, his fast-paced show with fancy dancing and pure showmanship was at odds with his slow, sad-tinged, country ballads which were dominating the country charts. He scored another Top 10 hit with **I Thought It Was You** (1991), then showed off his ability with an uptempo, honky-tonker in his second chart-topper, **A Jukebox With A Country Song** (1991). The hectic life on the road took its toll on Doug's health, and on the day of the 1992 ACM Awards Show, with him nominated for Top Male Artist and Top Song, he was undergoing emergency quadruple heart bypass surgery. Suitably recovered, Stone has continued in his hit-making way with a mixture of songs about romance carved in song, many with a witty twang about them. He scored Top 10 with **Made For Lovin' You** and **Warning Labels** (1992), and another No.1 with **Too Busy Being In**

Mel Street's Greatest Hits. Courtesy GRT Records.

dozen records reaching No.1, including: **Fool Hearted Memory** (1982), **A Fire I Can't Put Out** (1983), **You Look So Good In Love, Does Fort Worth Ever Cross Your Mind** (1984), **The Chair** (1985), **It Ain't Cool To Be Crazy About You** (1986), **Ocean Front Property** (1987), **Famous Last Words Of A Fool** (1988), **Love Without End, Amen** (5 weeks, 1990) and **I've Come To Expect It From You** (5 weeks, 1990). He also amassed a huge number of gold and platinum albums, and was named CMA Male Vocalist Of The Year in 1985 and 1986, and Entertainer Of The Year in 1988 and 1990.

It was Strait's first album, **Strait Country**, that persuaded a rock-crazy kid named Garth Brooks to switch to country when he was in high school. From the beginning Strait has kept to his image of cowboy hat, straight-legged jeans and tailored western shirts, his sound and look becoming a much-duplicated symbol in late '80s country. There's never been any great themes in his many albums, just a 'Strait' country mix of those twin fiddles, steel guitar, Texas two-steps and sparsely produced ballads. He's never allowed the new crop of performers to affect his popularity, and the chart-topping singles have continued with **You Know Me Better Than That** (1991), **So Much Like My Dad** (1992) and **Heartland** (1993).

Strait reached a new plateau in his career when he took his first serious steps into the movies to star as country singer Rusty Wyatt Chandler in 'Pure Country', a 1992 film specially written for him. It became a major box office success and the soundtrack album, the first of his recordings to be produced by Tony Brown, became his biggest seller. He remains the biggest star of country music, with a level of consistency second-to-none. He grosses $10 million a year and broke Elvis' record for consecutive sell-out shows in Las Vegas.

Recommended:
Something Special (MCA/MCA)
Strait From The Heart (MCA/MCA)
Does Fort Worth Ever Cross Your Mind (MCA/MCA)
Holdin' My Own (MCA/MCA)
Chill Of An Early Fall (MCA/MCA)
Beyond The Blue Neon (MCA/MCA)
Livin' It Up (MCA/MCA)
Ocean Front Property (MCA/MCA)

Mel Street

One of the finest country singers to emerge in the '70s, Mel (born on October 21, 1933 in Grundy, West Virginia), never really achieved the success or recognition he so richly deserved.

Scotty (fiddle), Jim (bass), Van (guitar), Donna (mandolin) and Roni (banjo), the last-named becoming a star on the Hee Haw TV show.

However, a stomach ailment began to affect Pop and he died in Nashville on June 14, 1968, his last recording session having taken place that day.

Although the Stonemans were considered one of the finest semi-bluegrass bands, Pop's early record output with his Dixie Mountaineers featured nineteenth-century sentimental ballads, British traditional melodies, dance tunes, religious material and even a number of

humorous sketches. He was reputed to have been the first musician to record with an autoharp.

Recommended:
In The Family (MGM/–)
The Stoneman Family (Folkways/–)
The Stonemans (MGM/–)
Stoneman's Country (MGM/–)
Tribute To Pop Stoneman (MGM/–)

George Strait

George Strait, born May 18, 1952, in Pearsall, Texas, emerged in the early '80s as one of the best exponents of unvarnished, clean-cut country music. When he first started recording in 1981, his authentic country sound, with twin fiddle breaks and strong steel guitar, seemed to breathe fresh air into the somewhat stale Nashville scene.

Born the second son of a junior high school teacher, George was raised on a ranch in Texas. After a short spell at

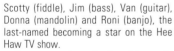

Something Special, George Strait. Courtesy MCA Records.

Above: George Strait is a huge star with a string of hits to his credit in the '80s and '90s.

college, George eloped with his high school sweetheart, Norma, and then joined the US Army.

While stationed in Hawaii, George started singing with a country band, using the songs of Merle Haggard, Bob Wills, George Jones and Hank Williams.

After his discharge in 1975, George returned to Texas and attended the Southwest Texas State University to complete his degree in agriculture. By this time he had been bitten by the music bug and, assembling his Ace In The Hole Band, was soon living a double life, attending classes by day and playing the clubs at night.

George and his band had built up a strong following on the southwest Texas honky-tonk circuit when, through the efforts of Erv Woolsey, a one-time MCA promotions man, he landed an MCA recording contract in early 1981. His first single, **Unwound**, reached the Top 10 in the country charts.

Strait spent more time at the top of the country singles charts than any other performer in the '80s, with more than two

He started out singing on local radio shows in the early '50s and, following his marriage, moved to Niagara Falls, New York. For several years he sang in a local night spot and eventually had enough money saved to return to West Virginia, where he opened his own automobile workshop.

With his four-piece band, Mel had his own television show in Bluefield, West Virginia called Country Showcase, at the same time working in local clubs and honky-tonks. Eventually he gained a recording contract with the small Tandem Records, releasing his first single, **House Of Pride**, in 1970.

It was the other side of the record, Mel's self-penned **Borrowed Angel**, that gained most response from the public, eventually making the country Top 10 during 1972. During the next few years, Mel recorded for a variety of labels, achieving Top 20 hits with **Lovin' On Back Streets** (1972), **Walk Softly On The Bridges** (1973), **Forbidden Angel** (1974), **Smokey Mountain Memories** (1975), **I Met A Friend Of Yours Today** (1976) and **Close Enough For Lonesome** (1977).

An excellent song stylist who specialized in honky-tonk sagas and bar-room ditties, Mel was the first singer to record the songs of such writers as Eddie Rabbitt, Earl Thomas Conley and John Schweers, and was one of the best intrepreters of Bob McDill material, scoring with **Shady Rest**, **Barbara Don't Let Me Be The Last To Know** and filling his albums with McDill's songs.

Depressed due to a heavy workload and personal problems, Mel shot himself at his Hendersonville home on October 21, 1978 – his 45th birthday.

Recommended:
Smokey Mountain Memories (GRT/–)
Country Soul (Polydor/–)
Many Moods Of Mel Street (Sunbird/–)

Stringbean

Born in Annville, Kentucky, on June 17, 1915, Stringbean's real name was David Akeman, and he was the son of a fine banjo player. Stringbean made his own first banjo at the age of 12 and began playing professionally six years later in the Lexington area, eventually working with Cy Rogers' Lonesome Pine Fiddlers on radio station WLAP.

It was during this period that the performer became dubbed Stringbean and adopted a more comic direction with his act. During the late '30s, he worked with Charlie Monroe, then joined Bill Monroe on the Grand Ole Opry in July, 1942, staying with Monroe for three years.

Also known as the 'Kentucky Wonder', Stringbean was an outstanding banjo player in the style of Uncle Dave Macon and a long-time member of the Opry, but perhaps won even more fame through his appearances on the Hee Haw TV series. He died on November 10, 1973, he and his wife Estelle being brutally murdered on returning home from the Opry and discovering burglars in their house.

Recommended:
Salute To Uncle Dave Macon (Starday/–)
Me And My Old Crow (Nugget/–)

Marty Stuart

Proud to be a hillbilly singer, John Marty Stuart was born on September 30, 1958, in Philadelphia, Missouri. A multi-instrumentalist who is at home on guitar, bass, mandolin, fiddle and upright bass, he

Below: Marty Stuart keeps traditions while maintaining a contemporary edge in his music.

was raised on country and made his first professional appearance at 13 with Carl and Pearl Butler. A few months later Marty was touring with Lester Flatt And The Nashville Grass, making his debut on the Grand Ole Opry before he was 14. He stayed with Flatt for eight years, until the bluegrass legend died in 1979. Stuart opted then to stay in Nashville, where he built his reputation as a studio musician, before joining Johnny Cash's band in the early '80s. He married Cash's daughter, Cindy, but it was a short-lived and turbulent liaison and they were soon divorced.

Stuart produced his first solo album, **Busy Bee Café**, in 1982. Released on the independent Sugar Hill label, the session band used attested to his reputation as picker, and included Doc Watson, Merle Watson and Johnny Cash on guitars, Jerry Douglas on dobro and Carl Jackson on banjo. Marty was on the road with Johnny Cash for the best part of six years, but he will managed to cram studio and concert work into his busy schedule, working for Bob Dylan, Billy Joel, Roger Miller, Willie Nelson, Emmylou Harris and others. He signed with Columbia Records in 1986, making the Top 20 with **Arlene**, but subsequent singles were only minor hits. His **Marty Stuart** album did poorly, and a follow-up, **Let There Be Country**, was never issued at the time. Deciding to get back to his roots, Marty hooked up with the Sullivans, a family gospel group with whom he had previously sung as a child. He played on and produced their **A Joyful Noise** album.

In 1989, he was signed by MCA Records, at this time building a high-profile image with his puffed-up, long, ebony hair – possibly the longest among country music performers. Initially his MCA recordings didn't take off, but with the help of videos that put across the visual side of Marty Stuart, he enjoyed Top 10 singles with **Hillbilly Rock**, **Little Things** (1990) and **Tempted** (1991). He made the headlines for his unique collection of country mementoes – he has a silver eagle tour bus (E.T.), which once belonged to Ernest Tubb, a trio of guitars that were originally owned by Lester Flatt, Hank Williams Sr and Clarence White, and sparkly rhinestone suits that were popular in the '50s and '60s. Far from trendy, Stuart describes himself as looking like "a cross between Roy Rogers, Porter Wagoner and Gene Autry", and his music as "rocking hillbilly music with a thump".

His career was given a big boost after he wrote **The Whiskey Ain't Workin'**, and sent it to Warner Brothers for Hank Williams Jr or Travis Tritt to record. The young Tritt decided to cut it, calling in Stuart to harmonize, and the result was a No.2 country smash in early 1992. Stuart and Tritt then got together for a highly successful 'No Hats Tour' that ran all the way through 1992. This helped Stuart's second MCA album, **Tempted**, to build up sales of more than 300,000, while his solo singles **Burn Me Down** and **Now That's Country** charted highly in 1992. A third MCA album, **This One's Gonna Hurt You**, found Stuart achieving a near flawless integration of southern rock, bluegrass, blues, honky-tonk, boogie and rockabilly. Travis dropped by to duet on the title song, another big-selling single. In the meantime, Marty Stuart is fulfilling his long-held ambition of taking country music, its legends and history, to a new younger audience. An accomplished writer and photographer, he has had his photos

published in country music magazines and contributed several articles to music publications.

Recommended:
This One's Gonna Hurt You (MCA/–)
Hillbilly Rock (MCA/–)
Busy Bee Café (Sugar Hill/–)
Tempted (MCA/–)

Nat Stuckey

Perhaps an underrated performer – though he has been a consistent supplier of medium-sized hits – Nat Stuckey was born in Cass County, Texas, on December 17, 1937. Employed for some considerable time as a radio announcer, Stuckey also worked with a jazz group in 1957–58, becoming leader of a country band, the Corn Huskers, in 1958–59.

In 1966, Buck Owens recorded his fellow Texan's **Waitin' In The Welfare Line**. At this stage Stuckey, who had been working with the Louisiana Hayriders and recording for the Sims label, switched to Paula Records, scoring his own Top 10 hit with **Sweet Thang**.

Seven chart records later, in 1968, he label-hopped once more, this time signing for RCA and immediately scoring five major disc successes with **Plastic Saddle** (1968). **Joe And Mabel's 12th Street Bar And Grill**, **Cut Across Shorty**, **Sweet Thang And Cisco** and **Young Love** (all 1969), the last a duet with Connie Smith.

Stuckey never really enjoyed the quota of potent singles expected of him, only **She Wakes Every Morning With A Kiss** (1970) and **Take Time To Love Her** (1973) establishing his name in the upper regions of the charts.

During the mid-'70s, he became an MCA artist, scoring Top 20 hits with **Sun Comin' Up** (1976) and **The Days Of Sand And Shovels** (1978), and producing **Independence**, an album acclaimed by the critics. However, he still failed to achieve the kind of commercial success that his talent deserved. He recorded for a variety of small labels and even worked as a jingle singer. Nat Stuckey died of lung cancer on August 24, 1988.

Recommended:
Independence (MCA/MCA)
She Wakes Me With A Kiss Every Morning (RCA/RCA)

Joe Sun

Joe Sun is one of a talented breed of singer-songwriters who have unselfconsciously absorbed influences across the spectrum from Hank Williams to Waylon Jennings.

In his music, he mixes soul, blues, honky-tonk, rock'n'roll, contemporary and traditional country into a sound that he describes as blues/country. Joe was born James Paulson on September 25, 1943, in Rochester, Minnesota. He arrived in Nashville in 1972 after spending time in college, the Air Force and in various jobs, which included a DJ stint at Radio WMAD in Madison, Wisconsin, and two years with a computer firm in Chicago.

While in Chicago he sang with a variety of semi-pro bands, working under the name Jack Daniels. Once in Nashville he gave himself five years to make it. For a

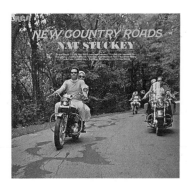

New Country Roads, Nat Stuckey. Courtesy RCA Records.

time he ran a small graphics business called The Sun Shop, then took up independent record promotions, which led to signing with Ovation towards the end of 1977.

His first single, **Old Flames (Can't Hold A Candle To You)**, came out in May 1978 and climbed steadily up the country charts, reaching the Top 20. Further hits followed with **I Came On Business For The King**, **I'd Rather Go On Hurtin'** and **Shotgun Rider** (1980). Then with his third album, **Livin' On Honky Tonk Time**, just released, Ovation closed down its record division.

Joe signed with Elektra in 1981, and though he has continued to make some fine records, gain rave reviews for his dynamic stage show and command a huge cult following in Britain, he has failed to achieve the commercial success he deserves.

Recommended:
The Sun Never Sets (–/Sonet)
Out Of Your Mind (Ovation/Ovation)
Hank Dogart Still Lives (–/Dixie Frog)

Billy Swan

A comparative unknown when his **I Can Help** single hit the charts in 1974, Swan turned out to have a long pedigree in southern music. Born on May 12, 1942, in Cape Giradeau, Missouri, he had written **Lover Please** at the age of 16. The song

Above: Sweethearts sisters Kristine and Janis started out in the '70s.

was recorded by his band of that time, Mirt Mirley And The Rhythm Steppers, but Clyde McPhatter made it a huge R&B hit.

Swan eventually tried his luck in Nashville and, taking odd jobs, he followed Kris Kristofferson as janitor at Columbia's studios. While working for Columbia Music, Swan became involved with Tony Joe White and produced that artist's first three, and most important, albums. He also backed Kris Kristofferson at the 1970 Isle of Wight Festival. Some time later he was to join Kinky Friedman's band for a while.

The 1974 album release of **I Can Help** revealed an artist with a liking for country, rock'n'roll and R&B. Swan made an

I Can Help, Billy Swan. Courtesy Monument Records.

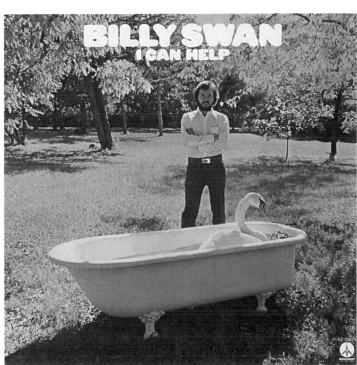

impressive version of Presley's **Don't Be Cruel** and in 1975 he was successful with another pop single hit with **Everything's The Same**.

In the summer of 1978, Swan joined A&M Records, then in 1981 moved on to Epic Records, recording some fine country-rock sides and touring with such highly respected Nashville musicians as Kenny Buttrey and Charlie McCoy as backing musicians.

Billy was back in the musical headlines in the summer of 1986 when he tamed up with Randy Meisner, Jimmy Griffin and Robb Royer, plus other musicians, to form a new band, Black Tie, recording an album, **When The Night Falls**, for Bench Records. Swan now mostly tours with Kris Kristofferson.

Recommended:
I'm Into Lovin' You (Epic/–)
At His Best (Monument/–)
Rock'n'Roll Moon (Monument/Monument)
I Can Help (Monument/Monument)

Sweethearts Of The Rodeo

A modern duo that mixes strains of contemporary and traditional country into a rich musical sound of their very own, Sweethearts Of The Rodeo comprise sisters Janis Gill and Kristine Arnold, who grew up in southern California and started out harmonizing together in their early teens. They performed at shopping malls, pizza parlours and honky-tonks in the early '70s as the Oliver Sisters. In 1976, Emmylou Harris saw their act and invited the girls to sit in on one of her gigs, so they sang with the original Hot Band. Both girls married and put their musical ambitions to one side as they started to raise families. In 1983 Janis moved to Nashville with her husband, singer Vince Gill, and after a few months urged Kristine to move to Music City, convinced that this time the sisters could make an impact with their music. Kristine was the lead singer for the group,

while Janis had been writing songs for a number of years.

Taking their name from the Byrds' country-rock album, Sweethearts Of The Rodeo entered the 1985 Wrangler Country Music Showdown, the world's largest talent contest, and were chosen as grand prize winners. This didn't net the expected recording contract, but a showcase gig at Nashville's Bluebird Café did the trick, and in 1986 they were signed to Columbia Records. They made their debut on the country charts with **Hey Doll Baby**, followed by such top 10 entries as **Since I Found You** (1986), **Midnight Girl/Sunset Town**, **Chains Of Gold** and **Gotta Get Away** (1987), as well as **Satisfy You**, **Blue To The Bone** (1988) and **I Feel Fine** (1989).

Their music, characterized by Kristine's distinct lead vocals and Janis' memorable harmony and guitar work, had a contemporary sound, but it still sounded hard country. Their recordings reverberated with swirling harmonies, staccato electric guitar and a driving rhythm section. Both are high-profile and dramatic-yet-playful onstage, with strong influences from the more colourful aspects of America's western heritage. Their stage costumes, which have played a big role in their image development, are designed and made by the girls themselves. When performing, Sweethearts Of The Rodeo present a kaleidoscope of colour in costumes which usually have a southwestern look. Due to their family commitments, Janis and Kristine are not able to tour as much as most country acts, and this has affected their record sales. They scored a handful of minor hits during 1990 and 1991, but, after cutting four high-quality albums, Sweethearts Of The Rodeo were dropped by Columbia in 1992. The following year they were signed to the independent Sugar Hill label, who are more interested in releasing quality music, than achieving mega-bucks with every release.

Recommended:
One Time, One Night (Columbia/CBS)
Sisters (Columbia/–)
Buffalo Zone (Columbia/CBS)

Sylvia

One of the most attractive young ladies to have emerged on the Nashville scene in the early '80s, Sylvia was born Sylvia Kirby Allen, on December 9, 1956, in the small town of Kokomo, Indiana.

After graduating from high school in 1975, she headed for Nashville, armed with *a capella* demonstration tapes she had made. Sylvia took a part-time secretarial position with Tom Collins, at that time producer of Barbara Mandrell.

She soon persuaded Collins to use her on demo tapes of new songs being written by the songwriters under contract to the producer, and this led to her being used as a back-up vocalist on recording sessions by Ronnie Milsap, Barbara Mandrell and Dave And Sugar. Sylvia was finally offered an RCA contract in the summer of 1979, and her first release, **You Don't Miss A Thing**, made the country charts.

Further hits followed with **It Don't Hurt To Dream** and **Tumbleweed** (both 1980), then Sylvia hit the top of the charts with **Drifter** at the beginning of 1981, consolidating that success with **The Matador** (another No.1), **Heart On The Mend** and the attractive, pop-styled **Nobody**, a pop cross-over hit in 1982, which went on to win Sylvia a gold disc.

She maintained her stature as a pop-country star with such hits as **Like Nothing Ever Happened** (1982), **Snapshot** (1983), **I Never Quite Got Back (From Loving You)** (1984), **Fallin' In Love**, **Cry Just A Little Bit** (1985) and **I Love You By Heart** (a duet with Michael Johnson, 1986). Sylvia was not at ease with her pop-flavoured country. Her idol was Patsy Cline, and she wanted to move away from the disco-beat of **Nobody**. In 1986 she married and moved out of music. Then, as Sylvia Hutton, she returned to Nashville in 1992, writing with Craig Bickhardt and Verlon Thompson, and touring with a five-piece acoustic band.

Recommended:
Sweet Yesterday (RCA/RCA)
One Step Closer (RCA/–)
Drifter (RCA/–)

One Step Closer, Sylvia. Courtesy RCA Records.

James Talley

A musical maverick, singer-songwriter James Talley, from Oklahoma, traded his carpentry skill for studio time to produce his breakthrough album, **Got No Bread, No Milk, No Money, But We Sure Got A Lot Of Love**, which he put out on his own label in 1975. Aided by some of Nashville's best session players, who donated their time, the response to the record was enthusiastic, with several major labels bidding for Talley's contract.

He signed with Capitol Records and during the next three years produced some timeless albums that pre-dated the 'New Traditionalist' movement of a dozen years later. Talley's music was steeped in rural traditions with threads of Jimmie Rodgers, Texas swing bands, country blues and Woody Guthrie all running through his work. However, his warm musical remembrances were considered revolutionary in the face of pop-country, and his recordings were shunned by Nashville, as if it was ashamed of its rich musical past. Undisturbed by this, Talley built up a cult following, very much in the mainstream of American troubadours. In many ways, his compositions marked a return to the sincerity of early country music, where attention was paid to the personal statement of the working man.

Talley carried this off with further conviction in his next album, **Tryin' Like The Devil**, in which every song related in one way or another to the plight of the worker and the enormous disparity between the rich and the poor. Not as mournful as it may sound, and like all of Talley's music, there was a warmth and humour as he utilized familiar musical forms — western swing, blues, classic rock'n'roll and country honky-tonk. He was to record two more albums for Capitol, but lack of airplay restricted sales and in 1978 the label dropped him. Talley has continued to write and make the occasional album, usually self-marketed, though a couple have surfaced on Bear

Family Records in Germany. In 1992, he recorded his most unusual collection, **The Road To Torreon**. The result of a 20-year project with photographer Cavalliere Ketchum, the album centres upon the Hispanic culture of New Mexico.

Recommended:
Blackjack Choir/Ain't It Something
  (–/Bear Family)
Got No Bread/Tryin' Like The Devil
  (–/Bear Family)
American Originals (–/Bear Family)

Jimmie Tarlton

Though his name is now almost forgotten it was John James Rimbert Tarlton (born in Chesterfield County, South Carolina, 1892) who first recorded and arranged the old folk song **Birmingham Jail**.

The son of a sharecropper, Tarlton became proficient on banjo, guitar and harmonica while still a boy, his repertoire being drawn not only from the traditional material learned from his mother but also from the blues songs of the black workers. During his twenties, he began hoboing his way around the country, his route taking him to New York, Chicago and Texas, where he became an oil-field worker. After a spell in the cotton mills of Carolina and a trek through the Midwest with a medicine show, he opted for a full-time career in music. A 1926 partnership with Georgian guitarist Tom Darby proved eminently successful and resulted in a recording session for Columbia. In November, 1927, Darby and Tarlton recorded **Birmingham Jail** and **Columbus Stockade Blues**, the ensuing disc attaining impressive sales figures.

For the next three years, the duo continued to provide Columbia with discs, their contract finally terminating in 1930. And, though no recordings were made in 1931, dates with Victor (1932) and ARC (1933) followed. The partnership dissolved in 1933 when Darby returned to farming.

Tarlton, however, remained an active musician for many years, at one time

Back In The Swing Of Things, Hank Thompson. Courtesy MCA Records.

working with Hank Williams in a medicine show. He was re-discovered by a new generation during the 1960s and began playing club dates and festivals, even cutting an album, **Steel Guitar Rag**, perhaps reminding everyone of his claim to be the first country steel guitar player. But it proved to be his final gesture: he died in 1973.

Recommended:
Darby And Tarlton (Old Timey/Bear Family)

Texas Tornados

A Tex-Mex quartet of veteran South Texas artists Freddy Fender (born June 4, 1937, San Benito, Texas), Flaco Jimenez (born March 11, 1939, San Antonio, Texas), Doug Sahm (born November 6, 1941, San Antonio, Texas) and Augie Meyers (born May 31, 1940, San Antonio, Texas), the Texas Tornados came together in December 1989, when they performed at a club in San Francisco as the Tex-Mex Revue. Such was their impact that by the following April they were recording their eponymous debut, having signed to Reprise Records. The foursome incorporated a wide variety of musical styles into a basic Tex-Mex structure that saw their first album garner a Grammy award in 1991. The follow-up, **Zone Of Our Own**, brought in a second nomination. An exciting live act, the Tornados attracted the same sort of unprecedented cross-cultural audience that Willie Nelson once bred, successfully blending Hispanics and Caucasians into a loyal group of fans.

All four members had enjoyed musical careers stretching back to the late '50s. Sahm and Meyers had been part of the Sir Douglas Quintet, while Fender had started out as a local R&B artist in Texas in 1957, and 20 years later had become a major country star. Jimenez, a legendary accordionist, is perhaps the best-known voice of Conjunto, a form of dance music that borrows from polkas and waltzes. Down through the years they had occasionally appeared at the same concerts and guested on each other's recordings. The core of the Tornados' success is their hypnotic blend of South

Texas' Mexican and Gringo musical cultures, such as blues, bar-room boogies, '50s rock'n'roll, doo-wop, swing, waltzes, polkas and Mexican folk.

The wide appeal of the group marked something of a comeback for the individual members, who all landed solo contracts with Reprise, producing solo albums of differing quality in an even wider cross-fusion of musical styles and sounds.

Recommended:
Texas Tornados (Warner Bros/Warner Bros)
Hanging On By A Thread (Reprise/–)
Zone Of Our Own (Reprise/–)
Flaco Jimenez – Partners (Reprise/Reprise)

B.J. Thomas

Born Billy Joe Thomas on August 27, 1942, in Hugo, Oklahoma, B.J. started out as a rocker, joining the Triumphs, a local band in Houston, Texas, at the age of 15. His first record with the group was titled **Lazy Man**, but it was with a Hank Williams song, **I'm So Lonesome I Could Cry** (a Scepter label release in 1966), that he obtained his first pop Top 10 hit.

Throughout the 1960s, Thomas continued logging pop Top 40 hits on Hickory and Scepter, the biggest of these being **Raindrops Keep Fallin' On My Head**, from the movie 'Butch Cassidy And The Sundance Kid', a US No. 1 in 1969, and a multi-award winner. From 1970 through to 1972, when he recorded **Rock And Roll Lullaby**, a single that featured the guitar of Duane Eddy, Thomas' name was a constant in the pop charts.

A switch from Scepter to Paramount signalled disaster for the Texan. His records failed to sell, and he was using

Above: Hank Thompson took western swing to the masses from the late '40s to the '70s.

everything from pills to cocaine. One of his lungs was pierced in a stabbing and by the mid-'70s he was bankrupt. Then came a turnabout. Billy Joe moved back into country and recorded Chips Moman and Larry Butler's **(Hey Won't You Play) Another Somebody Done Somebody Wrong Song**, a 1975 ABC Records release that became another pop No. 1. But B.J. was still on drugs when he cut the record and, in his autobiography 'Home Where I Belong', claims that he hardly remembers the session because he was using around 3,000 dollars worth of drugs each week during that period.

However, in January 1976, he became a born-again Christian and opted for a drug-free life. In 1977 he made a gospel album, also called **Home Where I Belong**, that saw him gaining a Grammy award. For a while, his name remained absent from the

Below: A guitar named Hank with its clean-shaven owner.

secular charts, but gradually his MCA releases began edging their way into the country Top 30 once more, via such singles as **Everybody Loves A Rain Song** (1978), **Some Love Songs Never Die** and **I Recall A Gypsy Woman** (1981). By 1983 he was back at the top. Signed to the Cleveland International label, he headed the country charts with **Whatever Happened To Old-Fashioned Love?** and **New Looks From An Old Lover**, following these with a Top 5 single in **She Meant Forever When She Said Goodbye**. And in 1984 he added to his tally with **The Whole World's In Love When You're Lonely** and **Rock And Roll Shoes**, a duet with Ray Charles.

Now a Grammy and Dove award-winner for his gospel releases, B.J. Thomas seems able to slot both sacred and secular songs into his repertoire and is equally happy playing both religious and country venues.

Recommended:
New Looks (Cleveland Int./Epic)
Home Where I Belong (Myrrh/Myrrh)
New Looks (Epic/Epic)
Midnight Minute (Reprise/–)

Hank Thompson

For 13 consecutive years (1953–1965), Thompson's Brazos Valley Boys won just about every western band poll and even today Thompson's influence pervades the country-rock scene.

Born Henry William Thompson in Waco, Texas, on September 3, 1925, he initially became a harmonica ace, winning many talent contests by his playing. Later he graduated to guitar, learning to play on a second-hand instrument costing only four dollars. During the early 1940s he began broadcasting on a local radio station and found a sponsor in a flour company. A few months later, in 1943, Thompson joined the Navy for a period of three years, upon discharge winning a spot on Waco station KWTX. He also formed a western swing band, the Brazos Valley Boys, and began recording for Globe Records in August

The Sue Thompson Story. Courtesy DJM Records.

1946. The results of the session provided **Whoa Sailor**, a regional hit. This reached the ears of Tex Ritter, who then suggested to Capitol that they sign the Waco singer. In 1948, Thompson commenced a career with the label that was to last 18 years, scoring immediately with national hits in **Humpty Dumpty Heart** and **Today**, following these with **Green Light** and a remake of **Whoa Sailor** (1949). From then on came a perpetual stream of hits, the biggest being Thompson's version of a Carter-Warren song, **The Wild Side Of Life**, which became a million-seller in 1952. Though his last appearance on the US pop charts was with **She's A Whole Lot Like You**, back in mid-1960, Thompson continued to provide a non-stop flow of country chart winners for several years, these including **Oklahoma Hills**, **Hangover Tavern** (1961), **On Tap, In the Can Or In The Bottle, Smokey The Bear** (1968), **I've Come Awful Close** (1971), **Cab Driver** (1972) **The Older The Violin The Sweeter The Tune**, and **Who Left The Door To Heaven Open?** (1974). He quit Capitol for Warner Brothers in 1966, and then moved on to Dot in 1968.

Although record buyers have veered away from the western swing style that first brought Hank into prominence, he and his Brazos Valley Boys have continued to play an abundance of dates worldwide, also logging the occasional chart entry on such labels as ABC, MCA and Churchill. Hank has made a major contribution to country music, which was recognized when he was inducted into the Country Music Hall Of Fame in 1989.

Recommended:
The Best Of (Capitol/Capitol)
Sings The Gold Standards (Capitol/Capitol)
A Six Pack To Go (Capitol/Capitol)
Back In The Swing Of Things (Dot/ABC)
Capitol Collectors Series (Capitol/Capitol)
Songs For Rounders (Capitol/Stetson)

Sue Thompson

Known as the lady with the itty-bitty voice, Sue Thompson always sounded like a teeny-bopper. Born Eva Sue McKee on July 19, 1926, in Nevada, Missouri, she grew

up on a farm listening to country music or viewing western films. At seven she began playing guitar, After winning a San José talent contest during her high school days, she played a two-week engagement at a local theatre as a reward. Later she became a regular on Dude Martin's Hometown Hayride show, over San Francisco KGO-TV. And, after cutting sides with Martin's Round-Up Gang (she was married to Dude Martin for a time and later spent some years as the wife of Hank Penny), she signed to Mercury as a solo act.

Moving to LA, she appeared in cabaret and, in the late 1950s, on Red Foley's portion of the Opry. Following record dates with Columbia and Decca, Sue signed for Hickory Records in 1960 and had an initial hit with **Sad Movies**, a gold disc winner. Others followed including **Norman** (another million-seller), **James (Hold The Ladder Steady)**, **Paper Tiger**, **Have A Good Time** and **Angel, Angel**, most of her songs in pure pop vein, though she became increasingly country-oriented during the late 1960s. Her last hit of any size was **Never Naughty Rosie** in 1976.

Recommended:
The Sue Thompson Story (–/DJM)
Sweet Memories (–/Sundown)

Mel Tillis

Though Tillis has always had problems with his speech (having a life-long stutter), he has had little trouble putting words (and music) down on paper. His songwriting efforts include: **Detroit City**, **Honky Tonk Song**, **Ruby, Don't Take Your Love To Town**, **I'm Tired**, **One More Time**, **Crazy Wild Desire**, **A Thousand Miles Ago** and many other Top 10 entries.

Born in Tampa, Florida, on August 8, 1932, Tillis grew up in Tahokee, Florida. A drummer in the high school band, he later studied violin but opted out to become a footballer of some distinction. Next came a spell in the US Air Force, followed by a stint on the railroad. During this time Tillis developed his writing and performing ability and in 1957 headed for Nashville with three of his songs – all became hits for other singers. Tillis' own first hit disc came later in 1958 with **The Violet And The Rose**, a Columbia release. This was followed by **Finally** (1959), **Sawmill** (1959) and **Georgia Town Blues**, a duet with Bill Phillips (1960).

Following a switch to the Ric label and a Top 10 debut with **Wine** (1965), Mel became signed to Kapp (later Decca). He obtained Top 10 hits with: **Who's Julie?** (1968), **These Lonely Hands Of Mine** (1969), **She'll Be Hangin' Round**

Heart Over Mind, Mel Tillis. Courtesy CBS Records.

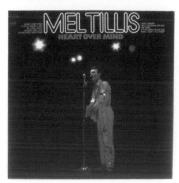

Old Faithful, Mel Tillis. Courtesy MCA Records.

Somewhere, **Heart Over Mind** (both 1970). He then moved to MGM to continue his personal hit parade with: **Commercial Affection**, **Heaven Everyday** (1970), **Brand New Mister Me** (1971), **I Ain't Never** (1972), **Neon Rose**, **Sawmill** (1973), **Memory Maker** (1974) and **Woman In The Back Of My Mind** (1975), among others. To this can be added two hit duets with Sherry Bryce and **How Come Your Dog Don't Bite Nobody But Me?**, a diverting duet with Webb Pierce that hit the charts during 1963.

Adjudged CMA Entertainer Of The Year 1976, Mel moved to the MCA label and celebrated by logging a No. 1 single with **Good Woman Blues**, following this with other chart-toppers in **Heart Healer** (1977), **I Believe In You** (19789), **Coca Cola Cowboy** (1979) and, on the Elektra label, **Southern Rains** (1980). During 1981 he teamed with Nancy Sinatra for a duet album, **Mel and Nancy**. He switched back to MCA and went Top 10 with **In The Middle Of The Night** (1983) and **New Patches** (1984), also recording some sides with Glen Campbell.

One of the most prolific writers in country music, Mel is a versatile performer and one who has always been able to turn his speech impediment to good use, becoming, unbelievably, an in-demand guest on all of TV's top chat shows. Also a movie actor, he has appeared in several films, including 'WW And The Dixie Dance Kings' (1975) and 'Uphill All The Way' (1985).

Recommended:
New Patches (MCA/MCA)
I Believe In You (MCA/MCA)
The Best Of Mel Tillis And The Statesiders (Polydor/–)
American Originals (Columbia/–)

Pam Tillis

Born on July 24, 1957, in Plant City, Florida, Pam Tillis is the eldest of five children by country singer Mel Tillis and his wife Doris. She grew up in Nashville and made her first stage appearance at the age of eight, singing with Mel on the Grand Ole Opry. In high school and at the University of Tennessee in Knoxville, Pam was attracted to rock acts like the Eagles, Linda Ronstadt and Little Feat, rather than pure country music. During her teen years she began a short-lived career in country music, as a Stutterette, one of the back-up vocalists for Mel Tillis, but, being a rebel child she teamed up with a jazz pianist to form a fusion band and moved to California. Although her plans didn't work out, she began songwriting. She moved back to Nashville and signed a writer's

contract with Tree Music in 1983. Occasionally Pam would play the Nashville clubs, and this resulted in her landing a record deal with Warner Brothers in 1984. Recording an album of pop songs, mainly self-written, Pam scored some country hits over a three-year period. However, it was as a songwriter and session singer that she was enjoying her biggest success.

Pam was in the studio working on a demo for **Someone Else's Trouble Now** (eventually a hit for Highway 101), when she was offered a recording contract with the newly opened Nashville office of Arista Records. The debut single, **Don't Tell Me What To Do**, raced up the charts in 1991, peaking at No. 4, and the album, **Put Yourself In My Place**, gained a gold disc. The album yielded more Top 10 singles with **One Of Those Things** and **Maybe It Was Memphis**. Rather surprisingly, the mandolin madrigal autobiography, **Melancholy Child**, was not released as a single. Overall, though, this was one of the best albums by a female singer in years. A package loaded with personality and the high gleam of experience, it served as an invigorating introduction to Pam. Proving that this was not to be a one-off experience, the next album, **Homeward Looking Angel**, was just as impressive, and Tillis enjoyed further chart success with **Shake The Sugar Tree** (1992) and **Let That Pony Run** (1993).

Girlish and garrulous, but with a gutsy poise unmatched in modern country music, and with her band the Mystic Biscuits, Pam Tillis has a knock-'em dead live show that is a powerhouse blend of rockabilly, country and blues, seasoned with a quick-witted dialogue she's obviously picked up from her father.

Recommended:
Put Yourself In My Place (Arista/–)
Homeward Looking Angel (Arista/–)

Floyd Tillman

One of country music's most successful songwriters, Floyd Tillman was born in Ryan, Oklahoma on December 8, 1914. He became singer, guitarist, mandolin and banjo player with the Mark Clark Orchestra

and the Blue Ridge Playboys during the 1930s, signing for Decca in 1939 and cutting the self-written **It Makes No Difference Now**, a country classic.

During the late 1940s, Tillman, who became a Columbia recording artist in 1946, wrote such compositions as **I Love You So Much It Hurts** (1948), **Slipping Around** (1949) and **I'll Never Slip Around Again** (1949). The songs became even bigger hits when recorded by Jimmy Wakely, with big band vocalist Margaret Whiting duetting.

Though his name remained absent from the record charts during the 1950s, in 1960 Tillman scored with **It Just Tore Me Up**.

A honky-tonk hero and among the first to utilize electric guitar, Tillman was also responsible for such songs as **Each Night At Nine**, **I'll Keep On Lovin' You** and **Daisy Mae**. He was elected into the Nashville Songwriter's Hall Of Fame in 1970, and received an even greater honour when he was inducted into the Country Music Hall Of Fame in 1984.

Recommended:
Country Music Hall Of Fame (MCA/–)
Greatest Hits (Crazy Cajun/–)

Aaron Tippin

A former competitive bodybuilder, Aaron Tippin, born July 3, 1958, in Pensacola, Florida, is a real hillbilly singer with an ear-jarring South Carolina twang, which he developed while living in Traveler's Rest, near Greenville, South Carolina, where his pilot father moved his family in the mid-'60s. When he was ten, Aaron got his first guitar and later played banjo, but at the time was more intent on following in his father's footsteps and took to flying planes. He flew solo at 16 and by 19 had his multi-engine commercial licence, but when airlines started laying-off pilots in the late '70s, Tippin decided to try music full-time. By 1978 he was playing in local bluegrass bands the Dixie Ridge Runners and Tip And The Darby Hill Band. After completion of his aviation course, he found

Put Yourself In My Place, Pam Tillis. Courtesy Arista Records.

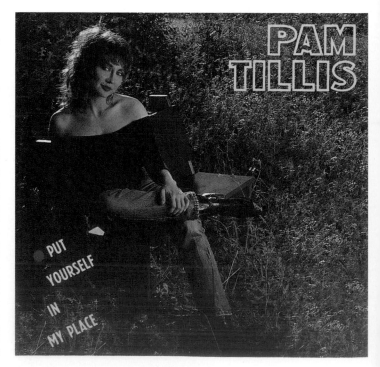

The Wonder Of It All, Tompall Glaser. Courtesy MCA Records.

work as a farm hand, truck driver and heavy equipment operator in an effort to support his family, while working the bars at weekends. His marriage disintegrated, so, in the mid-'80s, Aaron started regular trips to Nashville trying to break into music. He was working in an aluminium-rolling mill in Russellville, Kentucky by night, driving to Nashville to write songs by day. Signed to Acuff-Rose, he slowly started to get songs recorded by Charley Pride, Josh Logan and the Kingsmen.

In 1989, to save a few dollars, he recorded his own vocals for a new set of demos which were sent to RCA. They were impressed as much by the singer as the songs, and immediately signed Tippin to a recording contract. His first single, **You've Got To Stand For Something**, made the

You've Got To Stand For Something, Aaron Tippin. Courtesy RCA Records.

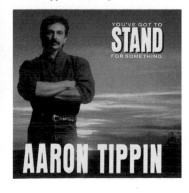

country Top 10 in 1990, and his debut album, carrying the same title, contained all his own songs and gained Tippin a gold album. Though this album received rave reviews, his follow-up singles were only minor hits. His vocal style, a raw blend of howls, yodels, bluesy slides and throaty crooning, didn't quite fit radio programming, but the fans decided that, regardless of radio, they were going to buy Tippin's records and watch his concerts. In 1992 he was back in the Top 10 with **There Ain't Nothing Wrong With The Radio**, a real uptempo number which was his first No.1, and **I Wouldn't Have It Any Other Way**. His second album, **Read Between The Lines**, also went gold.

Recommended:
You've Got To Stand For Something (RCA/RCA)
Read Between The Lines (RCA/–)

Tompall And The Glaser Brothers

Born on a ranch in Spalding, Nebraska (Tompall Glaser on September 3, 1933, Charles 'Chuck' Glaser on February 3, 1936 and James Glaser on December 16, 1937), the brothers' early interest in music was generated by their parents, who were both country music devotees. During the early 1950s they formed a band and played local clubs and dance halls. As their reputation spread, they gained a 13-week series on KHAS, Hastings, Nebraska. Later,

following a win on the Arthur Godfrey Talent Show, they travelled to Nashville in 1958 and were soon on tour with Marty Robbins. Signed by Decca, they recorded folk music (while performing country onstage) and were not entirely happy with their debut album, **This Land**.

But in 1962 they became members of the Grand Ole Opry and followed a country direction from then on. Also that year they toured with Johnny Cash, and the dates this package played at Las Vegas and Carnegie Hall provided the Glasers with an even wider audience.

By 1966 they had signed to MGM Records and begun a noteworthy recording career. Their delightful harmony vocals and acoustic guitar work were particularly suited to the more melodic country material and they kept abreast of the latest songwriting trends too. Their first hits came with songs like **Gone On The Other Hand** (1966) and **Through The Eyes Of Love** (1967), their first Top 10 being **Rings** (1971). Multi-award winners, they proved a popular live group and stopped the show at the 1970 Wembley Festival. But, after working seven days a week as a band and also trying to run a studio and an office, the brothers developed differences and split in 1972. Tompall cut a solo album called **Charlie** (1973) that indicated a change of direction, particularly in terms of lyrics. The title song spoke of a man's past and future lives and seemed prophetic.

Later albums saw Tompall in much the same mood, exploring themes that would not have been possible with the more melodic Glaser Brothers. He formed his Outlaw Band and appeared on the million-

selling **The Outlaws**, along with Waylon Jennings and Willie Nelson, providing that album's grittiest track with a stomping version of Jimmie Rodgers' **T For Texas**.

Meanwhile, both Jim and Chuck were having some success in more mainstream country, all three Glaser brothers appearing in the country charts during 1974; Chuck with **Gypsy Queen**, Jim with **Fool Passin' Through** and **Forgettin' All About You**, and Tompall with **Texas Law Sez** and **Musical Chairs**.

Chuck, however, became increasingly involved in record production and management, but suffered a stroke that put him out of action for some time.

Although Tompall had a critically acclaimed solo career, there remained a bigger demand for the brothers as a threesome. So, in 1978, they got back together again, resuming their joint chart activities with a brace of mid-chart hits for Elektra in 1980. This time, it seemed, they were really going to achieve a breakthrough in record sales. Their 1981 version of Kris Kristofferson's **Lovin' Her Was Easier (Than Anything I'll Ever Do Again)** went to No.2 in the charts. There were other Top 20 records with **Just One Time** (1981) and **It'll Be Her** (1982). Then

Charlie, Tompall Glaser. Courtesy MGM Records.

the Glasers split once again, Jim – who, with Jimmy Payne, had earlier penned the million-selling hit **Woman, Woman** for Gary Puckett – releasing a single on a new independent label, Noble Vision. Titled **When You're Not A Lady**, it not only went Top 20 in the charts, but, after a stay of 22 weeks, became the all-time longest-running debut release by a new record company in the history of those charts.

Proffering a soft, romantic line in country that contrasts with Tompall's method, Jim logged a country No. 1 with **You're Getting To Me Again** (1984) along with several other major chart climbers. In 1985, Noble Vision was absorbed into the MCA label, and, after scoring minor hits during the next two years, Jim's brief run of success came to an end.

Recommended:
Sing Great Hits From Two Decades (MGM/MGM)
The Award Winners (MGM/MGM)

Jim Glaser:
The Man In The Mirror (Noble Vision/–)

Tompall Glaser:
Charlie (MGM/MGM)
The Great Tompall And His Outlaw Band (MGM/MGM)
Tompall Glaser And His Outlaw Band (ABC/ABC)
The Outlaw (–/Bear Family)
The Rogue (–/Bear Family)

Diana Trask

An Australian who made it big in Nashville during the late 1960s and early 1970s, Diana Trask was born in Melbourne, Australia, on June 23, 1940. Winner of the top talent award at 16, she toured with a group before going to the US in 1959.

Then a pop vocalist, she later signed to Columbia Records, appeared on major TV shows and was even offered a film contract. However, she got married and returned to Australia. In the late 1960s, during a trip to the CMA convention, she became bitten by the country bug and stayed on in Nashville, having her first country hit with **Lock, Stock And Barrel**, a Dial release. She then joined Dot and cut an album, **Miss Country Soul**, and had Top 20 entries with **Say When**, **It's A Man's World**, **When I Get My Hands On You** (1973) and **Lean It All On Me** (1974).

She returned to Australia once more in 1975 and had her first hit there in 14 years with **Oh Boy**, a Festival release which went to No.2. Signed to Australian RCA in 1977 and Polydor in 1980, Diana was back in the US charts in '81 with **This Must be My Ship** and **Stirrin' Up Feelings**.

Recommended:
Diana's Country (Dot/–)
Miss Country Soul (Dot/–)

Merle Travis

Easily one of the most, if not *the* most, multi-talented men ever to enter the music business was Merle Travis, born in Rosewood, Mulenberg County, Kentucky, on November 29, 1917.

A singer and songwriter of major proportions and guitar stylist of monumental influence, he also proved adept as an actor, author and even cartoonist.

Merle learned the basics of his celebrated guitar style from Mose Rager,

Miss Country Soul, Diana Trask. Courtesy MCA-Dot.

who, in turn, learned it from black railroad hand, fiddler and guitarist, Arnold Shultz. Merle adapted the finger style to a degree of complexity unknown in that era (it was to prove extremely influential to Chet Atkins and many others). His renown won him a job with a group called the Tennessee Tomcats before joining Clayton McMichen's Georgia Wildcats on WLW's Boone County Jamboree.

After a stint in the Marines, Travis relocated on the West Coast, perfecting his songwriting, appearing in minor roles in a host of westerns. He also signed with Capitol Records and had several of the biggest hits of the era: **Divorce Me C.O.D.** (1946), **So Round, So Firm, So Fully Packed** (1947) and several others which ranked on the charts, these including **Dark As A Dungeon** (1947) and **Sixteen Tons** (1947), a 1955 hit for Tennessee Ernie Ford.

Writer or co-writer of all his hits, he also co-wrote **No Vacancy** with Cliffie Stone and **Smoke! Smoke! Smoke!** with Tex Williams. He was equally adept at reworking folk tunes, and **John Henry**, **I Am A Pilgrim** and **Nine Pound Hammer** were all adapted by and integrated into the Travis style.

In the 1950s, Merle became a southern California fixture, appearing regularly on the Hometown Jamboree and Town Hall Party, making a striking appearance as a guitar-strumming sailor in the movie 'From Here To Eternity', where he introduced the song **Re-Enlistment Blues**. He moved to Nashville for a short while in the 1960s but later returned to California, using it as a base for frequent tours up to the time of his death in Tahlequah, Oklahoma, on October 20, 1983. Travis, whose last film appearance was in Clint Eastwood's 'Honky Tonk Man', was inducted into the Nashville Songwriters Hall Of Fame in

The Atkins-Travis Traveling Show. Courtesy RCA Records.

Above: Merle Travis parades a blues or two in 'From Here To Eternity'.

1970. Both Doc Watson and Chet Atkins named sons after him.

Recommended:
The Atkins-Travis Traveling Show – with Chet Atkins (RCA/RCA)
Walkin' The Strings (Capitol/Pathe Marconi)
Travis! (Capitol/Capitol)
Merle Travis And Joe Maphis (Capitol/Capitol)
Folk Songs Of The Hills (–/Bear Family)

Randy Travis

When Randy Travis hit Nashville with his **Storms Of Life** platinum album in 1986, country music was fumbling for a pop-flavoured identity as record sales had

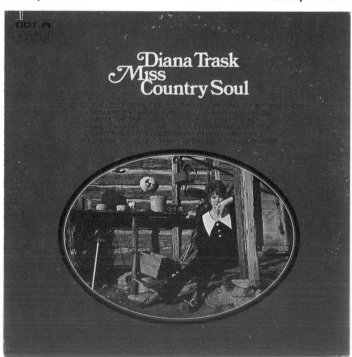

plummeted and the music had become very stale and cliché-ridden. Travis, sang straight-ahead country music with warmth and conviction, and, though he wasn't the best, he was young, good-looking, and in the right place at the right time.

Born Randy Bruce Traywick on May 4, 1959 in Marshville, North Carolina, Travis started singing and playing guitar when he was nine. Randy teamed up with his brothers Ricky and David, and, with their father arranging dates, they performed at local clubs. Frequently in trouble with the law, Travis appeared, while on probation, in a talent show at a Charlotte club owned by Lib Hatcher. Taking responsibility for the youngster as manager and guardian, Lib financed his first recordings as Randy Traywick, which were produced by Joe Stampley in Nashville and released on Paula Records. The single, **She's My Woman**, became a minor hit in 1979. Two years later Lib moved to Nashville to open a new club, The Nashville Palace, and develop Randy's career. Now working as Randy Ray, in 1982 he recorded his first album, **Randy Ray At The Nashville Palace**, while Hatcher took his demos around to every major label in Nashville. Eventually she persuaded Warner Brothers A&R executive Martha Sharp to see Randy performing. The label was looking for a new young artist to compete with George Strait and Ricky Skaggs and Martha signed him to a recording contract in 1985, suggesting a name change to Randy Travis.

The single **On The Other Hand**, released that summer, only did marginally better than his Paula release, but the next one, **1982**, made the Top 10 in 1986. The album **Storms Of Life** gained critical approval. **On The Other Hand** was singled out for special mention, so it was re-released and promptly climbed to the top of the charts. With his low-key, Lefty Frizzell-flavoured, pure traditional honky-tonk country vocals, Travis now dominated the charts with further No.1s, including: **Diggin' Up Bones** (1986), **Forever And Ever, Amen** (1987), **Too Gone Too Long** (1988), **Deeper Than The Holler** and **It's Just A Matter Of Time** (1989). With this success, Randy gained the CMA Horizon Award in 1986, and picking up both album and single award in 1987 for **Always And Forever** and **Forever And Ever, Amen**. His album sales sky-rocketed into platinum status, as Travis started attracting younger, female fans to country music.

Randy Travis was named CMA Male Vocalist in 1988, and also picked up his second Grammy. Initially not a great stage performer, he has gradually grown in confidence. Travis opened the floodgates for the 'New Traditionalists' who have dominated country music since the late '80s and given Nashville a new golden age. Randy has developed his songwriting, working closely with Don Schlitz and Alan Jackson, and maintained his success on the charts with singles **Hard Rock Bottom Of Your Heart** (1990), **Forever Together** (1991) and **If I Didn't Have You** (1992). Albums **Old 8 x 10**, **No Holding Back** and **High Lonesome** have each sold in excess of one million copies.

Recommended:
Old 8 × 10 (Warner Bros/Warner Bros)
Storms Of Life (Warner Bros/Warner Bros)
Heroes And Friends (Warner Bros/Warner Bros)
No Holding Back (Warner Bros/Warner Bros)
High Lonesome (Warner Bros/Warner Bros)

Above: In 1947 Ernest Tubb headed the first country show at Carnegie Hall.

Travis Tritt

Long-haired, blue-collar, biker-hero Travis Tritt was born on February 9, 1963 in Marietta, Georgia. With his rockin' country that celebrates the working-class South, his solid rock roots and influences that range from George Jones and Merle Haggard to the Allman Brothers and Lynyrd Skynyrd, Travis became one of country music's hottest acts of the early '90s. After graduation from high school in 1981, he went to work loading trucks, and within four years had worked his way up to a management position. By this time he was married, but, when the marriage didn't work out, he quit his job and began playing solo at various clubs. He worked Atlanta dinner clubs, rowdy honky-tonks and backroad greasy joints. Wherever he could, he worked his songs into his act, and it was through this that Tritt came to the attention of Danny Davenport, a local representative for Warner Brothers. Initially interested in some of Tritt's songs, Danny realized Tritt's potential as an entertainer when he saw him in front of an audience. Together at Davenport's home studio they began working on an album. When executives at Warners heard the

Country Hit Time, Ernest Tubb. Courtesy MCA Records.

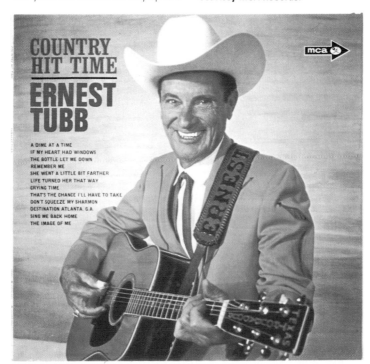

tapes, they offered Travis Tritt a recording contract in early 1989.

His debut single, **Country Club**, went to No.9 on the country charts in late 1989. **Help Me Hold On** climbed to the top and Tritt enjoyed further big hits with **I'm Gonna Be Somebody** (1990), **Here's A Quarter (Call Someone Who Cares)** and **Anymore** (both 1991), as well as **Lord Have Mercy On The Working Man** and **Can I Trust You With My Heart** (both 1992). He picked up the CMA Horizon award in 1991, while **Country Club**, **It's All About To Change** and **T-R-O-U-B-L-E** have all gone platinum. In early 1992 he became the youngest member of the Grand Ole Opry. Following duet success with Marty Stuart on **The Whiskey Ain't Workin'**, the pair put together a 'No Hats Tour' that garnered so much critical acclaim that a national pay-per-view concert was filmed. **Bible Belt**, his rocking collaboration with Little Feat, was heard in Joe Pesci's 1992 film 'My Cousin Vinnie'. His white-hot version of the Elvis classic **Burnin' Love** was included in the soundtrack album for the motion picture 'Honeymoon In Vegas'. **Texas Flyer**, a song he originally recorded as **Dixie Flyer**, was re-recorded by him in honour of US Olympic athlete Lance Armstrong, and included on the **Barcelona Gold** album.

Recommended:
T-R-O-U-B-L-E (Warner Bros/–)
Country Club (Warner Bros/–)
It's All About To Change (Warner Bros/–)

Ernest Tubb

The sixth member to be elected to the Country Music Hall Of Fame and a regular member of the Opry from 1943 to the time of his death, Ernest Dale Tubb, the son of a Texas cotton farm overseer, was born in Crisp, Texas on February 9, 1914. Tubb's boyhood hero was the great Jimmie

Rodgers. Although he had dreams of emulating Rodgers and sang at various local get-togethers during his early teens, Tubb was almost 20 before he owned his first guitar. The year 1934 proved important to him, Tubb obtaining his initial dates on San Antonio KONO. During this period he married Lois Elaine Cook.

In 1935 Tubb's eldest son Justin was born and Ernest met Carrie Rodgers (Jimmie's widow). She and Ernest became good friends, Mrs Rodgers loaning him her husband's original guitar and also arranging an RCA recording session at which Tubb cut two sides: **The Passing Of Jimmie Rodgers** and **Jimmie Rodgers' Last Thoughts**. However, Tubb's luck was not always that good. His second son, Rodger Dale, was born in July 1938, but died after just a few weeks. Things began to look brighter after the birth of a daughter, Violet Elaine; Decca offered him a new record contract and he obtained a job on Fort Worth's KGKO.

It was at this stage that he became the Gold Chain Troubadour, earning 75 dollars a week promoting Universal's wares. It was a nickname which preceded his famous Texas Troubadour image. By 1941 he had also moved into movies, appearing in 'Fightin' Buckaroos'.

Next came his recording of **Walking The Floor Over You**, a self-penned composition. Released in autumn 1942, it became a million-seller, helping Tubb gain his first appearance on the Opry in December. He was to gain regular membership during 1943.

He continued logging successful discs and film appearances. Also, in 1947, he opened the first of his now famous record shops and commenced his Midnight Jamboree programme over WSM, advertising the shop and showcasing the talents of up and coming country artists.

Tubb married again in 1949, his new wife being Olene Adams, mother of Erlene, Olene, Ernest Jr, Larry and Karen Tubb. That year he appeared on hit records with the Andrews Sisters and Red Foley. He also achieved Top 10 placings with no less than five of his solo efforts, the biggest of these being **Slippin' Around** and **Blue Christmas**. From then through to 1969 he became the charts' Mr Consistency, thanks to such discs as **Goodnight Irene** (with Red Foley, 1950), **I Love You Because** (1950), **Missing In Action** (1952). **Two Glasses Joe** (1954), **Half A Mind** (1958), **Thanks A Lot** (1963), **Mr and Mrs Used-To-Be** (with Loretta Lynn, 1964) and **Another Story, Another Place** (1966). His only real absence from hit listing was between 1952 and 1954 when, following an exhausting Far East tour, Tubb suffered from an illness that kept him off the Opry.

An inveterate tourer, he and his Texas Troubadours played around 300 dates a year. An honest singer rather than a great one – emotionally he was a 10-point man, technically he came a lot further down the scale – when ET performed honky-tonk you could almost smell the booze. Much loved, when he set out to record his **Legend And Legacy** album for First Generation records in 1979, virtually everyone who was anyone in Nashville dropped by to see if they could help out. The album line-up eventually featured the names of Willie Nelson, Loretta Lynn, Vern Gosdin, Chet Atkins, Merle Haggard, Johnny Cash, Charlie Rich, Johnny Paycheck, Linda Hargrove, Marty Robbins, Conway Twitty, the Wilburn Brothers, Ferlin Husky, Waylon Jennings, Charlie Daniels, George Jones and many, many others. When he died, on

September 6, 1984, the whole of Music City mourned the man writer Chet Flippo once accurately described as "honky-tonk music personified".

Recommended:

The Legend And The Legacy (First Generation/–)
The Ernest Tubb Story (MCA/MCA)
Honky Tonk Classics (Rounder/–)
The Country Hall Of Fame (–/MCA)
Let's Say Goodbye Like We Said Hello (–/Bear Family)
Live 1963 (Rhino/–)
The Yellow Rose Of Texas (–/Bear Family)

Justin Tubb

Eldest son of Ernest Tubb, singer-songwriter-guitarist Justin Tubb was born in San Antonio, Texas, on August 20, 1935. His father recorded one of his songs in 1952, and that year he and two of his cousins formed a group and began playing clubs in the Austin area, where Tubb was attending the University of Texas. But after just a year of college came the inevitable move to Nashville and a DJ job on a radio station in nearby Gallatin, Tennessee. Tubb not only spun discs, but also entertained his listeners with his own songs on air.

In 1953 he signed with Decca, the following year logging two hits, **Looking Back To See** and **Sure Fire Kisses**, both duets with Goldie Hill. Although Tubb became an Opry regular in 1955, his records sold only moderately well and he began to label hop, leaving Decca in 1959 and cutting sides for Challenge and Starday. Then, after a Top 10 Groove release in **Take A Letter Miss Gray** (1963), came a long association with RCA and some so-so chart visits with **Hurry, Mr Peters** (1965), **We've Gone Too Far Again** (1966) – both duets with Lorene Mann – and **But Wait There's More**, a solo item from 1967.

Once an inveterate tourer, Tubb has played in all but two states and has also appeared in several countries. During 1967 he took a show to the Far East, entertaining servicemen in Vietnam and other areas. Nowadays he tours less regularly but still appears on various country TV shows and is something of a fixture on the Opry. He has also enjoyed success as a writer, his most notable composition being **Lonesome 7-7203**, a No.1 for Hawkshaw Hawkins in 1963.

Recommended:

Justin Tubb, Star Of The Grand Ole Opry (Starday/–)
Justin Tubb (MCA–Dot/–)

Tanya Tucker

When she was nine years old, people at both MGM and RCA Records wanted to sign her. At 14 she had gained a Top 10 hit and a year later her face bedecked the cover of 'Rolling Stone'. Shortly after, she came up with the biggest country single in the land, also acquiring a reputation as a musical Lolita because of her penchant for songs equipped with provocative lyrics.

Born in Seminole, Texas on October 10, 1958, Tanya Denise Tucker, the daughter of a construction worker, spent her early years in Wilcox, Arizona, moving to Phoenix in 1967. There, Tanya and her father began attending as many country

concerts as possible, visiting local fairs to hear Mel Tillis, Leroy Van Dyke, Ernest Tubb and others, Tanya often joining the stars onstage for an impromptu song.

Following a cameo role in the movie 'Jeremiah Johnson', Tanya, then 13, cut a demo tape that included her renditions of **For The Good Times**, **Put Your Hand In The Hand** and other songs. The results impressed Columbia's Billy Sherrill, who signed Tanya to the label and promptly produced her recording of Alex Harvey's **Delta Dawn**. The result was a 1972 Top 10 single, after which the Tucker–Sherrill partnership moved into further action to provide such chart-busters as **Love's The Answer**, **What's Your Mama's Name?**, **Blood Red And Going Down** (1973), **Would You Lay With Me (In A Field Of Stone)** and **The Man Who Turned My Mama On** (1974). **Would You Lay With Me**, one of the year's most controversial singles, also proved a hit of international proportions.

In 1976, following a million-dollar deal, Tanya signed for MCA, thus terminating her association with Sherill and creating some doubts as to her ability to survive without the guiding hand of the Columbia Svengali. But the doubts were quickly dispelled when **Lizzie And The Rainman**, **San Antonio Stroll** (1975), **You've Got Me To Hold On To** (1976), **Here's Some Love** (No.1, 1976), **It's A Cowboy Lovin' Night** (1977) and **Texas (When I Die)** (1978) all went Top 10.

In the late '70s, Tanya attempted to move further into the higher stakes of the

Strong Enough To Bend, Tanya Tucker. Courtesy Capitol Records.

Above: Single-parent and country star Tanya Tucker successfully balances family and showbiz.

rock field, but, even though she donned red tights for a highly publicized **TNT** album, things began falling apart a little. Equally publicized was her affair with Glen Campbell, with whom she recorded some duets before the twosome parted in 1981. Nevertheless, she had further solo Top 10 hits in 1980 with **Pecos Promenade** and **Can I See You Tonight**, then switched to Arista Records in 1982 for a disastrous association that saw her career plummet as a country star. To make matters worse, Tucker had also become addicted to alcohol and cocaine, and entered the Betty Ford clinic for treatment.

After a three-year absence from the charts, Tanya signed with Capitol Records and enjoyed the most successful period of her long career. She hit the charts with such No.1s as **Just Another Love** (1986), **I Won't Take Less Than Your Love** (with Paul Davis and Paul Overstreet, 1987), **If It Don't Come Easy**, **Strong Enough To Bend** (1988), **My Arms Stay Open All Night** (No.2, 1989), **Walking Shoes** (No.3, 1990), **Down To My Last Teardrop** (No.2, 1991) and **Two Sparrows In A Hurricane** (No.2, 1992). One of the most exciting female performers in country music, Tanya Tucker was named the CMA Female Vocalist Of The Year in 1991, but had to miss attending, as she was in hospital giving birth to her second child, Beau Grayson. A single mother, Tanya, or 'T' as she prefers to be known, carved her success in the late '80s by refusing to compromise. Her outstanding talent and distinctive vocal hiccup showed audiences that the little girl of **Delta Dawn** fame had blossomed into a forthright and beautiful woman.

Recommended:

Delta Dawn (Columbia/CBS)
Would You Lay With Me (Columbia/CBS)
Here's Some Love (MCA/MCA)
Strong Enough To Bend (Capitol/Capitol)
Can't Run From Yourself (Liberty/Liberty)
Tennessee Woman (Capitol/Capitol)
Love Me Like You Used To (Capitol/Capitol)
Lizzie And The Rainman (–/Cottage)

Conway Twitty

Real name Harold Lloyd Jenkins, born in Friars Point, Mississippi, on September 1, 1933, Twitty learned guitar onboard a riverboat piloted by his country music-loving father. Almost signed by the Philadelphia baseball team, Twitty was drafted before the contract could be concluded and spent two years in the Army instead.

During the mid-1950s, he became a rock'n'roll singer, working on many radio stations and charting with a Mercury single **I Need Your Lovin'** (1957). Shortly after, he joined MGM Records and won a gold disc for **It's Only Make Believe**, one of 1958's biggest sellers. Extremely Presley-influenced at this point in his career, Twitty was hardly out of the pop charts between September 1958 and April 1961, also finding time to appear in three teen-angled movies – 'Sex Kittens Go To College', 'Platinum High School' and 'College Confidential'.

It was at this time that Twitty began writing country songs. His **Walk Me To The Door** was recorded by Ray Price in 1960. By June 1965, he himself was cutting country sides under Decca's Owen Bradley, at the same time settling down in Oklahoma City playing with a band known as the Lonely Blue Boys and (in June, 1966) commencing his own syndicated TV programme. During the late 1960s, Twitty moved to Nashville and began amassing an incredible number of hits – his solo chart-toppers alone including: **Next In Line** (1968), **I Love You More Today, To See The Want To In Your Eyes** (1974), **Linda On My Mind, Touch The Hand, This Time I've Hurt Her More Than She Loves Me** (1975), **After All The Good Is Gone, The Game That Daddies Play, I Can't Believe She Gives It All To Me** (1976), **Don't Take It Away, I May Never Get To Heaven, Happy Birthday Darlin'** (1979), **I'd Love To Lay You Down** (1980), **Rest Your Love On Me, Tight Fittin' Jeans** and **Red Neckin' Love Makin' Night** (1981), all Decca/MCA releases.

Additionally during this period, Conway, who became a vastly superior singer to the one known only to pop audiences, also fashioned an equally impressive number of hit duets with Loretta Lynn, hitting the No.1 spot with **After The Fire Is Gone, Lead Me On** (1971), **Louisiana Woman, Mississippi Man** (1973), **As Soon As I Hang Up The Phone** (1974) and **Feelin's** (1975). Voted Vocal Duo Of The Year by the CMA for four straight years in a row (1972–1975), Conway and Loretta also shared several business interests. An astute businessman, Twitty owned a music promotion company, a large slice of real estate and the Twitty City complex (a kind of theme park that included the homes of Conway, his four children and his mother), one of Nashville's major attractions since it opened in 1982.

Also in 1982 Conway quit MCA and moved to Elektra Records, immediately claiming three No.1s (with **The Clown, Slow Hand** and **The Rose**) in his first year with his new label. Switching to Warner Brothers in 1983, Twitty again obliged with three No.1s in a year during 1984, with **Somebody's Needin' Somebody, Ain't She Somethin' Else** and **I Don't Know About Love (The Moon Song)** – the last named featuring Conway's daughter, Joni Lee Twitty.

Twitty's success on the charts continued throughout the '80s. the most notable successes being **Don't Call Him A Cowboy** (1985) and **Desperado Love** (1986). He then re-joined MCA and continued with **I Want To Know You Before We Make Love** (1987), **I Wish I Was Still In Your Dreams** (1988), **She's Got A Single Thing In Mind** (1989), **Crazy In Love** (1990) and **I Couldn't See You Leavin'** (1991). In 1992 he felt his many business interests were getting in the way of his music. So, the tousle-haired tycoon put almost everything on the market. Twitty had just completed a new album, but, after an appearance at Branson, Missouri, was taken ill on his tour bus. Rushed to the Cox Medical Center in Springfield, Missouri, he had surgery to repair an abdominal aortic aneurysm, but he died on June 5, 1993.

Originally named after a famous silent film comedian, Twitty took his stage name from the towns of Conway (in Arkansas) and Twitty (in Texas). Made an honorary chief of the Choctaw nation in the early 1970s, he was also awarded the Indian name Hatako-Chtokchito-A-Yakni-Toloa – which translates into 'Great Man Of Country Music'. Apt for a singer who has, despite his pop heritage, never opted for cross-over appeal.

Recommended:
Classic Conway (MCA/MCA)
Songwriter (MCA/MCA)
Georgia Keeps Pulling On My Ring (MCA/MCA)
Conway (MCA/MCA)
Cross Winds (MCA/MCA)
Crazy In Love (MCA/–)
Even Now (MCA/–)
House On Old Lonesome Road (MCA/–)
Making Believe – with Loretta Lynn (MCA/–)
Borderline (MCA/–)

T. Texas Tyler

Tyler, real name David Luke Myrick, was born on June 20, 1916, near Mena, Arkansas. Educated in Philadelphia, he began his career at the age of 14, heading east and appearing on the Major Bowes Amateur Hour in New York during the 1930s. He became widely known as the 'Man With The Million Friends'.

Later came a further move to West Virginia, while in 1942 Tyler was in Louisiana, becoming a member of Shreveport KWKH's Hayride show. A period in the armed forces followed, Tyler settling down in the Hollywood area upon discharge and forming the T. Texas Western Dance Band, a popular unit.

It was during this period that Tyler wrote and recorded **Deck Of Cards**, a hit for Four Stars in 1948. A somewhat sentimental but ingenious monologue regarding a soldier who employed a deck of cards as his Bible, prayer book and almanac, Tyler's creation became a million-seller when recorded by Wink Martindale. The song also became a hit for Tex Ritter and British comedian Max Bygraves. Following this record, which won the 'Cashbox' award for the best country disc of 1948, Tyler came up with several more winners, the most potent of these being **Dad Gave The Dog Away** (1948),

His Great Hits, T. Texas Tyler.
Courtesy Hilltop Records.

Above: The late Conway Twitty and his Twitty City, which celebrated its 10th birthday in 1992.

Bumming Around (1953), **Courting In The Rain** (1954) and his theme song, **Remember Me**.

During 1949, the Arkansas traveller appeared in 'Horseman Of The Sierras', a Columbia movie, and won a fair amount of acclaim from Range Round Up, his Los Angeles TV show. During the 1950s and 1960s he continued performing, both live and on TV. However, despite some worthwhile Starday releases, Tyler failed to place his name on the record charts during the later stages of his career. He died from natural causes on January 28, 1972, in Springfield, Missouri.

Recommended:
T. Texas Tyler – His Great Hits (Hilltop/–)

Leroy Van Dyke

Van Dyke (born in Spring Fork, Missouri on October 4, 1929) was co-writer (with Buddy Black) and singer of **The Auctioneer**, a 1956 gold disc winner that incorporated a genuine high-speed auctioneering routine. He originally decided on a career in agriculture, obtaining a BS degree in that subject at the University of Missouri. After serving with Army intelligence during the Korean War, he became a livestock auctioneer and agricultural correspondent, utilizing his writing skills to pen songs. He sang **The Auctioneer** on a talent show and subsequently won a contract with Dot Records, his song providing his first release – ultimately a two and half million-seller.

A regular on the Red Foley TV Show, he later signed for Mercury, providing that label with **Walk On By**, yet another million-seller, in 1961. He followed this with **If A Woman Answers** and **Black Cloud**, both hits during the following year. After that his releases rarely charted impressively, only **Louisville** (1968) really making the grade.

Leroy Van Dyke

Van Dyke, who made his film debut in 'What Am I Bid?' (1967), recorded for Warner Bros, Kapp, Decca and ABC-Dot after leaving Mercury in 1965, his last chart record of any size being **Texas Tea**, an ABC-Dot release in 1977.

Recommended:
Greatest Hits (MCA/–)
The Original Auctioneer (–/Bear Family)
The Auctioneer (–/Ace)

Townes Van Zandt

Legendary singer, songwriter and guitarist, Van Zandt, from Fort Worth, Texas, is very highly regarded for such classic songs as **Pancho And Lefty** (a hit duet for Willie Nelson and Merle Haggard) and **If I Needed You** (an Emmylou Harris and Don Williams duet). The son of a prominent oil family, he pursued a beatnik-like lifestyle in the early '60s and started performing in clubs in Houston.

In 1967 he was signed by the small Poppy Records label and recorded such albums as **Our Mother The Mountain**, which contained his own quirky folk-country songs. For a while he joined a trio called the Delta Mama Boys, but preferred to work solo. He then joined the Peace Corp, but returned to music in the late '70s. He has built up a cult following as a member of the thriving Texas singer-songwriter community. He cut an acclaimed **Live At The Old Quarter** album in 1977, but generally lived a reclusive life in a cabin in Tennessee. He was tempted back into music and recorded his first all-new album in Nashville with production by Jack Clement and Jim Rooney. Van Zandt has toured extensively, especially in Europe.

Recommended:
At My Window (Sugar Hill/Heartland)
High, Low And In Between (Tomato/Charly)
The Late Great (Tomato/Charly)
Live At The Old Quarter (–/Decal)

Randy Vanwarmer

Singer-songwriter Randy was born Randall Van Wormer on March 30, 1955, in Indian Hills, Colorado, but spent much of his life living in Cornwall, England. His father died in a car accident when Randy was ten, and his mother decided to get away from unhappy memories, uprooting the family and moving to Looe in Cornwall in 1967. It was at this time that young Randy started to play guitar and write songs, and in his teens he met up with Roger Moss, the pair working for several years as a duo. Endless trips to London with his song demos led to some songs being taken to Nashville, and in 1977 he signed with American independent Bearsville Records through Warner Bros, their London licensee. He began cutting an album, but just before the album was due for release, Bearsville pulled out of England, and Randy was left high-and-dry. He hopped on a plane and settled in Woodstock, New York, and signed directly to Bearsville in America. Several singles were released, and in 1979 Randy made a big breakthrough with the self-penned **Just When I Needed You Most**, which hit No.4 on the pop charts and crossed into the lower regions of the country listings. He recorded three albums during the next few years, but was unable to repeat that commercial success.

A move to Los Angeles saw Randy sign to a publishing company that had affiliations in Nashville, and in 1984 the Oak Ridge Boys took his **I Guess It Never Hurts To Hurt Sometimes** to the top of the country charts. The following year Randy moved to Nashville and had more writing success with **I Will Whisper Your Name** (Michael Johnson) and **Bridges And Walls** (Oak Ridge Boys). He also signed a recording contract with 16th Avenue Records, scoring a minor country hit with **I Will Hold You** (1988).

Recommended:
Every Now And Then (–/Etude)

Porter Wagoner

Once a grocery store clerk, Wagoner (born in West Plains, Missouri, on August 12, 1930) used slow trading periods to pick guitar and sing. He was so impressive that he was engaged to promote the business over an early morning radio show.

His popularity on radio eventually led to a weekly series on KWTO, Springfield, in 1951. Wagoner later moved on to TV when KWTO became the home of Red Foley's Ozark Jubilee show. In August, 1952, he signed with RCA Records and, following several flops, had his first Top 5 hit with **A Satisfied Mind** three years later. Following two similarly successful singles in **Eat, Drink And Be Merry** (1955) and **What Would You Do (If Jesus Came To Your House)** (1956), the Missourian joined the Opry (1957). In 1960 he moved on to formulate his own TV show with singer Norma Jean (later replaced by Dolly Parton) and his band, the Wagonmasters.

Filmed in Nashville and initially syndicated to 18 stations, by the late '60s the programme was screened to over 100 outlets throughout the USA and Canada, establishing Wagoner's touring show as one of the most popular on the circuit.

Above: Porter Wagoner had a long association with Dolly Parton.

Predominantly straight country in his own musical approach, although sometimes seemingly a catalyst for more startling innovations (Buck Trent first began playing electric banjo on the Wagoner programme while Porter had also been involved in some of Dolly Parton's more contemporary moves), he managed to gain a consistent foothold in the upper reaches of the charts throughout the years. He had Top 10 solo hits with: **Your Old Love Letters** (1961), **Misery Loves Company** (1962), **Cold Dark Waters** (1962), **I've Enjoyed As Much Of This As I Can Stand** (1962), **Sorrow On The Rocks** (1964), **Green, Green Grass Of Home** (1965), **Skid Row Joe** (1965), **The Cold Hard Facts Of Life** (1967), **Carroll County Accident** (1968) and **Big Wind** (1969). He also shared an impressive number of hit duets with Dolly Parton, including **Burning The Midnight Oil**

(1971), **Please Don't Stop Loving Me** (1974) and **Is Forever Longer Than Always?** (1976).

Wagoner's albums have included 'live' recordings made in 1964 and 1966; a bluegrass offering, cut in 1965; some 'downer' sessions, typified by such releases as **The Cold Hard Facts Of Life** and **Confessions Of A Broken Man**, both releases dealing with the seamier side of humanity; and a number of duet LPs with Skeeter Davis and Dolly Parton.

The successful partnership with Dolly Parton came to an end in 1974. Porter didn't want her to leave, but Dolly wanted to be free to develop her career. This parting marked Porter's rapid fall from the top and, with his records failing to make the Top 10, he finally left RCA in 1981. He recorded briefly for Warner/Viva during 1982 and 1983. Today, Porter is a very successful Nashville businessman, though

The Farmer, Porter Wagoner's 1973 tribute. Courtesy RCA Records.

178

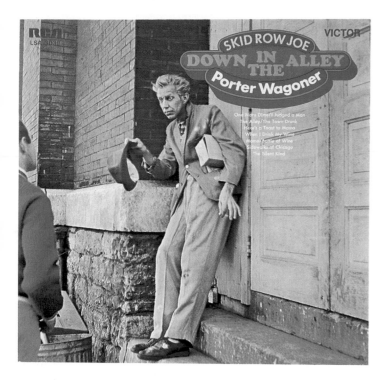

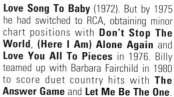

Down In The Alley, Porter Wagoner.
Courtesy RCA Records.

he continues to be active in country music, both recording and performing.

Recommended:
Carroll County Accident (RCA/–)
Today (RCA/–)
Highway Heading South (RCA/RCA)
The Thin Man From The West Plains
  (–/Bear Family)

With Dolly Parton:
Porter And Dolly (RCA/RCA)
Two Of A Kind (RCA/RCA)

Jimmy Wakely

One of country music's major stars during the '40s and early '50s, James Clarence Wakely was born in a log cabin at Mineola, Arkansas, on February 16, 1914.

Raised and schooled in Oklahoma, where he took such jobs as a sharecropper, journalist and filling station manager, he became a professional musician during the mid-'30s, forming the Jimmy Wakely Trio with Johnny Bond and Scotty Harrell in 1937. The group appeared daily on Oklahoma City's WKY radio station. In 1940, Gene Autry guested on the show, liked the trio and signed them for his Melody Ranch CBS radio programme.

On Melody Ranch, Wakely quickly established himself as a star in his own right – eventually securing parts in over 50 movies (in 1948 he was nominated as the fourth most popular western film actor – only Roy Rogers, Gene Autry and Charles Starrett being rated higher).

After two years on the Autry show, he left to form his own band, employing such musicians as Cliffie Stone, Spade Cooley, Merle Travis and Wesley Tuttle. By 1949 he had become so popular that he beat both Frank Sinatra and Bing Crosby in the 'Billboard' pop vocalist poll, enjoying a huge hit with his version of Floyd Tillman's **Slippin' Around**. Recorded as a duet with pop vocalist Margaret Whiting, the disc soon became a million-seller for Capitol Records. Other hits with Margaret Whiting

followed (including **I'll Never Slip Around Again**), the duo logging no less than seven Top 10 discs within two years.

Meanwhile, Wakely also did well in a solo capacity, such records as **I Love You So Much It Hurts** (1949), **I Wish I Had A Nickel** (1949), **My Heart Cries For You** (1950) and **Beautiful Brown Eyes** (1951) charting impressively. His 1948 hit, **One Has My Name, The Other Has My Heart**, in fact, started a whole cycle of 'cheatin' songs'

But during the mid-'50s, Wakely's career seemed to run out of steam, and though he had a CBS networked radio show until 1958 and co-hosted a TV series with Tex Ritter in 1961, his record sales diminished, Wakely forming his own label, Shasta. However, in the mid-'70s, Wakely was still in showbiz, mainly playing to clubs in Los Angeles and Las Vegas, using an act that featured his children, Johnny and Linda Lee. Following a prolonged illness, Jimmy Wakely died on September 23, 1982, in Mission Hills, California.

Recommended:
Jimmy Wakely Country (Shasta/–)
Slippin' Around (Dot/–)
Big Country Songs (Vocalion/–)
Sante Fe Trail (–/Stetson)

Billy Walker

Once billed as the 'Travelling Texan – The Masked Singer Of Country Songs', William Marvin Walker was born in Ralls, Texas on January 14, 1929.

In 1944, at the age of 15, while Walker was attending Whiteface High School, New Mexico, he won an amateur talent show. The contest also gained him his own 15-minute Saturday radio show on KICA, Clovis, New Mexico, Walker hitchhiking 80 miles to play on the programme, then hitching his way home again.

Joining the Big D Jamboree in Dallas during 1949, he adopted his masked singer guise; the ploy worked, gaining the Texan a considerable following and a subsequent record contract from Columbia.

Other shows followed, Walker appearing on the Louisiana Hayride in the early '50s, the Ozark Jubilee between 1955 and 1960, and joining the Opry in 1960. His first hit disc came in 1954 with **Thank You For Calling**, but it was not until 1962 and the release of **Charlie's Shoes**, a nationwide No.1, that Walker began to dominate the charts.

The majority of his discs became Top 20 entries during the following decade, providing Columbia with such hits as **Willie The Weeper** (1962), **Circumstances** (1964), **Cross The Brazos At Waco** (1964) and **Matamoros** (1965), before signing with Monument and scoring with **A Million And One** (1966), **Bear With Me A Little Longer** (1966), **Anything Your Heart Desires** (1967), **Ramona** (1968) and **Thinking About You, Baby** (1969).

By 1970 Walker had joined MGM, gaining high chart placings with **When A Man Loves A Woman** (1970), **I'm Gonna Keep On Loving You** (1971) and **Sing A**

The Hand Of Love, Billy Walker.
Courtesy MGM Records.

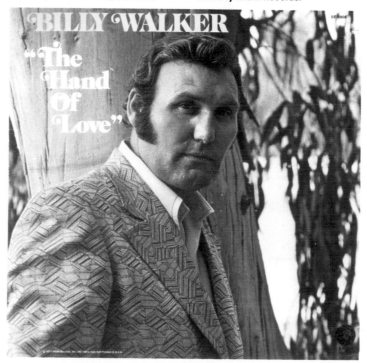

Love Song To Baby (1972). But by 1975 he had switched to RCA, obtaining minor chart positions with **Don't Stop The World, (Here I Am) Alone Again** and **Love You All To Pieces** in 1976. Billy teamed up with Barbara Fairchild in 1980 to score duet country hits with **The Answer Game** and **Let Me Be The One**.

Though he has failed to score Top 10 hits for many years, he has continued to record regularly for such minor labels as MRC, Scorpion, Caprice, Dimension and his own Tall Texan Records. Due to regular visits to Britain, he built up a whole new following in the 1980s, the likeable singer scoring with his Mexican-flavoured ballads that have played a major role in his long career. Walker has also made some film appearances, two of which were in 'Second Fiddle To A Steel Guitar' and 'Red River Round-Up'.

Recommended:
Alone Again (RCA/–)
Waking Up To Sunshine (Golden
  Memories/–)
Star Of The Grand Ole Opry (First
  Generation/–)
The Answer Game – with Barbara
  Fairchild (–/RCA)
Fine As Wine (MGM/–)
For My Friends (–/Bulldog)
Precious Memories (–/Word)

Charlie Walker

Born in Collins County, Texas, on November 2, 1926, Walker was a precocious singing and writing talent, becoming a good musician in his teens and joining Bill Boyd's Cowboy Ramblers in 1943. Later he was successful on radio, his announcing style sought after and getting him rated in 'Billboard's Top 10 Country Music Disc Jockey listing.

He signed with Columbia Records in the mid-'50s and in 1958 had his first big hit with **Pick Me Up On Your Way Down**. During the '60s and early '70s, he recorded for Columbia and Epic. Some of his hits were **Who'll Buy The Wine?** (1960), **Wild As A Wild Cat** (1965) and **Don't Squeeze My Sharmon** (1967). He also cut a series of honky-tonk titles that

I Don't Mind Goin' Under, Charlie
Walker. Courtesy RCA Records.

included **Close All The Honky Tonks** (1964), **Honky Tonk Season** (1969) and **Honky Tonk Women** (1970).

His announcing capabilities helped him gain many cabaret residencies, most notably at the Las Vegas Golden Nugget. A capable golfer, Walker has won respect as a knowledgeable golfing broadcaster.

In 1972 he became an RCA recording artist. His albums for the label included **Break Out The Bottle** and **I Don't Mind**

Charlie Walker

Going Under. A short spell with Capitol in 1974 proved fruitless, and since recording a couple of albums for Shelby Singleton's Plantation label in the late '70s, Charlie has concentrated on broadcasting.

Recommended:
Charlie Walker (MCA–Dot/–)

Jerry Jeff Walker

Originally a folkie operating out of New York, Jerry Jeff (real name Paul Crosby, born in Oneonta, New York, on March 16, 1942) became closely associated with the New Wave country movement emanating from Austin, Texas during the mid-'70s.

In 1966 he formed a rock group, Circus Maximus, with Austin songwriter Rob Runo, the band recording for Vanguard. However, Walker opted to become a solo act in 1968 and cut the self-penned **Mr Bojangles**, a memorable song regarding a street dancer he once met in a New Orleans jail, also providing Atco with an album of the same title. But although **Mr Bojangles** became a much-covered song and provided the Dirt Band with a Top 10 hit in 1970, Walker's career seemed to remain fairly stationary.

Signed to MCA in the early '70s, he mixed with fellow Texas singer-songwriters Guy Clark and Townes Van Zandt. With his own back-up unit, the Lost Gonzo Band, he recorded a series of good-timey, country albums that brought him a huge following across Texas.

Jerry Jeff split from the Lost Gonzo Band in 1977, but continued to record for MCA, later joining Elektra and forming the Bandito Band. In more recent years he has preferred to work as a solo performer, and has carved a new career as host of the popular TV series Austin City Limits.

Recommended:
Viva Terlingua (MCA/–)
Walker's Collectables (MCA/MCA)
It's A Good Night For Singing (MCA/MCA)
Too Old To Change (Elektra/–)
Hill Country Rain (Rykodisc/–)
Live At Gruene Hall (Rykodisc/–)
Navajo Rug (Rykodisc/–)

Jerry Wallace

Billed as 'Mr Smooth' – though he has been known to rock – Wallace is a one-time pop vocalist who swung into country music during the mid-'60s.

Born in Kansas City on December 15, 1933, singer-songwriter-guitarist Wallace was raised and educated in California. Following a brief term of service in the Navy, he made his first chart impact in 1958 when his recording of **How The Time Flies**, on Challenge, reached 11th place in the pop charts. The following year brought even more success when Wallace's version of **Primrose Lane**, a number later used as a theme for Henry Fonda's Smith Family TV series, became a million-seller.

After providing Challenge with 11 hit discs, Wallace signed for Mercury and cut more country-oriented material. **Life's Gone And Slipped Away** (1965) gained him his first country chart entry.

Since that time, he has cut sides for such labels as Liberty, Decca, MCA, MGM,

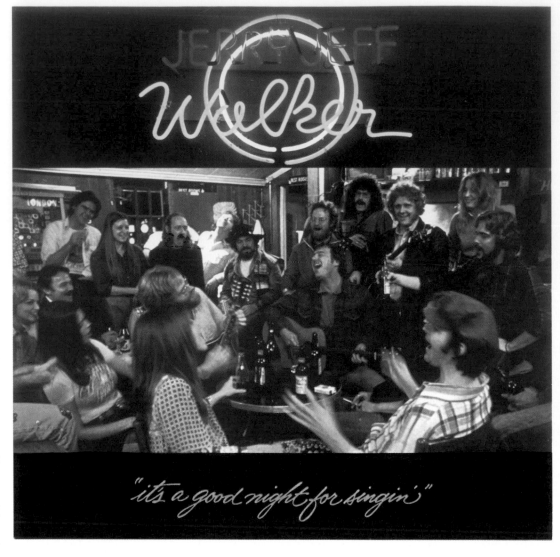

"it's a good night for singin'"

4-Star, Door Knob and BMA. His major country hits include: **The Morning After** (1971), **If You Leave Me Tonight, I'll Cry** (a No.1 in 1972), **Do You Know What It's Like To Be Lonesome?** (1973), **My Wife's House** (1974) and **I Miss You Already** (1977).

A performer on many top TV programmes, Wallace's voice has been heard on myriad commercials, while he has also turned up in such top-rated television shows as Hec Ramsey and Rod Serling's Night Gallery.

Recommended:
I Miss You Already (BMA/–)
The Golden Hits (4-Star/–)

Steve Wariner

Born in Kentucky on Christmas Day in 1954, Steve Noel Wariner grew up in a musical environment, with his father, a foundry worker, playing in a number of country bands in Indiana, where the family moved when Steve was young.

Before reaching his teens, Steve was playing bass in a little country band along with his father and an uncle. Although he was influenced by the music of George Jones and Merle Haggard, Steve's idol was guitar virtuoso Chet Atkins. When he finally signed a recording contract with RCA at the end of 1977, it was Chet who was to act as Steve's producer.

Prior to his move to Nashville and joining RCA, Steve had worked the road for three years with Dottie West and spent

little more than two years as front-man for Bob Luman's band. An overlooked but very talented songwriter, Steve wrote his first RCA release, **I'm Already Taken**, which was later recorded by Conway Twitty.

Between April, 1978 and the end of 1982, Steve scored a series of minor

I Am Ready, Steve Wariner. Courtesy Arista Records.

It's A Good Night For Singin', Jerry Jeff Walker's 1976 album. Courtesy MCA Records.

country hits such as **So Sad (To Watch Good Love Go Bad)**, **Forget Me Not**, **The Easy Part's Over**, **Your Memory** and **By Now**, finally hitting the jackpot with **All Roads Lead To You**, a 1982 No.1. At this time Steve's recordings were

**Midnight Fire, Steve Wariner.
Courtesy RCA Records.**

much like the Glen Campbell/Jimmy Webb pop-country classics of the '60s and were produced by Tom Collins.

A change of producer, with Norro Wilson and Tony Brown guiding Steve's recordings, led to a more country-styled approach and such Top 10 hits as **Don't Your Mem'ry Ever Sleep At Night**, **Midnight Fire** (both 1983) and **Lonely Women Make Good Lovers** (1984). When his contract with RCA came up for renewal at the end of 1984, he decided to make a move to MCA. For the first time he was allowed to play lead guitar on his own recordings, being turned loose on guitar solos, which proved to be nothing flashy but certainly well-executed and in keeping with the tone of the pieces.

The result has been such Top 10 hits as **Heart Trouble** and **What I Didn't Do** (both 1985), and No.1s with **Some Fools Never Learn** (1985), **You Can Dream Of Me**, **Life's Highway** (1986), **Smalltown Girl**, **The Weekend** and **Lynda** (all 1987). Wariner's wholesome good looks and pleasing personality made him a natural for such TV shows as Austin City Limits, Hee Haw, That Nashville Music and Country Music Comes Home. The hits continued with Top 10 winners **Baby I'm Yours**, **I Should Be With You** (1988) and two more No.1s with **Where Did I Go Wrong** and **I Got Dreams** (1989). In 1991 he teamed up with Mark O'Connor and the New Nashville Cats, vocalizing on the CMA award-winning **Restless**. He also moved over to Arista Records, with further Top 10 successes – **Leave Him Out Of This** (1991), **The Tips Of My Fingers** (1992) and **A Woman Loves** (1993).

Recommended:
Midnight Fire (RCA/–)
Life's Highway (MCA/–)
One Good Night Deserves Another (MCA/–)
I Am Ready (Arista/–)
Drive (Arista/–)
It's A Crazy World (MCA/MCA)
I Got Dreams (MCA/–)
I Should Be With You (MCA/–)

Doc Watson

Folk legend and heir to an old-time country tradition, guitarist-banjoist-singer Arthel (Doc) Watson was rediscovered in the boom folk years of the '60s and again in the '70s when the Nitty Gritty Dirt Band brought his music to the newly enthusiastic country-rock public.

Born in Deep Gap, North Carolina, on March 2, 1923, Doc was the son of a farmer who was prominent in the singing activities of the local Baptist church. Doc's grandparents lived with his immediately family and they taught the boy many traditional folk songs.

His first appearance was at the Boone, North Carolina, Fiddlers' Convention. He achieved fame locally but with country music 'smartening up' and with rock'n'roll finally hitting the scene, the mountain tradition was not foremost in the nation.

In 1960, some East Coast recording executives came to cut Clarence Ashley's String Band, and Ashley then appeared on a New York 'Friends Of Old Time Music' bill in 1961. Doc was invited along on the bill. As a consequence, he scored a solo gig at Gerde's Folk City in Greenwich Village, being rapturously received. In 1963, he consolidated his reputation considerably with an appearance on the Newport Folk Festival.

Doc relies heavily on traditional material. His voice, his guitar and banjo playing have a simplicity and intense profundity, almost making songs like **Tom Dooley** and **Shady Grove** his own.

During the '60s he recorded for Folkways and Vanguard Records. He has variously been heard on record with his mother, Mrs G. D. Watson, Jean Ritchie, his brother Arnold, Arnold's father-in-law Gaither Carlton and, most fruitfully, with son Merle, who sadly died when a tractor overturned on him at the Watson farm in Lenoir, North Carolina on October 23, 1985.

Although welded to an acoustic style which has been emulated widely by

Two Days In November, Doc and Merle Watson. Courtesy UA.

country-rock guitarists, Doc is no purist. His material runs the gamut of styles from bluegrass through western swing to a more commercial country-pop. During the 1970s he recorded for United Artists in Nashville with such session players as Joe Allen, Chuck Cochran, Johnny Gimble, Norman Blake and Jim Isbell, and even allowed his producer Jack Clement to surround him with strings on occasion.

A revered figure among old and young alike, drawing wild receptions quite out of keeping with his down-home musical style, Doc's concerts are virtually short courses in the history of American music, put across by using elements of field hollers, black blues, sacred music, mountain songs, gospel, bluegrass and even traces of jazz.

Recommended:
Memories (UA/–)
Two Days In November (UA/UA)
Lonesome Road (UA/–)
The Watson Family Tradition (–/Topic)
In The Pines (–/Sundown)
Guitar Album (Flying Fish/–)
Ballads From Deep (Vanguard/Vanguard)
Songs For Little Pickers (Sugar Hill/–)

Gene Watson

A singer with an easy-flowing style and a penchant for tear-stained ballads, Watson (born on October 11, 1943 in Palestine, Texas) initially worked out of Houston, becoming a resident singer at the Dynasty Club and recording for various independent record labels, such as Resco and Wide World, during the early '70s.

Obtaining a regional hit with **Love In The Hot Afternoon** (previously recorded by Waylon Jennings, but never released), Gene signed with Capitol Records, who made the record into a Top 5 country chart success in 1975. One of those country singers, well-equipped vocally, who found it a long and difficult task to win any real recognition, Gene is not a man to be thrown off balance by the recurrence of his name on the charts. In a five-year association with Capitol he enjoyed more than a dozen Top 5 hits, including: **Paper Rosie** (1977), **Farewell Party** (1979), **Nothing Sure Looked Good On You** and **Bedroom Ballad** (both 1980).

Working both on the road and in the studio with his Farewell Party Band, Gene moved over to MCA Records in 1981. He continued to produce first-rate country recordings, choosing his material with meticulous care and singing in a kind of mellow style, but with enough distinctiveness to make it much more than easy-listening. As well as scoring Top 10 country hits with such songs as **Maybe I Should Have Been Listening** (1981), **This Dream's On Me** (1982), **Sometimes I Get Lucky And Forget** (1983), **Forever Again** (19894) and **Got No Reason Now For Going Home** (1985), he has endeared himself to British country fans.

Towards the end of 1985, Gene changed labels once again, moving to Epic Records and scoring a Top 10 hit with **Memories To Burn** (1985). Several minor hits and a change to Warner Brothers followed, seeing him back in the Top 10 with **Don't Waste It On The Blues** (1989). This success was short-lived, and one of country music's finest honky-tonk balladeers ended up without a major label deal. He was recording for the Canadian

Above: Gene Watson cut his first record at 18 years old.

Broadland label in 1992, still maintaining that quality of straight country music.

Recommended:
Beautiful Country (Capitol/–)
Old Loves Never Die (MCA/–)
Little By Little (MCA/–)
Memories To Burn (Epic/–)
Heartaches, Love And Stuff (MCA/–)
In Other Words (Broadland Canada/–)
At Last (Warner Bros/–)

Kevin Welch

One of Nashville's most respected songwriters, Kevin Welch (born on August 17, 1955, in Long Beach, California) established his reputation as a songwriter par excellence by penning hits for the Judds, Ricky Skaggs, Sweethearts Of The Rodeo and Don Williams. This Oklahoma-raised performer was restless in his youth,

Because You Believed In Me, Gene Watson. Courtesy Capitol Records.

leaving home when he was 17 and dropping out of a college course to join a bluegrass band. By his mid-20s he'd already put a lot of miles on the road, that experience having paid off in a performance style and ear for powerful music that distinguish his work.

Moving to Nashville in the mid-'80s, Welch rapidly made his mark as a writer while still honing his skills as a performer. Working with his band, the Overtones, a unit comprised of crack studio musicians, he played the Nashville club circuit. He gained critical raves that landed him a recording contract with Warner/Reprise in 1988. One of country music's more inventive performers, Kevin's songs strive to recapture the romance and disillusionment of the road in lyrics full of stories about life-like characters. His eponymous debut album provided Welch with some minor country hits, including **Stay November** (1989), **Till I See You Again** (1990) and **True Love Never Dies** (1991). Touring with such diverse acts as the Oak Ridge Boys, Billy Bragg and Joe Ely also helped his reputation. During his 1991 European tour, his music was described as 'Western Beat'. It was a label that appealed precisely because of its subtle references. His music is western, not in a cowboy or swing sense, but because it is well-grounded in the roots of North America, and captures the heartbeat of American music. His second album was suitably titled **Western Beat**, and, as well as drawing critical praise from a wide cross-section of the media, has become a best-seller.

Recommended:
Western Beat (Reprise/–)
Kevin Welch (Reprise/–)

Freddy Weller

Born on September 9, 1947 in Atlanta, Georgia, Weller first achieved a fair degree of fame in the field of pop, both as a member of hit-parading rock group, Paul Revere And The Raiders, and as co-writer of many songs with Tommy Roe, including the million-sellers **Dizzy** (1968) and **Jam Up, Jelly Tight** (1969).

Once a bassist and guitarist with Joe South, Weller has also worked as a studio musician in Atlanta and toured as part of Billy Joe Royal's backup group. He became a country artist and signed to Columbia.

After achieving a Top 10 country hit with **Games People Play** in 1969, Weller enjoyed a successful patch through to 1971. **These Are Not My People**, **Promised Land**, **Indiana Lake** and **Another Night Of Love** all charted impressively during this period. In late 1974, Weller signed for Dot, scoring a couple of minor country hits.

He re-joined Columbia at the beginning of 1976, but was unable to make it back to the Top 10, only reaching the Top 30 with **Love Got In The Way** (1978) and **Fantasy Island** (1979), leading to him being dropped by the label in 1980.

Recommended:
Go For The Night (Columbia/–)
Roadmaster (Columbia/–)
The Promised Land (Columbia/–)
Back On The Street (–/Bulldog)

Kitty Wells

The acknowledged 'Queen Of Country Music', Kitty Wells (real name Muriel Deason) was born in Nashville, Tennessee, on August 30, 1918. As a child she sang gospel music at the neighbourhood church, at 14 learning to play guitar. Within a year

A Bouquet Of Country Hits, Kitty Wells. Courtesy MCA Records.

she was playing at local dances, some time later obtaining her first radio dates.

While appearing on station WXIX's Dixie Early Birds show, she met Johnny Wright (Johnny And Jack), whom she married two years later (1938). By this time she had become a featured artist on the Johnny And Jack touring show, adopting the name Kitty Wells from a folk song called **Sweet Kitty Wells**.

With their backup unit the Tennessee Mountain Boys, Johnny And Jack and Kitty Wells toured widely during the late '30s and the war years of the '40s, their biggest breaks on radio coming in 1940 on WBIG, Greensboro, North Carolina, then later on WNOX Knoxville's Mid-Day Merry-Go-Round.

In 1947 came Johnny, Jack and Kitty's membership on Grand Ole Opry, after which they moved to Shreveport to become the stars of KWKH's new Louisiana Hayride. Five years later came an offer of a regular spot on the Opry, plus a record contract from Decca (she had previously recorded with RCA-Victor). The same year saw the release of **It Wasn't God Who Made Honky Tonk Angels**, an answer disc to Hank Thompson's **Wild Side Of Life**. This enabled Kitty to become the first female to have a No.1 country hit – although Patsy Montana's **I Wanna Be A Cowboy's Sweetheart** would have reached No.1 if charts had existed in 1935.

Since that time, Kitty Wells has amassed an amazing number of chart entries, including duets with Roy Drusky, Red Foley, Roy Acuff, Johnny Wright and Webb Pierce. The biggest of her solo successes were: **Paying For That Back Street Affair** (1953), **Making Believe** (1955), **Searching** (1956), **Jealousy** (1958), **Mommy For A Day** (1959), **Amigo's Guitar** (1959), **Left To Right** (1960), **Heartbreak U.S.A.** (1961), **Unloved, Unwanted** (1962), **Password** (1964) and **You Don't Hear** (1965).

Her awards are equally numerous and include 'Billboard's No.1 Country Music Female Artist Of The Year 1954–65, a 1974 Woman Of The Year award from the Nashville Association of Business and Professional Women, plus a citation for the Most Outstanding Tennessee Citizen in 1954.

Kitty, who has three children – Ruby, Carol Sue and Bobby – eventually

Above. Kitty Wells, the first woman to have a No.1 country hit.

Dottie West

Known as the 'Country Sunshine' girl after writing and recording a song of that title for a Coke commercial, Dottie was born in McMinnville, Tennessee, on October 11, 1932, one of ten children. Farm raised, Dorothy Marie still had time to gain a college degree while helping to work the cotton and sugar cane fields.

She later incorporated these experiences into her songs, but one of Dottie's strengths has also been her ability to adapt pop stylings.

In the early 1950s, she studied music at Tennessee Tech and there met Bill West, her future husband. Bill was studying engineering but he played steel guitar and accompanied Dottie at college concerts. They later moved to Ohio where they appeared as a duo on local TV in the Cleveland area.

While visiting relatives in Nashville in 1959, they met some executives from Starday Records and were given a record contract. This resulted in local live appearances but little else.

Success eluded her until 1963 when Dottie, by this time signed to RCA, recorded **Let Me Off At The Corner**, a Top 30 disc. A year later came the big one – **Here Comes My Baby** – a West original that became covered by Perry Como, providing him with a pop hit and also earning Dottie a Grammy award.

Dottie then became an Opry regular (1964), arranged and worked with the Memphis and Kansas City Symphony Orchestra and provided RCA with such major solo hits as: **Would You Hold It Against Me?** (1966), **Paper Mansions** (1967), **Country Girl** (1968), **Forever Yours** (1970), **Country Sunshine** (1973) and **Last Time I Saw Him** (1974). She also recorded hit duets with Jim Reeves (**Love Is No Excuse** – 1964) and Don Gibson (**Rings Of Gold** and **There's A Story Goin' Round** – both 1969).

Between collecting numerous awards, making a few films, writing some 400 songs and commercials, and fitting in recording dates and several tours, she also found time to raise four children and marry again – her second husband was drummer Byron Metcalf.

In 1978 Dottie teamed up with Kenny Rogers for a successful duet partnership which resulted in the Top 10 hits, **Everytime Two Fools Collide** (1978) and **All I Ever Need Is You** (1979). The pair were named CMA Vocal Duo in both 1978 and 1979. Dottie had signed with United Artists Records in 1976 and continued to score major country hits.

The red-haired beauty, who had helped launch the careers of Larry Gatlin and Steve Wariner, found herself something of a country sex queen in her late 40s, with full-colour centrespreads in several of the leading American magazines. Remaining a member of the Opry, Dottie notched up a few minor hits for the Permian label in 1984–85, then her career went into a sharp decline. She became caught up in a tragic spiral of disasters before a car wreck took her life on September 4, 1991. Hell-bent on destruction, Dottie was hooked on drugs and booze and reportedly owed over $1 million in back taxes, with the IRS taking many of her possessions, and for a time she lived in a parking lot on her tour bus.

terminated her long association with Decca during the mid-'70s, signing for the Macon-based Capricorn label and cutting an album, aptly named **Forever Young**. In 1976 she received the supreme accolade – being elected to the Country Music Hall Of Fame. Kitty still continues to tour all over

Special Delivery, Dottie West. Courtesy UA Records.

America and records for her own Ruboca Records label, maintaining the style for which she is best known and refusing to be drawn into a modern pop-country sound.

Recommended:
Early Classics (Golden Country/–)
The Kitty Wells Story (MCA/MCA)
The Golden Years (Rounder/–)
Forever Young (Capricorn/–)
The Queen Of Country Music, 1949–1958 (–/Bear Family)
Country Music Hall Of Fame (MCA/–)

If It's All Right With You, Dottie West. Courtesy RCA Records.

Recommended:
High Times (Liberty/–)
Wild West (Liberty/–)
Special Delivery (UA/UA)
Carolina Cousins (RCA/RCA)
Everytime Two Fools Collide – with Kenny Rogers (UA/UA)

Shelly West

Daughter of Dottie West and her first husband, steel guitarist Bill West, Shelly (born on May 23, 1958 in Nashville, Tennessee) initially made an impression as the duet partner of David Frizzell on the 1981 chart-topper, **You're The Reason God Made Oklahoma**.

Shelly began performing in Dottie's shows in 1975, soon after her graduation from Nashville's Hillsboro High School. During her year and a half with Dottie, Shelly gradually worked her way up from harmony singing to her own solo spot.

Towards the end of 1977, she and Allen Frizzell (David and Lefty's younger brother who was employed as Dottie's front-man and guitarist) moved to California to pursue their own solo careers. They teamed up with David and worked honky-tonk club circuits.

Eventually David and Shelly began singing together and recorded a duet album featuring **You're The Reason God Made Oklahoma**, a song that Clint Eastwood insisted on using in his film, 'Any Which Way You Can'. Frizzell and West continued with such duet hits as: **Texas State Of Mind** (1981), **Another Honky Tonk Night On Broadway** (1982), **Cajun Invitation** (1983), **Another Dawn Breaking Over Georgia** (1984) and **Do Me Right** (1985).

These duets paved the way for Shelly's solo career, and she made her mark on the charts with **Jose Cuervo** and **Another Motel Memory** (both 1983), **Flight 309 To Nashville** (1984), **Now There's You** and **Don't Make Me Wait On The Moon** (both 1985). For a while Shelly was married to Allen Frizzell, but the couple separated and were divorced in 1985.

In Session, Shelly West and David Frizzell. Courtesy WEA-Viva Records.

Billy Edd Wheeler

Born in Whitesville, West Virginia, on December 9, 1932, Billy Edd is a college-educated country artist. He has a BA degree from Berea College, Kentucky, attended Yale Drama School and has been, variously, an editor, a music business executive, a Navy pilot and an instructor at Berea College.

The Kingston Trio had a Top 10 pop hit with his **Reverend Mr. Black** in 1963 and Wheeler himself enjoyed a rare hit single with **The Little Brown Shack Out Back**, which nearly (but not quite) topped the country charts in 1964, helping him earn an ASCAP writer's award.

Despite various changes of record company (he has been with such labels as Monitor, Kapp, UA and RCA), his only real influence upon the charts has been through songwriting. Johnny Cash and June Carter added to Wheeler's royalty cheque by recording his **Jackson**, a cross-over hit in 1967, and Kenny Rogers recorded the multi-million-selling pop-country smash **Coward Of The County** in 1979.

A collector of folk material – and author of a folk play – Billy Edd Wheeler was responsible for creating a special music room in the Mountain Hall Of Fame, Richwood, West Virginia.

Clarence White

A rock musician with a bluegrass background, guitarist Clarence White was born in Lewiston, Maine on June 7, 1944. Raised in California, he played with the Country Boys at the age of ten, the group's other members being his brothers, Roland (16) and Eric (12).

A bluegrass unit, working at various barn dances and local functions in the Burbank area, the Country Boys materialized into the Kentucky Colonels in 1962. The line-up then was: Clarence (guitar), Roland (mandolin), Roger Bush (bass), Billy Ray Latham (banjo) and Leroy Mack (dobro).

Two albums were recorded before Clarence left in 1965 to become a session-man, appearing on disc with Ricky Nelson, the Everlys, the Byrds, Gene Clark, the Flying Burritos, Wynn Stewart and others.

After cutting a never-released solo album for the Bakersfield International label and working sporadically with Cajun Gib And Gene (Gib Guilbeau and Gene Parsons), White formed Nashville West, a short-lived country-rock unit that featured both Guilbeau and Parsons plus bassist Wayne Moore. But in September 1968, he became a regular member of the Byrds.

Returning to session work once more, White began fashioning a new solo album, also putting in some gigs with the re-

formed Kentucky Colonels. However, the solo album was never completed; White was knocked down and killed by a drunken woman driver while loading equipment on to a van following a gig on July 14, 1973.

Joy White

Red-headed Joy White is one of the new faces of country music who has brought years of experience to Nashville. Many country music authorities have predicted a bright future for this gutsy firecracker.

Joy was born in the small farming town of Turrell, Arkansas, but grew up in Mishawaka, Indiana. Her father was a guitar player and all of the family would get together to sing and play music. Joy sang in church as a child, harmonized on country songs at family picnics and by her teenage years was belting out rock'n'roll songs on the back of flatbed trucks. With her own bands, she toured extensively in the region around her hometown and also earned extra money performing jingles and commercials for local radio and TV.

Eventually Joy moved to Nashville in the late '80s, rapidly making an impact singing on demos and back-up vocals on recording sessions. In 1991 she landed a recording contract with Columbia Records, and those years of singing paid off with her debut album, **Between Midnight And Hindsight**. This dynamic set showed Joy to be a passionate vocalist, capable of delivering her own brand of hot-blooded country. The rockin' **Little Things** became a minor country hit at the end of 1992, in the first phase of establishing Joy White as one of the brightest talents of the '90s.

The White Brothers, Clarence, Eric and Roland White. Courtesy Rounder Records.

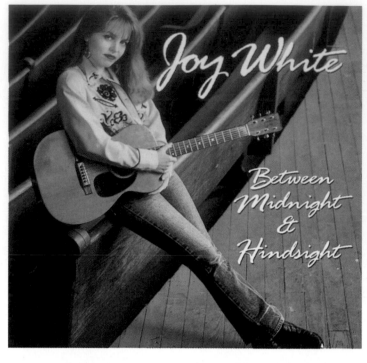

Between Midnight And Hindsight, Joy White. Courtesy Columbia Records.

The Whites

Buck White, piano, mandolin; Cheryl White Warren, acoustic bass; Sharon White Skaggs, acoustic guitar.

Although a distinctive and fascinating new group who emerged in the '80s, the Whites, in fact, go back a long way, with father Buck White having roots in western swing music and the distinction of playing piano on the original recording of Slim Willet's **Don't Let The Stars Get In Your Eyes** (1952).

Buck, who grew up in Texas, met his wife Pat in the early '50s, and music played a major role in their family life. At that time he played piano for various swing bands in and around the Wichita Falls area. In 1962 the family uprooted and moved to Arkansas where Buck became involved in bluegrass.

Working as Buck White And The Down Home Folks, the family group, consisting of Buck, Pat and their two daughters, Cheryl

and Sharon, became popular on the bluegrass festival and other country circuits. In the early '70s, a move to Nashville was made and they recorded their first album, **Buck White And The Down Home Folks**, for County Records in April, 1972. It was to be another five years before they recorded a second album, **In Person**, by which time Cheryl and Sharon were able to work full-time with the group.

These were hard times for the family group, though, as bluegrass music was not exactly popular, and the two girls had to find various jobs to supplement their meagre showbusiness earnings. They were still recording regularly for Ridge Runner and Sugar Hill.

A short-lived recording contract with Capitol Records in 1982 came at the same time as they decided to change their name to the Whites. One single was released, **Send Me The Pillow You Dream On**, which made the charts, but Capitol decided not to release any further records.

Emmylou Harris and Ricky Skaggs eventually became involved in the group's career, with Emmylou inviting them to open her tour in support of her **Blue Kentucky Girl** album, and Ricky offering to produce an album for Warner-Curb. This resulted in the Whites being nominated in the CMA 1983 awards as Vocal Group Of The Year and achieving Top 10 country hits with **You Put The Blue In Me**, **Hangin' Around** (both 1983) and **I Wonder Who's Holding My Baby Tonight** (1984).

Curb Records amalgamated with MCA in 1984 and the Whites continued to score Top 10 hits on that label, with **Pins And Needles** (1984) and **If It Ain't Love (Let's Leave It Alone)** (1965). Members of the Grand Ole Opry since 1984, their style is based upon the distinctive harmonies of Cheryl and Sharon, the expert mandolin playing of Buck and the dobro work of Jerry Douglas, who has been playing with the Whites since the late '70s. In 1989 they moved on to the gospel-based Canaan Records.

Above: The Whites – the group consists of Buck White and his daughters Cheryl and Sharon. Buck is a fine blues pianist and expert mandolinist.

Whole New World (MCA-Curb/MCA)
Poor Folks Pleasure (–/Sundown)

Keith Whitley

Keith Whitley, one of the purest honky-tonk singers to make it to the top in country music in the '80s, was a sad victim of his own drinking excesses, which saw his career come to an end when he had finally made that long-awaited breakthrough to international acclaim and chart-topping records.

Though he was considered a 'New Traditionalist', Whitley, who was born on July 1, 1955, in Sandy Hook, Kentucky, had been around the scene for years before most of the newcomers had even picked up a guitar. Something of a child prodigy, he learned to play guitar at six and was on the radio with Buddy Starcher in Charleston, West Virginia, when eight. His real roots lay with honky-tonk music gleaned through his mother's record collection, but when young Keith started to play music, there were no honky-tonk musicians around, so he turned to bluegrass. In the late '60s, at age 13, together with his brother Dwight and fellow Kentuckian Ricky Skaggs, he formed the Lonesome Mountain Boys, a bluegrass group that rapidly built up a local reputation. They did a few shows with Ralph Stanley and the Clinch Mountain Boys, and in early 1971 Keith and Ricky joined the legendary band, recording a half dozen or so albums with Stanley, including a gospel collection called **Cry From The Cross**, which was named Bluegrass Album Of The Year in 1971.

Two years later Whitley formed his own band, the New Tradition, which enabled

him to stretch the boundaries of bluegrass. As he branched out from bluegrass, he changed the band's name to the Country Store. In 1977 he was invited to join J.D. Crowe And The New South, a country/bluegrass fusion band. He often took lead vocals, both onstage and on recordings, leading to many recommending that he take his work to Nashville.

By this time he was married and also had a reputation for being a heavy drinker, but he heeded the advice, and signed with RCA Records in late 1982, but was still living in Kentucky. A year later he did move to Nashville, in order to actively pursue a solo career. He signed a writer's contract with Tree Music and worked as a writer and demo singer, waiting for his recording deal to take shape. Finally Whitley made his chart debut with **Turn Me To Love** (1984), followed in 1985 with a mini-LP, **A Hard Act To Follow**, which hardly set the world alight. He scored his first Top 20 hit with the lightweight **Miami, My Amy** at the end of 1985, followed by three Top 10 entries in **Ten Feet Away**, **Homecoming '63** (1986) and **Hard Livin'** (1987). In 1986, following a messy divorce, he married Lorrie Morgan, who was also struggling to establish herself as a country music performer, and, like her husband, was signed to RCA.

Working with various producers, Keith Whitley had recorded extensively, and though he had cut some fine material, including **Does Fort Worth Ever Cross Your Mind**, which was never released, his career seemed to be faltering. A new producer, Garth Fundis, was brought into the picture, and RCA gave Keith Whitley one last shot at making it. His third album, **Don't Close Your Eyes**, captured his hard honky-tonk country sound to perfection. Whether it was sad, tear-stained ballads or kickin' uptempo songs, Whitley was in top vocal form. The result was a gold album and chart-topping singles with **Don't Close Your Eyes** (Billboard's No.1 Country Hit, 1988), **When You Say**

Nothing At All (1988) and **I'm No Stranger To The Rain** (1989).

By rights Whitley should have been on top of the world, but he was still drinking heavily. He lost his last battle with the bottle, on May 9, 1989, when an accidental overdose in his home at Brentwood took his life; the cruel irony was that he drank his life away at the very time his musical

Below: Keith Whitley made a huge impact in the '80s, but died in 1989 due to an alcohol overdose.

career seemed poised, after so many long years, for real stardom.

A week before his death, he had completed a new album, **I Wonder Do You Think Of Me**, which became a posthumous success with both the title song and **It Ain't Nothing'** topping the singles chart and **I'm Over You** making Top 5, while the album gained another gold disc. That album, plus the subsequent **Kentucky Bluebird**, a superb set put together by Garth Fundis in 1991 from previously unreleased tracks taken from original song demos or recordings that were not included on the singer's previous four albums, prove conclusively that country music was robbed of one of the finest pure-country song stylists, a singer who had never realized his vast unfulfilled potential.

The success of his recordings have continued long after his death with a **Greatest Hits** set in 1990 gaining a third gold disc, while a duet with Lorrie Morgan of **'Til A Tear Becomes A Rose** went Top 20 and was also named the CMA Vocal Event Of The Year in 1990. Another duet recording, **Brotherly Love**, recorded in 1987 with Earl Thomas Conley, but never issued, rose to No.2 on the charts in 1991. The question now remains as to how many more Keith Whitley recordings can RCA 'polish' up for release. There is little doubt that Keith Whitley is a singer whose music and memory will continue to endure for many years.

Recommended:
Don't Close Your Eyes (RCA/RCA)
I Wonder Do You Think Of Me (RCA/RCA)
Kentucky Bluebird (RCA/RCA)

Ray Whitley

Despite a late start, Ray Whitley became a quite successful jack-of-all-trades in the era of the singing cowboy. Born on December 5, 1901, near Atlanta, Georgia,

Later, in 1952, he signed for Imperial Records and staked an immediate claim to stardom with his semi-yodelled version of **Indian Love Call**. This was followed by **Rose Marie**, a massive seller. It provided Whitman with a gold disc and an audience ready to snap up such other offerings as **Secret Love** (1954), **Cattle Call** (1955), **More Than Yesterday** (1965), **Guess Who?** (1970) and **Something Beautiful** (1971).

Whitman's reliance on mainly sweet, romantic ballads, purveyed in a rich voice that switches easily to falsetto, had made him a worldwide favourite. But nowhere is he more popular than in Britain where he became the first country vocalist to perform at the London Palladium. His British tours are usually in the SRO bracket while such albums as **The Very Best Of Slim Whitman** and **Red River Valley** topped the UK charts in 1976 and 1977 respectively.

A special TV-advertised set of his most popular numbers became a big seller in America in 1983, introducing Slim to a whole new audience, while he has continued to record regularly for United Artists, Cleveland International and Epic.

Recommended:

15th Anniversary (Imperial/Liberty)
Yodeling (Imperial/Liberty)
Slim Whitman Collection (–/UA)
Songs I Love To Sing (Epic/Epic)
Angeline (Epic/Epic)
25th Anniversary Concert (–/UA)
Country Style (–/Music For Pleasure)
Rose Marie & Other Love Songs (–/Pickwick)
50 Original Tracks (–/Liberty)

Henry Whitter

One of the earliest of the country musicians to be recorded – it is claimed that his earliest recordings were pre-dated only by those of Eck Robertson – William Henry Whitter was born near Fries, Virginia, on April 6, 1892.

Working in a cotton mill to earn a living, he learned guitar, fiddle, piano, harmonica

A Portrait, Wilburn Brothers. Courtesy MCA Records.

Red River Valley, Slim Whitman. Courtesy UA Records. Slim is a huge country figure in the US, where his albums are regularly advertised on television.

Whitley spent some time in the Navy and in Philadelphia and New York, where he pursued music as a hobby.

He auditioned for radio in New York City, and rapidly rose to co-host the WHN Barn Dance in the mid-1930s. Here he also recorded for the American Record Company complex, and also for Decca, his biggest hits being his theme song, **Blue Yodel Blues**, and **The Last Flight Of Wiley Post**.

One of the earliest singing cowboys to invade Hollywood, he appeared in films as early as 1936. He spent 1938–42 at RKO, where he made 18 musical shorts of his own and was the singing sidekick to George O'Brien and Tim Holt. His last role was as Watts, James Dean's manager in 'Giant'. Whitley was active musically during his film period, both as a cowboy singer and fronting a western swing band.

An active songwriter, he wrote or co-wrote with Fred Rose many of Gene Autry's big hits, including **Back In The Saddle Again**, **Lonely River**, **I Hang My Head And Cry** and **Ages And Ages Ago**.

In addition, Whitley also managed both the Sons Of The Pioneers and Jimmy Wakely for a time, and helped Gibson design and build their first J-200 guitar.

He was still turning up at western film festivals, singing and doing tricks with his bullwhip until shortly before his death in California on February 21, 1979.

Slim Whitman

Born Otis Dewey Whitman Jr in Tampa, Florida, on January 20, 1924, Whitman's early interest was in sport rather than music. He became a star pitcher with his Tampa high school team and hoped to make a career in baseball. However, on leaving school, he took a job in a meat-packing plant, where he met his wife.

Just prior to Pearl Harbor, Whitman became a shipyard fitter in Tampa, enlisting in the Navy during 1943. While in the Navy he learned guitar and entertained at shipboard events, upon return to civilian life splitting his time between baseball and entertaining when not working.

In 1946 he gained a contract with the Plant City Berries of the Orange Belt League – but his musical career also

Country Style, Slim Whitman. Courtesy Music For Pleasure.

prospered via radio spots on Tampa WDAE and many local club bookings. It was at this point that Whitman opted for music as a full-time occupation and began establishing his reputation beyond the bounds of Tampa, in 1949 winning a record contract with RCA. After gaining some attention with **Casting My Lasso To The Sky**, he moved to Shreveport, becoming a regular on the Louisiana Hayride.

Right: A consistent Top 10 hit-maker, Don Williams is known as the 'Gentle Giant Of Country Music'.

and organ, and began performing around the Fries area. In March 1923, he visited New York, gaining an audition with the General Phonograph Company and recording two numbers which were promptly shelved.

However, in the wake of Fiddlin' John Carson's success with his Okeh sides, Whitter was recalled to New York in December, 1923, there waxing nine numbers for Okeh release. The first of these, **The Wreck On The Southern Old '97**, backed with **Lonesome Road Blues**, was issued in January, 1924. Later that year, **Old '97** was to be recorded in the slightly different version by Vernon Dalhart.

Whitter continued to record as a soloist, an accompanist and as a bandleader, with Whitter's Virginia Breakdowners. He also formed a successful musical alliance with blind fiddler George Banman Grayson, recording with him several times between 1927 and 1929.

This partnership terminated when Grayson died in a road accident during the mid-'30s, and though Whitter continued in a solo role until the commencement of the 1940s, his health gradually deteriorated. He died from diabetes in North Carolina on November 10, 1941.

Wilburn Brothers

Once part of a family act that included their father, mother, elder brothers and a sister, Doyle (born in Thayer, Missouri, on July 7, 1930) and Teddy Wilburn (born in Thayer on November 30, 1931) began as hometown street corner singers. The Wilburn Family eventually toured the South and established a reputation that led to an Opry signing in 1941.

In the wake of the Korean War, Teddy and Doyle began working as a duo, touring with Webb Pierce and Faron Young. Obtaining a record contract with Decca, they scored a Top 10 disc in 1956 with **Go Away With Me**. This was the first of an impressive tally of hits that extended into the early '70s.

The Wilburns appealed to a wide audience, a fact reflected in their record sales of 1959 when three of their releases, **Which One Is To Blame?**, **Somebody Back In Town** and **A Woman's Intuition**, were major hits.

Founders of the Wil-Helm Talent Agency in conjunction with Smiley Wilson, the Wilburns found themselves representing many of Nashville's leading talents – including Loretta Lynn, whom they featured on their own highly popular TV show and for whom they obtained a recording contract with Decca.

Owners of Surefire Music, a publishing company, they have published the songs of Loretta Lynn, Johnny Russell and Patty Loveless, having no fewer than seven songs in the 'Coalminer's Daughter' film. They have enjoyed such Top 10 discs as **Trouble's Back In Town** (1962), **Tell Her No** (1963), **It's Another World** (1965) and **Hurt Her Once For Me** (1966). They continued to work the Opry throughout the '70s. Doyle Wilburn died from cancer on October 16, 1982, in Nashville. The family tradition has been maintained, Teddy still

appearing on the Opry, occasionally accompanied by brothers Lester and Leslie.

Recommended:
A Portrait Of The Wilburn Brothers (MCA/–)
Sing Your Heart Out (Decca/–)
Country Gold (Decca/Stetson)

Doc Williams

Although he has never had a hit record, Doc Williams has been one of the most popular regional acts in country music. Along with his wife Chickie and their band the Border Riders, they still play hundreds of dates a year, filling houses in the Northeast and in the Canadian Maritimes, largely on the strength of their long-time association with WWVA and the Wheeling Jamboree.

Born Andrew J. Smik, of Bohemian descent, on June 26, 1914 Doc grew up in the musically rich area of eastern Pennsylvania. Except for brief stays at WREC in Memphis (1939) and WFMD in Frederick, Maryland (1945), he has remained in that area: Cleveland from 1934 to 1936, then Pittsburgh and finally Wheeling, from 1937.

In 1948 he married Jessie Wanda Crupe, who became known as Chickie, and they have had many regionally popular records on their own label, Wheeling: **Beyond The Sunset, Mary Of The Wild Moor, Silver Bells** and Doc's own song **Willie Roy, The Crippled Boy**.

A staunch traditionalist and a long-time spokesman for Wheeling, WWVA and the

Wheeling Jamboree, Doc Williams has never achieved national success or huge record sales, but has been a great influence in the northeast and in Canada.

Recommended:
From Out Of The Beautiful Hills Of West Virginia (Wheeling/–)
Doc 'n' Chickie Together (Wheeling/–)
Wheeling Back To Wheeling (Wheeling/–)

Don Williams

Voted Country Artist Of The Decade by British fans in a 1980 poll, Don (born on May 27, 1939, near Plainview, Texas) has been called the 'Gentle Giant of Country Music', due to his laid-back personality and singing style. He first came to prominence with the pop-folk group, the Pozo Seco singers, in 1965. The group (comprised of Williams, Susan Taylor and Lofton Cline) had a major hit the following year with **Time**.

Between 1966 and 1967, the Pozos also had best-sellers with **I'll Be Gone, I Can Make It With You, Look What You've Done, I Believed It All** and **Louisiana Man**. But gradually their popularity waned and in 1971 Williams returned to Texas to join his father-in-law in his business.

A solo recording venture by former Pozo Susan Taylor had Don return to Nashville in a writing capacity, but he soon began singing once more. A solo album, **Don Williams Volume 1**, was released on Jack Clements' independent JMI label during 1973.

His debut solo single had been **Don't You Believe** (June, 1972) but it was his second, **The Shelter Of Your Eyes**, that gave him his first major bite at the county charts. Don finally made the country Top 10 with **We Should Be Together** and he topped the charts a few months later with **I Wouldn't Want To Live If You Didn't Love Me**.

He also hit the top spot with such songs as: **You're My Best Friend** and **Love Me Tonight** (both 1975); **'Til The Rivers All Run Dry** and **Say It Again** (both 1976); **Some Broken Hearts Never Mend** and **I'm Just A Country Boy** (both 1977); **Tulsa Time** (1978); **It Must Be Love** (1979); **I Believe In You** (a pop cross-over which hit No.24 on the pop charts in 1980); **Lord I Hope This Day Is Good** (1981); **If Hollywood Don't Need You** (1982); **Love Is On A Roll** (1983); **Stay Young** (1984) and **Walking A Broken Heart** (1985).

Harmony, Don Williams. Courtesy MCA Records.

Don Williams

Surprisingly he made a British breakthrough with **I Recall A Gypsy Woman**, which made the British Top 10 in 1976, yet was never released as a single in America. He emerged as the British No.1 album-seller in 1978 (outselling every rock, country and pop act).

Don tries to keep his public appearances down to a minimum and spends much of his time writing songs, recording or tending his farm near Ashland City, Tennessee. He keeps his private life very much detached from his showbiz career, which resulted in him being dubbed the 'Reluctant Superstar'. In 1986 he made a label change, moving from MCA (formerly ABC-Dot) to Capitol, maintaining the familiar Don Williams' sound for such Top 10 entries as **Heartbeat In The Darkness** (No.1, 1986), **I'll Never Be In Love Again** (1987) and **Another Place, Another Time** (1988). He then moved on to RCA, scoring with **One Good Well** (1989), **Back In My Younger Days** (1990) and **Lord Have Mercy On A Country Boy** (1991).

Recommended:

The Best Of The Pozo Seco Singers (–/CBS Embassy)
Visions (ABC/ABC)
Portrait (MCA/MCA)
Listen To The Radio (MCA/MCA)
Café Carolina (MCA/MCA)
New Moves (Capitol/Capitol)
True Love (RCA/RCA)
It's Gotta Be Magic (–/Pickwick)
Traces (Capitol/Capitol)

Hank Williams Sr

One of the most charismatic figures in country music – his Opry performance of June 11, 1949, when his audience required him to reprise **Lovesick Blues** several times, is still considered as the Ryman's greatest moment – Hank was born Hiram King Williams in Georgia, Alabama, on September 17, 1923.

A member of the church choir at six, he was given a guitar by his mother a year later, receiving some tuition from Tee-Tot (Rufe Payne), an elderly black street musician. When barely a teenager he won $15 singing **WPA Blues** at a Montgomery amateur contest, then formed a band, the Drifting Cowboys, which played on station WSFA, Montgomery, for over a decade.

In 1946 Williams signed with Sterling Records, switching to the newly formed MGM label in 1947. Though virtually an alcoholic, he was booked as a regular on KWKH's Louisiana Hayride. After having scored with his recording of **Lovesick Blues**, he signed a contract with the Grand Ole Opry in 1949.

An early recording, **Move It On Over**, had already been a minor hit for Williams, but, after the runaway success of **Lovesick Blues** (a song waxed by yodeller Emmett Miller in 1925), he began cutting Top 10 singles with almost monotonous regularity.

With Fred Rose masterminding every Williams' recording session, arranging, playing, producing and often participating in the songwriting, such hits as **Wedding Belles**, **Mind Your Own Business**, **You're Gonna Change** and **My Bucket's Got A Hole In It** all charted during 1949. The following year provided: **I Just Don't Like This Kind Of Living'**, **Long Gone Lonesome Blues**, **Why Don't You Love**

Me?, Why Should We Try Anymore? and **Moaning The Blues**.

These were followed by: **Cold, Cold Heart**, **Howlin' At The Moon**, **Hey Good Lookin'**, **Crazy Love**, **Baby We're Really In Love** (1951), **Honky Tonk Blues**, **Half As Much**, **Jambalaya**, **Settin' The Wood On Fire** and **I'll Never Get Out Of This World Alive** (1952). The last was ironically released just before his death (from a heart attack brought on by drinking) on New Year's Day, 1953.

He and his Drifting Cowboys had been booked to play a show in Canton, Ohio, and Williams hired a driver to chauffeur him through a snowstorm to the gig. He fell asleep along the way – but when the driver tried to rouse him at Oak Hill, Virginia, he was found to be dead. After his death, his records continued to sell in massive quantities. **Your Cheatin' Heart**, **Take These Chains From My Heart**, **I Won't Be Home No More** and **Weary Blue From Waitin'** all charted during the year that followed.

The last months of Williams' life – though financially rewarding – were ultra-tragic. A drug user in order to combat a spinal ailment caused by being thrown from a horse at the age of 17, he was fired from the Grand Ole Opry in August 1952 because of perpetual drunkenness. He was also divorced by his wife Audrey Sheppard – though he re-married to Billie Jean Jones soon after.

A difficult man to work with, being moody and uncommunicative, he was much respected and well loved by the country music fraternity. Over 20,000 people attended his funeral in Montgomery, at which Roy Acuff, Carl

Smith, Red Foley and Ernest Tubb paid tribute in song.

His songs were well accepted in pop music as well – his compositions providing million-selling discs for Joni James (**Your Cheatin' Heart** – 1953), Tony Bennett (**Cold, Cold Heart** – 1951), Jo Stafford (**Jambalaya** – 1952). Williams' material has been recorded by rock bands, folk singers and black music acts.

Elected to the Country Music Hall Of Fame in 1961, his plaque reads: "The simple, beautiful melodies and straightforward plaintive stories in his lyrics of life as he knew it will never die."

His son, Hank Williams Jr. still carries on the tradition today and in 1964 provided the music to 'Your Cheatin' Heart', a Hollywood scripted film biography, in which George Hamilton portrayed Hank Sr.

Recommended:

Rare Takes And Radio Cuts (Polydor/–)
The Essential Hank Williams (–/MGM)
The Collector's Hank Williams (–/MGM)
Live At The Grand Ole Opry (MGM/MGM)
I Ain't Got Nothin' But Time (Polydor/Polydor)
Country Store (–/Starblend)

Hank Williams Jr

Son of the late Hank Williams and his wife Audrey, Hank Jr was born in Shreveport, Louisiana, on May 26, 1949 – though he was taken to Nashville when only three months old and grew up there.

Just Me And My Guitar. Rare sides of Hank Williams. Courtesy CMF Records.

During his high school days he excelled in sports. When barely a teenager he toured with his mother's 'Caravan Of Stars' show, at the age of 15 having national hits via MGM releases **Long Gone Lonesome Blues** and **Endless Sleep**.

For many years he was forced to follow in his famous father's footsteps by doing endless versions of Hank Sr's songs. He fought against this in songs like **Standing In The Shadows (Of A Very Famous Man)**, which gave him a Top 5 country hit in 1966. Further major hits followed with: **It's All Over But The Crying** (1968), **Cajun Baby**, **I'd Rather Be Gone** (both 1969), **All For The Love Of Sunshine** (No.1 1970), **Ain't That A Shame** and **Eleven Roses** (both 1972), and **The Last Love Song** (1973).

In 1974 he moved from Nashville to Alabama, linked up with an old buddy named James R. Smith and began to forge a new Hank Williams Jr sound. He recorded the acclaimed **Hank Williams Jr And Friends** album, which featured country-rock musicians, including Charlie Daniels and Toy Caldwell.

On August 8, 1975 – about the time the album was being released – Hank Jr was involved in a climbing accident on a Montana mountain, suffering appalling head injuries. After two years of recuperation he re-emerged even stronger and made it back to the top with a series of gritty, best-selling country albums.

He changed labels in 1977, moving from MGM to Warner Bros. Although his singles failed to make much impression initially he

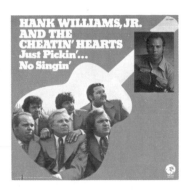

Just Pickin' ... No Singin', Hank Williams Jr And The Cheatin' Hearts.

finally made it back to the country Top 20 with **I Fought The Law** (1978) and scored Top 5 with **Family Tradition** and **Whiskey Bent And Hell Bound** (both 1979). He teamed up with Waylon Jennings on **The Conversation** (1979) and had such solo hits as **Women I've Never Had**, **Old Habits** (both 1980), **All My Rowdy Friends** (1981) and **A Country Boy Can Survive** (1982).

His brash, southern-styled country-rock, with macho lyrics, saw Hank Jr dominating the charts throughout the '80s with virtually every single making the Top 10. The most notable were **Leave Them Boys Alone** (with guest vocals by Waylon Jennings and Ernest Tubb, 1983), **Man Of Steel** (1984), **I'm For Love** (1985), **Mind Your Own Business** (1986), **Born To Boogie** (1987) and **If The South Woulda Won** (1988). This level of success, with many albums going gold or platinum and his shows being the wildest supported in country music, led to Hank Williams Jr finally gaining country music's top award, the CMA Entertainer Of The Year, in 1987 and 1988. Still unable to shake off the influence of his famous father, he duetted with Hank Sr on **There's A Tear In My Beer**, an obscure demo record from the early '50s that was discovered in 1988, and hit the Top 10 in 1989. However, the '90s found Hank Jr unable to score such major hits again, and in 1992 he signed with the re-activated Capricorn Records, though still working within the WEA family of labels.

Recommended:
Hank Williams Jr And Friends (MGM/MGM)
The New South (Warner Bros/–)
Habits Old And New (Elektra/–)
Man Of Steel (Warner Bros/–)
Are You Sure Hank Done It This Way (–/Warner Bros)
Five-O (Warner Bros/Warner Bros)
Maverick (Capricorn/–)
High Notes (Warner Bros/Warner Bros)
The Bocephus Box (Curb-Capricorn/–)

Lucinda Williams

Louisiana-born Lucinda Williams is a gutsy folk-country-blues performer, who is known more for her songs than her singing. Something of a folk troubadour, she has travelled extensively in America, playing music in the style to suit the region in which she was living at the time. Over the years this has given her music a rich, rootsy quality.

Lucinda's father is the well-known poet Miller Williams, and her mother was a pianist, though she never played professionally. During her childhood Lucinda mastered piano, zither, Hammond organ and guitar, and also started writing poetry and songs. By her teens she had become influenced by folk music, and later she absorbed folk-rock and the blues. Music became her way of making a living as she moved around from town to town to perform, living in such places as New Orleans, Los Angeles, Houston, Greenwich Village and Macon, Georgia.

Lucinda's first recordings were made for Smithsonian Folkways in the late '70s. They were mainly cover versions of country and blues classics with no definite sound of her own. Vocally she was a cross between Emmylou Harris and Bonnie Raitt. Already a prolific songwriter, from then on she was to record mainly her own songs, beginning with **Happy Woman Blues**, recorded in Houston, Texas, in 1980. A fine example of the country-blues style she was developing, this marked the first step towards wider acceptance. Later she moved to Los Angeles and in 1988 recorded a self-titled album for Rough Trade, which had her taking on a more contemporary edge. By now she was working with a band that included Gurf Morlix on various guitars, Donald Lindley on drums and Dr John Ciambotti on bass, a group of musicians who played with Lucinda for a number of years. This eponymous album contained the original versions of **Passionate Kisses**, which became a country hit for Mary-Chapin Carpenter, and **The Night's Too Long**, a Top 20 entry for Patty Loveless. A fourth album, **Sweet Old World**, for Chameleon Records, gained wider distribution through Elektra in 1992 and brought Lucinda much closer to country music. Her songs get right to the heart of people's emotions, heartaches and disasters, and her music is a fusion of roots that draws upon Williams' experiences of spending so many years on the road, honing and perfecting her musical craft.

Recommended:
Lucinda Williams (Rough Trade/Rough Trade)
Sweet Old World (Chameleon/Chameleon)

Tex Williams

Writer (with Merle Travis) and performer of **Smoke, Smoke, Smoke (That Cigarette)**, a 1947 hit that sold around two and a half million copies, Williams was predominantly a West Coast-based bandleader, who appeared in many films during the 1940s.

Born Sol Williams in Ramsey, Fayette County, Illinois, on August 23, 1917, he had his own one-man band and vocal show on radio WJBL, Decatur, Illinois, at the age of 13. He later toured throughout the States, Canada and Mexico with various western and hillbilly aggregations.

During the late 1930s he became Hollywood-based, there befriending Tex Ritter and working in films. After a long stay as lead vocalist and bass player with Spade Cooley, he formed his own band, the Western Caravan, in 1946, signing to the Capitol label.

Following the success of **Smoke, Smoke, Smoke**, the band's third release, Williams became a star and worked on scores of TV and radio shows, his band playing to capacity audiences at choice venues. Although his run of record successes seemed to peter out following the release of **Bluebird On Your Windowsill** (1949), he continued

Above: Lucinda Williams has provided hit songs for many country stars, including Patty Loveless.

recording for such labels as Decca and Liberty in the '50s.

A record deal with a Kentucky company, Boone, renewed Williams' acquaintance with the charts once more – albeit on a lower level. The singer accrued good sales with **Too Many Tigers** (1965), **Bottom Of A Mountain** (1966), **Smoke, Smoke, Smoke** (1968) and several other titles. 1970 saw him signed to Monument, obtaining a Top 30 disc in 1971 with **The Night Miss Nancy Ann's Hotel For Single Girls Burned Down**. By the mid-'70s Williams had teamed up once more with Cliffie Stone, who had produced his Capitol recordings, and on Stone's Granite

Those Lazy Hazy Days, Tex Williams. Courtesy PRT Records.

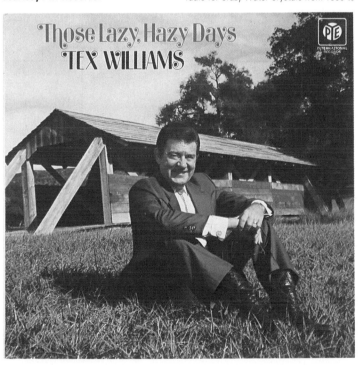

label came up with the album, **Those Lazy Hazy Days**. He died of lung cancer at his home in New Hall, California on October 11, 1985.

Recommended:
In Las Vegas (–/Sunset)
Oklahoma Stomp – with Spade Cooley (Club Of Spades/–)
Those Lazy Hazy Days (Granite/Pye)
Smoke, Smoke, Smoke (Capitol/Stetson)

Foy Willing

Born Foy Willingham in Bosque County, Texas in 1915, Foy aspired to a musical career while still in high school, appearing on radio as a solo singer and with a gospel quartet. He eventually found his way to New York City, where he appeared on radio for Crazy Water Crystals from 1933 to

1935, when he returned to Texas to work in radio as an executive and announcer.

Willing moved to California in 1940 and founded the Riders Of The Purple Sage, originally composed of himself, Al Sloey and Jimmy Dean, although later members included Scotty Harrell, Fiddler Johnny Paul, accordionist/arranger Billy Leibert, accordionist Paul Sellers, guitarist Jerry Vaughn, clarinetist Neely Plumb and steel guitarist Freddy Traveres.

The group was formed in 1943 as cast members of the Hollywood Barn Dance, and throughout the rest of the 1940s they appeared on many radio shows including All Star Western Theater, the Andrews Sisters Show, the Roy Rogers Quaker Oats Show, and appeared in many Republic films with Monte Hale and Roy Rogers.

They recorded for Decca, Capitol, Columbia and Majestic Records. Their biggest hits were **No One To Cry To** and **Cool Water** on Majestic and **Texas Blues** and **Ghost Riders In The Sky** on Capitol. The Riders of The Purple Sage disbanded in 1952 when Willing left active performing, although there were a couple of quick albums on Roulette and Jubilee and a 1959 tour with Gene Autry.

Foy Willing was still recording, writing songs and appearing at western film festivals up until shortly before his death on June 24, 1978.

Willis Brothers

The Willis Brothers (Guy, born in Alex, Arkansas on July 15, 1915; Skeeter, born in Coalton, Oklahoma on December 20, 1917 and Vic, born in Schulter, Oklahoma on May 31, 1922) were originally known as the Oklahoma Wranglers. Their radio career commenced on KGEF, Shawnee, Oklahoma. In 1940, the trio moved on to become featured artists on the Brush Creek Follies Show on KMBC, Kansas City, Missouri.

With Guy as front-man and guitarist, Vic on accordion and piano, and Skeeter appearing in his role as the 'smilin' fiddler', the brothers appeared to be on the way to establishing a healthy reputation, but

Below: Foy Willing and the Riders Of The Purple Sage.

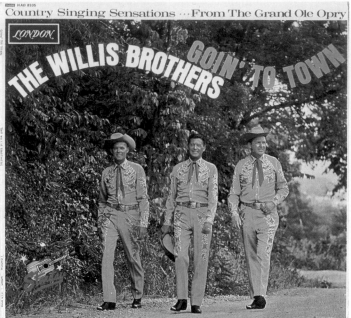

Ain't It Funny What A Little Drink Can Do · Show Her Lots Of Gold · Ruby Ann
Behind The Footlights · Diamonds For Ruby · One Man's Sugar · Goin' To Town
Bringing Mary Home · She's My Anti-Biotic · and others

World War II intervened and the Willis Brothers joined the forces for four years.

They regrouped in 1946 and became Opry members until 1949, striking up an association with Eddy Arnold, on whose show they appeared for some eight years. Also during this period they became the first group to back Hank Williams on Sterling Records, and in a sense were the original Drifting Cowboys.

Rejoining the Opry in 1960, the group enjoyed some hit Starday singles throughout the '60s via such titles as **Give Me Forty Acres** (1964), **A Six Foot Two By Four** (1965), **Bob** (1967) and **Somebody Loves My Dog** (1967).

Often employed as session musicians, the Willis Brothers have recorded for several labels including RCA-Victor, Mercury, Sterling, Coral, Starday and MGM. They were the first featured act on the Jubilee USA shows in Springfield, Missouri. The brothers, who often impersonated other groups as part of their set, also had the distinction of being the initial country act to play a concert at Washington DC's Constitution Hall.

Goin' To Town, Willis Brothers. Courtesy London Records.

Following Skeeter's death from cancer in 1976 and Guy's retirement, younger brother Vic formed the Vic Willis Trio, using his accordion as lead instrument and performing modern country favourites in a close harmony style, which proved very popular at the Opry. Guy Willis died in Nashville on April 13, 1981.

Recommended:
Best Of The Willis Brothers (Starday/–)

Bob Wills

Leader of the finest western swing band ever to grace country music, and in fact the originator of the style, the late Bob Wills is acknowledged as having been one of the most influential performers in country music. Merle Haggard, Asleep At The Wheel, Alvin Crow and Red Steagall all borrowed from his repertoire, and Waylon Jennings payed tribute to the Texas fiddle man with the anthem, **Bob Wills Is Still The King**.

Born near Kosse, Limestone County, Texas on March 6, 1905, James Robert Wills was the first of ten children of a fiddle-playing father. In 1913 the Wills family moved to Memphis, Texas, where Jim Rob began playing fiddle at square dances, his initial instrument having been mandolin.

He lived on a West Texas family farm until 1929, when he went to Fort Worth, and became 'Bob' Wills after working in a medicine show that possessed one too many Jims. Forming a duo, the Wills Fiddle Band, with guitarist Herman Arnspiger during the summer of 1929, the fiddler and his band began playing for dances in the Fort Worth area.

During 1930 he added vocalist Milton Brown, the unit later metamorphosing into the Light Crust Doughboys. The Doughboys recorded for Victor in February, 1932, Brown leaving soon after, to be replaced by Tommy Duncan, a vocalist selected from over 70 other applicants.

Fired from the Doughboys in August 1933 – due to excessive drinking and his

inability to get along with Doughboys' leader W. Lee O'Daniel – Wills took Duncan and his banjo-playing brother Johnnie Lee Wills with him, forming his own outfit, Bob Wills And His Playboys and gaining a regular spot on WACO in Waco. Although beset by legal problems, activated by Wills' ex-sponsors, the Burrus Mill and Elevator Company (the makers of Light Crust flour), the band struggled on, eventually making a base in Tulsa, where they became an institution on KVOO.

Now known as Bob Wills And His Texas Playboys, the band began recording for

Hall Of Fame, Bob Wills and Tommy Duncan. Courtesy UA Records.

Brunswick, cutting some sides in Dallas during September, 1935. The record success, KVOO programmes and regular dances at Cain's Academy made their Tulsa years their most memorable.

A swing band with country overtones – the Playboys comprised 13 musicians by the mid-'30s and grew into an 18-piece during the 1940s – Wills' outfit played a miscellany of country ballads, blues and riffy jazz items with horns and fiddles vying for the front-line positions.

This sound proved tremendously popular and when, in April 1940, WIlls recorded his self-penned **San Antonio Rose** as a vehicle for Tommy Duncan's vocal artistry, the resulting disc became a million-seller.

Many more hits followed, but with the advent of Pearl Harbor, the band began to break up as its various members enlisted in the forces. Wills himself joined the Army in late 1942. Physically unfit for service life, he was discharged the following July, at which time he headed for California where he appeared on radio shows and made several films.

During the post-war period, with big bands generally fading, Wills was forced to use a smaller band, and began featuring fiddles, electric steel guitar and string instruments more prominently. He used Leon McAuliffe on steel much in the manner of jazz horn soloists. Again, the

Remembering The Greatest Hits Of Bob Wills. Courtesy MCA Records. Wills was the leader of the finest western swing band.

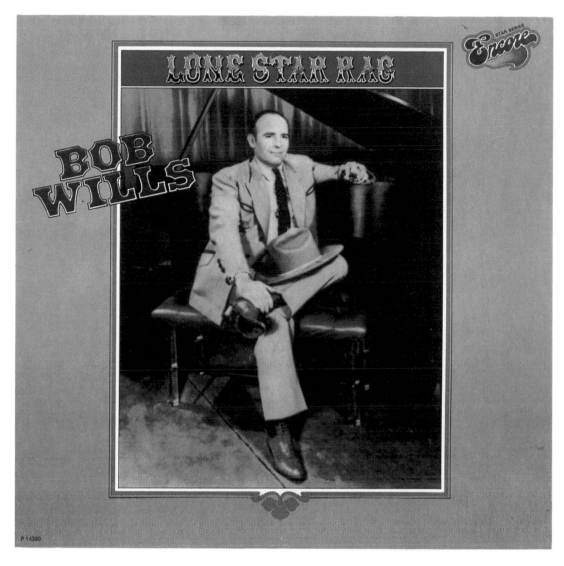

Shenandoah Valley in which Mac was raised was very much a folk art, and Mac learned music from people around him.

He has become known as a bluegrass artist, although his music also encompasses old-time, modern and even pop styles as well. Mac has floated in and out of the accepted Monroe–Earl Scruggs bluegrass style in his time and has indeed specialized in more traditional, sentimental material, such as **Jimmy Brown, The Newsboy** and **Letter Edged In Black**.

He attended the Shenandoah Conservatory of Music in Dayton, Virginia, and then joined the announcing staff of radio station WSVA in Harrisburg, Virginia, as newscaster and disc jockey. At this time he also wrote copy for station advertisements and worked nights with local country bands.

Possessing a warm, clear, tenor voice, Mac has been eagerly utilized by some of the top names in bluegrass, notably Bill Monroe and Flatt And Scruggs. Both acts included him live and on record. Mac began his career with another country music legend, Molly O'Day.

He has starred on Shreveport's Louisiana Hayride, Atlanta's WSB Barn Dance and Knoxville Tennessee Barn Dance, and has also guested on the Opry. He began recording on Dot Records in 1951 and his hits included: **'Tis Sweet To Be Remembered, Jimmy Brown, The Newsboy, Ballad Of Davy Crockett** and **Love Letters In The Sand**.

In 1957, Mac became Dot's Country A&R director and also ran the company's country music division for a few years. He recorded for Capitol Records during the early '60s, then moved back to Dot where he experimented with a string-filled album. Mac enjoyed a resurgence of popularity when he teamed up with Lester Flatt for some earthy bluegrass albums for RCA during the early '70s, and also built a large following in Britain with regular tours and record releases.

Apart from the bluegrass festivals he plays, Mac has been active behind the

public loved the sound, but Wills was unsure where he was heading.

His health began to fail and during 1962 Wills suffered his first heart attack. Still he continued to tour with the Playboys, but in 1964 came another heart attack and he was forced to call a halt to his bandleading days.

Nevertheless, he still made a more limited number of appearances as a solo artist and continued making records, and he was honoured in the Country Music Hall Of Fame in October, 1968.

Also honoured by the State of Texas on May 30, 1969, Wills was paralysed by a stroke the very next day. But, although bedridden for many months, he fought back, and by 1972 began to appear at various functions, albeit in a wheelchair.

In December, 1973, he attended his last record date, many of the original Texas Playboys, plus Merle Haggard, taking part. In two days, 27 titles were cut for UA – but Wills was only present for a portion of the time, suffering a severe stroke after the first day. He never regained consciousness, although his actual death did not occur until 17 months later on May 13, 1975.

However, though Wills has gone his music lives on, the Playboys reforming several times since his death and many younger singers and bands recreating the Wills' sound both on record and in live shows.

Recommended:
Papa's Jumping (–/Bear Family)
Bob Wills (Columbia/CBS)
San Antonio Rose (Lariat/–)
Anthology (Columbia/CBS)

The Last Time (UA/–)
Leon McAuliffe Leads The Texas Playboys (Capitol/–)
Anthology, 1935–1973 (Rhino/–)

Johnnie Lee Wills

Although often cast in the shadow of his elder brother Bob, Johnnie Lee Wills actually carved out quite a long and successful career of his own. Born in east Texas in 1912, Johnnie Lee got his start playing tenor banjo with Bob as a member of the Light Crust Doughboys and left the band with him when Bob formed the Playboys.

Business got so good for Bob around 1940 that he formed a second band around Johnnie Lee, which grew to as many as 14 or 15 pieces. Called Johnnie Lee Wills And His Boys, they became extremely popular in the Tulsa area, and at one time or another contained many of the finest swing musicians of the era, including Leon Huff, Joe Holley and Jesse Ashlock.

They signed with Bullet Records in 1940 and had hits with **Rag Mop** and **Peter Cottontail**. They also recorded for Decca, Sims, RCA and a few smaller labels.

When western swing slumped in popularity in the 1950s, Johnnie Lee continued to run his famous Tulsa Stampede and opened a thriving western wear shop. He continued to appear at various western swing reunions until ill-health got the better of him in 1982, and

he subsequently passed away on October 15, 1984.

Mac Wiseman

Malcolm B. Wiseman was born near Waynesboro, Virginia, on May 23, 1925. Country music in the area of the

Sheb Wooley

A highly versatile performer, Wooley was voted CMA Comedian Of The Year in 1968 for his alter ego character Ben Colder. In 1964 he won a 'Cashbox' magazine award for "his outstanding contributions to country and popular music as a writer, recording artist and entertainer".

In the role of Pete Nolan, he co-starred in the TV series Rawhide. As Ben Colder he has scored with such recorded comedy hits as: **Don't Go Near The Eskimos** (1962), **Almost Persuaded No.2** (1966), **Harper Valley PTA (Later That Same Day)** (1968) and **15 Beers Ago** (1971).

Born in Erick, Oklahoma on April 10, 1921, Wooley spent his early years on his father's farm, becoming a competent horseman at the age of four and a rodeo rider during his teens. He formed his own band while still at school, later having his own network radio show for three years. In 1948, he was awarded his first major recording contract by MGM.

It was at this stage that Wooley moved to California and began working on 'Rocky Mountain', a film starring Errol Flynn. He has since been featured in more than 30 films. Wooley received considerable acclaim for his performance as the whiskey-drinking killer Ben Miller in 'High Noon'.

Co-star in 105 episodes of Rawhide, Wooley has appeared on countless TV shows. As a recording star under his own name (as opposed to releases using his Colder identity), he has enjoyed a six-week stay at the top the pop charts with his 1959 **Purple People Eater**, three years later toping the country charts with **That's My Pa**.

Recommended:
Blue Guitar (–/Bear Family)
Best Of Ben Colder (–/MGM)

Johnny Wright

Wright (born in Mt Juliet, Tennessee, on May 13, 1914) came from a musical family, his grandfather being a champion old-time fiddler and his father a five-string banjo player.

In 1933 he moved to nearby Nashville, there meeting and marrying Kitty Wells, also working with singer-guitarist Jack Anglin (born in Columbia, Tennessee on May 13, 1916) on radio station WSIX, Nashville and forming a duo, Johnny And Jack, with Anglin in 1938.

During the early '40s, Johnny And Jack toured with their band, the Tennessee Mountain Boys, playing on WBIG, Greensboro, North Carolina, WNOX, Knoxville and many other radio stations. By 1948 they joined the Grand Ole Opry, then left to become stars of Shreveport's Louisiana Hayride. Their popularity on the show led to an opportunity to rejoin Opry members in 1952, and Kitty, Johnny and Jack became regulars on the Opry for a period of 15 years.

Signed initially to Apollo, an R&B label (there cutting such sides as **Jolie Blon** and **Paper Boy**), Johnny And Jack switched to the more country-oriented RCA in the late '40s, scoring Top 20 hits with: **Poison Love** (1951), **Crying Heart Blues** (1951), **Oh Baby Mine (I Get So Lonely)** (1954), **Beware Of It** (1954), **Goodnight, Sweetheart, Goodnight** (1954), **Stop**

scenes in the industry. In recent years he has recorded for Churchill Records and CMH, maintaining a traditional bluegrass styling.

Recommended:
Early Dot Recordings Volume 1 (Country/–)
Golden Classics (Gusto/–)
Shenandoah Valley Memories (Canaan/Canaan)
Mac Wiseman Story (CMH/-)
Concert Favorites (RCA/RCA)
Lester'n'Mac – with Lester Flatt (RCA/RCA)
Grass Roots To Bluegrass (CMH/–)
Sings Gordon Lightfoot (CMH/–)

Del Wood

Probably the second (after Maybelle Carter) female country instrumentalist to achieve any real degree of fame, pianist Del Wood recorded a corny, ragtime version of **Down Yonder** (previously in a 1934 hit for Gid Tanner of the Skillet Lickers) on the Tennessee label in 1951 and came up with a million-seller.

Born Adelaide Hazelwood on February 22, 1920 in Nashville, Tennessee, Del Wood became an Opry member in 1951.

Above: Mac Wiseman, an outstanding bluegrass guitarist.

She remained with the show until shortly before her death on October 3, 1989, following a stroke on September 22. Perpetuator of several other best-selling discs in heavy-handed ragtime/honky-tonk style, Del has recorded for RCA, Mercury, Class, Decca and Lamb & Lion.

Recommended:
Ragtime Glory Special (Lamb & Lion/Lamb & Lion)
Tavern In The Town (Vocalion/–)

The World (1958), Lonely Island Pearl (1958) and Sailor Man (1959). Other hits included Ashes Of Love and I Can't Tell My Heart That.

Shortly after one last success with Slow Poison, a 1962 Decca release, Jack Anglin was killed (on March 8, 1963) in a car crash en route to a funeral service for Patsy Cline – at which point Wright formed a new roadshow and became a solo recording act, notching a chart No.1 in 1965 with Hello Vietnam.

His son Bobby proved a success during the late '60s. Wright formed the Kitty Wells–Johnny Wright Family Show in 1969, doing extensive tours, and he and Bobby recorded an album of Johnny And Jack material for Starday during 1977.

Recommended:
Here's Johnny And Jack (Vocalion/–)
All The Best Of Johnny And Jack (RCA/–)
Johnny And Jack And The Tennessee Mountain Boys (–/Bear Family)

Michelle Wright

Michelle Wright, a sensual, sexy lady, is one of only a handful of Canadian performers who have succeeded in making a big impact on the American country music scene. Born on July 1, 1961, in Merlin, Ontario, a small Canadian farming community, Michelle was bred on American music. She heard the rhythm and blues and Motown hits coming out of Detroit, just 45 minutes away, but especially she heard the strains of country music. Her mother was the singer in a country band called the Reflections for ten years, and her father played in a traditional country band with steel guitar, rhinestone suits and all the works. As a child she would often get up on the bandstand and sing, and by college days was working with a local band. This was followed by several years out on the road, working with pick-up bands, playing small clubs across Canada. In 1986, she won the CJBX

London, Ontario 'Country Roads Talent Search'. That led to her signing to Canadian label Savannah Records and scoring several Canadian hits including I Want To Count On You, New Fool At An Old Game and Rock Me Gently.

She started gaining nominations from the Canadian Country Music Association in 1986, but it was not until 1989 that she really made a breakthrough, picking up her first Female Vocalist Of The Year award. It was a feat she was to repeat for the next three years. In 1992 she was also named Country Music Person Of The Year in recognition of her success in America. That success occurred because of the involvement of Nashville songwriters Rick Giles and Steve Bogard. The pair started providing Michelle with quality song material and also produced her recordings in Canada and Nashville. Her breakthrough in the States started to get under way when Michelle was signed to Arista Records in Nashville in early 1990, resulting in New Kind Of Love becoming her first US hit during that summer. Still based in Canada, Michelle scored a few minor hits during the next couple of years, then made a move to Nashville in order to develop her career further. The result was a Top 10 hit with Take It Like A Man (1992), and further success with One Time Around (1992), He Would Be Sixteen and The Change (1993).

A self-confessed one-time alcoholic, the husky-voiced songstress with the soulful edge possesses a strong ear for music that works best for her throaty voice, resulting in her second album, Now And Then, making a big impact on both the country and pop charts, gaining Michelle a gold disc in 1993.

Recommended:
Now And Then (Arista/Arista)
Do Right By Me (Savannah/Savannah)

Right: Canadian Michelle Wright gained a gold disc for her 1993 album Now And Then. The album made an impact on pop and country charts.

Left: Sheb Wooley played the killer Ben Miller in 'High Noon' and co-starred in the TV series Rawhide.

Tammy Wynette

One of the most successful female country singers of all time, Tammy Wynette was adjudged CMA Female Vocalist Of The Year for three consecutive years (1968–70), while her recording of Stand By Your Man, a No.1 in the US during 1968 and a major British hit in 1975, was the biggest selling single by a woman in the entire history of country music.

Tammy began life as Virginia Wynette Pugh, born near Tupelo, Mississippi on May 5, 1942. Her father died when she was but a few months old and her mother moved to Birmingham, Alabama, leaving her in the care of grandparents until the end of World War II. Brought up on a farm, Tammy learned to play the collection of instruments owned by her father, taking a lengthy series of music lessons with a view to a career in singing.

But, getting married at 17, she had little time for music during the next three years. Instead she became the mother of three children, her marriage breaking up before the third child was born. The baby, a girl, developed spinal meningitis, and Tammy had to supplement her earnings as a Birmingham beautician in order to pay off various bills incurred as a result of the child's ill health. She turned to music once more, becoming featured vocalist on station WBRC-TV's Country Boy Eddy Show during the mid-'60s, following this with

some appearances on Porter Wagoner's syndicated TV programme.

Soon she began making the rounds of the Nashville-based record companies, in the meantime working as a club singer and a song-plugger in order to support her children. Following auditions for UA, Hickory and Kapp, Tammy was signed by Epic's Billy Sherrill and recorded Apartment No.9, a song written by Johnny Paycheck and Bobby Austin. Released in 1966, the disc proved a great success. The next release, Your Good Girl's Gonna Go Bad (1967), proved to be even stronger, becoming a Top 5 item. From then on it was plain sailing throughout the '60s as I Don't Wanna Play House (1967), My Elusive Dreams (with David Houston, 1967), Take Me To Your World, D-I-V-O-R-C-E, Stand By Your Man (all 1968), Singing My Song and The Ways To Love A Man (both 1969) qualified as chart-toppers.

Married five times, Tammy had several well publicized relationships with other partners, including Burt Reynolds and Rudy Gatlin of the Gatlin Brothers, but it was her marriage to singer George Jones that made most headlines. The pair announced their marriage on August 22, 1968 in order to silence gossips, but they were not in fact married until February 16, 1969. For several years they toured together and recorded several big-selling duets, but Jones' regular drinking bouts and Tammy's career aspirations but did not mix too well and they were divorced on March 13, 1975.

However, on disc, Tammy could do little wrong – Run, Woman Run (1970), Good Lovin' (1971) 'Til I Get It Right (1973), Woman To Woman (1974), 'Til I Can

Make It On My Own (1976), **Womanhood** (1978), **They Call It Making Love** (1979), **Another Chance** (1982), **Sometimes When We Touch** (a duet with Mark Gray, 1985) – being just some of her major hits during the 1970s and 1980s. Her **Greatest Hits** album (which remained in the charts for over 60 weeks) earned a platinum disc for sales in excess of one million.

Tammy married her longtime friend, and, for a time, record producer, George Richey, at her Florida home on July 6, 1978. In 1982 Tammy's career was captured in her biography 'Stand By Your Man' and made into a successful film.

Throughout the rest of the '80s Tammy seemed to be dogged by ill-health as her records began to fall off the charts. In 1986 she entered the Betty Ford Clinic for drug addiction, and also had several stomach operations. Even duet recordings with Ricky Skaggs, Randy Travis and Emmylou Harris failed to return her to the top. However, in 1992, when she recorded a strange duet with pop duo KLF and appeared in the group's video of **Justified**

Below: Tammy Wynette recently moved into pop music with KLF.

And Ancient, Tammy found herself high on the pop charts in both Britain and America again.

Recommended:
Soft Touch (Epic/Epic)
Just Tammy (Epic/Epic)
No Charge (–/Embassy)
One Of A Kind (Epic/Epic)
Superb Country Sounds (–/Embassy)
Tears Of Fire (Epic/Epic)
Heart Over Mind (Epic/Epic)
Higher Ground (Epic/Epic)
Next To You (Epic/Epic)

With George Jones:
We're Gonna Hold On (Epic/Epic)
Let's Build A World Together (Epic/Epic)
Together Again (Epic/Epic)

Wynonna

The daughter of the Judds, country music's most popular duo of the '80s, Wynonna, who was born Christina Criminella on May 30, 1964 in Ashland, Kentucky, embarked on a highly successful solo career at the beginning of 1992. Signed to MCA/Curb,

MCAD-10529

Wynonna's eponymously titled debut solo album. Courtesy MCA Records.

her debut album, simply titled, **Wynonna**, soared high on both the pop and country charts as it raced to a multi-platinum award.

A rebellious, but determined young lady, Wynonna had unwittingly been groomed for this success from her teenage years growing up in Kentucky, where her musical influences were very eclectic. They ranged from bluegrass, through mountain harmonies, big band music and Bonnie Raitt, whom she cites as one of the biggest influences on her own vocal style. She moved with her mother and younger sister Ashley to Franklin, Tennessee, near Nashville, at the age of 15. Her mother, Naomi Judd, encouraged her music, singing harmonies and trying to further her daughter's musical ambitions. After a high school talent contest came the now famous live audition in RCA's Joe Galante's office, when mother and daughter, backed only by Wynonna's guitar, impressed the Nashville veterans. Then there was the first show, playing to an audience of 10,000 people opening for the Statler Brothers in 1984. The Judds really took off during the next seven years. The hits started and kept coming – 23 of them – and the awards kept picking up. The Country Music Association's Award for Vocal Group in 1984 was the first of their seven CMA awards. They won the first of four Grammies in 1985. Album sales soared to over 10 million worldwide.

The Judds' career came to an end when Naomi announced plans to retire, due to chronic hepatitis. Musically, as well as emotionally, Wynonna had to face the world alone. It marked a complete new beginning with a new producer in Tony Brown, and a new studio band. Developing more of a white blues sound than the mountain country of the Judds, Wynonna immediately made an impact. Her first three singles, **She Is His Only Need, I Saw The Light** and **No One Else On Earth**, all became No.1s during 1992. A fourth, **My Strongest Weakness**, made the Top 5 in early 1993. Taking her music in different directions, Wynonna succeeded in keeping her own distinctive

voice at the forefront of her new music, so that every song on her debut album, from the haunting gospel of **Live With Jesus** to the powerfully upbeat **I Saw The Light**, and the hard-edged **What It Takes** to the broken-hearted ballad **My Strongest Weakness**, sounds unmistakeably Wynonna.

She teamed up with Clint Black for the duet hit **A Bad Goodbye** in early 1993, then came a second album, **Tell Me Why**, which showcased the growing maturity, depth of feeling and emotion of Wynonna in a sparkling set of performances, highlighted yet again by the sheer strength of song material. The title song immediately became another Top 10 country hit, while the album passed the million sales mark within a few weeks of release.

Recommended:
Wynonna (MCA-Curb/Epic-Curb)
Tell Me Why (MCA-Curb/–)

Trisha Yearwood

Chic-looking Trisha Yearwood, who zoomed to stardom in 1991 with **She's In Love With The Boy**, is a country girl born on September 19, 1964, in Monticello, Georgia. The younger of two daughters of a banker father and school teacher mother, she grew up on a farm in the small central Georgia community, about an hour's drive from Atlanta, Athens and Macon. The music of Linda Ronstadt, Emmylou Harris and the Eagles were major influences during her teen years as she developed her own vocal style, making the rounds of area talent contests.

In 1985, after a stint at the University of Georgia, Trisha moved to Nashville to attend Belmont College, where she completed a music business course. Her first introduction to the music business was when she landed a job in the publicity department at MTM Records. Then came demo work for publishers. At this time she met a struggling Garth Brooks, who promised they'd work together if he ever made it big. True to his word, when Garth was recording his first album, Trisha was

TRISHA YEARWOOD

Trisha Yearwood's 1991 debut album. Courtesy MCA Records.

Below: Dwight Yoakam has recorded duets with various female partners.

called in to provide back-up vocals, and later Garth sang on her recordings, and also provided her with some songs.

With the help of Garth Fundis, a Nashville producer who had worked with Don Williams and Keith Whitley, Trisha played a showcase for Nashville's record industry and was signed to MCA Records in late 1990. The first single, **She's In Love With The Boy**, accompanied by a stunning video, raced to No.1 on the charts in 1991, followed by Top 10 entries with **Like We Never Had A Broken Heart** (1991), **That's What I Like About You**, **The Woman Before Me** and **The Wrong Side Of Memphis** (1992). The debut album, **Trisha Yearwood**, a stunning set of quality songs, had an extra edge that is absent from much of country music, giving her the added appeal to a younger audience. The end result is a powerful musical statement that saw the album make both the pop and country charts during 1991 as it eventually reached multi-platinum status. Sales of the album were obviously helped when Garth Brooks invited Trisha to be his opening act during his 1991 tour, but from then on this determined and talented young lady has made it to the top on her own terms. There have been further Top 10 entries with **Walkaway Joe** and **You Say You Will** (1993), while her second album, **Hearts In Armor**, featuring guest appearances by Garth Brooks, Don Henley, Vince Gill, Emmylou Harris and Raul Malo, has also reached platinum status.

Recommended:
Trisha (MCA/MCA)
Hearts In Armor (MCA/MCA)

Dwight Yoakam

A singer whose debut album for Reprise immediately climbed into the pop charts, Yoakam caught the attention of traditionalists and even punk rockers.

Born in Pikeville, Kentucky on October 23, 1956, Yoakam honed his style of

country in bars and roadhouses along Route 23 in southern Ohio, then headed for L.A. because he felt Nashville music had become too slick; he claimed, "Those Buck Owens records in the late 1950s and 1960s were some of the hippest hillbilly stuff known to man – and Nashville has all but abandoned it."

He became an opener for roots-oriented rock acts like Los Lobos, the Blasters and Lone Justice, and released a six-track EP titled **Guitars, Cadillacs, Etc** on Oak Records during 1985. He then moved on to provide Reprise (practically a dead label after Sinatra and Neil Young moved off) with an attention-grabbing album.

Yoakam, who first sang what he calls 'hillbilly hymns' in a Pikeville church, found grudging acceptance in Nashville when singles such as **Honky Tonk Man** (1986), **Little Sister** (1987) and **Always Late With Your Kisses** (1988) all went Top 10 on the country charts. He teased Buck Owens out of premature retirement, and the pair enjoyed a chart-topping duet with **Streets Of Bakersfield** (1988), while Yoakam had his own solo hits with **I Sang Dixie** (No.1, 1989) and **I Got You** (1989). Albums **Hillbilly Deluxe** and **Buenas Noches From A Lonely Road** went platinum as Yoakam's uncompromising approach to country won over a whole legion of younger, rock-oriented fans.

The risk-taking nature of his country style can be perceived in his choice of duet partners, which includes Patty Loveless, k.d. lang, Maria McKee and the neo-folk-rock duo, the Indigo Girls. He has also cut a diverse range of songs and styles, from a stormy, swamp, rockin' **I Hear You Knockin'** to **Truckin'** on the Grateful Dead tribute album, **Deadicated**, to the Elvis signature tune **Suspicious Minds** on the 'Honeymoon In Vegas' soundtrack. Yet he has maintained country radio play, resulting in such country Top 10 entries as **You're The One** (1991) and **Ain't That Lonely Yet** (1993).

Recommended:
Guitars, Cadillacs, Etc (Reprise/Reprise)
Hillbilly Deluxe (Reprise/Reprise)
If There Was A Way (Reprise/Reprise)
Buenas Noches From A Lonely Room (Reprise/Reprise)
This Time (Reprise/Reprise)

Faron Young

Affectionately known as 'The Sheriff' Faron has been a stalwart of the country music industry for some three decades.

Born in Shreveport, Louisiana on February 25, 1932, he was raised on a farm

This Time, Dwight Yoakam. Courtesy Reprise Records.

outside the town and spent his boyhood days picking up guitar chords while out with the family's cows. He formed his first band at school.

After college he found that he had gained something of a reputation in Louisiana and was invited to join KWKH and subsequently the Louisiana Hayride itself. It was then that Webb Pierce employed him as a featured vocalist.

In 1951 he was signed by Capitol Records and had country hits with **Tattle Tale Eyes** and **Have I Waited Too Long?**. Joining the Opry in 1952, Young then spent from 1952 to 1954 in the US Army, touring widely to entertain the troops. His first major success came with the Ted Daffan song **I've Got Five Dollars And It's Saturday Night**, and with his bid for the teenage market in **Going Steady**.

The '50s saw him gaining many hits and massive popularity, obtaining a No.1 disc

with **Sweet Dreams** and later with **Country Girl** (1959), following this in 1961 with another chart-topper in **Hello Walls**.

Throughout the '60s, the hits continued to flow. **Backtrack** (1961), **Three Days, The Comeback, Down By The River** (1962), **The Yellow Bandana, You'll Drive Me Back (Into Her Arms Again)** (1963), **Walk Tall** (1965), **Unmitigated Gall** (1966), **I Just Came To Get My Baby** (1968), **Wine Me Up** (1969) and **Keeping Up With The Joneses**, a 1964 duet with Margie Singleton, figured among his Top 10 successes for the Mercury label, to which Faron Young became contracted in 1961.

A versatile entertainer who presents an alive and amusing show with his own witty comments, Young retained his popularity over an extensive period, as such major '70s hits as **It's Four In The Morning, This Little Girl Of Mine** and **Just What I Had In Mind** clearly demonstrated.

He has appeared in a number of low-budget film productions, while his out-of-showbiz interests include a booking agency, a music publishing firm and magazine publishing – Young has been the owner of the monthly publication Music City News. He has even contributed to Nashville's rising skyline, owning the Faron Young Executive Building near Music Row.

Recommended:
The Man And His Music (Mercury/–)
Free And Easy (MCA/–)
The Capitol Years (–/Bear Family)
Sweethearts Or Strangers (Capitol/Stetson)

Neil Young

A Canadian singer-songwriter, born on November 12, 1945 in Toronto, Neil worked as a folk singer in Canada in the early '60s before moving to California where he became involved in the West Coast pop movement.

He was a key member of country-rock band Buffalo Springfield, then became part of the soft-rock group Crosby, Stills, Nash And Young. Embarking on a solo career in the early '70s, he formed Crazy Horse, a multi-instrumental unit that mixed strands of country, blues, jazz and rock in a repertoire that proved highly successful in terms of the huge number of albums sold.

The eclectic Young surprised many when he travelled to Nashville at the beginning of 1985 to record a new album, **Old Ways**, which brought him widespread country acclaim. Teaming up with Willie Nelson, Waylon Jennings and several notable Music City musicians, he recorded **The Wayward Wind**, once a hit for Tex Ritter, plus a number of originals all in country mould, the result being a best-selling album. "Rock'n'roll has let me down," he claimed later. "It doesn't leave you a way to grow old gracefully."

He subsequently took to the road with a traditional country band, utilizing fiddles, banjo, steel and mandolin. It was a short-lived flirtation with country, and soon Young was flitting between musical styles, seemingly playing whatever kind of music he fancied from album to album. He moved once again closer to a country sound for his **Harvest Moon** album in 1992, which gained enthusiastic reviews and became his biggest-selling album in years.

Recommended:
Old Ways (Geffen/Geffen)
Harvest Moon (Warner Bros/Warner Bros)

Below: Neil Young gained plaudits from critics with his 1985 Old Ways and moved close to country again with his 1992 offering, Harvest Moon.

Appendix

Lack of space prevents us from including a full entry on the following people, organizations and places, etc. Nevertheless, here is a brief run-down on the contributions they have made to country music.

A

WENDELL ADKINS – Born in Kentucky. Raised in Ohio, Wendell was a rock'n'roll teenage singer. Later he toured the Midwest with a band, moved to Florida, got noticed and ended up in Vegas. Following chunks of aid from Willie Nelson and David Allan Coe, he began an association with Gilley's club. He has recorded prolifically, but never made a major breakthrough.

BUDDY ALAN – Buck Owens' son, born in Tempe, Arizona, 1948, and a singer rarely out of the charts in the late '60s and early '70s. But when Dad stopped having hits, so too did 6'4" Buddy.

DANIELLE ALEXANDER – A singer-songwriter from Fort Worth, Texas, who enjoyed notable success in the late '80s, including a duet hit with Butch Baker. She started out singing jazz standards with her father in West Virginia, then sang in Texas bands, finally moving to Nashville, where she became a staff songwriter. Harold Shedd signed her to a Mercury contract in 1989, and since then Danielle has developed her own distinctive style.

SUSIE ALLANSON – A pop-styled country singer born in Minnesota in 1952, she performed in the musicals 'Hair' and 'Jesus Christ Superstar', before switching to country. Enjoyed several major country hits during the late '70s and early '80s, the biggest, **We Belong Together**, spending two weeks at No.2 in 1978.

TERRY ALLEN – Born in Wichita, Kansas in 1953, Allen became an art school teacher and singer. His first album (1975) was an incredible concept affair titled **Juarez**. Released by Fate Records of Chicago, the album became a cult

record among country and rock fans alike. Later he cut an essential double album, **Lubbock (On Everything)**, which saw him working with the Joe Ely Band and adding to his reputation as a country songwriter of some piquancy.

AMAZING RHYTHM ACES – A Memphis-based country-rock band formed in the early 1970s, best known for **Third Rate Romance**, a Top 20 pop and country hit in 1975. They enjoyed further country hits with **Amazing Grace (Used To Be Her Favorite Song)** and **The End Is Not In Sight**, and released several critically acclaimed albums before disbanding in 1981.

AMERICAN RECORD COMPANY – A company that owned five labels of its own and, in addition, recorded material for Conqueror, the Sears-Roebuck label. Once owner of the finest country music catalogue in America, it eventually was taken over by Columbia.

LIZ ANDERSON – Famed country singer and songwriter, Liz, from Minnesota, was born in 1930 and at 16 married Casey Anderson. Parents of Lynn Anderson, they wrote country hits for Roy Drusky, Merle Haggard and others. Liz recorded extensively throughout the '60s and '70s and by the late '80s was hosting a country show on cable television in Nashville.

AREA CODE 615 – A supergroup comprising Nashville and Muscle Shoals sessionmen. Area Code 615 was originally formed by Mike Nesmith, who still owns unreleased tapes of Code's initial sessions. They later made two albums for Polydor, including **Stone Fox Chase**, which became the theme for BBC-TV's rock programme The Old Grey Whistle Test. Eventually they split up, and three members went on to form Barefoot Jerry.

JERRY ARHELGER – A Christian country music singer who has worked all over the world, although his base is in Wewahitchka, Florida. His CB/trucking song, **Breaker, Breaker, Sweet Jesus**, is reputed to have once logged over 250

Bluer Than Midnight, Delia Bell. Courtesy County Records.

call-in requests in one night on a Mississippi radio station.

ARKIE THE ARKANSAS WOODCHOPPER – Longtime fixture on the National Barn Dance (1928–1970), his real name was Luther Ossenbrink. He was an all-rounder – a singer, guitarist, MC and square dance caller.

AUSTIN – A Texan city that, during the turn of the 1960s, became a centre for a new contemporary 'outlaw' form of country music. The changes evolved around Threadgill's Bar, where, around 1962, students from the university and musicians searching for an identity (such as Janis Joplin) gathered to play folk and country music. Later performers such as Michael Murphey, Steve Fromholtz and B. W. Stevenson came on like young, homespun idealists, using poetic imagery in their songs, while Kinky Friedman guyed country sounds and Commander Cody presented the whole of the southern music rainbow. The home of Willie Nelson, Austin – whose place in country music history is the subject of Jan Reid's fine book 'The Improbable Rise Of Redneck Rock' – still offers an alternative scene from that promulgated by Nashville.

B

DeFORD BAILEY – A black harmonica player, who opened the WSM Barn Dance on the night George D. Hay named the show 'The Grand Ole Opry'. Born in Carthage, Tennessee, in 1899, he remained on the Opry until 1941, but later drifted into obscurity. He operated a shoeshine stall in Nashville and made a brief television appearance on a blues show in the '60s. He died on July, 1982, and several Opry members were present at the funeral.

CARROLL BAKER – Born in Bridgewater, Nova Scotia, for many years she was Canada's 'Queen Of Country Music'. The winner of every award her country can offer, her record sales passed the million mark in 1983. Her main audience is, however, Canadian.

BAKERSFIELD – A Californian town touted as 'Nashville West' during the mid-1960s, when residents such as Buck Owens, Merle Haggard and Wynn Stewart achieved a fair degree in chart domination. The 'Bakersfield Sound' has been a major influence on West Coast country acts of the '80s and '90s.

EARL BALL – Born in Foxworth, Mississippi in 1941, Ball became a notable session pianist and producer who toured with the Johnny Cash Show for many years.

BANDANA – This Nashville-based band was formed in 1981 in the wake of Alabama's success. Signed to Warner Brothers they enjoyed several Top 20 country hits with their tight harmonies and smooth rock-based instrumental work. Following several personnel changes, the band split up in 1988.

AVA BARBER – A singer, born in Knoxville, Tennessee, 1954, who made it on the Lawrence Welk show in the mid 1970s. Signed to Ranwood Records, she had several hits, the biggest being a version of Gail Davis' **Bucket To The South** in 1978. In 1981 she signed with Oak Records.

GLENN BARBER – From Hollis, Oklahoma (born in 1935) but raised in Texas, Barber was a skilled carpenter who built his own recording studio. A multi-instrumentalist and singer-songwriter, he had hits for Sims and Starday in the mid-1960s before moving to Hickory and continuing his hit-making to the mid-1970s. By 1980 he had stopped having hit records and, in more recent times, has become a successful portrait painter.

BAREFOOT JERRY – Formed from the remnants of Area Code 615, Barefoot Jerry were headed by Wayne Moss who fashioned the band into an often inventive country-rock outfit that recorded variously for Capitol, Warner Bros and Monument, 1971–76.

RANDY BARLOW – A Detroit-born singer, Barlow worked as MC with Dick Clark's Caravan Of Stars in the mid-1960s. Then came a stint as a solo singer on the lounge circuit in California. The transition to country music came in the early 1970s, and by 1978 he was enjoying Top 10 success on Gene Autry's Republic Records, but within ten years he had faded from the country music scene.

SHANE BARMBY – A singer who was raised near Sacramento, California, Barmby, born in 1955, was named after the Alan Ladd movie 'Shane'. As a child he sang at rodeos and is a skilled trick ropester. In the early 1980s he landed bit parts in television series, but music was his first love. In 1987 he moved to Nashville, opened shows for Randy Travis, and signed with Mercury Records two years later.

J. J. BARRIE – A Canadian singer who became a genuine one-hit wonder in 1976 when his version of **No Charge** went to the top of the UK pop charts.

MOLLY BEE – Something of a child prodigy, Molly, who was born Molly Beachboard in Oklahoma City in 1939, appeared on Rex Allen's

Stacked Deck, Amazing Rhythm Aces. Courtesy ABC Records.

radio show in Tucson when only ten. In 1950 she became a regular on Cliffie Stone's Hometown Jamboree TV show. A successful actress and vocalist, she recorded for Capitol and MGM during the '60s and appeared in several musicals and TV variety shows. In the mid-1970s Molly recorded for Cliffie Stone's Granite label.

PHILOMENA BEGLEY – A superstar on the Irish country scene, Philomena was born in 1946 in County Tyrone, and her K-Tel album, **The Best Of Philomena Begley**, went platinum in her homeland. She has recorded duets with Ray Lynam, the pair frequently having appeared together onstage at Wembley. Philomena has remained a major star in Europe in a career that has spanned more than 30 years.

DELIA BELL – A bluegrass lady from Texas, who was raised in Hugo, Oklahoma, Delia possesses a voice that harks back to country's golden era. Loved by those who search the minor label catalogues, she came to the attention of Emmylou Harris in the early '80s and, unbelievably, got signed by Warner Brothers who released an album in 1983.

PINTO BENNETT – Bigger in Europe than the USA, Bennett, from Idaho, grew up on a ranch, listening to the music of Hank Williams and Lefty Frizzell. With his band, the Famous Motel Cowboys, he has been fusing honky-tonk with more contemporary sounds, mainly performing his own songs throughout Europe.

BEVERLY HILLBILLIES – This early California outfit had a radio show on KEJK, later KMPC, in 1928 and released a hit single the following year, **When The Bloom Is On The Sage/Red River Valley**. Zeke and Tom Manners, Hank Skillet, Elton Britt, Stuart Hamblen, Wesley Tuttle and Glen Rice were all members at various times.

BIG TOM – Born Tom McBride in Castleblaney, Ireland, he became a star in his native country where the song **Big Tom Is Still The King** topped the pop charts in 1980.

THE BINKLEY BROTHERS' DIXIE CLODHOPPERS – An early Grand Ole Opry string band that was severely under-recorded, they appeared on Nashville radio well into the mid-1930s, but only recorded during Victor's field trip to Nashville in 1928.

BILL BLACK COMBO – A rock'n'roll band formed in 1959 by bassist Bill Black, who was a regular sideman with Elvis Presley. They enjoyed pop success in the late '50s and the '60s. Black died of a brain tumor in 1965, but the band continued under the leadership of Bob Tucker, eventually edging towards country. By 1975 they cut their first country album, **Solid And Country**, with one track, **Boilin' Cabbage**, becoming the biggest instrumental of the year.

BLACKWOOD BROTHERS – The most famous gospel quartet in country music, formed in Mississippi in 1934. Originally comprising Roy, Doyle, James and Roy's son R.W., they regrouped after R.W. died in a 1954 plane crash, J. D. Sumner becoming the group's bass singer. All the original Blackwoods have died but the group continues on its highly successful way.

JACK BLANCHARD & MISTY MORGAN – A husband and wife team, both born in Buffalo, New York, they played mainly big band music prior to moving to Nashville in 1967, when Jack started producing records, songwriting and working as a newspaper cartoonist. He came up with the chart-topping **Tennessee Bird Walk** in 1969, which established the pair as a top-ranking act. Further hits came during the next six years, then the twosome faded from the scene.

BLASTERS – California-based rock/rockabilly band formed by Phil and Dave Alvin in 1979. They were brought up on Sun rockabilly and Chess R&B, and the band play an eclectic blend of roots music. Signed to Slash Records in 1981, their songs on albums **Non Fiction** and **Hard Line** dealt with the oppressed and under-privileged, combining downbeat lyrics with rock'n'roll excitement. Their **Long White Cadillac** is the story of Hank Williams' death.

BLUEGRASS – A development of traditional string band music formulated and popularized by Bill Monroe and his Blue Grass Boys. This music form was revitalized during the folk boom of the 1960s when a youthful element added touches of pop, the result being tagged 'New Grass'.

TONY BOOTH – From Tampa, Florida, a former member of Buck Owens' Buckaroos, Booth enjoyed consistent chart success throughout the '70s with his smooth honky-tonk style. His biggest hits came with **The Key's In The Mailbox** and **Lonesome 7-7203** in 1972.

JIMMY BOWEN – Once a hit-making rockabilly with Buddy Knox, Bowen became president of MCA Nashville in 1984 after a successful period as a Warner Brothers Nashville executive. By the early '90s he was heading up EMI's Nashville operations at Capitol-Liberty.

BOY HOWDY – A young four-man band formed in Los Angeles in 1991 comprising Jeffrey Steele (vocals, bass), Cary and Larry Park (guitars and vocals) and drummer Hugh Wright. Survivors of the tough Hollywood bar circuit, they play country music with a modernistic feel. Signed to Curb Records, their first album was **Welcome to Howdywood** in 1992.

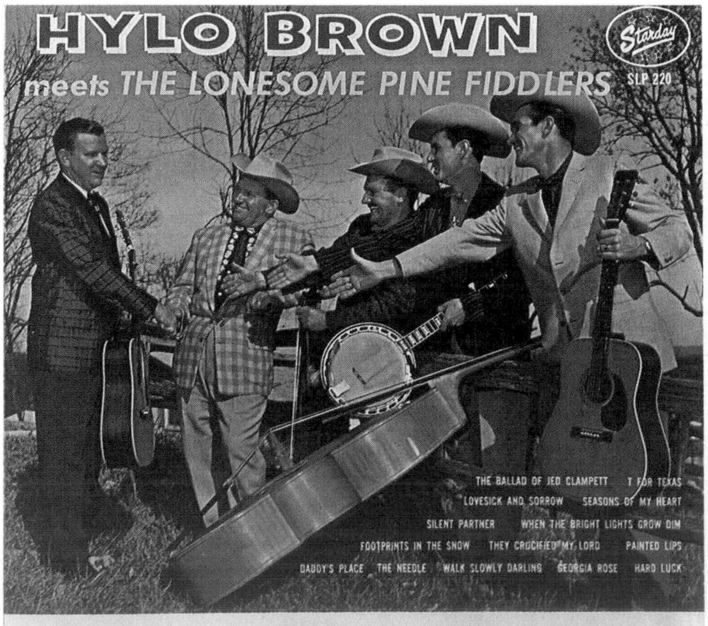

Hylo Brown Meets The Lonesome Pine Fiddlers. Courtesy Starday Records.

KAREN BROOKS – A professional team roper and barrel racer on the rodeo circuit, Dallas-born Karen Brooks first established a reputation as a songwriter. She sang on the Austin, Texas scene in 1975, at the time married to singer-songwriter Gary P. Nunn. A few years later she moved to Nashville and signed with Warners, scoring several hits during the '80s. Later she joined up with Randy Sharp for a successful duet team.

CLARENCE 'GATEMOUTH' BROWN – A hugely talented black singer and multi-instrumentalist, Brown was born in Orange, Texas in 1924. Though often thought of as a bluesman, he plays great bluegrass and Cajun fiddle and has appeared at several international country festivals.

FRANK 'HYLO' BROWN – Guitarist and singer of impressive range who once worked with Flatt And Scruggs. His folksy style was well suited to bluegrass and his **Hylo Brown Meets The Lonesome Pine Fiddlers**, a Starday album reissued in 1985 by Gusto, is well worth hanging on to.

JANN BROWNE – California-based singer, born in Anderson, Indiana, in 1955 and raised in Shelbyville, Indiana. Her parents were professional square dancers and Jann was playing in local bands during her high school days. She moved to southern California in 1977, where she played the rough and rowdy honky-tonk circuit. From 1981 to 1983 she was the featured vocalist with Asleep At The Wheel. Later she worked sessions, including back-up vocals on Rosie Flores' LP. In 1988 she was signed to Curb Records, her sandpaper voice gaining her a hip, young country following.

ANITA BRYANT – Born in Barnsdall, Oklahoma in 1940, Anita was a former Miss Oklahoma (1958), who started out as a country singer. She had a million-seller with **Paper Roses** in 1960, the song that many years later was to prove a country hit for Marie Osmond. These days Anita is best known as a battler against gay rights.

WILMA BURGESS – Born in Orlando, Florida in 1939, Wilma attended Stetson University, Orlando, majoring in physical education, but opted for a music career. She moved to Nashville in 1960 and worked as a demo singer, eventually gaining a record deal with Decca. Specializing in dramatic ballads, Wilma enjoyed major chart success with **Baby** and **Misty Blue**.

T-BONE BURNETT – Born in Tokyo and raised in Fort Worth, Texas, Burnett entered the music business as a producer and sessionman. In 1980 he released his own album, **Truth Decay**, and has continued to record spasmodically since. He produced Elvis Costello's **King Of America**, and was half of the Coward Brothers with Costello.

DORSEY BURNETTE – A country rockabilly musician born in Memphis in 1932. Along with his younger bother Johnny, he helped form the Johnny Burnette Rock'n'Roll Trio in 1954. The two brothers wrote hit songs for Ricky Nelson, then embarked on solo careers. Dorsey scored some pop hits in 1960 and continued recording for several labels, producing minor country hits until he died of a heart attack in 1979.

TRACY BYRD – Born in Beaumont, Texas in 1967, but raised in nearby Vidor, Tracy is a Texas honky-tonk singer who performed in Texas clubs while studying at Lamar University, Beaumont. He replaced Mark Chesnutt at Cutter's night-club in Beaumont when the latter signed a Nashville record deal. Three years later, Tracy followed suit and in 1991 signed with MCA Records.

C

CACTUS BROTHERS – Combine an old-time seven-piece string band with rock'n'roll energy who can play everything from aged fiddle tunes to sweet soul classics, and there you have the Cactus Brothers, who played the Nashville clubs for several years prior to landing a Liberty Records contract in 1992. They appeared in the George Strait movie 'Pure Country', and have been described as "Nashville's answer to the Pogues". In their line-up is world-class dulcimer player David Schnaufer, who has several acclaimed solo albums to his credit.

CAJUN MUSIC – A product of Louisiana bayou area which merges jazz, blues, country and French folk music. Fiddle and accordion dominate with most vocals still in French.

J. J. CALE – A singer, songwriter and guitarist born in Oklahoma City in 1938, Cale's lazy country-blues, laid-back singing and understated guitar work have gained him a cult following and have also proved influential, most noticeably in much of Eric Clapton and Mark Knopfler's style. His songs have been well-covered in country music and his albums have a wonderful timeless country appeal.

STACY DEAN CAMPBELL – Born in New Mexico and raised in Texas and Oklahoma, Campbell has that modern-day James Dean glow about him that spills over into his music, which owes much to '50s rock'n'roll and rockabilly. He started out with a local Texas outfit, the Nickels, playing Southwest clubs before gaining Nashville attention in 1990. Signed to Columbia Records in 1991, Stacey Dean is on the threshold of a major career.

JUDY CANOVA – A sort of slicked-up Minnie Pearl of the 1940s, Judy Canova, born in Jacksonville, Florida in 1916, was a country comedienne successful on Broadway and in some two dozen movies. She also had a long-running radio show (1943–53) and recorded regularly into the 1950s.

CANYON – A Texas-based band featuring Steve 'Coop' Cooper on lead vocals, Canyon played the bar-room circuit for a number of years before landing a record deal with the Nashville-based 16th Avenue Records in 1987. With their smoothly executed country-rock sound, they scored a number of minor hits without breaking through to the Top 20.

WAYNE CARSON – A versatile songwriter, singer and guitarist, Wayne Carson Thompson, born in Denver in 1946, played in rock'n'roll and R&B bands during high school days, and for a time played lead guitar for Red Foley in the early '60s. He toured for two years with the All Star Hoot Nanny Road Show, then in 1967 he moved to Nashville, where he made an impact as a songwriter and session player. He has penned more than 100 country hits, his best-known song, **Always On My Mind**, was a CMA winner in 1982. Carson has recorded for Monument, Elektra and EMH without too much commercial success.

WILF CARTER – A pioneer of Canadian country music, singer-songwriter-guitarist Wilf Carter, a one-time Canadian cowboy, was born in Nova Scotia in 1904. He branched out from rodeo to radio in the early 1930s. He signed with RCA Victor at the same time and has sustained a recording career for more than 50 years, cutting sides for Bluebird, Decca, Starday and RCA, resulting in more than 40 albums. One of the many yodelling singers influenced by Jimmie Rodgers, he adopted the guise of 'Montana Slim' while working on a New York CBS radio show.

JOHNNY CARVER – A pop-styled country singer who started out in a gospel group with two aunts and an uncle, Carver was born in Jackson, Mississippi in 1940. The featured singer in the house band at the famed Palomino Club in California, he started scoring minor country hits in the late '60s, eventually making it into the Top 10 in the '70s. The warm-voiced Carver specialized in covers of pop hits such as **Tie A Yellow Ribbon** and **Afternoon Delight**.

PETE CASSELL – Cassell was a long-popular blind singer with a fine, smooth voice which anticipated the likes of Jim Reeves. Most popular in the '40s and early '50s, Pete recorded for Decca, Majestic and Mercury, but died all too young in 1953, a few years too early to cash in on the smooth Nashville Sound for which his voice was so well suited.

CONNIE CATO – Born in Carlinville, Illinois in 1955, Connie signed to Capitol at 17. This singer's big moment came in 1975 when her version of **Hurt** (one of her three hits that year) went Top 20. She was once known as 'Superskirt' and 'Superkitten' following 1974 hits of those titles.

BRYAN CHALKER – Excellent, deep-voiced British singer and guitarist who made several above-average albums, but became disenchanted with the UK club scene and eventually opted to become a country DJ on a Bristol radio station. For a while, Chalker also published one of Britain's leading country music magazines.

JEFF CHANCE – From El Campo, Texas, vocalist-guitarist-fiddler Jeff Barosh, along with his drummer brother Mick Barosh, formed Texas Pride. In 1985 the five-piece band changed its name to Chance and, signed to Mercury, enjoyed some notable country chart success. In 1988 Jeff Chance embarked on a solo career. Though his rugged good looks and dynamic stage show should have led to instant success, his breakthrough is still waiting to happen.

MARSHALL CHAPMAN – From Spartanburg, South Carolina, where she was born in 1949, Chapman moved to Nashville in 1973 and made an impact as a songwriter. Signed to Epic Records three years later, she came on tough and rocky as she performed in a slow, bluesy powerhouse way. Her best-known number, **Somewhere South Of Macon**, scraped into the country charts in 1977, but she was too different or ahead of her time, and Epic let her go.

THE CHIEFTAINS – Formed in the early '60s and one of the most influential and long-lived Irish folk bands, the Chieftains helped to spearhead a revival of Irish traditional music, and they have built up an international following. In 1992 they made a country music connection, appearing in concert in Nashville and recording **Another Country**, an album of country songs featuring guest stars Ricky Skaggs, Chet Atkins, Emmylou Harris, Don Williams, the Nitty Gritty Dirt Band and several other Nashville musicians.

LEW CHILDRE – A veteran of vaudeville, 'Doctor Lew', who was born in Opp, Alabama in 1901, was a Hawaiian guitar player and sophisticated rural comedian. A regular on the Opry from 1945 until shortly before his death in 1961, he worked with Stringbean between 1945–48 and was also an adept singer who sang old standards like **I'm Looking Over A Four Leaf Clover**.

CIMMARON – A sextet from Roanake, Virginia, Cimmaron were formed in 1979 by lead vocalist Bobby Smith. They play a rich blend of country-rock, honky-tonk and high-powered neo-traditional with superb country picking and bluegrass-flavoured vocal harmonies. Having released an album on their own labels, they signed with Alpine Records in 1992, immediately making the CMI and TNN video rotations with such numbers as **Can't You Just Stay Gone** and **Detroit Diesel**, which quickly generated its own country dance.

YODELLING SLIM CLARK – Born Raymond LeRoy Clark in Springfield, Massachusetts in 1917, Yodelling Slim worked for a long period as a woodman. Winner of the World Yodelling Championship in 1947, he began recording for such labels are Continental, Remington, Wheeling and Palomino, his albums including **Yodel Songs** (1960) and **Jimmie Rodgers Songs** (1965).

LEE CLAYTON – A product of the Nashville 'underground', Clayton, born in Russelville, Alabama in 1942, also played it tough and rough. Much of the time he was over-produced when all he really needed was his voice and his songs. He wrote **Ladies Love Outlaws**, a biggie for Waylon Jennings, and recorded several albums for Capitol during the '70s.

PAUL COHEN – A Decca talent scout, Cohen (born in 1908, died in 1970) was the first to recognize the potential of Nashville as a recording centre. He was elected to the Country Music Hall Of Fame in 1976.

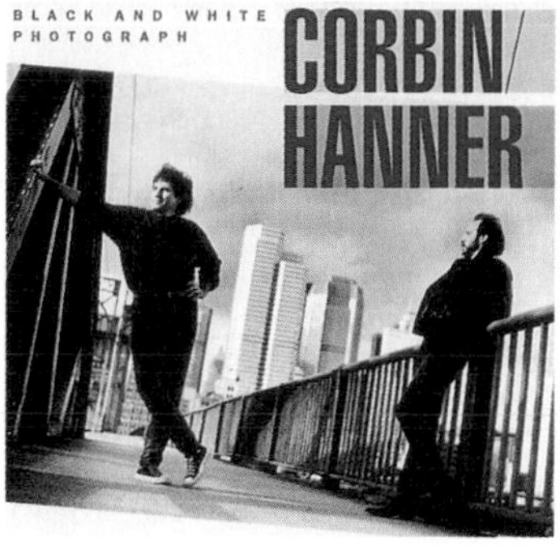

Black And White Photograph, Corbin/ Hanner. Courtesy PolyGram Records.

B. J. COLE – Unquestionably the most successful sessionman in British country music, steelie Bryan Cole has played on hundreds of pop, rock and country records. He also formed his own label, Cow Pie.

COLLINS KIDS – Lorrie and Larry Collins from Oklahoma were a country-pop duo signed to Columbia Records in 1955, when they were still in their early teens. They recorded classic rockabilly singles and were regulars on Town Hall Party in Los Angeles. They split in 1964 and Larry became a successful country songwriter – **Delta Dawn** and **You're The Reason God Made Oklahoma**.

COLORADO – A five-piece band from Sutherland, Scotland. One of the most respected British bands, they have toured with many US stars, including Jean Shepard, Boxcar Willie, Melba Montgomery and Vernon Oxford. Voted Top British Country Group many times during the '80s, Colorado changed direction to encompass their Scottish roots music and have now become known as Caledonia.

COMPTON BROTHERS – Harry and Bill Compton, from St Louis, Missouri, won a 1965 talent contest that resulted in a Columbia recording contract. However, they later became associated with the Dot label, supplying minor hits during the late '60s and early '70s.

BILL CONLON – An Irish balladeer originally from Portaferry, County Down, but since 1987 based in North London. Bill Conlon has made a big impact throughout Europe with successful appearances in Germany, Switzerland and Holland, plus several albums which put him on par with some of Nashville's top country vocalists. He always surrounds himself with good musicians and his recordings have gained extensive BBC Radio 2 plays, with **I Don't Have Far To Fall** being chosen as Record Of The Week in 1991.

MERVYN CONN – The producer of the prestigious series of Wembley Country Festivals plus numerous European tours featuring just about every worthwhile name in country music. Often criticized, Conn is, nevertheless, the man who has done most to popularize country sounds in Britain.

CORBIN-HANNER BAND – Bob Corbin and Dave Hanner, from Ford City, Pennsylvania, met while at high school. They formed the Gravel Band and worked the Pittsburgh clubs. Later they moved to Nashville where they recorded for numerous labels from 1978, finally making an impact when they linked up with Mercury Records as Corbin-Hanner in 1990.

ELVIS COSTELLO – Born Declan McManus, Elvis changed his name and built up a strong following after an unsuccessful stint in a country-rock band. The Irish-born pop star fulfilled a life-long ambition when he appeared on the Grand Ole Opry in 1982 during an American tour. An ardent admirer of George Jones, Elvis took his band, the Attractions, to Nashville to record **Almost Blue**, an album of country standards produced by Billy Sherrill in 1980. He scored a British chart-topper with an update of George Jones' **A Good Year For The Roses**, and recorded a duet with Jones of **A Stranger In The House**.

COUNTRY MUSIC ASSOCIATION – The CMA is a trade association formed in 1958 by a cadre of businessmen, artists and DJs to further the cause of country music. The CMA Awards, which take place in Nashville each October, are the most prestigious in country music, the premier accolade being Entertainer Of The Year.

COUNTRY MUSIC FOUNDATION – A non-profit organization which operates Nashville's Country Music Hall Of Fame and Museum, plus the Country Music Foundation Library, etc. It sums up its goals as being "dedicated to the study and interpretation of country music's past through the display of artifacts and the collection and dissemination of data found on discs, tape, film and in printed material".

COUNTRY MUSIC HALL OF FAME – Country music's major shrine, based in Nashville, in which the greats of the past and present are honoured for their contributions to their chosen form of music. Two or three members are elected annually. Jimmie Rodgers, Bob Wills, Eddy Arnold, Roy Acuff, Kitty Wells, Minnie Pearl, Hank Williams, Uncle Dave Macon, Tex Ritter and Jimmie Davis are among those who have a commemorative plaque and portrait in the Hall, which is actually part of a larger museum.

COUNTRY-ROCK – A trend that grew out of late 1960s West Coast rock, particularly around LA. Gram Parsons can be credited as acting as a catalyst to many of the part-time mandolin players and steel guitarists who were scraping a living in rock-oriented California, while Bob Dylan also helped to encouraged the trend with his **Nashville Skyline** album, also leaking the fact that Hank Williams had always been one of his favourite singers.

BRENDAN CROKER – Yorkshire-born singer-songwriter, Brendan Croker started out in the late '60s playing country-blues in Yorkshire pubs with Steve Phillips and Mark Knopfler. A few years later he formed his own group, the Five O'Clock Shadows. Then in 1989 he reunited with Phillips and Knopfler in the Notting Hillbillies. A trip to Nashville in 1991 saw him recording with top Nashville pickers for the solo LP **The Great Indoors**. Wynonna Judd included his **What It Takes** on her first solo album.

HUGH CROSS – One of country music's earliest professional entertainers, Hugh Cross, born in eastern Tennessee in 1904, joined a medicine show at 16 and by the mid-1920s was a popular singer on radio and record. A guitarist, banjoist and songwriter, he joined the Cumberland Ridge Runners on the National Barn Dance from 1930–33, then he struck out on his own, appearing on several radio stations, eventually drifting into executive capacities.

J. C. CROWLEY – A songwriter, guitarist and singer from Galveston Bay, Texas, Crowley was a member of the pop group Player during the late '70s. He co-wrote their No.1 pop hit **Baby Come Back**. Moving towards country, he signed with RCA Nashville in 1988, making Top 20 on the country charts with **Paint The Town And Hang The Moon Tonight**.

MAC CURTIS – A hillbilly singer who became a leading rockabilly with the King label, Curtis (from Olney, Texas) still cuts fine country sides from time to time. During the mid-1970s he produced some of Ava Barber's sides for Ranwood.

Beneath The Texas Moon, J.C. Crowley. Courtesy RCA Records.

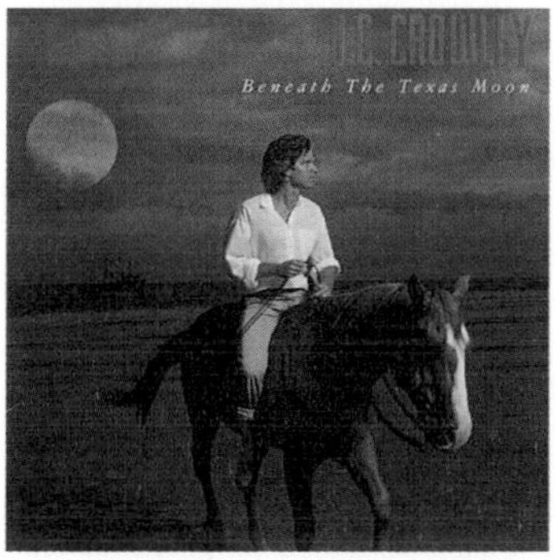

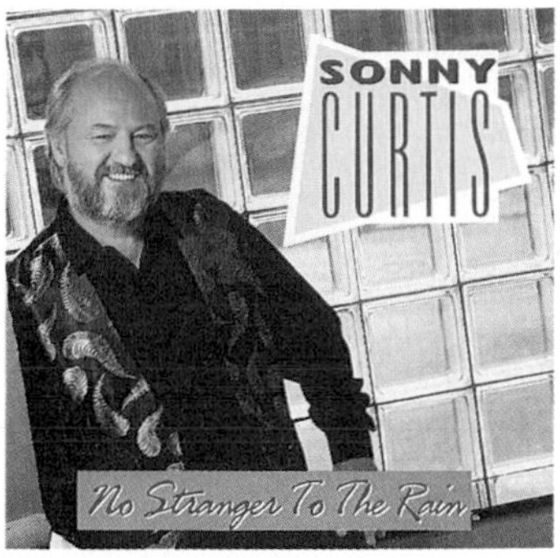

No Stranger To The Rain, Sonny Curtis. Courtesy Ritz Records.

SONNY CURTIS – Born in Meadow, Texas in 1937, singer, songwriter and guitarist Sonny Curtis will always be closely associated with Buddy Holly and the Crickets. He worked with Holly in 1956, then left to join Slim Whitman's group. A move to the West Coast in 1959 saw Curtis in the Crickets and penning pop/country hits for the Everly Brothers, Bobby Vee, Buddy Knox and others. Working both as a solo and occasional member of the Crickets, Curtis has recorded prolifically for various labels, making the country Top 20 with **Good Ol' Girls** in 1981. He has also penned such country hits as **I'm No Stranger To The Rain** (Keith Whitley) and **He Was On To Something** (Ricky Skaggs).

D

DICK DAMRON – A Canadian singer-songwriter, born in Bentley, Alberta, Damron is best known for his song, **Countryfied**, which became a US hit for George Hamilton IV in 1971.

DAVIS DANIEL – With his blonde hair, youthful features and light hearted attitude, Davis Daniel seems like he could have walked straight off a California beach, surfboard in hand. In fact, he grew up in Illinois, lived for a while in Nebraska and Denver, before moving to Nashville in 1987. His real name is Daniel Davis, but he changed it to avoid confusion with Danny Davis and the Nashville Brass. He was driving a truck for Miller Beer Company when he landed a recording contract with Mercury in 1990. With his southern-flavoured vocal punch he made the Top 20 with **Crying Out Loud** in 1991.

JOHNNY DARRELL – Once a motel manager, Darrell (born in Cleburne County, Alabama, 1940) cut the original version of **Green, Green Grass Of Home** and also had the first hit renditions of **The Son Of Hickory Hollers Tramp** (1967) and **With Pen In Hand** (1968).

PAUL DAVIS – Born in Meridian, Mississippi in 1948, this singer-songwriter first made an impact as a contemporary country act with the self-penned **Ride 'Em Cowboy**, a pop hit on Bang Records in 1975. He enjoyed further pop success, then started to make an impression as a country writer. Based in Nashville he recorded chart-topping duets with Marie Osmond and Tanya Tucker and by the late '80s had established himself as an in-demand producer.

LAZY JIM DAY – Born in Creek, Kentucky in 1911, died in 1959, Day was one of the early stars of country radio. A singer, banjoist and guitarist, he originated the singing news routine and by the late 1930s was the leading comedian on the Opry.

EDDIE DEAN – A cowboy film star of the '40s, Edgar Dean Glossup was born in Posey, Texas in 1907 and began his musical career as a gospel singer in the early '30s. His older brother Jimmy appeared on the WLS National Barn Dance in Chicago in 1936 then they headed west to try their luck in films. Eddie joined Judy Canova's Radio Show and appeared in scores of films before gaining his own series of 20 films with PRC from 1946–48. He recorded prolifically for Decca, Mercury, Sage And Sand and Capitol, his biggest hits, **One Has My Name, The Other My Heart** (1948) and **I Dreamed Of A Hillbilly Heaven** (1955) are two genuine country classics which he co-wrote.

MARTIN DELRAY – A guitarist-singer from Texarkana, Arkansas, Martin Delray spent years working the clubs and honky-tonks before landing a recording contract with Atlantic Records in 1990. A hard country stylist with '50s rockabilly overtones, he tempted Johnny Cash along to the studios to add vocals to an update of his **Get Rhythm** in 1991.

IRIS DeMENT – A traditional-sounding singer-songwriter, Iris was born in Paragould, Arkansas in 1961. She grew up in a musical household in California. Her father played fiddle, mother sang and her elder sisters formed a group, the DeMent Sisters. In 1984 Iris was performing at folk clubs in Kansas City, later moving to Nashville where she sang on sessions for Emmylou Harris, Jann Brown and Nanci Griffith. Signed to Philo/Rounder Records, Jim Rooney produced her debut album, **Infamous Angel** (1992), which gained good reviews, but the traditional lilt of the music and Iris's hill-country vocals gained virtually no radio plays in America. British DJ Wally Whyton played a track on his BBC Radio Country Club programme and was inundated for requests for more. Warner Brothers in Nashville picked up her contract and re-promoted the album in 1993.

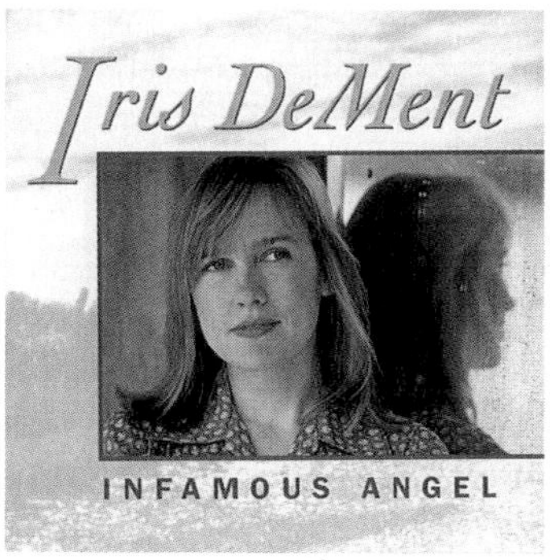

Infamous Angel, Iris DeMent. Courtesy Warner Bros Records.

JAMES DENNY – A one-time mail clerk, Denny was born in Buffalo Valley, Tennessee in 1911 and died in Nashville, 1963. He worked his way up the ladder to become talent director at Nashville's WSM radio. He also ran a booking agency business, at one point handling over 3,200 personal appearances throughout the world. He was elected to the Country Music Hall Of Fame in 1966.

KARL DENVER TRIO – This British country trio achieved pop group-styled stardom in 1961 when their Decca single, **Marcheta**, went Top 10 in the UK charts, to be followed by **Mexicali Rose** (1961), **Wimoweh** and **Never Goodbye** (both 1962). Two of the original threesome still work with the group.

SYDNEY DEVINE – Scotland's most successful country singer and a would-be Elvis, his **Doubly Devine** double-album on Philips went Top 20 in the UK during 1976, some 21 years after Devine first began his onstage career.

DIXIANA – From the heartlands of Greenville, South Carolina, Dixiana was formed in 1986. Lead singer Cindy Murphy was a longtime member of bluegrass outfit the Wooden Nickel Band, while brothers Mark and Phil Lister, as the Listers, hosted their own regional TV show in the mid-1970s. The other two members are Randall Griffith and Colonel Shuford. Signed to Epic Records in 1991, Dixiana have a hip image and traditional-flavoured contemporary country style, which ensures a bright future.

DOTTSY – For a while Dottsy Brodt (born in Seguin, Texas, 1953) swept all before her. A talent show winner at 12, by 14 she had her own weekly TV series, San Antonio. After quitting college in 1972 she appeared at Happy Shahan's Alamo Village in Bracketville, Texas, playing five shows a day. Later came tours with Johnny Rodriguez, and in 1974 she signed with RCA Records. Cute and country, petite and sweet, Dottsy seemed set to become a superstar. She had several major hits, the biggest being **(After Sweet Memories) Play Born To Lose Again** in 1977. Four years later she packed the music in to work with autistic and retarded children.

RUSTY DRAPER – Born Farrell Draper in Kirksville, Missouri, Rusty worked radio stations in Tulsa, Oklahoma, Des Moines, Iowa and Quincy, Illinois during his teens, then became singing MC at a club in San Francisco. A record deal with Mercury in 1951 resulted in his biggest hit, **Gambler's Guitar**, a pop and country Top 10 entry in 1953. He enjoyed further pop success in '50s, gaining several gold discs, but never made a major impact on the country charts, though he has recorded regularly in Nashville.

MARY DUFF – From Lobinstown, County Meath, Irish beauty Mary Duff has been one of Europe's top female country vocalists since linking up with Ritz Records in 1988, the following year winning the Euro Country Music Masters in Switzerland. Six years earlier she had started appearing with John Collier and New Dimension and Irish chart group Jukebox. Winning the Cavan Song Contest led to her signing with Ritz Records, tours with Daniel O'Donnell and her own bill-topping shows.

DUFFY BROTHERS – Ray and Leo Duffy, a British comedy duo from Peterborough, England, won the Marlboro Country Music competition and then went on tour with Marty Robbins and Tammy Wynette. Since then they have been voted Best British Country Duo for three years in a row, and also toured the word for two years as part of the Charley Pride road show.

JOHNNY DUNCAN – John Franklin Duncan from Oliver Springs, near Knoxville, Tennessee (where he was born in 1931), is better known in England, where he had a big pop hit with **Last Train To San Fernando** in 1957, and Australia, where he has lived since 1974. While in the US army he married an English woman and moved to England in 1955. Two years later he formed the Blue Grass Boys, in homage to Bill Monroe, and promoted as a skiffle band. He appeared on shows such as 6.5 Special and enjoyed several British pop hits in the late 1950s.

SLIM DUSTY – Australia's top-ranking country singer for four decades, Slim Dusty, born David Gordon Kirkpatrick in Dempsey, NSW, Australia in 1927, has sold more locally made records in his own land than any other artist. A champion of frontier ballads and music of the bush country, he has fought for survival since the beginning of his career. He rose to worldwide prominence with **A Pub With No Beer** (1958) and was made an MBE in 1970. He was still actively recording in the early 1990s.

BOB DYLAN – Born May 24, 1941, in Duluth, Minnesota, Dylan initially made the country connection through songwriting, with Johnny Cash and June Carter scoring his **It Ain't Me Babe** in 1964. He made two albums in Nashville – **John Wesley Harding** and **Nashville Skyline**, the latter providing his last hit single, **Lay Lady Lay**, in 1969. His music continues to touch on country, and many country performers have recorded his songs. In 1992 he co-wrote and duetted with Willie Nelson on their song about the plight of farmers, **Heartland**.

E

RAY EDENTON – A frequent winner of the NARAS Superpicker Band Rhythm Guitar award, Ray was born in Mineral, Virginia. He began playing professionally in 1946 and from 1952 to 1962 played on the Grand Ole Opry along with road shows for several stars. He is now a sought-after Nashville sideman.

DON EDWARDS – A pure cowboy singer, Edwards is America's modern cowboy troubadour. He performs authentic cowboy songs

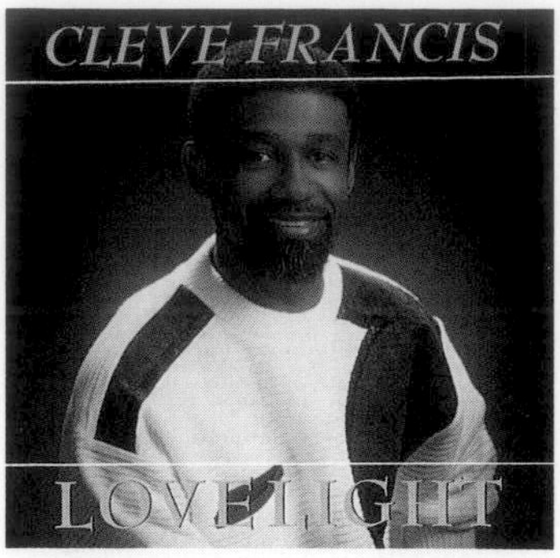

Lovelight, Cleve Francis. Courtesy Cottage Records.

and writes modern classics full of the wit and wisdom of the West. He has been performing around the Southwest since the early 1960s and was signed to the new Warner Western label in 1992.

JONATHAN EDWARDS – From Minnesota, where he was born in 1946, Edwards found success on the pop charts with **Sunshine**, a Top 20 entry in 1972. Labelled as part of the singer-songwriter genre, he always leaned towards country, having formed a bluegrass band, Sugar Creek, in 1965. He cut one of the first versions of **Honky Tonk Stardust Cowboy** in 1971. With his smooth tenor and delicate songs, he has record regularly for such labels as Atco, Atlantic and MCA, scoring some minor country hits in the late '80s.

RAMBLING JACK ELLIOTT – Born in Brooklyn, New York in 1931, Rambling Jack became known as an idealistic, bohemian folk singer, and a travelling troubadour. He flunked college to live in Greenwich Village, where he met Woody Guthrie, a friendship that proved fruitful in gaining him recognition. He played the Newport Festival in 1963, and continues to play colleges, coffee houses and folk festivals. He has been well received in Europe and enjoyed TV exposure and successful club bookings.

DARRYL AND DON ELLIS – This brother duo grew up in tiny Beaver Falls, Pennsylvania. Raised on a traditional country diet, they have had their own bands since Darryl was 15 and Don was 11. They made a move to Nashville in 1987, their airtight harmonies and insightful songwriting leading to a record deal with Epic four years later.

F

CHARLIE FEATHERS – An early Sun rockabilly artist, Feathers is still active in a family group in the Memphis area. Born in Hollow Springs, Mississippi, in 1932, he recorded for Flip, Sun, King, Kay, Memphis, Holiday Inn and Elektra Records, and is thought of as an artistic influence who somehow never found the right rockabilly record.

DICK FELLER – A singer-songwriter with a humorous cutting edge, Feller was born in Bronaugh, Missouri in 1943. A talented guitarist, he moved to Nashville in 1966, where he found work playing sessions or on the road with stars such as Mel Tillis and Warner Mack. He made an impact as a writer of hits for Johnny Cash and Jerry Reed, then came recordings with United Artists and Asylum in the '70s and such country hits as **The Credit Card Song**. A brilliant club performer, Dick Feller has built up a cult following in Europe.

DICK FORAN – Possessed of a fine voice – which sounded more at home on the Broadway stage than on the range – Foran was born in New Jersey in 1910, the son of a US Senator. He aspired to a career on the stage and later on film, but despite his singing cowboy films for Warner and Universal, he was also quite successful in high budget westerns and in other types of films. He retired at the start of the 1970s and lived in California up to the time of his death in 1979.

GERRY FORD – One of Scotland's most popular country performers, Gerry Ford was actually born in Athlone, County Westmeath, Eire in 1943. He moved to England in 1959, a few years later settling in Edinburgh where he joined the police force. A knowledgeable country music fanatic, he started singing seriously in the late '60s and has recorded prolifically since 1977, mainly in Nashville, where he is held in high esteem. Gerry is also a popular and successful DJ on BBC Radio Scotland.

LLOYD DAVID FOSTER – Texan singer-guitarist born in Wills Point in 1952, Foster played clubs on weekends, while driving a beer truck in Dallas by day. His first recordings were made for small Texas labels, then came stints with MCA and Columbia during the early 1980s, but that major breakthrough seems to have eluded him.

WALLY FOWLER – Cheerful, gladhanding Wally Fowler was born in Bartow County, Georgia in 1917. He first achieved success as a singer and songwriter, leading an Opry band called the Georgia Clodhoppers. He turned to gospel music, forming the Oak Ridge Quartet, forerunner of the Oak Ridge Boys, in the late '40s. In later years he turned his hand to gospel show promotion.

CLEVE FRANCIS – A practising cardiologist in Washington DC, hailing from Jennings, Louisiana, Cleve sang in a black gospel group during high school days. During medical college he sang in coffee and road houses, and recorded three independent label albums before making a breakthrough in 1992 when he was signed to Capitol/Liberty. Initially it was a video on CMT and TNN that brought Cleve Francis recognition and his first country hits.

J. L. FRANK – One of the great promoters of country music, Frank was born in Rossai, Alabama in 1900 and died in Detroit, 1952. Known as the 'Flo Ziegfeld of Country Music', he was instrumental in furthering the careers of Gene Autry, Roy Acuff, Ernest Tubb and many others. He was elected to the Country Music Hall of Fame in 1967.

RAYMOND FROGGATT – A distinctive British country singer-songwriter who started out as a pop writer, penning **Red Balloon**, a massive hit for the Dave Clark Five in 1968. A gritty, still slightly rock-oriented performer from Birmingham, he inspires fan adulation that is rare in British country music. He tours regularly, and performs his own, often excellent, material.

G

GEORGIA SATELLITES – An Atlanta-based rock band, the Georgia Satellites draw from a rich traditional American heritage with their guitar-heavy roots-type music. Influenced by a mixture of Dylan, Chuck Berry, George Jones and even ZZ Top, their music, which rocks with a fervour, made a commercial breakthrough in the late 1980s.

TERRI GIBBS – Born blind (in Augusta, Georgia, 1954), she was once a member of a group called Sound Dimension. A bluesy singer and pianist, Terri formed her own group in 1975 and gained a regular gig at Augusta's Steak and Ale House,

Where There's Smoke, Gibson/Miller Band. Courtesy Sony Music.

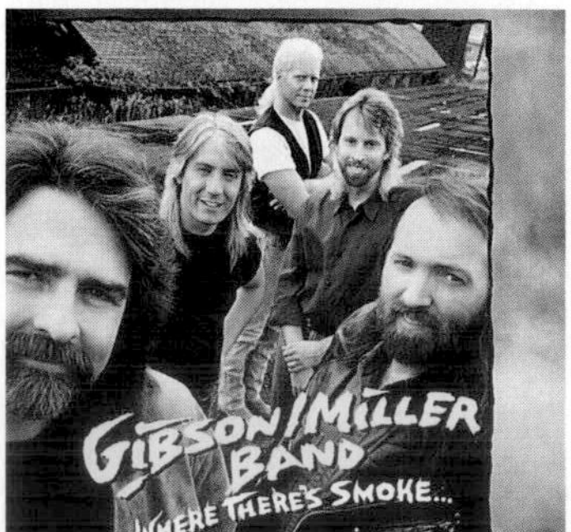

performing 50 songs a night. Signed to MCA in 1980, she came up with a Top 10 single **Somebody's Knockin'** later that year and won the CMA Horizon Award in 1981. For the next three years she maintained a steady flow of chart records without ever gaining the hit she undoubtedly deserved.

GIBSON-MILLER BAND – Five-man band led by Nashville songwriter Dave Gibson and Detroit rock guitarist Blue Miller, along with Bryan Grassmeyer, Steve Grossman and Mike Daly. They play what has been described as 'turbo-twang' country'. Gibson is a noted Nashville songwriter with hits for Alabama, Tanya Tucker and Joe Diffie to his credit. Miller is a one-time guitar player with Bob Seger, while the other members have worked in bands with Vince Gill, Suzy Bogguss and Sweethearts Of The Rodeo. Signed to Epic Records in 1992, they have brought varied country and rock musical elements together for an exciting '90s country sound.

BRIAN GOLBEY – Sussex-born British singer, songwriter and multi-instrumentalist, Brian Golbey is one of Britain's finest country music entertainers. He first came to prominence in the mid-1960s at the Folk Voice conventions. He often teams up with banjo player Pete Stanley to play bluegrass, but is at his best with his own self-penned albums. He recorded many albums as a soloist, and in the mid-1970s was a member of folk-rock trio Cajun Moon for a short time.

TONY GOODACRE – A British perennial who started out on a Carrol Lewis talent show in 1957. Like many others, he has indulged in 'cover' albums of US hits (**Thanks To The Hanks**, **Roaming Round In Nashville**) but redeemed himself with **Written In Britain**, a release containing all British material by Terry McKenna and Pete Sayers.

GRAND OLE OPRY – The greatest show in country music, the Opry has been broadcast on Saturday nights over WSM since 1927 (though it formerly ran as the WSM Barn Dance from 1925). The show has survived many changes of location, first being housed in a WSM studio, then in a larger studio, then in the Hillboro Theater, before moving to the Dixie Tabernacle and, for a short spell, to the War Memorial Auditorium, before settling down for over 30 years at the Ryman Auditorium. It is today situated in the modern Grand Ole Opry house in the grounds of a huge amusement complex.

CLAUDE GRAY – A popular singer, guitarist and bandleader who was born in Henderson, Texas in 1932, he enjoyed a spate of best-selling singles in the early '60s when signed to Mercury Records. With his deep voice and impressive stature he had his biggest hit with **I'll Just Have Another Cup Of Coffee** in 1961, but was still charting as recently as 1982.

OTTO GRAY – Influential bandleader from Oklahoma, Gray organized the Oklahoma Cowboys, one of the very early professional country bands, in 1924, and the band lasted through to the mid-1940s. They presented a slick, very rehearsed show and achieved their greatest success in the Northeast, particularly over WGY in Schenectady, New York. They recorded for Gennett, Vocalion and Okeh.

GREAT PLAINS – This Minnesota/Oregon quartet, high on rock energy and cool with country twang, first got together as a band through playing with Michael Johnson in 1986. Jack Sundrud (lead singer, guitar), Russ Pahl (lead/steel guitar), Danny Dadmun-Bixby (bass) and Michael Young (drums) were all impeccable musicians with credits on albums and tours by George Jones, Mary-Chapin Carpenter, etc. Signed to Columbia Records in 1991, they were just starting to get established when Pahl and Young left in May 1993, leaving the band's future in doubt.

RICKY LYNN GREGG – A former rock singer from Longview, Texas, long-haired Gregg built up a regional following in the Dallas/Fort Worth area. In 1983 he formed the Ricky Lynn Project and started touring. Three years later he joined rock band Head East as lead singer and wrote most of their 1989 album **Choice Of Weapons**.

Above: The Georgia Satellites mix up a popular brand of country-rock.

Then he moved towards country and formed a new outfit, Cherokee Thunder, in 1990, blending his rock roots with a solid country base. Jimmy Bowen signed him to Liberty Records in 1992.

CLINTON GREGORY – A vocalist and fiddle player from Martinsville in the backwoods of Virginia, Clinton Gregory is the son of a champion fiddle player and bootlegger. A former member of Suzy Bogguss' back-up band, he embarked on a fully fledged solo career signing with Step One Records in 1990 and scoring several country hits, the biggest being **(If It Weren't For Country Music) I'd Go Crazy**.

REX GRIFFIN – A popular singer, guitarist and songwriter best known for his composition **The Last Letter**, Rex (born in 1912) became popular over WSB in Atlanta and as host of the KRLD Texas Roundup. Probably the most fascinating aspect of his career was that he recorded **Lovesick Blues** for Decca, a record which went nowhere; nearly a decade later Hank Williams recorded Griffin's version identically, with tremendous success. Plagued with ill-health due to a lifelong drinking problem, Griffin died in 1959.

LEWIS GRIZZARD – Looking like a cross between Groucho Marx and Ernie Kovacs, Grizzard is a celebrated columnist, comedian, author and social commentator. With his southern-drenched humour he hits on such themes as southern living, religion and sex. Signed to Columbia Records he has been named country comedian by the CMA and is a popular concert performer.

ARLO GUTHRIE – Eldest child of Woody Guthrie, singer, guitarist and songwriter Arlo was born in Coney Island, New York in 1947. Though, broadly speaking, a folkie, he has always worked closely with country. His 1972 Top 20 pop hit was with Steve Goodman's **City Of New Orleans**, and the album **Last Of The Brooklyn Cowboys** (1973) featured country songs backed up by Buck Owens' Buckaroos.

H

THE HACKBERRY RAMBLERS – An early and influential Cajun band whose records, both in English and Cajun-French, helped win the music a wider audience in the '30s. In their prime they recorded mainly for Bluebird. They disbanded in 1939, but in the '60s leader Luderin Darbone

reformed the group for appearances at folk festivals and weekend dances in local taverns.

THE HAGERS – Identical twins born in Chicago, Jim and John signed to Capitol in 1969 and notched minor hits through to 1971. Versatile and equipped with ready-to-please comedy routines, they made many appearances on Hee Haw, then headed for Hollywood.

MONTE HALE – Singing cowboy Monte Hale, born in San Angelo, Texas in 1921, starred in some 19 Republic westerns from 1945–51, making him one of the last singing cowboys in chronological terms. Although possessed of a strong, smooth voice, his records were not particularly successful. He toured as a singer with rodeos before bowing out of musical and acting careers while still a young man.

THERON HALE AND DAUGHTERS – Theron Hale (1883–1954) led one of the most interesting and popular of the early Opry bands from 1926 until the early 1930s. Unlike most of the raucous hoedown bands, their music was gentle and reminiscent of parlour music of the preceding century, highlighted by lovely twin fiddling.

THE HALEYS – Sisters Jo-Ann and Becky Haley from the West Yorkshire village of Harden, England, were still teenagers when they became professional country singers, initially as part of a trio, Applejack, in 1989, then as self-contained duo, the Haley Sisters, the following year. The British Country Music Association voted them Top British Duo in 1991 and 1992. Performing a wide variety of material, both girls share lead and harmony vocals. In 1993 they formed a back-up band and became known as the Haleys.

GEORGE HEGE HAMILTON V – Son of George Hamilton IV, Hege was born in Nashville in 1960 and has always been surrounded by country music. While attending the University of North Carolina he played in several college rock bands. Then he linked up with his father as guitarist and back-up vocalist in a package tour in 1983 that included Faron Young, Leroy Van Dyke and Dave Dudley, followed by many Opry appearances. In 1987 he landed a record deal with MTM Records. His album, **House Of Tears**, gained rave reviews as the lanky youngster took off on an epic promotional tour in a '65 Cadillac hearse. His folkabilly single, **She Says**, made the country charts in early 1988, then MTM closed down, leaving the talented singer-songwriter high and dry. He has since built up a cult following on the British circuit with country band Fever.

GUS HARDIN – A gutsy singer, Gus spent 11 years singing in Tulsa clubs. One-time mentor Leon Russell described her voice as "a cross

between Otis Redding, Tammy Wynette and a truck driver". Signed to RCA in the early 1980s, she began logging a tally of Top 40 singles, gaining Top 10 records with **After The Last Goodbye** (1983) and **All Tangled Up In Love**, a duet with Earl Thomas Conley (1984).

JONI HARMS – Born and raised in Canby, Oregon, Joni Harms is a hometown beauty who won the Miss Northwest Rodeo title in 1979. Performing in clubs since a teenager, this talented singer-songwriter finally made the Nashville connection in 1988, when Jimmy Bowen signed her to the short-lived Universal Records. Her contract was switched to Capitol and she chalked up a sizeable hit with **I Need A Wife** in 1989.

ALEX HARVEY – Successful songwriter and quality soulful country vocalist, Alex Harvey was born in Brownsville, Tennessee, 1945. He obtained a degree in music at Murray State University, Kentucky, moved to Nashville in 1966 and established himself as a songwriter with such hits as **Delta Dawn**, **Reuben James** and **Tulsa Turnaround**. He gained a Capitol recording contract, but has had most success as a songwriter. His songs have been recorded by such stars as Helen Reddy, Tanya Tucker, Waylon Jennings and others.

HEE HAW – A syndicated TV show established in the summer of 1969. Full of cornporn humour supplied over the years by such funny men as Archie Campbell and Junior Samples plus musicians such as Buck Owens and Roy Clark, the show has continued to be highly popular, despite – or maybe because of – its total lack of anything that seems in the least sophisticated.

KELVIN HENDERSON – British, Bristol-born (1947) and -based singer, bandleader and radio broadcaster, Kelvin has been winning polls in the UK and various European countries for many years. He recorded several acclaimed albums, the best being **Black Magic Gun** in 1977, which perfectly captured the contemporary outlaw movement of the time. He had his own TV series, Country Comes West, and is an outspoken expert on country music.

TARI HENSLEY – Born Tari Dean Hodges in Independence, Missouri in 1953, her name is pronounced 'Terry'. An amateur singer as a teenager, she married bandleader Dan Hensley in 1972 and toured with his band for more than ten years. Eventually she landed a contract with Mercury Records in 1983 and scored several minor hits, but failed to make it into the Top 20.

GOLDIE HILL – Born in Karmes County, Texas in 1933, Goldie began her professional career during the early '50s, signing with Decca, appearing on Shreveport's Louisiana Hayride and having a Top 5 country hit with **Don't Let The Stars Get In Your Eyes** in 1953. She went into semi-retirement shortly after her marriage to Carl Smith in 1957, but is still remembered as one of the most popular female country singers of the '50s.

THE HILLSIDERS – A British band that began their long stay at the top in 1965. A Liverpool outfit, they have recorded a Chet Atkins-produced album with Bobby Bare and another with George Hamilton IV. They have had their own BBC-TV show, played a Royal Albert Hall date and even played a two-week engagement at the London Palladium.

STAN HITCHCOCK – A former DJ in Springfield, Missouri, Hitchcock, who was born in Pleasant Hope, Missouri in 1937, moved to Nashville in 1962. He landed a record deal with Epic in 1967 due to his successful TV series and made it into the country Top 20 with **Honey, I'm Home** in 1969. He continued recording well into the '70s, then switched to television backroom work and by the late '80s was programme director for Country Music Television.

BECKY HOBBS – Rebecca Hobbs was born in Bartlesville, Oklahoma in 1950. During high school she formed an all-girl band, the Four Faces Of Eve. She attended Tulsa University and became a member of another all-girl band, Surprise Package. A move to Baton Rouge in 1971 found her in a bar band, Swamp Fox. Two years later she moved to Los Angeles, writing songs and recording for MCA. She signed to Mercury in 1978 but didn't make Top 20 until she duetted with Moe Bandy on **Let's Get Over Them Together** in 1983. A vastly talented musician, singer and songwriter, Becky has never made the commercial impact she deserves. Her self-penned **Jones On The Jukebox** is a real classic country song.

ADOLPH HOFNER – A native Texan of German-Slavic descent, Adolph Hofner has had a long and fascinating career playing both western swing and ethnic dance music for Texas' large German-American community. He began his career in San Antonio in the '30s and continues, to this day, travelling five days a week within the Texas state line, sponsored by Pearl Beer.

DOYLE HOLLY – Born in Perkins, Oklahoma in 1936, he was a Kansas oilfield worker at 13 and joined the US army in 1953. Following discharge, he moved to Bakersfield, California, where he played in Johnny Burnette's band. He became a regular member of Buck Owens' Buckaroos from 1963–70. With his own band, the Vanishing Breed, he signed with Barnaby Records in the early '70s, registering several low-level hits.

BRUCE HORNSBY – Raised in Williamsburg, Virginia, singer, songwriter and pianist Bruce Hornsby leads the Range, a piano-based, jazz-influenced pop quintet which was formed in Los Angeles in 1982. Eclectic in their musical styles, they lean heavily towards country-rock and scored a country Top 40 entry with **Mandolin Rain** in 1987.

STEPHEN WAYNE HORTON – A singer-guitarist from Memphis, Horton is a throwback to '50s rock'n'roll. Playing the clubs in and around Memphis finally led to a recording contract with Capitol in 1988. Though his first album was critically acclaimed, he has failed to impress record buyers with his turbo-charged country-rock.

15.25, The Hillsiders. Courtesy of the Hillsiders.

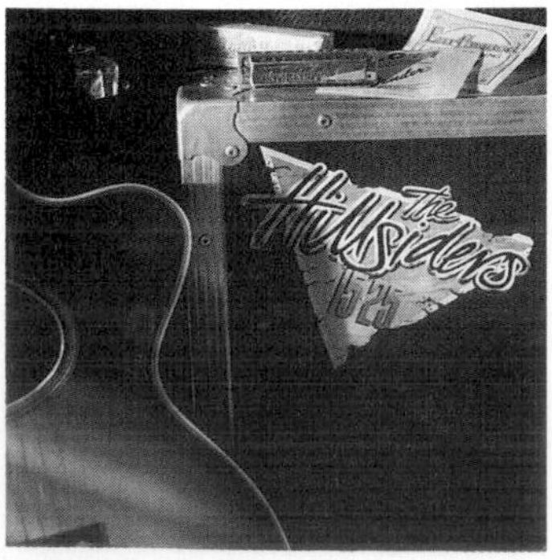

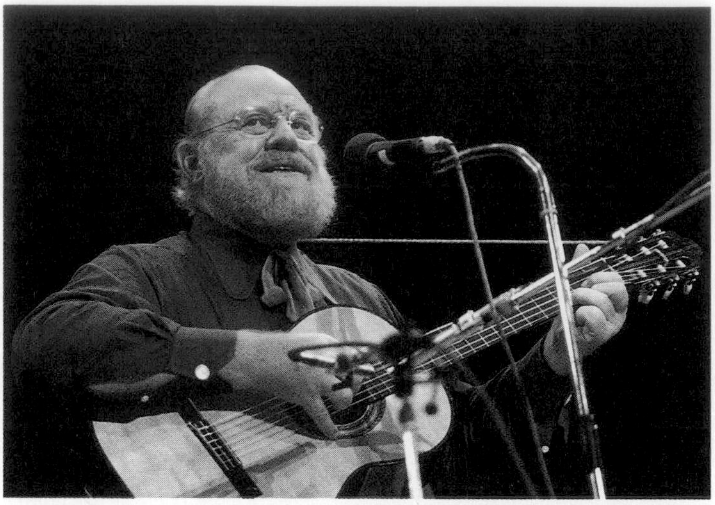

Above: Burl Ives, also an actor, had country hits from the '40s to the '60s.

JAMES HOUSE – A singer-songwriter from Sacramento, California, James began playing clubs as a single acoustic act at 18, eventually putting together the House Band to back up his country-rock repertoire. He became a staff writer with Unicity Publishing in Los Angeles and some of his country song demos reached Nashville. In 1988 he was signed to MCA. He has concentrated on his writing, penning hits for several major stars, while still touring and developing his own career.

RAY WYLIE HUBBARD – Born in Hugo, Oklahoma in 1946, Ray is a singer-songwriter whose **Up Against The Wall Redneck Mother** became the anthem of the Texas outlaw movement during the 1970s. His **Off The Wall** album, made for Willie Nelson's Lone Star label in 1978, is worthy of reasonable outlay – or even unreasonable outlay.

I

IDA RED – A British band based in Wales, Ida Red have successfully blended the best of traditional country into a multi-faceted contemporary styling. Bobbie Barnwell, a lady with several years experience as a singer and musician, plays guitar and accordion, her teenage daughter Sarah plays fiddle and harmonizes with her mother. Henry Nurdin is a master of every stringed instrument in sight, but is at his best as he dances about playing mandolin. The final member is Tim Smith, who plays mandolin, guitar, harmonica and adds vocals. The group have been building a healthy following since 1990.

FRANK IFIELD – A UK pop singer born in Coventry in 1937, but emigrated to Australia with his parents during World War II. He started working tent shows in 1950 and by 1955 had his own radio and TV shows and was recording straight country for the local Regal-Zonophone label. Within a few years he had become Australia's biggest recording star. He moved to England in 1959 and signed to Columbia (EMI), expanded his style to country-pop and within three years topped the UK pop charts with **I Remember You**. Utilizing his yodelling-falsetto developed in Australia, he enjoyed further pop success throughout the '60s, often updating country songs, and also broke into American pop and country charts. He toured regularly until a serious operation curtailed his singing activities in 1990.

THE IMPERIALS – A country gospel group that, during the mid-1960s, became back-up group for Elvis Presley. SInce 1975, they have been recording Christian music exclusively.

JERRY INMAN – Lead singer with the resident band at Hollywood's Palomino for several years, Jerry notched his first hit with the Chelsea label in 1974 and in the late '70s had a brace of mini-hits on Elektra before fading.

CHRIS ISAAK – A singer-songwriter born in Stockton, California in 1956, Isaak first made an impact as a member of rockabilly quartet Silvertone in the mid-1980s. As a solo performer he gained extensive radio plays for the haunting rockabilly anthem **Blue Hotel**, while an instrumental version of his **Wicked Game** was used in David Lynch's 'Wild At Heart' film. He has since provided incidental music for TV shows and films, while his parallel movie career has gathered strength with roles in 'Married To The Mob' and 'The Silence Of The Lambs'.

BURL IVES – Folksinger, actor, broadcaster and author, Burl Ives was born in Huntington Township, Illinois in 1909. He helped to keep folk music alive during the '40s with his radio broadcasts as the 'Wayfaring Stranger'. For a time a member of the Weavers, he has successfully balanced a career as actor ('East Of Eden', etc) and singer, registering country hits with **Riders In The Sky** (1949) **and Wild Side Of Life** (1952). He recorded in Nashville in the early '60s scoring his biggest hits with **A Little Bitty Tear** and **Call Me Mr In-Between**.

J

AUNT MOLLIE JACKSON – An early protest singer, Aunt Mollie was born Mary Magdalene Garland in Clay County, Kentucky in 1880. A member of a mining family, her mother died of starvation in 1886. Her brother, husband and son all died in pit accidents, and her father and another brother were blinded in the mines. She became a union organizer, singing at meetings and on picket lines, moving to New York in 1936 because she was blacklisted in Kentucky. Along with her sister, Sarah Ogan Gunning, she recorded a great wealth of material for the Library of Congress, though her only commercial disc was **Kentucky Miner's Wife**, a Columbia single. She died in 1960.

SHOT JACKSON – Owner of Sho-Bud guitar company, Shot was born in Wilmington, North Carolina. Previously a sideman with Johnny And Jack, Kitty Wells and Roy Acuff, Jackson remained with the latter until he and Acuff were injured in a near-fatal auto accident in 1965.

JANA JAE – A beautiful and talented fiddler, Jana won the National Lady's Fiddling Championship in 1973 and 1974. A part of the Buck Owens Show for a long period, she has since appeared on many top TV shows, including Hee Haw and has even played the Montreux Jazz Festival.

JASON AND THE SCORCHERS – A cowpunk outfit from Sheffield, Illinois and headed by Jason Ringenberg (vocals, guitar, harmonica). Nashville-based, they displayed a wild, breakneck-paced style of rock-oriented country on two EPs for the local Praxis label and in 1984 signed to EMI America, cutting an album **Lost And Found**. After moving closer to hard rock, the Scorchers split up in 1990 with Jason launching a solo career as 'Jason' and a hard-edged traditional country sound that has yet to find favour with country radio.

FRANK JENNINGS – A British singer, heavily influenced by Faron Young, his band, the Frank Jennings Syndicate, came into existence in 1970 and rose to be the best country unit in the UK, gaining a deal with EMI which did not last as long as it might have done.

JJ WHITE – Sisters Janice and Jayne White from northern California have been singing together most of their lives. Harmonizing was second nature as they sang in high school and performed at amateur talent nights. In 1990 they landed a recording contract with Curb Records and started charting country hit entries in the lower regions of the chart.

LOIS JOHNSON – From Knoxville, Tennessee, Lois Johnson worked on local radio from the age of 11 and was a regular on the WWVA Jamboree in Wheeling during her teen years. She joined the Hank Williams Jr Road Show in 1969, the pair recording several successful duets. Her biggest solo success came with **Loving You Will Never Grow Old**, a Top 10 entry in 1975.

ANTHONY ARMSTRONG JONES – Born Ronnie Jones in Ada, Oklahoma, 1950, something of a local child star, he was discovered by Conway Twitty in 1962 and worked shows with him for many years. His stage name came from the English photographer who married Princess Margaret. He has recorded for Chart, Epic and Air, making regular chart entries from 1969–86, the most notable being **Take A Letter Maria** in 1970.

K

BUELL KAZEE – Born in Burton Fork, Kentucky in 1900, Kazee was a college-educated, fully ordained minister of the church. He recorded during 1927–29 for Brunswick, singing and playing five-string banjo on such songs as **Hobo's Last Ride** and **Rock Island Line**. Author of a book, 'Faith In The Victory', he performed at many folk concerts and recorded some material for the Library of Congress. He died in 1976.

ROBERT EARL KEEN JR – A Texas singer-songwriter, born in Houston, 1956, Keen was at University with Lyle Lovett; the pair often performed together. Later he formed a bluegrass outfit, the Front Porch Boys, but has since become an acclaimed contemporary singer-songwriter. His song, **Sing One For Sister**, was picked up by Nanci Griffith. His own album, **West Textures**, about life in Texas, proved to be the ideal vehicle for his rough, gruff vocals.

TOBY KEITH – An emerging singer-songwriter from Oklahoma, this one-time cowboy signed with Mercury Records in 1992. Along with label-buddies John Brannen and Shania Twain, he was part of the 'Triple Play Tour', a whirlwind 1993 promotional tour to establish the acts. It worked for Toby Keith, as his self-penned single, **Should've Been A Cowboy**, soared to No.1 on the country charts. Definitely a major star of the future.

SANDY KELLY – Pretty Irish colleen from County Sligo, Sandy Kelly has been a major star in Ireland since the late '80s. A revival of Patsy Cline's **Crazy** topped the Irish charts and led to her own RTE TV series, which has been on air since 1990. Sandy has also made her mark in America, appearing at Fan Fair and in Branson, with Johnny Cash duetting with her on record and in concert. A past winner of the Country Euro-Masters, in 1993 Sandy embarked on her most ambitious project – 'Patsy Cline: A Musical Tribute', a show which was touring provincial theatres throughout Great Britain.

ANITA KERR – A singer born in Memphis, Tennessee in 1927 who got into the vocal group business early in life and later led the Anita Kerr Singers on records by Eddy Arnold, Jim Reeves, Chet Atkins, Skeeter Davis, Floyd Cramer and many other artists. By the 1970s she was based in Europe providing mainly MOR albums.

DON KING – A talented singer-songwriter-guitarist, Don was born in Omaha, Nebraska in 1954. He has never quite made the breakthrough to the big time. He moved to Nashville in 1974 and had a couple of Top 20 entries for Con Brio Records in 1977. He has since recorded for Epic, Bench Mark and 615, and written many hit songs for other major acts. He has his own thriving Don King Music Group publishing company in Nashville.

SID KING – Real name Sidney Erwin, Sid was born in Denton, Texas in 1936. He became leader of the Five Strings, a country outfit that started out as the Western Melodymakers. They edged into rockabilly, recorded for Starday , their repertoire including **Who Put The Turtle In Myrtle's Girdle** and, in late 1954, they gained a Columbia contract, staying five years. Some of the Five Strings' radio shots can be heard on the Rollercoaster album, **Rockin' On The Radio.**

EDDIE KIRK – A one-time singer and guitarist with the Beverly Hillbillies, Kirk was an amateur flyweight boxer whose yodelling ability won him the National Yodelling Championship in 1935 and 1936. Born in Greeley, Colorado in 1919, he was a singer much in the smooth style of Eddy Arnold. Signed to Capitol Records, his biggest hits were **Candy Kisses** (a version of George Morgan's hit song) and **The Gods Were Angry With Me** in 1949.

L

SLEEPY LA BEEF – The man mountain of rockabilly. a b b singer-guitarist who once played the Swamp Monster in the movie 'The Exotic Ones'. The possessor of an amazing baritone voice, La Beef (from Smackover, Arkansas) has recorded for Starday, Columbia, Sun, Plantation, Rounder and other labels.

LaCOSTA – Elder sister of Tanya Tucker, LaCosta Tucker, born in Seminole, Texas in 1951, was working as a medical records technician in Toltrec, Arizona when Tanya hit with **Delta Dawn** in 1972. She joined her younger sister in Las Vegas and in 1974 LaCosta was signed to Capitol Records, scoring her biggest hit with **Get On My Love Train**, a Top 3 hit in 1974. More Top 20 hits came during the next few years, but by 1982, working as LaCosta Tucker, the hits stopped flowing and eventually she left the music business.

JOHN LAIR – A country music pioneer, Lair was born in Livingston, Kentucky in 1894 and died in 1985. He produced many country radio shows, formed the Cumberland Ridge Runners and, in

Above: Sleepy La Beef found a rockabilly audience in the late '70s.

1937, together with the Duke Of Paducah, Red Foley and his brother Cotton Foley, bought and built the Renfro Valley Barn Dance.

CHARLIE LANDSBOROUGH – A British singer-songwriter born in Wrexham, Wales in 1941, but raised mainly in Birkenhead on Merseyside. He played in the Top Spots, a beat group in Liverpool in the early 1960s. Developing a soft, romantic style, he has provided hit songs for Foster And Allen and recorded occasionally since 1982. Signed to Ritz Records in 1992, Landsborough has his best opportunity to break through as both a songwriter and major British act.

CRISTY LANE – Born Eleanor Johnston in Peoria, Illinois in 1940, Cristy Lane has been one of the best-sold singers in country music, with her albums advertised on TV and in national magazines. Her husband, Lee Stoller, masterminded his wife's career, forming LS Records in 1972, with several major country hits following. In 1979 she signed with UA and scored

Left: Jason And The Scorchers split up in 1989 and Jason went solo.

a No.1 with **One Day At A Time** the next year. Cristy's album of the same title is reputed to be the biggest-selling gospel album of all time.

RED LANE – Born in Dogalusa, Louisiana in 1939, this singer-songwriter and award-winning guitarist has worked on Merle Haggard's Strangers. He had a few hits of his own while recording for RCA in 1971–72.

NICOLETTE LARSON – A lady who initially found fame as back-up vocalist for Hoyt Axton and Linda Ronstadt, Larson was born in Helena, Montana in 1952 and raised in Kansas City. She moved to L.A. in 1974 and worked with the Nocturnes. Session work followed and a recording contract with Warner Brothers resulted in a Top 10 pop hit, **Lotta Love**, in 1979. A fan of country music, she moved to Nashville in 1984, signed to MCA, and started registering country hits. The most successful, **That's How You Know When Love's Right**, featured Steve Wariner and made the Top 10 in 1986.

ALBERT LEE – Simply the finest country-rock guitarist ever to come out of Britain, he was born in Leominster, Herefordshire, 1943, but spent his teen years in London, where he played in various pop, rock and R&B bands. He appeared at London's Royal Albert Hall with Chet Atkins in 1969, played with the group Heads, Hands And Feet in the early '70s, and gained true recognition as a member of Emmylou Harris' Hot Band. Now living in America, he is a well-established Nashville session musician.

DICKEY LEE – A teenage Sun rockabilly who wrote **She Thinks I Still Care**, a country classic for George Jones, Dickey Lipscomb was born in Memphis, Tennessee in 1936. After recording for Sun Records in 1957–58, he went on to score pop hits for Smash in the early '60s with **Patches** being the biggest. A move to Nashville in 1970 saw him sign to RCA and enjoy an incredible run of country hits, including **Rocky**, a 1975 No.1. He had further hits for Mercury in the '80s, but has since devoted his time to his successful songwriting.

ROBIN LEE – Born Robin Irwin in Nashville, it was only natural for this young lady to follow a country music career. At high school she sang with rock group the Practical Stylists, then she sang demos for music publishers. While still a teenager she signed with Evergreen Records, registering several low-level hits between 1983–86. She joined Atlantic Records in 1988 and broke into the Top 20 with the song **Black Velvet** in 1990.

ZELLA LEHR – A versatile entertainer, Zella Lehr, who was born in Burbank, California in 1951, worked in the family vaudeville act. the Crazy Lehrs, from the age of six. When the act split up she became a regular on TV's Hee Haw, from which she built a country music career. Playing club dates in Nashville led to a RCA recording contract and a Top 10 hit with Dolly Parton's **Two Doors Down** in 1978. She has registered further hits for Columbia and Compleat.

GORDON LIGHTFOOT – A Canadian folk singer born in Orilla, Ontario in 1938. Lightfoot was a major influence on the Nashville folk-country of the mid-1960s with his songs recorded by George Hamilton IV, Marty Robbins, Waylon Jennings, etc. He broke through as a recording star in the '70s with platinum albums and hit singles **If You Could Read My Mind**, **Sundown** and **Carefree Highway**.

THE LILLY BROTHERS – Mitchell 'Bea' B and Everett Lilly (born in Clear Creek, West Virginia in 1921 and 1924 respectively) are a bluegrass duo who began as the Lonesome Holler Boys on a Charleston radio show in 1939 but became residents in the Boston area, where they played for around 18 years. During 1973 they visited Japan, cutting several albums.

GEORGE LINDSAY – Comedian-character actor known to the world as 'Goober'. He was a regular on Hee Haw.

LaWANDA LINDSEY – Once a singer with her father's band, Chart Records at 14 and had several hits in 1969–72. Later she moved on to Capitol, Mercury, etc., her biggest single to date being **Hello Out There** (1974).

LITTLE GINNY – An energetic British singer, born Ginnette Brown in Kingston-upon-Thames, England, she started out at 13 singing in country music clubs and in the Ivy Benson All-Girl Band. She had her own BBC-TV shows, then married Liverpool bass player Paul Kirkby and developed into a fine contemporary entertainer with her Room Service band. In 1986 she teamed up with Tammy Cline to form Two Hearts, a superb country duo with fast-moving stage show. She returned to a solo career in 1992.

HUBERT LONG – Born in 1923 and died in 1972, Long was elected to the Country Music Hall of Fame in 1979. Long began his career in a Texas dime store record department and later founded Nashville's first talent agency. He was the first person to serve as both president and chairman of the CMA.

LOUISIANA HAYRIDE – An influential show that originated on station KWKH, Shreveport, Louisiana, in 1948. The first programme featured Johnny And Jack, Kitty Wells, Bailes Brothers, etc. One of the first cast members to attain stardom was Hank Williams.

RAY LYNAM – Arguably Ireland's finest male country singer, he broke onto the scene in 1970 with a hard-country style developed from listening to Buck Owens and George Jones. Has recorded many duets with Philomena Begley. In 1980 he cut the **Music Man** album, which some hailed as "a milestone in Irish country music".

JUDY LYNN – A one-time teenage rodeo rider, national yodelling champion and beauty queen, Judy Lynn was born in Boise, Idaho, in 1936, the daughter of Joe Voiten, an ex-bandleader. She joined the Opry touring show in 1956 and began touring with her own eight-piece band four years later. Dressed in flamboyant western attire, she was a popular performer on the Nevada casino circuit for more than 20 years. Recorded for many labels from 1957–80, when she retired to become a church minister. She had only one major hit, with **Footsteps Of A Fool** in 1962.

M

DALE McBRIDE – A regional country star in Texas who never quite made the breakthrough to national stardom. Born in Bell County, Texas and raised in nearby Lampasas, McBride played guitar at 13 and was an original member of the Downbeats. For some time he worked in Jimmy Heap's Melody Masters. He recorded for Con Brio throughout the '70s, registering a dozen low-chart entries. His son, Terry McBride, is in McBride And The Ride.

MARY McCASLIN – A singer who grew up in California and became part of Linda Ronstadt's Stone Poneys before going solo and cutting a classic album for Barnaby. Her later albums of western-styled songs for Philo are exceptional.

DELBERT McCLINTON – Singer, songwriter, guitarist and harmonica player from Lubbock, Texas (born 1940), whose bluesy style has proved influential in country music. He played harp on Bruce Channel's 1962 pop hit **Hey! Baby**, and had songs covered by Waylon Jennings, Emmylou Harris, Vince Gill, etc. He duetted with Tanya Tucker on the 1993 country hit, **Tell Me About It**.

SKEETS McDONALD – A popular singer on the West Coast, McDonald is best known for his 1952 hit **Don't Let The Stars Get In Your Eyes**. Born in Greenaway, Arkansas in 1915, he began his career on local radio stations in Michigan before migrating to the West Coast after his World War II service. A longtime fixture on the Town Hall Party, he recorded for Capitol (1952–59) and Columbia (1959–67). He died of a heart attack in 1968.

PAKE McENTIRE – Dale Stanley McEntire, elder brother of Reba, was born in Chockie, Oklahoma in 1953. He sang at rodeos with Reba and another sister, Susie, as the Singing McEntires. Member of the Professional Cowboy Association since 1971, Pake continues to compete in roping events. Signed to RCA Records in 1985, he made Top 10 with **Savin' My Love For You** the following year.

WES McGHEE – Underrated in Britain where homegrown original country talent is ignored, this UK singer-songwriter, born in 1948, has made his mark in Texas, working with Ponty Bone, Butch Hancock and Kimmie Rhodes. He has recorded several invigorating albums on his own self-financed labels since the late '70s.

TIM McGRAW – Of Irish and Italian stock, the son of legendary baseball pitcher Tug McGraw, Tim was born in Delhi, Louisiana in 1969, but raised in Start, Louisiana. He moved to Nashville in 1989, played clubs and worked as a demo singer. He signed to Curb Records in 1990, and made his country chart debut with **Welcome To The Club** in 1992 and landed the opening spot in 1993's Honky Tonk Attitude Tour with Joe Diffie.

DON McLEAN – This talented singer-songwriter was born in New Rochelle, New York in 1945. He found overnight success in 1971 with **American Pie**, a pop classic that disguised his affection for country music. His 1973 album, **Playin' Favorites**, found him exploring his folk-country roots and since 1980 he has recorded in Nashville, making country Top 10 with **Cryin'** in 1981. A male version of Patsy Cline's **He's Got You** was a minor chart entry six years later.

TERRY McMILLAN – The man who has replaced Charlie McCoy as the most sought-after harmonica player. A NARAS Super Picker in 1975, his name appears on scores of records.

THE MAINES BROTHERS BAND – This country-rock family group from Texas have played a major role in the Lubbock music scene. The band began in the '50s with current members' father and uncle, James and Sonny Maines. The four brothers – Lloyd, Kenny, Steve and Donnie, got together in the late '70s with Richard Bowden, Gary Banks and Jerry Brownlow to record several albums for Texas Soul records. They linked up with Mercury in 1983, scoring their biggest hit with **Everybody Needs Love On Saturday Night** in 1985.

TIM MALCHAK – Originally a folksinger from Binghamton, New York, he worked in New York City and California before moving into country music in the early '80s. He teamed up with Dwight Rucker in 1980, and, as Malchak And Rucker, were the only country white/black duo to make the country charts. He went solo in 1986 and registered several Top 40 country entries, including **Colorado Moon**.

JAY DEE MANESS – Steel guitar supersessionman, born in Loma Linda, California in 1945, Maness has worked on hundreds of sides and with Buck Owens and Ray Stevens.

LINDA MARTELL – The first black female singer to appear on the Grand Ole Opry, she was initially a R&B singer born in Leesville, South Carolina, who included country material in her act. Shelby Singleton signed her to his Plantation Records and she registered three country hits, the biggest being **Color Him Father** in 1969.

WAYNE MASSEY – A singer-actor from Glendale, California, he played Johnny Drummond in TV's One Life To Live soap opera in the early '80s, which led to a recording contract with Polydor. He registered minor hits, but after he married Charly McClain and cut some duets, he made it into the Top 10 on Epic with **Just One Look In Your Eyes**.

MATHEWS, WRIGHT AND KING – A trio comprising Raymond Mathews, Woody Wright and Tony King. With their blend of three-part southern harmony with a bluegrass ring and a gospel spirit, they made an impact in 1992, gaining a Columbia record contract and several minor hits. Woody Wright was a former member of the Tennesseans, a Capitol act in 1979 and lead singer of Memphis, who charted in 1984.

THE MAVERICKS – A four-man, country-rock outfit from Miami, comprising lead singer Raul Malo, bassist Robert Reynolds, drummer Paul Deakin and guitarist David Lee Holt. Showcases in Nashville led to an MCA recording contract in 1992. Hard driving, hard country and hard nosed, their songs and their music exhibit great passion. Malo is a distinctive singer who is in great demand on Nashville sessions.

DONNA MEADE – Born in Chase City, Virginia in 1953, after building a regional following, Donna moved to Nashville and became a club singer at Buddy Killen's Bullpen Lounge. Signed to Mercury in 1987, she has registered several minor hits, but has yet to find that one song to take her into the big time.

TIM MENSY – A native of Virginia, this talented singer, songwriter and guitarist moved to Nashville in 1980 when he was 20 and joined Bandana. He spent several years on the fringes of mainstream country flirting with big time success. He wrote hit songs for Shenandoah, T. G. Sheppard, etc, played sessions and worked as a demo singer. Signed to Columbia Records in 1988, he had some minor success, but has made a bigger impact since joining Giant in 1992.

Dream Seekers, Matthews Wright And King. Courtesy Sony Music.

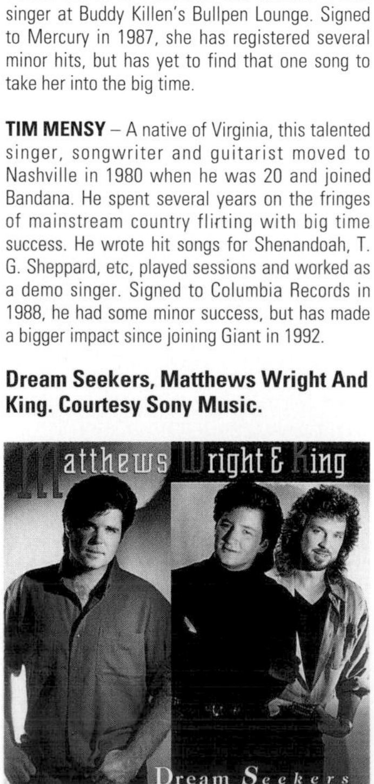

NED MILLER – A reluctant star, who refused to perform on stage, even when he had major hits, Miller made his mark initially as a songwriter. Born in Raines, Utah in 1925, he moved to California in the mid-1950s where he joined Fabor Records and wrote **Dark Moon** and **A Fallen Star**, two major country-pop hits. His original recording of **From A Jack To A King** in 1957 flopped, but when reissued in 1962 it became a massive pop-country seller in Britain and America. Further success followed with **Invisible Tears** and **Do What You Do Do Well**, but by the early '70s he had completely withdrawn from singing and songwriting.

BILLY MIZE – An ACM vice-president who was once host on Gene Autry's Melody Ranch show, Mize (born in Kansas City, Kansas in 1929) has always had TV connections, eventually heading his own production company. But he still tours with his Tennesseans and from 1966 through to 1974 charted consistently.

MOLLY AND THE HEYMAKERS – A quartet from Hayward, Wisconsin, comprising Molly Scheer, Andy Dee, Jeff Nelson and Joe Lindzius, they spent three years touring through Wisconsin, Minnesota and the usually rock-dominated Minneapolis, before gaining a Reprise record deal in 1989. With a blend of bluegrass, '60s California pop, rockabilly, honky-tonk, Cajun and western swing, they produce a lot of energy.

TINY MOORE – Another instrumental near-genius, born in Hamilton County, Texas in 1920, who plays both mandolin and fiddle, switching with ease from pure jazz to downhomey country. Once a Bob Wills Playboy, he later worked with Billy Jack Wills but these days plays many dates with Merle Haggard's Strangers.

THE MORRIS BROTHERS – Wiley and Zeke Morris comprised one of the fine duet acts which flooded country music in the mid-1930s. They became well-known for their smooth harmony singing and songs like **Salty Dog** and **Tragic Romance**. Their career lasted well into the '40s, although they retired to their native North Carolina and remained relatively inactive in later years. Wiley had a longer career playing mandolin and guitar for a number of bands, including Wade and J. E. Mainer, and with Charlie Monroe and his Kentucky Pardners.

TEX MORTON – One of Australia's greatest country artists, Morton was actually born in Nelson, New Zealand, in 1916. A fine singer and yodeller, he moved to Australia in 1932, making his first records for Regal Zonophone four years later and gaining instant popularity. In 1948 he settled in Canada, there becoming 'The Great Morton – The World's Greatest Hypnotist', also continuing with his singing career. In 1959 he returned to Australia, maintaining his reputation as a top-line entertainer until his death in Sydney in 1983.

JOHNNY AND JONIE MOSBY – Popular husband and wife duet team in the 1960s, Johnny from Arkansas and Jonie (born Janice Shields, 1940) from California had their own 'Country Music Time' on Los Angeles television and enjoyed several Top 20 hits for both Columbia and Capitol before fading from the scene to raise their family.

MOON MULLICAN – The originator of a highly personal two-finger piano style, Aubrey 'Moon' Mullican, born near Corrigan, Polk County, Texas, in 1909, influenced many later keyboard players, including Mickey Gilley and Jerry Lee Lewis. He gained his nickname 'Moon' because he slept by day and worked the clubs in Houston by night, then later appearing on radio and at clubs in the Louisiana-Texas area. By the mid-1940s Mullican had become a major solo attraction, his 1947 recording of **New Jole Blon** selling three million copies. He had another million-seller with **I'll Sail My Ship Alone** (1950) and joined the Grand Ole Opry. Later he toured as part of Governor Jimmie Davis' staff and band. Dogged by ill-health, the king of pumpin' piano died from a heart attack on January 1, 1967.

HEATHER MYLES – From Riverside, California, but raised in Texas, of Scottish-Canadian ancestry, this West Coast singer-songwriter

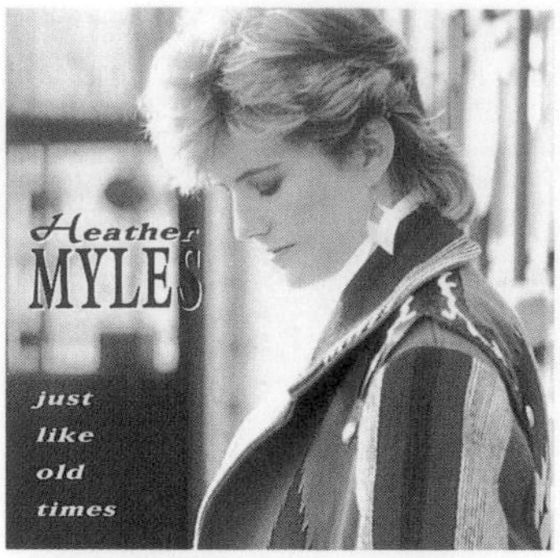

Just Like Old Times, Heather Myles. Courtesy HighTone Records.

started building a European following in 1992 after her debut album, **Just Like Old Times**, gained rave reviews. Re-interpreting the '60s Bakersfield Sound in her own distinctive way, Heather spent years playing the Texas honky-tonk circuit before relocating to California and forming the Cadillac Cowboys.

N

NASHVILLE – Known as Music City or the Country Capital, this Tennessee city started out as the Mecca of country music in 1925 when WSM began its Barn Dance. The first major artist to record in Nashville was Eddy Arnold in 1944, while Capitol was the first major label to commence a Nashville operation (1950). During the late '50s and '60s the famed 'Nashville Sound' took over and the producers, musicians and studios came up with a formula that not only saw such artists as Jim Reeves, Eddy Arnold, Chet Atkins and Floyd Cramer selling huge amounts of records to pop audiences, but also had scores of pop idols heading towards Tennessee in order to add a touch of saleable Nashville magic to their own wares. In 1974 came the opening of Opryland, a modern auditorium amid an extensive amusement park just a few miles outside the city.

NASHVILLE BLUEGRASS BAND – A five-man band that takes a bit of the twang out of bluegrass, they came to the fore in the late '80s, initially on Rounder, then later Sugar Hill Records. Mainstays of the group are Stuart Duncan, Pat Enright, Gene Libbea, Alan O'Bryant and Roland White, who produce modern bluegrass with hot picking.

BUCK AND TEX ANN NATION – To Buck (born Muskogee, Oklahoma, 1910) and Tex Ann (born Chanute, Kansas, 1916) goes the credit for starting the now popular country music parks, where Sunday afternoon crowds can picnic, relax and listen to country music. Active in the Northeast, Buck and Tex Ann opened their first park in 1934 and found their greatest success in Maine, of all the unlikely places.

NATIONAL BARN DANCE – One of the earliest and most influential of all radio barn dances for some years. Begun in 1924, it was later overshadowed by the Grand Ole Opry but survived until 1970. Early stars include Bradley Kincaid, Grace Wilson and Arkie The Woodchopper, these being followed by John Lair and the Cumberland Ridge Runners, Mac And Bob, Lulu Belle And Scotty and Red Foley.

TRACY NELSON – A bluesy country vocalist, born in Madison, Wisconsin in 1944, Tracy started out as a local folksinger, then joined R&B outfit the Fabulous Initiations. As founder member of Mother Earth in San Francisco in 1967, she became heavily country-oriented, and the band often recorded in Nashville. In 1973 she embarked on a solo career and duetted with Willie Nelson on the Grammy-nominated **After The Fire Is Gone**. Tracy has continued to record for MCA, Atlantic, Flying Fish and Adelphi.

OLIVIA NEWTON-JOHN – Lightweight English pop singer from Cambridge (born 1948), who grew up in Australia, but moved back to England in the late '60s. She enjoyed British and American pop success with country-flavoured songs in the early '70s, many crossing into the country charts. She won the CMA Female Vocalist Of The Year award in 1974, amid uproar from established country stars, but she soon turned her back on country and embarked upon a more lucrative film and pop-dance career.

EDDIE NOACK – A Texan honky-tonk singer and songwriter, Noack, who was born in Houston in 1930, never received due recognition during his lifetime. He recorded prolifically from 1949 up until shortly before his death in 1978, but gained more success as a writer, penning hits for Hank Snow, George Jones, Ernest Tubb, etc. He became an executive for the Nashville Songwriters' Association and has had several compilations of his early recordings released since his death.

NORMA JEAN – A highly regarded performer during the '60s, Norma Jean Beasler was born in Willston, Oklahoma in 1938 and raised in Oklahoma City, where she learned guitar and performed at square dances. By 1958 she had become a regular on Red Foley's Ozark Jubilee TV show – two years later she joined the Opry and also became a regular on Porter Wagoner's TV show. Soon her pure country voice was heard regularly in the charts, her biggest hit being **Let's Go All The Way** (1964). Replaced on the Wagoner show by Dolly Parton in 1967, Norma Jean's record sales dropped accordingly.

O

TIM O'BRIEN – A multi-talented bluegrass musician, singer and songwriter, from Wheeling, West Virginia, O'Brien started out in his early teens and throughout the '80s was lead vocalist with Hot Rize, with whom he also played mandolin, guitar and fiddle. Based in Colorado, the band recorded for Flying Fish and Sugar Hill before disbanding in 1990. Since then O'Brien has embarked on a solo career, with his own group, the O'Boys. He has also recorded duets with his older sister Mollie O'Brien and Kathy Mattea, who has turned some of his songs into country hits.

W. LEE O'DANIEL – Wilbert Lee O'Daniel, born in Malta, Ohio in 1890, became the first of many politicians to use the grass roots appeal of country music to propel him to high political office. An executive in the Burrus Mills Company, maker of Light Crust Flour, in 1930 he formed a band around a group of struggling musicians, the Light Crust Doughboys, to advertise the product over radio. Later he set up his own company and brand, Hillbilly Flour, and a new band, the Hillbilly Boys. In 1938 he waged a grass roots campaign for Governor of Texas, winning easily, and went on to serve a term in the US Senate.

JAMES O'GWYNN – Known as the 'Smiling Irishman Of Country Music', O'Gwynn was born in Winchester, Mississippi in 1928 and enjoyed considerable chart success in the late '50s and early '60s, making the Top 10 with **My Name Is Mud** in 1962 and appearing regularly on the Houston Jamboree, Louisiana Hayride and Grand Ole Opry.

Palomino Road's eponymous album. Courtesy Liberty Records.

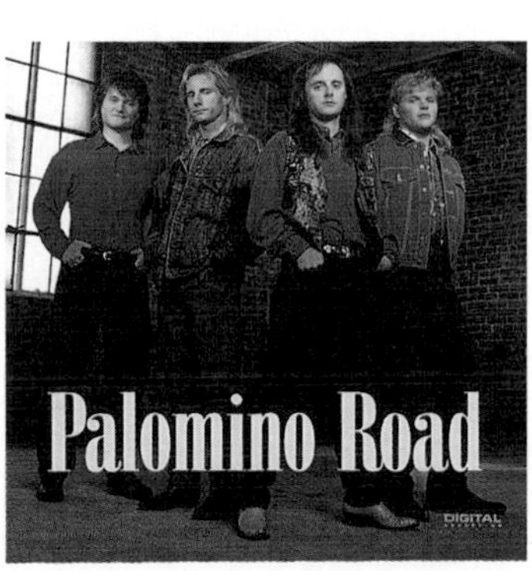

ORION – Masked mystery man who is the ultimate Elvis Presley clone, his real name is Jimmy Ellis from Orrville, Alabama. He was, naturally, recorded by Sun (revived by Shelby Singleton) from 1977 through to 1982, his albums being pressed as 'Collector's Edition Special Gold Vinyl'.

ROBERT ELLIS ORRALL – Singer, songwriter, pianist from Lynnfield, Massachusetts, Orrall first made an impact penning hits for Shenandoah, Carlene Carter, etc. Signed to RCA in 1992, he is building into one of the new major country acts of the future.

MARIE OSMOND – A member of the famous Osmond family, born Olive Marie Osmond in Ogden, Utah in 1959, she began appearing with her brothers at 14, and scored a major pop-country hit with **Paper Roses** at the same time. She co-starred with brother Donny in their own musical-variety TV series from 1976–80, and made a return to country in 1985 with Top 10 hits for Capitol. A tireless charity worker, Marie was bestowed with the prestigious Roy Acuff Community Service award.

JIM OWEN – Franklin, Tennessee singer-songwriter who is not only a Hank Williams soundalike but also an incredible lookalike. During the '80s, he logged a few hits for Sun.

TEX OWENS – Born in the Lone Star State in 1892, Owens was a popular star and co-host of several radio shows, but is best known and remembered for writing and singing his 1935 hit **Cattle Call**, on Decca. Owens died at his home in Baden, Texas in 1962. From a musical family, his daughter, Laura Lee, had a long career as Bob Wills' first girl singer, and in addition his sister was Texas Ruby, longtime Opry star.

P

TOM PACHECO – The 'Storyteller of the '90s', Tom Pacheco was born in Dartmouth, Massachusetts. His father, Tony, was a music store owner and guitar tutor, who had previously played in Europe with Django Reinhardt. Tom played folk music in Greenwich Village in the '60s and a few years later recorded for RCA and Columbia in a very modern country style, eventually moving on to play rock music. He travelled around playing music in Woodstock, Austin, Nashville and California, then settled in Ireland in 1987. Since then he has built a cult following as a singer-songwriter touring Europe and also working in and around Austin, Texas.

PATTI PAGE – Hardly a true country vocalist, Patti (born Clara Ann Fowler in Claremore, Oklahoma, 1927), had one of the biggest all-time country hits with **Tennessee Waltz**, in 1951. Really a pop singer, she switched to country at the start of the '70s and has since had a fair degree of success in the country charts, particularly during her stay with Shelby Singleton's Plantation label in the early '80s.

STU PAGE – A gritty British country singer born in Leeds, Yorkshire in 1954. He played with American bluegrass outfit the Warren Wilkeson Band in the mid-1970s, then formed Stu Page And Remuda in 1984, becoming one of Britain's most acclaimed modern country performers, mixing in fine original material with inspired covers of American country hits.

KEITH PALMER – A Missouri-born singer-songwriter, the adopted son of a fundamentalist, church-going farming couple, Palmer was raised in Corning, Arkansas. He moved to Nashville in 1989 and worked as a songwriter and demo singer. He penned **For My Broken Heart**, a No.1 for Reba McEntire, and he signed to Epic Records in 1991.

PALOMINO ROAD – High-energy country band of the '90s. Lead singer Ronnie Guilbeau, bassist David Frazier, guitarist J.T. Corenflo and drummer Chip Lewis had all been honing their skills in other bands, writing and playing sessions when they got together in early 1992. Following a showcase, they were signed by Jimmy Bowen to Liberty Records. Vocal blend harmonies, dynamic instrumental energy and rare songwriting skills make Palomino Road a band with a great future.

ANDY PARKER AND THE PLAINSMEN – Born near Mangum, Oklahoma in 1913, Andy Parker began his radio career at 16 in Elk City, Oklahoma. He assumed the role of singing cowboy on NBC's Death Valley Days from 1937–41. By 1946 he was based in L.A. and had formed a western harmony group, Andy Parker And The Plainsmen. They appeared in some eight films with Eddie Dean and signed with Capitol Records in 1947. The band had no particular big-selling records and Parker was forced to retire, suffering from a heart condition.

JIMMY PAYNE – A fine songwriter born in Arkansas in 1939, he played guitar with the Glaser Brothers' band and made his mark in Nashville as a writer of such hits as **Woman, Woman** (Gary Puckett & Union Gap, and the Glasers), **What Does It Take** (Skeeter Davis) and **My Eyes Can Only See As Far As You** (Charley Pride). He has recorded regularly since 1962, but has only achieved a few minor chart entries with **L.A. Angels** (1969), **Ramblin' Man** (1973) and **Turning My Love On** (1981).

PEARL RIVER – This Mississippi-based sextet have a bluesy, energy-laden vocal sound developed during a ten-year stint working small clubs and playing a mix of rock, R&B and country. Originally called the Toys, they took their new name from the river that runs through Mississippi. After being selected to appear at the Nashville Entertainments 'Music City Music Event' in 1992 they were signed to Liberty Records.

HERB PEDERSEN – Born in Berkeley, California in 1944, Pedersen is a singer-banjoist who has played with Flatt And Scruggs, the Dillards, Linda Ronstadt, Emmylou Harris, etc. He recorded solo albums for Epic and Sugar Hill, then joined the Desert Rose Band in 1986.

RALPH PEER – The most notable talent scout of the 1920s (born in Kansas City, Missouri in 1892; died in Hollywood, California in 1960). Peer discovered Jimmie Rodgers and the Carter Family, his 1923 sessions with Fiddlin' John Carson proving a landmark in country music history. In 1928 he formed Southern Music, a publishing company heavily involved in the publication of country songs.

PEGGY SUE – Younger sister of Loretta Lynn, born Peggy Sue Webb in Butcher's Hollow, Kentucky. For many years she toured with Loretta and co-wrote **Don't Come Home A'Drinkin'**. Signed to Decca Records in 1969, she had several minor hits. She later joined Door Knob Records and cut duets with her husband Sonny Wright, a one-time vocalist with Loretta's show.

RAY PENNINGTON – A talented singer, songwriter, record producer and executive, Pennington was born in Clay County, Kentucky in 1933. He made his TV debut in Cincinnati at the age of 16 and formed his own band in 1952, working local TV shows in such states as Kentucky, Indiana and Ohio. He moved to Nashville in 1964 and has recorded for Capitol, Monument and MRC, and has also been active as an executive at Step One Records.

BILL PHILLIPS – Longtime member of the Kitty Wells–Johnny Wright Roadshow, William Clarence Phillips was born in Canton, North Carolina in 1936. He moved to Nashville in 1957, making his mark as a songwriter, then signing with Columbia Records the following year. He appeared on the Grand Ole Opry, then moved over to Decca Records and began accruing chart entries, the most successful being **Put It Off Until Tomorrow** (1966) and **Little Boy Sad** (1969).

STU PHILLIPS – Longtime member of the Grand Ole Opry, Phillips was born in Montreal, Canada in 1933, but has lived in Nashville since 1964. He enjoyed several major hits on RCA during the late '60s, the most successful being **Juanita Jones** in 1967, the year he joined the Opry. He has remained a member ever since, though he has not recorded since 1970.

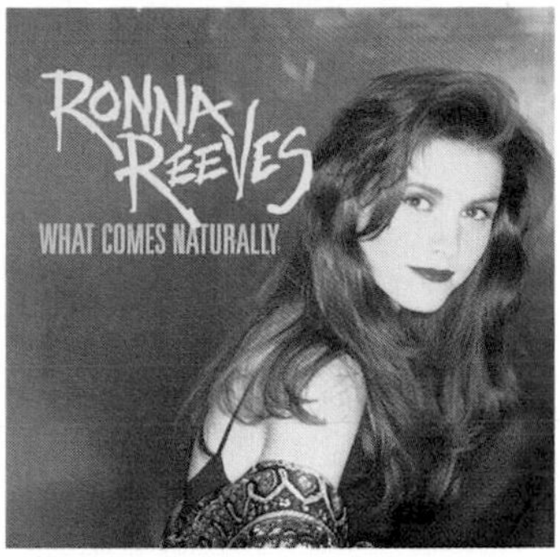

What Comes Naturally, Ronna Reeves. Courtesy PolyGram Records.

PIRATES OF MISSISSIPPI – This five-man outfit take the basic ingredients of country music and brand it with their own electric style. Named ACM's Top New Vocal Group in 1991, they played local gigs just for fun and unexpectedly landed a Capitol-Liberty recording contract, making it into the Top 20 with **Feed Jake**.

MARY K. PLACE – Born in Tulsa, Oklahoma, this actress portrayed a country singer called Loretta Haggers in the US TV series Mary Hartman, Mary Hartman (1976). Accepted as the real thing, she cut an album with Emmylou Harris and the Hot Band, and had a Top 5 hit with **Baby Boy** (1976).

POACHER – A British band who won the New Faces TV talent show in 1978. From Warrington, Lancashire, they became sponsored by the local vodka company and threatened an unbelievable breakthrough when, also in 1978, their version of **Darling**, on Republic, entered the US charts.

SANDY POSEY – Born in Jasper, Alabama in 1947, Sandy worked as a session singer in Nashville and Memphis before making an impact on the pop charts with **Single Girl** and **Born A Woman** in 1966. Country success came during the '70s when recording for Columbia, Monument and Warners. Nowadays Sandy works as a back-up vocalist on the Nashville Network.

PRAIRIE OYSTER – This Canadian sextet play a cross between swamp rock, rockabilly and honky-tonk in a style described as 'Rock meets the twang of steel'. Having established themselves in Canada, where they were first formed in the mid-1970s, they regrouped in 1983 and made a breakthrough in America when they signed with RCA Records in Nashville in 1990 and started scoring country hits.

MALCOLM PRICE – A perennial on the UK country circuit, where he is warmly regarded. His albums for Decca, made in the early '60s with the Malcolm Price Trio, are ranked highly.

R

RED RECTOR – One of country music's top mandolin players, he was born in Marshall, North Carolina in 1929 and worked in the bands of Johnny And Jack, Bill Clifton, Charlie Monroe and Flatt And Scruggs. Throughout the '50s and '60s he played recording sessions, and by the '70s he took centre stage at festivals and was a recording star in his own right.

RONNA REEVES – A diminutive singer with sensually gravelly vocals from Big Springs, Texas, this lady put her first band together at 11. In the mid-1980s she opened shows for George Strait, then in 1991 landed a recording contract with Mercury. This led to touring with Billy Ray Cyrus as she has started to make an impact with her recordings.

KIMMIE RHODES – A multi-faceted Texas singer-songwriter, Kimmie started out in a gospel trio when she was six and by her late teens was playing the Austin clubs with the Jackalope Bros (Bobby Earl Smith and Joe Gracey). She toured with Al Dressen's Swing Revue in 1983–84, but now mainly works solo. Kimmie is something of an actress, painter, poet, dancer and writer and has appeared in films, videos and has sung and played on sessions in Austin. Her reflective **I Just Drove By** was picked up by Wynonna in 1993.

BOBBY G. RICE – A former rock'n'roller who turned to country, born in Boscobel, Wisconsin in 1944, Rice was part of a family band that had their own radio show on WRCO Richmond from 1957–64. He went solo and formed the Bobby Rice Band, scoring with country versions of pop oldies on Royal American in the early '70s. With his commercial, pop-slanted style, he had his biggest success with **You Lay So Easy On My Mind** (1972) on Metromedia, and has since placed hits for GRT, Republic, Sunbird and Charta.

TONY RICE – Acoustic guitarist and vocalist born in Danville, Virginia in 1951 into a musical family, he joined brothers Larry and Ronnie when he was nine as the Rice Brothers. Later came stints with J.D. Crowe's New South, Ricky Skaggs and Emmylou Harris. He has recorded regularly, both as a solo and with his own Tony Rice Unit for Rounder, Sugar Hill and Kaleidoscope.

PAUL RICHEY – Born in Promised Lane, Arkansas, Richey is a singer-songwriter, music publisher and Tammy Wynette's brother-in-law. As Wyley McPherson he broke into the charts with **Jedediah Jones** and **The Devil Inside** in 1982.

RIDERS IN THE SKY – A current-day cowboy trio who offer loving (if frequently tongue-in-cheek) renditions of Sons Of The Pioneers' songs plus material of a similar bent. Nashville-based, the group comprises Ranger Doug (guitar, vocals), Woody Paul Chrisman (fiddle, vocals) and Fred 'Too Slim' LaBour (bass, vocals). Ranger Doug in reality being Doug E. Green, the noted country music historian. Regulars on the Grand Ole Opry, Riders In The Sky also host 'Tumbleweed Theatre' a western movie programme on TNN, and have recorded for both Rounder and MCA.

BILLY LEE RILEY – Rockabilly singer and multi-instrumentalist from Pochantas, Arkansas, he recorded for Sun Records in mid-1950s, but never had any big hits. He was a powerful rock'n'roll singer and his influence has been immeasurable.

DENNIS ROBBINS – A gifted singer, songwriter and slide guitarist from Hazelwood, North Carolina, this one-time member of the Michigan pop group the Rockets made his initial impact in country in 1987 when he cut the original **Two Of A Kind (Workin' On A Full House)** on MCA Records. Two years later he was lead singer of Billy Hill, a band of Nashville sessionmen-songwriters. Robbins picked up his solo career again in 1991, signed to Giant Records, and has started to make a bigger impression.

HARGUS 'PIG' ROBBINS – CMA Instrumentalist Of The Year in 1976. A blind pianist from Spring City, Tennessee, he gained attention while playing Nashville clubs and became a top sessionman.

KENNY ROBERTS – A super yodeller known best in the North and Northeast, although he was actually born in Lenoir City, Tennessee in 1927. He has recorded for Decca, Coral, Dot, King and Starday, his biggest hits being the yodelling extravaganzas, **Chimebells** and **She Taught Me How To Yodel**.

ROCKABILLY – The first link between country and rock. Carl Perkins has demonstrated the link between the rhythms of certain Hank Williams' songs and early rock as part of his act, while chunks of pure rockabilly occur on the Ernie Ford boogies of the late '40s and early '50s.

FRED ROSE – Founder of the Acuff-Rose Music Publishing Co., Rose (born Evansville, Indiana in 1897, died in Nashville in 1954) was a one-time honky-tonk pianist who set up the publishing company in 1942. A fine songwriter – his credits include **Be Honest With Me**, **Blue Eyes Crying In The Rain**, **Take These Chains From My Heart**, **Tears On My Pillow**, **Settin' The Woods On Fire** and others – he often wrote in partnership with such people as Hank Williams, Ray Whitley and Hy Heath. In 1961 he posthumously became one of the first members of the Country Music Hall Of Fame, sharing the honour with Jimmie Rodgers and Hank Williams.

WESLEY ROSE – The son of Fred Rose, born in Chicago, Illinois in 1918, he has been responsible for expanding the whole horizon of Acuff-Rose's business and making it one of the most successful publishing companies in the world. Initially he moved into the world of record production, at the outset fashioning material for major labels but later forming his own Hickory Records. A music industry leader, Wesley Rose was one of the founder members of the CMA.

PETER ROWAN – Singer-songwriter and brilliant mandolinist, once a member of the Rowan Brothers but, in more recent times, the leader of his own band, switching from folk-rock through to bluegrass, pure country and Cajun. He often works with accordionist Flaco Jimenez.

LEON RUSSELL – Vocalist, songwriter, multi-instrumentalist, sessionman, producer and label chief, Russell was born in Lawton, Oklahoma in 1941. During the early '60s he played numerous sessions in California from Phil Spector through Bobby Vee, the Crickets to Frank Sinatra. He formed Shelter Records with British producer Denny Cordell in 1970, and recorded as Hank Wilson in a pseudo country-rock style. In 1976 he started his own Paradise Records, recorded duet hits with Willie Nelson, and also teamed up with New Grass Revival for shows and recordings.

TIM RYAN – Singer-guitarist from Montana, whose first taste of the big-time came at age 12 when he played lead guitar for Tex Williams. A move to Nashville in 1988 found him teaming up with veteran songwriter Alex Harvey. With his matinee idol looks, solid songwriting skills and an identifiable voice that can bend notes and slip into falsetto, he has registered several minor hits for Epic Records.

JOHN WESLEY RYLES – An in-demand Nashville-based singer, Ryles was born in Bastrop, Louisiana in 1950. He sang in the family gospel group the Ryles Singers, appearing on local radio while still a child. A regular on the Cowtown Hoedown Show in Fort Worth and the Big D Jamboree in Dallas, he then moved to Nashville in 1966. He has recorded prolifically since 1967 for Columbia (as John Wesley Ryles I), Plantation, ABC-Dot, MCA and Warners, scoring several Top 20 hits. He is also kept busy as a back-up singer on Nashville sessions.

S

JUNIOR SAMPLES – From Cumming, Georgia, Alvin Junior Samples (born in 1927) weighed nearly 300 lbs and was proud of being dubbed 'the world's biggest liar'. A country comedian who relied on storytelling, his single, **The World's Biggest Whopper**, became a mild hit in 1967 and opened the doors for a highly successful career. He was a regular on the Hee Haw Show until shortly before he died of a heart attack in 1983.

ART SATHERLEY – During the 1930s, Satherly (born in Bristol, England in 1889; died in 1986) helped provide ARC with one of the strongest country music catalogues in America, his signings including Gene Autry (1931). In 1938, when ARC became Columbia, Satherley was retained by the company and continued in an A&R role until his retirement in 1952, having added such acts as Lefty Frizzell, Marty Robbins, Little Jimmy Dickens, Bill Monroe and Carl Smith to the Columbia roster. Known as 'Uncle Art' he was elected to the Country Music Hall Of Fame in 1971 for his work as a record pioneer.

PETE SAYERS – Versatile British performer (born in Bath, Somerset, 1942) whose finest hour came in 1980 when he compered the Wembley Festival, gaining plaudits from even the most acid critics. A multi-instrumentalist of considerable ability and creator of such characters as the Phantom Of The Opry and the Lovely LaWanda, Sayers has headed his own BBC series, Pete Sayers Entertains.

DON SCHLITZ – The most successful Nashville songwriter of the '80s, Schlitz was born in Durham, North Carolina in 1952. He started pitching his songs in Nashville in the early '70s without too much success. Eventually he recorded **The Gambler** on the small Crazy Mammas label in 1978. Many covers came out with Kenny Rogers scoring a million-selling country-pop smash. Schlitz landed a short-lived Capitol recording contract, but has emerged as a highly inventive, commercial country writer.

JACK SCOTT – Rock'n'roll/country singer born Jack Scafone Jr in Windsor, Canada in 1936, but raised in Detroit. He formed a band, the Southern Drifters in early '50s and made his first recording for ABC-Paramount in 1957. Later Scott enjoyed notable pop success with country-flavoured rock-ballads. Though his recordings for Groove in 1963–64 veered closer to country, he has always been considered strictly a rock'n'roller.

TROY SEALS – One of Nashville's most consistent songwriters, Seals was born in Big Hill, Kentucky in 1938. He formed a band that played both rock and country in the late '50s and met and married pop singer Jo Ann Campbell, forming a duo. Later they moved to Nashville where he worked as a session guitarist and songwriter. He recorded in the '70s for Atlantic and Columbia, and, though his recordings were critically acclaimed, they flopped commercially. Writing with various partners, he has penned more than 200 Top 10 country hits.

DAWN SEARS – A petite lady with enormous vocal strength, she was a drummer in a band as a teenager and played the clubs in and around Minnesota. A move to Nashville in 1987 saw her become a regular on Ralph Emery's Early Morning TV show. This exposure resulted in a Warners' contract in 1992, but that breakthrough record has yet to surface.

SELDOM SCENE – A 'newgrass' supergroup formed by the Country Gentlemen's John Duffey in 1971, they played in the Washington D.C. area. Named the Seldom Scene because of their infrequent concert appearances, the group merged both traditional and current chart material, proving popular with the younger set. The original members along with Duffey were Mike Audridge (dobro), Ben Eldridge (banjo), John Sterling (guitars and vocals), plus former Country Gentlemen bassist Tom Gray.

KENNY SERRATT – Classic honky-tonk singer who missed out on the big-time. Born in Manila, Arkansas, he played at the Ramada in Hemet, California for 11 years, then moved to Montana from 1967 to 1972, where he worked as a lumberjack and rancher. Merle Haggard enticed him back into music and wrote and produced some of his initial hits in the early 1970s. He has recorded for MGM, Melodyland, Hitsville and MDJ, clocking up minor hits between 1972–81.

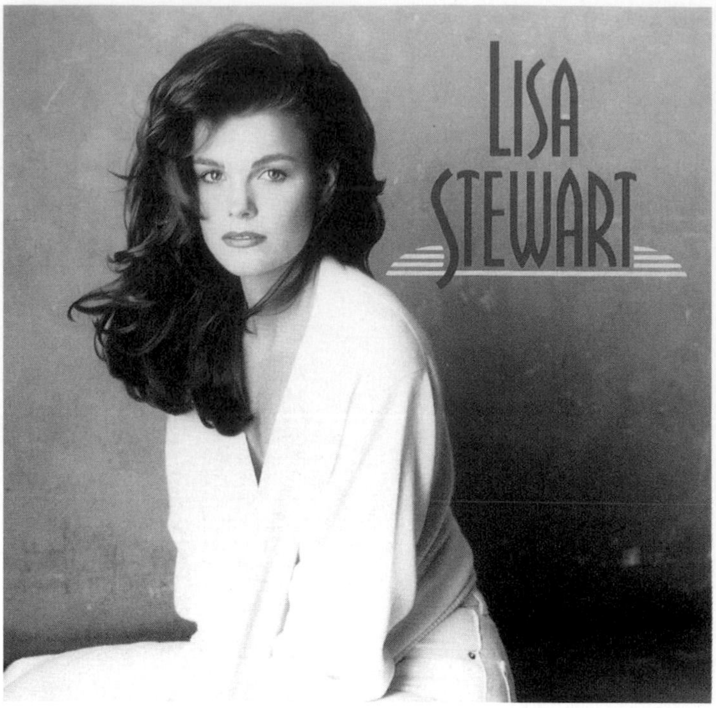

Lisa Stewart's first album. Courtesy BNA Records.

DOROTHY SHAY – Known as the Park Avenue Hillbilly, Dorothy's gimmick was to attire herself in exquisite gowns, then perform incongruous novelty hillbilly numbers. Very popular in the '40s, her biggest hit being **Feudin' And Fightin'** (1947). Born in 1923, she appeared in an Abbott and Costello movie 'Comin' Round The Mountain' in 1951 and in later life played a recurring role in the TV series The Waltons, but died in Santa Monica, California in 1978.

STEVE SHOLES – A&R manager for RCA's Country Music and R&B Division, Sholes (born in Washington DC in 1911; died in Nashville in 1968) was responsible for the label accumulating one of the most impressive country rosters in the world, signing Jim Reeves, Hank Snow, the Browns, Elvis Presley and Chet Atkins, the last eventually becoming Sholes' A&R assistant. He was elected to the Country Music Hall Of Fame in 1967.

RED SIMPSON – Singer-songwriter-impressionist, multi-instrumentalist and comedian who in the early '70s became associated with the Bakersfield crowd. Winner of Cashbox's New Male Vocalist award in 1972, he came up with an array of trucking songs and by 1979 could still be found charting with **The Flying Saucer Man And The Truck Driver**.

SHELBY SINGLETON – One of the shrewdest businessmen in Nashville, Singleton (born in Waskom, Texas in 1931) worked with Mercury Records and became vice-president, signing Jerry Lee Lewis and Charlie Rich along the way. In 1966 he resigned and formed his own production company, having his biggest success in 1968 when he produced Jeannie C. Riley's **Harper Valley PTA** for his own Plantation label. He has also set up other labels including SSS and Silver Fox, and in 1969 acquired Sun Records.

SIX SHOOTER – A teenage Nashville country band blessed with youthful good looks and barn-storming energy. Mainstays are Ronnie McDowell's son Ronnie Dean McDowell and his nephew Chris McDowell. They have toured with McDowell senior and appeared on the prime time sit-com Evening Shade. Their rock-rolled country is bringing in the younger generation as well as amazing the older country fans.

JIMMIE SKINNER – Born near Berea, Kentucky, his first taste of success came as a songwriter while working as a DJ in Knoxville, Tennessee. He signed as a performer with Mercury Records in the mid-1950s and had two Top 10 hits in 1957. Since then he recorded for Decca, Starday, King and Vetco and operated his successful Jimmie Skinner Music Center in Cincinnati for many years before moving to Nashville in the mid-1970s. He died in Hendersonville in 1979.

RUSSELL SMITH – Howard Russell Smith, from Lafayette, Tennessee, worked on local radio as a teenager. He formed the Amazing Rhythm Aces in the early '70s and was lead singer and main songwriter. He embarked on a solo career in Nashville in 1982, but though he has a distinctive soulful voice and recorded for Capitol and Epic, he has not made the impact expected. He has written dozens of country hits and helped form the quirky Run C&W group in 1992.

SISSY SPACEK – Award-winning movie actress (born in Quitman, Texas in 1950), who in her early days recorded for Roulette as Rainbo. Cast as Loretta Lynn in the film 'Coal Miner's Daughter' (1980), she did all the singing for the soundtrack and promptly got signed by Atlantic, cutting an above-average album **Hangin' Up My Heart**.

BUDDY SPICHER – Session fiddle-player whose career took off as a member of Area Code 615 in 1969. An in-demand picker ever since – he has even worked with Henry Mancini and the Pointer Sisters – he has recorded albums under his own name for Flying Fish and CMH Records.

BOBBY LEE SPRINGFIELD – Singer-songwriter born in Amarillo, Texas in 1953, who moved to Nashville as a teenager. He made his mark as a songwriter, penning hits for Marty Robbins, the Oak Ridge Boys, etc. As Bobby Springfield he signed to Kat Family Records, then adopted his full name when he joined Epic Records in 1986.

TERRY STAFFORD – A pop singer who returned to his country roots, Stafford was born in Hollis, Oklahoma and was raised in Amarillo, Texas. He worked in the Eugene Nelson Band in Texas as a teenager and moved to California in 1960 where he played with pop bands. Signed to Crusader Records, he had a massive pop hit with **Suspicion** in 1964. He began writing songs, with Buck Owens scoring with **Big In Vegas**. His own **Amarillo By Morning** was well-recorded in the '70s, before becoming a hit for George Strait in 1984. He recorded for Atlantic and Casino throughout the '70s.

KENNY STARR – A Loretta Lynn protégé, Starr was born in Topeka, Kansas in 1953. By the age of nine he was leading his own band, the Rockin' Rebels. Later he became a country entertainer with the Country Showmen, and was offered a job in Loretta Lynn's roadshow. A singer-songwriter-guitarist, he had a No.1 country hit with his own **The Blind Man In Bleachers** in 1976, following with some minor hits before mysteriously fading from the limelight.

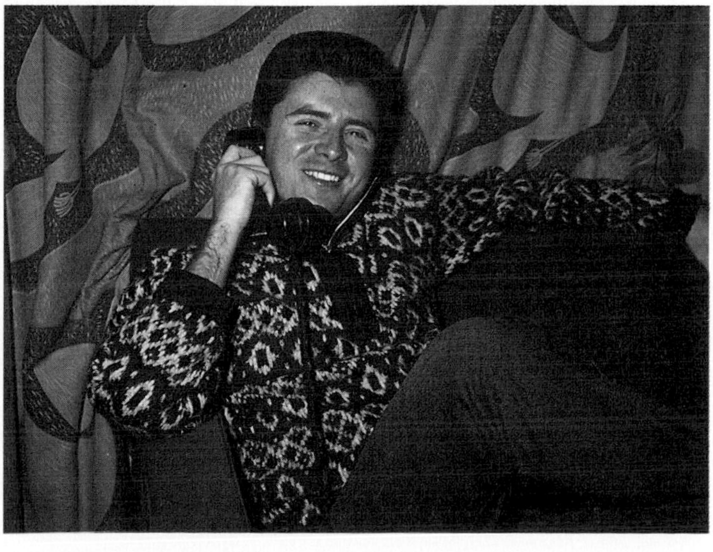

Below: Johnny Tillotson penned several classic country ballads.

STU STEVENS – British singer who, from time to time, looked likely to cross over and gain recognition from the pop fraternity, predominantly in 1979 when his version of Shel Silverstein and Even Steven's **Man From Outer Space** was picked up by MCA.

LISA STEWART – A Louisville, Mississippi native, this young lady, who was signed to BNA Records in 1991, has a wonderfully expressive vocal style with an alluring smoky quality that could see her emerge as one of the top female stars of the future.

CLIFFIE STONE – Born Clifford Gilpin Snyder in Burbank, California in 1917, Cliffie Stone has mainly been involved in the executive end of the music business. His father was a well-known banjo player-comedian known as Herman The Hermit, though Cliffie began his musical career as a bassist for big bands. He served as a DJ, MC and performer on several Los Angeles-area radio stations, and was bandleader and featured comedian on the Hollywood Barn Dance. In 1946 he linked up with the newly formed Capitol Records and stayed for over two decades, recording a half dozen albums and guiding the careers of Tennessee Ernie Ford and others. Owner of his own Central Songs publishing company, he co-wrote several hits, including **No Vacancy** and **Divorce Me C.O.D**. In the mid-1970s Cliffie Stone formed Granite Records in California. His son Curtis Stone was bassist with Highway 101.

J.D. SUMNER AND THE STAMPS – Legendary gospel group that grew out of the Stamps Quartet (formed in 1920). Headed by bass-voiced singer Sumner, they worked with Elvis Presley from 1971 up to the time of his death. Dave Rowland (of Dave And Sugar) and Richard Sterban (Oak Ridge Boys) both are former members of the Stamps Quartet.

JIMMY SWAGGART – Cousin of Jerry Lee Lewis and Mickey Gilley (born in Ferriday, Louisiana in 1935) who plays the same pumping piano but has aimed his music at the vast country-gospel audience, recording over 50 albums to date.

T

CARMOL TAYLOR – An underrated honky-tonk songwriter and singer, Taylor was born in Brilliant, Alabama in 1931 and worked at local shows and square dances from the age of 15. He tried his luck in Nashville in the mid-1960s and joined Al Gallico Music as a staff writer, penning hits for Charlie Walker, George Jones and David Wills. He recorded briefly for Elektra Records and others. He died of lung cancer in 1986.

CHIP TAYLOR – Brother of actor Jon Voight (born in New York in 1940), this singer-songwriter has penned hits for Waylon Jennings, Bobby Bare, Eddy Arnold, Jim Ed Brown and Floyd Cramer. Once a rockabilly singer with King, he did some excellent country-oriented albums with Warner Bros and Columbia.

TUT TAYLOR – A multi-instrumentalist (born in Milledgeville, Georgia in 1923), Robert 'Tut' Taylor is noted for his flat-picking dobro style. Also proficient on mandolin, fiddle, guitar, dulcimer, autoharp and banjo, he has provided back-up on scores of records and is renowned as a collector, builder and dealer in stringed instruments.

KAREN TAYLOR-GOOD – From El Paso, Texas, a singer-songwriter who worked her way up through the jingle jungle to work on sessions with George Jones, Dolly Parton, Conway Twitty and others, also working on the soundtracks of 'Best Little Whorehouse In Texas' and 'Smokey And The Bandit II'. In 1982 she and her manager formed Mesa Records, since when she has supplied a regular flow of mid-chart singles.

THE TENNEVA RAMBLERS – A relatively popular band of the late '20s and early '30s, originally known as the Jimmie Rodgers Entertainers, they were set to record for Ralph Peer in that historic week in August, 1927. At the last moment they defected from Rodgers and made up the new band name, which reflected the location of the session: Bristol, a city divided in half by the state line between Tennessee and Virginia. They were moderately successful in their recording efforts, but their decision to go it alone helped Rodgers' solo career.

AL TERRY – A Cajun-rocker born Alison Joseph Theriot in 1922, he hit it big when rockabilly came along with his **Good Deal Lucille**, which provided him with a tour with Red Foley and work with country package shows. However, despite the wide acceptance provided by the monster hit, Terry has remained pretty much a regional favourite.

UNCLE JIMMY THOMPSON – The first featured performer on the Saturday night barn dance show, which was to develop into the Grand Ole Opry, was Uncle Jimmy Thompson, born in Smith County, Tennessee in 1848. Primarily a farmer, he was frequent winner of a nationwide fiddle contest. Excited by the then new medium of radio, he applied – at the age of 78! – for a spot on WSM, and in 1925 his Saturday night show first came on the air. He stayed with the Opry (then still known as the WSM Barn Dance) until 1928, then toured a bit and recorded for both Columbia and Vocalion before passing away on February 17, 1931.

MARSHA THORNTON – A former singer with Country Music USA at Opryland, Marsha Thornton was born in Killen, Alabama in 1955. She left the Opryland show in 1988 and signed with MCA Records, scoring several minor chart entries, the best known being **A Bottle Of Wine And Patsy Cline** in 1990.

SONNY THROCKMORTON – A phenomenally successful country tunesmith, he was born James Fron Throckmorton in Carlsbad, New Mexico in 1941. He moved to Nashville in 1964 and worked as a staff writer with Tree Music, but it was to be ten years before he hit top gear, and has since penned more than 200 country hits. He recorded for Starcrest, Mercury and MCA in the late '70s, but has wisely concentrated on his writing – **Last Cheater's Waltz**, **Middle-Age Crazy** and **Can't You Hear That Whistle Blow** are just three of his classics.

JOHNNY TILLOTSON – A pop-country singer and songwriter, who is more country than many credit him. Born in Jacksonville, Florida in 1939, he was on local radio's Young Folks Revue from the age of nine. He appeared on the Toby Dowdy show in Jacksonville in his teens, leading to a recording contract with Cadence in 1958. He enjoyed several teen pop hits from 1959–65 but preferred country. Penned classic country ballads **It Keeps Right On A-Hurtin'** and **Out Of My Mind**, recorded in Nashville with album of country standards in 1962 that featured a young Charlie McCoy on harmonica. Continued to chart country on MGM, UA and Reward into the '80s.

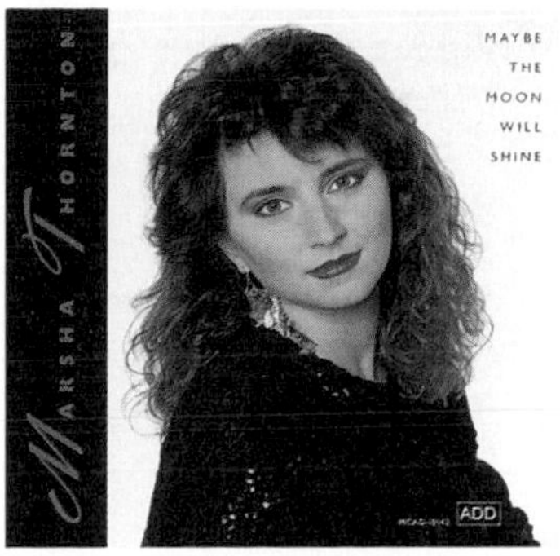

Maybe The Moon Will Shine, Marsha Thornton. Courtesy MCA Records.

MITCHELL TOROK – Writer and singer of novelty country songs, Torok was born in Houston, Texas in 1929 and started playing guitar when he was 12. He first recorded in 1948 for small Texas labels, then in 1951 was signed to Abbott Records, producing the pop-country smash **Caribbean** in 1953 and writing **Mexican Joe**, a biggie for Jim Reeves.

BUCK TRENT – One of country's most proficient banjoists (born Charles Wilburn Trent in Spartanburg, South Carolina). He worked with Bill Carlisle in the late '50s and early '60s then moved on to become a member of Porter Wagoner's Wagonmasters. During 1973 Trent teamed up with Roy Clark and put out a number of albums for ABC. Some of these albums were solo and some all-banjo duets with Clark.

GRANT TURNER – Born in Abilene, Texas in 1912, Turner was the Dean of Opry announcers from 1945. He began his radio career at the age of 16 and joined Nashville's WSM in 1944. Elected to the Country Music Hall Of Fame in 1981, he died in Nashville on October 19, 1991.

WESLEY TUTTLE – Born in Lamar, Colorado, he became West Coast-based after several radio stints in the Midwest. He was signed to Capitol Records in 1945, one of his biggest selling records being **Crying In The Chapel**. He also recorded several duets with his wife Marilyn, later fading from the mainstream country scene when he began working as an evangelist.

U

DONNA ULISSE – Fashion-model beauty with a strong, sultry voice, Donna initially had plans for a modelling career, then opted for music. She was a regular weekend performer at a popular Virginia night-club before moving to Nashville in 1989. She sang back-up vocals on Nashville sessions, worked as a demo and commercial jingle singer, then landed an Atlantic Records contract in 1990.

UNCLE HENRY'S ORIGINAL KENTUCKY MOUNTAINEERS – A fine and popular old-time string band which, by making certain concessions to modernity, remained active well into the 1940s. 'Uncle Henry' Warren was born in Taylor County, Kentucky in 1903. The band began as early as 1928 and for the next 20 years played radio stations throughout the South. Uncle Henry's son, Jimmy Dale Warren, moved to the West Coast when the band split up and became lead singer with the Sons Of The Pioneers.

V

THE VAGABONDS – A smooth harmony trio who were with the Grand Ole Opry from 1931–38. They were unique at the time – they were all non-Southerners (all from the Midwest), and had acquired formal musical training. They were best known for their extremely popular **When It's Lamp Lighting Time In The Valley**, and they recorded a host of similar sentimental tunes for Bluebird and other smaller labels.

Rick Vincent

RICK VINCENT – A true native of Bakersfield, Vincent is a throwback to the '60s and Buck Owens and Merle Haggard, yet with a real '90s energy to his music. This singer, songwriter and guitarist began playing in bands at 15 and worked clubs and colleges from California to the Carolinas, making several stops in Nashville to plug his songs. Eventually he moved to Nashville in 1989. After playing showcases and club dates, he gained a recording contract with Curb Records in 1991, making his debut on the charts with **Best Mistakes I Ever Made** (1992).

W

THE WAGONEERS – An Austin-based quartet formed in 1987 that rapidly gained an A&M recording contract for their blend of '50s-brand rockabilly and straight-ahead '60s country. Led by singer-songwriter Monte Warden, a veteran of the Austin music scene, they appeared in Austin City Limits and made a dent on the country charts with **I Wanna Know Her Again** in 1988.

HANK WANGFORD – Born Henry Hardman, he is also Dr Sam Hutt, an English gynaecologist. After befriending Gram Parsons, he formed a country band that became increasingly nutty, such monikers as Irma Cetas (the Vera Lynn of Vera Cruz), Brad Breath and Manley Footwear hiding the identities of various well-known sessioneers. A singer who has a love-hate relationship with country and its more 'sincere' aspects, he always seems just on the verge of making a breakthrough into commercial acceptance but, to date, has not quite made it.

B.B. WATSON – The first act signed to Nashville's new BNA label in 1991, B.B. (Bad Boy) Watson, whose real surname is Haskell, was raised in Shreveport, Louisiana. He has fronted his own Gulf Coast Cowboys Band in the Texas–Louisiana area since graduating from high school. His southern raspy voice with a gripping

soulfulness is ideal for the powerful country themes he constructs in his songs. He has scored a major success with **Light At The End Of The Tunnel**.

JIM WEATHERLY – Singer-songwriter born in Pontotoc, Mississippi in 1943, Jim moved to Nashville in the late '60s. Though country acts cut his songs, it was soul singer Gladys Knight who put him on the map, scoring major pop hits with **Midnight Train To Georgia** and **The Best Thing That Ever Happened To Me**. Signed to Buddah Records, he recorded some great country-styled albums, making the country Top 10 with **I'll Still Love You**. He continues as a successful country tunesmith today, often co-writing with many of the new young hopefuls in Nashville.

DENNIS WEAVER – A character actor best known for his TV roles in Gunsmoke and McCloud, the easy-going Weaver acquired both a western image and a reasonable reputation as a country singer. Born in 1924, he hails from Joplin, Missouri. Following graduation from Oklahoma University he started on an acting career, appearing in several top films during the '50s. Recording his first country album for the Impress label in 1972, he subsequently signed for Ovation, recording in Nashville under the direction of Ray Pennington. Failing to come up with a hit single, Dennis Weaver returned to his first love, acting.

GORDIE WEST – Popular Canadian singer – though he was born in Skipton, England. A one-time power engineer, he worked with several country bands but eventually went solo, cutting his first album, **Alberta Bound**, during 1978.

SPEEDY WEST – One of the most recorded steelies in country music (born in Missouri in 1924). Once resident on Cliffie Stone's Hometown Jamboree, his 1955 Capitol album with Jimmy Bryant, **2 Guitars Country Style**, remains an indispensable instrumental item.

MICHAEL WHITE – The son of noted country tunesmith L.E. White (he wrote several of Conway Twitty's hits), Michael was born in

Knoxville, Tennessee, but raised in Nashville. Following in his father's footsteps, he wrote his first songs at age 12, with two being recorded by Conway Twitty. He attended Lee College in Cleveland, Tennessee, pursuing a career in the Ministry, then opted for music. He sang lead in Gold Rush (a Top 40 covers band), then formed Fresh Horses (a southern rock outfit). Finally he returned to his musical roots, working as a demo singer and songwriter in Nashville. A record deal with Reprise in 1991 saw him placing his own versions of his songs on the charts.

WILD ROSE – All-girl, five-piece, Nashville-based band comprising well-established session singers/musicians Wanda Vick, Nancy Given-Prout, Kathy Mac, Pam Perry and Pamela Gadd. Following showcases and club dates around Nashville, they signed with Universal Records in 1989 and made the country Top 20 with **Breaking New Ground**.

LITTLE DAVID WILKINS – Born in Parsons, Tennessee. Another mail-order guitar player who started out with Sun Records in Memphis at 15. A chubby entertainer, perpetually on a diet, he has had hits for such labels as Plantation, MCA, Playboy and Epic.

CURLY WILLIAMS – Leader of the Georgia Peach Pickers, a popular Grand Ole Opry band in the '40s, he is best known for having written **Half As Much**, which, because it was popularized by Hank Williams, is frequently thought of as Hank's song. In the '50s he drifted out of performing.

LAWTON WILLIAMS – A former DJ in Detroit and Dearborn in the '40s, Williams (born in Troy, Tennessee in 1922) is best known as the writer of **Fraulein** and **Geisha Girl**. A talented singer, he had his own TV series in Fort Worth in the late '40s. Has recorded for several labels including Mercury and RCA, and was still touring regularly in the late '80s.

LEONA WILLIAMS – Born Leona Helton in Vienna, Missouri in 1943, she became part of the Helton family band at an early age. At 15 she married bass player Ron Williams, the duo becoming members of Loretta Lynn's back-up unit. In 1968 she signed with Hickory Records, this association lasting until 1974, when she joined MCA. A straight-down-the-line country singer, she joined the Merle Haggard roadshow as backing vocalist in 1975 and became not only Merle's duet partner, but his third wife (1978). It turned out to be a stormy marriage, and five years later they were divorced.

KELLY WILLIS – A young lady with a promising future, Kelly Willis was born in Virginia in 1969, but her music owes more to Texas dance music – roadhouse style. She joined her first band at 16, later moving to Austin, Texas, where Nanci Griffith put her in touch with MCA A&R chief Tony Brown, who immediately signed her up. Blending rockabilly abandon, hard-country emotion, Kelly uses her voice as another instrument, sliding and bending notes in classic country fashion.

DAVID WILLS – A classic honky-tonk singer who was born ten years ahead of his time in Pulaski, Tennessee in 1951. A prolific songwriter he was 'New Traditional' years before it was fashionable. Discovered by Charlie Rich, he gained an Epic recording contract in 1973, hitting Top 10 with **There's A Song On The Jukebox** and **From Barrooms To Bedrooms**. He has since recorded for UA, RCA and back to Epic, registering more than 20 minor hits.

NORRO WILSON – Norris Wilson, outstanding songwriter, singer, producer and music executive, was born in Scotsville, Kentucky in 1938. He enjoyed some regional success in the late '50s, then moved to Nashville in the early '60s, signing as a writer with Al Gallico Music, and recording for Mercury/Smash. He has cut records for several labels over the years, but it is as a writer of hits for Charlie Rich, Joe Stampley, Tammy Wynette, etc, that Wilson has built his reputation.

STEPHANIE WINSLOW – This accomplished fiddler and singer was born in Yankton, South

Dakota in 1956. A child prodigy, she made her professional debut at age ten, and leans towards the showbiz/cabaret style of country. She has recorded for Warners, Primero and MCA throughout the '80s, making the Top 10 with **Say You Love Me**.

TOM WOPAT – Singer-actor who played Luke in the TV series Dukes Of Hazzard, Wopat (from Lodi, Wisconsin) recorded for EMI-America in Nashville during the late '80s, scoring several Top 20 country hits, including **The Rock And Roll Of Love**.

BOBBY WRIGHT – The son of Johnny Wright and Kitty Wells, Bobby was born in Charleston, West Virginia in 1942. He started making show business appearances while still a child, and gained the part of Willie in the TV series McHale's Navy, remaining with the show for a four-year run. A member of his parents' family show, he has recorded regularly since the late '60s, his most successful record, **Here I Go Again**, a Top 20 entry in 1971.

X

X-STATIONS – Powerful radio stations that operated just inside the Mexican border, cutting in on wavelengths used by US and Canadian stations. Many country singers including the Carter Family were helped on their way through border radio.

Y

SKEETS YANEY – One of country music's great regional stars, Skeets, who was a spectacular yodeller, was born Clyde Yaney in Mitchell, Indiana. A longtime star on KMOX in St Louis, he was one of the main members of the KMOX Barn Dance in the '30s and '40s. He died of cancer in 1978.

JONNY YOUNG – A British singer who possesses one of the sweetest, most distinctive voices in British country music. He started out in the early '60s in pop bands, forming the Jonny Young Four in 1967 with tight harmonies, and signed to RCA. The group was set for the big time, but a car accident, in which the bass player was killed, held up their career. They worked behind many American stars and recorded for several labels during the '70s. They re-formed as the Jonny Young Band and took on a more contemporary stance, still working the scene in the '90s.

Below: Jonny Young has one of the most distinctive voices in UK country.

Broken Heartland, Zaca Creek. Courtesy Giant Records.

Z

ZACA CREEK – West Coast quartet of the Foss Brothers – Gates (vocals), Scot (guitar), Jeff (keyboards) and James (bass). Their name comes from an underground stream in their hometown of Santa Ynez, California. Signed to Columbia in 1989, they scored some country hits, but have yet to make a big impact.